The American People and Their Education

A Social History

RICHARD J. ALTENBAUGH

Slippery Rock University

Merrill
Prentice Hall

Upper Saddle River, New Jersey
Columbus, Ohio

Library of Congress Cataloging-in-Publication Data

Altenbaugh, Richard J.
 The American people and their education : a social history / Richard J. Altenbaugh.—
 1st ed.
  p. cm.
 Includes bibliographical references and index.
 ISBN 0-13-525379-9
 1. Education–United States–History. I. Title.
LA205 .A43 2003
370′.973′09–dc21

2002070970

Vice President and Publisher: Jeffery W. Johnston
Executive Editor: Debra A. Stollenwerk
Assistant Editor: Daniel J. Parker
Editorial Assistant: Mary Morrill
Production Editor: Mary Harlan
Production Coordination: Cliff Kallemeyn, Clarinda Publication Services
Design Coordinator: Diane C. Lorenzo
Cover Design: Jason Moore
Cover Image: SuperStock
Text Design: Clarinda Publication Services
Production Manager: Laura Messerly
Director of Marketing: Ann Castel Davis
Marketing Manager: Krista Groshong
Marketing Coordinator: Tyra Cooper

This book was set in Berkeley Book by The Clarinda Company. It was printed and bound by R. R. Donnelley & Sons Company. The cover was printed by Phoenix Color Corp.

Pearson Education Ltd.
Pearson Education Australia Pty. Limited
Pearson Education Singapore Pte. Ltd.
Pearson Education North Asia Ltd.
Pearson Education Canada, Ltd.
Pearson Educación de Mexico, S.A. de C.V.
Pearson Education—Japan
Pearson Education Malaysia Pte. Ltd.
Pearson Education, *Upper Saddle River, New Jersey*

Merrill
Prentice Hall

10 9 8 7 6 5 4 3
ISBN: 0-13-525379-9

P R E F A C E

Why is the historical view important? History opens the mind to our social world. Through it, we can better understand today's events, crises, and issues, because we gain a sense of perspective and a realization of the complexity and impact of change. Human events and educational activities and institutions have changed over time, arriving at the present state.

This is especially true with education. If they focus only on great school leaders, historians may overlook the roles that other people, through their ideas about education and through their activities and institutions, played in shaping the educational experience. For example, observers rarely comment on the fact that it was teachers who ran the schools on a daily basis, defining pedagogy and influencing policy. And what about the experiences of those being educated?

The American People and Their Education: A Social History attempts to bring history alive, to make it real by connecting the reader to the historical actors—families, teachers, and children—as well as teaching processes and the classroom settings, and by describing and analyzing their lives and routines and their successes, frustrations, and failures. Within that context, this text stresses complexity and conflict as well as consensus. And whenever possible, it draws on autobiographies and biographies, providing a personal kaleidoscope to enliven the descriptive narrative and personalize historical experiences. The unfolding of the history of childhood through different experiences at various times undergirds the narrative. *The American People and Their Education* therefore has four primary goals:

- It introduces students to a broad and comprehensive definition of education and how it changed over time.
- It analyzes the impact of race, ethnicity, social class, gender, and religion on education.
- It examines the conflict between the American public school ideal and its reality, focusing on early childhood, elementary, and secondary levels.
- And, finally, it attempts to engage students in an active intellectual manner.

ORGANIZATIONAL FRAMEWORK

The American People and Their Education may be used in two different ways—chronologically and conceptually.

The four parts, or units, take the reader on a historical odyssey through the institutionalization and formalization of the American educational process, a search for the

iii

public school ideal. Each chapter follows a chronological approach, but the treatment within chapters maintains a conceptual or thematic focus. The chapter titles reflect a chronological progression, while each chapter's subheadings follow a topical approach. This gives the instructor complete freedom to approach American educational history in a flexible manner.

Thus, on the one hand, and if the instructor prefers, this text has a traditional chronological structure. Each chapter provides a narrative and analysis of consecutive historical periods and experiences. On the other hand, the instructor may take a conceptual approach and focus on sections within different chapters that deal with Native Americans, African Americans, immigrants, teachers—their lives, pedagogy, organizations, and so on. Within each time period, a variety of educational institutions, issues, and ideas emerged, re-emerged, or became marginalized. Therefore, the instructor can focus on the historical development of current topics and conflicts in education, giving students a perspective of depth and complexity.

CLASSROOM USES

Pedagogy and technology can create, between instructor and students, a "community of scholars" or "knowledge-building communities," resulting in a highly interactive environment.[1] Research into the use of technology in college-level classrooms indicates a clear increase in "student interest" and "student learning." Web-based methods can be used to retrieve primary documents, statistics, and additional secondary information, as well as photographs, illustrations, and audio and video sources. Guided exposure to these primary and secondary sources expands students' thinking and analysis and deepens their appreciation of the value of the historical perspective in grasping contemporary social and educational issues and problems.[2] This textbook attempts to capture this approach, relying heavily as well on reading, writing, and discourse.

The activities at the end of each chapter use individual, small-group, cooperative learning, and whole-class activities to explore primary documents and databases and to debate fundamental educational questions within a historical context. Each chapter also includes a list of films that will provide additional information and elicit various perspectives and that can be used to study cultural artifacts. In the case of Web sites, I have provided only the URLs. The incredibly rich "History Matters" Web site includes many titles, some of which I have listed. The site has an abundance of contextual material as well as specific treatments of education in both text and audio versions.

Textbooks too often possess many liabilities: Descriptive narrative seems to dominate, hagiography too often prevails, facts appear to be supreme, chronological organization supersedes conceptual considerations, objectivity subsumes interpretation or polemics replaces narrative; and a reductionist approach to history is maintained, oversimplifying it. *The American People and Their Education* represents a modest response to these problems.

ACKNOWLEDGMENTS

I have had the great fortune and privilege of teaching social and educational history for twenty-eight years at a variety of institutions, at the undergraduate and graduate levels, in colleges of education and of liberal arts and sciences. I owe a great deal to my students, both past and present. Their questions and challenges over the years have helped to refine my thinking about many of the issues and topics treated in this book. Their willingness to participate and then assess various classroom activities proved to be invaluable.

I accumulated many other debts in the process of compiling this textbook. Debbie Stollenwerk, Executive Editor at Merrill, demonstrated incredible faith in me by offering me a contract and guiding me over the years. Heather Doyle Fraser and Dan Parker displayed exceptional patience as the due date came and went while I continued to toil.

My debts encompass many others. Bruce C. Nelson, Managing Editor, *History of Education Quarterly*, provided important comments on an early draft of the manuscript. Barbara Beatty, Robert A. Levin, and Victoria-Maria MacDonald kindly read a later draft of this entire manuscript, unselfishly donating their time, and offered insightful improvements. I also thank the following reviewers: Judy Arnold, Lincoln Memorial University; Carlton E. Beck, University of Wisconsin–Milwaukee; Carrine H. Bishop, Jackson State University; Malcolm B. Campbell, Bowling Green State University; Louise E. Fleming, Ashland University; Patricia A. Gross, Ursinus College; W. Thomas Jamison, Appalachian State University; James Kauffman, University of South Carolina–Aiken; Averil E. McClelland, Kent State University; Nancy McKinley, Laramee County Community College; Janet McNellis, Troy State University; Mumbi Mwangi, Iowa State University; Emmanuel C. Nwagwu, Texas Southern University; Alan F. Quick, Central Michigan University; Stanley W. Rothstein, California State University; Karen L. Sanchez, Nova Southeastern University; Ann H. Stoddard, University of North Florida. These good folks are not responsible for any interpretations or errors; those are solely mine.

I could not have assembled a synthetic work of this nature without profound intellectual influences and rich secondary sources. During my graduate years, and throughout my career, the works of David Montgomery, Herbert Gutman, and E. P. Thompson, among other social and labor historians, shaped my intellectual outlook. Early in my career, Howard Zinn's *A People's History of the United States* (New York: Harper & Row, 1980) presented me with a fundamentally different model of a history textbook; that influence endures. We also have witnessed a golden era in scholarship during the past thirty-five years in the field of social and educational history, expanding our notions of the historical development and influence of the family, religion, work, and schools; the significance of human agency; and the roles of race, gender, ethnicity, and social class in shaping our existence. I hope that I have sufficiently and properly provided adequate attributions both in the narrative and endnotes for all of this fine work.

I am further grateful to the Routledge/Falmer Press, which gave me permission to use sections from previous publications. For Chapters 5 and 11, I used revised versions of material from Richard J. Altenbaugh, ed., *The Teacher's Voice: A Social History of Teaching in Twentieth Century America* (London: Falmer Press, 1992), pp. 8–11, 60–61, 61–62; and for Chapters 6, 7, 8, and 9, Richard J. Altenbaugh, David E. Engel, and Don T. Martin, *Caring About Kids: A Critical Study of Urban School Leavers* (London: Falmer Press, 1995), scattered material from pp. 31–42.

The many fine images and photographs in this book represent the kind and thoughtful efforts of archivists. I owe a debt of gratitude to the good folks in the Photograph and Print Division of the Library of Congress; Rich Casey, Blackwell Museum, Northern Illinois University; Patricia J. Albright, Mount Holyoke College; James Huffman, the Schomburg Center for Research in Black Culture; David Ment and his staff, Milbank Library, Teachers

College, Columbia University; Lucinda Manning and Evan Daniel, United Federation of Teachers Archives; and Tedd Levy, an enthusiastic collector of educational prints and images.

Finally, as always, I have had the steadfast love of my family, Marianne, Ian, Colin, and the indomitable Protocol Bluebonnet, as I spent countless hours in my study, the University of Pittsburgh's Hillman Library, or Princeton University's Firestone Library researching, reading, and writing this book.

NOTES AND SOURCES

1. Ann Wyne, "History Instruction and the Internet: A Literature Review," in *History.edu: Essays on Teaching with Technology*, eds. Dennis A Trinkle and Scott A. Merriman (Armonk, NY: M. E. Sharpe, 2001), pp. 29, 30.
2. Larry Easley and Steven Hoffman, "Reinventing the American History Survey," in *History.edu: Essays on Teaching with Technology*, eds. Dennis A Trinkle and Scott A. Merriman (Armonk, NY: M. E. Sharpe, 2001), pp. 62, 63. See as well Gary J. Kornblith, "Venturing into the Civil War, Virtually: A Review," *Journal of American History* 88 (June 2001): 145–151.

BRIEF CONTENTS

C O N T E N T S

The American People
and Their Education

1

The Role of Clio: How the Past Influences the Present

What Is Education?

The Social History Perspective

A Multicultural Approach

Clio, one of the nine daughters of the ancient Greek god Zeus, was the Muse of History. Her name "simply means 'fame,' 'renown.' She is thus a proclaimer of deeds of renown."[1] History began as an oral tradition in many different cultures, times, and places. It was, in a sense, a form of storytelling: It proclaimed great human accomplishments and failures, heroic and evil alike; celebrated the human spirit; created an enduring heritage and culture; and explained the human condition and it continues to relate the past to the present, only now through the printed word, pictures, and electronically recorded voices and images. History explains how our present society has come about and why we have adopted certain practices, roles, institutions, and ideologies. This text attempts to tell the history of America's educational traditions, the good and the bad, the victories and the setbacks, the protagonists and the antagonists. This story is not a simple one, reflecting consensus, but is riddled with conflict, contradictions, and frustrations.

Two competing perspectives on the purpose of American public schooling exist:

- The ideal perspective is the vision of equal opportunity for all. From this point of view, schooling serves as a liberating force, socially, politically, and intellectually.
- The critical view sees schooling as a means of restricting opportunities and maintaining the status quo by stressing conformity rather than freedom.[2]

What, then, is the true function of schooling in America? The many and continuous struggles to establish the ideal of public schooling will be the focus of this text.

WHAT IS EDUCATION?

The meaning of education has become distorted overtime in American society, which now tends to equate it with schooling. It is true that today without school credentials, work and social advancement appear to be extremely limited. However, in the past schooling was haphazard and marginal, with the majority of students abandoning it after only a few years. Lawrence Cremin, a leading educational historian, defines education as a cultural experience, consisting of a configuration of social and political institutions, such as the family, church, work training, cultural institutions, print and nonprint media, and military service, among others. Placed within this pervasive educational context, schooling in the past played a very different role in the educational process.[3] Because education is such a broad and ongoing experience, institutions other than schools are considered in this text. The narrative describes and analyzes how the different educational institutions interacted, focusing on the family, religion, and work.

According to the 1990 and 2000 Censuses, the American family is experiencing profound change, but not unlike changes occurring in many other developed countries. The family structure idealized a generation ago in such popular television shows as *Father Knows Best* and *Leave It to Beaver* is now rare. Only 3 percent of families consist of a working husband and homemaker with two children; 25 percent of children live in single-parent households.[4] Because of its changing structure and the stresses placed upon it, the modern American family appears to play only a marginal role in the education of its children. According to some social critics and politicians, this was not always the case—or was it? It is true that in Puritan New England the family was the primary educator, instilling religious doctrine, teaching literacy, and training children for a vocation. We will examine how and why the family's educational role gradually shifted over time.

Religion also has a marginal role, if any, in today's schooling process. During the early nineteenth century, however, the **common schools** were established to promote **Pan-Protantism**, a sectarianism that offended many immigrant Roman Catholic parents, giving rise to the parochial school system, which flourished during the early decades of the twentieth century. Today, public schools, in order to avoid religious conflict, now attempt to remain neutral regarding religion. This text chronicles these changes.

Finally, in the past American parents and their children viewed work as wholesome and, more important, educational. Children often left school to work or learn how to work through an apprenticeship, which many perceived as a more valuable form of education. Today, the relationship between schooling and work has completely changed. Students in today's world stay in school to learn how to work or see schooling as a bridge to at worst a job or at best meaningful work. Thus, schooling is now seen as directly related to work, not separate from it.

This historical exploration of the changing and increasingly complex relationships among all of these educational institutions will inform us about today's seemingly insurmountable educational problems. It will also acknowledge the conflicts that often exist between some of these institutions, such as between religion and schooling, family and schooling, media and religion—a list that can obviously be extended.

THE SOCIAL HISTORY PERSPECTIVE

History textbooks, at all levels, are the bane of historians. James Loewen argues in his controversial study that traditional secondary textbooks distort history.[5] Like many college texts, they suffer from "herofication," the oversimplifying of the lives of individuals and their relationships to historical events. Loewen points to Woodrow Wilson as an example. Wilson, the leading proponent of European self-determination and democracy, implemented and enforced an undemocratic, if not downright colonial, foreign policy in Latin America. Further, Wilson, a progressive Democrat, was also a white supremacist and created segregation policies regarding federal offices and practices. The whole process of promoting "wartless stereotypes" obfuscates, according to Loewen, the sense of historical cause and effect, producing a history that does not remotely reflect reality and sanitizes it by creating the "ideal" not the "real" person in textbooks. Loewen addresses the serious consequences resulting from such an approach: Herofication can be "potentially crippling," producing "intellectual immaturity" and impeding informed political debate. College-level history texts attempt to take a more complex and balanced approach but too often condense, if not likewise oversimplify, matters (often to meet word limits set by well-meaning, but cost-conscious, editors).

I do not boast that *The American People and Their Education* will overcome all of the shortcomings of textbook writing, an activity that is more complex, sophisticated, and intellectually challenging than I first anticipated. However, I humbly hope that it addresses complexity and conflict and uncovers the role of cause and effect in the history of American education. Criticisms of today's public schools—by politicians, the media, and the public—reflect the cynicism produced by the erosion of a nonexistent ideal. To avoid disillusionment and to be able to grapple with today's educational challenges, fresh, eager, preprofessional teachers, as well as parents and policymakers and society as a whole, need history to provide perspective and assist in interpreting contemporary issues and guiding solutions.

The history of education is a rich and fascinating subject, deep in texture. It reveals that individuals who have typically been hailed as heroes are not so heroic, while people who have rarely received mention are the true historical actors. This textbook therefore relies on a social history framework, focusing on preschool through adolescent children, and pursues two goals in its treatment of American educational history:

- First, it attempts to be inclusive, going beyond the usual "movers and shakers" to focus on the efforts and accomplishments of other, different groups. As a result, the threads of race, ethnicity, gender, and social class are woven throughout the text.
- Second, it traces the changes in the relationships among various social and educational institutions and asks many questions: Why has the family's educational role seemingly shrunk? What has been the role of religion in American schooling? Why do schools now operate as "the" educational institution in our society? How do we account for the profound change in the relationship between schooling and work? Nothing has happened by accident; human beings have shaped history daily through their "ordinary lives and everyday events."[6]

This emphasis on the historical roles and processes of educational institutions other than schools should allow the reader to bring an informed perspective to current debates and issues in education. This text therefore operates from the notion that education is a broad experience, encompassing many cultures and institutions. It transcends the traditional history of a single, evolving institution established for the good of all, for many individuals and groups struggled to shape American education in general and public schooling in particular. This is their educational history.

A MULTICULTURAL APPROACH

Multiculturalism has been criticized as faddish, divisive, and "politically correct." However, these attacks fly in the face of reality: Diversity in America is increasing dramatically and will profoundly transform American society. According to Sam Roberts's analysis of the 1990 Census, "at no time in the nation's history have so many born abroad been residents of the U.S." According to the 2000 Census, "Hispanics" now represent 11 percent of the population, the same percentage as African Americans. If these trends continue, and there is every indication that they will, Anglo Americans will "again" become a minority sometime during the middle of this century, and "no ethnic or racial group will constitute a majority."[7] Unfortunately, as society grows ever more diverse, it is becoming less inclusive—albeit in subtle ways. The cover of a special issue of *Time* magazine proclaimed in the fall of 1993: "The New Face of America: How Immigrants Are Shaping the World's First Multicultural Society." The editors dedicated the entire issue to a description and analysis of these significant ethnic and racial changes. The title of the lead article screamed: "Not Quite So Welcome Anymore." It cited polls that revealed a disturbing and increasing mood of intolerance.[8] And in the aftermath of the terrorist attacks on September 11, 2001, the ugliness of intolerance in America was unveiled in the victimization of many Americans from the Middle East and India. Rather than ridicule and demean multiculturalism as merely politically correct, therefore, its detractors should recognize it as part of political and social reality and that we are a diverse society which harbors prejudice.

The themes of race, ethnicity, gender, and social class occur throughout this narrative. Native Americans, African Americans, Latinos, women, and working-class and poor people possessed their own educational views and occasionally created their own educational institutions. At the time of European contact, the First Americans had their own unique child-rearing goals and practices. Their educational views clashed with European instructional priorities and practices, and Native Americans resisted European-style schooling. African American education was purposefully limited in this country.[9] In the slave quarters, masters emphasized training in manual skills and a socialization process emphasizing obedience and subordination. The slave community resisted much of the socialization aspect of this educational process. Emancipation did not bring equality, however. Although African Americans placed a great deal of faith in American schools to produce their leaders, extend equality, and increase opportunities, then as well as now, they struggled against first **de jure segregation** and second **de facto segregation**.

Race remains a divisive issue in American society and in its schools. A 1996 issue of *Time* magazine declared "back to segregation" on its cover. It devoted a major article, titled "The End of Integration," to an analysis of why, four decades after the landmark *Brown v. Board of Education of Topeka* Supreme Court case, the schools have returned to the concept

*"How about a decent school
for me?" (c. 1942-1957)
Courtesy Library of Congress,
NAACP Collection*

of "separate but equal." Segregation and integration represent old social experiences in this society. As we shall see, in the fall of 1855 Boston became the first American city to desegregate its schools. But after almost a century and a half of struggle, a series of court cases, and numerous civil rights protests, this society is still grappling with this educational problem. The courts appear to be willing to accept stubborn residential segregation patterns. The number of separate schools is increasing rather than decreasing. The *Time* article pointed out, "Nationally, fully a third of black public school students attend schools where the enrollment is 90 to 100 percent minority—that is, black, Hispanic, Asian, and Native American"; the cause is persistent racism in which European Americans employ a variety of legal tactics or use residential patterns to avoid integration.[10]

Descendants of the Spanish, the first Europeans to settle on the North American continent, have also experienced segregation. Education on the Spanish-speaking frontier, much like that in the Plymouth Colony, maintained a religious focus and relied largely on the family and religious institutions. When Anglo European settlers expropriated Mexican property and political power after the Mexican War of 1846–1848, the Hispanic population became an "occupied" people. Protestant Anglo European missionaries attempted to convert the Roman Catholic Mexicans by means of frontier schools. During the early decades of the twentieth century, with a resurgence of Mexican migration, Mexican children faced school segregation throughout the Southwest. During the late 1960s and early 1970s, Mexican Americans fought against segregation and an Anglocentric curriculum. Although bilingual education compensated for this somewhat, a great deal of controversy has characterized the bilingual movement and has generated Anglo resistance.[11]

Like Native Americans, African Americans, and Spanish-speaking minorities, females have struggled to receive appropriate education. Female students during the colonial period found it very difficult to obtain any schooling beyond basic literacy training. Later, the egalitarianism of the American Revolution led to some limited schooling opportunities for girls, and these greatly expanded with the advent of the common schools, state-supported free schools open to all, in the nineteenth century. By the end of the nineteenth century, **coeducation** had become commonplace in most American public schools, unlike in other Western societies. Some people opposed this, however, and as a result, with the spread of high school education during the Progressive Era of 1890–1920, female students found themselves placed, at worst, in vocational, domestic tracks or, at best, in general education classes. In the 1960s, researchers brought to light a hidden curriculum in the schools that subtly taught traditional social roles to young girls and boys. Although since then female students have gained significant access to the entire curriculum, recent research indicates that the hidden curriculum is still operative.[12]

Like racial and ethnic minorities, poor and working-class children have not generally fared well in American public schools. They often had to abandon schooling because of family needs; the family's economic survival often superseded schooling. Only the children of affluent parents could afford to remain in school. Furthermore, poor and working-class children found more rewarding and useful education through apprenticeships as well as in the workplace itself. In 1900, only 10 percent of school-aged children completed high school. Even vocational education programs failed to attract many poor and working-class children, and school leaving rates remained over 50 percent until the 1950s and reached their lowest levels during the 1960s. They still plague the public schools. Although national rates hover around 25 percent, some urban school systems report that 40–60 percent of minority students leave school before graduation. In some localities, 78 percent of Hispanic students abandon school, and rates are as high as 90 percent among Native Americans. Poor children, regardless of gender, race, or ethnicity, leave school more often.[13]

CONCLUSIONS

"Progress" and "reform" too often carry the connotation of positive change, and history is often portrayed as a long, steady march toward some preexisting ideal. But this is not necessarily the case. Change represents progress for some and a setback for others; that is, it can be positive as well as negative.

This textbook stresses the complex and dynamic historical relationship between society and education. As different subcultures in particular and American society in general changed, educational goals and institutions were likewise altered. Each of the following chapters will describe American society at a particular time and analyze its educational goals, processes, and institutions. Throughout the text, the reader will encounter attributions, because this is a synthetic work, blending different sources of information and perspectives, and because I think it is important the reader understand that all written history is based on evidence and corroboration. Each chapter also includes several activities and suggestions, many of which have been classroom tested. Finally, each chapter concludes with notes and sources, which also suggest further, in-depth reading.

ACTIVITIES FOR FURTHER EXPLORATION

1. Write a brief explanation of the function of public schooling.
2. For additional and current data about ethnic and racial populations, family structure, gender issues, and the extent of poverty, refer to the U.S. Census Bureau's Web site: http://www.census.gov.
3. Specific educational statistics can be found at the Web site for the National Center for Education Statistics: http://nces.ed.gov.

NOTES AND SOURCES

1. Adrian Room, *NTC's Classical Dictionary: The Origins of the Names of Characters in Classical Mythology* (Lincolnwood, IL: National Textbook Co., 1990), p. 98; Michael Grant and John Hazel, *Who's Who in Classical Mythology* (New York: Oxford University Press, 1993), p. 225.

2. See James D. Anderson, *The Education of Blacks in the South, 1860–1935* (Chapel Hill, NC: University of North Carolina Press, 1988), particularly pp. 1–2; Lawrence A. Cremin, *The Genius of American Education* (New York: Vintage Books, 1965); Clarence J. Karier, Paul Violas, and Joel Spring, eds., *Roots of Crisis: American Education in the Twentieth Century* (Chicago: Rand McNally, 1973); Clarence J. Karier, ed., *Shaping the American Educational State: 1900 to the Present* (New York: Free Press, 1975); Michael B. Katz, *The Irony of Early School Reform: Educational Innovation in Mid-Nineteenth-Century Massachusetts* (Boston: Beacon Press, 1968); Joel H. Spring, *Education and the Rise of the Corporate State* (Boston: Beacon Press, 1972); Paul C. Violas, *The Training of the Urban Working Class: A History of Twentieth-Century American Education* (Chicago: Rand McNally, 1978).

3. Lawrence A. Cremin first provided his definition of education in *American Education: The Colonial Experience, 1607–1783* (New York: Harper & Row, 1970), p. xi, and began to formalize it in *Traditions of American Education* (New York: Basic Books, 1976), p. viii. His refined definition is in *American Education: The National Experience, 1783–1876* (New York: Harper & Row, 1980).

4. Sam Roberts, *Who We Are: A Portrait of America Based on the Latest U.S. Census* (New York: Times Books, 1993), p. 30.

5. James W. Loewen, *Lies My Teacher Told Me: Everything Your American History Textbook Got Wrong* (New York: New Press, 1995), pp. 12–22, 23, 25.

6. See James B. Gardner and George Rollie Adams, eds., *Ordinary People and Everyday Life: Perspectives on the New Social History* (Nashville, TN: American Association for State and Local History, 1983), for a comprehensive overview of the social history framework. Also see David Montgomery, "History as Human Agency," *Monthly Review* 33 (Oct. 1981), pp. 42–48.

7. Roberts, *Who We Are*, pp. 5, 246.

8. See *Time* 142 (Fall 1993).

9. See, for example, James Anderson, "Northern Foundations and the Shaping of Southern Black Rural Education, 1902–1935," *History of Education Quarterly* 18 (Winter 1978): 371–396.

10. James S. Kunen, "The End of Integration," *Time*, April 29, 1996, p. 39.

11. Rodolfo Acuña, *Occupied America: A History of Chicanos* (New York: Harper & Row, 1981).

12. David Tyack and Elisabeth Hansot, *Learning Together: A History of Coeducation in American Public Schools* (New Haven, CT: Yale University Press, 1990).

13. Richard J. Altenbaugh, David E. Engel, and Don T. Martin, *Caring for Kids: A Critical Study of Urban School Leavers* (London: Falmer Press, 1995); see Chapter 1 for a literature overview.

Education as Informal Experience

2

Family, Religion, and Education in Colonial America

". . . you will act wisely, if, from the beginning, you convince all your Scholars which you may easily do, of your abilities in the several branches, which you shall profess to teach . . . ."[1] Thus wrote Philip Fithian, a former Virginia tutor, to his successor in 1774. Whether conducted by a tutor, parent, religious leader, master craftsman, or school teacher, education represents a cultural experience and as such can be broadly defined. The primary social and educational institution in any traditional culture is the family. In the past, through its informal, day-to-day interactions and obligations, it introduced children to folkways and traditions, developed their language skills, and ensured their sheer survival through teaching valuable vocational skills. Religion served as the core knowledge.

This chapter focuses on those informal, and amorphous, educational processes used by both the First Americans and the colonists at the time of European contact and settlement. Both Native Americans and Europeans relied on the family as their main educational institution. Contact between these two profoundly different cultures altered the educational processes and outcomes for both groups. By the close of the colonial period, both groups moved, willingly or unwillingly, toward the more formal, institutionalized education commonly embodied in schooling.

THE FIRST AMERICANS AND THEIR CHILDREN

The First Americans, who inhabited the North American continent for some 30,000 years prior to the arrival of the Europeans, established diverse and rich cultures, with many types of languages, foods, shelters, and lifestyles. According to historian Gary Nash, "about 2,000 languages were spoken by the native Americans—a greater linguistic diversity than in any other part of the world." Estimates range and debates persist over how many Native Americans actually occupied the precontact North American continent, but the accepted figure is that ten million lived north of present-day Mexico. European conquests and diseases accounted for a 90 percent attrition rate, however.

Tribes developed sophisticated cultures based on cultivated food production, large settlements, and social institutions. Hopis and Zunis in the Southwest constructed large "apartment house" structures, with some 800 rooms accommodating 1,000 residents. "By the time of the Spanish arrival, the Hopis and Zunis were also using irrigation canals, check-dams, and hillside terracing as techniques for bringing water to what had been for centuries an arid, agriculturally marginal area." In the Northeast, the Iroquois Confederation represented the largest and most powerful tribe at the beginning of the seventeenth century. The Iroquois maintained a matrilineal society in social as well as in political and economic organization. Family structure and membership followed the female line; women played important political roles by appointing male representatives, and they assumed responsibility for agricultural production. "Thus power was shared between the sexes, and the European idea of male dominancy and female subordination in all things was conspicuously absent in Iroquois society."[2]

Traditional Native American Education

Traditional Native American child-rearing goals, philosophy, and practices continued through the colonial period. In spite of the diversity and richness of individual tribal cultures, "several common practices did cut across cultural boundaries." These had three goals. First, "economic skills" were stressed; which ones depended on the region, however. In the Great Lakes area, tribes focused on hunting abilities, while in other places farming techniques assumed primacy, as in the "maize-oriented society of the Hopi." Such training began for boys as soon as they learned to walk. Second, "cultural heritage" was conveyed. Native Americans depended on oral tradition to pass on this information, usually through elders, "medicine men or ritual leaders." "Storytelling was one of the strongest means of imparting the culture to children." Tribes commonly used tales to teach values like courage, generosity, kindness, obedience, respect, and diligence. Huron parents, for example, inspired their children through stories of honor and famous exploits. Third, children were imbued with spiritual awareness, which permeated the whole childhood experience.

Native American educational philosophy differed markedly from its European counterpart. Parents emphasized cooperation and sharing rather than competition and acquisition. Also, even according to seventeenth- and eighteenth-century European observers, Native Americans dearly loved their children.[3] This deep and visible affection guided child-rearing practices.

The educational process, although informal, was systematic, growing more abstract and demanding as children matured. Native Americans relied on the oral tradition and an experiential approach, that is, children learned by doing through "imitation." Children were daily engaged with adults and elders as well as their social and physical environment and were tested through challenges and contests. The "child was surrounded by expanding concentric circles of people who cared for him or her." This included the nuclear family, which "assumed basic guidance," as well as the extended family. Next came the "clan or lineage groupings." Instruction, therefore, represented a "community" responsibility.[4]

The educational process dominated childhood, yet, in addition to it being "a time of learning and a time of testing," childhood also included play, "from tobogganing and games of tag and wrestling to foot races, hoop games, ball games, and swimming—as well as play which centered on imitating adult life." Puberty marked the onset of adulthood. Rituals involving years of preparation symbolized this transition. For example, "the length of initiation varied among the eastern or Rio Grande pueblos. At San Juan, it lasted for four days, while at Taos the boys' training spanned a period of a year and half. During this time, boys were separated from their homes and lived in the kiva, where they were trained by spiritual leaders."[5]

Examples illustrate the connection between the specific tribal culture and education. Iroquois parents stressed the "autonomous individual, loyal to the group but independent and aloof." With power equally shared among men and women, young and old, Iroquois children also learned an egalitarian notion of social interaction, not hierarchical in a European sense. Furthermore, they did not hold private property and material wealth to be supreme. Iroquois parents also proved to be "permissive" and tolerant, avoiding "harsh physical punishment." Children basically followed adult examples.[6]

Cherokee parents used reason to "guide" their children, also avoiding harshness and authoritarianism. For historian David DeJong, "among the Cherokees, the unwillingness to exercise authority in dealing with their children was but a natural consequence of their intense love of liberty." They ensured an "orderly" society and government through kindness to their children and others. Since the Cherokee, like the Iroquois, maintained a matrilineal culture, fathers rarely participated in the educational process. "The mother, the maternal uncles, and the old men of the tribe were the child's early mentors." Ridicule represented the only sanction imposed against both wayward children and adults. Otherwise, boys' mentors used praise, ceremony, and symbolism to mark a Cherokee child's learning accomplishments, such as a successful hunt. Girls faced a demanding tribal experience, first assisting in housekeeping work and then assuming agricultural duties.[7]

In sum, Native Americans maintained clear educational goals, philosophy, and practices. The reluctance to use corporal punishment, or its total absence, stemmed from fundamental cultural beliefs, as historian Margaret Szasz points out: "Because most native cultures idealized the ability to withstand pain, it was logical that they should weave this societal ideal into their patterns for child rearing. Thus, a youth's ability to endure pain and suffering without flinching was almost universally touted as a sign of maturity."[8] One way male youths learned to endure pain was by remaining submerged neck deep in an ice-cold stream or lake, under an elder's supervision. However, the lack of corporal punishment did not mean there was a lack of discipline. Delaware children received "a dash of cold water in the face, a ducking in the stream, or a rubbing of the tongue with a bitter root."[9] Parents resorted to other means, like the supernatural, to control the behavior of young children. They spread the belief that creatures, such as the screech owl, "carried away naughty children." Ridicule, as with the Cherokee, also proved to be a common practice. Szazs has described how this occurred among the Blackfeet:

> If a Blackfeet youth committed an ill advised act, the incident became the subject of community verbal abuse. Shouted from one tipi at night, the story was picked up and repeated by a chorus of voices until the night reverberated with the sound; and the youth compelled to remain hidden until he had completed some great feat to erase the memory of his disgrace.

This public humiliation usually produced the desired effect on the mortified individual, with little backsliding. Native American parents also employed positive incentives. "A Yakima boy was given a feast in honor of his first deer; a Wishram girl gave away her first significant gathering of huckleberries to the old women of the community called together for the occasion." In these cases, the family and the tribe validated a child's acquisition of economic skills. In other cases, the tribe conferred honors with a new name, which held spiritual power. "Particular clans among the Creek owned war titles, which were assigned to men in recognition of their bravery."[10]

European Influences

European contact prompted a gradual yet profound transformation in traditional Native American educational goals, philosophy, and practices. The colonists simplistically viewed

Native American culture and education as inferior and savage and attempted acculturation. As historian James Axtell asserts, European colonists, especially in New England,
attempted to "remake" the Native American "in their own image through the time-honored
but formal institutions of English education—the church, the school, and the college."[11]
Few Native Americans accepted this strategy, with most resisting in order to preserve their
tribal cultures. Ethnocentrism appeared to be as strong among Native Americans as it was
among the colonists. Europeans successfully recruited some Native American students, but
they coerced others. Although the French appeared to be tolerant and benign, English and
Spanish colonials kidnapped Native American children, "indoctrinating them in the rigors
of English culture or the complexities of Spanish theology."

What drove European educational efforts among Native Americans was religious zeal.
In the Spanish Southwest, Franciscan missionaries labored at converting Native
Americans, stressing farming skills rather than academic knowledge. French Jesuit missionaries working in the Great Lakes region, the Mississippi valley, and along the
St. Lawrence River used a more subtle approach, cultivating a rapport with various tribes
yet stressing religious training. The Dutch sought only economic relationships, "ignoring
conversion efforts and avoiding integration with the Indians."

Institutionalized European education clashed with Native American child-rearing
practices in every way. As DeJong summarizes it,

> Concepts such as individualism, competition, and time—all of which were foreign to most
> Indian communities—were thrust upon the Indian students along with Europeans' man-
> ners and styles of clothing and hair dress. Educational methods, such as the use of the
> written word, daily classroom routine, and indoor study, soon became a burden to many
> Indian students, who were used to oral tradition and experiential learning. Moreover, the
> Europeans attempted to change the Indian's spiritual orientation.

Worse yet, this educational experience proved to have few, if any, benefits for Native
American students. Such "educated Indians" rarely found employment among Europeans,
except as servants or maids, and often "reverted" to their "former habits and customs."
Nevertheless, in a relative sense, the English proved to be the most successful in training
Native American children, while the French, Spanish, and Dutch appeared to be "less
interested in educating the Indians than in acculturating, converting, and exploiting
them."[12]

Along the Atlantic seacoast, European efforts to educate Native Americans lacked any
uniform pattern and usually followed the general attitude toward schooling in each colony,
as Szasz has pointed out. New England, which maintained the "strongest area of formal
schooling in colonial America, also opened the greatest number of Indian schools." The
South, specifically the Carolinas and Georgia, sponsored "the fewest number of schools
and the highest rate of illiteracy" and likewise rarely created schools for Native
Americans.[13] In Virginia's Tidewater region, religion was the center of cultural conflict
between the English settlers and Algonquians. The English there failed to establish any formal schooling for Virginia's Tidewater natives during the seventeenth century. However,
after Virginia colonials brutally subdued the Algonquian uprisings of 1622 and 1644, as
well as the 1676 Bacon's Rebellion, Governor Alexander Spotswood, demanded, beginning
in 1711, two children from each tribe as hostages to extract promises of peace and enrolled
them at the Brafferton School for Native American Students at the College of William and

Mary. "Many of the children in the boarding [school] facilities perished from the changed environment, diet, and manner of living; disease was always prevalent."[14]

Pennsylvania's Moravian missionary efforts best illustrate attempts to educate Native Americans in the Middle Colonies and also reveal a historical irony. The Moravian approach involved "total immersion" to assimilate Native Americans.[15] To this end, they established agricultural settlements, complete with mills, shops, and a school. The Christianized Native Americans who inhabited them even dressed like European colonists. To all intents and purposes, these European conversion and educational efforts appeared to be quite effective. However, frustrated by brutal Native American raids during Pontiac's War, "fifty-seven armed settlers," on December 15, 1764, sought revenge and attacked one such peaceful village at Conestoga Manor near Lancaster. These "Paxton Boys," as they called themselves, shot and hacked the unsuspecting and innocent villagers and rode away to celebrate their victory. Later, on March 6, 1782, as a reprisal against Native American attacks on the frontier, 160 unsympathetic and indiscriminate Pittsburgh militiamen, some of them former Paxton Boys, descended upon another missionized Native American village, called Gnadenhutten, in the Ohio country, along the Muskingum River. They massacred approximately 100 men, women, and children there. Two boys escaped and warned the inhabitants of Schoenbrunn, another Moravian settlement. These episodes revealed, as DeJong argues, that European acculturation did not imply assimilation, guarantee tolerance, or abate violence.[16]

In 1644, the Massachusetts Bay Colony passed a law encouraging Native Americans "to attend religious services on Sundays." However, John Eliot's famous "praying villages" best characterized this first period. Eliot began his missionary work converting Native Americans as soon as he arrived in 1631. He, like "most of the Puritan missionaries believed that Algonquian culture was totally devoid of 'civilization.' His persistence achieved substantial inroads. "Between 1651 and 1674, he founded fourteen praying villages radiating outward from Boston toward western Massachusetts and Connecticut." Each village stressed farming skills and supported a school with a Native American schoolmaster. Eliot also relied on a largely bilingual approach, printing his "Indian Bible" as well as other works in the Algonguin language.

In 1675, a variety of Native American tribes in New England united to drive European colonists off their land. King Philip's War, according to Szasz, "served as a rough dividing line between the two eras in New England schooling." It ended in a bloody defeat of the tribes involved and virtually obliterated the praying villages. Thereafter, educational efforts between the 1690s and 1730s relied on blatant Anglicization, since English colonists "viewed language as an integral expression of culture." They therefore gave the Algonquians a double dose of education, through Christianity and the English language. Such educational efforts also became official colonial policy. In the spring of 1717, the General Assembly of Connecticut "passed a measure declaring that the Indians falling under their jurisdiction should be gathered into villages, encouraged to farm, and taught Christianity." Finally, the Connecticut colony subsidized a modest schoolhouse, opened in 1726 and run by missionaries, boarding Mohegan children.[17] In this and other schooling efforts, DeJong asserts, New England colonists attempted to usurp the authority of the Native American family, the heart of the educational process, by marginalizing and ultimately manipulating it. Some colonists proposed boarding schools in order to eliminate Native American parents altogether. This practice represented the "forerunner of the nineteenth-century outing system, in which Indian children were distributed among white families for the purpose of 'civilizing' them."[18]

Between the 1730s and 1760s, missionaries opened numerous schools to educate Native Americans throughout New England and the Middle Colonies. The Great Awakening, an evangelical movement among Protestant sects, gave impetus to these schooling efforts. Eleazar Wheelock, a strong proponent of the Great Awakening, founded and ran the Moor's Charity School in Lebanon, Connecticut, between 1754 and 1759. It became the most active and publicized Native American school, and, when relocated to Hanover, New Hampshire, it "formed the nucleus for Dartmouth College."[19] His paternalistic approach maintained two "missionary goals," as Axtell points out, "to save the Indians from themselves and to save the English from the Indian. The best way to accomplish both was, as [Wheelock] stated so facilely, to turn the Indians into Englishmen." Wheelock's boarding school removed children from their Native American parents. Boys were trained to return to their tribes as "preachers, teachers, and interpreters of the English way." Thus, like John Eliot, Wheelock wanted his students to convert other Native Americans and act as agents of civilization. His coeducational emphasis required that girls be "apprenticed to local women" to become literate and learn European domestic skills.[20]

Boys in Wheelock's school faced an intense daily regimen. They began each day with a prayer and catechism and "remained in the classroom until noon, where they received a classical training in Latin and Greek, and sometimes Hebrew." They worked for several hours during the afternoon. "Just before dark, they attended evening prayers and public worship, and then studied until bedtime." This rigid routine only varied on Sundays, "when they spent the day in meetings and catechism classes." Native American boys chafed under this demanding and overbearing approach and protested by misbehaving or running away. Wheelock became disappointed with the girls as well. As Szasz writes, he "provided these girls with a practical skill, minimum reading and writing ability and a Calvinist view of life, but he failed to convince them that they should adopt the cultural traits of his own people."[21]

Therefore, the early colonial boarding school concept, that is, the removal of Native American children from their parents, largely failed. Native American parents, "especially the Iroquois," objected to the traditional, harsh English methods of education employed by Wheelock. Axtell summarizes this resentment: "The sting of the rod was perhaps the sharpest indignity the Indians suffered, but it was not the only one nor the worst. The school's work program aimed at teaching the boys in play time to farm, seemed to the boys little more than an elaborate ruse for getting the master's chores done at no expense." In addition to feeling exploited, Wheelock's students objected to his ethnocentric prejudices, which constantly demeaned his Native American charges and fell "clearly into the category of racism."[22] Finally, the effects of traditional Native American education endured; this, "the learning acquired at Moor's School was merely superimposed on their earlier education." In spite of this limited impact, the boarding school approach not only continued but, as we shall see, became official federal policy during the nineteenth century.[23]

In sum, the traditional Native American child-rearing process, while seemingly casual, was constant, pervasive, and effective. Colonial education efforts largely failed due to Native American resistance. In this matter, they acted as other cultural groups have. Religion and language serve as the pillars of any culture. Alter either of these, and that culture will experience profound change, if not disappear altogether. The historical contest between dominant and subordinate cultural groups usually centers on these two elements. In lieu of physical eradication, the best way for a majority group to erase a subgroup's culture, or to assert its authority over that subgroup, is to transform its religion or language, or both, through an education process. Conversely, the best strategy a minority group can use to preserve its culture is to protect its religion or language by resisting the dominant group's educational process or institution. This was precisely what Native Americans did. As Axtell concludes, "by the close of the colonial period, very few if any Indians had been transformed into civilized Englishmen."[24]

Cultural Barter

Nevertheless, early Native American tribes, while preserving their own cultures, learned from European colonists. "When the Iroquois combined European guns and Native-American tactics to smash the Hurons, they controlled their own culture and chose which elements of European culture to incorporate, which to modify, which to ignore." This "syncretic" process extended to languages as well, with Native Americans learning Spanish, English, French, or Dutch, often becoming proficient in two of the languages. "British colonists sometimes used Natives as interpreters when dealing with the Spanish or French, not just with other Native-American nations."[25]

The educational process was two-way, for Europeans learned a great deal from Native Americans. The education of the Puritans represents a case in point. "The Indian served as a teacher to the New English in three guises: as neighbor (their hospitable welcomer and unihibited visitor), as warrior (their mortal enemy or supportive comrade in arms), and as example (a tempting model of a different way of life)." Squanto taught the colonists vital agricultural information, and they absorbed many Native American place names, labels (moose, skunk, and racoon), and "cultural artifacts" such as moccasins, hominy, and toboggans into their language and culture. New Englanders, furthermore, gradually incorporated "Indian warfare" tactics, learning to rely on stealth.[26]

Many Europeans also chose to live among Native Americans or adopted their lifestyle. "Hernando de Soto had to post guards to keep his men and women from defecting to Native societies."[27] In New England, Axtell says that "beside the doleful failure of English education to 'civilize' and Christianize the Indians stands the impressive success with which the Indians converted the English to their 'barbarous' way of living." His thesis maintains that Native Americans "were not only proficient in educating their own children without resorting to physical compulsion or emotional undercutting, but also in converting enemies—Indian and white, young and old—to their way of life."

The education process for Europeans captured by Native Americans involved total immersion in Native American culture and ways. The captors immediately gave their European prisoners moccasins and snowshoes to facilitate travel through rough terrain and shared food to ensure their survival. The captors, as they entered the village, painted their prisoners' faces. "Belts of wampum were hung around their necks, Indian clothes were substituted for English, and the men and boys had their hair plucked or shaved in Indian fashion." This "physical transformation" proved to be effective. The prisoners immediately joined in the tribe's victory celebration, singing and dancing. The initiation rite followed, which involved purging "whiteness," through running the gauntlet and bathing, culminating with the adoption ceremony. "Most young captives assumed the places of Indian sons and daughters." Their new families welcomed them by presenting gifts. These new tribal members were treated with equality and "given freedom of movement within and without the Indian villages." Young children rarely took more than a few months to learn and adopt tribal language and customs. "Since the Indians generally assumed that whites were physically inferior to themselves, captive boys were often prepared for the hardy life of hunters and warriors by a rigorous program of physical training."[28]

Thousands of captured Christian New Englanders remained with their "pagan" Native American captors, or, what was worse in the eyes of Puritan ministers, became Roman Catholics when sold in French Canada. "Between 1689 and 1713, the years of heaviest Indian depredation along the northern and eastern frontiers of New England, about 600 men, women, and children were taken by the Indians and less frequently the French and marched northward into captivity." Only 29 percent chose to return to New England. They abandoned Puritan life, embracing "Indianization," as Axtell terms it, for several reasons. First, they saw Native Americans as more moral than their New England compatriots. Second, Native Americans, unlike their European counterparts, completely integrated captives into their families and tribes through adoption, creating a "social bond." Third, and most important, converted colonists preferred Native American life because they found freedom from the oppressive conformity of Puritan society.[29] Loewen adds that "women were accorded more status and power in most Native societies than in white societies, which white women noted with envy." He also asserts that Native American culture appealed to many Europeans because it lacked a clear hierarchy. "Although leadership was substantially hereditary in some nations, most Indian societies north of Mexico were much more democratic than Spain, France, or England in the seventeenth and eighteenth centuries." Indianization, therefore, represented a common experience among Europeans both early on and later, as thousands—among them, Daniel Boone—adopted many facets of native lifestyle.[30]

Nevertheless, for DeJong, colonial educational activities among Native Americans became a grim legacy. With charitable donations and government grants to subsidize missionary endeavors, the stage was set for an eventual centralized federal education policy for Native Americans. In virtually all cases, education became acculturation. The teaching of the Christian religion and basic literacy was purposefully designed to obliterate tribal customs, a process began when the colonists adopted the boarding school concept.[31] Formal, institutionalized European learning would eventually supplant the informal and naturalistic family-centered approach of Native American education.

EDUCACIÓN EN NUEVO ESPAÑA

The North American Spanish frontier, known as the Borderlands, stretched from Florida to Texas and westward to California, although Spanish explorers had explored and mapped the entire Atlantic seacoast. The European history of the Borderlands began on Easter Sunday in 1513 when Juan Ponce de León, who had conquered and governed Puerto Rico, landed in present-day Florida and named it *Pascua Florida*. After several failed attempts, Hernando de Soto established another temporary colony in *Las Floridas* in 1539. His North American explorations during the next three years, before his death, also covered parts of modern-day Georgia, the Carolinas, Arkansas, Mississippi, and Tennessee. The

Spanish ultimately established permanent villages in Florida through the relentless and often brutal military tactics in the 1560s and 1570s of Don Pedro Menéndez de Avilés, who murdered the French inhabitants of a tiny fort and subdued various Native American tribes, and through the devout and redoubtable conversion efforts of the Franciscan friars. These colonies never attracted many eager settlers, but the western Borderlands did, although slowly at first. Between 1540 and 1542, Spanish conquistadores led by Francisco Vásquez de Coronado explored much of the Southwest. In 1542, Juan Rodríquez Cabrillo, explored the California coast, sailing as far north as Oregon. Juan de Oñate colonized New Mexico in 1598. He at first persuaded Native Americans to accept Spanish rule but eventually resorted to enforced fealty.[32]

The Spanish, relying heavily on the crown's authority and royal edicts as well as its whims, took a serious and ponderous approach to settling and governing their vast colony. "The frontier was carefully planned, minutely organized, and regularly oversupervised," in contrast to the largely laissez-faire approach that dominated the later Anglo westward movement into this territory, according to John Francis Bannon's historical analysis, and "conversion, if possible assimilation, of the Native American was a Spanish aim of almost equal importance to wealth-gathering and other secular advantage."

Jesuits led the "Christianization-civilization process" in California throughout the 1590s, and the Franciscans in the rest of the western Borderlands and Florida well into the 1600s. "Most, if not all, of the Borderlands were mission frontiers." Franciscans introduced missions throughout New Mexico in the West, and Alabama, Florida, Georgia, and South Carolina in the Southeast. The friars attempted to convert Native Americans, teach them literacy, and acculturate them. This pattern in many ways prefigured English colonial efforts among Native Americans along the Atlantic seacoast. "From the beginning of Spanish occupation, the Spaniards, friars and officials, had made a concerted effort to stamp out traditional Indian beliefs and religious practices." In 1612, Friar Francisco del Pareja published the first bilingual catechism, in Castilian and Timucuan, printed in Mexico City. Others soon followed.

Like their eastern counterparts later on, Native American tribes in New Mexico resented this acculturation effort. After years of forced labor, enslavement, abuse, exploitation, domination, and cultural obliteration, the Native Americans fought back. Following a series of minor armed eruptions in Florida and New Mexico, the Pueblos united to wage a serious and major revolt in 1680, which marked a turning point on the Spanish frontier. Through a carefully planned and coordinated military operation, the Pueblos drove some 1,000 Spaniards from Santa Fe; ultimately, all Spanish colonists in the New Mexican territory retreated to the Rio Grande River. This uprising represented the only reversal to European colonial expansion on the North American continent. After liberating the territory, the Pueblos purged Spanish culture as well, including language, customs, buildings, and, of course, Christianity.

But after colonial diversions and royal delays, the *reconquista* began in 1692. Diego de Vargas struck out from El Paso and reconquered New Mexican territory. By 1694, by means of brutal military tactics and mass baptizings of Pueblos, Vargas occupied Santa Fe. He likewise quelled another, smaller Pueblo revolt in 1696. The Spanish had finally and permanently secured a peaceful New Mexico, and by 1767 the "Spanish frontier had reached its limits into the Borderlands in all areas save California, whose occupation was still several years into the future."[33]

Religion, Family, and Education

With a peaceful northern Spanish frontier, the process of educating Native Americans unfolded in earnest. Both informally and formally, the Spanish attacked the basis of Native American culture: religion and language. Spanish officials maintained a rigid allegiance to Western heritage and Roman Catholicism and flogged or sentenced to servitude any Native American who reverted to tribal culture.

Conversion

The colonial Spanish based their education on a caste system that reflected racial and social position. Spain instituted a "racialization" policy first and foremost. The Spanish Roman Catholic Church used formal schools with a traditional approach and the doctrina "to acculturate and evangelize the Indians." The first elementary school opened in Mexico City in 1523.[34] By 1744, friars had either introduced or "reestablished missions in most of the pueblos" throughout New Mexico. In Santa Fe, the daily regimen for Native American children consisted of attending mass, reciting the catechism, reading the Scripture, and singing hymns. Latin served as the language of instruction. The educational process involved attendance at mass on Saturdays and Sundays as well. Yet this "institutional" approach remained haphazard, relying solely on the narrow talents and infrequent availability of a teaching friar.[35] Furthermore, after 1575 the doctrina, a less institutional approach to catechizing Native American children, became the main system of education because Spanish colonials chose not to invest too many resources in the children. Franciscans focused more on the memorization of prayers and less on literacy. Thus, in many cases, natives could recite their prayers perfectly but could neither read nor write.

Roman Catholic missionaries also converted and acculturated Native Americans by creating "Christian rancherios." "This conversion process, in some cases, took months or years; however, the transformation of Indian villages into Christian rancherios occurred only after the Indians voluntarily agreed to be baptized, to adapt to Spanish customs—that is, to believe in Catholic doctrines, to speak Spanish, and to wear Spanish clothing—and to register the rancherios in the presidios as ally settlements." This system further required that Native American tribes send a male youth as a hostage to the mission, a policy similar to that followed in the English colonies on the Atlantic seaboard.[36]

La Familia

Among Spanish colonists, the nuclear family served as the principal educational institution, teaching the rudiments of literacy and conveying cultural values. The family also took responsibility for vocational skills. Apprenticeship training, as we shall see, involved a formal contract between the boy's father and the artisan, and literacy became the main requirement for this training. Literacy remained the primary educational goal by far, but it served as a means to an end, since it facilitated religious instruction. Relying on signatures on enlistment records, historian Bernardo Gallegos estimates that the literacy rate in colonial New Mexico reached approximately 33 percent by the early 1800s, with Santa Fe boasting a much higher rate. He concludes that "if we assume . . . that there was not a consistent drive for schooling throughout the period, the rate is not remarkably low." Informal education proved to be effective, given the scarce resources on the colonial Spanish frontier.

Nevertheless, according to Gallegos, the teaching of literacy was a two-edged sword. On the one hand, it served as an acculturating mechanism throughout New Spain, that is, friars used it to not only eradicate Native American culture but to preserve Spanish heritage among the colonials, which usually entailed nothing more than reciting prayers and learning and memorizing Roman Catholic doctrine. The Spanish clergy believed that too much literacy spelled danger and consciously limited knowledge. "In the Spanish colonies, it was the Inquisition which had charge of maintaining religious hegemony, and thus keeping a check on the possible misuses of literacy." After 1569, the Inquisition controlled religious orthodoxy by censoring reading materials exported to New Spain, restricting theatrical performances, and indicting heretical colonial writers. The clergy remained committed, in short, to obliterating heresy among Spanish colonials at any cost, including the manipulation of knowledge. For Native Americans, this largely focused on the "Hispanicization" process.[37]

Schooling

Formal education appeared to be rare in New Spain because of the crude frontier conditions, scattered settlements, and scarce resources. It also adhered to the rigid caste system. Children of Spanish officials attended private mission schools, paying a fee, or were sent to schools in the "interior of Mexico, a form of private school unavailable to the commoner." The first formal school in Texas, which opened in San Antonio in 1746, was both private and Roman Catholic.[38]

Girls rarely, if ever, attended school. Roman Catholic convents represented the only educational opportunities for girls in New Spain. The convent experience was neither an uncomfortable nor deprived life by some accounts. For girls, "education was not universally bestowed but mostly limited to the aristocratic classes." **Mestizas** received some education while "*Indias* probably received little, if any, formal education."[39]

In 1793, a royal decree "ordered local governments in the Southwest to establish public schools." These were to be compulsory and funded by a combination of taxation and private fees. In 1803, Texas established compulsory attendance. "Although Texas required school attendance, resources were scarce and there were more students than there were schools in which to teach them." The educational record in the rest of New Spain proved to be equally uneven, if not haphazard. The 1793 decree appeared to be most successful in California, which established five public schools within five years. However, as in Texas, school supplies, such as slates, paper, and books, remained scarce. No public schools existed in Arizona. By 1812, the Spanish crown had abolished caste restrictions in all walks of life, except for African American slaves, and "public education was to be made available to all free children, irrespective of their parents' ability to pay."[40] New Mexico sponsored public schools in the early 1800s only after being prodded by Spain. The first opened at the Santa Fe presidio for the children of soldiers and officers. According to Gallegos, by 1812, public schools existed in Albuquerque, Taos, Belar, San Miguel, and Santa Cruz. However, the term *public* remained broadly defined, meaning that public funds subsidized the salary of the teacher or, more often, supported a priest-instructor. "In Santa Fe, the teacher was paid 500 pesos a year; in Albuquerque and Santa Cruz, 300 pesos a year; and the rest were paid 250 pesos a year." As in the rest of the Spanish frontier, instructional materials remained "scarce." Schools primarily relied on missals and catechisms for reading materials.

In sum, Spanish colonials largely relied on military might, the family, and Roman Catholic clergy, not schooling, to maintain and spread their culture under frontier conditions. The Borderlands remained fragile nonetheless. English traders and raiders, competing for North American land and wealth, encouraged natives to revolt against the Spanish in Florida. English colonists from the Carolinas also launched numerous attacks on Spanish missions and forts in Florid. By the early 1700s, therefore, the Spanish maintained only precarious control over Florida.[41]

Literacy had a very limited role in New Spain and a sustained drive for formal schooling never materialized. Many of the educational practices and institutions used by Spanish colonials were also used in other European settlements in North America. This was not surprising since these colonists, regardless of where they settled on the North American continent, brought their European traditions, including education, with them.

THE EDUCATIONAL MOSAIC OF THE ATLANTIC SEACOAST

The colonies along the Atlantic seacoast had a variety of educational approaches, and colonial New England in particular profoundly influenced subsequent educational philosophies and practices. According to historian Gary Nash, "the initial arrival of the Pilgrims on the western edge of the Atlantic in 1620 marked the beginning of a movement of English Protestantism whose ideas, values, and institutions did more to shape the contours of colonial society than any other groups."[42]

This section first addresses "community-building by the Puritans and their communitarian values" and how these beliefs shaped and influenced their social institutions and daily behavior. It focuses on the family, the "key institution in socializing the individual within the Puritan community."[43] Second, it highlights the role of religion as a source of values and the church as an educational institution. Third, it analyzes how the educational configuration operated during this period, stressing the tight bonds between the family, church, and schools in Puritan New England.

The Puritans maintained a clear vision of their community, seeing themselves as a corporal body of believers. As Governor John Winthrop proclaimed in 1630:

1. First, this loue among Christians is a reall thing not Imaginarie.
2ly. This loue is as absolutely necessary to the being of the body of Christ, as the sinewes and other ligaments of a naturall body are to the being of that body.
3ly. This loue is a divine spirituall nature free, actiue strong Couragious permanent vnder valueing all things . . . .
4ly. It restes in the loue and wellfare of its beloued, for the full and certaine knowledge of these truthes concerning the nature vse, [and] excellency of this grace, that which the holy ghost left recorded . . . .

Winthrop likened the Puritan community to a single "body" with "sinewes" and "ligaments," painting a clear picture of a group of believers working in concert. In this setting, conformity and consensus became all-important. He also alluded to the source of all knowledge, the Bible, thus narrowly and dogmatically defining knowledge. Finally, this community existed in a sea of iniquity, and Puritans self-righteously declared themselves, in Winthrop's words, "as a City upon a Hill, the eies of all people are upon us."[44] Hence, New England society served, not very humbly, as a model for all others to emulate.

How would the Puritans preserve as well as expand this ideal world? "Convinced that man [sic] was fallen and could be saved from endless damnation only by the infusion of god's grace—a gift he vouchsafed only to the elect—the Puritans sought a knowledge inseparable from faith and a faith inseparable from regeneration and saintly conduct."[45] Religious training and education appeared to be synonymous and permeated the moral and cultural development of the child. "Life was deadly serious, predestination inhumanly grim, and New England prepared its children accordingly."[46] What is crucial to grasping this context and in analyzing the resulting educational process is that the Puritans saw children as inherently evil and naturally "wayward," carrying Adam's original sin with them. "Through the diaries of many Puritan parents runs a common note of concern for their children's spiritual health, of worry at times that their children might be too cheerful and carefree."[47]

The Colonial Family

The family served as the fundamental unit in Puritan society. The migration from Europe to New England consisted largely of nuclear families. And in Puritan society the Scriptures were regarded in a literal sense, as God's inflexible prescriptions for human behavior. The Fifth Commandment, "honor thy father and mother . . . ," was the key and had far-reaching repercussions. It was taken to mean obedience to all superiors, in the family, in society, and, of course, in the church, where ultimate authority of the minister represented God's preordained order. Thus, a sin committed by an individual automatically cast guilt upon the entire community of believers. And a sin committed by a child naturally reflected on the family. The enormous responsibility for the child's conversion initially fell on parents' shoulders, which was not a unique role, reflecting as it did traditional European practice. However, this responsibility became intensified in the crude and rudimentary conditions of early New England settlements.

Puritan family structure followed typical Western patterns, stressing nuclear arrangements. Most colonial households claimed six or more members by the late seventeenth century, including parents, children, apprentices, servants, and slaves, although the majority of families lacked servants or slaves. Everyone in Puritan New England "had" to live in a family. "If a single man could not afford to hire servants and so set up a household of 'family' of his own, he was obliged to enter another family, either as a servant or as a boarder, subjecting himself to the domestic government of its head."[48]

In this patriarchal setting, the father served as the "governor" and "priest" of the family. All mates came from within the congregation and had the same social status. Once the couple formally married, the wife forfeited all property to her husband, with his home becoming her sole responsibility. Although she remained totally submissive to her husband, this type of relationship often did not deteriorate into cruel or abusive treatment. Their relationship remained reserved, avoiding effusive displays of emotion and passion. The paternal parent also assumed chief responsibility for secular and religious instruction as well as for social matters. He approved the marriages of his children and determined the division of property among his children at his death.[49] Generally speaking, this familial role proved to be quite common along the colonial seacoast. " 'Puritan' fathers of seventeenth-century New England were not indistinguishable from their counterparts in the southern colonies or along the Appalachian frontier. . . ."[50]

Nevertheless, within this strict institution of marriage, divorce did occur. In fact, America's propensity for divorce, a civil matter according to Puritan theologians, dates back to this period; the first recorded divorce, because of bigamy, occurred in 1639. To be sure, divorces grew out of other reasons. Some displeased ministers forced couples to marry because of premarital fornication and/or pregnancy, a not uncommon occurrence. Beginning as they did, these unions often ended in separation. In other cases, spousal abuse, adultery, and desertion served as catalysts for separation. These situations, according to the Puritans, produced social instability, which the dissolution of such unhappy marriages could rectify. New England had the highest divorce rate; divorce appeared to be less common in the Middle Colonies, which gradually developed a system of marital separation as this period progressed; and seemed to be totally absent in the largely Anglican Southern Colonies. However, by the time of the American Revolution, a clear custom of divorce had emerged in the majority of the colonies. In the post-Revolutionary era, spousal breakups certainly conformed to American notions of "democracy and individualism." But in spite of present-day periodic handwringing over this nation's divorce rate, the American family has remained intact and vital.[51]

Family Education

According to Axtell, the Puritan family operated as "a little church and a little commonwealth"; the family served, in short, as a little school. By the "clergy's own admission, the home was supreme." The family taught literacy, transmitted religious morals, and oversaw vocational training. "In colonial New England the child's world, like his parents, was a tightly ordered, highly reticulated organism." Law validated the family's central position, and the courts enforced it. In 1649, the Massachusetts General Court issued a law that condemned to death any son, older than sixteen, who was "STUBBORNE or REBELLIOUS." The historical record indicates that no colonial magistrates actually executed any such insubordinate children, but in 1664 they ordered young John Porter to the gallows, placed a noose around his neck for an hour, removed it and whipped him, and finally imprisoned him for his persistent disobedient and disrespectful behavior toward his parents. This intimidation proved to be effective since he enthusiastically repented.

The educational experience began as soon as possible, with parents bringing their infants to church within days of birth, in spite of the risk from inclement weather, for baptism. The baptismal name, such as Hannah and Prudence for girls and Joseph and Solomon for boys, itself assumed religious symbolism. "Parental feelings and expectations were frequently expressed in such names as Truegrace, Reform, Hoped For, Promise, More Mercy, Restore, Preserved, Thanks, Desire, Hope, Joy, Rejoice, Patience, and Love." Training was by parental instruction through daily "piecemeal moralizing." Children also experienced public preaching in towns as they accompanied their parents or ran errands, both reinforcing and deepening their religious knowledge. Children also participated in regular and frequent family prayer and worship. Literacy became necessary for every individual in order to read and interpret the Bible, in the best Protestant tradition. It was read aloud to young children at the dinner table.[52] According to historian John Demos, "there was no idea that each generation required separate spheres of work or recreation. Children learned the behavior appropriate to their sex and station by sharing in the activities of their parents." And education was not confined to spiritual or vocational topics—even in this religiously dogmatic setting, sexual conversations proved to be frank and detailed in front of children.

Literacy Training.   Although males during early colonial times appeared to be more literate than females, some equity was achieved by the post-Revolutionary period. Between 1650 and 1670, 60 percent of adult males and 33 percent of females in colonial New England were able to write. However, female literacy gradually increased as their participation in church affairs expanded and male church attendance waned. Furthermore, virtually all females could read, and by the 1780s, some 80 percent of women could write, as well. Generally speaking, this society deemphasized the formal education of women because it viewed them as intellectually inferior and morally vulnerable, carrying the sin of Eve with them.[53] Literacy only served as a means to an end, that is, to facilitate religious training.

The Inculcation of Values.   The catechism experience began in the home and was conducted at least once a week, usually on Sunday, and continued there until the child was seven or eight years of age. At that point, older children received their catechism training at church, where girls and boys were separated. This informal home experience failed to produce a uniform degree of inculcation, as Axtell points out:

> Catechizing brought into the church a highly variable group of children, both in knowledge and age. In 1676, for example, 173 "children" of ages stretching from seven to thirty-one, presented themselves to the First Church in Dorchester for instruction. There were 88 under twelve, 85 over twelve, and 35 over twenty years of age, all groups evenly divided between girls and boys.[54]

Training in the catechism appeared to be standard and straightforward. Families and congregations had over 500 different catechisms at their disposal, and these maintained a rigid question-and-answer format. The *Young Child's Catechism*, by Isaac Watts, was commonly used with three- and four-year-old children: "Have you learnt to know who God is? What must you do to escape God's Anger, which your Sins have deserved?" Another question, with its prescribed answer, was the following:

Q: What must become of you if you are wicked?
A: If I am wicked, I shall be sent down to everlasting Fire in Hell among wicked and miserable creatures.

Initially the child usually memorized the entire catechism, drilled by parents and elders. Probing questions to gauge in-depth understanding followed in later years. For the most part, and in spite of highly irregular training, catechizing ended at sixteen years of age, when a test for church membership was conducted.[55]

Work.   Parents also guided their children's vocational pursuits. Regardless of location, the entire colonial seacoast operated largely as a "small-scale" agricultural society. Children thus worked from a young age, often assuming farm chores as early as seven.[56] In towns, parents assumed responsibility for their children's work pursuits through apprenticeship arrangements, as we have seen. Apprenticeship represented a direct relationship between families, children, and work, with the master craftsman serving as a "co-parent."[57] This indentured relationship traditionally lasted for seven years, beginning at fourteen years of age. "The most important elements in the contract were the youngster's promise to serve the master in all lawful commands and capacities over a stipulated period of time and the master's promise in turn to teach the youngster the arts and mysteries associated with a particular craft or trade."[58] This arrangement implied systematic and comprehensive instruction in the workplace, with the young apprentice residing with his surrogate family. Historian W. J. Rorabaugh adds that while apprenticeship did not fulfill all of its objectives, "it provided a safe passage from childhood to adulthood in psychological, social, and economic ways for a large number of people over a long period of time."[59] However, in New England, as in the rest of the seacoast colonies, apprenticeship only extended for a few years, as Axtell reports: "Labor in general and skilled labor in particular was scarce, and therefore according to the laws of supply and demand, wages were high, from 30 to 100 percent higher than the wages of contemporary English workmen. During the first half century, poverty was scarce."[60] Regardless of its length, "apprenticeship remained the most common form of craft training."[61]

However ideal all of this may seem, the Puritan family did not always fulfill its educational obligations to the complete satisfaction of religious elders. "New England," Axtell stresses, "felt that the family was in a precipitate decline." In 1648, the Massachusetts General Court passed a law requiring catechism training, and Connecticut followed seven years later. By 1669, frustrated by the family's inability to effectively and consistently catechize children, Boston's religious leaders "empowered" church elders to visit homes and examine the children.[62] Furthermore, as early as the mid-seventeenth century, colonial demographics, interfered with family education. According to Szasz, northern seacoast towns like Boston, Newport, New York, and Philadelphia hosted dense populations, up to 6 percent of the colonial populations creating conditions that eroded the family's ability to instruct its children. "Here, family education was at a disadvantage because it could not compete with the availability of two phenomena: the presence of adequate schools and a thriving industry in trades and crafts."[63] Finally, and generally speaking, the colonial family did not represent a stable institution. "High mortality rates meant that the average length of a marriage was less than a dozen years. One-third to one-half of all children lost at least one parent before the age of twenty-one; in the South, more than half of all children aged thirteen or under had lost at least one parent."[64] Thus, in a relatively short period of time, the church had moved from reinforcing the family to usurping its religious and instructional role.

Religion as Education

The Puritan church maintained an important educational role. A clear and purposeful relationship existed among education, the family, and religion. For Axtell, the church

> . . . provided a form of weekly drama, austere yet sentient, like its congregations. When newspapers were scarce, it was the community center of information and entertainment. In an age which knew the tension of a new printed culture and an older oral one, the

minister was the personal link between the homely conversation of rural New England and the literary sophistication of Boston, New York, and London. Most important, the church was the locus of the deep layer of common values shared by New Englanders, the physical center that gave point and structure to their various lives.[65]

It operated as an educational institution and social center and facilitated a sense of community. The minister served as a "town officer." "He examined the children in the catechism and their knowledge of the Bible, and sometimes questioned them on the sermon of the preceding Sunday." He also visited the schools and prayed with the students. Finally, "the rural minister also often rendered service as a teacher, especially as a teacher of Latin in towns that had no grammar school."[66]

The meetinghouses reflected the rigidity of Puritan society. Seating arrangements separated men, women, and children. Congregations also assigned seating based on social status. But by the early 1700s families began to sit together.[67]

Colonial Schools

Schooling fit into New England's educational configuration but played a complementary role, reinforcing the religious instruction given by the family and the church. According to Axtell, "the educational function of the family began to diminish in the second half of the seventeenth century and was supplemented by other institutions, many of which were new to American society." By the end of the 1600s, schools and masters had accepted responsibility for catechizing, and so schooling assumed both the informal and formal aspects of education.

Dame Schools

The **dame school** emerged as a private venture, a "domestic enterprise," with a local mother, often a widow, caring for children as young as two years old and teaching them some basic literacy.[68] It therefore had two purposes: child care and instruction. The former was an important function, especially during the summer months when everyone, except children younger than six years, worked in the fields. Dame schools also served an academic purpose: "to prepare boys for entry into the district grammar school by starting them on their ABCs and to give girls the basic literacy they would need to fulfill their religious and family duties." The dame schools relied on a basic "curriculum," stressing the alphabet and some simple spelling and religious training. The mother occasionally taught the boys some writing and "perhaps some oral arithmetic illustrated by numbers scratched in the sand of the floor with a stick." While girls certainly learned how to knit and sew in this homey setting, they also mastered reading and writing skills.[69]

Historian Clifton Johnson describes a typical scene in a dame school: "While she heard the smaller pupils recite their letters, and the older ones read and spell from their primers, she busied her fingers with knitting and sewing, and in the intervals between lessons sometimes worked at the spinning-wheel." They often used a hornbook, a paddle-shaped instrument about three inches wide and four inches long holding a printed page covered by a translucent sheet of horn to protect it. This page contained the alphabet, capitals and small letters, vowels, other sound combinations, and occasionally Roman numerals, and concluded with the Lord's Prayer.[70] A Virginian recalled her teacher and experiences in a Norfolk dame school in the 1750s in less-than-romantic terms: "a poor old dame by the name of Mrs. Drudge, and, to be sure, she did drudge to teach me my letters—spelling and reading after a fashion."[71] These mothers often rewarded good behavior with gingerbread but also punished bad behavior by thumping the children's heads with a thimble. In some cases, to deter whispering, they inserted a bridlelike instrument, made from a stick and string, into their student's mouth, and tied it around the poor offender's head.[72] By the mid-1700s, families had begun to relinquish basic literacy instruction to these informal school settings.

In many villages, dame schools represented the only source of elementary instruction. Because of the popularity of the schools, "an increasing number of towns," as historians David Tyack and Elisabeth Hansot point out, "began to underwrite the primary education first of poor children and then of all boys and girls in summer schools taught by women." This "institutional change" proved to be profound because it "blurred two familiar institutions, the family and the school." "Goodwives," or female instructors, eased this transition. They became increasingly popular as teachers since they "cost less" and were more available than male instructors. "Instead of the older practice in which parents bargained on an ad hoc and occasional basis with individual dame-school teachers, towns began to use part of

A typical hornbook. The front is standard, with the alphabet, vowels, and Lord's Prayer, while the back is covered with leather and has an incised image of a figure on horseback. Courtesy of the Blackwell History of Education Museum. Northern Illinois University.

the regular school appropriations to hire women to teach young children while continuing to employ men to instruct the older boys during the winter season." Therefore, according to Tyack and Hansot, the dame school proved to be a complex phenomenon. First, the dame school became the "forerunner of the American public primary school." Second, it hinted at the fully coeducational system that was to come. This simple effort in **coeducation** "made the integration of girls into common schools in the decades after the American Revolution seem part of a gradual evolution rather than a sharp new departure." Third, the dame school introduced the schoolmistress into American education, providing a "foothold" for women to be ultimately and fully integrated into teaching during the nineteenth-century common school era.[73] Finally, the teaching of values in the dame school began a long-term shift in educational institutions, from the family, to the semi-formal dame school setting, and finally to the institutionalization of values in formal school.

The Classroom Setting

New England was the only area in colonial North America where schooling "achieved some degree of consistency."[74] Colonial schooling began to take shape with the Massachusetts school law of 1642 in which the Massachusetts General Court (legislature) expressed concern over the "great neglect of many parents and masters [i.e., artisans] in training up their children in learning, and labor, and other implyments which may be proffitable to the common wealth." It ordered selectmen in each town to oversee the children's literacy training and gave them power to levy "fines for the neglect thereof." In compliance with Puritan culture, the Court stressed the children's need "to read and understand the principles of religion and the capitall lawes of this country." The law, however, did not mention schools; thus, the educational process referred to could occur in families.[75] The Court passed another act, the "old deluder Satan" law, after five frustrating years of, as Axtell expresses it, "trying to place the sole responsibility for education on the family's already stooping shoulders."[76] The 1647 law established the foundation for Massachusetts schools. It required towns of at least fifty families to hire a master, who was to be paid by the parents and the artisans who sent their apprentices. In towns of at least 100 "households," the community had to not only employ a teacher but also "set up a gramer schoole, ye master thereof being able to instruct youth so farr as they may be fitted for ye university [i.e., Harvard College]." Connecticut enacted a similar measure three years later. What is significant is that the community began to assume a larger educational responsibility by subsidizing this formal schooling process.[77]

As Tyack cautions, while these laws "sought to buttress traditional family structure and the system of apprenticeship by requiring compulsory literacy and job training," they did not mandate "compulsory schooling." This distinction is critical: The Puritan community, even as it moved to supplement the family, still regarded the family and the informal education process as supreme. By 1677, the Connecticut, New Haven, and Plymouth colonies had enacted similar statutes. Although some historians have asserted that these acts established the groundwork for the public school system, Tyack offers this important qualification:

> The Puritans' new self-consciousness about the importance of schooling, their cautious new departure in "public" financing and control of schools, prefigured changes to come in American education. But the Puritan achievement in education is inseparable from their

religious world view and from the trials they encountered in establishing a city upon a hill; it is misleading to read present views of public education into the Puritan experiment. The founding of public education as it is known today would stem from a new world view and new trials in the nineteenth century.[78]

Dedham, Massachusetts, became the first town to build and support its school through taxation in 1649, but financial support proved to be largely unstable and varied in other villages. Johnson summarizes this experience:

> The early schools were supported partly by the subscriptions of the well-to-do, partly by the rentals of lands set aside for the purpose, partly by tuition fees, and partly by taxes. . . . Each town in Massachusetts had full control of its own schools, and the people voted in their regular town meetings what they would spend on them, how to raise the money, who should teach, and what should be the amount of compensation.

This crude, haphazard, and irregular approach to school funding caused many communities, in their frugalness, to often seek exemptions or simply scrimp when it came to building schoolhouses, which were usually crude, small, and cramped log cabins. By the early eighteenth century, and because some towns appeared to be unable to meet their financial obligations, "moving schools," which literally traveled to a different vicinity on a regular schedule, were created. "The Massachusetts town of Scituate ordered the school to be kept one-third at each end of the town and one-third in the middle; Yarmouth decided to have the school in five places varying from one to four months each; and in Sutton, where a more scanty education was provided, the school was kept at the discretion of the selectmen in four places, one month each."[79]

Instruction.   Children would assemble for their lessons in the local meetinghouse or in the schoolmaster's home. "Although some of the larger communities provided Latin grammar schools for youths who planned to attend Harvard, the vast majority of towns taught boys only such subjects as reading, writing, and arithmetic." By the middle of the seventeenth century, English grammar schools had largely replaced Latin grammar schools. Many towns constructed a **grammar school** before they built a primary school because residents presumed that children could already read. While eighteenth-century grammar schools continued to teach the classical curriculum, academies, or private secondary schools, offered them competition.[80]

The typical colonial school day droned on with monotonous and tedious drill and rote memorization, motivated by frequent and severe does of corporal punishment. The school rules for Dorchester, Massachusetts, in 1645 explicitly defined the schoolmaster's power to instill correct behavior in his charges:

> The rod of correction is a rule of God necessary sometimes to be used upon the children. The schoolmaster shall have full power to punish all or any of his scholars, no matter who they are. No parent or other person living in the place shall go about to hinder the master in this. But if any parent or others shall think there is just cause for complaint against the master for too much severity, they shall have liberty to tell him so in friendly and loving way.

The ferrule, a three-foot long thick wooden stick, served as the standard instrument of punishment. Some masters liberally used a rattan or cowhide and caning was widely practiced.[81]

Students. The typical schoolboy possessed a "catechism or primer, a Psalter, and a Testament, or a Bible." *The New England Primer*, which first appeared during the late seventeenth century, became the most popular and famous school text during the colonial period. Its structure reflected its English predecessors. It devoted one page to the alphabet, with other pages including word fragments and syllables. "The rest of the book was almost entirely a religious and moral miscellany of verse and prose gathered from all sorts of sources." Even the picture alphabet contained rhymes like: "In Adam's Fall/We sinned all." In "Lessons for Youth," precepts typically warned: "Foolishness is bound up in the Heart of a Child, but the Rod of correction shall drive it from him." The *Primer* achieved virtually universal circulation, with approximately 3 million sold, and appeared in Boston's dame schools as late as 1806. As Johnson concludes: "This humble little primer was a chief tool for making sure that the children, or, as Jonathan Edwards called them, 'young vipers and infinitely more hateful than vipers to God' should grow up into sober and Christian men and women."[82] By today's standards, some of the school child's reading material would be provocative, to say the least. "Eighteenth-century spelling and grammar books routinely used fornication as an example of a four-syllable word, and preachers detailed sexual offenses in astonishingly explicit terms."[83] Classroom pedagogy placed a great deal of responsibility on the student. The catechism required memorization. Students had to study; the schoolmaster merely drilled them. Thus, the burden of learning fell "almost entirely on the students."[84]

Not all students were welcome. Boys entered grammar schools at seven or eight years of age, but girls experienced irregular and infrequent opportunities to participate in formal schooling. Their families provided them with an informal education instead; the dame schools, as we saw earlier, were the only semiformal environment offered. As we shall see, tutors sometimes taught the daughters of prosperous families. In New England, there were a few isolated cases of girls attending grammar school, but in "sexually-segregated settings." "Here and there a town schoolmaster taught a small group of girls before or after the regular boys' sessions in grammar school or at noontime, usually for tuition paid by parents but sometimes for free." Only Quakers sponsored classes and schools for African American children.[85]

Schoolmasters The religious background and general character of teachers, rather than their intellectual ability and preparation, were their key qualifications, and denominational orthodoxy remained foremost, regardless of the colony. In Pennsylvania, the Quakers required membership in the Society of Friends, and "among the Swedes in New Jersey and Delaware, education was largely determined by the church and its ministers." Masters in Virginia and the Carolinas had to demonstrate church affiliation as well. This colonial requirement was a durable legacy. For decades, if not centuries, as we shall see, communities demanded upright and moral teachers; parents often prescribed higher moral standards for their children's instructors than for themselves. Political fidelity represented another requirement for teaching. In 1760, New Jersey's governor mandated that all masters swear allegiance to the crown. Like moral purity, political fealty would be required of American instructors up to and through the twentieth century, with loyalty oaths required as recently as the Cold War era.

While religious and political devotion remained immutable and consistent, the requirements for academic preparation of teachers appeared to be uneven, ranging from bare literacy to a college education. Younger children were the least fortunate. Since they only needed rudimentary knowledge, they usually had teachers who were barely literate. Rural schools "found it difficult to attract and retain competent schoolmasters." Some towns hired the physically handicapped as instructors to provide them with a livelihood. However, as historian Willard Elsbree indicates, some communities insisted on masters with respectable academic preparation, such as Dedham, Massachusetts, which hired only candidates with some college background. "Of sixty-six schoolmasters who taught in Dedham, between 1644 and 1757, thirty-three were graduates of some college and eighteen of these had their master's degrees." Francis Daniel Pastorius, "the first schoolmaster" hired in Germantown, Pennsylvania, in 1701, knew several languages and was educated in science and philosophy.

The typical schoolmaster was a young, single male, who rarely taught for more than two years. Ages varied, but most teachers were very young. The ages of thirty-four masters who taught in Dedham ranged from sixteen to seventy, with an average of twenty-three. For economic reasons, communities preferred single men because married ones had families to support and, consequently, demanded higher compensation. Rural settlements also saved money by requiring that single male instructors "board around," that is, spend several days, or even a few weeks, residing with a local family. However, some villages shunned single men as masters because they deemed them "transient" or unreliable. "In those towns where married men were employed, the locality frequently provided a house and several acres of land over and above the regular salary." Teachers usually had short tenures. "The average length of time taught by sixty-six schoolmasters employed in Dedham, Massachusetts, between 1644 and 1757 was one year and ten months." Ezekial Cheever was the most famous exception to this pattern. He taught for a total of seventy years, spending the last thirty-eight years of his life as a master at the Boston Latin Grammar School. He died in 1708, still teaching, at age ninety-four.

Masters seldom taught for long since teaching itself only represented a "stepping stone to more respectable or remunerative positions." Most aspired to become ministers. They taught briefly after graduating from college to earn tuition money for ministerial studies. Moreover, schoolmasters' incomes varied greatly among colonies and from community to community. Parents often paid tuition fees, but many appeared to be delinquent, forcing the teacher to cajole, if not actually pursue, his debtors. Colonial communities operating on a barter system rarely paid teachers in money and usually gave them "country pay," that is, crops like wheat, corn, barley, peas, and rye or livestock, such as pigs and chickens. Teachers also received wampum, manure, or firewood. On a comparative basis, colonial instructors earned much less than ministers and physicians, somewhat less than skilled artisans, and slightly more than common laborers.

These teachers had neither regular hours of employment nor uniform duties—they had to perform a myriad of tasks for this modest remuneration. The school calendar followed the seasons. "In New England, in 1667, a six-hour teaching day was fairly common during September, October, March, and April; a four-hour day during November, December, January, and February; and during May, June, July, and August school was kept eight hours, from 7:00 a.m. to 5:00 p.m., with a two-hour lunch period." The school day also varied because time was not standardized, since schoolhouses lacked clocks and few instructors owned watches. Furthermore, masters rarely just taught. The schoolmaster often served as a community's preacher. At the very least, he assumed many church-related duties. In Flatbush, Long Island, in 1682, the teacher cleaned the church, rang the bell for services, read Bible passages to the congregation, sang hymns, catechized the children every Sunday, provided water for baptism, supplied bread and water for communion, and dug graves, among a host of other jobs. In other communities, instructors toiled at civic duties, acting as court messengers, serving summonses, and assuming responsibility as town criers. Finally, teaching was often part-time work, done to supplement other sources of income. In Maine, most schoolmasters worked as small farmers, while teachers elsewhere worked as innkeepers, shoemakers, and tailors.[86]

Tutors

Tutoring was another, entirely different manifestation of formal education. Throughout the Atlantic seacoast, affluent colonial families hired tutors, but the Southern plantation class used them the most. Some planters sent their children to England to receive their education. However, most planters deliberately employed tutors to educate their children in the home rather than at school. They preferred this for several reasons. First, on isolated plantations, the household served as the center of education, with the tutor residing in the home. Second, intent on reproducing the lifestyle of English country gentlemen, Southern planters "emulated the English aristocracy where tutors were commonly employed."[87] Third, few grammar schools existed. Even if schools had been available, it is doubtful that planter families would have sent their children. They simply preferred to interact with their "social equals." As Tyack remarks, "The planter's chief education was his socialization in his family and in association with his peers, his performance in the political, social and economic roles assigned to his class as the ruling elite in tidewater Virginia."[88]

Affluent families hired tutors mainly to teach their sons and, on occasion, to teach their daughters but the latter were a tiny minority, since most Southern women during the seventeenth century remained illiterate. Philip Fithian served as a tutor in the Robert Carter family of Virginia in 1773. "The Carter sisters, pupils of Fithian, learned basic reading, writing, and arithmetic from him while their brothers were being taught advanced grammar, Latin, and Greek." However, lessons in music and dancing superseded academic subjects for the sisters, reflecting Southern priorities for daughters, who faced marriage and eventual motherhood.[89]

Tutors were often redemptioners, teaching in order to subsidize their ship passage, or even criminals deported to the colonies from England. "When one of these unfortunates could read and write, he sometimes was purchased for a schoolmaster, and teachers of this kind were common both in the Southern and Middle colonies." George Washington's father bought such a bondsman to educate his son. Given this background, they often fled as soon as they had an opportunity.[90]

Since tutors served only the Southern elite and few schools existed, only a small group of children in the Southern Colonies actually received any formal education. "With the exception of a few charity schools, the poor had few opportunities for education and the rate of illiteracy was much higher in Virginia than in New England."[91]

The Loosening of Institutional Bonds

By the early eighteenth century, New England culture had undergone many changes. Kenneth Lockridge's careful study of Dedham, Massachusetts, between 1640 and 1740 reveals gradual and subtle, yet profound, change. Internecine religious battles, the seductive attraction of economic wealth, the allure of the rich frontier wilderness, and a growing and increasingly heterogeneous population created a fluid environment. "Together, by the middle of the eighteenth century, they had shattered the old politics of Christian corporatism. In place of obedience to a narrow clique of divinely ordained leaders they had put a politics of diverse, frank, and contending interests."[92] Because of these broad social changes, the tight bonds between the educational institutions of the family, work training, the church, and schools began to disappear, even among the Puritans, and there was now only a loose interplay among them. Serendipity played a role, and individual talents and predilections likewise influenced the educational process.

Benjamin Franklin's early life reflected this change in culture. His autobiography reveals a fragmented and disjointed educational experience with some false starts. Born in 1706 in Boston, Franklin was the fifteenth of seventeen children; he was the youngest of ten sons. His father, a candlemaker and soapmaker, had apprenticed all of his sons, in Franklin's words, "to different trades." Franklin's father intended that his youngest son would become a minister. Franklin began grammar school at eight years of age, although he could already read. As he recalled, "I continued . . . at the grammar school not quite one year, though in that time I had risen gradually from the middle of the class of that year to be the head of it, and farther was removed into the third at the end of the year." But Franklin's father withdrew him from grammar school because he could not afford to subsidize his youngest son's Harvard College education, which was necessary to become a minister. He enrolled Franklin instead at a "school for writing and arithmetic" for a year.

Young Franklin's schooling ended at age ten, when he joined his father in his trade. Franklin described his tasks: "I was employed in cutting wick for the candles, filling the dipping mold, and the molds for cast candles, attending the shop, going of errands, etc." He strongly "disliked" this craft, but toiled at it for two years. Cognizant of his son's aversion to this work, Franklin's father expanded his son's craft knowledge by taking him to different artisans, eventually apprenticing Franklin to his cousin, a cutter, in an unsuccessful attempt to find the boy another vocation. Franklin, meanwhile, dearly loved to read and exhausted his father's personal library.

Taking advantage of this interest, Franklin's father apprenticed him to Ben's brother James, a Boston printer. Franklin hesitated yet agreed: "I stood out some time, but at last was persuaded and signed the indentures, when I was yet but twelve years old. I was to serve as an apprentice till I was twenty-one years of age, only I was allowed journeyman's wages during the last year." With ready access to books, Franklin took advantage of the situation and began a long process of self-education. He eagerly consumed books, borrowing them from a bookseller's apprentice and reading them overnight. A regular customer of the print shop even loaned books to Franklin from his personal library. Franklin appeared to be delighted: "I now took a fancy to poetry, and made some little pieces." James, his master, encouraged him, hoping to earn some profit from his apprentice, but his father squelched this budding author's writing career. In order to avoid further trouble with

James and his father, Franklin resorted to writing secretly, taking great care to improve himself by comparing his with other writers' works. Also, using the excuse that he worked in the printing shop on Sundays, Franklin was able both to practice his writing, which he passionately loved, and avoid church, which he detested. He continued his self-studies, expanding to arithmetic, geometry, and navigation and acquainting himself with the works of John Locke, the famous English philosopher. In 1720, when James began to publish *The New England Courant*, America's "second" newspaper, Franklin started to submit articles by secretly slipping them under the print shop's door at night, using the pseudonymn "Silence Dogood." James published these as well as other articles by authors who, fearing religious persecution and legal retribution, likewise employed aliases. The "Puritan Establishment," intolerant of criticism, arrested James, censuring and imprisoning him for a month, and in early January, 1723, forbade him to print the newspaper.

Franklin and his brother who often feuding, which resulted in frequent beatings of the young apprentice, and their relationship deteriorated. Franklin believed that he should have been treated more as a brother and less as an apprentice; James thought otherwise, asserting his authority as a master. Their differences proved to be irreconcilable, and a frustrated seventeen-year-old Franklin deliberately broke his indenture contract and secretly fled by ship to Philadelphia, where he found work with a printer.[93] Thus Franklin's early education ended.

What becomes clear from Franklin's educational odyssey is the marginal role of schooling and the central role of work training by means of apprenticeship. His father, like many others, deemed schooling expendable when he realized that he could not afford to pay Franklin's college tuition. Private colonial schooling thus existed largely as a means to some higher calling and was reserved for the affluent elite. After all, Franklin could already read when he began grammar school, revealing the family's role in literacy training. Other than this, his family, through his father, played a mediating role in guiding this youngest son through different work choices and admonishing him for seemingly frivolous activities, like writing. Apprenticeship assured a viable work skill, and this, through a steady and sufficient income, provided economic security. Finally, and perhaps the most subtle point, Franklin's *Autobiography* reveals the significant role of self-education. Franklin exploited his father's library, covertly borrowed books from a bookseller, and spent countless hours studying. Franklin's educational experience, in sum, appeared to be fragmented and informal, and although it proved to be successful in his case, this was not always so.

CONCLUSIONS

Informal education of children was practiced by both Native Americans and European colonists. For both groups, the family was the primary educational institution, conveying cultural traditions and values and overseeing the acquisition of vocational skills. For Europeans, education also included literacy training. But whether in colonial New Mexico or in New England, literacy restricted rather than liberated students, according to Gallegos. In both cases, "religion and the spread of literacy went hand in hand."[94] Thus, education largely operated as a mechanism of socialization. It reinforced a narrow, ethnocentric, and theocentric definition of culture. Europeans imposed their culture on Native Americans through education. Education thus became acculturation. Conflicts inevitably arose as Native American families resisted submitting their children to European culture.

Two key developments emerged from the colonial period. First, attitudes toward education began to change and a gradual and irrevocable trend toward institutionalized, formal education developed. In New England, all aspects of the early educational system changed. The family slowly began to relinquish some of its educational responsibilities while schools quietly assumed more. Schooling, nevertheless, remained irregular and lacked any institutional credibility during the colonial period. Szasz summarizes the experience along the Atlantic seacoast:

> In the colonies, schooling was frequently selective, sometimes haphazard, and often nonexistent. Its substance and character depended not only on the individual colony, but it was also determined by density of population, community attitudes towards schooling, and the chronology of events between 1607 and 1783."[95]

Second, a crude and limited concept of free schooling began to unfold. As early as 1635, Boston's leaders supplied "free school" through donations and tax levies. "By the mid-1640s tax support for public schooling had become one of the town's largest expenditures." This appeared to be typical in many Massachusetts towns and villages. Boston continued to expand its free schools through the early 1700s. "In colonial urban America, Boston led the way in public schooling." This free schooling experience was available only to poor children whose parents could not afford to pay private school tuition. The political distractions and the diversion of financial resources from the civilian sector to military needs during the Revolution, however, abruptly ended this educational activity.[96] But with the coming of national independence, the concept of schooling in general and free, universal schooling in particular began again to take hold and spread.

ACTIVITIES FOR FURTHER EXPLORATION

1. Do you want to read the "first" Native American autobiography? What did colonists learn from Native Americans? Go to http://chnm.gmu.edu/us/many.taf and read "Black Hawk Remembers Village Life Along the Mississippi" and "Captured by Indians: Mary Jemison Becomes an Indian."

2. What did the Puritans expect children to learn? Cotton Mather, a famous Puritan writer, expounded on this in "The Duties of Children to Their Parents," "The Duties of Parents to Their Children," and "The Education of Children," among others. Go to http://www.gty.org/~phil/mather.htm to read these documents. Also, for a broader picture of colonial life and childhood culture, consult primary documents at http://www.ogram.org/17the/images.shtml.

3. Can you imagine what Benjamin Franklin felt as he escaped from his Boston apprenticeship to Philadelphia? Read " 'A Most Awkward, Ridiculous Appearance:' Benjamin Franklin Enters Philadelphia" among excerpts of Franklin's autobiography at http://chnm.gmu.edu/us/many.taf. This sequel to the brief biography described and quoted in this chapter provides a context for colonial Philadelphia and reveals the importance of the knowledge and skills obtained from his apprenticeship experience. You can also explore his works at http://www.law.ou.edu/hist.

4. What is the educational role of the modern American family? Create a list of these responsibilities. Which are ideal goals? Which represent reality?

5. What are modern manifestations of informal education? How does this list compare with informal education during the colonial period?

VIDEO EXPLORATION

Clips from the video *Surviving Columbus* (Alexandria, VA: PBS Home Video, 1992) illustrate the cultural impact of European exploration and settlement on the North American Pueblo culture. The first segment of this two-hour film treats, in particular, the Spanish and Mexican periods in what is now the American Southwest. This penetrating film reveals the toll of conflicts over culture, including the 1680 Pueblo Revolt, and raises several potential discussion questions: How do we define who is civilized? Does might make right? What lessons have we learned? Exploring the Iroquois Constitution may offer further insight into Native American culture; see http://www.law.ou.edu/hist.

NOTES AND SOURCES

In order to condense endnotes, the first work cited is the primary one, usually the source of any direct quotes. Subsequent references serve as supplementary, or additional, sources of paraphrased information and/or alternative historical interpretations.

1. Fithian is quoted in David B. Tyack, *Turning Points in American Educational History* (New York: Wiley & Sons, 1967), p. 45.

2. Gary Nash, *Red, White, and Black: The Peoples of Early America* (Englewood Cliffs, NJ: Prentice-Hall, Inc., 1982), pp. 9, 11, 17, 21. Refer as well to James W. Loewen, *Lies My Teacher Told Me: Everything Your American History Textbook Got Wrong* (New York: New Press, 1995), pp. 70–79; David J. Weber, *The Spanish Frontier in North American* (New Haven, CT: Yale University Press, 1992), pp. 17, 18, 31.

3. Margaret Connell Szasz, *Indian Education in the American Colonies, 1607–1783* (Albuquerque, NM: University of New Mexico Press, 1988), pp. 7–9, 11–12, 14, 15. Also see Michael C. Coleman, *American Indian Children at School, 1850–1930* (Jackson, MS: University Press of Mississippi, 1993), p. 30; David H. DeJong, *Promises of the Past: A History of Indian Education in the United States* (Golden, CO: North American Press, 1993), pp.

5–6; and Jon Reyhner and Jeanne Eder, *A History of Indian Education* (Billings, MT: Native American Studies, Eastern Montana College, 1983), pp. 9–10.

4. Coleman, *American Indian Children at School*, pp. 15, 16–19, 22. Also refer to DeJong, *Promises of the Past*, pp. 5, 10, 22; Linda, Peavy and Ursula Smith. *Frontier Children*, (Norman, OK: University of Oklahoma Press, 1999), p. 9; Szasz, *Indian Education*, p. 11.

5. Szasz, *Indian Education*, pp. 16, 23.

6. Nash, *Red, White, and Black*, pp. 21, 22.

7. DeJong, *Promises of the Past*, pp. 15, 16–17. The second quote in this paragraph is quoted in DeJong, p. 15. Refer as well to Coleman, *American Indian Children at School*, pp. 24, 25, 26.

8. Szasz, *Indian Education*, p. 18.

9. Paul A. W. Wallace, *Indians in Pennsylvania* (Harrisburg, PA: Pennsylvania Historical and Museum Commission, 1993), p. 62. Refer as well to Szasz, *Indian Education*, p. 19.

10. Szasz, *Indian Education*, pp. 17, 18, 20–22. Refer as well to Coleman, *American Indian Children at School*, p. 23; DeJong, *Promises of the Past*, p. 16. See Wallace, *Indians in Pennsylvania*, p. 63, about the threat of the supernatural among Delaware parents and children.

11. James Axtell, *The School Upon a Hill: Education and Society in Colonial New England* (New York: W.W. Norton, 1974), p. 246. Also, see Szasz, *Indian Education*, p. 53: "In early Stuart England, Christianization and civilization (or civility) were mutually interdependent, and when these concepts were applied to the Indians they often came under the general rubric of 'education.' " Coleman, *American Indian Children at School*, p. 37, sees acculturation as a "deculturation" process. Joel Spring, *Deculturalization and the Struggle for Equality: A Brief History of the Education of Dominated Cultures in the United States* (New York: McGraw-Hill, 1997), in Chapter 1 argues that "[d]eculturalization refers to the stripping away of a people's culture and replacing it with a new culture."

12. This information and quotes in these two paragraphs draw heavily on DeJong, *Promises of the Past*, pp. xiii, 22, 23–24, 26. Refer as well to Reyhner and Eder, *A History of Indian Education*, p. 11; Szasz, *Indian Education*, p. 55.

13. Szasz, *Indian Education*, pp. 4, 5.

14. DeJong, *Promises of the Past*, p. 26. Refer also to Szasz, *Indian Education*, pp. 50, 62, 69–70, 77; Reyhner and Eder, *A History of Indian Education*, p. 9.

15. Szasz, *Indian Education*, quoted on p. 203; also refer to p. 204.

16. Thomas P. Slaughter, *The Whiskey Rebellion: Frontier Epilogue to the American Revolution* (New York: Oxford University Press, 1986), pp. 28–29, 75–78. Also, see Szasz, *Indian Education*, p. 204; DeJong, *Promises of the Past*, pp. 26, 28.

17. Szasz, *Indian Education*, pp. 103, 111, 173, 178, 183, 186, 258. Refer as well to James Axtell, *The European and the Indian: Essays in the Ethnohistory of Colonial North America* (Oxford, UK: Oxford University Press, 1981), pp. 65–66; Coleman, *American Indian Children at School*, pp. 36–37; DeJong, *Promises of the Past*, p. 25; Reyhner and Eder, *A History of Indian Education*, pp. 15, 16–17.

18. DeJong, *Promises of the Past*, p. 30. Refer as well to Axtell, *The European and the Indian*, p. 66.

19. Szasz, *Indian Education*, pp. 191, 200, 218.

20. Axtell, *The European and the Indian*, pp. 97, 99. Also refer to Szasz, *Indian Education*, pp. 8, 220, 222, and Reyhner and Eder, *A History of Indian Education*, pp. 16–17.

21. Szasz, *Indian Education*, pp. 223, 229.

22. Axtell, *The European and the Indian*, pp. 98, 100, 102.

23. Szasz, *Indian Education*, p. 230. Refer as well to Coleman, *American Indian Children at School*, p. 37; DeJong, *Promises of the Past*, p. 24.

24. Axtell, *The European and the Indian*, p. 170.

25. Loewen, *Lies My Teacher Told Me*, pp. 95–96.

26. Axtell, *The European and the Indian*, pp. 133–135, 136–137, 138–139.

27. Loewen, *Lies My Teacher Told Me*, p. 101. See Weber, *Spanish Frontier in North America*, pp. 49–55, for details of De Soto's ill-fated expedition.

28. The quotes in this and the preceding paragraph are from Axtell, *The European and the Indian*, pp. 161, 168, 184, 188, 190, 198, 200.

29. Axtell, *School Upon a Hill*, pp. 276, 277, 278, 280. Refer as well to Axtell, *The European and the Indian*, pp. 162–166.

30. Loewen, *Lies My Teacher Told Me*, pp. 101–102.

31. DeJong, *Promises of the Past*, p. 33. See also Coleman, *American Indian Children at School*, pp. 39, 40.

32. Weber, *Spanish Frontier in North America*, pp. 7, 8, comes to grips with the "Spanish borderlands" interpretation of colonial America pioneered by Herbert Eugene Bolton, *The Spanish Borderlands: A Chronicle of Old Florida and the Southwest*, as early as 1921. John Francis Bannon, in *The Spanish Borderlands Frontier, 1513–1821* (New York: Holt, Rinehart and Winston, 1970), fits into this provocative historiographical school of thought; see, in particular, pp. 8, 17–21, 22, 23, 26, 45–48 for the extent of Spanish exploration of the North American continent. Weber likewise provides detailed analysis of the scope of Spanish exploration in North America on pp. 33–54, 61–63, 70, 71–72, 77, 82–87. Also, refer to Guadalupe San Miguel, Jr., *"Let All of Them Take Heed": Mexican Americans and the Campaign for Educational Equality in Texas, 1910–1981* (Austin, TX: University of Texas Press, 1987), p. 1. Finally,

for historiographical background, see Victoria-Maria MacDonald, "Hispanic, Latino, Chicano, or 'Other?' ": Deconstructing the Relationship between Historians and Hispanic-American Educational History," *History of Education Quarterly*, 41 (Fall 2001), p. 373.

33. The quotes in this and the preceding three paragraphs are from Bannon, *Spanish Borderlands Frontier*, pp. 5, 56–57, 71, 79, 81, 86, 91, 172. Refer as well to Bernardo P. Gallegos, *Literacy, Education, and Society in New Mexico, 1693–1821* (Albuquerque, NM: University of New Mexico Press, 1992), p. 11; MacDonald, "Hispanic, Chicano, or 'Other?' ", pp. 390–391; Weber, *Spanish Frontier in North America*, pp. 92, 95, 105, 108–110, 122, 125–127, 133–140, 175–176.

34. Martha Menchaca, "The Treaty of Guadalupe Hidalgo and the Racialization of the Mexican Population," in *The Elusive Quest for Equality: 150 Years of Chicano/Chicana Education*, ed. Jose F. Moreno (Cambridge, MA: Harvard Educational Review, 1999), pp. 5–6.

35. Gallegos, *Literacy, Education, and Society in New Mexico*, pp. 24, 25–27.

36. Menchaca, "The Treaty of Guadalupe Hidalgo," pp. 3, 11, 12. See also Weber, *Spanish Frontier in North America*, pp. 105, 106.

37. Gallegos, *Literacy, Education, and Society in New Mexico*, pp. 38–40, 53, 63, 67–68, 69, 70, 92. Weber, *Spanish Frontier in North America*, p. 121, likewise refers to the Hispanicization process. Refer as well to Alfredo Mirande and Evangelina Enriquez, *La Chicana: The Mexican-American Woman* (Chicago: University of Chicago Press, 1979), p. 59.

38. Menchaca, "The Treaty of Guadalupe Hidalgo," p. 12.

39. Mirande and Enriquez, *La Chicana*, pp. 44–45, 59.

40. Menchaca, "The Treaty of Guadalupe Hidalgo," pp. 12, 13, 14.

41. Gallegos, *Literacy, Education, and Society in New Mexico*, pp. 30, 32, 92. Also see Menchaca, "The Treaty of Guadalupe Hidalgo," p. 14, who argues that the first public school in New Mexico opened in 1813, and Weber, *Spanish Frontier in North America*, pp. 141, 145, 159.

42. Nash, *Red, White, and Black*, p. 17.

43. Gerald N. Grob and George Athan Billias, eds., *Interpretations of American History: Patterns and Perspectives*. Volume I: to 1877. 5th ed. (New York: Free Press, 1982), pp. 42, 44. See Lawrence A. Cremin, *American Education: The Colonial Experience, 1607–1783* (New York: Harper & Row, 1970), for his valuable concept of an educational configuration consisting of a variety of social institutions, like the family, religion, work, etc.

44. John Winthrop, "A Modell of Christian Charity," in David B. Tyack, ed., *Turning Points in American Educational History* (New York: John Wiley & Sons, 1967), pp. 11, 14. Tyack's *Turning Points* is a compilation of primary documents.

45. Tyack, *Turning Points*, p. 2.

46. James Axtell, *School Upon a Hill*, p. 49. Szasz, *Indian Education*, states on p. 35: "The Puritans viewed education as one of the many steps leading toward salvation. . . . they deemed salvation impossible without Christian knowledge and understanding."

47. Tyack, *Turning Points*, p. 3. See as well John Demos, *Past, Present, and Personal: The Family and the Life Course in American History* (New York: Oxford University Press, 1986), p. 45; Edmund S. Morgan, *The Puritan Family: Religion and Domestic Relations in Seventeenth-Century New England* (New York: Harper & Row, 1966), pp. 92, 97.

48. Morgan, *The Puritan Family*, pp. 10–11, 12, 15, 16, 19, 27, 97, 136, 143, 145. Refer likewise to John Demos, *A Little Commonwealth: Family Life in Plymouth Colony* (London: Oxford University Press, 1970), pp. 62, 63, 64, 74, and *Past, Present, and Personal*, pp. 28, 76.

49. Tyack and Hansot, *Learning Together*, pp. 14, 15, 16. Also, see Demos, *Past, Present, and Personal*, p. 44; Morgan, *Puritan Family*, pp. 33, 35, 42–43, 45, 51, 53, 55, 66, 117.

50. Demos, *Past, Present, and Personal*, p. 48.

51. Glenda Riley, *Divorce: An American Tradition* (Lincoln, NE: University of Nebraska Press, 1991), pp. 3, 6, 7, 9–10, 11, 12, 21, 22, 23–24, 25.

52. This and the quotes in the preceding paragraph are from Axtell, *School Upon a Hill*, pp. 8, 10, 11, 14, 15, 20, 53, 135, 146, 155–159. See also Demos, *A Little Commonwealth*, pp. 100–101, and *Past, Present, and Personal*, pp. 29–30; Morgan, *The Puritan Family*, pp. 97–98; Tyack, *Turning Points*, p. 3; and David Tyack and Elisabeth Hansot, *Learning Together: A History of Coeducation in American Public Schools* (New Haven, CT: Yale University Press, 1990), p. 14.

53. Demos, *Past, Present, and Personal*, p. 48, 139–140. Refer as well to Stephanie Coontz, *The Way We Never Were: American Families and the Nostalgia Trap* (Basic Books, 1992), p. 10; Kenneth A. Lockridge, *Literacy in Colonial New England: An Enquiry into the Social Context of Literacy in the Early Modern West* (New York: W. W. Norton & Company, 1974), pp. 38–39; Morgan, *The Puritan Family*, p. 89; Joel Perlmann, Silvana R. Siddali, and Keith Whitescarver, "Literacy, Schooling, and Teaching among New England Women, 1730–1820," *History of Education Quarterly* 37 (Summer 1997), pp. 120, 123.

54. Axtell, *School Upon a Hill*, pp. 37, 39–40.

55. The quote is from Clifton Johnson, *Old-Time Schools and School-books* (Macmillan Company, 1904; reprint ed., New York: Dover Publications, 1963), p. 13. Also, see Axtell, *School Upon a Hill*, pp. 36–38, 45; Morgan, *The Puritan Family*, p. 98.

56. Demos, *Past, Present, and Personal*, p. 97.

57. Coontz, *The Way We Never Were*, p. 211.

58. Lawrence A. Cremin, *American Education: The National Experience, 1783–1876* (New York: Harper & Row, 1980), p. 343. Refer also to W. J. Rorabaugh, *The Craft Apprentice: From Franklin to the Machine Age in America* (New York: Oxford University Press, 1986), p. vii, and Richard J. Altenbaugh, David E. Engel, and Don T. Martin, *Caring for Kids: A Critical Study of Urban School Leavers* (London: Falmer, 1995), pp. 29–30.

59. Rorabaugh, *The Craft Apprentice*, p. vii.

60. Axtell, *School Upon a Hill*, p. 119.

61. Cremin *American Education: The National Experience*, p. 344.

62. Axtell, *School Upon a Hill*, pp. 22–23, 30–31, 32, 34. Refer also to Tyack, *Turning Points*, p. 3.

63. Szazs, *Indian Education*, p. 32.

64. Coontz, *The Way We Never Were*, p. 10.

65. Axtell, *School Upon a Hill*, p. 49.

66. Johnson, *Old-Time Schools*, p. 24.

67. Demos, *Past, Present, and Personal*, p. 29; Tyack and Hansot, *Learning Together*, p. 14.

68. Axtell, *School Upon a Hill*, pp. 35, 132, 175. Refer also to Morgan, *The Puritan Family*, pp. 100, 101.

69. Tyack and Hansot, *Learning Together*, p. 19. See as well Perlmann, Siddali, and Whitescarver, "Literacy, Schooling, and Teaching among New England Women," pp. 126–128.

70. Johnson, *Old-Time Schools*, pp. 25–28.

71. Quoted in Mary Beth Norton, *Liberty's Daughters: The Revolutionary Experience of American Women, 1750–1800* (Boston: Little, Brown and Company, 1980), p. 259; see also pp. 140–141.

72. Johnson, *Old-Time Schools*, p. 44.

73. Tyack and Hansot, *Learning Together*, pp. 13, 14, 18, 20. Also, refer to Jo Ann Preston, "Feminization of an Occupation: Teaching Becomes Women's Work in Nineteenth-Century New England" (Ph.D. diss., Brandeis University, 1982), especially Chapter 2.

74. Szasz, *Indian Education*, p. 26.

75. Tyack, *Turning Points*, pp. 14–15. Also, refer to Axtell, *School Upon a Hill*, p. 156.

76. Axtell, *School Upon a Hill*, pp. 169, 170.

77. The quote is from Johnson, *Old-Time Schools*, pp. 1–2. Also, refer to Axtell, *School Upon a Hill*, pp. 169, 170; Lorraine Smith Pangle and Thomas L. Pangle, *The Learning of Liberty: The Educational Ideas of the American Founders* (Lawrence KS: University Press of Kansas, 1993), p. 76; Szasz, *Indian Education*, p. 36.

78. Tyack, *Turning Points*, pp. 4, 5. Emphasis is Tyack's.

79. Johnson, *Old-Time Schools*, pp. 4, 31, 36.

80. Tyack and Hansot, *Learning Together*, p. 18. Also, see Axtell, *School Upon a Hill*, pp. 178, 186–187; Johnson, *Old-Time Schools*, p. 10; Szasz, *Indian Education*, p. 37.

81. The quote is from Johnson, *Old-Time Schools*, pp. 11–12. Refer as well to pp. 43 and 44 in Johnson.

82. The quotes in this paragraph are taken from Johnson, *Old-Time Schools*, p. 14, 71–72, 76, 77, 82, 99. Refer as well to Morgan, *The Puritan Family*, p. 101.

83. Coontz, *The Way We Never Were*, p. 10.

84. Barbara Finkelstein, *Governing the Young: Teacher Behavior in Popular Primary Schools in Nineteenth-Century United States* (New York: Falmer Press, 1989), p. 44.

85. Tyack and Hansot, *Learning Together*, p. 26. Also, see Szasz, *Indian Education*, pp. 37, 38; Johnson, *Old-Time Schools*, p. 13.

86. All the quotes and much of the information in this section are from Willard S. Elsbree, *The American Teacher: Evolution of a Profession in a Democracy* (New York: American Book Company, 1939; reprint ed., New York: Greenwood Press, 1970), pp. 34, 35, 37, 39, 42, 44, 58, 63–64, 66, 81, 84, 89, 97, 99. Refer as well to Richard J. Altenbaugh, ed., *The Teacher's Voice: A Social History of Teaching in Twentieth-Century America* (London: Falmer Press, 1992), p. 64; Axtell, *School Upon a Hill*, pp.

187–188, 190; Johnson, *Old-Time Schools*, pp. 5–6, 14; Michael W. Sedlak, " 'Let Us Go and Buy a School Master': Historical Perspectives on the Hiring of Teachers in the United States, 1750–1980," in *American Teachers: Histories of a Profession at Work*, ed. Donald Warren (New York: Macmillan Publishing Co., 1989), p. 260; Szasz, *Indian Education*, p. 38; Tyack and Hansot, *Learning Together*, p. 16.

87. Szasz, *Indian Education*, p. 44. Refer as well to Johnson, *Old-Time Schools*, p. 32; Tyack, *Turning Points*, pp. 28, 31.

88. Tyack, *Turning Points*, p. 34.

89. Mary Beth Norton, *Liberty's Daughters*, pp. 260, 261. Also, refer to Szasz, *Indian Education*, p. 44; Richard D. Brown, *Knowledge Is Power: The Diffusion of Information in Early America, 1700–1865* (New York: Oxford University Press, 1989), p. 62. For an excerpt from Fithian's letter to his successor, see Tyack, *Turning Points*, pp. 41–49.

90. Johnson, *Old-Time Schools*, pp. 32, 33.

91. Tyack, *Turning Points*, p. 34.

92. Kenneth A. Lockridge, *A New England Town: The First Hundred Years* (New York: W. W. Norton, 1985), p. 172.

93. Quotes and facts concerning Franklin's early life taken From Esmond Wright, ed., *Benjamin Franklin: His Life As He Wrote It* (Cambridge, MA: Harvard University Press, 1990), pp. 1, 18, 19, 23–24, 42, 44. Both Rorabaugh, *Craft Apprentice*, pp. 2–15, and Lawrence A. Cremin, *American Education: The Colonial Experience*, pp. 371–378, also use Franklin's life as an illustration of colonial education.

94. Gallegos, *Literacy, Education, and Society in New Mexico*, p. 63.

95. Szasz, *Indian Education*, pp. 26, 44.

96. Stanley K. Schultz, *The Culture Factory: Boston Public Schools, 1789–1860* (New York: Oxford University Press, 1973), pp. 5, 7–8.

3

Early Nationalism and Education

Although the trend toward formal, institutionalized education began to form during the colonial period, it underwent a profound transition, not so much institutionally but conceptually, during the early days of the republic. Many of the Founders and early national leaders expressed concern about the ability of the family to successfully prepare citizens for the new United States. They saw a need for mass education that would be systematized and consistent, that is, for free schooling sponsored by some level of government, schooling that would serve a nation-building purpose and include the education of females.

The early decades of the nineteenth century also saw the development of cultural confrontation, especially through schooling. As the new nation aggressively expanded westward, uprooting Native Americans and pushing them farther west—with tragic consequences—Anglo Americans began the long, government-sponsored institutionalization of Native American education in an attempt to eradicate their culture. In Mexico, which won its independence from Spain in 1821, the new constitution provided for schooling, but schooling failed to evolve as quickly in the Mexican republic as it did in the American republic; few funds were made available and thus many of the colonial patterns endured on the Mexican frontier, although schooling did gradually become more secular. Here, too, however, as Anglo Americans encroached on Mexican territory, cultural domination followed in the wake of military supremacy.

This chapter treats the impact of early nationalism on education by describing and analyzing the perceived need for a more systematic and institutionalized approach and for the control of knowledge, not for insidious reasons, but in response to the traditional informality and haphazardness of education. Early national leaders' blueprints for schooling in many ways laid the philosophical foundation for the American public school. In addition, the perception of a new, unique, "American" character also led to intolerance of other, more-established cultures on the North American continent.

THE UNCERTAIN NATION

In January 1794, the American government struggled with an apparent national crisis. Congress assembled for a new session in Philadelphia under threats of war with Great Britain and Spain as well as domestic strife on the western frontier. As historian Thomas Slaughter points out, Great Britain had seized 250 American ships in the Caribbean and appeared intent on initiating hostilities on the frontier by "supplying" Native Americans with arms and "encouraging" them to attack American settlers.

"Canadian officials and Tory refugees had collaborated since 1783 with disaffected citizens in western Pennsylvania for secession of the region and reunion with Great Britain." Spain, too, became involved in frontier intrigue, threatening to annex, in alliance with Great Britain, vast stretches of the American frontier "west of the Alleghenies." Finally, the young government faced the possibility of the armed insurrection of western Pennsylvanians, who for several years defiantly threatened, regularly tarred and feathered, and occasionally attacked federal tax collectors and generally defied the national government's authority. In October and November of 1794, President George Washington mobilized 12,950 troops, more than he had commanded during the Revolutionary War, to smother this perceived civil war. Only eight years before armed forced had to be used to suppress Shay's Rebellion in Massachusetts.

The Watermelon Army

Many sections of the frontier had contemplated independent statehood, if not outright secession. Settlers saw the central government as ineffective and unresponsive to their needs, much in the same way the rebellious colonists had viewed the British Crown. They expressed their distrust and disaffection through protests and independence movements. In 1794, Whiskey Rebellion protestors, or "whiskey rebels," evoked revolutionary memories by employing an important symbol: the liberty pole. As early as 1776, parts of western Pennsylvania and northern Virginia seriously considered becoming the autonomous state of Westsylvania. Three western counties of North Carolina endeavored to become the sovereign state of Franklin during the 1780s. Vermonters negotiated with Canada and Great Britain in 1786, and Kentucky sought its freedom that same year. The United States maintained a fragile unity and flirted with fragmentation. "Eruptions on the frontier—Indian attacks, British and Spanish intrigues, and anti-excise [tax] violence—all seemed to national officials strands in a seamless web threatening to envelop the nation and doom the republican enterprise."

Although Great Britain and Spain became distracted by other international events and the Whiskey Rebellion eventually fizzled in an anticlimatic fashion, with federal troops, derisively called the "watermelon army," having nothing more to do than scour the Pennsylvania countryside for would-be traitors, early national leaders believed that they faced a series of external threats and internal disorders. Some, like Alexander Hamilton, a federalist, held mixed feelings of hope and anxiety about conferring political power on the people.[1]

The future of the young country appeared to be precarious, indeed. Americans needed to stand united against foreign conspiracies. Government officials could not always resort to armed suppression to ensure the power of the state and federal governments. The entire republican process seemed to be vulnerable unless a literate, informed, and patriotic electorate peacefully and wisely chose judicious, competent, and loyal political leaders. A nationalistic spirit needed to be created and nurtured in order to ensure a sense of social and political harmony and cohesiveness. Only this would guarantee the survival of the new nation-state. There was no precedent for building this new and unique national identity, and the leaders turned to education to accomplish the task.

POLITICAL EDUCATION

Several early leaders proposed education as a means to instill in Americans a strong sense of civic duty, or, as Noah Webster expressed it, a "national character."[2] This meant that former allegiances to the Crown and current loyalties to individual colonies, or states, had to be replaced by "a new unity, a common citizenship and culture, and an appeal to a common future," a daunting challenge since "order and liberty" had to be kept in balance, that is, political indoctrination had to coexist with political freedom.[3]

Although numerous educational statutes and proposals with a variety of emphases were put forward, three common threads ran through all of them: utilitarianism, moral training, and government sponsorship. The new American nation represented the Founders' notion of a blend of classical republicanism, inherited from the ancient Greek and Roman civilizations, and modern republicanism, shaped by the European Enlightenment and such thinkers as John Locke. Classical republicanism encouraged civic virtue; modern republicanism emphasized a progressive mindset, promoting inquiry of all kinds. This latter idea in particular was seized upon by early American leaders. The traditional European classical curriculum appeared to be mired in the past. Locke's ideas of practical schooling were more appealing. Students should learn arithmetic, the English language, drawing, and natural philosophy (the sciences) rather than Latin, Greek, and Hebrew and moral philosophy. However, public speaking and the study of history, part of the classical tradition, should remain.

Nevertheless, moral training remained important to the early leaders. Breaking from the colonial past, however, they no longer saw moral training as the purpose of schooling, but merely as a means of ensuring a civil and stable society, one in which citizens willingly obeyed laws. The Puritans had certainly valued schooling and liberty, but their religious doctrine required a sense of "hierarchy and exclusivity." Likewise, early leaders were deeply suspicious, if not fearful, of Roman Catholicism and its grounding in absolutism. Finally, many Founders, like Thomas Jefferson, James Madison, and George Mason, generally opposed any established religion, even Anglicanism. Presidents Jefferson and Madison resisted such measures and practices as the appointment of congressional and military chaplains, tax exemptions for churches, and the designation of national religious holidays, such as Thanksgiving. Still, while they avoided establishing a direct relationship between government and religion, they supported moral instruction in order to develop loyal and law-abiding citizens for a new nation, that is, piety without religion. Locke's influence was evident. To shape the morals of the young, Locke would rely less on the use of the Bible in particular, and religion in general, and instead promote reasoning. Duty, honor, and noble behavior formed the habits of virtue, that is, a sense of "civility".[4]

Half of the states that ratified their constitutions before 1800 "adopted articles or clauses calling for public aid to education."[5] Republican principles influenced these state constitutions. The idea of government support for education, whether central or state, represented a sharp break from the general European tradition of private schools. Universal access to schooling also proved to be a departure. In this, the early American leaders, such as George Washington, John Adams, Benjamin Rush, and Noah Webster, rejected the influence of Locke, who did not support universal schooling. Behind all of these ideas was a sense of "equalitarianism"; "equality" was at least "implicit" in all of them, as reflected in Locke's notion of educating girls as well as boys.[6]

The Continental Congress, under the Articles of Confederation, established a precedent for the federal government's role in educational policy and the building of an education infrastructure. The 1785 Land Ordinance stipulated that one square mile in every township in the Old Northwest Territory (all of the land north of the Ohio River and east of the Mississippi River) be sold and the revenue set aside for, as it stated, the "maintenance of public schools."[7] Although the Constitutional Convention did not include federal responsibility for education in the new Constitution, political leaders still promoted the concept. President Washington recommended in 1790 "that the federal government grant aid to schools throughout the several states."[8] He especially supported the idea of a government-funded national university to promote unity. In 1796, the year Washington retired as President, Samuel Harrison Smith and Samuel Knox, two proponents of a "national system of education," won an essay contest on education sponsored by the Philadelphia-based American Philosophical Society, led by Thomas Jefferson. The concept of a coherent, publicly financed, and sequenced system of schooling was evident in both proposals. Smith proposed a national board to oversee the curriculum and teachers in a public system for boys that would extend from primary school through the university level. Knox, too, recommended a national board, as well as stressed secular education and discipline in his proposed system, which would include local primary schools, county academies, state colleges, and a national university. Girls, in Knox's scheme, would attend the primary schools but would not advance beyond the basic literacy level. Knox saw a close relationship between education, literacy, and equality. He blamed the paucity of educational opportunities in England and that country's high rate of illiteracy on class barriers—only the wealthy and privileged had access to education. Despite the various actions by the states and the support of national leaders, however, "the idea of federal control of education never did overcome the state and local loyalties and the private and religious values of the majority of the American people."[9]

A closer look at the educational proposals of three early leaders gives clear insight into the goals, scope, and curricula they felt were needed to build a new nation. Whether federalist or antifederalist, these leaders felt strongly that education would preserve the young republic. The ideas and schemes, taken together, of Thomas Jefferson, an antifederalist worried about absolutism, Benjamin Rush, a liberal federalist committed to preserving freedom, and Noah Webster, a conservative federalist who feared anarchy, constitute a unique, republican form of education and offer an outline of what would later emerge as part of the rationale for the American public school. First, they felt that Americans should be educated, at all levels, in the United States. Education abroad, a common practice during the colonial period, ran the risk of contaminating American students with antirepublican notions. They rejected "exclusive" and "aristocratic" European culture and institutions.[10] Second, they supported the concept of a new institution, that is, publicly financed schooling, to produce "homogeneous" Americans. The European model of private, tuition-driven schooling would not serve their needs. "Webster, Rush, and Jefferson believed that education must be systematic, useful, and uniformly republican in aim." Students who attended these schools would be imbued with American "language, geography, and history." Third, knowledge had to be diffused among the masses. Everyone would receive at least basic training in reading, writing, and ciphering. For Jefferson, ever suspicious of an intrusive government, this translated into knowledge serving to protect naturally ordained individual rights (in contrast to James Madison and Alexander

Hamilton, to whom this meant creating loyal and patriotic subjects). In any event, the United States needed a literate citizenry in order to ensure full and active participation in the process of selecting wise and judicious political leaders, who would be identified and prepared for their important roles through universal, free, public education, provided even through the university level.[11] Mass schooling, in sum, was a key element in the nation-building process.

"Raking a Few Geniuses from the Rubbish"

Thomas Jefferson's pyramidal approach to schooling in his 1779 *Bill for the More General Diffusion of Knowledge*, presented to the Virginia Assembly, had two main goals: a literate electorate and an enlightened leadership. His scheme divided each county into 100 wards, with each hosting a free primary school. The curriculum, for Jefferson, would consist of "reading, writing, and common arithmetick [sic], and the books which shall be used therin for instructing the children to read shall be such as will at the same time make them acquainted with Graecian, Roman, English, and American history." But the Bible was excluded. All European American male and female children would attend these schools for free for three years. The county would subsidize the school building, as well as the salary, board, and lodging for the teacher. The teacher, in Jefferson's scheme, was to be unquestionably loyal to the commonwealth. Overseers would periodically visit the schools and test the "scholars" through oral drills, and the best scholars would be permitted to attend the next level, the grammar school. The remaining children had two choices: terminate their schooling or continue to attend primary school. If parents wanted their children to attend primary school for more than three years, then they had to pay tuition. In sum, using Jefferson's words, each such village school would serve as a "little republic."[12]

Each grammar school or academy, built by three or more counties, would provide secondary education. Each, according to Jefferson, "shall contain a room for the school, a hall to dine in, four rooms for a master and usher, and ten or twelve lodging rooms for the scholars." This boarding school concept seemingly echoed the English model; it certainly removed children from their families and seemed to purposely usurp the family's educational role. Emphasizing college preparation, Jefferson's proposed curriculum included "Latin and Greek languages, English Grammar, geography, and the higher part of numerical arithmetick, to wit, vulgar and decimal fractions, and the extrication of the square and cube roots." Two annual examinations by overseers would sort out the best students, who would be permitted to continue for four additional years. Overseers would again test this group, and the best scholars would attend William and Mary College for three years at public expense.[13]

Jefferson's proposal contained several noteworthy points. First, every white male and female citizen had to be literate in order to actively participate in the political process—albeit only white males who owned property could vote. The primary schools supplied this literacy training. Second, the system was sequenced and would gradually sort out future political, economic, and intellectual leaders, or, as Jefferson stated it, would amount to "raking a few geniuses from the rubbish."[14] Third, this entire educational experience, from the primary to the college level, was, for the most part, free. The only partial exception occurred at the grammar school level: "The maintenance of the schools was to be paid for by private tuition, but the best students from the elementary schools were to be selected and sent to the grammar schools at public expense."[15] Fourth, Jefferson, who remained "passionately anti-clerical" all of his life, stressed secularism in his educational plan. Sectarianism bred "religious bigotry," which he fought against. He was, at the same time, equally intolerant of "political heresy." In this sense, Jefferson saw political ideology as a religion to be taught in the schools.[16]

"One Great, and Equally Enlightened Family"

Benjamin Rush, who graduated from the College of New Jersey (Princeton) in 1760 and studied medicine at the University of Edinburgh and College of Philadelphia (University of Pennsylvania), taught chemistry at the University of Pennsylvania, "helped to found Dickinson College," signed the Declaration of Independence, and opposed slavery and capital punishment, was a physician and social reformer. In order to ensure the very survival of the young United States, Rush wanted to produce, as he expressed it, "republican machines." While the "American war" had ended, he saw the "American Revolution" as continuing with the creation of a new culture and institutions. The only means of accomplishing this rested on, again in his words, "one general, and uniform system of education." Private schools, a European legacy, would prove to be inadequate, since they often reflected sectarian influences that stressed different values and excluded most children by charging tuition. All schools had to teach the same set of values and be available to everyone. This required a new approach to education, and for Rush, "the only social agency capable of creating such an educational system was the government, whether state or national."[17]

Rush's position became clear in his 1786 educational proposal, "A Plan for the Establishment of Public Schools and the Diffusion of Knowledge in Pennsylvania: to Which are Added, Thoughts upon the Mode of Education, Proper in a Republic." He saw this model of republican education as a prototype for the new nation. His educational goal was the diffusion of knowledge to unify the state and, ultimately, the republic; he wanted to produce "one great, and equally enlightened family." He continued: "Our Schools of Learning, by producing one general, and uniform system of education, will render the mass of the people more homogeneous, and thereby fit them more easily for uniform and peaceable government." Rush, of course, wanted the schools in his scheme to instill patriotism: "Let our pupil be taught that he does not belong to himself, but that he is public property. Let him be taught to love his family, but let him be taught at the same time, that he must forsake them . . . when the welfare of his country requires it."[18] Thus, a political entity seemed to supersede the emotional bonds of family. Rush's emphasis on the child being the "property" of the state is crucial here and will be reflected in subsequent rhetoric supporting public schooling and its expanding role. Children represented political and economic assets too important for the state to ignore.

In his "simple plan," Rush wanted "free schools established in every township, or in districts consisting of one hundred families." The curriculum would ensure literacy by teaching "English and German languages and the use of figures." He included the German language because Pennsylvania hosted a large population of German immigrants as well as descendants of Germans. At the next level, each county would host an academy, in Rush's words, "for the purpose of instructing youth in preparing them to enter college." There they would study the "learned languages." His scheme stressed accessibility and called for four colleges to be located in different parts of the state, at Philadelphia, Carlisle, and Manheim, "for the benefit of our German fellow citizens." He further recommended that later a fourth college be located in Pittsburgh, on the western frontier. "In these colleges," Rush continued, "let young men be instructed in mathematics and the higher branches of science." Finally, his comprehensive proposal included a university located in the state capital. At the university level, Rush wanted the curriculum to cover "law, physic divinity, the law of nature and nations, economy." He insisted that the "professors receive such salaries from the state as will enable them to deliver lectures at a moderate price." In sum, Rush proposed a sequential and interrelated, semipublic system and one that accounted for a crude form of teacher preparation: "The university will in turn furnish masters of the colleges, and the colleges will furnish masters for the academies and free schools, while the free Schools, in their turn, will supply the academies—the colleges, and the university with scholars—students and pupils."[19]

Rush, unlike Jefferson, argued for the teaching of Christianity in his proposed schools, since "man is naturally an ungovernable animal." The moral training of children through schooling would produce upright citizens and, ultimately, ensure a stable republic. Without religion, he asserted, "there can be no virtue, and without virtue there can be no liberty, and liberty is the object and life of all republican governments." Rush equated Christianity with republicanism; thus, religion served an important role. The Bible would serve as a "school book," and the schoolmaster would reinforce all of this. Rush also wanted a stern approach to schooling in order to offset the family's inability to properly socialize the child. As Rush declared, "In the education of youth, let the authority of our masters be as *absolute* as possible."

Rush's means of subsidizing this system drew directly upon the resources of the state government. The state would hold land sales and the revenue from those would be allocated to establishing the colleges in Manheim and Pittsburgh, as well as the country academies and free schools. The already-existing Dickinson College would become one of the four colleges, while the University of Pennsylvania would be absorbed as "the" state university. In the beginning, however, each county would be taxed to support its academies, and individual families would pay taxes to support the free schools. Everyone in Rush's scheme paid taxes to support the schools, including single people and couples who had no children.

Rush saw this state system of schooling as an investment that in the long run would save money. The benefit would exceed mere monetary costs—a literate citizenry would ensure economic prosperity, material and scientific progress, and, most important, social and political stability. As Rush summarized it, "I believe it could be proved that the expenses of confining, trying, and executing criminals amount every year, in most counties, to more money than would be sufficient to maintain all the schools that would be necessary in each county."[20]

"Every Class of People Should Know and Love the Laws"

Noah Webster graduated from Yale in 1778 planning to become an attorney. However, due to the economic upheavals of post-Revolutionary America, he turned instead to teaching school. Four years later, he published his highly successful spelling book, which proved to be so popular that he and his family lived on the royalties while he compiled his famous dictionary. Seeking cultural autonomy from Great Britain to reinforce political independence, he wrote a series of articles between 1787 and 1788 on educational reform, which were published together in a 1790 pamphlet titled "On the Education of Youth in America." In it, Webster supported both universal education and "linguistic reform." He, like Rush, stressed a utilitarian approach to the curriculum and the practical education of girls. Webster's proposed curriculum, a clear break from British tradition, reflected national chauvinism, stressing American history and geography, for, he asserted, "Here every class of people should know and love the laws." Unlike Rush, he opposed the Bible as a school reader but still emphasized the learning of Christian moral virtues: "The only practicable method to reform mankind, is to begin with children; to banish, if possible, from their company, every low bred, drunken, immoral character. . . . The great act of correcting mankind therefore, consists of prepossessing the mind with good principles." Webster's teachers would serve as intellectual and moral models, and he insisted on "good teachers," that is, "men of unblemished reputation, and possessed of abilities, competent to their stations." In addition to these traits, "teachers should possess good breeding and agreeable manners."[21]

Like Rush, Webster believed that the "teacher should be an absolute monarch." Discipline, therefore, played a crucial role in Webster's ideal classroom.

> The rod is often necessary in school; especially after the children have been accustomed to disobedience and a licentious behavior at home. All government originates in families, and if neglected there, it will hardly exist in society; but the want of it must be supplied by the rod in school, the penal laws of the state, and the terrors of divine wrath from the pulpit. The government both of families and schools should be absolute. . . . In schools the master should be absolute in command. . . . A proper subordination in families would generally supersede the necessity of severity in schools; and a strict discipline in both is the best foundation of good order in political society.[22]

Webster's concern over the deteriorating social and educational role of the family in the post-Revolutionary period is apparent throughout this passage. His stern words strike a familiar chord in terms of present-day anxieties over the family as a viable social institution. Time and again, especially during the early nineteenth and twentieth centuries, other reformers would express alarm over the decline of the American family. To compensate, they would assert the need to expand the school's institutional role in socializing and educating the nation's children. Either the family should willingly surrender its responsibilities, they argued, or well-meaning reformers and educators would usurp it, assigning yet more tasks to the public schools. Webster and Rush both believed that moral and disciplined students ensured a stable political society. Thus, for them, schools should serve a significant socialization role.

Webster also saw a common language as a unifying force; as he stated it, "a *national language* is a band of *national union*."[23] His focus on language stressed uniform "spelling, pronunciation, and political and economic principles."[24] A common spelling and dialect not only reduced a sense of regionalism but blurred social-class lines. "Europeans used language to divide people; Americans should use it to bring them together." Webster therefore "demanded an American revolution at the linguistic level."[25] He attempted to accomplish this task through his famous speller, *The American Spelling Book*, later retitled *The*

Elementary Spelling Book, which had an immediate impact, making spelling the basis of reading instruction and spelling bees a "craze." Students competed to "spell down" their classmates. The victor received instant recognition and rewards, such as a written certificate or a coin. "Each prize coin was drilled and hung on a string, and the winners in the afternoon spelling lessons were entitled to carry a coin suspended from their necks until the next morning, when these decorations were turned over to the teacher to be again contended for."[26] These school contests, absorbing whole afternoons, occurred on a weekly basis, usually on Friday afternoons, and orthographic champions participated in spell downs between schools during dreary winter evenings, with entire communities in attendance.

> The spelling bee dramatized equality: any person of any background could win and children and their parents could prove their ability to "use" language as well as any person of whatever background. That someone in their community could spell a word from the last pages of Webster's speller assured the people that their village was as good as any other place, whether village, or urban cultural center. It also proved that the promises of democracy were real: the most sophisticated and cultural "use" of language, the possession of only the upper classes in despotic Europe, was available to all in America.[27]

Thus was established a school tradition still in existence today. Only high school athletics, a nonacademic activity, has supplanted the spelling bee as a source of community pride in local schools.

Webster's speller attained almost universal general circulation and universal use in American schools. By the time of his death, in 1842, the speller had sold 24 million copies. As historian Clifton Johnson asserts, "For the first two or three years that the children attended school, during the earlier decades of the Republic, Webster's speller was their chief textbook."[28] It transcended simple spelling and language lessons for he added a "Moral Catechism" to it in 1794. Only the Bible outsold the speller nationwide. "It and the Bible were commonly the only two books a family owned."[29]

Webster, growing conservative after the French Revolution, appended the "Federal Catechism" to the 1798 edition of *The American Spelling Book*. He stressed law and order, seeing no difference between "instruction in the principles of government" and political "indoctrination." In the "Catechism," he told children of the advantages of republicanism and the defects of monarchy, aristocracy, and democracy.[30] The following excerpt severely criticizes democracy:

Q. *What are the defects of democracy?*

A. In democracy, where the people all meet for the purpose of making laws, there are commonly tumults and disorders. A small city may sometimes be governed in this manner; but if the citizens are numerous, their assemblies make a crowd or mob, where debates cannot be carried on with coolness and candor, nor can arguments be heard: Therefore a pure democracy is generally a very bad government. It is often the most tyrannical government on earth; for a multitude is often rash, and will not hear reason.[31]

This civics lesson reflects not only Webster's fears of popular rule but the concerns of other early national leaders who expressed grave doubts about the ability of the American people "to govern themselves."[32] A republican form of governance, in contrast to participatory democracy, removed a great deal of direct decision-making power from the American people.

What impact did these proposals have? None of them were actually implemented, but they established educational ideals that endured. They "argued that a democratic government must see that all its citizens could read and write and thus be capable of resisting demagogic appeals, which were thought to succeed only among the ignorant. None produced plans to equal Jefferson's in scope but, like Jefferson's, they all insisted that the new nation must look to the careful education of all its citizens if the fragile republic were to survive the many challenges it faced."[33] The rhetoric of the common-school movement, beginning in the 1830s, would echo these statements about need for mass schooling, supported by the state, to sustain the republic.

"REPUBLICAN MOTHERS"

The Revolution politicized colonial women. During the boycott of British products prior to the war, women adapted by producing their own goods or by shopping very carefully, buying only "American" wares. But they did not just abstain from drinking British tea; they also wrote "poems and essays" urging "patriotism and political principle." As historian Sara M. Evans points out, "because the war had given political overtones to domestic consumption, it offered increased opportunities for women to act politically and aggressively from within their role as housewives." In 1780, Philadelphia and New Jersey women solicited door-to-door for funds to help support the colonial military cause. Women were directly involved in the war as well, as refugees fleeing enemy troops and the danger of battles; as camp followers, some of whom "cooked and cleaned for the soldiers; others served as nurses; and still others disguised themselves as men and fought"; and finally, with men absent fighting the war, as the managers of farms or businesses.

"The political ideals of the Revolution raised new questions about women" and their political and social roles. Women had asserted themselves during the Revolution and raised their political profile, yet they were still viewed as incapable of independent thought and too delicate for participation in the political process. The dilemma over how to grant women a political function and maintain, at the same time, their traditional domestic responsibilities was resolved by a compromise. As Evans summarizes it, "The problem of female citizenship was solved by endowing domesticity itself with political meaning. The result was the idea and image of the republican mother. Her patriotic duty to educate her sons to be moral and virtuous citizens linked her to the state and gave her some degree of power over its future."[34] They had to, in short, assist in producing republican machines, as Rush termed it. This, of course, had educational implications.

Schemes for mass education during this period implied that all European Americans, including women, should acquire the rudiments of literacy at a minimum. The idea of female education encountered little opposition, since proponents based their arguments either on equalitarianism or nationalism. However, this represented only an illusive gain because the education of females rested on notions of traditional social roles for women. Although supporters made bold proposals, they did not want to "unsex" women.[35]

Judith Sargent Murray, a leading eighteenth-century proponent of female education, however, asserted the need for "educational equality" throughout her writings. The daughter of a Boston merchant, she led a privileged life yet received only a basic education from studying with her brother as a tutor prepared him for Harvard College. Otherwise, her life followed a traditional pattern; she married for a second time after being widowed. Nevertheless, in her 1779 essay "On the Equality of the Sexes," she attacked "male superiority on several fronts" and argued that "women did not lack brains but did lack instruction."[36] In a 1784 article, "Desultory Thoughts upon the Utility of Encouraging a Degree of Self-Complacency, Especially in Female Bosoms," Murray questioned basic literacy training by encouraging girls to seek a broader and more meaningful education to, in her words, "teach young minds to aspire."[37] Historians David Tyack and Elisabeth Hansot summarize Murray's position in this way: "Her ideal woman was not the dependent wife or fashionable maiden, but rather an educated and serious companion of her husband, a competent worker, and a mother who raised upright citizens."

Benjamin Rush also proposed a more practical approach to female education. In 1787, during the Constitutional Convention he presented his plan at the Young Ladies' Academy in Philadelphia, which he had helped to found. His address, titled "Thoughts upon Female Education," stressed a uniquely American approach and made a profound break from British precedents. He proposed utilitarianism, dispensing with the traditional emphasis on genteel accomplishments. "He wanted to train women in practical subjects so they could 'be the stewards and guardians of their husbands' property' and could 'discharge the duties of those offices with the most success and reputation.' " Thus, instead of teaching dancing, flower arranging, novel reading, and painting, "he would have girls study 'history, travels, poetry, and moral essays' as well as receiving 'regular instruction in the Christian religion.' " Although women could not participate in the political process themselves, they had to be literate and socialized to prepare their sons to do so. "While limiting their scope to the home, as wives and mothers, Rush nonetheless assigned women a civic role in creating a virtuous republic."[38]

Female Academies

The republican influence bore some fruit. In the 1780s and 1790s, some grammar schools began to accommodate girls and private **academies** were opened for female students, which "made higher education available to young American women from middling and well-to-do families." Largely located in the Northeast, especially New England, the academies included Poor's school in Philadelphia and Isabella Graham's school in New York City; others were in Boston and New Haven. Southern planter families often sent their daughters to these academies.

The republican academies assumed four basic characteristics. First, they taught academic subjects as well as "ornamental accomplishments," like "needlework, music, and dancing." Second, many academies were located in small towns as well as large cities, thus facilitating access to many girls. Third, operating as boarding schools, they provided formal, institutionalized education for women. Fourth, they were not ephemeral; rather, many academies endured, surviving "well into the nineteenth century and a few even have lineal descendants in operation today." Early republican educational reform therefore substantially expanded schooling opportunities for women. According to historian Mary Beth Norton, "Whereas their mothers, if they were fortunate, had had advanced training only in such ornamental accomplishments as music, dancing, French, and fancy needlework, republican girls from middling and well-to-do families could attend schools at which they were taught grammar, rhetoric, history, geography, mathematics, and some of the natural sciences."[39]

Emma Hart Willard, Catharine Beecher, and Mary Lyon, graduates of republican academies, became "pioneer educators" themselves, founding female seminaries to further expand educational opportunities for women.[40] Willard opened Troy Female Seminary in 1821 in New York, Beecher established the Hartford Female Seminary in 1823 in Connecticut, and Lyon founded Mt. Holyoke Seminary in 1837 in Northampton, Massachusetts. Guided largely by evangelical principles, "such reformers extolled a serious if not stern ideal of feminine character and called for 'professionalizing motherhood.'" Reflecting a belief in the equality between the male and female intellect, the curricula in these schools stressed academic subjects but retained traditional notions of women's roles as wives and mothers; they also included instruction in "moral character."

Willard, Beecher, and Lyon shared other common themes in their various writings and pronouncements. For example, female education should no longer rely on informal means and social institutions, like the family, but should be formal and institutionalized through schooling, stressing academic subjects. They also believed that the pedagogy in "secondary schooling for girls should be rigorous and systematic, but they criticized the mechanical

*Mary Lyon, c. early 1840s
(based on a daguerreotype)
Courtesy of the Mary Lyon
Collection, The Mt. Holyoke
College Archives and
Special Collections*

method of instruction common in men's academies and colleges." At the same time, they questioned the role of competition in a classroom setting and rejected outright the use of corporal punishment. Finally, they mantained that education, to some extent, liberated women. "[L]ike Murray, [these] women educators wanted marriage to be a choice, not a trap, and thus wished single women to have an honorable alternative to marriage (like teaching)."

Female seminaries left a valuable legacy, as Tyack and Hansot contend, influencing the common schools in several ways. First, they were the prototype, later adapted by common-school advocates, for the schooling of girls. "Second, the seminaries demonstrated that there was a large public demand among girls and their families for secondary education and provided a model of curriculum and instruction for public high schools." Third, Willard, Beecher, and Lyon set a precedent by hiring female instructors, who demonstrated their capabilities in full-time classroom settings; female teachers would serve as the backbone for the expansion of the common schools. Fourth, the seminaries introduced teacher training for women "long before the establishment of the more well known public normal schools." Fifth, seminary graduates spearheaded common schools in their local communities and on the western frontier. The alumnae of these schools became "pedagogical Jenny Appleseeds, planting seeds across the nation."[41] In these ways, the efforts to educate girls in general and prepare female teachers in particular influenced the common-school movement of the 1830s and 1840s.

American Women and Divorce

The post-Revolutionary period saw the formal and permanent establishment of divorce as part of American culture, thereby creating yet another opportunity for women. Although the Puritans had freely practiced divorce in seventeenth-century New England, American attitudes toward divorce in all regions shifted profoundly between 1776 and the 1850s. The South and the rapidly expanding western frontier adopted laws similar to those in the East. The western divorce rate, in fact, outstripped that of any other region throughout the nineteenth century. Furthermore, informal divorces, separations, and desertions appeared to be far more numerous in all regions during this period. Revolutionary principles of independence, the familial disruptions caused by industrialization, the many distractions of a growing urban culture, and the ease of the western migration fed this trend. This experience, however, appeared to be limited to "white Protestant Americans." Formal and legal divorce among Roman Catholic and African American couples proved to be rare.

Divorce thus grew to be quite acceptable, even attaining the status of a "national scandal" by the middle of the nineteenth century. "Opponents of divorce believed that the spread of divorce revealed decay in American society and breakdown of the American family." It was thought that children would be neglected and their education imperiled. On the other hand, "female divorce-seekers" saw this as a personal choice over submissiveness, abuse, and neglect, as a way to protect their children; marriage did not serve as a "lifetime contract."[42]

Thus, American women, through their participation in the colonial revolt and because of the heady ideals of the post-Revolutionary period, appeared to make modest gains during the early 1800s. Although not granted equal political rights, they gradually gained access to private and public schooling and began to assert their independence and individuality through the ever-growing practice of divorce. The former ensured them literacy, an important tool for active participation in the political arena; the latter, as a formalization of a colonial tradition, profoundly shaped the educational mission of the family, an influence that continues to this day.

THE GREAT WHITE FATHER

The federal government, although not directly involved in the education of European and African Americans, from the beginning played a major educational role among Native Americans. Drawing on colonial educational precedents, it formalized the educational process for this group as well as bureaucratized it. Between 1778 and 1871, the United States government signed "almost 400 treaties" with "various Indian nations." Most of these agreements contained some educational provisions. The 1825 treaty signed by the Choctaw is illustrative: "We wish our children educated. We wish to derive lasting, if not transient, benefits for the sale of our lands. The proceeds of those sales we are desirous should be applied for the instruction of our young countrymen. . . . We feel our ignorance, and we begin to see the benefits of education." In many cases, the federal government used the promise of education to persuade Native American nations to cede lands. In Oregon, the territorial governor in the 1850s told the Nisquallys; ". . . the Great Father wishes you to have homes, pasture for your horses and fishing places. He wants you to learn to farm and your children to go to a good school. . . . "Two types of Native American schools emerged. Schools funded by the U.S. government remained largely the responsibility of religious missions. In other cases, Native American tribes controlled their own schools. "Most notable among these tribes are the Choctaws and Cherokees, who combined had nearly 200 schools when the Indian Territory was dissolved in the early 1900s.[43]

Religion, Literacy, Work, and Civilization

Congress passed the Indian Civilization Fund Act in 1819, which subsidized religious groups' efforts to educate Native Americans. A variety of religious denominations—the Baptists, Quakers, Methodists, and Roman Catholics—sent missionaries among the Chippewa, Iroquois, Oneida, Seneca, and Winnebago and many other Eastern, Midwestern, and Western tribes. Twenty-one Native American schools existed by 1824 as a result. The Cherokee, in the Southeast, wanted education because, as a "Cherokee told the Baptists in 1824, 'We want our children to learn English so that the white man cannot cheat us.' " The Brainerd Mission, in Chickamauga, Georgia, relied on the **Lancasterian method** (which we will discuss in Chapter 4), drilling students in English reading and writing as well as Christian religion. Students received English names and boys learned farming while girls practiced domestic skills during their sixteen-hour days.[44] However, with the 1830 Indian Removal Act, the federal government forced the Cherokee to exchange their eastern lands for land west of the Mississippi River, and "as a side effect of removal, federal support for mission schools east of the Mississippi was ended in 1832, and generous subsidies were offered to move the missions west."[45]

Many of these missionary efforts achieved little success, according to David H. DeJong's historical analysis. First, many Native Americans, to protect their tribal religious traditions, resisted. Second, the federal government failed to set clear "standards" and provided little oversight. Finally, in 1873, when the government terminated its subsidy of missionary efforts, various Protestant denominations began to withdraw from the missions because they wanted to preserve the "separation between church and state." The Catholics, however, refused to give up the mission schools. But by the 1890s, the U.S. government had assumed full responsibility for Native American education.

"The Five Civilized Tribes"

As part of treaty negotiations, some tribes sought to pursue " 'white man's' education." The "Five Civilized Tribes," consisting of the Cherokee, Chickasaw, Choctaw, Creek, and Seminole, organized elaborate and successful educational systems. "Three types of schools existed, to some degree, among the Five Civilized Tribes. They were the tribal neighborhood schools, the tribal boarding schools, conducted under contracts with various religious denominations, and the male and female academies or seminaries operated under contract with religious denominations or private individuals."[46]

When the Cherokee were forced westward during the 1838–39 "Trail of Tears," which was engineered by President Andrew Jackson and which drove 11,500 Cherokee from their southern Appalachian homes to "Indian Territory" (later, Oklahoma Territory), with some 4,000 of them dying along the way of "dysentery, malnutrition, exposure, or exhaustion," the Cherokee became "disillusioned with Christianity" and the Christians who had forced them out of their land and inflicted such pain. They established their own schools; by 1842, Cherokee schools "taught reading, writing, arithmetic, bookkeeping, English grammar, geography, and history," in eleven schools, forming a "national school system." According to historians Jon Reyhner and Jeanne Eder, "[by] 1852, the Cherokee Nation had a better common school system than the neighboring states of Arkansas and Missouri." However, the Department of the Interior confiscated these schools in 1898, just as the federal government had earlier expropriated the land.[47]

The Chickasaw Nation, which established public schools in 1867, compiled the most remarkable educational record. It established community day schools that relied on Chickasaw teachers, who used both their native language and English in the classroom. The tribe also standardized all of its schools' textbooks. Finally, the Chickasaw permitted white children to attend these schools, although they had to pay tuition. The Chickasaw, according to observers created the "finest school system west of the Mississippi River."[48]

The Growth of Government Bureaucracy

The federal government gradually bureaucratized its influence over Native American education. The War Department oversaw Indian affairs as early as 1789. The government then established the Bureau of Indian Affairs in 1824, shifting it from the War Department to the Department of the Interior in 1849, and also created the position of Commissioner of Indian Affairs in 1832. In 1839, Congress formally established manual schools to teach Native American children "farming and homemaking." By 1871, 286 such schools existed with an enrollment of 6,061 students. "Nearly half of those schools were in the Cherokee, Choctaw, Chicasaw[sic], and Creek nations in Indian Territory, present-day Oklahoma."[49]

The constant flow of tens of thousands of European American settlers to the western frontier resulted in an increasing demand for land. The consequence of this was that in the 1880s the federal government began to withdraw its support of tribal education activities. The passage of the Dawes Act of 1887 dissolved tribal ownership of lands and eroded the tribes' authority over their own affairs. As a result, Native American tribes lost a great deal of land to homesteaders. Finally, the Curtis Act of 1898 ultimately "gave the United States supervision over the tribal schools."

The federal government would continue to shape and control Native American educational policy into the early decades of the twentieth century. These efforts, driven by national concerns, did not benefit Native American children, but rather worked to their detriment. The quality of the schooling offered declined. Another shift, from federal to state control, took place in the 1930s and 1940s; Native American education would subsequently deteriorate further.[50]

EDUCATION ON THE MEXICAN FRONTIER

The conflict and upheaval faced by Spain in the Borderlands culminated in Mexican independence in 1821. Before that event, during the first half of the 1700s, Spain's North American settlements had "stagnated," attracting few colonists. The bleak and often hostile frontier did not appeal to them, and Spain's clumsy rule of its colonies also hindered development. Its North American colonies, the subject of continental rivalry, proved to be highly unstable. In the east, English settlers encroached on Spanish territory in Florida, which covered much of present-day Florida, Georgia, Alabama, and Louisiana. With only 1,500 Spanish colonists in Florida, one-tenth of the English population of South Carolina, Spain's claim to present-day Georgia and Florida seemed precarious indeed, and in 1763, Britain assumed control of Florida. However, beginning in the late 1760s and early 1770s, to counter Russian incursions in the West, the Spanish aggressively settled California. By 1781, a series of Spanish missions, presidios, and towns, including San Francisco, San José, Santa Barbara, Los Angeles, and San Diego, occupied the coast of New California. The California Spanish population grew from 990 in 1790 to 3,200 in 1821.

Preoccupied with continental intrigue, Spain allowed its American colonies to fragment. From the 1790s until 1814, Spain first fought revolutionary France, then England, and then Napoleonic France. Spain drained its North American colonies of their already meager military and financial resources, and its largely neglected North American claims gradually eroded away to other powers or became independent. In 1790, Spain lost control of the Pacific Northwest coast to England; it surrendered the Ohio River Valley, in addition to other territorial concessions, to the United States in 1795; and in 1803 it ceded its Louisiana territory to France, which promptly sold it to the United States. Although Spain, which had sided with the American revolutionaries and had declared war on Britain in 1779, had recaptured Florida, Americans living in the western part of

West Florida—a territory which stretched as far as Louisiana—declared themselves independent and became absorbed into the United States in 1810. Spain lost East Florida, as well as the remainder of West Florida, to the United States in 1821. Texas immediately became a "defensive province" as the two frontiers, one Spanish and the other Anglo, clashed.[51]

With Mexican independence in 1821, the "Spanish Borderlands became the Mexican Borderlands."[52] Initially there were few significant political and cultural changes. As the years passed, though, the Mexican frontier became increasingly fluid. Mexico allowed Anglos to settle on the Texas frontier, and by the mid-1830s they outnumbered **Tejanos**, Mexicans who already resided on the Texas frontier. Warfare exacerbated this imbalance. In 1834, San Antonio, the largest Texas settlement and the site of the Alamo mission, hosted a population of 24,000, mostly Mexican, residents. Historian Richard Griswold del Castillo continues, "a year later, however, a large body of the population fled when the city was occupied by Mexican and Texan armies. Additional hundreds of families departed when the Texans finally occupied San Antonio after General Santa Anna's defeat at San Jacinto in 1836." Conflict and turmoil continued, resulting in the expropriation of Mexican possessions and land. Many *Tejanos* fled for their safety. "By 1845, on the eve of the Mexican War, the town's population numbered only about 700."

Santa Fe, New Mexico, the oldest Spanish pueblo and the northernmost administrative center of New Spain's vast frontier, developed its own unique culture, "one more oriented toward Spanish customs and traditions than the Mestizo Mexican." Griswold del Castillo further writes, "the northern New Mexicans, or **Hispanos**, had a long history of resistance to outsiders who challenged their independence and deep attachment to the land." In addition to the 1680 Pueblo Revolt, another Native American uprising occurred in 1837, "encouraged by Hispanos who were dissatisfied with their Mexican-appointed governor. A decade later the Pueblo Indians again allied themselves with Hispanos to resist the encroachment of the Americans," overthrowing the "newly established governor of Taos." United States troops subdued that rebellion. However, cultural resistance persisted after the conclusion of the Mexican War in 1848, with Mexican Americans, the majority of the population, struggling to preserve their heritage and traditions well into the twentieth century.[53]

Albert Camarillo's description of Santa Barbara and California in general paints a similar complex and dynamic picture of Mexican frontier life at this time. Heavily steeped in Spanish and Native American culture, colonial institutional patterns endured well into the early national period. "Throughout the colonial period, and for another decade after the beginning of the Mexican national period in 1821, the presidio-mission complex remained the bulwark of the northern Mexican borderlands frontier in California." However, presidios gradually became civilianized, were converted to pueblos, and eventually evolved into municipalities. The 1834 Secularization Proclamation marked the end of the colonial mission as well as the decline of its educational function. Mission secularization resulted in land redistribution and introduced the "Golden Age of the ranchos, the period from 1834 to 1846," throughout California. At the time of American occupation, three social classes of **Californios** lived in pueblos like Santa Barbara: "The ranchero and his family were at the top of the social ladder, while the mestizos made up the small working class. . . . The Native Americans served as the chief source of manual labor."[54]

Early Educational Developments

The educational process in the former Spanish colonies likewise began to undergo change. Mexican independence "guaranteed citizenship and equality" for all citizens. By 1829, this applied to African Americans as well, since Mexico had abolished slavery. The new Mexican government, although short of resources, promoted public elementary schooling, but the ultimate responsibility fell on the state and territorial governments. According to Martha Menchaca's research, in 1833 the Mexican federal government began to assume administrative control of public education and proceeded to secularize it. The government required certified teachers, reviewed textbooks, instituted compulsory attendance, and designated federal taxes for schools. "Though the taxes earmarked for public education were outrageously inadequate, the idea of federal funding for public education had finally begun." The Mexican government sent teachers to California to improve its schools. However, "[i]n New Mexico, the educational system did not expand during the Mexican period." Texas meanwhile hosted a rudimentary public school system, relying largely on the Lancasterian method, which we will examine in Chapter 4.

The 1846–1848 war between Mexico and the United States short-circuited any further educational developments.[55] The result of the War was that in 1848 the Mexican Borderlands became the American Southwest.[56] Beginning with the usurpation of political power and seizure of vast public and private Mexican landholdings, the long process of Americanization included the Mexican public schools. Educational changes continued to be made through a variety of public, private, and religious schools established on the southwestern frontier during the late nineteenth century, as we shall see in Chapter 6.

CONCLUSIONS

In both the young United States and Mexico, colonial educational patterns continued, for the most part, through the early 1800s. "During the [American] early national period, despite the desire of the revolutionary educational reformers for a homogeneous citizenry, education continued to be heterogeneous, maintaining much of its sectarian energy and social diversity."[57] Although none of the proposals by early American national leaders reached fruition, they did nevertheless establish a durable legacy that would influence the common-school movement during the early decades of the nineteenth century. Meanwhile, by the late 1820s and early 1830s, the Mexican federal government was attempting to establish public elementary schools on its frontier. The trend toward formalized schooling away from the system of informal education based on the family, and toward free schooling rather than private educational, and largely reli-

gious, institutions continued as notions of nationalism and equality were articulated in both countries.

There were some early, but rudimentary, manifestations of the trend toward state-supported public schools. John Adams, a federalist and largely responsible for the new Massachusetts constitution of 1780, had "for some years, promoted state-supported public education." Such schooling would produce loyal Americans, ensure moral training, and promote social stability. In 1789, the Massachusetts legislature, reflecting republican principles and somewhat echoing the colonial act of 1647, passed "the first comprehensive state school law in the new nation." It required town and township schools, as well as district schools in less populated areas. Boston enacted its own comprehensive education act, subsidized by tax revenue, that same year. In Boston, boys and girls were to attend school together and learn the same subjects.

"Yet, girls were required to be in school fewer hours per day—and only from April to October—while boys were to attend year around, except for a brief vacation." The Boston act also created district schools. Children younger than seven attended dame schools, began grammar school at age seven, and moved on to reading and writing schools or Greek or Latin schools to prepare for college. The law unified the curriculum, requiring the study of grammar, and it established uniform times for schools throughout the city. Finally, the act created a "permanent school committee." Thus, the rudiments of a defined system of schooling emerged in Boston. Nevertheless, only about 12 percent of school-aged children attended school. Others were either apprenticed, received tutoring at home, learned their literacy skills through their family, "or continued illiterate."[58] The common-school movement would represent a culmination of this early, publicly subsidized educational activity.

ACTIVITIES FOR FURTHER EXPLORATION

1. Who were the early national leaders? Investigate the biographical backgrounds of the delegates who attended the Constitutional Convention: www.nara.gov/exhall/charters/constitution/conmain.html.

2. What is the federal role in education? What do the Articles of Confederation and the U.S. Constitution say about education? These documents, including the Northwest Ordinance of 1787, can be found at the following Web site: http://www.law.ou.edu/hist/.

3. What provision does your state constitution make for education? Obtain a copy to find references to education.

4. How did early nineteenth-century girls live? See the memoir "Sarah Smith Emery— Memories of a Massachusetts Girlhood at the Turn of the Nineteenth Century" at http://chnm.gmu.edu/us/many.taf. Note Sarah's responsibilities. Compare them with contemporary women's lives. What has changed? What has remained the same?

5. When did the feminist movement begin? To gain insight into the rich history of women's accomplishments, check http://www.nwhp.org/events/events.html. Also see Sojourner Truth's famous speech, "Ain't I A Woman?" at http://chnm.gmu.edu/us/many.taf.

6. Has there been continuity in the government's policy toward Native Americans? To gain a better sense of the historical sequence of events regarding government policy, see http://digital.library.okstate.edu/kappler. For details on the tragic Cherokee experience, refer to http://www.powersource.com/nation/dates.html.

7. What role did religion play in Native American lives? European Americans staunchly denied that Native Americans' religion was a fundamental component of their culture. For a Native American perspective, see "Red Jacket Defends Native American Religion, 1805," http://chnm.gmu.edu/us/many.taf.

NOTES AND SOURCES

In order to condense endnotes, the first work cited is the primary one, usually the source of any direct quotes. Subsequent references serve as supplementary, or additional, sources of paraphrased information and/or alternative historical interpretations.

1. These two pages draw heavily on Thomas P. Slaughter, *The Whiskey Rebellion: Frontier Epilogue to the American Revolution* (New York: Oxford University Press, 1986), pp. 3, 31–33, 49, 51, 159–160, 171, 188, 190–191, 205–206. See especially Lorraine Smith Pangle and Thomas L. Pangle, *The Learning of Liberty: The Educational Ideas of the American Founders* (Lawrence, KS: University Press of Kansas, 1993), p. 1.

2. Quoted in David B. Tyack, ed., *Turning Points in American Educational History* (New York: John Wiley & Sons, 1967), p. 83. Tyack's collection consists of excerpts from key primary documents in American educational history, supplemented with an introduction and commentary by him. Also refer to Peter S. Onuf, "The Founders' Vision: Education in the Development of the Old Northwest," in "*. . . School and The Means of Education Shall Forever Be Encouraged*": *A History of Education in the Old Northwest, 1787–1880*, eds. Paul H. Mattingly and Edward W. Stevens (Athens, OH: Ohio University Libraries, 1987), p. 6. Onuf, on p. 13, uses the phrase, "political socialization." Finally, see Robert L. Church, *Education in the United States: An Interpretive History* (New York: Free Press, 1976), pp. 3–4.

3. Tyack, *Turning Points*, p. 84.

4. Pangle and Pangle, *Learning of Liberty*, pp. 15, 16, 17, 20–21, 22, 25, 32, 38, 63–64, 66, 67–68, 69, 70, 76, 78–82, 85, 188, 192, 201.

5. Rush Welter, *Popular Education and Democratic Thought in America* (New York: Columbia University Press, 1962), p. 24.

6. Frederick Rudolph, ed., *Essays on Education in the Early Republic* (Cambridge, MA: Harvard University Press, 1965), p. xi–xiii. See as well Pangle and Pangle, *The Learning of Liberty*, pp. 67–68, 91, 93, 96.

7. Quoted in Onuf, "The Founders' Vision," p. 5. Also see R. Freeman Butts, *Public Education in the United States: From Revolution to Reform* (New York: Holt, Rinehart and Winston, 1978), p. 16; Richard D. Brown, *Knowledge Is Power: The Diffusion of Information in Early America, 1700–1865* (New York: Oxford University Press, 1989), p. 287. David Tyack and Thomas James, "State Government and American Public Education: Exploring the 'Primeval Forest,' " *History of Education Quarterly*, 26 (Spring 1986), p. 57, argue that "the federal government became an early patron of public education through its grants of land for common schools. Between 1803 and 1896 the federal government gave more than 77 million acres to western and southern states to support common schools."

8. Welter, *Popular Education*, p. 25.

9. Butts, *Public Education*, pp. 37–38, 39–40, 41.

10. Onuf, "The Founders' Vision," p. 6; Butts, *Public Education*, pp. 19–20.

11. Tyack, *Turning Points*, pp. 85, 86, 87. Refer as well to Pangle and Pangle, *The Learning of Liberty*, pp. 108, 112.

12. Thomas Jefferson, "Bill for the More General Diffusion of Knowledge," in Tyack, *Turning Points*, p. 111. The "little republic" quote is from Pangle and Pangle, *The Learning of Liberty*, pp. 115–116, 118. Also refer to Butts, *Public Education*, pp. 26–27; Tyack, *Turning Points*, p. 87; Welter, *Popular Education*, p. 24.

13. Jefferson, "Bill for the More General Diffusion of Knowledge," pp. 114, 116.

14. Jefferson here is quoted by Tyack, *Turning Points*, p. 89. See likewise Pangle and Pangle, *The Learning of Liberty*, pp. 120–121.

15. Butts, *Public Education*, p. 27.

16. Jefferson's "political heresy" quote is by Tyack, *Turning Points*, p. 90.

17. "Republican machines" is a famous phrase of Rush and is quoted in Tyack, *Turning Points*, pp. 86–87; also see Onuf, "The Founders' Vision," p. 8. For brief biographical background, see Rudolph, *Essays on Education*, p. 1, and Butts, *Public Education*, p. 28. The "American war" and "American Revolution" quotes are taken from Pangle and Pangle, *Learning of Liberty*, pp. 12–13.

18. Rudolph, *Essays on Education*, contains all of Rush's proposals; see especially pp. 10, 14. Likewise, see Benjamin Rush's proposal in Tyack, *Turning Points*, pp. 100–106. Finally, refer to Pangle and Pangle, *The Learning of Liberty*, p. 32.

19. Rush, "A Plan for the Establishment of Public Schools," in Tyack, *Turning Points*, pp. 100–101. Also, refer to Butts, *Public Education*, p. 28.

20. Rush, "A Plan for the Establishment of Public Schools," in Rudolph, *Essays on Education*, pp. 5–7, 10–12, 16. Further refer to Rush, "A Plan for the Establishment of Public Schools," in Tyack, *Turning Points*, pp. 103, 104; Pangle and Pangle, *The Learning of Liberty*, pp. 30–31, 33.

21. Clifton Johnson, *Old-Time Schools and School-books* (Macmillan Company, 1904; reprint ed., New York: Dover Publications, 1963), pp. 167–169. Butts, *Public Education*, also includes some biographical background on Webster on pp. 31, 32. Noah Webster, "On the Education of Youth in America," in Tyack, *Turning Points*, p. 94, 97. Refer as well to Ruth Miller Elson, *Guardians of Tradition: American Schoolbooks of the Nineteenth Century* (Lincoln, NE: University of Nebraska Press, 1964), p. 221; Pangle and Pangle, *The Learning of Liberty*, pp. 12, 102–103, 126.

22. Noah Webster, "On the Education of Youth in America," in Tyack, *Turning Points*, pp. 88, 94–95.

23. Webster is quoted in Onuf, "The Founders' Vision," p. 8.

24. Tyack, *Turning Points*, p. 86.

25. Church, *Education in the United States*, p. 18. Refer likewise to Henry Steele Commager, ed., *Noah Webster's American Spelling Book* (New York: Teachers College Press, 1958), pp. 1–2.

26. Johnson, *Old-Time Schools*, pp. 169, 170, 172, 174, 175. See as well Barbara Finkelstein, *Governing the Young: Teacher Behavior in Popular Primary Schools in Nineteenth-Century United States* (New York: Falmer Press, 1989), pp. 50–52.

27. Church, *Education in the United States*, pp. 19–20.

28. Johnson, *Old-Time Schools*, pp. 169–170, 172–175. Also see Pangle and Pangle, *The Learning of Liberty*, p. 133.

29. Church, *Education in the United States*, p. 19. Refer as well to Pangle and Pangle, *The Learning of Liberty*, pp. 135–36.

30. Tyack, *Turning Points*, p. 88; Butts, *Public Education*, p. 32.

31. Noah Webster, "Federal Catechism," in Tyack, *Turning Points*, pp. 189–190.

32. Onuf, "The Founders' Vision," p. 8. Refer as well to Pangle and Pangle, *The Learning of Liberty*, pp. 133, 136.

33. Church, *Education in the United States*, p. 5.

34. These two paragraphs draw on Sara M. Evans, *Born for Liberty: A History of Women in America* (New York: Free Press, 1997), pp. 49–54, 56–57.

35. Quote is from Mary Beth Norton, *Liberty's Daughters: The Revolutionary Experience of American Women, 1750–1800* (Boston: Little, Brown and Company, 1980), p. 263. Also, see David B. Tyack

and Elisabeth Hansot, *Learning Together: A History of Coeducation in American Public Schools* (New Haven, CT: Yale University Press, 1990), p. 32.

36. Tyack and Hansot, *Learning Together*, p. 33. Refer to Evans, *Born for Liberty*, p. 58; Norton, *Liberty's Daughters*, p. 252.

37. Norton, *Liberty's Daughters*, pp. 252–254.

38. Quotes in these two paragraphs from Tyack and Hansot, *Learning Together*, p. 33, 34. Also, see Butts, *Public Education*, p. 30; Norton, *Liberty's Daughters*, pp. 267, 268, 271.

39. These two paragraphs quote Norton, *Liberty's Daughters*, pp. 256–257, 272–273, 274, 288. See also Evans, *Born for Liberty*, p. 65.

40. The first quote in this paragraph is from Norton, *Liberty's Daughters*, p. 282, while the second quote is from Tyack and Hansot, *Learning Together*, p. 37.

41. The quotes in these three paragraphs are from Tyack and Hansot, *Learning Together*, pp. 37, 40, 41, 43. Also, see Carol Ruth Berkin and Mary Beth Norton, *Women of America: A History* (Boston: Houghton Mifflin Company, 1979); Pangle and Pangle, *The Learning of Liberty*, p. 104; Anne Firor Scott, "The Ever Widening Circle: The Diffusion of Feminist Values from the Troy Female Seminary," *History of Education Quarterly*, 19 (Spring 1979), pp. 3–26; Kathryn Kish Sklar, *Catharine Beecher: A Study in American Domesticity* (New York: W. W. Norton & Company, 1976).

42. The quotations and facts in this and the preceeding paragraph are taken from Glenda Riley, *Divorce: An American Tradition* (Lincoln, NE: University of Nebraska Press, 1991), pp. 34, 47, 49, 53–55, 59.

43. David H. DeJong, *Promises of the Past: A History of Indian Education* (Golden, CO: North American Press, 1993), pp. 34–35. The Choctaw and governor's quotes are on pp. 41 and 48, respectively.

44. Reyhner and Jeanne Eder, *A History of Indian Education* (Billings, MT: Eastern Montana College, 1989), pp. 26–27. The quote can be found on p. 29. Refer as well to Lawrence A. Cremin, *American Education: The National Experience* (New York: Harper & Row, 1980), pp. 234–237; DeJong, *Promises of the Past*, pp. 57, 59, 61, 63, 67.

45. Reyhner and Eder, *A History of Indian Education*, pp. 31, 33.

46. DeJong, *Promises of the Past*, pp. 58–59, 74, 81, 86, 89.

47. Linda Peavy and Ursula Smith. *Frontier Children*, (Norman, OK: University of Oklahoma Press, 1999), p. 16; Reyhner and Eder, *A History of Indian Education*, pp. 6, 33, 34, 54.

48. DeJong, *Promises of the Past*, pp. 90, 91, 94, 103. The quote is on p. 105.

49. Reyhner and Eder, *A History of Indian Education*, pp. 36, 37. Also see Coleman, *American Indian Children at School*, p. 38.

50. DeJong, *Promises of the Past*, pp. 100–101, 104.

51. David J. Weber, *The Spanish Frontier in North America* (New Haven, CT: Yale University Press, 1992), pp. 11, 174, 175, 176, 177, 179, 182–183, 199, 200, 243, 259, 262, 265, 267–268, 270, 273, 275, 285, 289, 295, 297, 299, 300. See as well John Francis Bannon, *The Spanish Borderlands Frontier, 1513–1821* (New York: Holt, Rinehart and Winston, 1970), pp. 206, 207–208, 209, 210.

52. Bannon, *Spanish Borderlands*, pp. 206, 229.

53. Richard Griswold del Castillo, *La Familia: Chicano Families in the Urban Southwest: 1848 to the Present* (South Bend, IN: University of Notre Dame Press, 1984), pp. 11, 12–13. Also see Guadalupe San Miguel, Jr., *"Let All of Them Take Heed": Mexican Americans and the Campaign for Educational Equality in Texas, 1910–1981* (Austin, TX: University of Texas Press, 1987), p. 2.

54. Albert Camarillo, *Chicanos in a Changing Society: From Mexican Pueblos to American Barrios in Santa Barbara and Southern California, 1848–1930* (Cambridge, MA: Harvard University Press, 1979), pp. 8–9, 12. Weber, *The Spanish Frontier in North America*, in Chapter 11, treats the syncretic cultural experience in detail.

55. Martha Menchaca, "The Treaty of Guadalupe Hidalgo and the Racialization of the Mexican Population," in *The Elusive Quest for Equality: 150 Years of Chicano/Chicana Education*, ed. Jose F. Moreno (Cambridge, MA: *Harvard Educational Review*, 1999), pp. 17, 18–19.

56. Bannon, *Spanish Borderlands*, p. 229. Also refer to Jay P. Dolan and Giberto Hinojosa, eds., *Mexican Americans and the Catholic Church, 1900–1965* (South Bend, IN: University of Notre Dame Press, 1994), p. 84.

57. Tyack, *Turning Points*, p. 120.

58. Stanley K. Schultz, *The Culture Factory: Boston Public Schools, 1789–1860* (New York: Oxford University Press, 1973), pp. 8, 11, 15, 16, 23.

P A R T

II

The Early Years of Formalized Schooling

4

The Common-School Era

The American family, as we have seen, began to relinquish its educational responsibility as early as the colonial period. Religious authorities in Puritan New England, committed to a tight-knit religious community, expressed doubts about the family's ability to teach its children values, literacy, and a vocational skill. During the post-Revolutionary War period, early national leaders, concerned about the very survival of the new nation-state, supported systematic education, implicitly—and explicitly in some cases—criticizing the family's ability to prepare future citizens. Thus, over two centuries, American education had been experiencing a gradual and subtle transition, moving toward a greater reliance on formal, institutionalized education through schooling.

The inception of the common schools, beginning in Massachusetts in the 1830s, marked the culmination of this institutional shift. However, the consensus supporting these schools proved to be fragile. Although they included female students, the schools failed to be inclusive, contradicting the concept of "common." Because of their Pan-Protestant emphasis, proponents alienated Roman Catholic parents. Northern African American children went to separate school buildings, if they attended school at all; their Southern counterparts received training only for slavery. This chapter traces the origins of the American public school as a product of cultural and institutional forces and places education within the context of gender, ethnicity, and race.

"ALL WERE INSTRUCTED IN THE SAME SCHOOL"

As in other eras, during the early nineteenth century education reflected the needs and interests of society. The result was free schooling made available to most children. Social, economic, and political forces, as well as institutional changes, clearly shaped the need for this system. The American Revolution altered our culture, but the Industrial Revolution transformed it.

A World Turned Upside Down

The transformation of **mercantile capitalism** into **industrial capitalism** during the early nineteenth century shredded the social fabric of American culture. Lynn, Massachusetts, was a representative case. When President George Washington visited Lynn in the fall of 1789, he found a seemingly sleepy agricultural village of "several hundred households" with livestock grazing in nearby fields. This pastoral setting proved to be somewhat deceptive because only Philadelphia outstripped Lynn's manufacturing output in shoes in the young United States. As labor historian Alan Dawley points out, "little wooden outbuildings" stood near most dwellings. "Larger than privies, smaller than barns, these were the workshops of the shoe industry." Dubbed "ten-footers," these cramped quarters contained several people working under the direction of a master shoemaker. Dawley stresses that, "as the basic unit of production, the household was also the basic link between the economy and the social structure of the community."

Social roles based on class, gender, and age certainly existed but became blurred in this work setting. "In the master shoemaker's household, the work team normally included nonrelated journeymen and apprentices, plus wives, daughters, and sons." This genial setting combined the master's, and his family's, personal and work lives. "As a husband and father, the master superintended his wife and children; as the owner of a workshop and raw materials he set the tasks for the journeymen."

Not to present a romanticized view, but preindustrial work moved at a very distinct pace and maintained a different culture than industrial labor. First, the master and his family completely controlled their time. "Women decided when to boil tallow for candles, when to darn socks, and when to bind shoes. Men chose when to repair the front stoop, when to manure the garden, and when to bottom shoes." This sense of autonomy even extended to the children. Running errands, a boy exploited this time to play games with friends or joined them for some "youthful amusement," or prank, which seldom went unpunished. Second, the master supervised the entire production process. He owned, or rented, the ten-footer, the leather, or raw materials, and tools, or means of production. His "control extended into the character and quality of the product, since he determined when the leather had been hammered long enough, whether to make the instep snug or full, how much stiffening to put in the heel."[1] Work paused for relaxed meals, or when customers and visitors stopped to be fitted or simply to pass the time gossiping or debating politics. The master took care of his children if his wife had to run an errand or visit a neighbor or relative.

Such preindustrial notions of time and work followed "natural rhythms." As a result, work was task oriented. Social historian E. P. Thompson points out that farming communities based their routines on cycles of planting, cultivating, and harvesting: "Sheep must be attended at lambing time and guarded from predators; cows must be milked." Even preindustrial manufacturing processes maintained this natural pattern. Thompson describes charcoal and iron making: "the charcoal fire must be attended and not burn away through the turfs (and the charcoal burners must sleep beside it); once iron is in the making, the furnaces must not be allowed to fail." Because of task-oriented work, there was no standard length to the workday or workweek. The duration of work depended on the completion of the task. Such irregular work rhythms caused bouts of leisure to be followed by frenetic periods of labor. And no sharp demarcation existed between work and "social intercourse."[2]

During the early decades of the nineteenth century, market forces and mechanization profoundly altered the manufacturing process and setting, social relationships, and the household's culture. Shoe factories enforced a formal and rigid work schedule antithetical to the informal and irregular routine of the ten-footer. "The factory itself was a kind of supermachine—a gross, cacophonous exaggeration of the elegant principles of the clock." The transformation went beyond mere technology changes, however. Conformity replaced individualism and dependence supplanted autonomy and independence in this dirty, noisy, and often dangerous workplace. Clear economic and social lines were drawn between employers and employees. Workers now became wage laborers, selling their time instead of their skill. "Order rested on the power of the manufacturers, and harmony in the beehives of industry was founded on economic compulsion, rather than on some instinctive dronish desire on the part of wage earners to cooperate among themselves for the owners' benefit."[3]

Industrial capitalism therefore introduced a regimented and inflexible work culture. Employers, faced with production quotas and concerned about profits, saw seemingly casual preindustrial work habits and attitudes as "wasteful and lacking in urgency." They implemented a standardized concept of time in order to synchronize labor. They set the length of the workday and workweek, often twelve hours a day, six days a week; determined the pace of production, usually excessive; and established the wage scale, generally insufficient. Timed labor eradicated task-oriented work. Industrialists enforced this new "time-discipline" in the factory, "with the time-sheet, the time-keeper, the informers and fines."[4] But were there other, less external ways to socialize workers?

Industrial capitalism also wreaked havoc on the family. With the preindustrial household gradually and grudgingly surrendering its manufacturing abilities, the family fragmented, and personal and work lives became bifurcated. Paternal, and often maternal, parents now trudged to and from the factories and home in the dark instead of casually entering the ten-footer. If the children did not work in the factory, they had to largely fend for themselves, and so the urban common schools began to adopt a custodial role, assuming some of the absent parents' responsibilities.

Social commentators began to criticize the American family increasingly between the 1830s and the 1860s. "Articles in domestic popular magazines attested to growing doubts about the social worth of the family as the molder of virtuous youth." They pointed to the rapid pace and seductive allures characteristic of city life and the disruptions and insecurities wrought by industrial work as the causes. As historian Stanley Schultz summarizes it,

> Writers asserted that in the country, on farms, and in small, rural towns family stability was undisturbed by any wide separation among the places of work, recreation, and dwelling. Fathers remained close to home, worked side by side with their children in the fields, read to them and aided in their lessons when district schooling was in session. Family harmony and security in small towns was not disrupted by hurried commercial activity, or by children at work in factories, or by the temptations of European fashions of dress and recreation that were common in the city.

Child labor, working mothers, and "rising divorce rates" symbolized the travails of the urban American family. The notion of the family's decline had larger implications according to alarmed observers. "Believing in the organic nature of society, educators and reformers asserted that the lack of parental discipline within the family caused a failure of order and authority throughout society."

Organized religion, like the family, had lost much of its authority. Republican ideals caused state support for religion to wane in the post-Revolutionary period. Orthodoxy became suspect and the tradition of an established church faded. By the 1830s, in Massachusetts, "[f]ull equality of all denominations became law with citizens no longer required to support churches financially." Religion became a matter of individual, voluntary choice. "The organized church as a social institution was no longer a dynamic force." Many Protestant leaders worried that the moral foundation of society appeared to be eroding. "Some educators who worked to extend the common schools agreed, often linking together as inseparable public education, the preservation of social order, and Protestant Christianity." With the family seemingly fragmenting and church authority eroding, the informal education network seemed to be breaking down. Education had to become formal and institutionalized through the common schools. "By 1840, leading educators agreed that God had established two schools—the family and the church—but added that public schools must supplement, if not completely replace, these institutions."

Finally, the profound changes in the cultural context culminated in acceptance of the notion of childhood, a concept that had emerged during the early 1800s. Observers no longer saw children as inherently wayward, in need of salvation, as the Puritans had; children were innocents. "Most ministers, educators, physicians, and writers in the popular press advertised a new view of childhood as a separate and psychological stage of human life with problems and promises of its own." This view found expression in a variety of forms. First, a flood of children's literature began to pour forth, replacing the dour *New England Primer*. "Christian moral principles still challenged young readers, but now in the sugar-coated guise of fiction." Second, children's health and physical fitness received attention. Crowded, dirty, smoky cities limited physical activity and restricted space available for play. Crusaders began to campaign for gymnasiums and school playgrounds. Third, children were seen as malleable. They could be influenced, shaped, and molded intellectually, morally, and physically.[5] With the family and church relinquishing their traditional educational roles, free schools were now proposed to assume the responsibility for the education of children.

Schooling at the Local Levels

The common schools did not suddenly burst forth from an institutional vacuum. Rather, they gradually emerged out of a variety of ongoing rural and urban school experiences. "From the Revolution to the 1830s, educational institutions were fluid and heterogeneous: the lines between public and private institutions were blurred, for example, as were the distinctions between elementary and secondary levels."[6] One phenomenon was clear and undebatable, however—without mandatory attendance laws, without compulsion of any kind, school enrollment was increasing. Parents were willingly surrendering more and more educational responsibility to institutions.

Rural School Experiences

In spite of industrialization and urban growth, the United States remained a rural nation throughout the nineteenth century. In 1830, 91 percent of the population lived in rural areas. Most of these scattered and small communities informally organized quasipublic ventures in schooling, extending and modifying colonial educational patterns. Many Northeastern and Midwestern farming communities sponsored district schools, while Southern communities opened "old-field schools." "Some combination of property taxes, fuel contributions, tuition payments, and state aid" financed these schools. "The terms 'public' and 'private' did not have their present connotations, and most schools did not fit neatly into either of our modern categories." These district schools accounted for a steady increase in school enrollment. In New York between 1800 and 1825, school enrollment rose from 37 to 60 percent. "Long before the common-school reform movement and the creation of state free-school systems, beginning at least as early as the late eighteenth century, the proportion of children attending school each year was rising, particularly among girls and particularly in the Northeast." Rural children began school as early as two years of age, but usually around four, and continued until fourteen. The common-school concept therefore began as a largely informal, localized effort in rural areas, introducing the tradition of the neighborhood school. These district schools, in reality, were not the traditionally romanticized "little red schoolhouse."[7]

Warren Burton's colorful and wry account, first published in 1833, recalls bare and crude surroundings. The school structure, located in the exact center of the district, reflected how frugal communities were even then when it came to subsidizing their local schools. The edifice remained unpainted, with loose clapboards and cracked and patched windows. The roof barely kept the rain out, as Burton recounts it: "The shingles battered apart by a thousand rains; and excepting where the most defective had been exchanged for new ones, they were dingy with the mold and moss of time. The bricks of the chimney-top were losing their cement, and looked as if some high wind might hurl them from their smoky vocation." The doorstep, made from a "broad unhewn rock," proved to be slanted. "Icy times," Burton humorously recalls, in typical nineteenth-cenury rhetoric, "the scholars used to snatch from the scant declivity the transitory pleasure of a slide. . . . And once the most lofty and perpendicular pedagogue I ever knew, became suddenly horizontal on his egress."

The inside of the schoolroom itself only measured ten by twenty feet. The teacher's desk sat on a "platform a foot from the floor." An aisle led to the fireplace, and on each side of the aisle "were five or six long seats and writing benches." The older scholars sat in the rear of the room while the younger ones occupied the front benches. During the bitter cold winter months, the fireplace unevenly heated the room. The students who sat farthest from it suffered with "blue noses, chattering jaws, and aching toes" because of too little heat. Burton sat directly next to it and remembers how he suffered from too much heat: "The end of my seat was . . . oozy with melted pitch, and sometimes almost smoked with combustion. . . . It was a toil to exist. I truly ate the bread of instruction, or rather nibbled at it, in the sweat of my face."

District schools conducted both summer and winter sessions. Very young children, as young as two or three years, attended summer school while older children planted, cultivated, and harvested crops between May and October. Female instructors usually taught summer sessions because young children presented few, if any, discipline problems. Summer school therefore served a custodial purpose as well as provided literacy training. Children rarely attended summer school after ten years of age because they had to work on their farms. Winter school included older students, some as old as twenty-one, as well as young children. Thus, the typical school year—which we still largely maintain—was based on a nineteenth-century rural agricultural cycle.[8]

The district school proved to be highly parochial, transmitting community values—nothing more. It "sought to socialize children to a changeless community in which ties were tight, in which opportunity was fairly circumscribed, in which power relationships were clearly drawn." These schools reinforced "all the other institutions within the village." Schools literally and physically operated as the center of rural community life, serving as the site for Sunday services, town meetings, social gatherings, polling places, lectures, and general entertainment. Rural communities therefore remained complacent about their schools, content to maintain an anticosmopolitan, if not antiintellectual, attitude. "The common-school movement that began in the 1830s and continued for nearly a half century sought, among other reforms, to overcome problems of the district system by centralizing control at the township, county, and state levels."[9]

Attempts to overcome provincial attitudes and local control, however, proved to be slow and frustrating. And because of regional differences, the common-school movement developed unevenly. New England and the Middle Atlantic states organized their common schools first; the Midwest and West quickly followed as easterners moved farther and farther west. A few Southern states did commit to the common-school system, passing legislation and laying some groundwork, but the common school did not become prevalent until after the Civil War. "In 1850 the number of [southern] white children attending school was about half that in New England. Traditions of private schooling among the well-to-do were strong, and efforts to create public schools were sporadic and scattered."[10] Internal state politics also frustrated common-school reformers, as we shall see.

Urban School Experiences

In sharp contrast to rural America, urban schools were marked by diversity, if not chaos. In the cities, a variety of institutions existed to educate children from the entire social and economic spectrum. Cities basically hosted three levels of schooling.

Social Class and Schooling.   At the bottom, male and female children of poor and working-class parents either became apprentices or enrolled in **charity schools**. Apprenticeship patterns endured well into the early 1800s. However, with republican ideology spawning a new sense of freedom and independence, the mechanization of production, which began the long de-skilling process, and a persistent labor shortage throughout the nineteenth century, which maintained wage rates, the relationship between artisan and apprentice became less formal—if not more tenuous. Traditional apprenticeships shrank from seven to six, or even five, years. Nevertheless, "apprenticeship remained the most common form of craft training."[11] Many children continued to learn their job skills in the workplace, accounting for low school attendance. Only 45 percent of Boston's school-aged children attended primary and grammar schools in the late 1820s. Still, workplace education underwent steady change as apprenticeship further declined between the Revolution and the Civil War. "Like a glacier, the institution receded year by year, imperceptibly at first and more rapidly later." Master printers and shoemakers, for example, virtually disappeared by midcentury. Other crafts would soon follow.[12]

Charity schools, which were sponsored by different religious denominations, appeared to be prevalent in the cities and, through morals instruction, they served social goals. These schools, as historian Carl Kaestle points out, created "a network" through which "philanthropists laid the basis for the free school system of mid-nineteenth-century American cities." "New York had six such schools in 1796, and in Philadelphia there were at least twelve by 1810, including schools maintained by the Episcopal, Presbyterian,

Lutheran, Reformed, and Catholic churches for the children of their poor members." Educational activities for the "churchless poor" also increased as poverty and crime increased in the ever-expanding cities. The Quakers became the "most prominent" in serving these poor. They "established a school for Negro [sic] boys in Philadelphia in 1770, which was supplemented in 1787 by a school for girls and by an evening school for adults in 1789."

These sectarian educational efforts emphasized instruction in religious morals as a remedy for social problems, and so for the first time, social reform began to be associated with schooling. Many "advocates stressed collective goals—such as the reduction of crime and disruption—rather than individualistic or personal advancement."[13] Many charity school proponents simplistically believed poverty and crime existed because poor people and criminals lacked proper values. Thus, these social ills could be easily reduced, if not totally eradicated, by an infusion of religious principles.

New York City's Free School Society, a voluntary association created in 1805, was the most elaborate of these educational efforts. It avoided sectarian affiliation and, through a combination of philanthropic support and state aid, provided tuition-free schooling for the city's poor children. In 1825, it initiated a profound shift in scope that signaled the beginning of a gradual move toward the universal systematization of schooling. The Society "called for public schools for all children of the city, rich and poor, and . . . for an end of public assistance to denominational schools." The state legislature approved, and the following year the group changed its name to the Public School Society and endeavored to establish "common schools" in New York City.[14]

These early attempts at mass schooling required careful use of scarce financial resources. In the United States, the monitorial system represented the "initial response" to the growing need for cheap mass schooling in an urban setting. Joseph Lancaster, an English Quaker schoolmaster, created this "assembly-line technique," and it was introduced in America by the Free School Society in 1806. Most cities adopted this pedagogical approach, including Philadelphia and frontier towns like Pittsburgh, Detroit, and Louisville, among others. In 1829, over a dozen of Boston's primary and grammar schools employed the Lancaster method.[15]

Using the factory system as its model, the monitorial instructional system stressed regimentation, efficiency, and hierarchical relationships. There were male and female monitorial schools. Cavernous classrooms accommodated between 200 and 1,000 students who were taught by several monitors, who were, in turn, supervised by a master stationed on a raised platform to oversee the entire educational operation. The master dictated each day's lesson to the monitors for each level of scholars. Moral training was the main objective, with literacy training serving as the means to this end. Students marched to their lessons, memorized answers, and recited them to monitors. While many monitors punished inattentive, disobedient, or unruly students by boxing their ears or whipping or thrashing them, some clever monitors rewarded their studious and attentive scholars for learning their lessons and behaving. Once students demonstrated mastery, they could advance at their own rate, a crude form of individualized learning. Nevertheless, rote memorization and drill dominated Lancasterian pedagogy. The system thus controlled scholars' every physical, emotional, and intellectual action. This pedagogy would establish an enduring pattern for the public schools.[16]

Both the charity school and its pedagogical approach generated criticism. "For many poor children the charity schools offered the only available means of instruction." However, attending them was demeaning and demoralizing, since parents had to publicly declare themselves paupers in order to qualify their children for admission. As Schultz found in Boston, "[b]earing the stigma of pauperism, the schools attracted few lower-class children."[17] During the late 1820s and early 1830s, workingmen's associations in Pennsylvania decried the fact that the pauper schools were the only free schools available. The schools excluded the children of working people who could not afford private tuition but who were not poor and their children could only attend if the parents declared themselves to be paupers. Furthermore, these schools proved to be extremely limited, providing a truncated education for boys and girls alike. "In Pennsylvania, where free schools were sparse and designed only for the poor, the workingmen argued that common schools should be established, open to all without taint of pauperism and so good that the rich, who could afford private education for their children, could find not better."[18] The monitorial system that the charity schools often employed also received close scrutiny. Opponents criticized the emphasis on regimentation and conformity because this undermined republican ideals of individualism. No less an educator than Horace Mann opposed the Lancasterian approach.[19]

Voluntary associations sponsored a variety of other schools as well. Observers had become alarmed at the increasing number of children employed in factories, which, of course, prevented school attendance. In 1823, labor journals "found that 1,600 children between seven and sixteen years of age worked in the mills, most of them between thirteen and fourteen hours a day, with no opportunity for schooling save after eight thirty in the evening and on Sunday."[20] As early as 1790, the Philadelphia First Day School Society, sponsored by Benjamin Rush, had been created and by 1800 it served 2,000 children. An interdenominational, nonsectarian effort, replicating similar endeavors in England, it involved providing education to poor children on Sundays, putting their rare idle time to good use. The children, who attended morning and afternoon sessions, prayed, sang hymns, learned the alphabet, and memorized the Bible. This missionary approach for the children of the poor quickly spread to other cities, both North and South. "In Delaware the state legislature granted a per pupil subsidy to Sunday Schools throughout the state." Attendance, according to one estimate, reached 200,000 in the United States by 1827.[21] Sunday School activity even overlapped other educational efforts. In New York City, the Free School Society worked closely with the Sunday School Union. Many individuals supported both educational activities, and the Free School Society often made its buildings available for Sunday school use. "Whatever the overlap between these two agencies of moral instruction, clearly they were both working with the same general population in mind: the poor, and especially, the churchless poor."

In the 1830s, however, there occurred a twofold alteration in this arrangement. Kaestle focuses on New York City to illustrate the change. First, the Public School Society began to assume total responsibility for teaching literacy while the Sunday Schools concentrated on religious values. Various denominations created their own Sunday Schools, abandoning the nonsectarian approach. "Scripture memorization gave way to question-and-answer lessons and stories," shifting to "denominational catechism." The second change involved a shift away from exclusive focus on the poor, similar to what was happening in the free schools. "The Sunday Schools had adopted the public schools' policy of including children of all economic classes; at the same time, they differentiated their function from that of the public schools." Moral training, as a result, became institutionalized in an increasingly urbanized society.[22]

Infant schools, also imported from England, represented yet another philanthropic effort to save poor young children from corrupt and undesirable family environments, recognizing the "discovery of childhood as a separate stage of human development."[23] In the 1820s and 1830s, they appeared in major American cities, like Boston and Philadelphia. The *American Journal of Education* reported in 1826 that infant schools provided child care for working mothers and, more important, operated as a socializing mechanism to instill proper moral values in order to reduce juvenile delinquency and other social problems. The Infant School Society of New York, founded in 1827, appeared to be typical of such organizations in most Northern cities, teaching boys and girls between eighteen months and five years of age. "In Massachusetts, the state for which the most data on the infant schools are available, 40 to 50 percent of all three-year-olds were attending school in 1840."[24] Infant school promoters hoped to provide an alternative environment that would, they hoped, offset the negative influences of the parents. "As a result," Schultz says, "these children would be far better citizens than their parents."[25] Some primary schools eventually absorbed the infant schools but barred children younger than four years old. Thus began the first experiment in institutionalized early childhood education, culminating in, as we will see in Chapter 7, the kindergarten.[26]

Social reform served as the primary purpose of these many urban charity educational efforts. A stable, affluent, and well-run society required moral citizens. Illiterate and poor parents, according to some observers, could not be relied on to teach proper values, and so literacy was used to facilitate this objective. But the moral lessons taught by these various schools did not always conform to the parents' values, and these schools essentially marginalized the educational role of the poor and working-class family. "One of the central goals of charity-school workers," Kaestle asserts, "was to rescue children from an allegedly harmful family environment." In contrast, urban middle-income parents could send their children to a variety of pay schools, while elite families could hire tutors, patronize academies, or enroll their children in exclusive boarding schools. Unlike the "message" of the charity school, the "cultural message" in these private schools, "created and patronized by the middling and upper ranks, was more in harmony with the family's goals. . . . Such independent schools complemented and extended the educational role of the family."

Nevertheless, the early rudiments of the public school could be found in the urban charity school. From an organizational standpoint, single, coherent school systems began to emerge in the cities. The charity schools underwent a gradual process of formalization and institutionalization. As we have seen, the New York Free School Society changed its name to the Public School Society in 1826, although it continued to rely on a private, self-perpetuating board of trustees and to be supported by philanthropic donations and "private grants." Enrollment steadily increased in the charity schools while it waned in the "independent pay" schools, which became "progressively more elite and expensive." Finally, the concepts of "public" and "private," which had been ambiguous during the pre-common-school years, became distinct. Towns provided subsidies to some charity, or pauper, schools. "In some states, such as New York, academies received regular legislative grants, and their admirers considered them 'public' institutions, in the same sense that they provided the public with education and attempted to prepare children for responsible public life." However, and ever so gradually, a clear intellectual and political separation between the notions of public and private schooling began to appear. As a result, by the 1830s and 1840s, "in many cities, the charity schools literally became the public common schools."[27]

In sum, until this point, civil authority had certainly "encouraged" private schools and had subsidized semiprivate educational ventures, like New York City's Public School Society. Gradually, however, reformers began to support the notion of state-sponsored education, which would result in "universal schooling." "This change in attitude came about for a number of reasons, none more immediately compelling than the increased awareness that the church-sponsored schools and private academies were failing to provide for all children." Through the common schools, education became a "direct responsibility of the state," supplanting the family and the church.[28]

The Common Schools

The common-school movement "occurred in nearly every state in the Union, appearing earliest in New England, New York, and Pennsylvania." It had three goals. First, it provided "free elementary education" for every child. Second, it created "a trained educational profession." Third, it established "some form of state control over local schools." According to historian Robert Church,

> This last goal was the linchpin of the movement for, without central control, none of the other goals was possible. As long as the autonomy of the district or town school committees went unchallenged, uniform criteria relating to attendance, the quality of school building, curriculum, and teacher qualifications would be unenforceable. In the early years of the movement, especially, the lack of central authority repeatedly stymied the reformers' efforts.

States eventually centralized authority "by assuming financial leverage over the local school districts."[29]

Pennsylvania was typical. Pennsylvania's free school law, An Act to Establish a General System of Education by Common Schools, was approved on April 1, 1834. This sparked an immediate public reaction. Opposition came from religious denominations, such as the Society of Friends, the Lutherans, and so on, which preferred parochial schools, as well as from German residents, who, to protect their language, opposed public schools for cultural reasons. In April of 1835, the state Legislature considered repealing the 1834 bill.[30]

Thaddeus Stevens, a state legislator at that time, passionately, eloquently, and successfully defended the 1834 law in a famous speech. He equated the state public school concept with democratic principles because it promoted equality, and like Benjamin Rush, another Pennsylvanian, he regarded children as a public responsibility. Because of the 1834 legislation, Stevens proclaimed,

> all were instructed in the same school; all were placed on perfect equality, the rich and poor man's sons, for all were deemed children of the same parent—the Commonwealth. Indeed, where all have the means of knowledge placed within their reach, and meet at common schools on equal terms, the forms of government seem of less importance to the happiness of the people than is generally supposed; or rather, such a people are seldom in danger of having their rights invaded by their rulers.

The phrase "same school" can be understood in this context as meaning that every public school in the state would be alike or uniform—implying a schooling system. In his speech, Stevens echoed Rush as well concerning the political mission of schools, that is, to ensure a stable government:

> If an elective republic is to endure for any great length of time, every elector must have sufficient information, not only to accumulate wealth and take care of his pecuniary concerns, but to direct wisely the Legislature, the Ambassadors, and the Executive of the Nation; for some part of all these things, some agency in approving or disapproving of them, falls to every freeman. If, then, the permanency of our government depends upon such knowledge, it is the duty of the government to see that the means of information be diffused to every citizen.

Stevens concluded with an appeal for equality of opportunity as the legislators' legacy:

> and so cast our votes that the blessing of education shall be conferred on every son of Pennsylvania—shall be carried home to the poorest child of the poorest inhabitant of the meanest hut of your mountains, so that even he may be prepared to act well his part in this land of freedom, and lay on earth a broad and solid foundation for that enduring knowledge which goes on increasing through increasing eternity.[31]

For Stevens, the common-school experience provided equal opportunity that would have lasting effect on the individual and the state.

The Free School Law 1834 proved to be wholly inadequate, however, because it failed to take away local autonomy, thus undermining establishment of a cohesive state system. Participation was optional for the school districts, not mandatory, although only participants received state funds. In 1834, there were 987 school districts in Pennsylvania; by 1848 between 144 and 200 districts had refused to adopt the state system. "In 1848 the legislature ordered free schools in all districts" but failed to coerce them to participate. It would be another twenty-five years before "the last district gave in and accepted the law."[32] As of 1868, twenty-three districts still had "no common schools in operation." Consequently, considerable variation existed among community schools because of the 1834 law.[33] Finally, after protracted political conflict, local control and parochialism were overcome by the 1874 Pennsylvania State Constitution, which mandated a cohesive system of public schooling. The tension between local control and central authority exists to this day across the nation.

"Native-Protestant Ideology"

Massachusetts is universally credited with initiating the common-school movement and pioneering its legislation. In 1838, Massachusetts inaugurated a central state board of education and employed a full-time education secretary, Horace Mann. Mann, known as the "father of public education," is regarded as the quintessential common-school reformer. He spearheaded that state's common-school legislation in the Massachusetts legislature and served as the state's first Secretary of Education.[34]

Born in 1796 in Franklin, Massachusetts, a farming community, Mann grew up with orthodox **Calvinism**, which was stern and highly moralistic, but drifted to the "more liberal Unitarianism." Farm work also shaped his views. "Convinced of the values of hard work, diligence, and seriousness, he exemplified the Protestant work ethic, which saw industriousness and productivity as positive moral values." Mann attended the local district school, which, he later recalled, was marked by poor teaching, a limited curriculum, bare facilities, and ample corporal punishment. He graduated from Brown University in 1819 and read law, completing his legal studies in 1823. After practicing law in Dedham, Massachusetts, for four years, he was elected to the state House of Representatives, and in 1833, he won a four-year term to the state Senate.

So began Mann's distinguished career in public service, in which he became an advocate of "social improvement." As historian Gerald Gutek summarizes it, Mann's "humanitarian efforts led to an investigation by the legislature of conditions in prisons and in asylums for the insane. Mann sponsored legislation to improve the care of the insane and his efforts contributed to the establishment of the Worcester Asylum in 1833, a model institution." Mann supported the 1837 Massachusetts education bill, An Act Relating to Common Schools. As Secretary of Education, he issued annual reports on the state of education in Massachusetts. His first annual report (1838), "made clear he regarded, as did Jefferson, the state as having primary responsibility for supporting and governing public education." Mann's idea of the common school may be summed up in two points: He "saw the U.S. common school as an integrative social agency for bringing children of different social and economic classes and religions together in one institution. Mann's common school was also a completely public institution, supported by funds derived from public taxation, governed by publicly elected officials, and responsible to the community it served."[35]

Mann's leadership remains unquestioned in the field of education; his "writings, particularly the annual reports, were cited, quoted, reprinted, and plagiarized, throughout the United States."[36] Innumerable common-school proponents as well as legislators borrowed his rhetoric and ideas. Other states subsequently passed measures similar to the 1837 Massachusetts act. **"native-Protestant ideology,"** according to Kaestle's thorough study of this experience, *Pillars of the Republic: Common Schools and American Society, 1780–1860,* drove the common-school movement throughout the country. Mann's counterparts in other states, Connecticut's Henry Barnard, Ohio's Calvin Stowe and Samuel Lewis, Indiana's Caleb Mills, Michigan's John Pierce and Isaac Crary, Illinois's Ninian Edwards, Kentucky's Robert Breckinridge, North Carolina's Calvin Wiley, and California's John Swett, among others, all shared similar backgrounds. The majority of these school crusaders were born in New England and were Anglo American, middle class, and Protestant. They consequently shared the same beliefs embodied in this ideology, consisting of republicanism, capitalism, and Protestantism; these represented "three sources of social belief that were intertwined and mutually supporting"[37]

Republicanism.   As we saw in Chapter 3, the very survival of the American government depended on a common purpose and set of beliefs. "Cultural diversity and regional loyalties" were serious dangers. Early national leaders believed that the American people needed to be homogenized, to be led to embrace a common core of values, in order to ensure unity. With the rise of industrialization, class conflict, urban growth, increased immigration, and crime in the early nineteenth century, the republic faced many new and seemingly overwhelming challenges. As a result, in the common schools, "political education consisted of stressing common beliefs and glorifying the exercise of intelligence in a republic, while urging respect for laws and downplaying the very issues upon which citizens might exercise their intelligence."

Mann certainly supported the notion of citizenship training through schooling. He argued in his *Ninth Annual Report* (1845) and *Twelfth Annual Report* (1848) that schools should focus on future voters to preserve the republic. A "republican government," in his words, required the "universal education of the people" because "legislators will never far surpass their electors."[38] However, Mann also urged that teachers avoid teaching "controversial issues." As Kaestle summarizes, "schooling should stress unity, obedience, restraint, self-sacrifice, and the careful exercise of intelligence." This marked an alteration in political philosophy from that of Thomas Jefferson, who had envisioned a marketplace of political ideas that literate citizens could debate. Mann narrowed this in the direction of the indoctrination of political beliefs and permitting no political heresy.

Capitalism.   The reformers expected the schools to teach other, related virtues, like hard work, punctuality, temperance, and respect for private property. From their point of view, the frontier and industrial capitalism offered endless opportunities for the acquisition of land, property, and wealth. Poverty, they reasoned, grew not from economic instability and dislocation nor from a maldistribution of wealth and power, but from individual failure and reflected idleness, immorality, and intemperance, which children learned from their parents. "Their children, of course, had to be rescued and taught that industry was a central trait of the virtuous individual."[39] Schools as well inculcated the new industrial culture based on regulated time, focusing on habits of regularity and punctuality. "Once within the school gates, the child entered the new universe of disciplined time."[40] Bells summoned students to school, announced recess and lunch, and ended the school day, much as factory whistles organized their parents' workday. A sense of discipline was thus internalized and began to make the external coercions on the factory floor unnecessary, producing highly efficient workers.

Mann extolled the economic benefits of the common schools. Universal schooling prevented class conflict because it created opportunities for individual social advancement. He outlined this ideal in a famous passage from his *Twelfth Annual Report* (1848):

> Education, then, beyond all other devices of human origin, is the great equalizer of the conditions of men—the balance-wheel of the social machinery. I do not here mean that it so elevates the moral nature as to make men disdain and abhor the oppression of their fellow-men. . . . But I mean that it gives each man the independence and the means, by which he can resist the selfishness of other men. It does better than to disarm the poor of their hostility towards the rich; it prevents being poor.[41]

According to Mann's perspective, the common schools did not create equality, but they did provide equal educational opportunity. Common-school teachers were thus to inculcate the economic values of hard work, punctuality, obedience, and individual opportunity.

Protestantism.   The "chief purpose of public common schooling was moral education." Since all morality stemmed from religion, school crusaders equated Christianity with democracy. Furthermore, they narrowly identified Christianity with Protestantism. "They associated Protestant Christianity with republicanism, with economic progress, and with virtue."[42]

Mann saw the United States as "a Protestant and a Republican country," and he supported the teaching of Christianity in the common schools. "Children should be given," he declared, " 'so much religious instruction as is compatible with the rights of others and with the genius of our government.' " Mann also supported the use of the Bible in the classroom. For him, it remained "the great Protestant doctrine of the inviolability of conscience, the right and sanctity of private judgement without note or interpreter." He, in essence, embraced, "classical Protestant principles." According to historian Neil McCluskey, an important, if not contradictory, caveat existed: "Religion was to remain in the public schools, but it was not to be identifiable as Congregational or Episcopal or Methodist. It was simply to be 'nonsectarian.' "[43] This disingenuous notion of nonsectarianism proved to be a bone of contention for Roman Catholic parents.

School reformers persistently claimed the common schools were nonsectarian, but the schools clearly practiced Protestant rituals and imbued beliefs that would prove to be an affront to some. Each day began with a passage read from the **King James Bible** by a teacher, a layperson, and recitation of the Lord's Prayer. Jewish parents generally tolerated this clearly Christian practice, "following a policy of accommodation toward public schools while arranging Jewish religious education outside of school hours." Roman Catholic parents and clergy, however, objected to such sectarian practices in the public schools. Catholic liturgy required a priest, an anointed person, to read and interpret the Scriptures for parishioners. Religious conflict over public school policy and practices grew so intense, as we shall see, that Catholic immigrants eventually created another educational system, the parochial school. The religious emphasis of the common schools consequently generated an unintended outcome, a new type of religious schooling in America.

The common schools, to be sure, were an effective instrument for ensuring a stable society, but they were an institution in which social aims seemed to supersede academic ones. And this can be simply summed up, according to Kaestle, as representing the goals of native-Protestant ideology: "moral education to produce obedient children, reduce crime, and discourage vice; citizenship training to protect republican government; literacy for effective economic and political participation; and cultural education for assimilation and unity."[44] The common-school reform movement, therefore, was a mechanism of social reform based on a narrow set of beliefs. However, not everyone embraced these values, and conflict resulted.

"ALL CATHOLIC PARENTS ARE BOUND TO SEND THEIR CHILDREN TO THE PARISH SCHOOL"

The public schools and the parochial schools share a common history, "one cannot understand American education apart from it."[45] And immigration contributed to it. The first great wave of immigration occurred during the early decades of the nineteenth century. Between 1831 and 1860, 1,538,737 Germans emigrated to the United States. They eventually became the largest group of European immigrants to settle in this country, totaling 5,947,883 between 1820 and 1930. Nevertheless, Irish immigrants outnumbered their German counterparts between 1831 and 1860, totaling 1,902,492. In sum, "comparing

1840 with 1850, the total population increased 35 percent while the number of immigrants entering the country increased 240 percent."[46] The sheer volume of these immigrants created a cultural dialectic between Protestant Americans and new European settlers.

Language and religion represent the foundation of any culture, as we saw in Chapter 2. Native-born Americans proved to be less than hospitable to the newcomers and stressed assimilation through the acquisition of the English language and conversion to the Protestant religion. Immigrants meanwhile attempted to preserve their cultures. All of this set the stage for ethnic conflict and began a long tradition of ethnic intolerance on the part of native-born Americans.

Little Germany

Germans clung tenaciously to their language in particular and their culture in general. "In 1889 when Wisconsin and Illinois passed laws requiring some of the education of school-age children to be conducted in English, both Lutheran and Catholic Germans denounced the new measures" and successfully overturned those statutes. Wherever they settled, Germans established a *Deutschtum,* or counterculture. In their ethnic communities, they literally replicated their cultural institutions and traditions—German-language newspapers and publications, for example, and theaters, athletic groups, benevolent societies, beer gardens, picnics, music, churches, and schools.[47]

Milwaukee best illustrates this experience. It became the "preeminent German city" in antebellum America. According to the 1850 census, Germans comprised over 36 percent of that city's total population. Their cultural loyalty could be seen through their educational attitudes. "Throughout much of the antebellum period, from a third to over half of all children were not in the public school system." There are two explanations for this phenomenon. First, for pious Germans, much of their opposition fixed on language. German parents preferred that instruction be done in their native language, but they would even have settled for a bilingual approach. Although local law permitted this, insufficient funding aborted one brief effort. Lutheran and Roman Catholic German parents solved the problem by creating their own parochial schools, "which ensured religious orthodoxy as well as cultural and linguistic continuity." Second, freethinking German parents avoided public education because they simply considered it inferior. "While they approved of it on philosophical grounds, from a practical viewpoint they objected to its failure to include German instruction, the lack of secondary education before 1858, the minimum number of subjects taught, and what they felt to be mindless and mechanical cramming which passed for instruction in the public schools." **Freethinkers** organized and created a series of private schools for male and female students at the elementary and secondary levels.[48] Thus, Milwaukee's German residents, regardless of their religious beliefs, founded their own parochial and private schools because that city's public schools failed to meet their cultural demands and educational expectations.

Irish Catholics

Religion was the most strident and emotional source of conflict between native-born Americans and European immigrants, especially between American Protestants and Irish

Catholics. This hostility had long and deep roots, beginning with the colonial period. Vestiges of the bitterness of the European Reformation crossed over to North America. Anti-Catholicism among English settlers proved to be especially strong. "While disagreeing widely among themselves on religious matters, Anglicans, Congregationalists, Baptists, Methodists, and even Quakers all recognized 'the Papist' as the common enemy of all free-born Englishmen, and for such their could be small welcome on the shores of New Canaan." The colonies passed a variety of strict anti-Catholic laws that, among other things, forbade religious services and the formation of congregations and denied Catholics the right to vote and hold office. In 1704, Maryland passed An Act to Prevent the Growth of Popery outlawing Catholic schooling.[49] Such religious intolerance dissipated somewhat with the Revolution, but fear of Catholics endured. Even during the early national period, "only four of the original states gave Catholics the unrestricted right to vote and hold office."[50] Catholics nevertheless opened schools in Philadelphia, New York City, and Boston between 1783 and 1830. These largely decentralized efforts proved to be inadequate; they lacked sufficient funding and permanent teachers.

The massive immigration of the early nineteenth century rekindled intolerance and outright hostility. As we saw earlier, "the underlying issue revolved around the American belief that Roman Catholicism and American institutions, which were based on Protestant concepts, were incompatible." American institutions followed democratic principles while Catholic decision making depended on a concept based on ancient Roman imperial hierarchy. None other than Samuel F. B. Morse, who invented the telegraph, hysterically warned Americans to be vigilant and mobilize against the alleged Papist threat to national sovereignty. Writing in 1835, he beseeched his countrymen not to be "deceived by the pensioned Jesuits, who have surrounded your press, are now using it all over the country to stifle the cries of danger, and lull your fears by attributing your alarm to a false cause. . . . To your posts! . . . Fly to protect the vulnerable places of your Constitution and Laws. Place your guards; you will need them, and quickly too."[51] He like many others saw Irish immigration as a Jesuit plot to infiltrate and undermine the United States, ultimately creating a Papist state.

The intense feelings and shrill tone characterizing these verbal attacks occasionally manifested themselves in outright mob assaults on Catholic immigrants. Native-born Americans attacked Catholics in Baltimore, Boston, New York City, and Philadelphia. A Protestant mob burned a Catholic convent in Boston in 1834, and nativists burned two Catholic churches in Philadelphia in 1844. In the latter case, Catholics had campaigned to allow their children to use their own Bible rather than the **King James** version in the public schools. This led to three days of rioting in the Kensington community, resulting in thirteen dead and fifty wounded. There was little religious conflict in the Midwest, however, because of the sheer size of the Catholic population in cities like Chicago, Cincinnati, Detroit, Milwaukee, and St. Louis.[52]

This religious intolerance expressed itself in acrimony over ethnic values within institutions. In 1851, *The Massachusetts Teacher,* an educational publication, described the problems associated with the schooling of immigrants. While it saw Germans as "obstinate," they at least brought the positive characteristics of "industry, frugality, and pride" with them. Irish immigrants proved to be a different matter altogether. The report stereotyped the "priest-ridden" Irish as intemperate and lazy; it proclaimed "the great remedy is education":

The rising generation must be taught as our own children are taught. We say must be, because in many cases this can only be accomplished by coercion. In too many instances the parents are unfit guardians of their own children. . . . Nothing can operate effectually here but stringent legislation, thoroughly carried out by an efficient police; the children must be gathered up and forced into school, and those who resist or impede this plan, whether parents or *priests*, must be held accountable and punished.[53]

Nativist educators saw Catholics as idol worshipers, antidemocratic, and immoral. The American public schools from the educators' point of view operated as "culture factories" to assimilate this perceived cultural threat, inculcating Irish children with a sense of national loyalty and, more important, introducing them to Protestant values and religious practices. Irish Catholic leaders, on the other hand, "linked common schooling with Protestantism, atheism, sexual depravity, and social unrest."[54] These divergent cultural perspectives and educational goals resulted in institutional bifurcation, with the creation of the Roman Catholic parochial school system.

The Roman Catholic parochial school system grew directly out of cultural and religious conflict. Although the First Plenary Council of Baltimore, in 1852, and the Second Council, in 1866, urged, respectively, pastors and bishops, to establish parish schools, the Third Council in 1884 mandated this by ordering "that a school was to be established near every church 'within two years.' " The Council further declared that "all Catholic parents are bound to send their children to the parish school, unless it is evident that a sufficient training in religion is given either in their own homes, or in other Catholic schools; or when because of a sufficient reason, approved by the bishop."[55]

Chicago's Catholics actually began the process much earlier. According to historian James Sanders, "Protestant control of the public schools," through Protestant teachers, enforced reading of the King James Bible, and fiscal management, "constituted a major factor in Chicago Catholicism's commitment to parochial education." The growth of that city's parish schools was rapid. "By the early 1850s, attendance at the several elementary schools numbered about 900 pupils. In 1870, 10,000 pupils attended the city's fifteen parish schools." Sixteen percent of Chicago's school-aged children attended Catholic parochial schools in 1865. Not only did Chicago's Catholics create their own schools to protest public school sectarianism but they embarked on a long and bitter campaign to "de-Protestantize the public school curriculum." Focusing their attack on classroom Bible reading, they initially met strong opposition from the Protestant community. By the 1860s, however, they had acquired allies. "The City's Jews objected to reading the New Testament in the schools. Unitarians and Universalists, more liberal Protestants, and a handful of articulate atheists and agnostics also argued the case against religion in the public schools." In 1875, the school board banned the Bible by a decisive vote. This episode, in many ways, portended later conflicts over classroom Bible reading and ultimately the federal Supreme Court's decision in *Abington School District v Schempp* some ninety years later.

Chicago's experience reflected Catholic opposition to state authority over school matters nationwide. Catholic parents resorted to a variety of strategies, reflecting their dissatisfaction with the common schools. As in Chicago, many attempted to have their children "excused from classroom reading of the Protestant Bible and similar devotional practices." In other cases, Catholics lobbied to have their tax money diverted to their own religious schools, foreshadowing the contemporary school-voucher movement. Both tactics failed, generating even more hostility. "The great Protestant majority was easily persuaded that

Catholic efforts to eliminate the Protestant Bible from the schools and to get public money for their own schools represented a concerted attack on the foundations of the republic. It was simply taken for granted that the Bible and the flag symbolized America and that an attack on one was an assault on the other." Finally, as we have seen, frustrated and angry Irish and German Roman Catholics established their own schools. In the latter case, the German language as well as the Catholic religion were taught.[56]

No political or religious compromise appeared to be imminent. During the 1840s, protesting the Protestant mission of the schools, Bishop John Hughes of New York City saw them as teaching children that "Catholics are necessarily, morally, intellectually, infallibly, a stupid race." His campaign for a share of state funds for Catholic schools failed. The religious conflict continued. By the latter half of the nineteenth century, Bishop Bernard McQuaid of Rochester bluntly asserted: "The Catholic is unwilling to transfer the responsibility of the education of his children to the state. His conscience informs him that the state is an incompetent agent to fulfill his parental duties." In a similar vein, in 1877, the Bishop of Trenton (New Jersey) declared, "that the idea that the state has a right to teach . . . is not a Christian idea. It is a pagan one."[57] Common-school reform had thus created the conditions for the largest religious school system in the country.

German immigrants had led all ethnic groups in establishing parochial schools, both Catholic and Lutheran. Irish immigrants soon joined them. Even so, prior to the Civil War, the growth of parochial schools, which charged a tuition fee, proved to be modest and fitful. For example, the expansion of regular parish schools in Boston was retarded by the poverty of Irish immigrants. The parochial system in Boston started with the establishment of Catholic Sunday schools. By 1845, 4,000 Catholic children attended them. In New York City during the mid-1800s, Catholic schools were held in damp church basements.[58] Significant growth would not occur until after the Civil War.

Thus religion served as a source of discord in American public schools from the beginning, and confrontations over conflicting values would become more numerous and strident as the country grew more diverse. While voluntarily emigrating to this country, immigrant groups rarely surrendered their cultural heritage and institutions immediately or willingly. The early experiences would be repeated at the turn of the nineteenth century, with more intensity, with southern and eastern European immigrants and again during the mid-twentieth century with Chicanos. Immigrants, often resisting assimilation efforts by preserving their culture, that is, their language and religion, used the classroom as the battleground. The assimilation of girls into the common schools, in contrast, generated far less conflict and controversy.

COEDUCATION

In spite of the ideas of Benjamin Rush and Judith Sargent Murray and the establishment of the female seminaries, school-aged girls largely remained excluded from the grammar schools. During the common-school era, this changed, with significant results. "By 1870, girls aged ten to fourteen had surpassed boys in their rates of literacy and academic achievement."

America's rural schools were at the center of this transformation. In 1790, ninety-five percent of the U.S. population resided in rural areas; 80 percent still lived there in 1860. By midcentury, "more than 90 percent of all pupils" attended the common schools, and 80 percent of these "were one-room schools in rural communities." Therefore, sending girls to school represented a local decision, based on community culture rather than a state mandate.

Historians David Tyack and Elisabeth Hansot characterize the inclusion of girls as a "gradual, decentralized, and obscure process." First, with a scattered population, these frugal communities just found it cheaper to construct one schoolhouse and hire a single teacher to educate all of their children. In other words, duplicating construction, maintenance, and salary costs to separately educate girls was simply out of the question. Second, sending brothers and sisters together to school just seemed to be a natural extension of the family. They shared the same parents, house, and meals, and attended church together, why not walk or ride to school together and sit in the same classroom? "All three institutions—family, church, and school—were mixed-sex, and gender practices moved easily through the permeable membranes that joined the three social agencies in rural communities." Thus, the rationale to school girls did not flow from any idealized notions of or commitment to equal education. More important, schooling did not threaten, in the eyes of these communities, traditional social roles for males and females.

The schooling of city girls proved to be more varied, and in cities the practice of coeducation became contentious. Urban communities differed profoundly from their rural counterparts. First, they hosted dense populations, possessed large concentrations of wealth, and maintained a higher tax base. In 1842, cities like New York, Chicago, and Cincinnati claimed eleven-month school years.

> In 1880 in thirty-two of the thirty-eight states, urban schools were open more than 180 days, and in twenty-five states, for more than 190 days, compared with a national average of 130 days, and a school term in many rural schools of only a few weeks. In the same year, cities spent $12.62 per capita on education, compared with only $3.28 in rural areas. Teaching was not only a full-time job in cities but also paid from two to three times more than weekly salaries in the countryside. City teachers were generally older, better educated, and more experienced than those in one-room schools.

Second, cities consisted of heterogeneous populations, especially in terms of ethnicity and social class. As a result, rural and urban schools, although part of the same "common-school system," contrasted in institutional structure, clientele, and instruction, as Tyack and Hansot maintain. Given the location and with ample fiscal resources and clear biases, separate-sex schools could be rationalized and accommodated in cities. City dwellers thus debated the concept and practice of coeducation, since it appeared to be for them an option.

Critics feared that same-sex school would harm girls. "In some cities, middle- and upper-class parents claimed that their daughters needed to be protected against association with the sons of poor and immigrant families during what the parents regarded as a 'dangerous time of life.'" In other cases, opponents invoked religion. These conservatives "feared that coeducation might blur the God-ordained differences between the sexes; it led in their imagination to an absurd adult sameness." Some cities, such as Boston, New York,

Philadelphia, and Baltimore, as well as all Southern cities, responded to these concerns by maintaining separate-sex schools.

Other groups supported coeducation. Most teachers and many state superintendents believed, first, that coeducation benefitted both boys and girls because they learned from each other. "Uncouth and unruly boys became more gentle, while girls became less 'coyish and simpering' and more self-reliant and energetic in behavior." Second, proponents asserted that women deserved the right to an "equal education, and that meant the same education." A third and related point was that "leaders in the woman's movement" supported coeducation because it facilitated equal economic and political opportunities. Reinforcing all of this was the mounting evidence that girls outperformed boys academically. In Washington, DC, Cincinnati, and New York City, girls earned higher marks than boys in grammar, spelling, mathematics, reading, and writing.

The supporters of coeducation eventually prevailed and "identical coeducation," with boys and girls occupying the same classroom and learning the same subjects, became widely accepted at the urban grammar school level. Although coeducation took hold in the Northeast, Midwest, and West, the South followed a different path. "White southerners often favored separate-sex secondary private schools for their daughters and sons." But by 1870, these regional differences had disappeared. "Girls comprised 49 percent of all pupils in all public schools."[59] Coeducation had begun at the primary level in the colonial dame schools and became largely institutionalized throughout the elementary level during the common-school movement. It would continue to make inroads and become part of secondary education during the latter half of the nineteenth century. In spite of occasional criticism, therefore, gender integration continued. Girls would eventually excel in boys high school attendance, enrollment, graduation, and academic achievement.

African Americans, however, enjoyed no such success. In the South, as slaves, they faced a unique educational process that was dedicated to their subjugation. And racial segregation in Northern schools appeared to be intransigent, establishing an enduring and tragic legacy.

"OBEY YOUR OLD MASTER AND YOUR YOUNG MASTER— YOUR OLD MISTRESS AND YOUR YOUNG MISTRESS"

The African slave trade began in the Western hemisphere in 1502. At first, the North American colonies had fewer slaves than the Caribbean and South American colonies; in 1650, slaves comprised only 4 percent of the North American colonial population. But by 1770, this figure had grown to 22 percent, and some 1,750,000 slaves lived in the southern United States in 1825.[60] "On the eve of the Civil War, the more than 4,000,000 slaves and free blacks comprised more than 40 percent of the population in the South."[61] At that point, according to historians Robert Fogel and Stanley Engerman, the United States had become the "greatest slave power in the Western world . . . and the bulwark of resistance to the abolition of slavery."[62]

The Planter's Educational Agenda

Slave socialization proved to be harsh, cruel, and pervasive. There was no such thing as an idyllic or carefree childhood. Children faced the threat of the sale of one or more of their parents and the sting of the overseer's strap. They were terrified by the whippings they witnessed. "Other children saw their friends divested of a finger for attempting to learn to read, escapees tortured, and grandparents put off the plantation and told by the white authorities to fend for themselves." Finally, slave children began to work between the ages of six and ten, tending livestock, cooking, and running errands. The onset of back-bending field work occurred between the ages of ten and fourteen.[63]

Harriet A. Jacobs, born a slave in North Carolina around 1813, was eleven years old when she witnessed her first beating of another slave who had stolen some corn. Her master, Mr. Flint, hoisted the culprit from a beam in the workhouse, with his feet dangling just off of the floor. The whipping proved to be relentless and vicious, as she recalled: "I went into the workhouse next morning, and saw the cowhide still wet with blood, and the boards all covered with gore." Not long after that incident, she received her first punishment:

> My grandmother had taken my old shoes, and replaced them with a new pair. I needed them; for several inches of snow had fallen, and it still continued to fall. When I walked through Mrs. Flint's room, their creaking grated harshly on her refined nerves. She called me to her, and asked what I had about me that made such a horrid noise. I told her that it was my new shoes. "Take them off," she said; "and if you put them on again, I'll throw them into the fire."
>
> I took them off, and my stockings also. She then sent me a long distance, on an errand. As I went through the snow, my bare feet tingled. That night I was very hoarse; and I went to bed thinking the next day would find me sick, perhaps dead.

At age fifteen, Jacobs's fifty-nine-year-old master began to sexually harass her.

> He told me I was his property; that I must be subject to his will in all things. My soul revolted against the mean tyranny. But where could I turn for protection? No matter whether the slave girl be as black as ebony or as fair as her mistress. In either case, there is no shadow of law to protect her from insult, from violence, or even death; all of these are inflicted by fiends who bear the shape of men.[64]

Jacobs's childhood experiences as a slave consisted of stark lessons in terror, intimidation, and degradation.

In addition to this informal socialization process, as historian Thomas L. Webber points out in his careful study *Deep Like the Rivers: Education in the Slave Quarter Community,* plantation owners took a systematic approach toward achieving two clear educational goals: work skills and social control. Plantation life and products totally depended on slave labor. Slaves built and repaired the houses and other plantation buildings, cared for the livestock, manufactured iron implements and horseshoes, planted and cultivated gardens, made shoes, wove cloth, served as butlers, maids, and cooks, and, of course, toiled in the fields. These tasks required innumerable skills, for which slaves were trained. Therefore, the plantation operated, as Webber argues, as "an effective vocational or industrial school." Webber also points to a second, more important educational goal: slave socialization. Masters wanted to prevent uprisings, eliminate runaways, and develop efficient, devoted, and productive laborers. The planter class endeavored to have their slaves "internalize the knowledge, attitudes, values, skills, and sensibilities of the 'perfect servant.'" They wanted slaves to overflow "with awe, respect, and childlike affection for the planter and his family." In short, they strived for "unconditional submission."[65]

Slaveholders used a varied process to accomplish this goal. First, they exploited isolation whenever possible. Remote plantations insulated slaves from news of the outside world, especially news about the abolitionist campaign and slave insurrections. This became particularly crucial with the **Nat Turner Revolt** of 1831. Harriet Jacobs recalled the panic of Southern whites in her community. The local militia ransacked slave homes, stole their paltry possessions, and conducted a general reign of terror: "All day long these unfeeling wretches went round like a troop of demons, terrifying and tormenting the helpless. At night, they formed themselves into patrol bands, and went wherever they chose among the colored people, acting out their brutal will." Many slaves fled to hide in the woods while others were beaten. "Everywhere men, women, and children were whipped till the blood stood in puddles at their feet." Planters struggled to suppress or distort information about abolitionist thinking, that is, the fact that many whites opposed slavery. Jacobs recounted how slaveholders spread lies about the North and the circumstances of escaped slaves living there: "When they visit the North, and return home, they tell their slaves of the runaways they have seen, and describe them in the most deplorable condition."[66] The implication, of course, was that slavery, in which all were fed, clothed, and generally well-cared for, was benevolent. To reinforce their isolation, slaves rarely were permitted to leave their plantations to visit other slaves and other plantations. "Secret or unsupervised meetings where blacks could exchange information, views of their slave condition, and knowledge of the larger world were outlawed."

Second, to ensure compliant and obedient slaves, slaveholders relied on ignorance. Illiteracy inhibited communication with and about the outside world by further restricting the flow of information. "A slave able to read or write not only could forge passes for himself and his friends but could read incendiary literature."[67] South Carolina and Georgia pioneered antiliteracy laws in 1740 and 1770, respectively. Masters severely punished literate slaves through whippings, brandings, dismemberment, and even death. "Local ordinances supplemented state laws; in some places it became a crime merely to sell writing materials to slaves."[68]

Third, planters attempted to destroy the individual identity and cultural background of their slaves. Masters often named their slaves, giving them their own surname. Slaveholders also denigrated as well as attempted to eradicate African traditions and heritage. According to Webber, they forbade African songs, dances, and languages. "The very word 'African' was meant to invoke the image of ignorant savagery and the words 'black' and 'dark' (as in 'darkey') carried connotations of evil, immorality, and ugliness. Blacks were taught that their skin was ugly, that their lips and noses were unaesthetic and malformed, and that they carried a natural smell that was offensive."[69] This acculturation process proved to be pervasive and relentless.

Religion served as the final component in the process. Masters saw "Christianity primarily as a means of social control," especially after the Turner Revolt.[70] Planters set aside every Sunday as a holiday for slaves, when they attended sanctioned plantation services. These were led by the slaveholder, his wife, or an itinerant preacher—the latter was usually the case. Slave masters proved to be highly selective about the religious values they conveyed. These beliefs reinforced as well as validated slavery and the master–slave relationship. In order to ensure submissiveness and docility, the "religious instructor" invoked the "supreme power and authority of the God of Christianity" and the need for absolute obedience to his commands.[71] Failure to do so resulted in eternal damnation and punishment. Using God as a symbol of authority naturally transferred to the relationship between planter and slave. Jacobs recalled one particular sermon which illustrated this message: "Obey your old master and your young master—your old mistress and your young mistress. If you disobey your earthly master, you offend your heavenly Master. You must obey God's commandments."[72] Some planters even resorted to using slave preachers, threatened with flogging, or bribed with money, or relieved from labor, or promised manumission, to advocate obedience.[73]

Masters also used religion to rationalize slavery: "Slaves were taught that it was God's design, as decreed by the Holy Scriptures, that they, as the sons and daughters of Ham, be the servants of whites into eternity." These were highly selective Christian beliefs. Much of what was taught drew on the more severe parts of the Old Testament and sparingly tapped the New Testament. Planters and their ministers referred to Christ to convey meekness and submissiveness, but avoided His teachings about the harsh values and brutal structure of slavery. Webber carefully points out that slave masters were not necessarily being "devious" or "hypocritical"; they actually "believed" this. "Most slaveholders were convinced that God quite clearly sanctioned slavery in the Bible."

Masters certainly maintained clear educational goals, values, and methods. However, a fundamental question remains: What did slaves actually learn? In this regard, the slave community and its culture proved to be deep, rich, and resilient. Human agency clearly asserted itself. All the historical data dramatically reveal "just how little of white teaching was absorbed into the way members of the quarter community looked at the world."

Slave Values and Institutions

The slave quarter organized its own child-rearing practices. The community maintained a nursery for toddlers and young children, that is, children too young to work in the fields. "On many plantations the quarters contained a fenced-in yard where the children could play in safety. Their activities depended greatly upon the energy and inclination of the older children or 'nurses' watching them." The nursery teacher led the children in singing and dancing, told stories, and carved toys. Older children played "among themselves" or roamed "through the fields and woods of the plantation." In the evenings, according to Webber, they joined their parents for meals and completed chores, like gathering fire wood and carrying in water from the well. They would join the adult slave community for singing and storytelling outside around a fire. Older children also participated in nocturnal "clandestine" activities, like hunting and fishing. "As they grew older still, quarter children began attending their community's feasts of stolen food prepared deep in the woods, unsanctioned dances, voodoo ceremonies, and meetings of the clandestine congregation."

Sundays and holidays like Christmas, the Fourth of July, and Easter served as special days. "Besides church, the Sunday activities of most quarters involved singing and storytelling, various games and athletic contests, and visiting among friends and relatives. For children with fathers who lived on neighboring plantations Sundays were especially important as the one day father was certain to be able to visit." Social interactions on holidays fostered as well a strong sense of and commitment to the slave community. As Webber summarizes it: "Through their common experiences they learned the ways in which the community operated, how it made common decisions, planned secretive events, provided for common physical and recreational needs, and generally organized itself to be as independent as possible from the whims of the white personalities and the strictness of plantation rule and regulation."

The slave quarters therefore taught a strong and enduring sense of "group spirit, identification, and solidarity." Members of the slave community saw themselves as distinct, with a clear and unique history and culture. As a result, slaves rarely, if ever, betrayed, stole from, or abused each other. "Most members understood that it was to their mutual advantage to protect each other and that such group solidarity was a good which they believed to have moral force." They operated as an extended family and affection transcended blood relations. They assumed responsibility for the quarter's children and elderly, mutually providing food, protection, clothing, and shelter. Finally, the community took pride in its African heritage.[74]

Slave Families

The family operated as the single most critical social, emotional, and educational institution in the community. The nuclear family was the ideal and adults assumed traditional roles. Slaves remained committed to monogamous relationships in spite of the disruptions and trials of bondage; spouses maintained deep affection for one another. Hundreds suffered whipping and even death protecting their wives from the sexual advances of the planter. Many slaves refused to marry another after the master sold their mates. In other cases, some slaves ran away to find their sold spouses. A few slaves sacrificed rare opportunities to escape to freedom in order to stay with their mates. In these situations, love superseded freedom.[75]

Adults struggled to maintain a warm and affectionate environment for their children. John Blassingame's historical analysis of the slave community reveals that "[f]athers regaled their children with fascinating stories and songs and won their affection with little gifts." Mothers, by showering love and attention on their babies, built "much self-esteem" and a "sense of security." Grandparents too were honored, respected, and loved. "Grandmothers frequently prepared tidbits for the children, and grandfathers often told them stories about their lives in Africa."

Child rearing represented the family's most critical function, and survival skills served as its most important socialization goal. "Since slave parents were primarily responsible for training their children, they could cushion the shock of bondage for them, help them to understand their situation, teach them values different from those their masters tried to instill in them, and give them a referent for self-esteem other than the master." Parents attempted to "shield" their children from the horrors of slavery, teaching them when and how to defer to whites. "Learning to accept personal abuse and the punishment of loved ones passively was one of the most difficult lessons for a slave child."[76] This "racial etiquette," that is, the ability to exercise "self-control," represented the difference between life and death. Parents taught a strict sense of discipline and morality.[77] "If children disobeyed they were sometimes cautioned with tales of haunts, spirits, and the slave bogey man, Raw-Head-and-Bloody-Bones." Parents even

Slave Family (c. 1860s). Courtesy of the Schomburg Center for Research in Black Culture, New York City Public Library.

occasionally resorted to using a switch.[78] Finally, slave parents "did not teach unconditional submission."[79]

"Let My People Go"

Religion served an important educational role. In spite of efforts to censor religious beliefs, slaves embraced their own views. Many slave quarters supported clandestine congregations. These secret religious meetings occurred at least once a week and were usually held in the woods. "Often they would hear the white preachers or the master himself on Sunday morning, but the 'real meetin' and the 'real preachin' came later, among themselves."[80] At other times, in order to ensure security, they would announce a meeting by singing "Steal Away to Jesus" while they were working, meeting as late as eleven o'clock at night.

"This congregation of the religious faithful was an important instrument in the quarter community's ability to transmit and perpetuate not just its own religious ideals but crucial secular understandings, values, and beliefs." To begin with, African Americans saw slavery as anti-Christian. The "True Christian" simply did not own slaves; to do so—that is, to profess to be a follower of Christ and still possess slaves—represented a fundamental contradiction. "For those slaves who knew more of Christianity than what they heard from slaveholders, the principal tenants of true Christianity revolved around the complementary principles that God intended all men to be free and that, therefore, slavery was wrong."[81] They saw their masters as hypocrites. Furthermore, slave religion emphasized deliverance. Moses in Exodus and Christ as the Savior were durable themes. Slave "spirituals vibrated with the message: God will deliver us if we have faith in Him." A quiet sense of defiance grew out of these beliefs; God proved to be more powerful than the slave master.[82]

Frederick Douglass

Frederick Douglass's early life personifies much of this educational process. He was born a slave in February 1818 in the Chesapeake area of Maryland. His mother, who could read, died when he was young, and his grandmother raised him. His father was his white master. At age six, Frederick joined his brother and sisters at the Wye House, a typical isolated, self sufficient plantation, owned by the affluent Colonel Edward Lloyd. "On his thirteen farms, covering approximately ten thousand acres, his 550 slaves raised sufficient wheat to make him one of the largest producers of grain in the country." Lloyd's overseer maintained strict slave discipline through severe whippings, even shooting a disobedient slave. There was no leniency shown. "The Lloyds allowed no manumissions, no hope of freedom to disrupt the basic order of the world the slaves were ordained to inhabit. And food and clothing were kept sparse. . . ."

Young Frederick proved to be bright and curious. He played with Daniel Lloyd, the master's son, and explored the "house." "One of the wonders of the world of American slavery is that before puberty, the children of the slaves and those of the masters were often allowed to play together. In the grander establishments, a white family might arrange for a young slave child to be simultaneously an always available playmate and a step-and-fetch-it servant." This was Frederick's role. He hunted with the older Daniel, retrieving the dead birds for him. However, Frederick also sat with Daniel as a tutor taught him to read, write, and calculate. Frederick "imitated the patterns of speech" he heard exchanged between the teacher and the student. He mimicked "other 'cultured' white people" as well.[83]

At age eight, Frederick was sent to live in Baltimore. Here he encountered a profoundly different environment, typical of Southern cities. Richard Wade, an historian, argues that urban slavery prior to 1840 departed sharply from its rural plantation counterpart. Southern cities—New Orleans, Mobile, Richmond, Louisville, and, of course, Baltimore, among others—hosted large African American populations. In 1820, they composed 37 percent of Southern town dwellers. In Charleston alone, "the total black population exceeded 58 percent." The institution of slavery in such bustling, crowded, and fluid city settings assumed a more relaxed nature. Slaves moved freely on the streets as masters "hired" them out as domestics or skilled and unskilled laborers to households, businesses, and other employers. Many slaves who received an allowance even rented their own apartments and fended for themselves. Strict racial segregation also proved to be difficult, as slaves interacted with whites from other parts of the country and in coastal towns with visitors from different nations. Finally, slaves mingled with free African Americans; these outnumbered slaves in Baltimore by ten to one, for example. Free African Americans established strong communities. "They formed congregations and erected churches, established schools and aid societies, and organized improvement projects aimed at bringing some of the better things of life to their members."

A high literacy rate prevailed among Southern urban free African Americans and slaves. Cities provided a natural environment for literacy. "Newspapers abounded; signs lined streets and shops; books and pamphlets circulated freely." African American congregations conducted "Bible classes as part of church programs." Free African Americans, in defiance of Southern antiliteracy laws, opened schools, "which slaves attended; one slave taught another, and the more ingenious managed alone." Frederick Douglass, who carried a copy of Webster's spelling book in his pocket, recalled that "when sent on errands, or when playtime was allowed me, I would stop, with my young friends, aside, and take a lesson in spelling." He could read by thirteen years of age.[84]

Five years later, Frederick's master apprenticed him as a caulker in Baltimore's shipyard. By the age of twenty, as a journeyman caulker Frederick was permitted to hire himself out. He recalled the arrangements with his master: "I was to be allowed all my time; to make all bargains to work; to find my own employment, and to collect my own wages; and, in return for the liberty, I was required, or obliged, to pay him three dollars at the end of each week, and to board and clothe myself, and buy my own caulking tools."[85] Shortly thereafter, in September 1838, following a confrontation with his master, Frederick escaped to Philadelphia and the free North, where he became a famous, popular, and powerful abolitionist.

Education among the slaves transcended schooling, as we have seen. Slave masters knew this and resorted to other means to train slaves to be productive workers and socialize them to accept their exploited position. Slaves did not act as victims, however. They, too, knew that knowledge was power; they understood that Christianity, in its ideal sense, did not sanction the subjugation of people; and they preserved their African roots in spite of incredibly difficult conditions. Northern African Americans also faced a long educational struggle.

FREEDOM'S LAND?

Slavery dominated racial relations in the South, but racism was alive and well in the free North as well. Leon Litwack argues in his classic *North of Slavery: The Negro in the Free State, 1790–1860* that such racism resulted in both general segregation and separate schooling.[86] Traveling throughout the North to make antislavery speeches, Frederick Douglass had to contend with segregation. "Like other African-American abolitionists smarting under indignities, Douglass devoted a large portion of his speeches not to slavery, but to Jim Crow practices. The two injustices were inseparable in his mind." On two occasions in 1841, Douglass was physically removed from white railway cars while traveling in Massachusetts.[87]

Most Northern states during the early 1800s either excluded African American children from schooling altogether or "established separate schools for them." The New England states, Pennsylvania, Ohio, and New York had all passed legislation maintaining segregated schools. One of the provisions of Pennsylvania's 1854 School Law mandated "separate schools for Negro or mulatto children 'whenever schools could be so located as to accommodate twenty or more pupils.' "[88] This statute remained in effect until 1881, when it was repealed. States that lacked specific segregation laws relied on "custom" to exclude African American children from white schools. Northerners rationalized that African American children needed only the bare minimum in facilities, teachers, and curricula, because they possessed limited intellectual ability.[89] "In a speech to blacks in Ohio in 1852, Horace Mann said that 'in intellect, the blacks are inferior to whites, while in sentiment and affections, the whites are inferior to blacks.' "[90] Fear of African American settlers, especially in the Midwest, also drove some of the restrictions, in other words, "equal educational privileges" might attract African American migration. African Americans were therefore faced with a dilemma: "continue to attend segregated institutions or secure no education at all."

African American children as a result experienced "a poor educational environment." Students attended classes in overcrowded rooms or deteriorating buildings. Their white instructors usually lacked competence, often resented their work, frequently "faced insults and social ostracism," and always received "meager salaries." "In Providence, Rhode Island, a white teacher threatened to punish any of his African American students who dared to greet him in public." Also, the curriculum in these schools was constricted. Instructors rarely taught their students grammar. "To a large extent, this limitation reflected the exclusion of African Americans from the most professional pursuits and the prevailing belief that the average African American's intellectual capacity debarred him [sic] from advanced studies." Thus, segregated schooling merely prepared African American children for their limited work lives in a segregated society.

African Americans responded in a variety of ways to Northern segregated schools. Some established their own private schools: "In Ohio, African Americans organized the School Fund Society and established some educational centers." In other cases, the abolitionist movement, especially after 1831, "gave substantial support and encouragement to African American education." However, whites harassed and attacked African American schools in towns throughout the North. Enraged whites opposed to the education of African Americans destroyed an African American school building in Troy, Ohio, in 1840. Some African American leaders campaigned for separate schools in Hartford, Connecticut, and Providence, Rhode Island. Such settings, they reasoned, would shield African American children from insensitive white teachers and abusive white classmates. Further, some proponents argued that "separate schools afforded African Americans the opportunity to refute charges of inferiority by producing scholars superior to those in the best white schools." But many African Americans attacked the practice of segregated schooling. "Through convention appeals, petitions, court suits, and editorial campaigns, African Americans maintained a constant agitation in the 1840s and 1850s for the abolition of school segregation." As Frederick Douglass wrote, "The point which we must aim at is, to obtain admission for our children into the nearest schoolhouse, and the best schoolhouse in our respective neighborhoods."[91]

Boston became a focus of efforts to integrate the schools. Boston's pattern of segregation had begun in the 1790s when African American parents petitioned the city for separate schools. They wanted to "shield" their children from racist abuse, epithets, and the taunts of white children and teachers alike. A common form of punishment in school was to "sit in the 'nigger-seat,' the symbol of stupidity, the place of shame." By 1812, as Stanley Schultz sums up, African Americans "had succeeded in segregating their children into an all-Black school, one taught, since 1808, by Black instructors." This semiprivate institution received some public funds from the city (eventually, it was absorbed into Boston's unique public school system). By the late 1820, however, African American parents and leaders began to question the need for segregated schools.

David Walker served as an articulate spokesperson. Born a freedman in North Carolina in 1789, he settled in Boston during the 1820s. He soon became a writer for the *Freedman's Journal,* the nation's first African American newspaper. "By 1828 he was well known in Boston as a fiery writer and public speaker, a man dedicated to the extinction of slavery and racism." Walker published a pamphlet, "Appeal to the Coloured Citizens of the World," in 1829 that was a critique of broad social issues, including education. He attacked the North in general and Boston in particular for the "total inadequacy of educational facilities." He argued that a "conspiracy" existed to limit African American education. As Walker proclaimed, "I must truly say that ignorance, the mother of treachery and deceit, gnaws into our very vitals. . . . We are an unlettered people, brought up in ignorance, not one in a hundred can read or write, not one in a thousand has a liberal education." His pamphlet attained wide circulation, went through three editions, and proved to be influential in raising the consciousness of white Americans and mobilizing African Americans. Although Walker died in 1830, the campaign against separate schools continued.

The Boston School Committee itself reported in 1833 that separate schooling was unequal. "Not only was the quality of education inferior, but the physical accommodations were unhealthy and inadequate." The report saw no benefits in separate schools for either race. However, the only action the committee took was to erect a new school building for African American children, leaving the separate-school pattern intact.

The Origins of "Separate But Equal"

Beginning in the 1830s, African American parents and leaders and white abolitionists began "militant attacks" to integrate Boston's schools. They petitioned school and city officials, briefly boycotted the schools, and finally filed suit in a famous Massachusetts Supreme Court case, *Roberts v Boston*. The arguments and opinions connected with this case resonate to this day. In 1847, Benjamin Roberts attempted to enroll his five-year-old daughter Sarah in the primary school nearest to his home. This white school, along with three others, refused to admit her because a separate school existed for African American children. However, the closest such school required her to walk almost one-half mile, passing five white primary schools on the way.[92] In this case, neighborhood schools existed for white children but not for their African American counterparts. Roberts contended that Sarah was denied public schooling because of Boston's statutes mandating separate African American schools and filed suit. The case reached the Massachusetts Supreme Court in 1849.

Robert Morris, an African American attorney, and Charles Sumner, a leading abolitionist and later a congressman, represented the Roberts family. As Sumner argued for the plaintiff, Sarah Roberts: "On one side is the city of Boston, strong in its wealth, in its influence, in its character; on the other side is a little child. . . . This child asks at your hands her *personal rights*."[93] Sumner based his case on, first, the concept of equality, that is, equal rights and equal treatment. Second, he maintained that the Massachusetts constitution and state law regarding public schools made no distinction about race, only the city of Boston did. Hence, Boston's school segregation law, because it was predicated on race, "is in the nature of caste, and is a violation of equality." That law, he continued, "inflicts upon them the stigma of caste; and although the matters taught in the two schools may be precisely the same, a school exclusively devoted to one class must differ essentially, in its spirit and character, from that public school known to the law, where all classes meet together in equality." For Sumner, such segregation "tends to create a feeling of degradation in the blacks, and of prejudice and uncharitableness in whites."[94] Finally, Sumner eloquently and definitively described the "common school" concept.

> . . . there is but one kind of public school established by the laws of Massachusetts. This is the general Public School, free to all the inhabitants. There is nothing in these laws establishing any exclusive separate school for any particular class, whether rich or poor, whether Catholic or Protestant, whether white or black. In the eye of the law there is but *one* class, in which all interests, opinions, conditions, and colors comingle in harmony— excluding none, comprehending all.[95]

The court delivered its opinion in 1850 for the City of Boston, the defendant in this case. Justice Lemuel Shaw gave the unanimous opinion.

> The plaintiff had access to the school, set apart for colored children, as well conducted in all respects, and as well fitted, in point of capacity and qualification of the instructors, to advance the education of children under seven years old, as the other primary schools; the objection is, that the schools thus open to the plaintiff are exclusively appropriated to colored children, and are at a greater distance from her home. Under these circumstances, has the plaintiff been unlawfully excluded from public school instruction? Upon the best consideration we have been able to give the subject, the court are all of the opinion that she has not.[96]

Shaw simply deferred to local authority in this matter. What the justices overlooked is this: If the law cannot be used to alleviate, if not eliminate, the debilitating effects of racism, what can? The court also conveniently ignored the fact that the law was being used to institutionalize racism. The question remained, then as it does now, how can we change a racist culture?

Boston's African American leaders, undaunted, regrouped. They formed the Equal School Rights Committee and appealed to Massachusetts state legislators to overturn Boston's, school segregation law. The state assembly approved such a bill in 1855, and that fall Boston peacefully desegregated its public schools—a far cry from the racial conflict over school desegregation in Boston during the 1970s.

Buoyed by the Massachusetts victory, African American leaders led similar campaigns in Rhode Island, Pennsylvania, Ohio, and Indiana, but to no avail. "By 1860, some small and scattered communities agreed to integration, but the larger cities, including New York, Philadelphia, Cincinnati, Providence, and New Haven, hoped to stem increasing agitation by correcting existing abuses and making the African American schools equal to those of whites." Even in instances of apparent progress, white racism continued to manifest itself. "Some communities admitted African Americans to the public schools but seated them separately and frequently punished white offenders by forcing them to sit with African Americans." Frederick Douglass's daughter experienced such in-school segregation. Many Northern states did not legally desegregate their public schools until after the Civil War; in some cases, this took well into the 1870s.[97]

SPECIAL CHILDREN

African American students experienced segregation, but exceptional children found themselves excluded from the public schools. According to Margaret Winzer's historical analysis, the education of exceptional children has progressed from isolation to segregation to integration in the past 200 years. This section will focus on the first period; Chapters 7 and 10 will concentrate on their segregation and integration, respectively.

Institutional Isolation

During the colonial period, the care of exceptional children fell to relatives, the local community, and church-sponsored efforts. Usually, the children were provided just bare subsistence. Lacking systematization, these well-meant efforts proved to be haphazard and uneven.

The growth of cities during the early 1800s strained if not eliminated the voluntary and fragile efforts at care. A more purposeful approach was required and this resulted in "institutional reform." During the nineteenth century, such reform went through three stages. First, religious charitable and philanthropic ventures pioneered early but rudimentary organizational care. Then special institutions under state auspices became prominent by midcentury as part of the broader movement for social reform. By the century's end, the treatment of exceptional children had adopted a purely educational mission. In sum, largely private efforts in this area dominated the first half of the nineteenth century, whereas public-sponsored organizations assumed responsibility during the second half of the century.

European experiments in educating exceptional children exerted a strong influence on American teaching methods and institutions. In the United States, "[d]eaf children were the first to receive attention," followed in succession by the blind and mentally ill. After studying French treatments of the deaf for two years, Thomas Hopkins Gallaudet arrived in New York City in 1817 with his French colleague Laurent Clerc. The following year Gallaudet, with Clerc and Mason Fitch Cogswell, opened the Connecticut Asylum for the Educational Instruction of Deaf and Dumb Persons, renamed two years later as the American Asylum at Hartford for the Education and Instruction of the Deaf and Dumb. The Asylum relied on the French manual of methods of communication and survived on donations raised by public appeals and demonstrations of student progress. Other similar private, residential institutions quickly followed in other states; they numbered fifty-five by 1880.[98]

In the 1840s, Horace Mann and Samuel Gridley Howe began promoting German methods of educating exceptional children. Like Gallaudet, Howe had traveled to Europe to study the methods of pioneering institutions, and in 1832 he opened the New England Asylum for the Blind in Boston. It later was named the Perkins Institution and Massachusetts Asylum for the Blind, after a major benefactor. Horace Mann, a "close friend" of Howe, served as a school trustee. The Perkins Institution earned a national reputation. Howe believed every child had a right to schooling, and he relied on an enlightened, naturalistic approach to education. He allowed the learning process to follow the child's interests and heavily used tactile methods to teach blind students. Seven-year-old Laura Bridgman, both blind and deaf, became Howe's most famous student. "Thousands of tourists flocked to the Perkins school for its weekly fund-raising student exhibition, most of them coming specifically to see Laura Bridgman."[99] Howe even succeeded in negotiating some state support for the Perkins institute. "By 1875 there were thirty schools for blind persons serving 3,000 pupils."

The institutionalization of exceptional people began with Benjamin Rush. As we saw in Chapter 3, he was a proponent of state-financed education; he also campaigned for the institutionalization of the mentally ill. Rush viewed the practice of spectators paying an entrance fee to officials of lunatic hospitals to be entertained by the antics of inmates as inhumane. He banished such exploitative schemes in Philadelphia and, in the hope of curing patients, initiated a demanding regimen of hard work and "strict discipline." Although somewhat improved, institutional conditions for the mentally ill remained harsh, dominated by "patient restraint," until mid-century. Through the devoted efforts of Dorothea Lynde Dix, these conditions began to change. She vigorously lobbied the Massachusetts legislature for more humane treatment of the insane. "By 1847 she visited 128 penitentiaries, 300 county jails and houses of correction, and 500 almshouses . . . and was specifically responsible for improvements in hospitals in Rhode Island and New York and the establishment of insane hospitals in thirteen other states as well as the District of Columbia, Ontario, and Nova Scotia."

All of these activities had far-reaching and cumulative consequences. By midcentury, the idea of providing institutions for exceptional children had gained momentum. Horace Mann, as we have seen, was a strong proponent of special schooling. "Disability and dependence" were seen as linked. "Inevitably, it was argued, schooling for blind children would remove from society 'so many dead weights' and prevent them from becoming 'taxes on the community'. . . . Education would emancipate deaf children from 'the fetters imposed . . . by their deafness' so that 'the old ignorance, the old animism, the old brutishness are passed away'. . . . [S]chooling for mentally-retarded youngsters would serve to teach 'such habits as to render possible for them, life in a domestic relation.' "[100] The policy of isolation was thus dominant regarding exceptional children. In the absence of effective compulsory attendance laws, nothing compelled the public schools to retain, or for that matter attempt to teach, special education youngsters. "School order depended on exclusion."[101]

CONCLUSIONS

The education of young children during the first half of the nineteenth century gradually began to assume an institutional character. The scattered rural communities laid the foundation for local district control of schooling. Cities, with their dense and diverse populations, experimented with a wide variety of institutional forms in efforts to reform society in the face of rising crime and poverty, a growing number of immigrants, and the imposition of a new economic order and culture. All of this culminated in the establishment of the common schools, a state system of free schooling.

The common-school legacy continues to exert much influence. For Kaestle, the movement embodies the American search for social reform:

> School reformers believed that common schools could solve the problems of diversity, instability, and equal opportunity. That faith has been resilient in American history. Despite the periodic rediscovery that schools have not in fact solved our problems, and despite occasional periods of disillusionment with the education profession, the American common-school system has always revived, buoyed by Americans' faith that education is the best approach to most social problems.[102]

Public schooling, to be sure, has served as the "imperfect panacea."[103]

The legacy also includes conflict. Committed to native-Protestant ideology, the public schools were anything but neutral regarding values and the educational policies to be derived from them. Critics included

> taxpayers—urban landlords and dirt farmers alike—who could see no reason to educate the children of others; sectarian groups who attacked public schools as godless or covertly Protestant; patrons and proprietors of private schools; laborers who opposed education beyond the three R's as a subsidy of the wealthy; and patricians who clung to an elitism which was going out of style in Jacksonian America.[104]

Even to this day, the public school concept is supported by an uneasy consensus and is subject to many of these same criticisms.

The creation of the common schools marked a "shift of educational responsibility from the family to the school, a shift which accelerated between the Revolution and Civil War." American society began to socialize and educate its children less through an organic, family-centered approach, and more through formal, institutionalized means. "Despite the cultural cost involved in having a common public-school system, and despite the public schools' manifest failure to treat children equally, Americans widely share a belief in fairness and cohesion through common schools, a belief that is the core of the cosmopolitan solution."[105] In retrospect, common-school reform continues to present us with a dilemma. On the one hand, taken at face value, the rhetoric undergirding the common-school concept called for universal mass schooling to ensure literacy and opportunity as well as a stable society and an enduring nation-state—certainly an admirable ideals. On the other hand, clear support for the common schools came from a small, affluent, if not privileged, segment of society, whose arguments were often based on schooling as a mechanism of social control. Public schooling ameliorated economic, political, and social conflict by producing efficient and loyal workers, assimilating immigrants, and training devoted wives and mothers; in short, it operated to limit opportunities, thus ensuring inequality. Historians continue to ponder these contradictory interpretations; more important, all of this directly relates to the basic functions of public schooling, which educators and the general public hotly debate to this day.

In the beginning, the common school provided only a limited educational experience. Initially, it only applied to elementary schooling. Moreover, the idea of "common" was for the most part mere lofty rhetoric; it was seldom matched by social reality. In urban areas especially, the common schools acted as instruments of segregation, isolating Protestant native-born children from immigrant Catholic ones, European Americans from African Americans, and the rich from the poor, as well excluding special-needs children.[106] But the stage had been set: Through decades-long struggle and conflict, many different groups would strive to achieve the common-school ideal—schools open to all children and treating them equally. The ideal was achieved in small and gradual steps. Both as a concept and as an institution, public schooling expanded and grew throughout the nineteenth century, spread to secondary education, and came to include female students.

ACTIVITIES FOR FURTHER EXPLORATION

1. Relying principally on Carl Kaestle, ed., *Joseph Lancaster and the Monitorial School Movement: A Documentary History* (New York: Teachers College Press, 1973), create a simulation of short arithmetic and spelling lessons in a Lancaster setting. "Male" students must act as monitors. The "master" must select the lessons for the monitors, direct them to give rewards, handout punishments, and order "scholars" to march from one lesson to another.

2. Do you agree with Horace Mann's reasons for creating the common schools? See his 1848 annual report at http://usinfo.state.gov/usa/infousa/facts/democrac/16.htm and compile a list of them. Are these goals still in effect?

3. How did antebellum plantation owners control their slaves? See " 'The Happiest Laboring Class in the World': Two Virginia Slaveholders Debate Methods of Slave Management, 1837" at http://chnm.gmu.edu/us/many.taf.

4. What did slave children actually learn? For former slave recollections, consult the Gilder Lehrman Institute of American History Web site at http://vi.uh.edu/pages/mintz/primary.htm and review the "James W. C. Pennington" and "Lunsford Lane" excerpts from the "Slave Narratives." Additional slave narratives from the Federal Writers Project can be found at http://memory.loc.gov/ammem/doc.html. To gain further historical insight into the sequence of events in African American history, refer to the "Timeline of African-American History" at http://lcweb2.loc.gov/ammem/aap/timeline.html.

5. Did fleeing to the "Free North" always mean freedom for slaves? To better grasp how Northern white society limited options for African Americans, see the "Fugitive Slave Law" at http://www.law.ou.edu/hist/.

6. Engage fellow students in a debate over the following two questions: What is the single most important purpose of the public schools? Should the public schools practice social control?

NOTES AND SOURCES

In order to condense endnotes, the first work cited is the primary one, usually the source of any direct quotes. Subsequent references serve as supplementary, or additional, source of paraphrased information and/or alternative historical interpretations.

1. The quotes in these paragraphs are from Alan Dawley, *Class and Community: The Industrial Revolution in Lynn* (Cambridge, MA: Harvard University Press, 1976), pp. 16–18, 45–46. Samuel Bowles and Herbert Gintis, *Schooling in Capitalist America: Educational Reform and the Contradictions of Economic Life* (New York: Basic Books, 1976), rely on a political economy framework to explain school reform.

2. E. P. Thompson, "Time, Work-Discipline, and Industrial Capitalism," *Past and Present* 38 (1967), pp. 59, 60, 73.

3. Dawley, *Class and Community,* pp. 90, 92.

4. Thompson, "Time, Work-Discipline, and Industrial Capitalism," pp. 60, 61, 82. As Thompson states, "Time is now currency; it is not passed but spent."

5. The quotes in these paragraphs are from Stanley K. Schultz, *The Culture Factory: Boston Public Schools,*

1789–1860 (New York: Oxford University Press, 1973), pp. 50, 52–54, 57–58, 59, 62–64, 66. Refer as well to N. Ray Hiner and Joseph M. Hawes, eds., *Growing Up in America: Children in Historical Perspective* (Urbana, IL: University of Illinois Press, 1985), p. 83; Linda Peavy and Ursula Smith. *Frontier Children* (Norman, OK: University of Oklahoma Press, 1999), p. 9.

6. David Tyack and Elisabeth Hansot, *Learning Together: A History of Coeducation in American Public Schools* (New Havent, CT: Yale University Press, 1990), p. 31.

7. All quotes in this paragraph are from Carl Kaestle, *Pillars of the Republic: Common Schools and American Society, 1780–1860* (New York: Hill and Wang, 1983), pp. 13, 15, 24, 25, 27. Much of the organization of this section relies on Kaestle's fine study.

8. Warren Burton, *The District School As It Was, By One Who Went to It* (Boston: Phillips, Sampson and Co., 1850), pp. 2–3, 16, 23, 40.

9. Robert L. Church, *Education in the United States: An Interpretive History* (New York: Free Press, 1976), pp. 10, 20–21. Also refer to David B. Tyack, *The One Best System: A History of American Urban Education* (Cambridge, MA: Harvard University Press, 1974), pp. 14–16.

10. Tyack and Hansot, *Learning Together*, p. 50.

11. Lawrence A. Cremin, *American Education: The National Experience, 1783–1876* (New York: Harper & Row, 1980), p. 344. Parts of this section are taken from Richard J. Altenbaugh, David E. Engel, and Don T. Martin, *Caring for Kids: A Critical Study of Urban School Leavers* (London: Falmer Press, 1995), p. 29.

12. W. J. Rorabaugh, *The Craft Apprentice: From Franklin to the Machine Age in America* (New York: Oxford University Press, 1986), p. vii; Tyack and Hansot, *Learning Together*, p. 125; Schultz, *Culture Factory*, p. 70. Also, refer to Altenbaugh, Engel, and Martin, *Caring for Kids*, pp. 29–30.

13. Kaestle, *Pillars of the Republic*, p. 31–33, 37, 38.

14. Carl Kaestle, *The Evolution of an Urban School System: New York City, 1750–1850* (Cambridge, MA: Harvard University Press, 1973), p. 85.

15. Schultz, *Culture Factory*, p. 264; Kaestle, *Pillars of the Republic*, pp. 40, 42.

16. Kaestle, *Pillars of the Republic*, p. 41. Also, see Barbara Finkelstein, *Governing the Young: Teacher Behavior in Popular Primary Schools in Nineteenth-Century United States* (New York: Falmer Press, 1989), pp. 101–102, 121–123; David Hogan, "The Market Revolution and Disciplinary Power: Joseph Lancaster and the Psychology of the Early Classroom," *History of Education Quarterly* 29 (Fall 1989), pp. 382, 386, 398, 402–403; Carl Kaestle, ed., *Joseph Lancaster and the Monitorial School Movement: A Documentary History* (New York: Teachers College Press, 1973), pp. 4–9, 48–49.

17. Schultz, *Culture Factory*, pp. 25–26.

18. Tyack, *Turning Points*, pp. 122, 138, 139.

19. Schultz, *Culture Factory*, pp. 267–268.

20. Tyack, *Turning Points*, p. 123.

21. Kaestle, *Pillars of the Republic*, pp. 44, 45; Schultz, *Culture Factory*, pp. 26, 28.

22. The quotes is these two paragraphs are from Kaestle, *Evolution of an Urban School System*, pp. 121–122, 125, 126; See as well Tyack, *Turning Points*, p. 120.

23. Schultz, *Culture Factory*, pp. 271–272. Also see Caroline Winterer, "Avoiding a 'Hothouse System of Education': Nineteenth-Century Early Childhood Education from the Infant Schools to the Kindergartens," *History of Education Quarterly* (Fall 1992), pp. 291–292.

24. Winterer, "Avoiding a 'Hothouse System of Education", pp. 290, 293. Refer as well to Kaestle, *Pillars of the Republic*, p. 48. The *American Journal of Education* appears in Michael B. Katz, ed., *School Reform: Past and Present* (Boston: Little, Brown and Co., 1971), pp. 32–34.

25. Schultz, *Culture Factory*, p. 272.

26. Winterer, "Avoiding a 'Hothouse System of Education'," pp. 290, 293.

27. Kaestle, *Pillars of the Republic*, pp. 47, 51–52, 55, 57. See as well Barbara Finkelstein, *Governing the Young*, pp. 14, 15; Tyack, *Turning Points*, p. 120.

28. Neil G. McCluskey, *Catholic Education in America: A Documentary History* (New York: Teachers College Press, 1964), p. 8.

29. Church, *Education in the United States*, pp. 55–56.

30. J. P. Wickersham, *A History of Education in Pennsylvania.* (Lancaster, PA: Inquirer Publishing Company, 1886; rpt. New York: Arno Press, 1969), pp. 308–309, 312, 317, 319, 320, 332.

31. Stevens is quoted in Thomas F. Woodley, *Thaddeus Stevens* (Harrisburg, PA: Telegraph Press, 1934), pp. 154–155, 166–167. Also see Ralph Korngold, *Thaddeus Stevens: A Being Darkly Wise and Rudely Great* (New York: Harcourt, Brace & Co., 1955), p. 34.

32. Ellwood P. Cubberley, *Public Education in the United States: A Study and Interpretation of American Educational History* (Boston: Houghton Mifflin Company, 1919), pp. 142, 145. Consult as well Forest C. Ensign, *Compulsory School Attendance and Child Labor* (Iowa City, IA: Athens Press, 1921; rpt. New York: Arno Press, 1969), p. 170; Wickersham, *History of Education in Pennsylvania,* pp. 322, 369.

33. Wickersham, *History of Education in Pennsylvania,* p. 369. Also, refer to Cremin *American Education: The National Experience,* p. 172.

34. Lawrence A. Cremin, ed., *The Republic and the School: Horace Mann on the Education of Free Men* (New York: Teachers College Press, 1957), p. 26.

35. Gerald L. Gutek, *Historical and Philosophical Foundations of Education: A Biographical Introduction* (Upper Saddle River, NJ: Prentice-Hall, 1997), pp. 191, 194–206, 208.

36. The quote is from Cremin, *American Education: The National Experience,* p. 142. Also refer to Ensign, *Compulsory School Attendance,* p. 90.

37. Kaestle, *Pillars of the Republic,* pp. 75, 76. Schultz, *Culture Factory,* p. 3, refers to a similar triad, "piety, patriotism, and public order," to analyze the roots of the common schools in Boston. Also refer to David Tyack, ed., *Turning Points in American Educational History* (New York: John Wiley & Sons, 1967), p. 125.

38. All quotes are from Cremin, *The Republic and the School,* pp. 58, 91. See likewise Finkelstein, *Governing the Young,* pp. 16–17.

39. Kaestle, *Pillars of the Republic,* pp. 80, 81, 83. Refer as well to Cremin, The *Republic and the School,* p. 97; Cremin, *American Education,* pp. 137–138.

40. Thompson, "Time, Work-Discipline, and Industrial Capitalism," p. 84.

41. Cremin, *The Republic and the School,* p. 87.

42. Kaestle, *Pillars of the Republic,* pp. 93, 98.

43. McCluskey, *Catholic Education in America,* p. 6; Mann is quoted on pp. 6, 7. Also see Mann's statement about religion in his *Twelfth Annual Report* (1848) in Cremin, *The Republic and the School,* p. 106.

44. Kaestle, *Pillars of the Republic,* pp. 93, 98, 101.

45. This quote is from Lawrence Cremin, who wrote the Preface for McCluskey, *Catholic Education in America,* p. vii.

46. The quote is from Kaestle, *Pillars of the Republic,* p. 64, while the data are drawn from Leonard

Dinnerstein and David M. Reimers, *Ethnic Americans: A History of Immigration* (New York: Harper & Row, 1988), p. 16.

47. Dinnerstein and Reimers, *Ethnic Americans,* pp. 38, 39.

48. Kathleen Neils Conzen, *Immigrant Milwaukee, 1836–1860: Accommodation and Community in a Frontier City* (Cambridge, MA: Harvard University Press, 1976), pp. 7, 14, 180, 181, 182.

49. The quote is from McCluskey, *Catholic Education in America,* p. 3. Also, see Timothy Walch, *Parish School: American Catholic Parochial Education from Colonial Times to the Present* (New York: Crossroad Publishing Co., 1996), p. 13.

50. McCluskey, *Catholic Education in America,* p. 3; Walch, *Parish School* pp. 15, 19.

51. Morse is quoted in Dinnerstein and Reimers, *Ethnic Americans,* p. 35. Refer also to Walch, *Parish School,* p. 25.

52. Walch, *Parish School,* pp. 24–25, 44, 47, 49.

53. This excerpt from *The Massachusetts Teacher* appears in Katz, ed., *School Reform,* pp. 169–71.

54. The quote is from Dinnerstein and Reimers, *Ethnic Americans;* p. 37. The notion of "culture factory" is from Schultz, *Culture Factory.* Finally, see Walch, *Parish School,* p. 25.

55. McCluskey, *Catholic Education in America,* contains significant primary documents drawn from Catholic educational history; see pp. 30, 94. Also see Walch, *Parish School,* pp. 54, 61.

56. The quotes in these three paragraphs are from James W. Sanders, *The Education of an Urban Minority: Catholics in Chicago* (New York: Oxford University Press, 1977), pp. 4, 5, 13–15, 24–25.

57. Hughes is quoted in David B. Tyack, *The One Best System: A History of American Urban Education* (Cambridge, MA: Harvard University Press, 1974), p. 85. The other individuals are quoted in McCluskey, *Catholic Education in America,* pp. 9, 11.

58. Walch, *Parish School,* p. 37, 38, 39, 41, 42.

59. The most authoritative historical account of coeducation in American education is Tyack and Hansot, *Learning Together.* See in particular pp. 46, 48, 49, 50, 59, 79, 82–83, 100, 101, 111, 112. See Schultz, *Culture Factory,* pp. 118–119, for the coeducation debate in Boston.

60. Robert William Fogel and Stanley L. Engerman, *Time on the Cross: The Economics of American Negro Slavery* (Boston: Little, Brown and Co., 1974), pp. 15, 22.

61. Leon F. Litwack, *Been in the Storm So Long: The Aftermath of Slavery* (New York: Vintage Books, 1980), p. 3.

62. Fogel and Engerman, *Time on the Cross*, p. 29.

63. Thomas L. Webber, *Deep Like the Rivers: Education in the Slave Quarter Community, 1831–1865* (New York: W. W. Norton and Co., 1978), pp. 21, 22. Also, refer to Eugene D. Genovese, *Roll Jordan Roll: The World the Slaves Made* (New York: Vintage Books, 1976), p. 502.

64. Harriet A. Jacobs, *Incidents in the Life of a Slave Girl: Written by Herself,* ed. Jean Fagan Yellin (Cambridge, MA: Harvard University Press, 1987), pp. 13, 19, 27.

65. Webber, *Deep Like the Rivers*, pp. 26, 27, 36.

66. Jacobs, *Incidents in the Life of a Slave Girl*, pp. 43, 64. See as well Webber, *Deep Like the Rivers*, pp. 27, 45.

67. These quotes are from Webber, *Deep Like the Rivers*, p. 29.

68. Genovese, *Roll Jordan Roll*, pp. 562, 564. Also, see Webber, *Deep Like the Rivers*, p. 30.

69. Webber, *Deep Like the Rivers*, p. 35.

70. Genovese, *Roll Jordan Roll*, p. 186.

71. Webber, *Deep Like the Rivers*, pp. 47, 48–49, 52.

72. Jacobs, *Incidents in the Life of a Slave Girl*, p. 69.

73. John W. Blassingame, *The Slave Community: Plantation Life in the Antebellum South* (New York: Oxford University Press, 1979), pp. 132–133.

74. The quotes in these paragraphs are from Webber, *Deep Like the Rivers*, pp. 14–15, 17, 18–19, 49, 54, 56, 63–64, 67, 68, 69, 153. Also refer to Blassingame, *Slave Community*, pp. 147, 148; Genovese, *Roll Jordan Roll*, pp. 246, 508.

75. See Herbert G. Gutman, *The Black Family in Slavery and Freedom, 1750–1925* (New York: Vintage Books, 1977), Chapter 1; Blassingame, *Slave Community*, pp. 151, 171; John Demos, *Past, Present, and Personal: The Family and the Life Course in American History* (New York: Oxford University Press, 1986), p. 59; Genovese, *Roll Jordan Roll*, pp. 451–453, 484–484, 491–492; Webber, *Deep Like the Rivers*, pp. 111–112, 115.

76. The quotes in these paragraphs are from Blassingame, *Slave Community*, pp. 151, 181, 183, 186, 187. Also refer to Genovese, *Roll Jordan Roll*, pp. 522–523.

77. Genovese, *Roll Jordan Roll*, pp. 510–511. Also see Blassingame, *Slave Community*, p. 187.

78. Webber, *Deep Like the Rivers*, p. 165. Also refer to Genovese, *Roll Jordan Roll*, p. 511.

79. Blassingame, *Slave Community*, p. 188.

80. Genovese, *Roll Jordan Roll*, p. 237. Webber, *Deep Like the Rivers*, p. 194, makes similar observations.

81. Webber, *Deep Like the Rivers*, pp. 80, 82, 191, 196; Genovese, *Roll Jordan Roll*, p. 236.

82. Genovese, *Roll Jordan Roll*, pp. 244, 252, 253. Also see Blassingame, *Slave Community*, p. 147.

83. The information and quotes in these paragraphs draw on William S. McFeely, *Frederick Douglass* (New York: W. W. Norton, 1991), pp. 3, 5, 6, 7, 8, 10, 11, 14, 15, 21, 22.

84. Richard C. Wade, *Slavery in the Cities: The South, 1820–1860* (London: Oxford University Press, 1964), pp. 17, 173, 243, 248, 249–250. Douglass is quoted on pp. 92 and 174.

85. Douglass is quoted in McFeely, *Frederick Douglass*, pp. 64–65.

86. Leon Litwack, *North of Slavery: The Negro in the Free States, 1790–1860* (Chicago: University of Chicago Press, 1961).

87. McFeely, *Frederick Douglass*, pp. 92–93.

88. The first quote is from Litwack, *North of Slavery*, p. 114. The second quote about Pennsylvania's school segregation law is from James P. Wichersham, *A History of Education in Pennsylvania: Private and Public, Elementary and Higher* (Lancaster, PA: Inquirer Publishing Co., 1886; rpt., New York: Arno Press, 1969), p. 506.

89. Litwack, *North of Slavery*, pp. 114, 115.

90. Kaestle, *Pillars of the Republic*, p. 89.

91. The quotes and information in this and proceding paragraphs are from Litwack, *North of Slavery*, pp. 114–116, 120–122, 131–133, 136, 142. Douglass is quoted on pp. 142–143. I changed all of Litwack's references from "Negro" to "African-American."

92. The quotes and information in this and preceding paragraphs are from Schultz, *Culture Factory*, pp. 160, 162, 168–169, 172–176. Walker is quoted on p. 173.

93. Sumner is quoted in Litwack, *North of Slavery*, p. 147. Schultz, *Culture Factory*, p. 201.

94. *Roberts v City of Boston*, 5 Cush. 198 (1849), pp. 202, 203, 204.

95. Sumner is quoted in R. Freeman Butts, *Public Education in the United States: From Revolution to Reform* (New York: Holt, Rinehart and Winston, 1978), p. 141. Also see Katz, ed., *School Reform*, pp. 193–196, for a text of Sumner's argument.

96. *Roberts v City of Boston,* p. 209. See likewise Schultz, *Culture Factory,* pp. 200–203.

97. Litwack, *North of Slavery,* pp. 149–151. The quotes are from p. 151. Also see Butts, *Public Education in the United States,* p. 142; Schultz, *Culture Factory,* pp. 203, 205.

98. Margaret A. Winzer, *The History of Special Education: From Isolation to Integration* (Washington, DC: Gallaudet University Press, 1993), pp. 82–84, 85, 94–95, 100, 101, 102. See as well Paul H. Mattingly, *The Classless Profession: American Schoolmen in the Nineteenth Century* (New York: New York University Press, 1975), pp. 23, 25; Robert L. Osgood, *For "Children Who Vary from the Normal Type": Special Education in Boston, 1838–1930* (Washington, DC: Gallaudet University Press, 2000), pp. 43, 44.

99. Ernest Freeberg, " 'More Important Than a Rabble of Common Kings': Dr. Howe's Education of Laura Bridgemen," *History of Education Quarterly,* 34 (Fall 1994), pp. 307, 308, 317, 320, 309, 312. Also refer to Winzer, *History of Special Education,* pp. 97, 104.

100. Winzer, *History of Special Education,* pp. 93, 107–108, 110–111. See as well Osgood, *For "Children Who Vary from the Norm,"* pp. 46, 48–49.

101. Joseph L. Tropea, "Bureaucratic Order and Special Children: Urban Schools, 1890s–1940s," *History of Education Quarterly,* 27 (Spring 1987), pp. 30–31.

102. Kaestle, *Pillars of the Republic,* p. 222.

103. Henry J. Perkinson, *The Imperfect Panacea: American Faith in Education, 1865–1965* (New York: Random House, 1968).

104. Tyack, *Turning Points,* p. 121.

105. Kaestle, *Pillars of the Republic,* pp. 69, 222.

106. Finkelstein, *Governing the Young,* p. 23.

5

The Little Red One-Room Schoolhouse

Although the American public schools trace their institutional and philosophical roots to the early nineteenth century, the modern public schools as we know them did not emerge until the Progressive education movement, between 1890 and 1920. There is also some historical continuity between nineteenth-century schoolmasters and schoolmistresses and their modern counterparts. However, the classroom pedagogy and culture of the time followed colonial tradition. But during the 1800s, the creation and expansion—albeit uneven—of the common schools greatly increased the demand for teachers, which had a direct effect on bringing about changes in the teaching profession, including training, licensing, feminization, and compensation. Much of what occurred during this period established enduring precedents. This chapter describes what the day-to-day life of early nineteenth-century common schools was like by focusing on American teachers and their pedagogy.

ICHABODS AND SCHOOLMARMS

Teachers have often been stereotyped in a comical or negative manner. Washington Irving in his classic 1820 tale *The Legend of Sleepy Hollow* paints an unflattering picture of a schoolmaster. Ichabod Crane is described as "so tall and so thin" that he could be mistaken for a "scarecrow." Ichabod's personality proved to be equally undesirable. He beat little schoolchildren with a birch rod, coveted wealth, courted the innocent and beautiful Katrina Van Tassel for her inheritance alone, and fled in the face of danger, chased by the ghost of the headless horseman. This was anything but an ideal image of a man. Ichabod proved to be unmasculine, if not effeminate, in every way. His education, slight build, and refined manners set him apart from the other, more typical men, like Brom Bones, in the tale.[1]

The negative stereotype isolated the classroom instructor in the community, an enduring legacy through the middle of the twentieth century. Writing in 1932, sociologist Williard Waller concluded that "the community can never know what the teacher is really like because the community does not offer the teacher opportunities for normal social intercourse." Waller, reflecting on this long tradition, maintained that the segregation of teachers from mainstream society assumed gender and racial overtones: "It has been said that no woman and no Negro [sic] is ever fully admitted to the white man's world. Possibly we should add men teachers to the list of the excluded." Why did these communities spurn their school instructors? First, female teachers were perceived as sacrificing their adulthood and male teachers their masculinity through their association with children and devotion to a feminine occupation. Second, teaching was perceived as a "failure belt." Waller cited a popular saying in this regard: "Teaching was the refuge of unsalable men and unmarriageable women." The old and persistent labels "Ichabod" and "schoolmarm" hinted at a deep-seated American prejudice toward intellectualism as well as at the relegation of teaching to a quasi caste occupation.[2]

This section captures the experiences of nineteenth-century instructors by describing and analyzing teacher training, introduced during the nineteenth century and gradually formalized during that period; the certification of teachers, which began in a rudimentary fashion at the local level; the growing feminization of the teaching profession as the common schools expanded and spread to different states; and, finally, what teachers were paid, traditionally inadequate.

The Birth of Teacher Training

As reforms in the common schools grew and spread and with the establishment of state school systems and expanding enrollments, the new public schools required not only more teachers but competent ones who were uniformly trained. As education became formalized, so too did teacher training. The concept of teacher training originated in private seminaries and colleges, as we saw in Chapter 2. In 1823, Reverend Samuel R. Hall opened in Concord, Vermont, the first seminary to be solely devoted to teacher training. Semiprivate ventures in teacher training were undertaken as well as various states gave some financial support to private seminaries and academies. Indiana, New York, Pennsylvania, and Wisconsin pursued this approach during the 1830s.[3]

Publicly subsidized teacher training began when Massachusetts opened the first state **normal school** in Lexington in 1839. Other states followed, albeit in an uneven fashion. The Midwest and West outpaced all other regions in embracing the concept and institution of state normal schools, absorbing them into their public education systems and ultimately democratizing higher education. The South did not establish public normal schools until after the Civil War. "In 1860, only eleven modest normal schools existed nationwide." But the trend had begun nevertheless. "By 1898, the number of public normal schools had jumped to 166, graduating 8,188 students; private institutions numbered 165, graduating 3,067."[4] Municipal normal schools, a more localized attempt at publicly subsidized teacher training, first appeared in Boston in 1852. The New York City Board of Education followed suit four years later with the Daily Normal School for Females. "By the early sixties Philadelphia, San Francisco, Baltimore, St. Louis, Trenton, and several other towns had established full-time teacher-training institutions."[5]

Thus, the concept of coursework and institutions dedicated exclusively to teacher training emerged during the first half of the nineteenth century, and public normal schools began to appear conterminiously with the common schools. This did not mean, however, that all teachers who entered the classroom had been specifically prepared for their pedagogical responsibilities. "In Massachusetts alone, more than 60 percent of the teachers claimed no formal training of any kind."[6] Opponents, then as now, saw specialized preparation as lacking in intellectual rigor and substance, preferring immersion in a specific content area, and also then as now two questions remained: Who certifies teachers to enter the classroom? And based on what?

Certification

The young Ralph Harstook in Edward Eggleston's 1871 autobiographical novel nervously approached "old Jack Means," the school trustee, who was working in his front yard, and inquired about the teaching job available in that southern Indiana community. Means gruffly responded to the anxious applicant:

> Want to be a school-master, do you? You? Well, what would *you* do in Flat Crick deestrick, *I'd* like to know? Why, the boys have driv off the last two, and licked the one afore them like the blazes. You might teach a summer school, when nothin' but children come. But I 'low it takes a right smart *man* to be school-master in Flat Crick in the winter. They'd pitch you out of doors, sonny, neck and heels, afore Christmas.

Eggleston's novel caricatures school culture in mid-nineteenth-century rural America. Jack Means's mocking comment clearly reveals the key qualification for prospective school teachers: an intimidating *man*.[7]

In lieu of modern state certification laws, the selection process depended on highly subjective and questionable local practices; as historian Willard Elsbree recounts: "During the colonial period and well into the nineteenth century, the selection of teachers and determination of their qualifications rested almost entirely in the hands of selectmen and school committees." They relied on three basic qualifications: "a good moral character, capacity to govern a school, and suitable academic attainments."[8]

The first requirement continued to remain the most important, echoing a colonial legacy. *The Massachusetts Teacher* proclaimed in 1856 that teachers had to convey proper morals, not by teaching or preaching, but by "upright example . . . by a pure life, which is far more eloquent than words . . ."[9] Intemperance and the use of profanity were the greatest evils to be avoided in prospective schoolmasters. Experienced masters could account for their upstanding character through references from their previous schools. New candidates had to endure the tedious heat of scrutiny, responding to probing questions like the following: "What method or methods would you adopt in order to inculcate the principles of morality, justice, truth, humanity, industry, and temperance?" The second qualification, school governance, referred to the ability of the applicant to maintain classroom order. Experienced candidates again relied on their reputations. Local school committees judged new candidates by their size and age, reflecting Jack Means's superficial appraisal of young Ralph Harstook. School trustees generally hired men to teach the winter session when older, usually rowdy, boys attended district schools. Communities fully expected their schoolmasters to rely on corporal punishment, if not brute physical force, to maintain order—a practice sometimes referred to as "Muscular Christianity." The final requirement, academic ability, proved to be highly inconsistent. Since the hiring process, and ultimately the conferring of a certificate, depended on oral examinations—often conducted by semiliterate, or totally illiterate, rural school committee members—the quality of the screening process to determine the academic acumen of candidates was unreliable. Nevertheless, rural communities usually regarded their teachers as intellectuals.[10] The provincialism of local control contributed to a lack of standardization that made the certifying of teachers highly subjective, if not absurd in some situations. Local school committees annually subjected classroom instructors to these examinations, which were occasionally open to the public.

Certification authority did eventually become standardized, however, as it gradually moved from local to county to the state level during the nineteenth century. Pennsylvania's educational history reveals this pattern clearly. That state passed an act in 1840 assigning local school districts the authority to examine potential instructors and grant them certificates. Fourteen years later, the state legislature moved certification authority from local to county jurisdiction. In 1857, Pennsylvania, in "An Act to provide for the Due Training of Teachers for the common schools of the State," established normal schools to train teachers. These were not state institutions per se, but private ones that received state approval. In 1867 the legislature mandated a basic curriculum for teacher certification. Teacher certification finally became a function of Pennsylvania's state government with the passage of the 1911 School Code.[11]

"She Holds Her Commission From Nature"

Although schoolmasters madeup the majority of teachers through the early decades of the nineteenth century, women had taught during the colonial and early national periods. New England towns began to hire married women for teaching positions as early as 1700, but during the latter part of that century they employed single adolescent women who were completing their schooling. Towns preferred them to men because they lacked familial obligations and possessed more education. Nevertheless, for school officials "women were still considered inferior to men teachers," usually assigning women to the summer sessions and men to the longer, more prestigious winter school periods.[12]

Teaching became a feminized occupation in the United States with the advent of the common-school movement. Especially after the Civil War, women became classroom instructors in increasing numbers. Subsidized by tax revenue instead of tuition fees, the formalized common-school system required economy. It was commonly reasoned at that time that women did not have families to support, and therefore they could be hired for less money. Without overgeneralizing, it could be argued that female teachers, because of their cheap labor, largely subsidized the expansion of American public education.

Separate Spheres

The cult of domesticity, which extolled women's inherent nurturing ability, innocence, and submissiveness, ensured a favorable cultural environment for the entrance of females into teaching. Catherine Beecher, a strong nineteenth-century proponent of domesticity, essentially redefined the gender of the American teacher through her countless writings and speeches. Born on September 6, 1800, in East Hampton, Long Island, New York, she was the oldest of eight children. Her father was a leading Congregational minister. She attended Sarah Pierce's school in Litchfield, Connecticut, and began to teach in New London in 1821. In her writings, Beecher idealized the "value of women's domestic responsibilities." The home, family, and children represented the center of women's lives.[13] Thus, during the first half of the nineteenth century, the mother began to emerge as the "primary parent," which was a profound shift from family patterns of the colonial period. "It was woman's purity that, from a moral standpoint, elevated her far above men. It was also her purity that especially qualified her for motherhood." Meanwhile, the husband and father worked exclusively outside of the home and became largely detached, both physically and emotionally, from the family. The "Victorian patriarch" became a "part-time" caregiver. Finally, woman's purity augured her role as the ideal mentor of young children.[14]

Beecher also worked diligently to improve female education. As we saw in Chapter 3, she founded the Hartford Female Seminary in 1823. In her many publications, among them the influential *A Treatise on Domestic Economy for the Use of Young Ladies at Home and School* (1841), she advocated practical education for women. Her notions of female education, of course, were designed to train women for the domestic sphere, to better perform their social roles. "After 1837 Beecher traveled incessantly, lobbying, fund raising, and organizing for the training of women as teachers, especially in the West."[15] Beecher envisioned teaching as a vocation "dominated by—indeed, exclusively belonging to—women." Teaching enabled women to enlighten society and to exert their moral influence, thus adding the schoolhouse to women's "proper sphere."[16]

Horace Mann officially promoted this notion, particularly in the case of young children:

> She [the female instructor] holds her commission from nature. In the well developed female character there is always a preponderance of affection over intellect. However powerful and brilliant her reflective faculties may be, they are considered a deformity in her character unless overbalanced and tempered by womanly affections. The dispositions of young children of both sexes correspond with this ordination of Providence.[17]

Mann and others saw the schoolroom "as a continuation of the family." "The child," as historian Kathleen Weiler argues, "was viewed as developing first within the context of maternal care in the family, and then moved naturally to the care of the woman teacher."[18] Boston's Board of Education clearly supported this process in 1841 and celebrated the feminization of teaching:

> It is gratifying to observe that a change is rapidly taking place, both in public sentiment and action, in regard to the employment of female teachers. . . . That females are incomparably better teachers for young children than males, cannot admit of a doubt. Their manners are more mild and gentle, and hence more in consonance with the tenderness of childhood. They are endowed by nature with stronger parental impulses, and this makes the society of children delightful, and turns duty into pleasure. . . . They are also of purer morals.[19]

As Weiler concludes, "[i]nstead of seeing women teachers as waged workers, which would have threatened the separate sphere ideology, the work of teaching itself was redefined to be part of the private sphere."[20] Women, therefore, conformed to their traditional gender roles by pursuing work as a teachers.

Because of their subordinate social position and perceived submissive tendencies, women appeared to fit perfectly into the school hierarchy that emerged as the century wore on. If a discipline problem arose in an urban setting, the female instructor routinely sent the poor culprit to the male principal. When graded schools and increasingly centralized bureaucracy, run by male administrators, appeared on the scene, much of the teacher's previous autonomy was usurped. School "officials believed that women teachers would be more compliant in carrying out centralized directives."[21] In sum, according to Jo Anne Preston's historical analysis, males continued to retain "control."[22]

Finally, neither Beecher nor Mann, nor anyone else for that matter, regarded teaching as a career but rather as a "procession into marriage." "Thus, Victorian ideology about women's place made positive use of sex-typing to encourage women to enter teaching as an occupation and appealed to employers not wanting to undermine the family but wishing cheap and efficient teachers."[23]

The Schoolmarm

All of these factors changed the nature of teaching profoundly. By 1888, women comprised 63 percent of the teaching force nationwide, while in cities they constituted 90 percent. In Massachusetts, approximately one out of every five women had taught at some time in their lives. Teaching therefore became a universally accepted occupation for women. Yet the feminization process proved to be more complex and uneven than these figures indicate. There were, for example, regional variations. Social and economic conditions differed between rural and urban labor markets, with female instructors generally less common in rural areas. The domestic service of a daughter appeared to be more critical to farm families than to their city counterparts. Moreover, with few job opportunities for men in the countryside, males tended to abandon teaching at a slower rate than did urban males. Isolated one-room schoolhouses, with no male principals, also presented occasional discipline obstacles for women.[24]

Iowa was typical. Civil War enlistments quickly depleted the number of males available and willing to teach in that state. Only then did women teachers become the majority, amounting to 73 percent by 1865. However, women did not simply substitute for men, because the trend continued even after the conflict ended and many veterans had returned. By 1900, women accounted for 83 percent of Iowa's classroom instructors. Men chose not to teach, and for two reasons. First, low salaries drove males away from teaching. School reformers in Iowa, as earlier in Massachusetts, championed the employment of female instructors because they could be hired for a lower salary, saving local taxpayers money. Second, Iowa formalized teacher preparation after the war. A comprehensive school law required that every county offer a summer training institute and mandated that teachers attend at their own expense. Male instructors balked at the twin financial burdens of tuition fees and loss of summer income. Men no longer saw teaching as a stepping-stone to another career and now bypassed it completely, pursuing other, more lucrative occupations. Historian Thomas Morain summarizes the ironic outcome of Iowa's school reform efforts: ". . . the professionalization of medicine and law—formal educational requirements, examinations, state licensing laws, professional associations—had the effect of closing these pursuits to women. The professionalization of teaching had the opposite effect."[25] When teaching became a primary job instead of a secondary one, low wages and more credentials made it less attractive to men than women in rural areas.[26]

Teaching did liberate women to some extent by providing them more diverse and complex lives than their nonteaching peers had. It soon became the "aristocracy of women's labor."[27] "Taking a school offered a respectable and sometimes pleasant alternative to young women who needed to work and found few alternatives except textile mills or domestic service."[28] Compared with other women, schoolmistresses earned superior salaries, accrued pensions, enjoyed better working conditions, lived in comfortable surroundings, and achieved relatively high status. In Colorado during the late nineteenth and early twentieth centuries, female instructors attended college, gained economic independence, traveled frequently, and married later. Single and married women, as well as separated, divorced, and widowed ones, reaped financial benefits.[29]

Limitations did exist, however. "Teaching did not . . . revolutionize women's lives; the decisions they made frequently were shaped by the social and familial context within which they lived."[30] Teaching had become "women's high calling" but motherhood remained women's "crowning glory."[31] Thus, regardless of location and grade level, by the early twentieth century, female instructors taught only for a median of four years, while their male colleagues taught for a median of seven years. Given the relatively short work life of a female teacher, it appears questionable whether their work should be regarded as a career at all— at least in the same manner as males perceived it. Teaching for women seemed more like a " 'dead-end job,' one reserved for youth without prospect of promotion."[32]

Compensation

The colonial tradition of modest remuneration for schoolmasters continued through the nineteenth century and well into the twentieth. Horace Mann in 1843 wrote that teachers earned 50 to 100 percent less than shoemakers, carpenters, blacksmiths, and others. In state after state, instructors received less pay than the common foot soldier. Differentiation was also made on the basis of gender, position, and race. During the early nineteenth century, the typical Massachusetts schoolmaster received $10–12 per month, while schoolmistresses made $4–10.[33] Between 1841 and 1864, the average rural female teacher's salary amounted to no more than 62 percent of her male colleague's income; in cities, the average never exceeded 37 percent. In 1905, the typical "female high school teacher" still received only "69 percent of her male counterpart's pay," although many urban female instructors earned a higher income than rural male teachers. Salary differentiation based on gender also existed among building principals. Female principals generally earned half of what their male counterparts made. In 1860, San Francisco paid males $2000 and females only $800 per year. In St. Louis in 1862, male grammar school principals made $800, with females doing comparable work receiving $400.[34]

Salaries differed for several reasons. First, as we have seen, many believed in this era of domesticity that single, young women did not have families to support, even though many did and were the sole support for their widowed mothers and dependent siblings. Second, women earned less money simply because they remained in teaching for a short period of time. This partially explains why female salaries continued to lag behind those of male instructors. In the long run, women received less money because "they left the teaching force much sooner than their male colleagues."[35] They were coerced to leave in many cases since most nineteenth-century communities refused to employ married female teachers. This practice continued well into the twentieth century. By 1930, 77 percent of some 1,473 school districts refused to hire married women, and 62 percent compelled them to resign once they married. Because females taught for shorter periods than males, men tended to advance to school administrator posts.[36]

The sexual division of labor that developed during the nineteenth century—male administrators and female teachers—reflects the unevenness of the feminization of education. "New England led the nation in the feminization of teaching, while the South lagged far behind." City school districts feminized at a faster rate than rural areas, which usually relied on male teachers to maintain order in the one-room schools. Urban districts resorted to fundamentally different strategies. They employed age grading to segregate children.

This naturally concentrated women at the elementary levels where they could easily manage young children. City schools also hired male principals to supervise female teachers and discipline unruly children "Male managers in the nineteenth-century urban school regulated the core activities of instruction through standardized promotional examinations on the content of the prescribed curriculum and strict supervision to ensure that teachers were following mandated techniques. Rules were highly prescriptive."[37] All of this established and reinforced a paternalistic atmosphere, which is still largely in effect.

This sexual division of labor occurred within teaching as well. Women comprised only 50 percent of high school instructors by the turn of the century. School boards and administrators relegated them to elementary schools, both as teachers and administrators. But women's hold on even these administrative positions was not firm. While women accounted for 62 percent of elementary principalships in 1905, this figure would deteriorate to 20 percent by 1972. "When women 'took over' teaching in nineteenth-century New England, they 'took over' the jobs but not the institution."[38]

Preston offers a compelling conclusion about this differential treatment of women. Placing it in a broader context, that is, the treatment of female labor, not just the teaching occupation, she points out, "It has been argued that women are either hired for lower-paying jobs with poor working conditions or alternatively, the hiring of women causes the jobs to become low-wage, undesirable work. In the case of schoolteaching, neither occurred. As women were hired, they were offered low pay and the most undesirable positions because they were women."[39]

Salary differentiation profoundly affected African American teachers as well. European American male instructors earned the highest salary, followed by European American females, as we have seen. African American male teachers received the next-lowest salary; African American females, suffering from gender as well as racial discrimination, took home the lowest salary for teachers.

Until 1850, boarding around was a common form of partial remuneration. The diary of one rural Vermont teacher who boarded with a local family for a week illustrated the many liabilities of this experience. This young, eligible bachelor had to navigate around the dangerous shoals of puberty, adroitly avoiding the amorous overtures of the family's flirtatious daughter, Peggy. He also had to contend with a poor diet, for the family served him gander at virtually every meal. As he recorded it, "suppose from its size, the thickness of the skin and other venerable appearances it must have been one of the first settlers of Vermont." Although the family provided him with his own room and bed, considered a luxury, the window was broken. One morning he wrote, "very cool night, and couldn't keep warm; got up and stopped the broken window with my coat and vest; no use; froze the tip of my nose and one ear before morning." At the end of the week, he "grew alarmed" because he had lost six pounds. He moved in with another family.[40]

"SPARE THE ROD AND SPOIL THE CHILD"

Much of the nineteenth-century legacy in education remains. To this day, teachers continue to be criticized for inadequate training, toil in a low-status occupation, earn meager salaries and benefits, and long for respect. On the other hand, for the most part the relationship between classroom instructors and their students has changed.

In America, the idea persists of a golden era of schooling, when children eagerly sped to a humble and well-kept school, enthusiastically, cooperatively, and successfully learned their assignments, and teachers professionally and seriously conducted their business, nurturing their charges. According to this idea, schools performed their functions with a high degree of success, with outstanding student achievement, in a modest school building, and at a very low cost to the community. This fiction, if not mythology, usually congers up an idealized image of the little, nineteenth-century, one-room schoolhouse, romanticized by the media and poor memories. No such golden era ever existed.

Even Laura Ingalls Wilder's autobiographical *Little House* series paints a different picture of nineteenth-century schools. In *These Happy Golden Years*, she describes her first teaching experience. At fifteen years old and with no training, she began to teach at the Brewster settlement, twelve miles from her home. A drafty and perpetually cold shanty served as her schoolhouse; the family she boarded with acted rudely, if not outright inhospitably, toward her; and the students proved to be mischievous and uncooperative. Yet, somehow she survived.[41] This section taps a variety of secondary and primary sources, including diaries and recollections, to reconstruct the nineteenth-century classroom, focusing on student misbehavior and the art of schoolkeeping.

Student Misbehavior

Serious acts of student violence according to contemporary popular media have plagued only late twentieth- and early twenty-first-century public schools. While these events are frightening to be sure, student misbehavior claims a long history; it was a "prevalent problem" in nineteenth-century schools. "In 1837 . . . over 300 schools in Massachusetts alone were broken up by rebellious pupils." Rural school students occasionally threw bullets into the red-hot, potbellied stove as a joke.[42] Two types of mischief existed: "putting out" and assaulting the teacher.

Putting Out the Teacher

Also referred to as "turning out" and "barring out," putting out involved simply locking the master out of the school building. Horace Greeley recalls such an incident at the school he attended as a child:

> At the close of the morning session the first of January . . . the moment the master left the [school] house in quest of his dinner, the little ones were started homeward, the doors and windows suddenly and securely barricaded, and the older pupils, thus fortified against intrusion, proceeded to spend the afternoon in play and hilarity.

However, the clever young male teacher nimbly climbed to the roof and simply placed a board over the chimney, thus smoking out the hapless culprits. The combatants involved in such educational warfare obviously resorted to physical force as well as guile and stealth. Smoking them out, in this case, proved to be the best weapon in the schoolmaster's arsenal. Another instructor in Pennsylvania used an axe to pry open a window to crawl into the locked schoolhouse. The schoolmasters won in these cases, but on other occasions in other schools with the teachers unable to enter the building, the students earned a holiday, and the younger children and masters stoically retreated to their homes.[43]

Attacks on Teachers

In addition to mischievous conduct, student attacks on masters could be malicious. There were generally two reasons for assaults on teachers. First, if the instructor exercised excessive cruelty when punishing a scholar, the "big boys" confronted the bully. Warren Burton recollects one such student revolt. A group of older students retaliated against a sadistic schoolmaster, Mr. Starr, who had bloodied a young child. They forcibly removed Mr. Starr from the schoolroom, immediately following the incident and carried him to the crest of a steep hill.

> Now it so happened that the hill-side opposite the school-house door was crusted, and as smooth and slippery as pure ice, from a recent rain. To this pitch, then, he was borne, and in all haste that his violent struggles would permit. Over he was thrust. . . .[44]

With his dignity tarnished, his schoolkeeping abilities destroyed, and fearing parental retribution for his ruthless approach to teaching, Mr. Starr secretly escaped the community that night. Other such confrontations proved to be less comical. "In 1882 a schoolmaster in a country school in Guernsey County, Ohio, stabbed to death two of his students who attacked him after he insisted that they study their grammar lessons."[45]

The second cause of teacher attacks arose indirectly from innocent and good-natured physical contests, such as wrestling, between the master and students. Since physical size and prowess represented the basic assets of classroom control during this period, the defeat of an instructor in a seemingly meaningless contest spelled his doom. "A teacher who had been defeated in these encounters was likely to have difficulty restoring and maintaining order."[46] He usually lost his job. Thus, in these crude and isolated settings, the teacher almost played the role of gunslinger, grimly meeting and defeating potential enemies committed to his defeat. Both male and female teachers employed a variety of weapons and tactics.

Schoolkeeping

Because of such raucous behavior, nineteenth-century instructors often had to resort to "schoolkeeping" rather than "school teaching." They physically subdued their charges and usually relied on large doses of corporal punishment, often with the full approval of the community. This pedagogical tradition had a long history. A Sunderland, Massachusetts, "schoolhouse erected in 1793 contained a whipping post set firmly in the schoolroom floor."[47] Schoolmasters openly displayed and used two instruments of control: the "*ferrule*, a thick three-foot stick, and the "*heavy gad*, a flexible sapling about five feet in length." Instructors either threw the ferrule like a spear at an offender or used it to smack students' palms. The heavy gad served as a whip. Instructors also used rattans. In Boston in 1845, floggings "averaged sixty-five per day" in a typical school building hosting 400 students.[48]

"Schoolmaster About to Whip a Small Boy" (c. 1900) Cabinet of American Illustration, Courtesy of the Library of Congress, Prints and Photographs Division.

Regardless of the setting, "severity in a teacher was considered a virtue."[49] Burton recalls one terror, a female summer school teacher named Mehitabel Holt:

> She kept order; for her punishments were horrible, especially for us little ones. She dungeoned us in the windowless closet just for a whisper. She tied us to her chair post for an hour, because sportive nature tempted our fingers and toes into something like play. If we were restless on our seats, wearied of our posture, fretted by the heat, or sick of the unintelligible lesson, a twist of the ear, or a snap on the head from her thimbled finger, reminded us that sitting perfectly still was the most important virtue of a little boy in school.

Her main concern, typical of other teachers, appeared to be governance, as it was then called. Winter school, run by a male instructor, proved to be equally painful for Burton; this master appeared to be obsessed with punishment, employing a variety of techniques:

> Some were feruled on the hand; some were whipped with a rod on the back; some were compelled to hold out, at arm's length, the largest book which could be found, or a great

leaden inkstand, till muscle and nerve, bone and marrow, were tortured with the continued exertion. If the arm bent or inclined from the horizontal level, it was forced back again by a knock of the ruler on the elbow.

In the latter instance, tapping the funny bone usually renewed the suffering scholar's attention. Burton continues that this teacher also occasionally pulled hair, tweaked noses, and pinched or boxed ears. He devoted over half of his time to "keeping" school.[50]

Pedagogy relied on monotonous rote memorization and repetition. Throughout much of the 1800s, according to historian Barbara Finkelstein, most instruction relied on oral lessons. Chalkboards, slates, and precious paper remained scarce; pedagogues "simply called up students—singly or in classes—and with a pen, pencil, knife, or rattan, pointed out letters from A to Z, asked the students to pronounce them, and then instructed the student by themselves pronouncing the letter names."[51] This "dull and dry" routine, as Burton recollects, involved daily penmanship lessons, grammar recitations, and ciphering drills, with spelling bees as the only exciting learning activity. Writing instruction usually consisted of just penmanship. The student often laboriously traced the teachers' letters and words for practice. Each school year closed with an "examination." The examination committee usually consisted of the town's minister, the school committee, and some parents. Individual students participated in several hours of oral recitation drilled by the committee members. Some times this deteriorated into exercises in trivia. Burton remembers how one year the third class had completed their spelling examination, which focused on long and elaborate words to impress the audience, when the local minister spoke up as the students were about to return to their seats:

> "Please to let them stand a few minutes longer, I should like to put out a few words to them myself. . . . " Now look out. They expect words as long as their finger, from the widest columns of the spelling-book, or perhaps such as are found only in the dictionary. "Spell *wrist*," says he to the little sweller at the head. "O, what an easy word!" r-i-s-t, wrist. It is not right. The next, the next—they all try, or rather do not attempt the word; for if r-i-s-t does not spell *wrist*, they cannot conceive what does.

The minister continued his examination with *gown, penknife,* and *andiron,* with similar results. The minister had humbled the "mortified" master with this lesson in practicality.[52]

Other pedagogical ideas, in contrast to what was actually occurring in the schools, were beginning to emerge. In the spring of 1843, Horace Mann toured Europe inspecting schools. He shared his observations in his *Seventh Annual Report* (1843), lauding the theories of Johann Heinrich Pestalozzi in Prussian schools. Mann praised the "beautiful relation of harmony and affection which subsisted between teacher and pupil." He continued: ". . . I never saw a child struck, I never heard a sharp rebuke given. I never saw a child in tears, nor arraigned at the teacher's bar for any alleged misconduct . . . I heard no child ridiculed, sneered at, or scolded, for making a mistake . . . No child was disconcerted, disabled, or bereft of his senses, through fear." Mann had witnessed encouragement and a generally positive classroom environment created through a child-centered methodology. Too few early nineteenth-century instructors heeded Mann's recommendations. By the latter half of the 1800s, however, a more humanistic pedagogy was beginning to be adopted. Rural instructors gradually abandoned their odious role. In urban areas, the development of age grading, report cards, and rewards and recognition proved to be more powerful means of control.[53]

Recalcitrant Children

Many educators and social reformers saw the urban environment as detrimental to the moral development of children. In many city schools, principals merely solved the problem of children who repeatedly misbehaved by expelling them, leaving them to wander the streets as "vagrants." This seemed only to exacerbate behavior problems because these children often found refuge in gangs. If arrested for crimes, they suffered dearly. "Child offenders were dealt with in much the same way as adults—they were subjected to the same laws, their cases were heard in the same courts, and they suffered the same punishments," generally sentenced to prison terms.

Reform Schools

To mitigate these severe punishments and to protect these children from the unseemly and immoral influences of adult criminals, social reformers created reformatories to punish youths. Some also promoted "industrial schools" to instill the virtues and rewards of hard work in wayward youngsters. Thus, the state increasingly supplanted the family responsibility for children. "When parents directly or indirectly contributed to dereliction and criminality by failing to provide for a child's physical, moral, and intellectual well-being, then the state, as *parens patriae*, had the right to mediate between parents and child."[54]

Orphans

Social reformers resorted to other tactics as well. They attempted to mitigate the influence on innocent children of unwholesome urban life in general and corrupt families in particular by sending orphans to the West for adoption. The goal was to place these poor—and not always orphaned—children in bucolic rural areas and thereby expose them to a virtuous environment of fresh air, hard and honest work, and pious Protestant families, close to the purifying effects of nature—the perfect atmosphere in which a child could grow and develop morally and physically.

In 1853, Charles Loring Brace founded the Children's Aid Society (CAS) in New York City and began to ship deprived children West to save them from the ravages of city living. Similar efforts were made in other Eastern cities. For the next seventy-five years, the CAS sent between 100,000 and 150,000 children westward to be adopted. Some Western families lovingly chose children as they stood forlornly on train platforms; others were merely looking for free farm labor to exploit. Whether or not the outcome proved to be positive, in their overly romanticized efforts to save these children, the reformers often resorted to extreme measures, separating them—either by force or subterfuge—from their poor, or immigrant, or seemingly morally deficient parents.[55] To be sure, moral salvation also assumed other forms.

The classroom environment reflected the general culture of the time. Some parents complained about the excessive cruelty of teachers, but most endorsed it. They themselves physically punished their own children in ways that by today's standards would be deemed abusive. The authoritarian classrooms maintained by schoolmasters and schoolmistresses therefore were dictated by contemporary social mores. And during this period both teachers and institutions began to play a more important role in shaping children's lives and beliefs. They had a valuable ally in schoolbooks.

THE GOOD BOOK

Many observers during the post–Civil War period complained about what children of all ages read, especially outside of school. They saw boys' adventure stories, published in the new and popular dime novels, and the new penny newspapers as dangerous influences promoting immoral behavior. Some, like Anthony Comstock, even campaigned during the 1870s and 1880s to censor such obscene literature.[56] However, if children's reading matter could not be controlled in the public realm, it certainly could be circumscribed in the classroom.

Two modes of conveying a common set of values to nineteenth-century school children existed: teachers and books. Schoolmasters and, increasingly, schoolmistresses served as moral models. Their stellar behavior was supposed to inspire children to act accordingly. Of course, as we have seen, local communities ensured that these classroom instructors maintained spotless reputations, even dictating behaviors and prescribing conduct in their personal lives. This was never truer than for female teachers:

> In her high-buttoned shoes and long skirt, black apron and shirtwaist fringed with celluloid collared cuffs, she was expected to be and she was a symbol of rectitude. . . . She was frequently a Sunday school teacher . . . and regular in her church attendance, and her daily life was above reproach. Unlike her male counterpart, she virtually never had her teaching certificate rescinded for immorality.

Armed with her pure, virginal image, with Bible in hand, she served as the perfect role model for schoolchildren.[57] She also had other help, from the available schoolbooks, which supplemented the process of moral training. Ill-trained or untrained teachers relied heavily on them. They became the curriculum. Schoolmasters and schoolmistresses merely directed "textbook exercises" and in a highly rigid fashion.[58] The schoolbooks not only influenced pedagogy but shaped values. "Schoolbooks, central to the curriculum of the nineteenth-century school, offered both information and standards of behavior and belief that the adult world expected the child to make his own."

Teachers used many different kinds of books. The Bible, with few exceptions, was widely used in classrooms. Spellers, often the "first books" children used, contained the alphabet as well as lists of words, syllables, and vocabulary words. Most educators saw spelling as the first step toward learning how to read. Prior to the 1830s, school readers excerpted material from classical writers, such as Cicero and Shakespeare, but later drew more heavily on religious sources. "Arithmetics" emphasized practical problems, with applications to business and "surveying." Teachers slavishly followed the textbook in a highly linear fashion, requiring students to memorize mathematics rules and definitions and to be able to recite many of them orally, on demand. Geographies and histories typically "evaluated the civilization of the United States in relation to other countries." Masters and mistresses again assiduously adhered to the book. They required their students to orally define land masses and recite location names. The subject of United States history began to appear in the 1830s but became required study after the Civil War.

What values did these books convey? Ruth Miller Elson painstakingly catalogued them in her historical survey of "more than a thousand of the most popular textbooks." Some of them emphasized the rich bounty of the vast lands of the United States and the superiority of the white race. Authors of these books often ranked nations according to their racial stock. They portrayed the Irish as "ignorant," Italians as "degenerate," and Chinese as "deceitful." Books stressed that America represented the "best of all worlds; that American institutions and character are the hope of all mankind." These books also practiced hagiography, raising to Olympian heights American leaders, such as George Washington, Benjamin Franklin, and later Abraham Lincoln.[59]

McGuffey's Readers

No set of schoolbooks achieved such wide circulation and exerted such lasting influence in the nineteenth century as *The Eclectic Readers* written by William Holmes McGuffey. Over 120 million copies were sold between 1836 and 1920. McGuffey, born into a farm family on the Ohio frontier in 1800, was a religious conservative. He attended the local public school and began to teach school at age fourteen. He attended an academy for two years and in 1820 enrolled at Washington College in Western Pennsylvania. Before he graduated, McGuffey returned to teaching; eventually, at the age of twenty-six, he accepted a faculty position at Miami University in Oxford, Ohio, where he completed his college degree. He supported Ohio's common-school movement as well as worked to professionalize teacher training. According to historian John H. Westerhoff, III, "McGuffey considered the public schools the proper place for religious and moral instruction, or at least that is where he chose to exert his influence."

McGuffey published the *Eclectic First, Second, Third,* and *Fourth Readers* in 1836. He designated each for a different level of reading ability, which was distinctive. It was the first time schoolbooks facilitated the grouping of students, an uncommon practice in early nineteenth-century rural schools. The *First Reader* related best to the first and second grades, the *Second Reader* to the third and fourth grades, the *Third Reader* to the fifth and sixth grades, and the *Fourth Reader* to advanced students. Furthermore, McGuffey's phonetic approach in the readers strongly influenced reading instruction. The books also included instructions for teachers, collections of stories—many drawn straight from the Bible—and moral lessons, all followed by a section of questions for students. For example, in the *Fourth Reader*, he directed instructors to require students to read each story aloud, then retell it in their own words, write it, and answer the questions. Schoolmasters and mistresses grew to rely heavily on the readers to guide their classroom methodologies.

Generally speaking, McGuffey glorified God, who was "central" in his readers; God was "omnipresent, omnipotent, and omniscient." And he drew heavily on the Old and New Testaments of the Bible for material. As Westerhoff summarizes it, "McGuffey's Readers present us with a God-conscious, God-centered world, a world in which God reveals himself through nature, but most significantly through the Bible, as creator, preserver, and governor of all life. Our proper response is fear, obedience, and to be grateful to him for all his goodness to us." Proper conduct included a long list of expected behaviors: honesty, obedience, thrift, patriotism, cleanliness, meekness, industriousness, and piety, among others, all transmitted through highly moralistic and simplistic stories and lessons as well as prayers.

McGuffey's readers carefully and purposefully shaped students' beliefs in conformity to the prevalent set of Protestant values at that time. Religious morals, as a fixed set of laws, prescribed strict adherence to a code of conduct. For example, the *First Reader* included a story titled "John Jones." It related how the poor and illiterate boy began work at a very young age. Work was good; idleness was bad. John's "kind" employer spoke with him about God and how thankful John should be for everything he had. The boy should toil and pray hard every day. The spelling words that followed this short story included *pray, work, great,* and *good,* among others. Values such as these were intended to socialize children with a set of values acceptable to society, ensuring the status quo.

As Westerhoff concludes, the 1879 edition of the readers, revised after McGuffey's death in 1873, softened the religious overtone. Few Bible stories appeared but the Lord's Prayer remained. The revised edition also presented God more indirectly. God receded into the background, and human acts moved to the foreground. "The spirit of self-reliance, individualism, and competition fill the 1879 edition. Virtue is rarely its own reward, but material and physical rewards can be expected for good acts."[60] These changes reflected the changes being brought about as the frontier advanced, immigration increased, and a more fluid and diverse society emerged, one which relied less on a narrow and rigid set of religious beliefs. American society was gradually surrendering to a growing sense of humanism, a concern for social needs and human welfare, and the need for a universal set of beliefs to be shared by all. By the early twentieth century, all traces of Protestant religious dogma and references had disappeared from school textbooks. Schoolbooks certainly continued to instruct children in the same set of values, but they began to assume a more neutral, or secular, tone, devoid of religious sectarianism. However, some Christian religious rituals persisted in many public school classrooms: Bible reading and recitation of the Lord's Prayer. These too would disappear by the 1960s, as we will see in Chapter 10.

CONCLUSIONS

Modern critics often point nostalgically to the one-room schoolhouse as the exemplar of American education. We have attempted here to present a more complex and realistic interpretation and demythologize that overly romanticized educational symbol by stressing the micro level of schooling, the daily routines and experiences of teachers and students. "Not much learning occurred. There are, of course, exceptions, dearly beloved by those for whom the one-room schoolhouse represents the golden age of American education. These exceptions prove the rule." History thus teaches us that the one-room schoolhouse neither represented the best American schooling had

to offer nor was it the worst. It simply and modestly served the needs of frugal rural communities attempting to school their children. Like today's schools, it had warts. Moreover, it is impossible for us to return to that classroom setting—assuming that we would even want to.

Still, some of its legacy endures. Although their responsibilities have changed, teachers still shoulder a myriad of roles. In the nineteenth century, both rural and urban masters and mistresses served as moral role models. They also served an authoritarian function, demanding respect and imparting verbal and physical punishment. And teachers operated as surrogate parents. In rural areas, the schoolmaster or schoolmistress went so far as to prescribe student behavior outside of the classroom; in cities, they taught their charges about proper hygiene habits.

That era also established an enduring and stubborn tradition of provincialism. "These attacks on the master and his authority, in a smaller theater, reenacted the anticosmopolitanism and antiauthoritarian drama of the American revolt against Europe itself, and they manifested a profoundly anti-intellectual strain in the early American character. This anti-intellectualism, this need constantly to reaffirm that the community's standards were superior to those of the larger world, accounts in part for the people's willingness to tolerate an inferior educational system."[61] At the beginning of the twenty-first century, American society continues to belittle its teachers, the media and peers demean bright students, referring to them as "nerds" or "geeks," and parent and religious groups attempt to censor books and curricular materials. Finally, Americans continue to "do" schooling as cheaply as possible. Communities and politicians fight increases in school taxes yet criticize the schools for having failed their children.

But what is also clear is that the basic concept of schooling, as well as the culture of schooling, in that simpler time differed profoundly from its modern counterpart. Schooling represented "a matter of individual choice, with the decision left to the pupil and his family." Historian David Swift continues, "if he [sic] came to school, it was mainly because his parents wanted him to, and he was more or less willing to do so. As far as the school was concerned, it didn't really matter whether or not he attended but, if he did come, he had to abide by the teacher's demands or accept the frequently severe consequences." Given this laissez-faire atmosphere, schooling was expendable. Moreover, the schooling process appeared to be rigid and largely oblivious to the individual needs of children. "Thus, the traditional public school, when it existed at all, was a selective institution, accommodating only those hardy souls who were able to adapt to its inflexible demands."[62] The rest simply and casually left school. Finally, schooling possessed no practical value, disconnected as it was from the world of work. In cities, many school-aged children earned a living through apprenticeship or factory work; in rural areas, they inherited farms. Why did they "need" to go to school?

School enrollment and attendance nevertheless continued to grow throughout the nineteenth century. Formal schooling assumed an ever-larger educational role in children's lives, no matter the region, gender, or race.

ACTIVITIES FOR FURTHER EXPLORATION

1. Have you ever seen a one-room schoolhouse? To explore a variety of actual one-room schoolhouse images, refer to: http://history.cc.ukans.edu/heritage/orsh/graphics.

2. What content of nineteenth-century books did we not explore in this chapter? To further investigate the topic of nineteenth-century books and the role of print matter in a broader "educational" context, refer to: http://memory.lco.gov/ammem/indlpcoop/moahtml/mnchome.html. A common Gilded Age belief, widely promoted by Horatio Alger in a series of books geared to young boys, proclaimed that hard work led to success. One of these stories, "Horatio Alger's American Fable: 'The World Before Him,'" illustrated this idea perfectly. Not everyone, however, supported this notion. See, for example, "Gimme A Break! Mark Twain Lampoons the Horatio Alger Myth" and " 'Selfish wealth is never good:' A Worker's Definition of Success." All of these documents can be found at http://chnm.gmu.edu/us/many.taf. After analyzing these various views, do you agree with the "rags to riches" philosophy that young boys were taught?

3. What role did schooling play in mid-nineteenth-century America? Explore the rich Web site "The Valley of the Shadow: Two Communities in the American Civil War," which contains newspaper accounts, among other primary documents, at http://jefferson.village.virginia.edu/vshadow2/.

VIDEO EXPLORATION

The history of nineteenth-century childhood did not only involve the schools. The film *"The Orphan Trains"* (Alexandria, VA: PBS Home Video, 1995) gives a comprehensive visual portrayal of the massive child resettlement program engineered by Charles Loring Brace. This moving video, from the *American Experience* series, deftly uses the recollections of orphan survivors to recount their experiences as they were "saved" from deleterious urban environments and morally corrupt families. It also raises many questions: What is a morally dysfunctional family? Who judged those families to be dysfunctional?

NOTES AND SOURCES

In order to condense endnotes, the first work cited is the primary one, usually the source of any direct quotes. Subsequent references serve as supplementary, or additional, sources of paraphrased information and/or alternative historical interpretations.

1. See any edition of Irving's tale. This section relies on the following: Washington Irving, *The Legend of Sleepy Hollow,* adapted and illustrated by Robert Van Nutt (Westport, CT: Rabbit Ears Production, 1989).

2. This paragraph heavily taps Richard J. Altenbaugh, ed., *The Teacher's Voice: A Social History of Teaching in Twentieth-Century America* (London: Falmer Press, 1992), pp. 61–62. I retained the original sources. Willard Waller, *Sociology of Teaching* (1932; rpt. ed., New York: Russell and Russell, 1961) pp. 49, 50, 61. Also, refer to Richard Hofstadter, *Anti-Intellectualism in American Life* (New York: Vintage Books, 1963), pp. 309–322; Geraldine Joncich Clifford, "Man/Woman/Teacher: Gender, Family and Career in American Educational History," in *American Teachers: Histories of a Profession at Work,* ed. Donald Warren (1989), pp. 311–319.

3. Willard S. Elsbree, *The American Teacher: Evolution of a Profession in a Democracy* (New York: American Book Company, 1939; rpt ed., New York: Greenwood Press, 1970), pp. 138, 146.

4. Richard J. Altenbaugh and Kathleen Underwood, "The Evolution of Normal Schools," in *Places Where Teachers Are Taught* (San Francisco: Jossey-Bass Publishers, 1990), p. 143; See as well Elsbree, *American Teacher,* pp. 146, 150, 151; Jurgen Herbst, "Nineteenth-Century Normal Schools in the United States: A Fresh Look," *History of Education* 9 (1980), pp. 219–227; Louise Gilchiese Walsh and Matthew John Walsh, *History and Organization of Education in Pennsylvania* (Indiana, PA: R. S. Grosse Print Shop, 1930), pp. 174, 175, 176, 254–256; J. P. Wickersham, *A History of Education in Pennsylvania* (Lancaster, PA: Inquirer Publisher Company, 1986; rpt. ed., New York: Arno Press, 1969), pp. 505–508.

5. Elsbree, *American Teacher,* p. 153.

6. Altenbaugh and Underwood, "Evolution of Normal Schools," p. 143.

7. Edward Eggleston, *The Hoosier School-Master* (New York: Hill and Wang, 1957), p. 1. Also see David B. Tyack, *The One Best System: A History of American Urban Education* (Cambridge, MA: Harvard University Press, 1974), p. 13.

8. Elsbree, *American Teacher,* pp. 178, 179.

9. This excerpt from *The Massachusetts Teacher* appears in Michael B. Katz, ed., *School Reform: Past and Present* (Boston: Little, Brown and Co., 1971), pp. 93–96.

10. Elsbree, *American Teacher,* pp. 179–180, 181. The quote is on p. 180. Also, see Barbara Finkelstein, *Governing the Young: Teacher Behavior in Popular Primary Schools in Nineteenth-Century United States* (New York: Falmer Press, 1989), p. 96. "Muscular Christianity" is quoted on p. 100. Tyack, *The One Best System,* p. 20, for the intellectual status of the rural teacher.

11. *100 Years of Free Public Schools in Pennsylvania: 1834–1934* (Harrisburg, PA: Department of Public Instruction, 1934), pp. 80, 81; John A. Nietz, "The Constitutional and Legal Bases of the Public School System of Pennsylvania" (Ph.D. diss., Chicago, IL: University of Chicago, 1933); John A. Nietz, "The Constitutional Provisions and the Titles of the More Important Laws of Pennsylvania Relating to Schools and Education" (Ph.D. diss. summary, Pittsburgh, PA: University of Pittsburgh, 1933), p. 9, 11; Walsh and Walsh, *History and Organization of Education in Pennsylvania,* pp. 174–175, 193–193, 214–215, 254–256; Wickersham, *History of Education in Pennsylvania,* pp. 507–508, 521, 558.

12. Jo Anne Preston, "Feminization of an Occupation: Teaching Becomes Women's Work in Nineteenth-Century New England" (Ph.D. diss., Waltham, MA: Brandeis University, 1982), p. 29, 138. Parts of this section on the feminization of teaching draw heavily on Altenbaugh, *The Teacher's Voice,* pp. 8–11, and Richard J. Altenbaugh, "The Irony of Gender," in *The Politics of Educators' Work and Lives,* ed. Mark B. Ginsburg (New York: Garland Publishing, 1995), pp. 73–90.

13. Kathryn Kish Sklar, "Catharine Beecher," in *Portraits of American Women: From Settlement to the Present,* ed. G. J. Barker-Benfield and Catherine Clinton (New York: St. Martin's Press, 1991), p. 169, 178; Refer as well to Barbara Welter, "The Cult of True Womanhood: 1820–1860," *American Quarterly* 18 (Summer 1966), pp. 151–174.

14. John Demos, *Past, Present and, Personal: The Family and the Life Course in American History* (New York: Oxford University Press, 1986), pp. 48, 49, 51, 60.

15. Sklar, "Catharine Beecher," pp. 169, 177.

16. Kathryne Kish Sklar, *Catharine Beecher: A Study in American Domesticity* (New Haven, CT: Yale University Press, 1973), p. 97. The term "proper sphere" is from Welter, "The Cult of True Womanhood", p. 153.

17. Horace Mann, *Sixth Annual Report: Massachusetts Board of Education* (Boston: Dutton and Wentworth, 1843), p. 28.

18. Kathleen Weiler, "Women's History and the History of Women Teachers," *Journal of Education* 17 (1989), p. 17.

19. Quoted in Elsbree, *American Teacher,* p. 201.

20. Weiler, "Women's History," p. 18.

21. Myra Strober and Audri Gordon Lanford, "The Feminization of Public School Teaching: Cross-Sectional Analysis, 1850–1880," *Signs: Journal of Women in Culture and Society,* 11 (Winter 1986), p. 219.

22. Preston, "Feminization of an Occupation," p. 55.

23. Myra Strober and David B. Tyack, "Why Do Women Teach and Men Manage? A Report on Research on Schools," *Signs: Journal of Women in Culture and Society* 5 (Spring 1980), p. 496.

24. Richard M. Bernard and Maris A. Vinovskis, "The Female School Teacher in Antebellum Massachusetts," *Journal of Social History* 10 (Spring 1977), pp. 332–345; David B. Tyack, *The One Best System: A History of American Urban Education* (Cambridge, MA: Harvard University Press, 1974), p. 61; Lawrence A. Cremin, *American Education: The National Experience, 1783–1876* (New York: Harper & Row, 1980), pp. 144–147; Carl F. Kaestle and Maris A. Vinovskis, *Education and Social Change in Nineteenth-Century Massachusetts* (New York: Cambridge University Press, 1980) p. 206; John L. Rury, "Who Became Teachers? The Social Characteristics of Teachers in American History," in *American Teachers: Histories of a Profession at Work,* ed. Donald Warren (New York: Macmillan, 1989), p. 27; Sklar (1973), pp. xiv, 97, 172–173, 182. Also, refer to Preston, "Feminization of an Occupation."

25. Thomas Morain, "The Departure of Males from the Teaching Profession in Nineteenth-Century Iowa," *Civil War History* 26 (1980), pp. 165, 169–170. See as well Wayne E. Fuller, *The Old Country School: The Story of Rural Education in the Middle West* (Chicago, IL: University of Chicago Press, 1982), pp. 159–160.

26. See Strober and Lanford, "The Feminization of Public School Teaching"; Strober and Tyack, "Why Do Women Teach and Men Manage?"

27. Marjorie Murphy, "The Aristocracy of Women's Labor in America," *History Workshop* 22 (Autumn 1986), p. 58.

28. Keith Melder, "Woman's High Calling: The Teaching Profession in America, 1830–1860," *American Studies* 13 (Fall 1972), p. 25.

29. Clifford, "Man/Woman/Teacher," p. 302. Refer to Kathleen Underwood, "The Pace of Their Own Lives: Teacher Training and the Life Course of Western Women," *Pacific Historical Review* 55 (November 1986) for a fine historical overview.

30. Underwood, "The Pace of Their Own Lives," pp. 525, 530.

31. Melder, "Woman's High Calling," p. 20.

32. The quote is from John Rury, "Gender, Salaries, and Career: American Teachers, 1900–1910," *Issues in Education* 4 (1986), pp. 222–224, 229. Also see Lotus D. Coffman, *The Social Composition of the Teaching Profession* (New York: Teachers College Press, 1911), pp. 25–30; Altenbaugh, *The Teacher's Voice,* p. 10.

33. Clifton Johnson, *Old-Time Schools and School-Books* (New York: Dover Publications, 1963), p. 126.

34. James W. Fraser, "Agents of Democracy: Urban Elementary-School Teachers and the Conditions of Teaching," in *American Teachers: Histories of a Profession at Work,* ed. Donald Warren (New York: Macmillan, 1989), p. 131. Also, refer to Elsbree, *American Teacher,* pp. 274, 277–278, 279–281; Tyack, *The One Best System* (1974), p. 62; Also, refer to Altenbaugh, *The Teacher's Voice,* p. 10.

35. Rury, "Gender, Salaries, and Career," p. 215.

36. See Strober and Tyack, "Why Do Women Teach and Men Manage?"; Altenbaugh, *The Teacher's Voice,* p. 10.

37. Strober and Tyack, "Why Do Women Teach and Men Manage?," pp. 497–498, 500.

38. Preston, "Feminization of an Occupation," p. 70. Also refer to John L. Rury, "Who Became Teachers? The Social Characteristics of Teachers in American History," in *American Teachers: Histories of a Profession at Work,* ed. Donald Warren (New York: Macmillan, 1989), p. 27; Myra H. Strober and Laura Best, "The Female/Male Salary Differential in Public Schools: Some Lessons from San Francisco, 1879," *Economic Inquiry* 17 (April 1979), pp. 218–236; David B. Tyack and Elisabeth Hansot, *Managers of Virtue: Public School Leadership in America, 1820–1980* (New York: Basic Books, 1982), p. 183; Altenbaugh, *The Teacher's Voice,* pp. 10–11.

39. Preston, "Feminization of an Occupation," p. 147; Altenbaugh, *The Teacher's Voice,* p. 11. For information on the salaries of African-American instructors, refer to Susan B. Carter, "Incentives and Rewards to Teaching," in *American Teachers: Histories of a Profession at Work,* ed. Donald Warren (New York: Macmillan, 1989), p. 58.

40. Quoted in Johnson, *Old-Time Schools,* pp. 127–128.

41. Laura Ingalls Wilder, *These Happy Golden Years* (New York: Harper Collins Publishers, 1981).

42. David Swift, "The Problem of Control," in *Education and American Culture,* eds. Elizabeth Steiner, Robert Arnove, and B. Edward McClellan (New York: Macmillan Publishing Co., 1980), p. 320. Also, see Johnson, *Old-Time Schools,* p. 121.

43. Greeley is quoted in Johnson, *Old-Time Schools,* pp. 123–125, but Swift, "The Problem of Control," who relies on Johnson, also uses this same quote, p. 321. Refer as well to Finkelstein, *Governing the Young,* p. 121; Fuller, *Old Country School,* p. 209.

44. Warren Burton, *The District School As It Was, By One Who Went to It* (Boston: Phillips, Sampson and Co., 1850), p. 87. Also, refer to Swift, "The Problem of Control," p. 321.

45. Fuller, *Old Country School,* p. 209.

46. Swift, "The Problem of Control," p. 322.

47. The last quote is from Johnson, *Old-Time Schools,* pp. 122–123, while the "schoolkeeping" term is from Swift, "The Problem of Control," p. 322.

48. Finkelstein, *Governing the Young,* p. 96; Swift, "The Problem of Control," pp. 322, 323.

49. Swift, "The Problem of Control," pp. 322, 323. See as well Johnson, *Old-Time Schools,* pp. 121, 122.

50. Burton, *The District School,* pp. 21, 22, 36.

51. Finkelstein, *Governing the Young,* p. 47.

52. Burton, *The District School,* p. 104. Also see Finkelstein, *Governing the Young,* p. 67.

53. Lawrence A. Cremin, ed., *The Republic and the School: Horace Mann on the Education of Free Men* (New York: Teachers College Press, 1957), p. 55. Refer as well to Finkelstein, *Governing the Young,* pp. 100, 103, 104.

54. Margaret A. Winzer, *The History of Special Education: From Isolation to Integration* (Washington, DC: Gallaudet University Press, 1993), pp. 115–119.

55. Linda Peavy and Ursula Smith. *Frontier Children* (Norman, OK: University of Oklahoma Press, 1999), p. 79; Christine Stansell, *City of Women: Sex and Class in New York, 1789–1860* (Urbana, IL: University of Illinois Press, 1987), pp. 209–214.

56. Hawes, *Children in Urban Society,* pp. 123, 124, 125.

57. Fuller, *Old Country School,* pp. 200, 201.

58. Finkelstein, *Governing the Young,* p. 67.

59. Ruth Miller Elson, *Guardians of Tradition: American Schoolbooks of the Nineteenth Century* (Lincoln, NE: University of Nebraska Press, 1964), pp. viii, 2–3, 4–5, 11, 40, 67, 103, 124, 147, 162, 188. Also refer to Johnson, *Old-Time Schools and School-Books,* p. 233; and Finkelstein, *Governing the Young,* pp. 46, 74–75, 78, 81, 84–85, 87, for the teachers' pedagogical uses of schoolbooks.

60. The information and quotes in these paragraphs are from John H. Westerhoff, III, *McGuffey and His Readers: Piety, Morality, and Education in Nineteenth-Century America* (Nashville, TN: Abingdon Press, 1978), pp. 13, 14, 18, 30, 31, 32, 34, 42, 50, 51, 53, 57, 58, 59, 60, 76, 77, 80, 82, 94, 104–105, 106, 120–121. Also consult Finkelstein, *Governing the Young,* pp. 43, 44, 52–54, 67.

61. Church, *Education in the United States,* p. 12.

62. The information and quotes in these paragraphs draw from Swift, "The Problem of Control," p. 325.

C H A P T E R

6

Education in the Gilded Age

Race and *The Crisis* in the North
Northern Schooling
W.E.B. DuBois

The Emergence of the Urban High School
Early Patterns
Academies
The People's College
"What ye learn in school ain't no good"

The Public School Bureaucracy
Systemization of the Schooling Process
The Move from Local to State Control

Charlotte L. Forten, an abolitionist, African American teacher from Philadelphia, went to the South in 1862 to teach newly freed slaves on South Carolina's Sea Islands. She found both young and old anxious to learn:

> It is wonderful how a people who have been so long crushed to the earth, so imbruted as they have been,—and they are said to be among the most degraded negroes of the South,—can have so great a desire for knowledge, and such a capability for attaining it. One cannot believe that the haughty Anglo-Saxon race, after centuries of such an experience as these people have had, would be very much superior to them. And one's indignation increases against those who, North as well as South, taunt the colored race with inferiority while they themselves use every means in their power to crush and degrade them, denying them every right and privilege, closing against them every avenue of elevation and improvement.[1]

Up to this point, African Americans had been denied formal instruction even while the common schools in the North and East were already providing free schooling to most American children.

This chapter primarily focuses on national educational developments in the period following the Civil War. Schooling expanded throughout the West and South, where it assumed different and unique characteristics. In the growing cities, the schools were becoming mature institutions and the formalization of the educational process and school management began and the early outlines of modern school bureaucracies emerged.

There were a number of other developments in education during this period. As the Anglo frontier continued to roll west across the continent, schooling opportunities for pioneer children increased. Their education was not confined to the classroom, however. Also during this period, the federal government fully asserted its control over Native American education with an intense and intrusive emphasis on Americanization. This lengthy and conflict-ridden approach was likewise applied in earnest to the Mexican American population as Anglo settlers moved relentlessly into the Southwest. The South, during Reconstruction, ultimately embraced the public school concept and gradually implemented state systems of schooling. In addition to bringing about profound political and economic changes, Reconstruction brought education to former slaves and unique forms of schooling. The education provided, however, did not meet the hopes and expectations African Americans had for it as a means of economic and social liberation. Throughout the nation, as enrollments steadily increased at the grammar school level, a growing demand for secondary schooling emerged, although patterns of attendance and success varied widely. Finally, although mostly in urban areas, early patterns of centralized school governance began to appear as the common-school system matured.

TEACHING AND LEARNING ON THE WESTERN FRONTIER

The settlement of the western frontier proved to be a significant event in the shaping of American society. Tens of thousands of migrants journeyed across the North American continent. More than 300,000 people moved west to California, Colorado, Idaho, Montana, Oregon, and the Dakotas between 1840 and 1867 alone. The demographic transformation was profound. "By 1880, that half of the continent which forty years earlier had contained less than one percent of the nation's people boasted over 20 percent of the population." Indeed, for all intents and purposes, the frontier was no longer a frontier by the 1890s.[2]

The West hosted a highly diverse population. Native Americans, of course, already occupied much of the Great Plains as well as other areas. Mexican Americans had for centuries maintained settlements throughout the Southwest. African American sharecroppers fled their southern peonage to farm on the frontier. Europeans traveled westward to find precious farm and grazing land. And Asians moved eastward from California to work on the transcontinental railroad and establish businesses. "Many mining towns had far greater proportions of foreigners than any precinct of turn-of-the-century Chicago or New York." Farming communities likewise hosted a cosmopolitan group of pioneers; frontier towns proved to be multilingual.[3]

The settlement of the West deeply affected American culture. The pioneer spirit and the settling of the frontier have been romanticized in countless legends and rich folklore. The legends and folklore served to imbue individualism even deeper in the American psyche. For our purposes, how did this historical experience affect education in general and children in particular? We will focus on three stages: the journey, initial settlement, and community development.

Westward Trek

According to historian Julie Roy Jeffrey, the western "migration was a family affair" for European Americans. Most of the families came from the East. "Economically, emigrants were neither very rich nor very poor. Though family situations differed, all emigrants had to be financially solid enough to raise the substantial amount of cash necessary for the trip." The entire journey took between five and six months. Migrants, especially women and children, began their western trek filled with ambivalence. On the one hand, the West offered new opportunities and adventures for them. On the other hand, they had to abandon their relatives, friends, and homes—perhaps forever. The partings often assumed a mournful tone, as at the death of a loved one or friend.[4] Not many children embarked on this transcontinental journey; they "accounted for only 20 percent of the crowd, about half of the population found elsewhere in the country."[5]

The journey west proved to be exhausting; fatigue and stress were common. Slave women walked the entire way beside their master's wagon. Most Mormons pulled hand-carts weighing between 400 and 500 pounds. The work seemed endless. Women maintained traditional work duties, like cooking meals, watching children, and caring for the sick. Because of the treeless plains, they often had to collect dried buffalo dung, otherwise known as "meadow mushrooms," to fuel the campfires. "This caused many ladies," one observer remarked, "to act very cross and many were the rude phrases uttered, far more humiliating to refined ears than any mention of the material used for fuel could have been." Divisions of work between men and women blurred as the trip continued. "Women whose husbands became sick or died on the trail, of course, assumed all the responsibilities for the family's survival and welfare, unless they were lucky enough to fall under the protection of another man." Otherwise, widows drove wagons, looked after the livestock, and slept with guns beside them, fearing nocturnal intruders. Men occasionally cooked and did the wash.[6]

For children, the journey west began with high hopes and almost giddy feelings. The early expectations of the journey created a partylike atmosphere, as seventeen-year-old Susan Thompson recalled: "We were a happy, carefree lot of young people and the dangers and hardships found no resting place on our shoulders. It was a continuous picnic, and excitement was plentiful." As the journey continued, however, children found the trek tedious, rigorous, frightening, and dangerous. Each day passed monotonously with the same mind-numbing routine: traveling, camping, and foraging. Many children walked much of the way. With little close adult supervision, they would wander for miles from the wagons and then eventually catch up. The very young who rode in the wagons grew restless and cranky. Sudden violent thunderstorms on the Great Plains in the middle of the night created havoc, frightening oxen, blowing the camp into disarray, and terrifying children. Adults occasionally became lost, creating insecurity, or quarreled among themselves, generating anxiety.[7]

Work, danger, and death were ever present. Children performed an endless list of demanding chores: They herded and fed livestock; collected brush kindling, wood, and buffalo chips for the campfires; hunted game and fished for food; drove wagons; and stood guard at night. Accidents and illnesses also plagued children. Young ones fell from the wagons and under the wheels, breaking bones and in many cases dying. Older children occasionally became disoriented from walking for days and weeks behind the wagons and some became lost, never to be found. "The anxiety of mothers, some of whom kept their young on leashes while in camp, surely was communicated to the boys and girls." Children often clutched the wagon wheels while they rested or dozed. By doing this, they knew immediately when the wagon was resuming the journey. If they failed to do this, in their daze, they may have been left behind. All children fell prey to diseases, like diarrhea, and many died from them. And children witnessed adults, relatives, and parents dying because of strain, injuries, and disease. "Parents died quickly of mountain fever and cholera, lingered with pneumonia and dysentery, dropped from strokes and heart attacks and drowned in rivers." Many children were left parentless and were adopted by others. The emotionally stressed survivors merely dug a shallow grave along the trail, buried their loved ones, and moved on. "A young boy counted thirty-two graves in fourteen miles; a girl saw twenty-five in a day, lying in clusters of twelve, five, and eight." Because of wind and water erosion, as well as wild animals foraging for food, human bones and hair often protruded from these inadequate burial places. One child recalled finding human skulls during the journey: "We would pick them up and read the verses on them, then perhaps add a line or two and set them up to attract someone else as they passed by."[8] The entire journey proved to be a mix of awesome sights, adventure, and grisly nightmare for children.

Emigrant encounters with Native Americans were often friendly on both sides. Supplies were traded and "[b]ecause most of the wagon trains of California-bound emigrants were large, they were not attacked by hostile Indians as they crossed the Southwest." But both also had traumatic experiences. Native American children maintained their parents' traditional routes of migration, trailing herds of animals for food. At first they were awestruck by the whites but grew terrified as more and more European American settlers entered their territory. Sarah Winnemucca (náee Thoc-me-tony), a Piute, remembered her childhood experiences:

> What a fright we all got one morning to hear some white people were coming. Everyone ran as best they could. . . . My aunt said to my mother: 'Let us bury our girls, or we shall all be killed or eaten up.' . . . So our mothers buried me and my cousin, planted sage bushes over our faces to keep the sun from burning them, and there we were left.

These terrifying expectations were not fulfilled and Sarah and her cousin were released that night. On another occasion, a wagon party encountered on the trail a lost, starving, naked eight-year-old Native American girl. The majority of the party decided to abandon her, but two women strongly objected and remained with her as the wagons continued. Eventually, they too deserted her and rejoined the party. As a young male member of the party recalled: "One of the young men in charge of the horses felt so badly about leaving her, he went back and put a bullet through her head and put her out of her misery."[9]

Early Settlement

The migrants found little solace when they finally arrived at their destinations. Their clothes had been reduced to rags. They were filthy and exhausted, had brown leathery skin from the beating sun and ceaseless wind and heavily calloused feet from having walked thousands of miles, often without shoes. They were usually penniless. The emotional strain of leaving home and familiar surroundings, facing endless danger, and having lost loved ones on the trail often overwhelmed them at this point.[10]

In spite of the crude conditions, families attempted to re-create their former lives. They hastily erected some sort of shelter for themselves, which ranged from log cabins and traditional wood houses where timber was plentiful to tar-paper shanties, sod houses, and dugouts in dire cases or where wood was simply not available. Many settlers simply converted their wagons into homes or disassembled them for the wood. In an extreme case, an Oregon family resided in two hollow tree stumps. Generally speaking, these early abodes were small and overcrowded and there was little privacy. The dwellings were jammed with furnishings, when possible, to re-create the homelike environment the pioneers had abandoned back East. "Here fathers and mothers, daughters and sons, would pass time together, reading, talking, and playing games, all in a setting ostensibly little different from one in Vermont and Ohio."[11] But isolation and loneliness dominated the lives of the settlers, sometimes for years. Exposed to the elements, they also faced natural disasters—blizzards, deadly cold, drought, earthquakes, floods, lightning strikes, prairie fires, tornados, and wind storms. Rattlesnakes crawled into children's rooms, and families constantly feared cougar attacks on their little ones. Insects and skunks boldly invaded.

Contrary to popular myth, Western households were not large. "Young children who were unable to contribute to the frontier family's welfare in these crucial early years were not an asset but a burden." Frontier women relied on contraceptives and abortions to control the size of their families. In this, the Western rural households followed the national trend. The average number of children in European American families steadily declined during the nineteenth century, from 7.04 in 1800 to 6.14 in 1840, and finally to 4.24 in 1880.[12]

The frontier economy required all children to work. In other parts of the country during this time, children were gradually abandoning work for school. "On the frontier, however, the child's working sphere was expanding, not contracting. . . . Most families could not afford idle children." Children began work at a very young age and proved to be indispensable to the very survival of the family. In farming communities, they helped their parents clear the land, cutting and hauling trees, and then assisted them in planting, cultivating, and harvesting. Both boys and girls herded sheep and cows. When not working in the fields, girls cleaned, cooked meals, sewed, mended, washed clothes in boiling pots of water, and maintained gardens, among other domestic chores, while boys tended livestock, cut firewood, and repaired the house. Although some tasks crossed gender lines, such as boys washing dishes, most were allotted according to social norms. In mining towns, children panned for gold with their parents and their small, compact bodies allowed them to squeeze into the narrow sluices to clean them. "They hauled water and cared for the horses and mules that pulled the ore carts and wagons; they picked up tools; hung up brass for time keepers; and helped freight the machinery and supplies that fed elaborate operations." They also helped their families by earning money washing dishes, selling newspapers, and cleaning stables to cover family expenses. Children in all settings devoted much of their time to gathering wild berries and plants as well as hunting squirrels, rabbits, ducks, and other wild game. Childhood did not become extinct in the West, however; it existed, although altered by the demanding setting. Pioneer children played games they learned back East and eventually created new ones for their new environment, such as horseback riding. Families still nurtured their children.

In spite of a difficult journey and frontier conditions, literacy remained high. "In most of the West the literacy rate among youngsters over the age of ten was barely below that of the Ohio Valley and slightly above that of New England, regions that took great pride in their spread of learning." At first, education was informal. Families were its primary source. Parents taught their children religious morals, basic literacy, and work attitudes and skills, sometimes with the aid of a horsewhip. Modest home libraries boasted classic authors such as Plato and Shakespeare, the works of Charles Dickens, Sir Walter Scott, and other popular writers, and everyday reading, such as Sears, Roebuck and Company catalogues, newspapers, and magazines. There were rudimentary public libraries as well. Community activities such as spelling bees, literary societies, and public lectures provided additional educational opportunities.[13]

"Civilizing" the West

At the completion of the westward trek, women assumed the significant role of "civilizers," in accordance with Catherine Beecher's nineteenth-century notion of their proper domestic function. "In the earliest stages of community growth, married women often set up simple schools in their own houses. . . . These impromptu schools had little permanence, serving neighbors and family for a few months a year when nothing else was available." Children also assembled in dugout schools and "brush-arbor" schools, which literally consisted of a roof made of twigs and tree branches, a lean-to structure that seemed appropriate for the arid and hot Southwest. As a community's population rose, education became more formal. Churches, schools, and libraries were among the first "formal institutions" to be developed, and communities often expanded around them. Families either organized schools in their local communities themselves or appealed to the state for the establishment of common schools. "Although women were not listed on school boards in the West, or on the boards of trustees which founded early schools, they played a significant part both in establishing and serving educational institutions."[14]

Because of a shortage of qualified teachers and a lack of resources, the organization of formal schooling proved to be difficult. Nevertheless, there was progress, although it occurred at an uneven pace. California, Kansas, Nebraska, and Oregon saw a rapid growth of public schools, while Arizona and Wyoming lagged behind. By 1880, "public education was more accessible in the West than in any other part of the nation." Many western states, like Colorado and Idaho, had the highest attendance rates in the country, although the average academic year of 5.9 months was less than the national average of 6.4 and much less below the Northeast's average of 8.3 months. The shortage of male teachers resulted in female participation in western schools "even more than elsewhere in the nation." In 1847, Catharine Beecher established the National Popular Education Board to send women to the West to teach. By 1858, the board had succeeded in dispatching some 600 women, on two-year contracts. In other cases, communities relied on local women, some incredibly young. "School mistresses of fifteen were commonplace, thirteen-year-olds not unknown." Their tenure rarely exceeded a year, as they married or moved to a better-paying school district. They taught in crude buildings, often just dugouts and with dirt floors.[15] Mary S. Adams, a Missouri teacher, described her school to her former normal school instructor at Mount Holyoke Female Seminary in 1853: "Our schoolhouse to be sure, might be a better one, for when it rains the water comes in quite freely, but then the floor furnishes numerous facilities for it to run out again soon." She also commended her students and their parents: "I never before saw children so much interested in learning, and so desirous to please me. The parents visit me every week, and seem to partake of the spirit of the children."[16] Many of these women, particularly before the Civil War, saw frontier teaching as a "mission, of bringing Protestant evangelical religion and education to the West." They felt compelled "to serve God."[17]

Teaching methods remained the universal drill, repetition, and memorization with ample doses of corporal punishment. One teacher "locked his worst boys in a coal house, while another asserted command by periodically shooting a moose head hanging at the rear of the room." Schooling remained an erratic experience, with irregular attendance. "Children's varied experiences and their in-again, out-again attendance made them exceptionally independent and reluctant to accept the close regulation of a tightly disciplined schoolroom."[18]

Thus, the journey west created incredible hardships for pioneers and especially for children. But children still learned, whether by informal or formal means. The daily travails of life shaped their outlook and taught them survival skills. They endured family illnesses, deaths, and tragedies and had to adapt to new and challenging circumstances. And formal schooling began soon after settlement. All in all, children underwent a highly dynamic educational experience.

Anglo movement westward caused serious cultural conflicts. Asians and African Americans encountered widespread rejection on the frontier. The Chinese were excluded from all aspects of frontier life, and the children, especially the young girls smuggled into the United States as part of a highly profitable slave trade, were brutally exploited. African Americans too often confronted discrimination.[19] Native Americans experienced bitter upheavals because of Anglo land acquisition and had imposed on them an educational experience that proved to be highly disruptive and that directly assaulted their heritage and beliefs.

The White Man's Ways

The western military campaigns against Native Americans undertaken to facilitate the settlement of the West were successful. In 1851, the Sioux, Cheyenne, and Arapaho signed treaties under which they agreed to live within designated boundaries. Congress "confirmed" the reservation system in 1871. For economic, moral, and cultural reasons, official government policy then shifted from a focus on warfare to education as a means of control. Senator Henry L. Dawes estimated that it cost nearly $1 million to exterminate one Indian, and according to Secretary of the Interior Carl Schurz, the federal government could save a substantial amount of money through education rather than warfare because it cost only $1,200 to school a Native American child for eight years. Thus, the government chose to eradicate Indian religion, heritage, and language rather than the Native Americans themselves. The approach also proved to be more morally acceptable, as historian David Adams points out:

> The war against Indians had now entered a new phase. Conquering a continent and its aboriginal peoples had been a bloody business, and for a Christian people, not without

moral discomfort. Now the war against savagism would be waged in a gentler fashion. The next Indian war would be ideological and psychological, and it would be waged against children.

The cultural rationale for this policy reflected white ethnocentrism, which was based on a simple dichotomy: The European American was civilized; the Indian was savage. The civilizing process undertaken had three components. First, Native American children needed to be imbued with the notion of individuality and weaned away from tribal "communism." Second, Indian children needed to learn English, to the exclusion of their native languages, in order to operate within the dominant European American culture. Third, Native American children needed to be Christianized and saved from paganism. "All in all, the Indian child was to be transformed, all vestiges of his former self eradicated."[20] Of course, as we saw in Chapters 2 and 3, much of this agenda was not new.

Government officials estimated that their plan for assimilating Native Americans would take twenty years. In 1888, the Board of Indian Commissioners concluded: "Ten years of thorough training of all Indian children in industrial schools will take a large portion of them off our hands, and in twenty years there would be but few Indians needing the care and support of the government."[21] The blatant and purposeful destruction of Native American cultures would by then be completed. But they did not anticipate the unprecedented scale of implementing this policy. In 1877, Congress appropriated only $20,000 for Indian education; by 1900, this figure had climbed to $3 million. In that same twenty-five-year period, the school enrollment of Native American children increased from 3,598 to 21,568, a trend that would continue, for by 1926 83 percent of all Indian children were attending "American" schools. The growth in enrollment was assisted by Congress, which passed a series of compulsory attendance laws for Native American children, beginning in 1891.[22]

Reservation Day Schools and Boarding Schools

The Bureau of Indian Affairs, which assumed control of Native American education in 1870, sponsored three different types of schools: the reservation day school, the reservation boarding school, and eventually the off-reservation boarding school. The reservation day school proved to be the cheapest approach. "Lawrence Horn, a Blackfoot who attended the government school at Heart Butte, recalled students getting a stroke of a leather strap with holes in it every time they spoke Indian." In spite of such cruel efforts, these schools were the least successful in assimilating the children. The family's presence ensured the persistence of tribal culture.[23]

At the reservation boarding school, the second option, academics occupied half a day and work the other half. Boys raised stock and learned various craft skills, and girls completed domestic tasks. As in the South with African American children, industrial education predominated. Reservation boarding schools offered the clear advantage of greater institutional control over Native American children. The disadvantage was that many parents continued to visit their children at the schools. The tribal community thus continued to exert too much influence over the students, interfering with the school's acculturation agenda.[24]

Off-Reservation Boarding Schools

The off-reservation boarding school began as an experiment when sixty-two Indians were sent to Hampton Institute in 1878. It proved to be so successful at assimilation, according to proponents, that Richard Henry Pratt, an army officer, opened the first completely Indian boarding school in 1879 in a former barracks in Carlisle, Pennsylvania. With an initial enrollment of 136 students, Pratt committed the institution and the boarding school concept in general to the total and complete assimilation of Native American children. William P. Dole, Commissioner of Indian Affairs, wrote that in such off-reservation environments "the children are under the entire control of the teacher. . . . " Thus, separating children from their families represented the first stage of the assimilation process. By 1903, Commissioner William A. Jones asserted that this type of education "will exterminate the Indian but develop a man."[25]

The cultural transformation of the students began immediately at Carlisle under a rigid military-type of regimen. Upon arriving, the boys had their hair sheared by school employees. Long hair was perceived as a symbol of savagery; the boys were instantly traumatized because it was humiliating to lose their braids. Zitkala-Sa, a Nakota, recalled her rough treatment at White's Manual Labor Institute in Wabash, Indiana:

> I remember being dragged out, though I resisted by kicking and scratching wildly. In spite of myself, I was carried downstairs and tied fast in a chair.
> I cried aloud, shaking my head all the while, until I felt the cold blades of the scissors against my neck, and heard them gnaw off one of my thick braids. Then I lost my spirt.[26]

The school then issued "standard school uniforms": Boys wore suits and girls wore dresses. School officials further obliterated tribal identities by conferring new names on the students, basically English translations of their existing ones. The students adhered to a rigorous and strict schedule—one recalled a typical day:

> Early in the morning at 6 o'clock we rose at the sound of bugles. We washed and dressed; then we lined up in military formation and drilled in the yard. For breakfast, companies formed, and we marched to the dining room, where we all stood at attention with long tables before us. We recited grace aloud. . . .
> Some teachers and other workers weren't very friendly. When students made mistakes they often were slapped or whipped by the disciplinarian who usually carried a piece of rope in his hip pocket.

By 1887, Carlisle enrolled 617 students, whose average age was fifteen.

In all, twenty-three boarding schools opened throughout the West and Midwest. "Reservation schools became feeder elementary schools for off-reservation boarding schools, and the off-reservation schools that remained open changed from teaching only elementary subjects to teaching only secondary subjects in the twentieth century."[27] The educational program involved the usual academic subjects, like English, arithmetic, physical geography, and science, as well as citizenship training. As at Hampton Institute, for African American students, manual training at the Indian boarding schools involved agricultural and craft skills for boys and domestic chores for girls. Much of this quickly deteriorated into the drudgery of repetitive cleaning of toilets, washing of clothes, and making of uniforms. Irene Stewart, a Navajo, bitterly recollected her work experiences:

> I have never forgotten how the steam in the laundry made me sick; how standing and iron-
> ing for hours made my legs ache late into the night. By evening I was too tired to play and
> just fell asleep whenever I sat down. I think this is why the boys and girls ran away from
> school; why some became ill; why it was so hard to learn. We were too tired to study.

And many of the skills, such as blacksmithing and harness making, learned by the boys proved to be antiquated by this time. Nevertheless, by 1900, such industrial training pre-dominated at all of the federal boarding schools.[28]

At Carlisle, Pratt devised an "outing program," a type of apprenticeship. He placed Indian boys and girls with families, usually farmers, to live and work for various periods of time. The program theoretically provided opportunities for the students to refine their English and expand their work skills, to experience civilization firsthand. As Pratt argued, "I say that if we . . . place one in each American family . . . and train them up as children in those families, I defy you to find any Indian in them. . . . [They] would then be Anglo-Saxon in spirit and American in all . . . qualities. Color amounts to nothing. The fact that they are born Indians does not amount to anything." Through this outing system, by 1892 Pratt had placed some 662 Native American children with "American" families. This was the second stage of assimilation, that is, separating Native American children from each other. But aside from its clear purpose of acculturation, the program soon became an

"Six Boys Doing Laundry" (c. 1901–1903) United States Indian School, Carlisle, PA. Courtesy of Library of Congress, Prints and Photographs Division.

exploitative labor service. In New Mexico and California, the schools sent gangs of 50 to 100 students to fruit farmers to perform the monotonous work of picking crops in the fields for days.[29]

Failure

Some Native American parents and their children willingly participated in the federal school program. Conditions on government reservations were wretched. Disease, inadequate sanitation, overcrowding, and poor farming land increased mortality rates and made survival difficult. The formerly strong and communal nuclear family began to dissolve under such conditions. Some Native American families saw the boarding schools as the only salvation for their children. The death of a spouse spurred some now-single parents to relieve the family's burden by sharing child-raising responsibilities with boarding schools. In other cases, a few Native Americans willingly embraced assimilation. Geronomo sent his nephew to school to prepare a new generation of leaders to "compete" with the whites. And orphaned children went to boarding schools rather than face homelessness. Nevertheless, even "volunteering" often involved compulsion; one doomed Apache student recalled how the decision was made for him as he stood in a line: "I well remember that when Captain Pratt came to me he stopped, looked me up and down, and smiled. Then he seized my hand, held it up to show I volunteered. I only scowled; I didn't want to go at all."[30]

By the early 1900s and by all accounts, "the nation's Indian policy was a miserable failure." The Native American education program proved to be the biggest disappointment, for it was the policy that had met with the most resistance. Parents did not object to schooling per se, but were reluctant to conform to the federal government's educational policies for two reasons. First, some opposed the whole concept of acculturation. Second, others feared for the safety of their children under the cruelty that they would experience. Indian agents often had to resort to withholding rations from parents—literally starving them into submission—in order to coerce them into relinquishing custody of their children.[31] "The Tenth Calvary was called out during the winter of 1890–91 and again in the summer of 1891 from Fort Wingate near Gallup, New Mexico, to force Hopi parents living in the village of Oraibi to send their children to school."[32] On Navajo reservations, many children had to be hunted down by posses. A "Senate subcommittee investigation on the conditions of Indians" reported on such "kid catching" techniques: "The children are caught, often roped like cattle, and taken away from their parents, many times never to return." Parents also encouraged their intensely homesick children to run away from the boarding schools, which they did at an alarming rate. Unfortunately, some died during their escapes, found frozen to death.[33]

Students also resisted. Some actually burned school buildings in protest. Students at the Haskell Indian School organized an outright rebellion. Others practiced "passive resistance" by feigning illnesses, initiating "work slowdowns," creating "disruptive pranks," and generally not responding to teachers and authority figures. And parental influence endured despite physical separation. Children and their parents maintained close and frequent contact through extensive written correspondence. Finally, students opposed their forced, and often cruel, assimilation by secretly practicing tribal customs, often late at night in clandestine meetings.[34]

The failure of the off-reservation boarding schools was also brought about by inadequate living and educational conditions. A 1907 health report disclosed the following about the Haskell Indian School: "The people slept two, three, or more in single beds. Both pulmonary and glandular cases (of tuberculosis) were found occupying beds with supposedly healthy pupils. Common towels, common drinking cups, and no fresh air in the dormitories were the rule rather than the exception. No attention was paid to decayed teeth and tooth brushes were not regularly used or their use insisted upon." The students barely survived on poor diets and the classrooms had a chronic lack of educational materials. Because of overcrowding, poor sanitation, and insufficient diets, diseases like influenza, measles, smallpox, and trachoma, ravaged the students.[35] "Between 1885 and 1913, one hundred Indian students were buried in the Haskell cemetery along." Actually, more than 100 died since the school sent many students' bodies home to be buried by their parents. Serious emotional stress, such as fear, trauma, anxiety, and homesickness, certainly contributed to these illnesses and deaths.[36]

There were other signs of failure. Graduation rates remained chronically low, a frustrating disappointment for school proponents. At Carlisle in 1909, only one out of eight students received a diploma. More significant is the broader question of the success of cultural transformation. The historical record appears to be ambiguous at best. While "most homecomings were touching, affection-filled reunions," many returning students felt detached from their former tribal culture. Some parents rejected their converted children out of disgust. Most students reverted to traditional ways when they returned because tribal members would have otherwise ostracized them. A few graduates fled the tribe and worked with white missionaries. Thus, their educational experiences at the off-reservation boarding schools appeared to disrupt their lives significantly and jeopardize family and tribal ties, but they were never completely assimilated into the dominant European American culture.

Because the policy of acculturation through education had largely failed, the federal government began to close the institutions, abandoning especially the boarding-school concept. "Between 1900 and 1925, the total number of government schools dropped from 253 (25 off-reservation boarding, 81 reservation boarding, 147 day schools) to 209 (18 off-reservation boarding, 51 reservation boarding, 140 day schools)." Hampton Institute eliminated its Indian education program in 1912. Carlisle, "once the crown jewel of the Indian school service," had deteriorated and closed in 1918 on the pretext of war needs.[37] In spite of their failure, the boarding-school experience had a positive and unanticipated outcome. Native-American historians Jon Reyhner and Jeanne Eder point out that since the schools were coeducational, they unwittingly encouraged, or at least facilitated, "tribal intermarriage." Students also mingled with members of other tribes, developing friendships. Ironically, "[b]oarding schools which had been started to destroy tribal identity, ended up helping to create an Indian identity."[38] This would serve them well in future struggles, as we will see in Chapters 8 and 10.

Mexican American Education on the Frontier

Anglo expansion westward generated cultural conflict not only with Native Americans but with Mexican Americans as well. At the conclusion of the Mexican American War, "there were perhaps 5,000 Mexicans in Texas, 60,000 in New Mexico, not more than 1,000 in

Arizona, and perhaps 7,500 along the length of California."[39] The 1848 Treaty of Guadalupe Hidalgo, which officially ended the war, granted full citizenship to those Mexicans who chose to remain in the former territories of Mexico, now the American Southwest. Within a year of that agreement, the United States government revoked "citizenship equality" and began a "racialization" policy. "Much as Spain had done, the United States gave full citizenship to Mexicans who were considered white and ascribed inferior legal status to people of color on the basis of race." In California and Texas, "Indians, *mestizos*, and *afromestizos* were ineligible to vote and therefore stripped of most political rights." New Mexico managed to stall this racialization policy for a couple of decades but gradually acceded because of increased Anglo settlements and political pressure from the federal government and surrounding states, such as Texas.[40]

The cultural conflict had an added element in the Southwest in that Anglo Americans occupied legitimate Mexican territory in California, which was not yet part of the United States. Mexicans saw themselves as victimized by this and some of this feeling translated into outright hostility and contempt. Sometimes violence erupted between Anglos and Mexicans. In the 1870s, as historian Rodolfo Acuña notes, Mexican "youth were taught from the very cradle to look upon the American government as that of a foreign nation." *Californios* protested as unjust the appropriation of economic and political power by Anglos. Some newspapers, such as *El Clamor Público*, published by Francisco P. Ramírez in Los Angeles between 1855 and 1859, criticized the Anglo treatment of Mexicans. In 1856, he passionately editorialized: "California has fallen into the hands of the ambitious sons of North America who will not stop until they have satisfied their passions, by driving the first occupants of the land out of the country, vilifying their religion and disfiguring their customs."[41]

Education certainly became a battleground in this situation. As historian Guadalupe San Miguel analyzes it, "schools, especially public schools, became subtractive institutions, meaning that they sought to 'de-ethnicize' the Mexican-origin population and to remove all vestiges of ethnicity from their operations and curricula." He points to four Mexican American schooling experiences in the Southwest between 1848 and 1891. First, the Roman Catholic Church, as we saw in Chapter 2 and 3, had always assumed responsibility for education in New Spain as well as in the Mexican republic. Catholic schools in California, New Mexico, and Texas continued to emphasize religious education and literacy training. However, although those schools had accommodated themselves to Mexican culture, they began to gradually adopt an agenda of Americanization. Second, Protestant missionaries, mostly Presbyterians but also Baptists and Congregationalists, gradually introduced their own schools to the southwestern frontier and evangelized among the Spanish-speaking inhabitants. They focused on religious conversion and Americanization. At first intolerant of Mexican culture, Protestant instructors grew less so and adopted a "paternalistic" posture. Third, Mexican American communities throughout the Southwest created and maintained private, secular schools. (Their role remains obscure, however, since they left few records.) Finally, until about 1880 public schools were slow to develop in the Southwest. At that time, the "number of schools for Mexican children in general increased dramatically because of popular demand, legal mandates, increasing financial ability of local government, and a greater acceptance of the ideal of common schooling." As San Miguel adds, "despite the various forms of schooling in the Southwest, by the 1880s public education was emerging as the dominant form."

Early southwestern public schools "included Mexican cultural heritage in their curricula, and encouraged members of the Catholic and Mexican communities to participate in them." Gradually, Anglos "Americanized the public schools" and they "became increasingly subtractive institutions." They began, first, by marginalizing, if not completely eliminating, Mexican American participation, then they eradicated the use of the Spanish language in the schools, and finally they deleted Mexican culture from the curriculum.[42] Educational experiences in Texas and New Mexico were typical.

Texas

In the ten-year period between the Texas Revolution of 1836, in which Texas gained independence from Mexico, and the Mexican American War of 1846, when Texas became a part of the United States, the process of the political subordination of Mexicans began. The loss of economic power followed as **Tejanos** were dispossessed of their land. Following the Mexican American War, the process of subordination was completed. "Despised for being Mexican and suspected of harboring disloyal sentiments, this population was systematically deprived of whatever political and economic resources it had. The effort to relegate it to a subordinate position in the developing social order was effective and accomplished within three decades." Mexican American culture was included in the process. State legislation banned the use of Spanish in the schools, a highly selective and prejudicial action since the legislature permitted the use of the German language in education for children of that ethnic group. In all of the Southwest, Texas was the worst in its treatment of Mexicans.

By the latter half of the nineteenth century, *Tejanos* were attending Catholic parochial schools (girls attended convent schools), Presbyterian missionary schools, and private schools, which replicated the curriculum used in Mexico's classrooms, as well as public schools. Other educational facilities were used as well. In most cases, "[t]hese schools were usually segregated, overcrowded, and lacked adequately trained teachers and school equipment." Nevertheless, Mexican American parents, valuing education, most often insisted that their children attend the public schools. To overcome obvious language barriers, the *Tejano* community in El Paso established a private school "to teach English to their children to prepare them for the public schools." Rural Mexican American children rarely attended school at all; either the Anglo landowners "discouraged" it or schooling conditions, where they even existed, were extremely poor. *Tejano* parents sometimes sent their children to Mexico to attend schools, "when possible, or to the Mexican private schools, if any were available."[43]

New Mexico

Anglo American settlers in the Territory of New Mexico viewed the Spanish-speaking Roman Catholic inhabitants they encountered as hopelessly ignorant and backward. Anglo settlers found high illiteracy rates, inadequate elementary schooling, few secondary schools, ill-prepared teachers, and poor facilities. "From the 1850s through the 1920s, most Anglo-Americans insisted that it would benefit Hispanics to adopt American customs and beliefs. Anglo-American culture seemed to them to be the pinnacle of progress: English-speaking, Protestant, individualistic, acquisitive, hard-working, future-oriented, egalitarian, pragmatic."[44] Thus began a long and conflict-ridden Americanization process in the schools. It was a serious and intense social issue that exists to this day throughout the Southwest.

Between 1880 and 1910, an organized campaign unfolded to dispossess **Hispanos** of their land. As a result, they began to lose both economic status and political clout. *Hispanos* resisted through direct action and political organizing. In 1889, *Las Gorras Blancas* ("The White Caps") destroyed fences erected by Anglo cattle ranchers on land the *Hispanos* had formerly owned. And "in the early 1890s, *El Partido del Pueblo* ("The Party of the People"), an independent Hispanic political party, was organized. It called for ethnic unity and sought to organize the supporters of *Las Gorras Blancas*." The party's candidates won several local elections, but land ownership among *Hispanos* continued to decline.

Hispanos responded in the field of education as well to these profound economic and political changes. "Illiteracy, and inability to read English in particular, often led to the loss of land as landholders misunderstood or were unable to read statements of new laws concerning taxes and land."[45] A complex process of cultural negotiations unfolded. Although treated as a minority, *Hispanos* remained a majority of the population in New Mexico until World War II. They used this numerical strength in 1856 to oppose the first school law. They did not oppose schooling per se—as claimed by the Anglos—they simply wanted to retain some control over education. Subsequent school laws passed, beginning in 1860, and many *Hispanos* won elections as county commissioners, enabling them to raise funds, hire and pay teachers, set the school calendar, and regulate attendance.

Other, more fundamental, conflicts existed with schooling that reflected the larger issue of Americanization. *Hispanos* sharply differed with Protestant Anglos over the role of the Catholic Church in education. The Church, as we saw in Chapter 2 and 3, had always assumed responsibility for education in New Spain as well as in the Republic of Mexico. In New Mexico territory, priests and nuns "served as county school commissioners, superintendents, and teachers for the public schools." The public school system had simply absorbed the earlier church schools and had retained the priests and nuns as instructors. This "outraged" anti-Catholic Anglos. Disputes arose, too, over the use of Spanish in the classroom. Well into the late nineteenth century, during New Mexico's territorial period, both Anglos and *Hispanos* accepted bilingual instruction. Beginning in the early 1900s, however, state superintendents at first discouraged the use of Spanish in the schools and then eventually attempted to purge it altogether in 1907 through the adoption of English textbooks, citing the uniform textbook law. With statehood in 1912 and a constitution that protected the use of Spanish in public affairs, the legality of using Spanish in the schools remained ambiguous and unresolved, setting the stage for further conflict.

Hispanos thus faced a serious dilemma: school their children or preserve their culture. "Illiteracy which had stood at 78.5 percent of the adult population in 1870, had decreased to 24 percent in 1910, still much higher than the national average of 8 percent of the adult population for that year." Historian Lynne Marie Getz summarizes the choice that *Hispano* parents confronted: "[I]n New Mexico *Hispanos*, while they wished to learn English and American ways, had no desire to abandon their own cultural patterns. The paradoxical outcome was that educational conditions for *Hispanos* suffered, but they retained their ethnic identity. Such was the price paid for cultural integrity."[46] Southern Italian immigrants would replicate this same pattern, as we will see in Chapter 8.

Missionary Schools

Hispanos had at least one educational alternative to the public schools. During the late 1800s, Anglo American women, under the auspices of the Presbyterian church's Woman's Board of Home Missions, embarked on an evangelical campaign in New Mexico to educate, assimilate, and convert Roman Catholic *Hispanos*. Their missionary schools filled a significant educational void, for New Mexico's efforts to establish a public school system proved to be wholly inadequate; through the 1870s, the system was insufficiently funded. This unique New Mexican experience gives us an opportunity to take a look at cultural negotiation and its impact on both Anglos and Mexican Americans.

Presbyterian women staffed approximately forty one-room schools in small villages throughout northern New Mexico. By 1900, they had also opened two secondary boarding schools in Santa Fe and Albuquerque, one each for boys and girls. The curriculum relied heavily on the Bible, and the instructors acted as moral models, "as examples of Anglo-Protestant culture in all aspects of their lives—in their role as teacher, as housekeeper, as community leader." The results of this acculturation process proved to be surprising. While *Hispano* parents, in their eagerness for education, filled these schools with their children, "fewer than 10 percent became Protestant." Those parents faced fierce opposition from the Catholic Church, which attempted to discourage them through pamphlets and newspapers, and, most seriously, by threats of excommunication. But a complex process of cultural negotiation had unexpectedly unfolded in the meanwhile. *Hispano* parents accepted the schooling that Anglo Americans offered but rejected the imposition of Anglo culture. Anglo teachers could never exercise the degree of cultural "control" over the *Hispanos* that they desired. The missionaries, realizing this, retreated somewhat from their cultural goal by "deemphasizing conversion as a critical part of the Americanization process," opting for a more secular approach. Many of the women began to offer social services that complemented their educational mission. They combated poverty by providing meals for their students, by working to improve sanitation and health conditions in remote villages, by building windmills and digging wells, and generally by using the school as a social services community center. In the process, many of these missionary women themselves became sympathetic to, if not partially assimilated into, *Hispano* culture; that is, a sort of "cultural exchange" had occurred. The original paternalistic mission and ethnocentric perspective shifted to one of assistance in relieving poverty and to general acceptance of *Hispano* culture. *Hispanos*, in turn, adapted to the ever-encroaching Anglo culture while preserving the crucial elements of their own.[47] A temporary cultural compromise had been struck.

Anglo European social and educational patterns had thus become clear. Anglo settlers attempted to impose their culture on Native Americans and Mexican Americans already living in the region, and a great deal of conflict resulted. This cultural clash would persist in the Southwest: Native Americans and Mexican Americans would continue to resist the imposition of Anglo assimilation throughout the twentieth century, as we shall see in later chapters.

THE COMMON-SCHOOL MOVEMENT IN THE SOUTH

The South proved to be the last region, as a whole, to embrace the common-school concept. Exceptions existed, of course. To better grasp this complex experience, we must consider separately the three key chronological periods of Southern history: the "Old South," prior to the Civil War; the "New South," from Reconstruction through the mid-twentieth century; and the "American South," dating from the passage of the 1964 Civil Rights Act.[48] We will focus on the first two periods in this section. We will take up the American South, the third period, in Chapters 8 and 10.

The Old South

School reformers throughout the South had campaigned for state-subsidized education before the Civil War but, except for North Carolina, had achieved little success. In 1839, North Carolina began a local system of publicly financed schools, and in 1852 appointed the first state superintendent of common schools, Calvin Henderson Wiley. "By the time of the Civil War, those resources supported the instruction of more than 100,000 children—roughly half the white-aged population—enrolled in 3,488 districts scattered across the countryside."[49] Many other Southern states, such as Virginia, had managed only to institute a system of publicly subsidized charity schools. There are two basic reasons for this phenomenon. First, the absence of mass schooling preserved the social status quo. "Indeed, the Bourbon political leadership viewed illiteracy by and large as a virtue because it conserved and maintained traditional values" and hence social relationships. Second, the common-school concept connoted a sense of "Northernness." Southerners were suspicious, if not outright hostile, to Northern institutions like the public school.[50]

The South's port cities, in contrast, were strong adopters of Northern school reform. Common schools appeared in New Orleans, Louisiana, Mobile, Alabama, Savannah, and Charleston, during the antebellum period. Historian Joseph W. Newman sees three influences on this development. To begin with, Northern entrepreneurs who had assumed residence in those cities transplanted the "Yankee" notion of common schooling. "Yankees who moved south to the coastal cities often worked their way into prominent positions in business, society, and politics." The next two influences reflect the Native-Protestant ideology we explored in Chapter 4. Southern urban dwellers, who, like their Northern counterparts, became uneasy about the growing Roman Catholic population, had to assure the continuing dominance of Protestantism. "By 1860 more than one-third of New Orleans's residents, about one-fourth of Mobile's, and about one-fifth of Savannah's and Charleston's were foreign born, many of them Irish Catholics." Finally, common schools would assist the "commercial elite" in conveying the new values and social relationships of industrial capitalism by promising "social uplift" while ensuring "social control."

Southern cities largely replicated Northern patterns when they created their common schools. By the 1840s, New Orleans had become the "first" Southern city "to establish a common-school system," built "directly on the New England model." At first, that city relied on Northern teachers, textbooks, school furniture, and curricula. Horace Mann, the Massachusetts Secretary of Education, praised the New Orleans public schools. Charleston followed New Orleans in 1856. Henry Barnard, Connecticut's Secretary of Education, strongly supported that city's educational efforts. Both cities implemented comprehensive systems, which included primary, grammar, and high schools as well as normal programs to train teachers. Savannah and Mobile generally mimicked these efforts in the 1850s.[51]

Thus, by the outbreak of the Civil War, the concept of common schooling had taken root in Southern cities. But the powerful and predominantly rural regions, led by the planter class, successfully resisted common-school reform. As a result, "there was about one elementary school per fifty square miles in South Carolina. . . . "[52] Following the Civil War, however, the "port cities would serve as models for other southern states," becoming "educational exemplars."[53]

The New South

The Southern common-school movement began in earnest, albeit slowly, during Reconstruction. In a variety of ways, African Americans provided valuable, initial leadership for the development of Southern common schools. During the post–Civil War period, as we will see later in this chapter, African Americans made great sacrifices to establish their own schools. Former slaves opened the first free schools for African American children in Atlanta in 1865. By the late 1860s, four schools existed in Atlanta for African Americans: "These schools were viewed as a threat by white citizens, who urged the establishment of free education for white children." In 1869, a white public school was opened in Atlanta. African Americans also served on some Southern urban boards of education until the 1870s and 1880s,[54] and African American legislators supported the inclusion of publicly funded schools in the drafting of new state constitutions. Because of African American Republican leadership, North Carolina's Reconstruction Constitution of 1868 extended public schooling "to African-American children, and a tax-supported, four-month term was made a legal requirement rather than a local option." Public schools, nevertheless, remained largely a local responsibility.[55] As historian James D. Anderson points out, "surrounded by planters who were hostile to public education, middle-class professionals who allied themselves with planter interests, and lower-class whites who were largely alienated from mass education, ex-slaves were the only native group to forge ahead to commit the South to a system of universal schooling in the immediate post-war years." At first opposed, the initiative was then coopted by whites. "Even though the long-term gains of public education for ex-slaves proved to be small and slow, their organized efforts and ideological imperatives laid the foundation for universal education in the South." Southern free schooling began to become a reality in the 1880s and 1890s.[56]

As we have seen, the notion of Southern common schools dated to the antebellum period, and "[b]etween 1868 and 1870 the new plans were developed on paper in constitutional conventions and legislatures from Virginia to Georgia, as elsewhere in the South."[57] But actual implementation of public schooling encountered formidable resistance. During Reconstruction, most Southerners continued to see the common-school system as an instrument of "Yankee imposition," and there was some truth to this view. Historian Lawrence A. Cremin cogently points out, "public schooling was imposed on some regions as part of a political and military campaign."[58] As a consequence, no systematic and effective education authority at the state level existed in the South; local school districts proliferated. In North Carolina alone, "between 1880 and 1902, the number of white and black districts grew from 6,392 to an all-time high of 8,094." These isolated, rural communities assumed, for all intents and purposes, full autonomy, allocating resources, hiring teachers, and drawing district boundaries. Conformity to community values superseded academic content—"Parents insisted on sending their children to schools that mirrored their own sympathies and allegiances"—thus the localist tradition we discussed in Chapter 5 was largely perpetuated.

As a result, the South's public schools lagged behind those of other regions, particularly the Northeast. As they had in many other rural, one-room American schools of an earlier era, students found themselves subjected to bewildering, if not totally incomprehensible, lessons often led by semiliterate and semicompetent instructors. Memorization, drill, and corporal punishment dominated the daily routine. "Turning out" the teacher, as we saw in Chapter 5, continued, "particularly at Christmastime." Historian James L. Leloudis recounts that "a mock battle often ensued, especially if the teacher was a man. After an exchange of sticks and insults, the teacher usually gave in, much to the delight of parents who by this time gathered to witness the confrontation." This bit of theater held a deep symbolic meaning: "Students and parents took possession of the schoolhouse, reminding teachers that they owed their positions to local favor and approval."[59] As well, the Southern school calendar amounted to only half of that in New England, and only one-third of Southern children regularly attended school. Differences in expenditures also proved to be significant. "For each child of school age in South Carolina $1.80 was expended, and North Carolina $1.65; the amount in Massachusetts was $21.55, over twelve times as large." The development of high schools was especially retarded. "In 1903 Georgia had only seven, white four-year public high schools graduating ninety-four students; South Carolina in 1900 claimed thirty, Virginia twenty-eight, and North Carolina four." Southern teachers on average received less than a third of the salary of their Massachusetts counterparts. The consequences were serious. "With less than one-tenth of the nation's population, these states were burdened with one-fourth of the nation's illiterates."[60] These deficiencies in systemic development continued until the end of the century. Georgia's school funding was the subject of pitched battles between state and local interests. Virginia's legislators opposed school taxes because they refused to subsidize African American schools.[61]

However, beginning in the 1880s, significant economic progress came to the New South; the economy shifted from a largely agricultural to an industrially based one. Tobacco factories grew, cotton mills expanded, urbanization proliferated, railroad construction increased, and state and local governments subsidized "public improvements." As a result of these developments, Southern educational reform began to gain momentum in the late nineteenth century. In North Carolina, "by the late 1890s, more than two dozen communities had approved special taxes to support graded education, in most cases for black and white students alike." This movement was driven both by Southern school reformers and Northern philanthropists.

These late-century school reformers reflected a new generation: one too young to have fought in the Civil War and who "longed for the South's reunification with the North and its integration into the world of industry, commerce, and science." They disdained the old order and saw educational improvement as an important means of creating a new social, economic, and political South. At a series of high-profile annual meetings, beginning in Capon Springs, West Virginia, in 1898 and continuing throughout the South until 1914, "southern school reformers and northern philanthropists" planned long-term educational policy for the entire region: universal public schooling in general and industrial education in particular for African Americans. They consciously avoided challenging racial segregation as they embarked on their agenda of regional educational improvement.[62]

With strong support from John D. Rockefeller, Sr., Northern philanthropists created the Southern Education Board (SEB) in 1901 to direct the Southern school reform campaign. A year later Rockefeller subsidized the General Education Board (GEB) and, along with Robert Ogden, manager of New York City's Wanamaker's department store, banker George F. Peabody, and railroad president William H. Baldwin, Jr., "with help from Andrew Carnegie and the General Education Board, financed the [Southern Education] Board's modest budget," which was largely committed to a "propaganda" campaign for public schooling.[63] Baldwin "had helped shape the Capon Springs conferences on southern education and had served as a founding member of both the SEB and the GEB." Rockefeller created an interlocking directorate for these organizations and extended this linkage to the George Peabody and Slater funds. The Peabody Fund, founded in 1867, was the oldest Northern philanthropic effort in the South; John F. Slater, a Connecticut textile manufacturer, launched his altruistic efforts in 1882. "Backed by such potent resources, the SEB and GEB quickly established themselves as the arbiters of educational policy throughout the region, deftly shaping the actions of state lawmakers and local school districts."[64]

Southern school reform steadily moved that region's educational institutions from the common-school era to the modern era of the graded school. As part of the broader Progressive educational movement, as we will explore in Chapter 7, Southern white public schools became transformed. According to historian Louis R. Harlan, "educational expenditures in the southern seaboard increased 180 percent in the period 1900 to 1912." The number of elementary schools increased, school libraries expanded, the school year lengthened, enrollment climbed, teacher training improved, and instructors' salaries rose slightly. Even so, the South still lagged behind the rest of the nation in public education, in some cases spending less than half the average amount allocated for Northern school children. However, as Harlan concludes, "southern expenditure was destined to quadruple again in 1930, and yet again by 1945," eventually surpassing all other regions by the 1950s.[65]

African American Education in the South

Any discussion of Southern schooling must, of course, include an analysis of the African American experience, which proved to be significantly different. At the end of the Civil War, 4 million African Americans, comprising 40 percent of the South's population, resided in that region and 409,000 lived in the North. Freedom from slavery did not translate into social equality, however. On the social level, white Southerners wanted to avoid the "indignity" of mixing with African Americans, an "inferior people," as they saw them. Florida, Mississippi, and Texas passed "Jim Crow" laws in 1865 and 1866 to separate whites and African Americans on public conveyances. Leon Litwack summarizes this experience:

> In most instances, the "color line" simply perpetuated distinctions that had been made during slavery. On the city streetcars, blacks were forced to ride on the open platforms or in separate and specially marked cars. (In New Orleans, for example, blacks rode only on cars marked with a black star.) On the railroads, blacks were excluded from first-class

accommodations (the "ladies' car") and relegated to the smoking compartments or to freight boxcars in which seats or benches had been placed. On the steamboats plying the waterways and coasts, blacks were expected to sleep on the open deck and to eat with servants, although they paid the same fares as white passengers.

This legalization of racial separation established the framework for later, more efficient and thorough segregation laws.

In many locations, African Americans resisted this treatment. In Charleston, in 1867, they refused to accept separate accommodations on that city's streetcars, producing a confrontation. After a protest and the threat of a lawsuit, the streetcar company rescinded its racial practices. Similar successes occurred in Richmond and New Orleans. In other cases, Southern whites resorted to violence to express their anger and reassert their dominance. Beatings, shootings, and lynchings of African Americans steadily increased and intensified throughout the South. " 'The negro [sic] was murdered, beheaded, skinned, and his skin nailed to the barn,' a Freedmen's Bureau officer wrote of a case in Mississippi, as he supplied the names of the murderers and asked for an investigation." Through brutal intimidation, whites thus attempted to reassert their authority over freed African Americans.

Southern white control found further expression in the Black Codes. The codes, according to Litwack, represented a combination of "antebellum restrictions on free African Americans" and "lingering paternalism" as well as post–Civil War white fears and anxieties. "While the Codes defined the Freedman's civil and legal rights, permitting him to marry, hold and sell property, and sue and be sued, the key provisions were those which defined him as an agricultural laborer, barred or circumscribed any alternative occupations, and compelled him to work." Many of the restrictions and much of the language were haunting echoes of former masters' control over slaves. "Rather than expedite the slave's transition to freedom or help him to realize his aspirations, the Black Codes embodied in law the widely held assumption that he existed largely for the purpose of raising crops for a white employer. Although the ex-slave ceased to be the property of a master, he could not aspire to become his own master." White Southerners wanted African Americans to remain politically, economically, and socially dependent on whites, not independent of them.

Federal occupation authorities suspended the codes in most places, tolerated them in others, and completely ignored them in a few situations. "But if the Codes were dead, the sentiment which created them was still very much alive."[66] With the social context thus firmly established, with hostile racial attitudes well entrenched, what unfolded in the classroom was no surprise.

Native Schools

Generally speaking, the post–Civil War white South proved to be unreceptive to the notion of educating African Americans. The education of African Americans following the Civil War was shaped by three historical crosscurrents: human agency, white missionaries, and planter power.

Ex-slaves, barely literate themselves, opened "native schools."[67] Some of these had been in existence since 1860. "In Hampton, Virginia, an elderly black who had been a slave of ex-President John Tyler opened a school in the basement of the abandoned Tyler mansion, while in the same neighborhood Mary Peake, a free African American who had taught clandestinely before the war, seized the opportunity afforded by Union occupation to expand her teaching to include the newly created class of contrabands."[68] Former slaves opened and sustained Sabbath schools to provide elementary education. In 1865, African Americans created the Georgia Educational Association to support their own day and evening schools. The Freedmen's Bureau estimated in 1866 that 500 such schools existed throughout the South, especially in places where missionary societies and the bureau had failed to open schools. "Enrollment in such schools grew rapidly and actually exceeded the number registered in the bureau's system. In January 1867, there were about 65 private schools in New Orleans enrolling 2,967 pupils; the bureau maintained 56 schools with 2,527 pupils enrolled." The African American attendance rate proved to be impressive as well, with 82 percent in Virginia, 72 percent in Memphis, Tennessee, and 60 percent in Louisiana.[69] According to historian James D. Anderson, "the ex-slaves' educational movement became a test of their capacity to restructure their lives, to establish their freedom. Although they appreciated northern support, they resisted infringements that threatened to undermine their own initiative and self-reliance." Control was a major issue. Former slaves preferred to send their children to private African American schools rather than enroll them in free white schools opened by Northerners.[70]

Education connoted power to Southern African Americans. It would prevent them from being cheated in business dealings and enable them to participate in the political process. They stressed leadership training, relying on the classical, liberal arts curriculum. "They believed," Anderson stresses, "that the masses could not achieve political and economic independence or self-determination without first becoming organized, and organization was impossible without well-trained intellectuals—teachers, ministers, politicians, managers, administrators, and businessmen." To them, education was not for the purpose of maintaining the social status quo; rather, schooling would ensure economic freedom, social mobility, and political liberty.[71] The educational agenda of Northern white educators had less ambitious goals, and Southern whites opposed outright the concept of unrestricted schooling of African Americans.

Northern Missionaries

Northern civilian volunteers had hastily organized educational activities for African Americans during the Civil War; federally sponsored schooling efforts began after hostilities ceased. A variety of teachers participated in these schools. With the end of Reconstruction in 1877 and the withdrawal of federal occupation troops from the South, a new approach to institutionalized schooling, industrial education, which did *not* promote opportunities for advancement of any kind, came into being.

Northern efforts to educate former slaves occurred in two stages. While the Civil War was still being fought educational endeavors relied solely on religion-based, philanthropic support from abolitionists. The education of runaway slaves began in 1861 in Virginia with volunteers sent and supported by the American Missionary Association (AMA). Based in New York City, the AMA sponsored additional schools on the "coastal islands of Virginia, the Carolinas, and Georgia."[72] Early in 1862, the Boston Educational Commission, along with other, similar groups, joined the AMA in these activities. Not all of these associations were white. Northern African American religious groups created the African Civilization

Society and sponsored schools in many Southern states. Nevertheless, the AMA became the "most prominent of the northern freedmen's aid societies."[73] Because of these efforts, "by the end of 1865 there were schools in all eleven Confederate states plus Maryland, the District of Columbia, Kentucky, Kansas, and Missouri." The success of these well-intentioned early educational efforts were mixed. The educators faced a volatile social context and a fluid military situation.[74] The war's end, however, brought some stability to the educational scene.

Freedmen's Bureau

The second stage of schooling for newly freed slaves was more formal and systematic. Supported by the New England Freedmen's Aid Society, the National Relief Association of New York, the Pennsylvania Freemen's Relief Association, the Western Freedmen's Aid Committee, and other groups, the concept of using government authority and sponsorship of freedmen's activities was first presented to President Abraham Lincoln in November 1863. The Bureau of Refugees, Freedmen, and Abandoned Lands, generally known as the Freedmen's Bureau, became an official operation under the auspices of the Department of War in early 1865. In May, President Andrew Johnson appointed Major General Oliver Otis Howard as director of the bureau. The bureau provided facilities, materials, and transportation "while the northern freedmen's aid societies supplied and paid the teachers."[75] The educational goals proved to be modest. The purpose was simply to aid the transition between slavery and freedom, which involved basic literacy training, instruction in the basic notions of democracy, and normal school training. "By 1870, five years after the end of the war, there were about 7,000 teachers in the South, instructing some 250,000 black students."[76]

Yankee Schoolmarms?

It is commonly believed that only Northern whites served as bureau teachers. Indeed, they did play a crucial role, but African Americans and Southern whites participated as well.

Females comprised 65 to 85 percent of the total bureau instructional corps, in conformity with the nineteenth-century pattern of the feminization of teaching. "The 'average' Yankee teacher was a white, unmarried woman under forty years of age, quite likely living in Massachusetts, New York or Ohio at the time of her appointment." They all had to be professed Christians, even though the appointments were nonsectarian. However, the bureau banned Catholic candidates out of "fears that Rome was making a concerted effort to bring southern blacks into the Church." And the strong anti-Semitic feelings of the time also ruled out Jewish applicants. The overwhelming majority of these women had completed some form of higher education; most were drawn from a variety of Northern state normal schools while others were "recruited from such prestigious institutions as Harvard, Yale, Brown, Amherst, Williams, and Mt. Holyoke." They also came from a variety of backgrounds, but the majority appeared to have been involved in some way with social reform. A few had taught in Northern African American schools, and many others had been avowed abolitionists. Josephine S. Griffing, who had become a bureau teacher in Washington, D.C., had used her Ohio home as part of the underground railroad as well as actively participated in the feminist movement, campaigning for women's suffrage and equal rights.[77] These women proved to be highly committed and serious, as historian Nancy Hoffman asserts: "Whether the teachers believed that ultimately they were doing god's work by awakening the religious spirit or doing democracy's work by preparing the freed people to be landowners, office holders, voters, and friends, they made their decision to leave home with similar activities in mind—feeding the hungry, clothing and housing the refugees, and teaching reading and writing."[78]

African Americans were strongly represented in this group of teachers. "Between 1867 and 1870 the American Missionary Association's proportion of African-American teachers and missionaries jumped from 6 percent to 20 percent." Most came from the North but others were increasingly Southerners. Commissioner Howard subsidized teacher-training opportunities for African American candidates. Most were ministers, but "also included in the ranks of the freedmen's teachers were farmers, blacksmiths, mechanics, businessmen, lawyers, and even editors." Many were former slaves. As you may recall from Chapter 4, Harriet Jacobs, who had escaped to the North, returned to Alexandria, Virginia in 1862. By 1864, sponsored by New York Quakers, she and her daughter, Louisa, ran the most important African American school in that city.[79]

Although they shared the same mission, racial prejudice barred social equality between white and African American instructors. Some Northern white teachers, although they worked with African American colleagues, objected to interacting with them outside of the classroom. In Kentucky, white instructors refused to eat with their African American counterparts. In Virginia, North Carolina, and Mississippi, local supervisors organized segregated boarding arrangements. Many African American teachers had to board with local African American families. Numerous African American instructors complained to the AMA about the racist attitudes of some of their Northern white colleagues, but the AMA itself sent African American teachers to the "most undesirable locations, such as small rural schools, and assigned them to teach only primary grades."[80] Regardless, African American instructors established "an important leadership group not only in education but in religion and politics as well."[81]

A variety of Southern whites also worked as bureau teachers. Pragmatism, not idealism, was usually behind their participation. Some taught to gain control over what African American children learned. "In one school taught by two native whites, the children were not only whipped frequently but forced to address their teachers as 'massa' and 'missus.' "[82] Many others were Southern Unionists who could find no other employment in their communities, which had ostracized them for their political beliefs. And still others were Southern planters who "maintained schools to prevent their laborers from leaving the plantation in search of greater educational opportunities."[83]

Generally speaking, students and teachers had to overcome difficult, if not dangerous, conditions. One Northern white female instructor marveled at how adults and children walked up to six miles to attend school. Work demands prevented many African American children from attending day school; therefore they often attended evening school, usually after 8:00 P.M. Early school buildings were rudimentary; in some cases, stables and warehouses served as schoolhouses. Often, the local African American church hosted classes. "In Savannah, the Bryant Slave Mart was converted into a school; the windows in the three-story brick structure still had their iron grates, the handcuffs and whips found inside became museum pieces, and the children were taught in what had been the auction room."[84] Even when actual school buildings existed, they too proved to be crude, as one Northern white female teacher described it in 1865: "The school shed has no floor, and the rains sweep clear across it, through the places where the windows should be. I have to huddle the children first in one corner and then in another, to keep them from drowning or swamping."

Many Northern white teachers also faced serious racial barriers. Southern whites remained at best skeptical and some were outright hostile to educating newly freed slaves. They regarded the African American intellect as inferior and educational efforts as therefore useless. Whites burned schoolhouses throughout the rural South. Furthermore, many Southern whites ostracized and vilified Northern whites as "nigger teachers." Local storekeepers refused to give them credit. Other white Southerners harassed the instructors, even physically threatened them. Maria S. Waterbury, a Northern white who taught in the Deep South, recalled how she and her students responded to this danger: "In the upper story of the plantation house, we are guarded by freedmen . . . who build great bonfires, and we hear them in their night watches, talking and sometimes singing. They are paying dear for their first attempt at starting school."[85]

The Freedmen's Bureau's schools sponsored far less ambitious educational goals than African Americans themselves preferred. Bureau instructors taught basic literacy as well as social skills: "Obedience to law, respect for personal and property rights, honesty, industry, economy, sectional and racial harmony." Morris correctly labels this as a "conservative educational philosophy." Textbooks, such as *The Freedman's Third Reader*, "stressed racial accommodation" and were generally "moderate" in tone. Both Northerners and Southerners saw this type of socialization as crucial to save former slaves from "barbarism," "vice," and general social upheaval. This attitude eventually translated into "self-help" efforts among African Americans, which were expressed in such efforts as the Hampton Normal and Agricultural Institute, which we will turn to shortly.[86]

In sum, the bureau's largely paternalistic attitude and approach bred dependence rather than independence, subordination rather than equality. "From the outset, in fact, the movement to educate the freedmen had been biracial." Litwack elaborates: "The entrance of Union troops into a community often set in motion efforts among black residents to collect sufficient funds to build a school and hire a teacher." Many officials of the Northern freedmen's societies, however, saw African Americans as incapable of educating themselves and took over these efforts. They comfortably relied on the belief "that black people emerging from the debilitating thralldom of bondage would require for some time the counsel and direction of their white allies."[87] In short, they presumed they knew best what African Americans needed.

"By the early 1870s, the picture of black southern education was changing."[88] First, Northern aid societies, which had never made a permanent commitment to southern African American education, began to withdraw their support. "In 1870 the American Missionary Association sustained 157 common schools. That number had declined to 70 in 1871 and to 13 in 1874."[89] And the withdrawal of federal troops from the South in 1877 was largely the cause of the dismantling of the educational activities of the Freedmen's Bureau. Also, many of the freedmen's schools became absorbed into a segregated public school system. Finally, Northern and Southern whites began to support "a new group of institutions," ones committed to segregated industrial education. Hampton Normal and Agricultural Institute created in 1868 in Virginia was the prototype of these institutions, of which the most publicity was given to Tuskegee Normal and Industrial Institute, founded and led by Booker T. Washington.[90]

Southern Industrial Education

According to Anderson, "the freedmen's educational revolution bred a counterrevolution." The power and influence of the Southern planters remained largely intact after the Civil War. "In 1880, 75.4 percent of the South's labor force was in agriculture. Black agricultural laborers constituted more than 40 percent of the South's total agricultural force and formed a clear majority in several southern states." The planter class preferred to retain control over this labor force, and in this education played a vital role. "Their interest in the schooling of Afro-American children differed in social origin and purpose from the ex-slaves' educational movement and even from the interests of the most conservative missionary societies." For all intents and purposes, industrial education reflected the dual educational agenda of Southern planters during slavery: work skills training and social control.

Hampton Normal and Agricultural Institute

General Samuel Chapman Armstrong, a former Freedmen's Bureau agent who served as Hampton's principal between 1868 and 1893, profoundly shaped the institute's educational philosophy and program. He was an extreme social conservative, so much so that Hampton Institute endorsed Jim Crow laws and a picture of Robert E. Lee was displayed in the chapel. "He identified with the conservative wing of southern reconstructionists who supported new forms of external control over blacks, including disenfranchisement, segregation, and civil inequality." In short, Armstrong supported the notion of a subordinate role for African Americans in a segregated society. He viewed African Americans as "culturally and morally deficient and therefore unfit to vote and hold office in 'civilized' society." Sharing many of the same racial perspectives as Southern planters, he saw education as an important tool for preparing African Americans for their social and economic roles.[91]

Hampton Institute was the institutional manifestation of Armstrong's social and educational attitudes and philosophy. Hampton's boarding school approach was adopted to facilitate the socialization process. "The 'average Negro student,' according to Armstrong, needed a boarding school so that his teachers could 'control the entire twenty-four hours each day—only thus can old ideas and ways be pushed out and new ones take their place.' " The boarding school environment, eliminated, of course, the family's influence. Furthermore, Armstrong did not focus on training African American students in the skilled trades, which would give them economic independence and provide social mobility; rather, he stressed semiskilled or unskilled work training to reinforce a sense of general subordination.

Hampton's three-pronged educational program followed from this social goal. The academic program emphasized rudimentary literacy training. The work training part of the program required that all students perform a varying amount of manual work. This manual work was the core of the entire educational experience. Students toiled anywhere from two to six ten-hour days a week for three years. Farm laborers, students learning domestic skills, and sawmill hands worked the most. Finally, the school maintained a rigid routine. A typical day began at 5:45 A.M. and continued until 9:00 P.M. Work, prayer, study, and military drill monotonously filled students' days, with short breaks for meals. Little leisure time existed in this highly structured environment.[92]

The "Negro Moses"

In an 1895 address at Fisk University, Booker T. Washington lauded industrial education and criticized the abstractness of pure academic studies: "The educated colored men must, more and more, go to the farms, into the trades, start brick yards, sawmills, factories, open coal mines; in short, apply their education to conquering the forces of nature."[93] As he saw it, all education had to be utilitarian. No figure better symbolized the Southern industrial education movement than Washington. Not only a product of this educational model, he became its most visible and prominent advocate.

Washington was born into slavery in Franklin County, Virginia, sometime in the late 1850s. In his autobiography, *Up From Slavery*, he recalled growing up in meagre surroundings:

> The cabin was without glass windows; it had only openings in the side which let in the light, and also the cold, chilling air of winter. There was a door to the cabin—that is something that was called a door—but the uncertain hinges by which it was hung, and the large cracks in it, to say nothing of the fact that it was too small, made the room a very uncomfortable one.

He and his siblings "slept in and on a bundle of filthy rags laid upon a dirt floor." Washington received no schooling as a slave child, yet carried the books for the slave owner's children and waited for them outside the schoolhouse. His family moved to Malden, West Virginia, in 1865, where he worked in a salt mine and attended night school. Washington abandoned the salt mines for the coal mines but hated this job, fearing injury or death. He eventually became a house servant for the salt mine's owner. In 1871, Washington applied for admission to Hampton Institute. His entrance examination consisted of cleaning a room:

> I swept the recitation-room three times. Then I got a dusting-cloth and I dusted it four times. All the woodwork around the walls, every bench, table, and desk, I went over four times with my dusting cloth. Besides, every piece of furniture had been moved and every closet and corner in the room had been thoroughly cleaned.

Based on this thorough and conscientious effort, school officials admitted Washington. He worked as a school janitor to subsidize his board, toiling until late at night and rising at 4:00 A.M. to start the fires.

Washington recalled his Hampton experiences as positive and as shaping his entire life. He adored General Armstrong, who he perceived as "superhuman" and "Christlike." Washington saw the key benefit of his education as learning to work: "At Hampton I not only learned that it was not a disgrace to labour [sic] but learned to love labour. . . . " Following graduation, Washington returned to Malden and began a lifelong commitment to education by becoming a teacher. Armstrong invited him back to Hampton in 1879 in order to supervise the first class of Native Americans at the school. Two years later Washington accepted the principalship of Tuskegee Normal and Industrial Institute in Alabama.

Washington literally created Tuskegee out of nothing. There was no land or buildings and he began the school by renting a "dilapidated shanty near the coloured [sic] Methodist church, together with the church itself as a sort of assembly-room." During the first year, Washington managed to purchase an abandoned plantation and move the school to its new location. Teachers and students used the existing plantation buildings at first. Much of what followed conformed to the industrial education model pioneered at Hampton. Tuskegee's students constructed all of the new buildings, as Washington recalled:

> . . . I was determined to have the students do not only the agricultural and domestic work, but to have them erect their own buildings. My plan was to have them, while performing this service, taught the latest and best methods of labor, so that the school would not only get the benefit of their efforts, but the students themselves would be taught to see not only utility in labour, but beauty and dignity; would be taught, in fact, how to lift labour up from mere drudgery and toil, and would learn to love work for its own sake.

Student labor continued, resulting in the construction of some forty buildings. For Washington, "the same principle of industrial education has been carried out in the building of our wagons, carts, and buggies, from the first."

Manual labor was central to the Hampton–Tuskegee model of education and, in fact, racial relations. Equipped with proper work attitudes, African Americans trained at Tuskegee would become indispensable to society. These individuals would serve as shining examples for their race. For Washington, "the whole future of the Negro rested largely upon the question as to whether or not he should make himself, through his skill, intelligence, and character of such undeniable value to the community in which he lived that the community could not dispense with his presence."[94] Indispensability and respectability, in Washington's mind, would evolve into acceptability and eventually result in equality. The anti-intellectualism of this was clear. Abstract intellectual acuity and knowledge beyond basic literacy were simply ill-suited for a segregated world. Basic survival of African Americans in the short run with gradual racial tolerance in the long run through perseverance, hard work, and deference were Washington's social and educational goals.

Washington garnered significant and powerful moral and financial support for Tuskegee and for Southern industrial education in general. He raised funds by traveling throughout the North. John D. Rockefeller made contributions and Andrew Carnegie donated $20,000 to Tuskegee's library. "The Hampton Idea was supported actively by Ulysses S. Grant, Rutherford B. Hayes, James A. Garfield, Theodore Roosevelt, William Howard Taft, Woodrow Wilson, Julius Rosenwald, George Eastman, Charles W. Eliot, Jabez L. M. Curry, and Clark Howell, to name only a few." This support came at a high price. William H. Baldwin, Jr., Northern railroader, Southern educational leader, and Tuskegee trustee, advised Southern African Americans: "Avoid social questions; leave politics alone; continue to be patient; live moral lives; live simply; learn to work . . . know that it is a crime for any teacher, white or black, to educate the negro for positions which are not open to him." As we saw earlier, the John F. Slater Fund subsidized many industrial education efforts in the South, especially at Tuskegee. In addition to gaining the support of Northern politicians, businessmen, and philanthropists, the industrial education approach "constantly gained support" among "southern whites."[95]

Washington became a national figure with his renowned "Atlanta Exposition Address" on September 18, 1895. In it, he proclaimed his racial and educational philosophy to whites and African Americans alike. He saw the "agitation of questions of social equality" as "extremist folly." He urged that African Americans "learn to dignify and glorify common labour"; this would solve the social chasm between the races. An enthusiastic reporter for the *New York World* labeled Washington as the "Negro Moses" for his views.[96]

Opposition

But while Washington was advocating a patient and peaceful approach to raising the status of the African American, Southern Whites were lynching some 2,500 African Americans during the last two decades of the nineteenth century. In the face of this racial violence, Washington intertwined racial accommodation and industrial education. Many African Americans disagreed with him. In fact, the Hampton-Tuskegee concept of education had only a small number of supporters among African Americans.[97]

Washington faced internal as well as external conflict over his educational ideas. Many students at both Hampton and Tuskegee resented their education. In 1887, Hampton's male students protested being trained as handymen and not as skilled craftsmen, such as carpenters and bricklayers, and submitted a petition. African American writers and leaders criticized Hampton for its "Confederate orientation."[98] Similar problems arose at Tuskegee. Many students there objected, as Washington recalled, to "being taught to work." Their parents also lodged complaints. "Most of the new students," Washington further noted, "brought a written or a verbal request from their parents to the effect that they wanted their children taught nothing but books. The more books, the larger they were, and the larger the titles printed on them, the better pleased the students and their parents seemed to be."[99]

African American attacks on Washington, particularly on his educational theories and practices, intensified after his Atlanta speech. The Northern and Southern intelligentsia offered particularly strong opposition. They criticized him, first, for being too conciliatory toward Southern whites and, second, for not aggressively pursuing civil rights for his race. Some African American organization even threatened to boycott Tuskegee, the educational embodiment of Washington's racial philosophy. "In 1905 these black leaders organized themselves into the Niagara Movement, which aggressively and unconditionally demanded for blacks the same civil rights and privileges which other Americans enjoyed."[100] The most articulate and forceful voice of this organization came from W. E. B. DuBois.

Thus, during the latter half of the nineteenth century, Southern African Americans struggled long and persistently to secure schooling for their children. They sought knowledge, opportunity, and basic rights. Northern and Southern whites, for a variety of reasons, pursued a different educational agenda, one with limited intellectual, economic, social, and political goals. The situation proved to be different in the North, but not remarkably so.

RACE AND *THE CRISIS* IN THE NORTH

The North's long policy of segregation condemned most African American children to poor facilities, few resources, and ultimately an inferior education. Nevertheless, some educational experiences did exist that afforded a few African American youths unprecedented opportunities.

Northern Schooling

For decades following the Civil War, Northern urban school districts for the most part continued their policies of segregation. Between 1860 and 1874, the California legislature and judiciary either banned "mixed" schools or upheld segregated education. Although the state of Illinois outlawed segregated schools in 1889, most local educational officials flaunted the law by maintaining separate institutions. African American activists, protested such practices. "In integrated schools, Frederick Douglass said in 1872, black and white children 'will learn to know each other better, and be better able to cooperate for mutual benefit.' "[101] Many African Americans, however, defended separate schooling, for two reasons: first, to protect their children from insults, threats, and harassment from white teachers and classmates, and second, to provide teaching opportunities for the African American intelligentsia. In the latter case, "[b]ecause the job ceiling in white institutions and the poverty of African American communities severely restricted careers for the African American middle class, teaching had great prestige and frequently attracted highly educated African American men and women." Desegregated schools often meant the loss of job opportunities for these instructors. For example, no more African American teachers were employed after the New York City school district officially desegregated in 1873. By 1908, desegregated Northern cities rarely, if ever, hired African American instructors—Los Angeles and Pittsburgh employed no African American teachers while Boston claimed only three.

Despite the segregation, the often poor conditions, and the exclusion of African American teachers, African Americans maintained their faith in education. "In 1890 a larger percentage of African Americans as a proportion of the St. Louis African American population attended public school than whites—18.7 percent as opposed to 12.9 percent." The literacy rate among Philadelphia's African American youths, ages ten to twenty, reached 96 percent in 1897.[102]

W. E. B. DuBois

Some individual African Americans benefited from the somewhat more tolerant racial situation after the Civil War. W. E. B. DuBois was among them. His ideas about racial equality and in particular schooling for African Americans that aimed to preserve the status quo applied both to the South and the North, where African Americans continued to face persistent white resistance to desegregated schooling.

DuBois had an upbringing very different from Booker T. Washington's. Born in the small town of Great Barrington, Massachusetts, in 1868 and abandoned by his father, DuBois lived with his ill mother until she died in 1885. Thereafter, the local African American community and his aunt assumed responsibility for him. DuBois attended neighborhood schools and achieved a highly successful academic record at the town's integrated high school. While a student, he wrote occasional articles for local newspapers as well as New York's African American *Globe*.

With support from the town's white and African American churches, DuBois enrolled at Fisk University, an African American school located in Nashville, Tennessee. There he immersed himself in the classical curriculum, studying Latin, Greek, history, and natural sciences, among other subjects. He became editor of the school's newspaper and spent his summers teaching at a small, rural elementary school.

Fisk also injected him into a different social reality, that of an African American elite and the racially hostile South. DuBois's classmates were often the "sons and daughters of slaves," usually from Southern towns and cities. Although some were poor and others affluent, they "comprised an elite, confident, leadership class," who would face racial prejudice and segregation and struggle for their rights. DuBois was also introduced to blatant white Southern racism and its violent manifestations. He now lived in the South, where the long and brutal epidemic of lynchings of African Americans had begun. "Many fellow students went about armed when they left campus to go into the city."

After DuBois graduated from Fisk in 1888, he attended Harvard University to further his education but first had to complete additional undergraduate courses there. "Harvard and Yale traditionally required African American baccalaureates to repeat a portion of their undergraduate training, a requirement frequently imposed on white graduates of undistinguished colleges." DuBois majored in philosophy and graduated cum laude in 1890. He immediately pursued graduate work in history at Harvard, completing his studies in 1892. That same year DuBois received a rare two-year fellowship from the John F. Slater Fund to extend his graduate study at the University of Berlin, one of Europe's premier institutions of higher learning. After returning from highly successful study in Germany, DuBois taught classics at Wilberforce University in Ohio. He spent countless hours preparing for classes as well as completing his highly acclaimed doctoral dissertation, *Suppression of the African Slave Trade to the United States, 1638–1870*, which was published by Harvard in 1896.

Leaving Wilberforce in 1896 for a temporary appointment at the University of Pennsylvania, DuBois researched and published the renowned study *The Philadelphia Negro*. He interviewed some 2,500 families to compile the data for this project, which depicted the result of that city's racism: absolutely deplorable living conditions. Published in 1899 and highly praised at the time, it became a sociological classic.

In 1897, DuBois accepted a faculty position at Atlanta University, where he continued his prolific career. He edited the Atlanta University's Studies, which produced a series of publications between 1898 and 1910 treating different aspects of African American life and culture. As historian David Levering Lewis notes, "DuBois's professional research placed him in the vanguard of social-science scholarship in America." Although he remained at Atlanta University for twelve years, DuBois as early as 1899 began to grow increasingly uncomfortable with the pervasiveness of Southern white racism. He was shocked by the lynching and burning of a local African American, alarmed by the 1898 race riot led by whites in Wilmington, North Carolina, and tired of the persistent racial epithets hurled at him by whites as he and his wife harmlessly strolled down Atlanta's streets. During this period as well, DuBois grew anxious about Booker T. Washington's avoidance of the notion of racial equality. Although DuBois had corresponded with Washington over the years and visited Tuskegee on a couple of occasions, he began to see Washington's racial philosophy and educational practices as contributing to the erosion of equal rights. The publication of *Up From Slavery* created the ultimate ideological break between Washington and DuBois.[103]

In 1903, DuBois published *The Souls of Black Folk*, a landmark work. In it, he clearly outlined the issue of race in almost prophetic terms: "The problem of the twentieth century is the problem of the color line. . . ." He provided a context by briefly describing the historical struggles of African Americans: enslavement and resistance, emancipation but disenfranchisement, the frustration and hopelessness of sharecropping, and social subordination. DuBois devoted an entire chapter to a critique of Booker T. Washington. Although Washington was widely acclaimed and accepted by Southern and Northern whites, DuBois reported, he had met with strong opposition and rebuke among African Americans: ". . . there is among educated and thoughtful colored [sic] men in all parts of the land a feeling of deep regret, sorrow, and apprehension at the wide currency and ascendancy which some of Mr. Washington's theories have gained." DuBois was of the opinion that Washington accepted "submission" for his race because of its perceived "inferiority." In another chapter, in a swipe at Washington's educational scheme, DuBois argued that education in general and higher education in particular should serve to liberate minds and produce leaders, not suppress thinking and rationalize subordination. He encouraged the development of what he called the "Talented Tenth." The "Negro College," DuBois continued, "must maintain the standards of popular education, must seek the social regeneration of the Negro, and it must help in the solution of problems of race contact and cooperation. And finally, beyond all this, it must develop men."[104] Following the publication of *The Souls of Black Folk*, "DuBois was recognized as Washington's chief opponent."[105]

The opposition soon assumed institutional form. In 1905, DuBois mobilized twenty-nine African American leaders, who met in Fort Erie, Ontario, because discrimination prevented their meeting in Buffalo, to create the Niagara Movement to strive for equal rights. DuBois wrote the original draft of the "Declaration of Principles," which opposed **de jure segregation** and supported equal voting rights, housing, jobs, and education. This organization held annual meetings until 1910, when it merged with a group composed of "white socialists and liberals" to form the National Association of Colored People (NAACP). DuBois abandoned the intellectual life at Atlanta University and moved to New York City to found and edit *The Crisis*, the NAACP's "official organ," which he edited until 1934. Under his editorship, *The Crisis* served as a significant and effective voice for the NAACP. It decried lynchings, fought for race consciousness and pride, criticized establishment newspapers, like the *New York Times*, for poor coverage of African Americans, and included poetry and fiction.[106]

The North offered, in a relative sense, only slightly better educational opportunities than the South. African American parents encountered segregated schools for their children and some fought against them. The emergence of articulate and talented leaders like DuBois, the creation of newspapers and other publications, such as *The Crisis*, and the founding of advocacy organizations, such as the NAACP, laid the groundwork for future, more fruitful attempts to achieve educational equality. Nevertheless, secondary education remained virtually inaccessible to Southern and Northern African American children alike.

Until the early twentieth century, secondary education continued to be an elite institution, accommodating only a fraction of eligible students.

THE EMERGENCE OF THE URBAN HIGH SCHOOL

By the 1880s, the public high school had become an important urban educational institution, the culmination of decades of institution building. This higher form of learning grew directly from efforts of the elite to preserve the social and economic status quo in a highly stratified society.[107]

Early Patterns

Clear distinctions between levels of education did not exist during the colonial period. Colonials relied largely on European institutional traditions, and the Latin grammar school, through classical training, prepared students for direct admission to the professions or college. The classical curriculum included "Latin, Greek, rhetoric, logic, arithmetic, geometry, astronomy, natural and moral philosophy." Having completed this course of study, scholars would then have to pass rigorous, yet somewhat informal and unsystematic, oral examinations to gain admission to college; some of the applicants were as young as ten years of age.[108]

The first instance of an interstitial educational experience, one sandwiched between grammar school and college, grew out of the importance Puritans assigned to education. They created the Boston Latin School in 1636, which only enrolled the boys of wealthy and influential families to prepare Boston's privileged sons for admission to Harvard College. As a partially tax-supported school, Boston Latin stressed the European classical curriculum.[109]

Academies

The Latin grammar school remained dominant until the late eighteenth century, when the academy began to appear. "People no longer saw schooling as appropriate only for future professionals but as desirable also for tradesmen and farmers, businessmen and merchants." The typical academy encompassed a variety of levels of schooling, what we now call elementary, secondary, and higher education. Thus the schools were multipurpose institutions, including academic subjects as well as practical skills.[110]

Academies proliferated throughout the United States during the late 1700s and early 1800s; there were over 6,000 nationwide by 1850. Every region hosted them and in both urban and rural areas, but mostly they were located in the rural areas of the East and Midwest. As historian William J. Reese asserts, "Mixed academies and female seminaries boomed in Illinois and Ohio. Illinois chartered at least 125 academies and seminaries between 1818 and 1848; Ohio incorporated approximately 100 between 1803 and 1840." And the South particularly embraced private academies.[111]

Most academies maintained an affiliation with some religious denomination. "Chartered as quasi-public ventures, like banks or canals, these academies were generally controlled by private boards of trustees. But they often received public funds and eagerly accepted all students who would attend and could pay the fees." Until the end of the Civil War, private academies and public high schools competed for dominance in secondary education, with the latter ultimately victorious. Nonetheless, academies maintained a considerable presence until well into the late nineteenth century.[112]

The People's College

The high school, a largely urban development, was an outgrowth of the common school and was the successor to the academy. Boston pioneered publicly supported secondary education with the creation of the English Classical School for Boys in 1821, which changed its name to Boston English High School three years later. The Boston school offered a practical curriculum of English, geography, history, and other academic subjects. The establishment of English High marked the beginning of a new era and the apex of the academy system.

The campaign for the establishment of high schools unfolded in earnest between the 1830s and 1880s. Proponents invoked native-Protestant ideology (refer to Chapter 4) in support. Horace Mann, among other common-school reformers, attacked private schools, particularly academies, because they seemed to attract the better element of society, thus fragmenting it: "Mann believed that wealthy families always set the standard for education." Therefore, in order to draw them to the public school system and to persuade them to subsidize it willingly through public revenue, the private academies had to be eliminated. Thus a vigorous campaign against them began.

Private academies were decried by reformers as antirepublican; public high schools were promoted as fulfilling dual purposes: imbuing the individualistic values of a bourgeois society and ensuring the continuation of the republic. The high school would operate as part of a meritocracy in which only the talented few would advance. Jeffersonian notions of the necessity of a literate electorate and an enlightened leadership likewise prevailed. Reese summarizes this historical development: Whigs, and later Republicans, in state after state, "praised individual responsibility and merit in a land where dependency increased. . . . And they ultimately persuaded enough people that centralized, hierarchical institutions represented the fulfillment of republican ideas."

Cities became the centers of high school development and growth. "In larger cities and smaller towns, the northern middle classes sought to eliminate academies, to centralize town control over districts, and to build an educational system that would provide sound moral and intellectual training from the elementary through higher branches." Philadelphia opened its famous Central High School in 1838; Baltimore followed a year later, Cleveland in 1846, and Cincinnati and Hartford in 1847.[113] "By 1851, eighty cities had public high schools." They all maintained practical curricula.

Michigan's 1874 Kalamazoo court decision, according to historian Jurgen Herbst, served as the "magna carta" of the American public high school. Opponents of the public high school saw its program as narrow and serving a small elite. High schools therefore should charge tuition for those obviously best able to pay for this next level of education. Charles E. Stuart, a resident of Kalamazoo and former Democratic state representative and U.S. Senator, challenged the use of tax dollars to subsidize high schools by filing suit. The lower courts ruled against him; he appealed to the state supreme court, which, in

1874, likewise ruled against him. The public high school, both as concept and institution, thus had legal credibility, much to the joy of Republicans and school reformers everywhere.

In Search of an Identity

The demand for secondary education increased steadily during the last half of the century. Yet, by 1890, high schools "enrolled only 6.7 percent of the country's fourteen- to seventeen-years-olds." In the Midwest and West, high schools grew as an extension of the common-school tradition and as part of a "democratic imperative," as Herbst terms it. "Here the distinctions between people's college and connecting-link high school, between preparing for life and preparing for college, were unimportant. Having grown up, as it were, grade by grade out of the local district school, the high school began to be seen as an advanced common school." Still, by the late 1800s, high schools appeared to be rare in rural communities, largely remaining an urban institution.

In spite of an expanding enrollment, the dual mission of the high school remained quite unsettled. Did high schools prepare students for college, or did they prepare them for life? The Yale Report of 1827 promoted the concept of liberal education in secondary schools. The Committee of Ten addressed this notion once again in 1893 in an attempt to clearly identify the educational role of the high school. The National Education Association appointed an executive committee (the Committee of Ten) in 1892 to review the scholastic function of public high schools and more clearly articulate the differences between them and colleges and universities. Led by Charles W. Eliot, president of Harvard University, the committee completed its deliberations a year later; Eliot was the main author of its report, which for the most part "revived the spirit of the Yale Report with its definition of secondary education as training and disciplining the mind through academic studies and argued that the approach should be retained."[114] Although students could enroll in four different programs of study, the committee's report recommended a common set of courses: Latin, Greek, mathematics, English, modern languages, natural history, physical science, geography, and history. The committee declared "that every subject which is taught at all in a secondary school should be taught in the same way and to the same extent to every pupil . . . no matter what the probable destination of the pupil may be, or at what point his [sic] education is to cease." Even so, the Committee of Ten largely perceived the high school as an elite, academically oriented institution that was to prepare its students for higher education.[115]

The efforts of the Committee of Ten eventually led to the process of high school accreditation. This, in turn, enhanced articulation between high schools and colleges. The high school capped the public school institutional hierarchy. Nevertheless, and in spite of the democratic rhetoric declaring it the "people's college," it did not serve as a means of mass education during the late nineteenth century. The Committee of Ten in 1893 saw it serving "a small proportion of all the children in the country."[116]

According to Herbst, the American public viewed the high school differently: "Most Americans had come to view their schools as advanced common schools and servants of community interests." The committee emphasized academic preparation, while "school administrators and local school boards" saw the high school's mission as broader and more inclusive, embracing "practical training" and attracting ever more students.[117]

"What ye learn in school ain't no good"

The emergence of public high schools seemingly fulfilled the democratic ideal of free schooling for all, but they failed to serve the needs of the whole population. "In the 1830s far more non-farm youths entered apprenticeships than attended high schools that would have fitted them for a wider variety of careers in those segments of the economy that were growing most rapidly." The lure of mechanical pursuits, the reverence for tradition, and the promise of higher earnings continued to attract young people to apprenticeships. But the 1837 depression, according to historian W. J. Rorabaugh, marked a turning point. Many masters went bankrupt, business opportunities dried up, wages fell, and the standard of living declined.[118] Apprenticeship no longer offered the best promise of a secure future, but secondary education did. According to Carl Kaestle's analysis,

> precise studies of high schools in Chicago, New York, and Salem in the 1850s partially confirm that . . . [s]ons of clerks, merchants, proprietors, craftsmen, and professionals attended. . . . A few factory workers' sons appeared on the rolls, but the lower working class is severely underrepresented. The trend in graduates' careers was toward white-collar work, both clerical and professional, regardless of whether the boys' fathers worked in manual or non-manual jobs. The New York graduates of 1858 included a brass turner's son who became a lawyer, a machinist's son who became a bookkeeper.

The ongoing decline in the demand for skilled labor and the growing insecurity of work, Kaestle asserts, prompted craftsmen, more and more, to send their sons to high school instead of arranging an apprenticeship experience for them. "Some fathers with such artisan labels may have been substantial craftsmen or even proprietors of their own businesses; however, because of changes from craft to factory production, some members of this artisan group may have felt anxious about their positions and their sons' futures."[119]

The growing demand for unskilled labor in the workplace offered children of unskilled parents in contrast to those of the middle class endless opportunities. Some families needed the children's income to ensure their very survival; other parents saw work as educational, teaching values and skills necessary for economic survival. Ever so gradually, though, as attested to by mid-century attendance patterns among some craftsmen's sons, schooling was beginning to function as a bridge to a job. With the decline of crafts, schooling was seen as the source of new values, skills, and job security. Changes in the work process and the need to work, therefore, influenced family decisions concerning the importance of schooling.

The relationship between many poor and working-class parents and schooling was also characterized by resistance for other reasons. Families struggled to retain control of their children as work grew increasingly unskilled and the struggle for survival intensified. Some families resented the imposition of educational authority over their children. They confronted teachers and administrators about school values and procedures, and they withheld their children from the schools in protest. According to 1880 data from the St. Louis schools, "80 percent of sons of professional fathers and 64 percent of the sons of white-collar workers between the ages of thirteen and sixteen were in school, compared to only 32 percent of sons of unskilled workers." While many boys chose not to attend high school, girls did, and often in overwhelming numbers: One rough estimate for 1866 indicates that female secondary students outnumbered males by a margin of two to one.[120]

The declining demand for skilled work, which systematically, though unevenly, reduced the need for and number of skilled laborers, profoundly affected family income and roles. An 1893 statistical analysis of workers in the coal, iron, and steel industries, for example, revealed that the husband's average earnings only accounted for 85 percent of the total income necessary to support a family. This report included only the wages of skilled workers, such as "foremen, miners, engineers, masons, etc."[121] They, of course, received the highest wages, which allowed them to better support their families than their semi-skilled and unskilled counterparts. These latter groups faced serious financial difficulties. Yet, in spite of the disruptions of factory life, the working-class family remained intact and stable even as it grew increasingly unskilled and was often underemployed and unemployed. According to historian Virginia Yans-McLaughlin, the family functioned as a "working productive unit" in order to resolve the income shortfall of the paternal parent.[122] It employed a variety of strategies, either singly or in combination, such as taking in boarders, finding employment for mothers, and sending the children to work. The first two options often proved difficult, which left child labor as the only viable option to augment the income of the hard-pressed working-class family.

Family Strategies

In order to survive, poor and working-class parents chose to send their children to work when there was no other available option. Often, they saw little connection between schooling and the workplace. They had access to a source of extra income and exploited it. There were few obstacles in their way. "In 1899, there were still twenty-four states and the District of Columbia without a minimum-age requirement for children employed in manufacturing."[123] With the existence of weak state compulsory attendance laws, like those passed by Massachusetts in 1852 and Connecticut in 1871, which excused poor children from school in order to work, schooling became even more easily expendable.[124] Thus, schooling throughout the nineteenth and early twentieth centuries appeared to be a matter of choice rather than compulsion. Working children were common in rural, preindustrial, and early industrial life. Reinforcing all of this was the common belief that work at a young age was a virtue, not a vice, and taught children diligence, discipline, and responsibility: "Overwork . . . was a preferable alternative to over coddling."[125]

Rural children especially led "semi-autonomous" lives. "Boys of all ages were expected to be at home during the summers, in order to help their families with the heavy work of farming. But in the winter and spring they might well go off to look for work elsewhere, in activities such as lumbering or fishing, or clerking in one of the commercial towns that were sprouting so rapidly across the land." Schooling thus became an afterthought.[126]

Children were a source of labor in urban, industrial America as well. During a Senate investigation of relations between labor and capital in the 1880s, George Blair, a box manufacturer, testified that children produced between 40 and 50 percent of the manufactured goods in New York State, and a New York City tailor confessed that he saw six-year-olds working in the nation's largest cotton mill. In 1880, 29 percent of all males employed in the glass industry were under sixteen years of age. According to the 1910 census, an estimated 2 million children below the age of sixteen worked; 26 percent of cotton textile workers in 1907 claimed to be younger than sixteen. Schooling became so expendable that, in 1914, 60 to 65 percent of all children abandoned it as early as the fifth or sixth grades.[127] This trend assumed gender and social-class differences over time. During the first decade of the twentieth century, "17 percent more girls than boys completed elementary school." In ninth grade, girls comprised 63 percent of the high school student body, and by the twelfth grade they constituted 73 percent. Historians David B. Tyack and Elizabeth Hansot compared enrollments by social class and found "fewer working-class boys than working-class girls continued in school, suggesting that males dropped out more often to work."[128] Social class, more than any other variable, however, determined entry into the workforce. "Families opting to keep their children in school longer were 'better off' in a number of ways: their fathers had higher incomes and higher status jobs, they lived in less crowded homes which they were more likely to own, and they found it possible to live within their means."[129]

Child workers faced brutal conditions. While the majority of cotton textile workers earned between $5 and $6 per week in 1910, full-time working children younger than sixteen seldom made more than $3. Almost half of the children employed in industry worked at least ten hours a day. In the metal trades, 92 percent of the children under sixteen worked more than fifty-four hours a week, and 32 percent of these worked a sixty-hour week. Schooling, as they saw it, did little to increase their earning power. As one young factory worker expressed it to Helen Todd, a factory inspector, who published her 1909 survey of Chicago's child labor: "What ye learn in school ain't no good. Ye git paid as much in the factory if ye never was there. Our boss he never went to school."[130]

School offered long-term intangible rewards, while work, which remained easily accessible, guaranteed immediate monetary gains and potential future opportunities. A 1916 U.S. Department of Labor study of the conditions for child and women wage earners determined the value of this trade-off. The report, encompassing the cotton and silk textile, clothing, and glass industries, found that children aged fourteen and fifteen accounted for 18.3 percent of their family's incomes. For the majority of families, work demands too often superseded schooling. Thus, the cult of domesticity, the ideal of a tight-knit nuclear family with a working paternal parent and maternal parent remaining at home to serve as wife and mother and maintain the household, proved to be possible only for the affluent members of society:

> For every nineteenth-century middle-class family that protected its wife and child within the family circle, then, there was an Irish or a German girl scrubbing floors in that middle-class home, a Welsh boy mining coal to keep the home-baked goodies warm, a black girl doing the family laundry, a black mother and child picking cotton to be made into clothes for the family, and a Jewish or an Italian daughter in a sweatshop making "ladies" dresses or artificial flowers for the family to purchase.[131]

The relationship between the family, schooling, and work during the Victorian era, as is often the case today, depended on social-class background.

Divorce and Family Structure

The late-nineteenth-century family also appeared to be experiencing other strains, further shaping its attitudes toward schooling. "After mid-century, popular literature on domestic life poured out a long litany of complaints: divorce and desertion were increasing; child-rearing had become too casual and permissive; authority was generally disrupted; the family no longer did things together; women were more and more restless in their role as homemakers."[132] Between 1850 and 1880, there was a national furor over high divorce rates because the "number of divorces had increased faster than the population and faster than the married population." The United States led the world in divorce at that time. Many Americans, according to historian Glenda Riley, saw "their marriage vows as a dissolvable contract." For these Americans, divorce did not represent a "social problem," marriage did. In fact, a variety of organizations and advocates challenged the concept and practice of marriage. Utopian communities, such as the Shakers, rejected marriage altogether. Feminists like Elizabeth Cady Stanton viewed divorce as confronting the patriarchal family structure. Free love proponents saw marriage as a type of forced servitude.

By the late nineteenth century, several clear demographic patterns relating to divorce had emerged. Women applied for 67 percent of the divorces, largely on the grounds of cruelty. The Western states and territories led the nation in divorce rates, followed by the North and the South, respectively. By the 1890s, the Dakotas and Oklahoma had assumed a dubious reputation as "divorce mills." Western migration and settlement undertaken alone by husbands, causing them to be absent from their families for long periods of time, were disruptive to the traditional family structure and routine. In some instances, the deserted partner sued for abandonment. Despite the higher divorce rates in the West, divorces were more numerous in American cities. Finally, particularly in the West, courts usually awarded women, who were most often seen as natural nurturers, custody of their children as well as alimony payments. This trend reversed previous notions that fathers owned their children.[133]

As we have seen, public school enrollment steadily increased during the nineteenth century. However, just because parents signed their children up for school does not mean that they actually attended. The goal throughout the century was to maximize attendance. School completion was another matter. In the setting of the nineteenth century, graduation simply did not matter. Schooling was not then, as it is now, required for a job. Nineteenth-century and early twentieth-century youths could secure meaningful work without it. Students abandoned high school education, if they even progressed that far, because they preferred to work, or had to work.[134] Moreover, high school enrollment, attendance, and completion was a function of social-class expectations well into the twentieth century. Cultural tradition or sheer survival shaped families' decisions about schooling for their children.

In sum, the high school during the nineteenth century remained a modest, if not fledgling, institution, reserved for the social and economic elite. Although often "housed in a palatial building" in cities, by 1890 the average high school hosted a mere 80 students and 3.6 teachers. Attendance varied with location, of course. Small-town and rural high schools claimed only an average of 52 students and 2 instructors each while their urban counterparts typically consisted of 355 pupils and 12 teachers. Only 11 percent of all high-school-aged students graduated by 1890.[135] With the advent of the Progressive education movement, much of this would change.

THE PUBLIC SCHOOL BUREAUCRACY

The latter half of the nineteenth century saw the refinement and expansion of the public schools in the North, West, and South through regulatory laws. As we saw in Chapter 4, democratic localism had been the typical mode of school organization during the first half of the nineteenth century. Rural, largely homogeneous, communities assumed full responsibility for their local schools. They generally opposed state control and disapproved of the training and professionalization of teachers, especially through state-sponsored normal schools. This notion of school organization presumed an implicit "faith in the people."[136] In the growing cities, ward control, a "village pattern of schooling," dominated governance.[137] However this decentralized approach could produce conflict in the heterogeneous cities. As historian Michael B. Katz points out, local control in the wrong hands could promote tyranny by imposing a narrow set of religious or political views on a minority through the schools. By the second half of the nineteenth century, "incipient bureaucracy" began to supplant "democratic localism" as the model for school organization.[138]

Systemization of the Schooling Process

The nineteenth-century factory "inspired" many educators to reorganize and systemize urban schools. Graded schools were one manifestation of this industrial influence. Many educators, including Horace Mann of Massachusetts and Calvin Stowe of Ohio, acknowledging the lead of the Prussian state school system in implementing graded schools, relied on industrial jargon to promote the idea in the United States. Historian Stanley Schultz describes the rhetoric:

> It assumed that children arrived at school in pre-packaged units according to age and intellectual abilities. Those units could be grouped together for convenience and efficiency, and run through the school as though on an assembly line. When the children completed the last grade, they graduated—finished products as far as the school was concerned.

The schools thus served as factories and the children as products. This "mechanistic" approach was first introduced at the primary and grammar levels by the Boston School Committee (BCS) in 1847. The BCS attempted to rationalize the schooling process. "The graded school was to be one of the chief tools used in the process of manufacturing good Americans."[139] By the 1860s, most city schools were graded. The emergence of a sequenced and coherent curriculum with standard examinations followed. "Through an elaborate system of gradation, programmed curricula, examinations, and rules for 'deportment,' then, the pupil learned the meaning of obedience, regularity, and precision."[140]

Students' individual needs became subsumed to a rigid system of age grouping as they moved from one grade to another each year. If a child did not progress to the next level, then educators thought something was wrong with the student, not the system. The uniform approach did not tolerate purported laggards and slackers and diverse learners in general. Educators never questioned the inflexible graded routine. The mechanistic approach eventually produced a differentiated curriculum, separating academic students from their vocational counterparts and segregating "normal" children from those who had special needs, which seemed like the most efficient solution to the problem of students who did not fit well into the system.[141]

The Move from Local to State Control

The drive toward systemization had characteristics other than age grouping. The concepts of centralization and supervision ensured that there were state secretaries of education to over see the entire school system and district superintendents to operate at the local level. Furthermore, the development and expansion of state normal schools ensured standard training for teachers.[142] The gradual emergence of such a public school "system" reflected the twofold influence of school "legislation" and school "regulation."[143] The fact that legislation concerning schools was passed by state legislatures formalized the notion of a system and centralized authority in the state capital. This system then matured, spread, and became bureaucratized through subsequent state "regulation," which included state mandates regarding the school year, teaching certification, curricular matters, and, of course, funding. Finally, the development of a system was also related to needs of scale, that is, as enrollment increased and the number of teachers grew, coordination became a concern and this resulted in gradual centralization.

The shift of control of school matters from the local to the state level was clearly illustrated in Pennsylvania, a heavily populated and industrialized state, which only slowly and painstakingly instituted a state system of public education. From 1834 to 1850, because of state law, authority for school matters like teacher certification moved from the local level to the county level. Bureaucratic centralization at the state level did not occur until after the 1874 constitution, which eliminated any residual local power as well as county authority. The state grew more confident and assertive in school matters as it attempted to establish a uniform and standardized state public education system. Over the next fifty years, the state assembly passed an unprecedented series of laws and regulations addressing the academic month and year, teacher certification, salaries, and retirement, compulsory attendance, availability of free textbooks, and high schools. The 1911 Pennsylvania School Code, passed in the midst of the halcyon days of the Progressive education era, was followed by the 1920 Edmonds Act, both of which institutionalized the modern state public education system in Pennsylvania.[144] Generally speaking, the introduction of efficiency and centralization, among other reforms, would produce the modern system of school governance, as we will see in the next chapter.

By the end of the nineteenth century, the district school, appeared to be an anachronism. The modest and haphazard local community initiatives and support for schooling during the late eighteenth century were forced to yield to the process of formalization and rationalization through the next century by the growth in education. A rapidly industrializing and urbanizing society, increasing in racial and ethnic diversity, would require the public schools to expand their scope and function as well.

CONCLUSIONS

Nineteenth-century school culture was quite different from that of the present day. Tiny, isolated, rural common schools housed a single instructor and the community's children, who were usually all of the same ethnic and religious backgrounds. Teachers were ill-prepared and only informally supervised.

During the latter half of the nineteenth century, the public schools underwent significant changes. Schools assumed more and more responsibilities and became, with the westward movement, part of the acculturation process. Following the Civil War, public schools gradually expanded to include secondary education, and as the United States became an urban society, schooling and its administration gradually grew more formal. Increasing enrollment was a primary goal, but gradually, as enrollment figures rose, this shifted to attendance. The first state compulsory school laws passed during the latter half of the nineteenth century.

The American family continued to assert ultimate authority over its children, deciding whether to send them to work or school, but this too began to shift. The family's role and structure underwent changes that altered its relationship to schooling and ability to educate children.

Westward migrations, cultural conflicts, industrialization, urbanization, and changing ideas about marriage itself all shaped the family in profound ways. As a result, the local community and nuclear family gradually assumed less responsibility for the education of children, and the state began to formalize the expanding school system.

As American families changed, as the educational experiences of children became more formalized, as society grew more urban, schooling assumed an expanded role. Much of the institutionalization and expansion of schooling that began during this period would be refined and extended between 1890 and 1920, during the Progressive education movement.

ACTIVITIES FOR FURTHER EXPLORATION

1. What were the racial and ethnic backgrounds of the Western settlers? Southern African Americans and European immigrants emigrated, established settlements, and endured hardships. Three such experiences, "In Search of Eden: Black Utopias in the West," "A German Jewish Woman Settles in North Dakota," and "A Mormon Woman's Life in Southern Utah," can be found at http://chnm.gmu.edu/us/many.taf.

2. How did Native American and European American cultures differ? The expansion of European American settlements in the West profoundly disrupted Native American lifestyles and culture. An oral history, " 'We Didn't Have Flies Until the White Man Came': A Yankton Sioux Remembers Life on the Plains in the Late Nineteenth Century," recalls in both in text and audio form some of the routines of Native American culture: http://chnm.gmu.edu/us/many.taf.

3. Did all Native Americans resist the Americanization process? Two oral histories, at http://chnm.gmu.edu/us/many.taf, " 'The White Man's Road is Easier!': A Hidatsa Indian Takes up the Ways of the White Man in the Late Nineteenth Century" and " 'All That Is Passed Away': A Young Indian Praises U.S. Government Policy in the Late Nineteenth Century," illustrate compliance rather than resistance. Why did these individuals conform to government policy?

4. The Washington–DuBois debate represents a profound disagreement about educational and social philosophy and policy. Two excerpts, "Making the Atlanta Compromise" and "Equal and Exact Justice to Both Races," from Washington's autobiography, *Up From Slavery*, as well as a rare audio version of his famous speech, "Cast Down Your Bucket Where You Are" and DuBois's attack on Washington, "W.E.B.

DuBois Critiques Booker T. Washington," can be found at http://chnm.gmu.edu/us/many.taf.

5. To gain further historical insight into the sequence of events in African American history, refer to the "Timeline of African-American History": http://lcweb2.loc.gov/ammem/aap/timeline.html. See as well http://memory.loc.gov/ammem/ndlpedu/index.html. If you want to see an actual picture of a "Rosenwald School" and read about its history, refer to http://www.cr.nps.gov/nr/feature/afam/soo 1/nr_properties.htm.

6. How was racial violence justified? The white Southern rationale for the violence that was inflicted on African Americans can be found in the graphic " 'Their Own Hotheadedness': Senator Benjamin R. 'Pitchfork Ben' Tillman Justifies Violence Against Southern Blacks" at http://chnm.gmu.edu/us/many.taf. At this same web site you will find sharply contrasting views: "Burned in Memory: An African American Recalls Mob Violence in Early Twentieth-Century Florida" and "Defending Home and Hearth: Walter White Recalls the 1906 Atlanta Race Riot."

7. What was a sharecropper? How was the tenant farmer experience similar to slavery? Was it different? How did it affect children's lives? Read one tenant farmer's recollections, "A Georgia Sharecropper's Story of Forced Labor, c. 1900", or listen to the voices of two other sharecroppers, " 'Still Livin' Under the Bonds of Slavery': Minnie Whitney Describes Sharecropping at the Turn-of the-Century" and "A Year's Wage for Three Peaches: A Black Man Tells of Exploitation in the Late Nineteenth-Century South," at http://chnm.gmu.edu/us/many.taf.

VIDEO EXPLORATIONS

1. What dangers did the pioneers face moving West? See "The Donner Party" (Alexandria, VA: PBS Home Video, 1992), a video in the *American Experience* series. It illustrates, through primary documents, photographs, and diary narratives, the motives of these pioneers as well as the dangers and tragedies of this fatal journey. Pay special attention to the experiences of the company's children.

2. How did Anglo European settlement affect the North American Pueblos? A fourteen-minute (starting at 73 minutes and ending at 87 minutes) clip from the video, *Surviving Columbus* (Alexandria, VA: PBS Home Video, 1992), nicely illustrates the 1846–1912 period, including the 1847 Pueblo Revolt.

3. Should education serve an assimilationist agenda? The Indian boarding school experience is poignantly captured with oral histories and original photographs and film footage in an *American Experience* treatment "In the White Man's Image" (Alexandria, VA: PBS Home Video, 1992). Preface this with a reading from " 'Kill the Indian, and Save the Man': Capt. Richard C. Pratt on the Education of Native Americans," at http://chnm.gmu.edu/us/many.taf.

NOTES AND SOURCES

In order to condense endnotes, the first work cited is the primary one, usually the source of any direct quotes. Subsequent references serve as supplementary, or additional, sources of paraphrased information and/or alternative historical interpretations.

1. Forten is quoted in Nancy Hoffman, *Woman's "True" Profession: Voices from the History of Teaching* (Old Westbury, NY: Feminist Press, 1981), p. 149.

2. Julie Roy Jeffrey, *Frontier Women: The Trans-Mississippi West, 1840–1880* (New York: Hill and Wang, 1979), pp. xi–xii, 27; Elliot West, *Growing Up with the Century: Childhood on the Far Western Frontier* (Albuquerque, NM: University of New Mexico Press, 1989), p. 13.

3. West, *Growing Up*, p. 13. Also, see Jeffrey, *Frontier Women*, p. xi; Linda Peavy and Ursula Smith, *Frontier Children* (Norman, OK: University of Oklahoma Press, 1999), pp. 3–4, 11–12, 39.

4. Jeffrey, *Frontier Women*, pp. 3–4, 26, 28, 37.

5. West, *Growing Up*, p. 13. Also refer to Emmy E. Werner, *Pioneer Children on the Journey West* (Boulder, CO: Westview Press, 1995), p. 1.

6. Jeffrey, *Frontier Women*, pp. 39, 40, 41, 42, 44–45. See as well Linda Peavy and Ursula Smith, *Pioneer Women: The Lives of Women on the Frontier* (Norman, OK: University of Oklahoma Press, 1996), pp. 21–22, 23, 35, 44–45. The "meadow mushroom" reference is on pp. 30–31.

7. The quote is from Werner, *Pioneer Children*, p. 129. Refer, as well to Jeffrey, *Frontier Women*, p. 40; Peavy and Smith, *Frontier Children*, pp. 4, 17, 22, 24–25; West, *Growing Up*, pp. 29–32, 33–34.

8. West, *Growing Up*, pp. 35, 38, 39, 46. Also see Jeffrey, *Frontier Women*, p. 40; Peavy and Smith, *Pioneer Women*, pp. 40, 41; Peavy and Smith, *Frontier Children*, pp. 17, 18, 21, 24–25; Werner, *Pioneer Children*, p. 142. The skull quote is from Peavy and Smith, *Frontier Children*, p. 22.

9. Werner, *Pioneer Children*, pp. 21, 23, 129; Winnemucca is quoted on p. 23. Peavy and Smith, *Frontier Children*, pp. 15, 28, 31, 41, 45, also include Winnemucca's recollection.

10. Jeffrey, *Frontier Women*, pp. 44, 51; Peavy and Smith, *Frontier Children*, p. 18.

11. West, *Growing Up*, pp. 52, 54, 55, 63. Refer as well to Jeffrey, *Frontier Women*, p. 53; Peavy and Smith, *Pioneer Women*, pp. 47, 50–53; Peavy and Smith, *Frontier Children*, p. 51.

12. Jeffrey, *Frontier Women*, pp. 56, 57, 58. See likewise Peavy and Smith, *Pioneer Women*, pp. 60–63, 81–82; Peavy and Smith, *Frontier Children*, pp. 55–57.

13. The quotes in these paragraphs are from West, *Growing Up*, pp. 74, 76–78, 80, 105, 148, 180–181, 182, 184–185. Also, see Jeffrey, *Frontier Women*, pp. 70, 71; Peavy and Smith, *Frontier Children*, pp. 64–65; Werner, *Pioneer Women*, pp. 149, 150.

14. Jeffrey, *Frontier Women*, pp. 79, 80, 85, 87, 88. Refer also to Peavy and Smith, *Frontier Children*, p. 124.

15. West, *Growing Up*, pp. 189, 190, 191–192, 198, 199. See also Jeffrey, *Frontier Women*, pp. 87–88; Peavy and Smith, *Pioneer Women*, pp. 120, 122.

16. Quoted in Hoffman, *Woman's "True" Profession*, p. 63. Also, see Jeffrey, *Frontier Women*, pp. 89, 92.

17. Polly Welts Kaufman, *Women Teachers on the Frontier* (New Haven, CT: Yale University Press, 1984), pp. 17, 18.

18. West, *Growing Up*, pp. 201, 203, 204. Refer as well to Jeffrey, *Frontier Women*, p. 91.

19. Peavy and Smith, *Frontier Children*, pp. 37, 49, 133.

20. David Wallace Adams, *Education for Extinction: American Indians and the Boarding School Experience, 1875–1928* (Lawrence, KS: University of Kansas Press, 1995), pp. 7, 12, 18, 20, 21–24, 25, 26–27. Also refer to David H. DeJong, *Promises of the Past: A History of Indian Education* (Golden, CO: North American Press, 1993), p. 107; Jon Reyhner and Jeanne Eder, *A History of Indian Education* (Billings, MT: Eastern Montana College, 1992), pp. 42, 53–54; Margaret Connell Szasz, *Education and the American Indian: The Road to Self-Determination Since 1928* (Albuquerque, NM: University of New Mexico Press, 1999), pp. 8, 9.

21. The Commission's quote is from DeJong, *Promises of the Past*, pp. 108–109.

22. Adams, *Education for Extinction*, pp. 26–27. For missionary educational efforts, many subsidized by federal funds, refer to Michael C. Coleman, "The

Responses of American Indian Children to Presbyterian Schooling in the Nineteenth Century: An Analysis through Missionary Sources," *History of Education Quarterly,* 27 (Winter 1987), pp. 473–497, and *American Indian Children at School, 1850–1930* (Jackson, MS: University Press of Mississippi, 1993), pp. 41, 45.

23. Reyhner and Eder, *History of Indian Education,* p. 42. The quote is on p. 50. See also Adams, *Education for Extinction,* p. 30; Coleman, *American Indian Children at School,* p. 42; DeJong, *Promises of the Past,* p. 107; Szasz, *Education and the American Indian,* pp. 10–11.

24. Adams, *Education for Extinction* pp. 31–32; Szasz, *Education and the American Indian,* pp. 10–11.

25. Dole is quoted in Coleman, *American Indian Children at School,* pp. 42–43, and Jones is quoted on p. 46. Refer as well to Adams, *Education for Extinction,* pp. 36, 46; Brenda J. Child, *Boarding School Seasons: American Indian Families, 1900–1940* (Lincoln, NE: University of Nebraska Press, 1998), p. 6; DeJong, *Promises of the Past,* p. 107; Peavy and Smith, *Frontier Children,* pp. 119–123; Reyhner and Eder, *History of Indian Education,* pp. 79–80; Szasz, *Education and the American Indian,* pp. 9, 10.

26. Zitkala-Sa is quoted in Coleman, *American Indian Children at School,* p. 82; see also pp. 17, 79.

27. The long quote is from Reyhner and Eder, *History of Indian Education,* p. 87; also see pp. 79, 80, 82, 83, 85. See likewise Adams, *Education for Extinction,* pp. 36, 46, 97, 101, 103, 108; Child, *Boarding School Seasons,* pp. 5–6, 29, 30–31, 39, 40; Coleman, *American Indian Children at School,* p. 45; Szasz, *Education and the American Indian,* p. 10.

28. Stewart is quoted in Coleman, *American Indian Children at School,* pp. 112–113. Refer also to Adams, *Education for Extinction,* pp. 144, 145, 150, 153, 156. Child's interpretation in *Boarding School Seasons,* pp. 73, 75, 76, 79, 80, closely parallels that of Adams, although Coleman illustrates more student ambivalence.

29. Pratt is quoted in DeJong, *Promises of the Past,* pp. 110–111. See as well Adams, *Education for Extinction,* pp. 157, 163; Child, *Boarding School Seasons,* pp. 82, 85; Coleman, *American Indian Children at School,* p. 43.

30. Geronomo is quoted on p. 65 while the student is quoted on p. 61 of Coleman, *American Indian Children at School.* Refer likewise to Child, *Boarding School Seasons,* pp. 12, 15–16, 17; Szasz, *Education and the American Indian,* pp. 11, 12

31. The quote is from Adams, *Education for Extinction,* p. 307; also see pp. 211, 214, 223, 244. Refer as well to Child, *Boarding School Seasons,* pp. 12, 15–16, 17; Coleman, *American Indian Children at School,* p. 65; Szasz, *Education and the American Indian,* pp. 11, 12.

32. Reyhner and Eder, *History of Indian Education,* p. 89. Also refer to Adams, *Education for Extinction,* p. 216; Child, *Boarding School Seasons,* p. 13.

33. The Senate subcommittee is quoted in DeJong, *Promises of the Past,* p. 118. See as well Adams, *Education for Extinction,* pp. 212, 214; Child, *Boarding School Seasons,* pp. 43, 87; Coleman, *American Indian Children at School,* pp. 166–167.

34. Adams, *Education for Extinction,* pp. 231, 233–234; Child, *Boarding School Seasons,* pp. 27, 87, 93, 94.

35. The health report is quoted in DeJong, *Promises of the Past,* p. 108; also see p. 117. Likewise refer to Child, *Boarding School Seasons,* pp. 55, 56, 57, 62.

36. Child, *Boarding School Seasons,* pp. 66, 67. See as well Coleman, *American Indian Children at School,* p. 162.

37. The quotes in these paragraphs are from Adams, *Education for Extinction,* pp. 277, 278, 280, 291, 319, 326. Refer as well to Child, *Boarding School Seasons,* p. 97; Coleman, *American Indian Children at School,* pp. 179, 180, 182; DeJong, *Promises of the Past,* p. 111; Reyhner and Eder, *History of Indian Education,* p. 84, 90; Szasz, *Education and the American Indian,* p. 10.

38. Reyhner and Eder, *History of Indian Education,* p. 99; Child, *Boarding School Seasons,* p. 2, makes a similar claim.

39. Joan W. Moore, *Mexican Americans* (Englewood Cliffs, NJ: Prentice-Hall, Inc., 1976), p. 12.

40. Martha Menchaca, "The Treaty of Guadalupe Hidalgo and the Racialization of the Mexican Population," in *The Elusive Quest for Equality: 150 Years of Chicano/Chicana Education,* ed. Jose F. Moreno (Cambridge, MA: Harvard Educational Review, 1999), pp. 3, 19, 20–21, 23–24. See as well Victoria-Maria MacDonald, "Hispanic, Latino, Chicano, or 'Other?' ": Deconstructing the Relationship between Historians and Hispanic-American Educational History," *History of Education Quarterly,* 41 (Fall 2001), p. 394.

41. Rodolofo Acuña, *Occupied America: A History of Chicanos* (New York: Harper & Row, 1981), pp. 109, 111–114; Ramirez is quoted on p. 110.

42. The quotes in these paragraphs are from Guadalupe San Miguel, Jr., "The Schooling of Mexicanos in the Southwest, 1848–1891," in *The Elusive Quest for Equality: 150 Years of Chicano/Chicana Education*, ed. Jose F. Moreno (Cambridge, MA: Harvard Educational Review, 1999), pp. 32–33, 34, 35, 37, 39, 40–44. See also Acuña, *Occupied America*, pp. 114, 115; Eliot West, *Growing Up with the Century: Childhood on the Far Western Frontier* (Albuquerque, NM: University of New Mexico Press, 1989), pp. 188–189.

43. Guadalupe San Miguel, Jr., *"Let All of Them Take Heed": Mexican Americans and the Campaign for Educational Equality in Texas, 1910–1981* (Austin, TX: University of Texas Press, 1987), pp. 2, 3–4, 6–7, 9–10, 11, 12. Refer as well to Arnoldo De Leon, *The Tejano Community, 1836–1900* (Albuquerque, NM: University of New Mexico Press, 1982), pp. 187–194.

44. Lynne Marie Getz, *Schools of Their Own: The Education of Hispanos in New Mexico, 1850–1940* (Albuquerque, NM: University of New Mexico Press, 1997), pp. 5, 6, 7. Gilbert G. Gonzalez, *Chicano Education in the Era of Segregation* (Philadelphia: Blach Institute, 1990), p. 15, is careful to point out that New Mexico represents a unique case and, until the 1940s, did not necessarily typify Mexican American educational experiences throughout the Southwest. See MacDonald, "Hispanic, Chicano, or 'Other?' " p. 394, for her discussion of Getz.

45. Susan M. Yohn, "An Education in the Validity of Pluralism: The Meeting between Presbyterian Mission Teachers and Hispanic Catholics in New Mexico, 1870–1912," *History of Education Quarterly* 31 (Fall 1991), pp. 345, 346. Refer to MacDonald, "Hispanic, Chicano, or 'Other?,' " p. 395, and Acuña, *Occupied America*, pp. 52–54.

46. Getz, *Schools of Their Own* pp. 13–14, 15, 23, 34, 25.

47. Yohn, "An Education in the Validity of Pluralism," pp. 347, 349–350, 352, 353, 354, 355, 356–357, 359. See as well Susan M. Yohn, *A Contest of Faiths: Missionary Women and Pluralism in the American Southwest* (Ithaca, NY: Cornell University Press, 1995), pp. 77–78. Jay P. Dolan and Giberto Hinojosa, eds., *Mexican Americans and the Catholic Church, 1900–1965* (South Bend, IN: University of Notre Dame Press, 1994), pp. 42–43, also argue that few Catholic Mexican Americans converted. Their conversion figure is 5 percent.

48. John Hardin Best, "Education in the Forming of the American South," *History of Education Quarterly* 36 (Spring 1996), pp. 47, 48, provides solid periodization for Southern education history. Also refer to Harvey G. Neufeldt and Clinton B. Allison, "Education and the Rise of the New South: An Historiographical Essay," in *Education and the Rise of the New South*, eds. Ronald K. Goodenow and Arthur O. White (Boston: G. K. Hall, 1981), pp. 250–251; Wayne J. Urban, "History of Education: A Southern Exposure," *History of Education Quarterly* 21 (Summer 1981), pp. 131–146.

49. James L. Leloudis, *Schooling the New South: Pedagogy, Self, and Society in North Carolina, 1880–1920* (Chapel Hill, NC: University of North Carolina Press, 1996), p. 6.

50. Best, "Education in the Forming of the American South," p. 47. See also Joseph W. Newman, "Antebellum School Reform in the Port Cities of the Deep South," in *Southern Cities, Southern Schools: Public Education in the Urban South*, eds. David N. Plank and Rick Ginsberg (Westport, CT: Greenwood Press, 1990), p. 18; Lawrence A. Cremin, *American Education: The National Experience, 1783–1876* (New York: Harper & Row, 1980), p. 177.

51. Newman, "Antebellum School Reform," pp. 17, 18, 20–21, 23, 28.

52. Louis R. Harlan, *Separate and Unequal: Public School Campaigns and Racism in the Southern Seaboard States, 1901–1915* (New York: Atheneum, 1969), p. 4.

53. Newman, "Antebellum School Reform," p. 30.

54. Marcia E. Turner, "Black School Politics in Atlanta, Georgia, 1869–1943," in *Southern Cities, Southern Schools*, eds. David N. Plank and Rick Ginsberg, p. 179. Also see Michael W. Homel, "Two Worlds of Race? Urban Blacks and the Public Schools, North and South, 1865–1940," in *Southern Cities, Southern Schools*, eds. David N. Plank and Rick Ginsberg, p. 253.

55. Leloudis, *Schooling the New South*, p. 6.

56. James D. Anderson, *The Education of Blacks in the South, 1860–1935* (Chapel Hill, NC: University of North Carolina Press, 1988), pp. 18, 19, 25, 26,

27. Refer as well to Herbert G. Gutman, "Observations on Selected Trends in American Working-Class Historiography," in *Work, Youth and School: Historical Perspectives in Vocational Education, Proceedings of the Conference on the Historical Study of Education and Work*, eds. Harvey Kantor and David B. Tyack (Stanford, CA: Stanford University, August 17–18, 1979), pp. 486–499.

57. Harlan, *Separate* and *Unequal*, p. 5. Also see Cremin, *American Education: The National Experience*, p. 159.

58. Cremin, *American Education: The National Experience*, pp. 149, 159, 177.

59. Leloudis, *Schooling in the New South*, pp. 7, 9, 10, 17.

60. Harlan, *Separate* and *Unequal*, pp. 10, 11, 28.

61. Cremin, *American Education: The National Experience*, pp. 177–178; Harlan, *Separate* and *Unequal*, pp. 121, 136, 234.

62. The quotes in these paragraphs are from Leloudis, *Schooling in the New South*, pp. 18, 19, 20, 23, 37, 60, 145, 146, 147, 148, 182. See as well Anderson, *Education of Blacks*, pp. 83–84; Harlan, *Separate* and *Unequal*, pp. 75, 80, 93; Neufeldt and Allison, "Education and the Rise of the New South," pp. 260–261.

63. Harlan, *Separate* and *Unequal*, pp. 76, 89. Also refer to Leloudis, *Schooling in the New South*, pp. 146, 147, 149–150.

64. Leloudis, *Schooling in the New South*, pp. 150, 151, 181, 195, 213. See also Harvey G. Neufeldt, "Peabody Education Fund," in *Historical Dictionary of American Education*, ed. Richard J. Altenbaugh (Westport, CT: Greenwood Press, 1999), p. 282; Spencer J. Maxcy, "Progressivism and Rural Education in the Deep South, 1900–1950," in *Education and the Rise of the New South*, eds. Ronald K. Goodenow and Arthur O. White (Boston: G. K. Hall, 1981), p. 53.

65. Harlan, *Separate* and *Unequal*, pp. 245, 249, 253, 255, 268. Refer as well to Leloudis, *Schooling in the New South*, pp. 22, 74, 85, 90, 229; Maxcy, "Progressivism and Rural Education," p. 53.

66. All of the quotes in these paragraphs are taken from Leon F. Litwack, *Been in the Storm so Long: The Aftermath of Slavery* (New York: Vintage Books, 1980), pp. 262, 264, 277, 366, 367, 370.

67. Anderson, *Education of Blacks*, pp. 4, 6–7. Also refer to James D. Anderson, "Ex-Slaves and the Rise of Universal Education in the New South,

1860–1880," in *Education and the Rise of the New South*, eds. Ronald K. Goodenow and Arthur O. White, p. 3.

68. Litwack, *Been in the Storm*, p. 494. I substituted "African American" for "Negro" in this quote. See most importantly, Gutman, "Observations on Selected Trends in American Working-Class Historiography," pp. 485–486

69. Anderson, "Ex-Slaves and the Rise of Universal Education," pp. 7, 9, 12. Refer as well to Anderson *Education of Blacks*, pp. 6–7, 11, 12.

70. Anderson, *Education of Blacks*, pp. 12, 17. Also see Linda M. Perkins, "The History of Blacks in Teaching: Growth and Decline Within the Profession," in *American Teachers: Histories of a Profession at Work*, ed. Donald Warren (New York: Macmillan Publishing Company, 1989), p. 348.

71. Anderson, *Education of Blacks*, pp. 18, 28.

72. Hoffman, *Woman's "True" Profession*, p. 92. Refer also to Robert C. Morris, *Reading, 'Riting, and Reconstruction: The Education of Freedmen in the South, 1861–1870* (Chicago, IL: University of Chicago Press, 1981), pp. 2, 3–4.

73. Litwack, *Been in the Storm*, p. 477.

74. Morris, *Reading, 'Riting, and Reconstruction*, p. 12, 13–14, 32.

75. Litwack, *Been in the Storm*, p. 477. Also see Morris, *Reading, 'Riting, and Reconstruction*, pp. 32, 33, 35.

76. Hoffman, *Woman's "True" Profession*, p. 92.

77. Morris, *Reading, 'Riting, and Reconstruction*, pp. 57, 58, 59, 69–70, 71–73, 79, 82.

78. Hoffman, *Woman's "True" Profession*, pp. 92, 95.

79. Morris, *Reading, 'Riting, and Reconstruction*, pp. 85, 91–92, 107–108, 109, 111. Refer also to Litwack, *Been in the Storm*, pp. 495–496; Anderson, *Education of Blacks*, pp. 9–11; Harriet A. Jacobs, *Incidents in the Life of a Slave Girl: Written by Herself*, ed. Jean Fagan Yellin (Cambridge, MA: Harvard University Press, 1987), pp. 225, 249–251; Gutman, "Observations on Selected Trends in American Working-Class Historiography," pp. 486–487.

80. Perkins, "History of Blacks in Teaching," pp. 347, 348. Also, see Morris, *Reading, 'Riting, and Reconstruction*, pp. 126–127, 128, 129; Litwack, *Been in the Storm*, pp. 494–495, 496, 497.

81. Morris, *Reading, 'Riting, and Reconstruction*, p. 130.

82. Litwack, *Been in the Storm*, pp. 488, 489. Refer as well to Morris, *Reading, 'Riting, and Reconstruction*, p. 134.

83. Morris, *Reading, 'Riting, and Reconstruction*, pp. 136–137, 145.

84. Litwack, *Been in the Storm*, p. 475. Also, see Hoffman, *Woman's "True" Profession*, p. 112.

85. Hoffman, *Woman's "True" Profession*, pp. 97, 108, 110, 113, 116, quotes these teachers. Refer as well to Litwack, *Been in the Storm*, pp. 485, 486, 487; Morris, *Reading, 'Riting, and Reconstruction*, p. 65.

86. Morris, *Reading, 'Riting, and Reconstruction*, pp. 150–151, 199–200, 206.

87. Litwack, *Been in the Storm*, pp. 499, 500.

88. Hoffman, *Woman's "True" Profession*, p. 103.

89. Anderson, *Education of Blacks*, p. 30. Also, see Litwack, *Been in the Storm*, p. 493.

90. Hoffman, *Woman's "True" Profession*, pp. 103, 135. Refer as well to Litwack, *Been in the Storm*, p. 493.

91. Anderson has written extensively about the industrial school experience. See his *Education of Blacks*, pp. 20, 31, 36–38. See also Anderson, "Ex-Slaves and the Rise of Universal Education," pp. 15–17.

92. James D. Anderson, "The Hampton Model of Normal School Industrial Education, 1868–1900," in New Perspectives on *Black Educational History*, eds. Vincent P. Franklin and James D. Anderson (Boston: G. K. Hall, 1978), pp. 62, 63, 70–72, 75, 77. Refer as well to Morris, *Reading, 'Riting, and Reconstruction*, pp. 154, 155, 156, 160. See Chapter 2 in Anderson, *Education of Blacks*, for a comprehensive narrative and analysis of the Hampton–Tuskegee social and educational philosophy and program.

93. Booker T. Washington, "Extracts from Address Delivered at Fisk University," in *American Education and Vocationalism: A Documentary History, 1870–1970*, eds. Marvin Lazerson and W. Norton Grubb (New York: Teachers College Press, 1974), p. 68.

94. Booker T. Washington, *Up from Slavery* (New York: Oxford University Press, 1995), pp. 2–4, 19, 22, 23, 26, 31, 32, 34, 35, 43, 44, 62–64, 76, 87, 88, 90, 91, 118.

95. Anderson, *Education of Blacks*, pp. 66, 72, 78 88. Baldwin is quoted on p. 84 of Anderson. Harlan, *Separate* and *Unequal*, also quotes portions of Baldwin's "advice" on p. 78. Also see Washington, *Up from Slavery*, pp. 66, 112, 114, 174; James D. Anderson, "Northern Foundations and the Shaping of Southern Black Rural Education, 1902–1935,"

History of Education Quarterly (Winter 1978): 371–396.

96. Washington, *Up from Slavery*, pp. 121, 128, 131, 140. "Negro Moses" is quoted on p. 140.

97. Anderson, *Education of Blacks*, p. 67; John Hope Franklin, *From Slavery to Freedom: A History of Negro Americans* (New York: Alfred A. Knopf, 1980), p. 313.

98. Anderson, "Hampton Model of Normal School," pp. 78, 79, 80, 82. Refer as well to Anderson, *Education of Blacks*, p. 60.

99. Washington, *Up from Slavery*, p. 91.

100. Anderson, *Education of Blacks*, p. 105. Also, see Harlan, *Separate* and *Unequal*, p. 100; Washington, *Up from Slavery*, pp. 134–135.

101. Douglass is quoted in David B. Tyack, *The One Best System: A History of American Urban Education* (Cambridge, MA: Harvard University Press, 1974), p. 111; also refer to p. 115.

102. Tyack, *One Best System*, pp. 117, 118, 122–123. See also Homel, "Two Worlds of Race?", pp. 243, 244.

103. The quotes in these paragraphs are from a superb biography of DuBois, David Levering Lewis, *W.E.B. DuBois: Biography of a Race* (New York: Henry Holt & Co., 1993), pp. 1, 11, 39, 50, 53, 54–55, 59, 61, 62, 67, 69–70, 73–74, 82, 116–117, 151, 155, 180, 190, 205, 206–207, 208, 211, 212, 225–228, 233, 245, 256, 263–264. Refer as well to Manning Marable, *W.E.B. DuBois: Black Radical Democrat* (Boston: Twayne Publishers, 1986); Arnold Rampersad, *The Art and Imagination of W. E. B. DuBois* (New York: Schocken Books, 1990), pp. 41, 47, 49, 50–51, 53–54, 55; W. E. Burghardt DuBois, *The Souls of Black Folk: Essays and Sketches* (1903 rpt.; Greenwich, CT: Fawcett Books, 1961), pp. vii, viii.

104. DuBois, *Souls of Black Folk*, pp. 45, 46, 48, 58, 85, 87, 89. See Lewis's, *W.E.B. DuBois*, Chapter 11, and Rampersad's, *Art and Imagination of W.E.B. DuBois*, Chapter 4, for detailed analyses of *Souls of Black Folk*.

105. Anderson, *Education of Blacks*, p. 107. Likewise refer to Lewis, *W.E.B. DuBois*, pp. 261, 288.

106. Rampersad, *Art and Imagination of W.E.B. DuBois*, pp. 91, 99, 133, 139–150. Refer also to Anderson, *Education of Blacks*, p. 108; Harlan, *Separate* and *Unequal*, p. 99; Lewis, *W.E.B. DuBois*, pp. 316, 321, 330.

107. William J. Reese, *The Origins of the American High School* (New Haven, CT: Yale University Press, 1995), p. 6.

108. Jurgen Herbst, *The Once and Future School: Three Hundred and Fifty Years of American Secondary Education* (New York: Routledge, 1996), pp. 13, 20. Refer as well to Frederick Rudolph, *The American College and University: A History* (New York: Vintage Books, 1962), pp. 24–25.

109. Reese, *Origins of the American High School*, p. 3. Also see Robert L. Osgood, *For "Children Who Vary from the Normal Type": Special Education in Boston, 1838–1930* (Washington, DC: Gallaudet University Press, 2000), p. 21.

110. Herbst, *Once and Future School*, pp. 19, 20. For the latest historiographical interpretation of the impact and significance of the academy see Kim Tolley, Nancy Beadie, Margaret A. Nash, and Bruce Leslie, "Reappraisals of the Academy Movement," *History of Education Quarterly*, 41 (Summer 2001), 216–271.

111. Reese, *Origins of the American High School*, pp. 29, 30. See also Tyack, *One Best System*, pp. 57.

112. David B. Tyack, *Turning Points in American Educational History* (New York: John Wiley & Sons, 1967), p. 120. Also refer to Reese, *Origins of the American High School*, p. 33; Tolley et al., "Reappraisals of the Academy Movement."

113. The quotes in these paragraphs are from Reese, *Origins of the American High School*, pp. 2, 3, 28, 29, 33, 37, 40, 41, 48–49, 50, 51, 52, 53. See as well Herbst, *Once and Future School*, pp. 41, 42, 43, 45, 50, 53. Tolley et al., "Reappraisals of the Academy Movement," refute the commonly held notion of academies as elitist institutions. They, in fact, catered to a broad range of social classes, although they mainly served the rural and urban middle class.

114. The quotes in these paragraphs are from Herbst, *Once and Future School*, pp. 42, 45, 62, 63, 64, 65, 66, 107, 108. Also see Herbert M. Kliebard, *The Struggle for the American Curriculum: 1983–1958* (Boston: Routledge & Kegan Paul, 1986), pp. 9, 10; Edward A. Krug, ed., *Charles W. Eliot and Popular Education* (New York: Teachers College Press, 1961), pp. 7, 9; Reese, *Origins of the American High School*, pp. 69–70, 76–79; David B. Tyack and Elisabeth Hansot, *Learning Together: A History of Coeducation in American Public Schools* (New Haven, CT: Yale University Press 1990), p. 117. David F. Labaree, *The Making of an American High School: The Credentials Market and the Central High School of Philadelphia, 1838–1939* (New Haven, CT: Yale University Press, 1988), provides an excellent, in-depth analysis of Philadelphia's famous Central High School.

115. Krug, *Charles W. Eliot*, pp. 8–9. Krug, pp. 83–99, includes the entire committee's report. See also Herbst, *Once and Future School*, pp. 109, 116; Kliebard, *Struggle for the American Curriculum*, pp. 10, 12.

116. Tyack, *One Best System*, pp. 57, 58. The Committee of Ten is quoted on p. 58.

117. Herbst, *Once and Future School*, pp. 114, 115–116.

118. W. J. Rorabaugh, *The Craft Apprentice: From Franklin to the Machine Age in America* (New York: Oxford University Press, 1986), pp. 118–119. Parts of this section are taken from Richard J. Altenbaugh, David E. Engel, and Don T. Martin, *Caring for Kids: A Critical Study of Urban School Leavers* (London: Falmer Press, 1995), pp. 31–35.

119. Carl F. Kaestle, *Pillars of the Republic: Common Schools and American Society, 1780–1860* (New York: Hill and Wang, 1983), p. 121. See also Herbst, *Once and Future School*, p. 93; Reese, *Origins of the American High School*, pp. 167, 175; Tyack and Hansot, *Learning Together*, p. 125.

120. Tyack and Hansot, *Learning Together*, pp. 131, 143. Likewise refer to Reese, *Origins of the American High School*, pp. 167, 175.

121. E. R. L. Gould, *The Social Condition of Labor* (Baltimore, MD: Johns Hopkins University Press, 1893), pp. 17, 25.

122. Virginia Yans-McLaughlin, "Patterns of Work and Family Organization: Buffalo's Italians," *Journal of Interdisciplinary History* 2 (Autumn 1971), pp. 302, 308. Refer also to her study, *Family and Community: Italian Immigrants in Buffalo, 1880–1930* (Ithaca, NY: Cornell University Press, 1977).

123. Viviana Zelizer, *Pricing the Priceless Child: The Changing Social Value of Children* (New York: Basic Books, 1985), p. 75.

124. Forest C. Ensign, *Compulsory School Attendance and Child Labor* (1921; rpt., New York: Arno Press, 1969), pp. 68–69, 96–97.

125. Zelizer, *Pricing the Priceless Child*, pp. 59, 67, 100–101. Also see David L. Angus and Jeffrey E. Mirel, "From Spellers to Spindles: Workforce Entry by the Children of Textile Workers, 1888–1890," *Social Science History* 9 (Spring 1985), p. 139; David Nasaw, *Children of the City: At Work and At Play* (New York: Oxford University Press, 1985), p. 42; Joseph M. Hawes, *The Children's Rights Movement: A History of Advocacy and Protection* (Boston: Twayne Publishers, 1991), p. 41.

126. John Demos, *Past, Present, and Personal: The Family and the Life Course in American History* (New York: Oxford University Press, 1986), p. 99.

127. U.S. Senate, *Report Upon the Relations Between Labor and Capital*, (Washington, DC: Government Printing Office, 1885), Volume I, p. 851, Volume II, pp. 6, 67; Department of Labor, Bureau of Labor Statistics, *Summary of the Report on Conditions of Women and Child Wage Earners in the United States*, Bulletin No. 175 (Washington, DC: Government Printing Office, 1916), pp. 40, 130; Richard O. Boyer and Herbert M. Morais, *Labor's Untold Story* (New York: United Electrical, Radio & Machine Workers of America, 1976), p. 184; Zelizer, *Pricing the Priceless Child*, p. 57; S. Alexander Rippa, *Education in a Free Society: An American History* (New York: David McKay, 1976), pp. 157, 159; Stephanie Coontz, *The Way We Never Were: American Families and the Nostalgia Trap* (New York: Basic Books, 1992), p. 13.

128. Tyack and Hansot, *Learning Together*, p. 171. Also see Werner, *Pioneer Children*, p. 3: "By 1850 the United States could claim one of the highest female literacy rates in the world." Herbst, *Once and Future School*, p. 76, provides the attendance figures.

129. Angus and Mirel, "From Spellers to Spindles," p. 139.

130. Department of Labor, *Summary*, pp. 62, 283; Department of Labor, Bureau of Labor Statistics, *Report on the Condition of Women and Child Wage Earners in the United States: Employment of Women in Metal Trades*, Volume II (Washington, DC: Government Printing Office, 1911), p. 28. The quote is from Helen M. Todd, "Why Children Work: The Children's Answer," *McClure's Magazine*, 40 (Nov.–Apr. 1912/1913), p. 74.

131. Coontz, *The Way We Never Were*, pp. 11–12. See as well Department of Labor, *Summary*, p. 30.

132. John Demos, *Past, Present, and Personal*, pp. 30–32.

133. Glenda Riley, *Divorce: An American Tradition* (Lincoln, NE: University of Nebraska Press, 1991), pp. 62, 67, 68, 71, 73, 79–80, 83, 85–86, 87, 89, 91–92, 98, 102.

134. Tyack, *One Best System*, pp. 67–68.

135. Tyack and Hansot, *Learning Together*, p. 136.

136. Michael B. Katz, *Class, Bureacracy, and the Schools: The Illusion of Educational Change in America* (New York: Praeger Publishers, 1975), pp. 15, 18, 20.

137. Tyack, *One Best System*, p. 39.

138. Katz, *Class, Bureaucracy, and the Schools*, pp. 20, 28.

139. Stanley Schultz, *The Culture Factory: Boston Public Schools, 1789–1860* (New York: Oxford University Press, 1973), pp. 126, 131. Also see Tyack, *The One Best System*, p. 41.

140. Tyack, *The One Best System*, pp. 45, 55. Refer as well to Osgood, *For "Children Who Vary from the Normal Type,"* pp. 32, 33.

141. Osgood, *For "Children Who Vary from the Normal Type,"* pp. 35, 38–39, 40–41.

142. Katz, *Class, Bureaucracy, and the Schools*, pp. 33, 35, 36.

143. Carl Kaestle, *The Evolution of an Urban School System: New York City, 1750–1850* (Cambridge, MA: Harvard University Press, 1973), pp. 161–162.

144. Louise Gilchiese Walsh and Matthew John Walsh, *History and Organization of Education in Pennsylvania* (Indiana, PA: R. S. Grosse Print Shop, 1930), pp. 219, 220, 222, 224, 249, 254–256; *100 Years of Free Schooling in Pennsylvania: 1834–1934* (Harrisburg, PA: Department of Public Instruction, 1934), pp. 82, 83; John A Nietz, "The Constitutional Provisions and the Titles of the More Important Laws of Pennsylvania Relating to Schools and Education" (Ph.D. diss. summary, University of Pittsburgh, 1933), pp. 17, 37, 44, 47–51; Katz, *Class, Bureaucracy, and the Schools*, pp. 19–20, 33.

P A R T

III

The Emergence of the Modern American Public School

7

The Progressive Education Movement

J oseph Mayer Rice, a pediatrician and writer for *Forum* magazine in the early 1890s, reported his astonishment at what he discovered in a typical urban public school classroom:

> After entering the room containing the youngest pupils, the principal said to the teacher, "Begin with the mouth movements and go straight through." Complying with the request . . . the teacher directed her attention to the class, and said, "Now let us see how nicely you can make the mouth movements." About fifty pupils now began in concert to give utterance to the sounds of a (as in car), e, and oo, varying their order, thus: a, e, oo, a, e, oo; e, a oo, e, a, oo, . . . , etc.
>
> The mouth movements made by the pupils while uttering these sounds were as exaggerated as the mouths would permit. While uttering the sound "a" the mouth was stretched open as far as it would go; in "e" the corners were drawn as closely as possible to the ears, and in "oo" the lips were pointed. . . .
>
> When some time had been spent, the teacher remarked, "Your tongues are not loose." Fifty pupils, now put out their tongues and wagged them in all directions. . . .[1]

In spite of the many and profound changes in education during the nineteenth century, the modern American school as we know it did not emerge until the Progressive era when between 1890 and 1920 the philosophical foundation and institutional framework for our modern schools appeared. This chapter will first broadly outline the Progressive period and then relate the specific effects of the Progressive movement on education, focusing on its philosophy, pioneers, manifestations, and impact.

THE PROGRESSIVE ERA

The Progressive movement represented a broad response to the changes the country had experienced as it matured during the latter half of the nineteenth century. Industrial capitalism had profoundly altered our culture in the early 1800s, as we saw in Chapter 4. During the late 1800s, industrial capitalism began the transformation to **corporate capitalism**, which was characterized by large-scale industrial production and bureaucratic business organization. Textile mills, steel mills, and other factories now employed tens of thousands of workers instead of a few dozen. Corporations, the new form of business organization, relied on economies of scale to reduce production costs, a vertical hierarchy for decision making, and a large bureaucracy to formalize and manage the entire operation. In 1901, J. P. Morgan created a monopoly in steel with the United States Steel Corporation, capitalized at an unprecedented $1 billion. "Morgan monopolies included electrical machinery (General Electric), communications (American Telephone and Telegraph, Western Union), traction companies (Interborough Rapid Transit in New York,

Hudson and Manhatten), and insurance (Equitable Life)." Morgan interests also "organized super-trusts" in shipping and agricultural machinery.[2] Workers were at the bottom of the pyramid, and from an economic standpoint, survival became more tenuous. The typical employee now faced an overwhelmingly large and impersonal workplace, which contributed to alienation, anger, and confrontation.

The United States had also experienced a "transportation and communications revolution." After the Civil War, the existing railroad system expanded into a cheap and relatively efficient transportation system. "By 1915, when the railroads boasted some 250,000 miles of track, not an important community in the country lay outside this extensive system." Railroads united all "sectors of the economy" and all regions of the country. A national market now supplanted local ones. Communication developments had also "accelerated the tempo of economic life." The telegraph, introduced in 1844 by Samuel F. B. Morse, the rotary press, invented in 1875, and the telephone, patented in 1876 by Alexander Graham Bell, all facilitated communication by making it accessible, fast, and less expensive. "The new communication supplemented the new transportation in creating the highly integrated and complex human relationships inherent in modern industrialism."

The transportation and communications revolution brought about "radical change" in agriculture. The development of national and international markets prompted commercial farming on a mass scale, virtually eliminating subsistence farming. "Instead of producing most of the items needed for his livelihood, the farmer became a specialist, concentrating on those crops that climate, soil, and ability enabled him to produce profitably." Technology played a role as well. The steel plow, invented in 1847, replaced its cast-iron predecessor. The steam-driven reaper, self-binder, and combine increased production and reduced costs. "Between 1830 and 1896 these new implements almost cut in half the time and labor cost of production for all crops; for wheat it reduced the time worked to one-twentieth that required for hand labor, and the labor cost to a fifth of the previous figure." Scientific innovations likewise increased production and fed profits. Farmers began to utilize "specialized dairy cattle breedings, insect and disease control, fertilizer, improved plant varieties, and new methods of preserving perishables," such as refrigeration. As historian Samuel B. Hays summarizes it: "Markets, machinery, and science, then transformed American agricultural from a relatively simple operation, requiring little capital and less knowledge, into a highly complex affair, demanding increasing amounts of investment, equipment, scientific information, and close attention to markets."[3] Farmers now toiled in a world market, in which the individual was dwarfed by scale, dominated by impersonal forces, and increasingly dependent.

The closing of the frontier during this period caused Americans to focus on cities and their inhabitants. "Urbanization proceeded at a faster rate between 1820 and 1860 than any other period of American history."[4] The 1920 census revealed that more than half of all Americans resided in cities. According to Hays,

> [c]ities served as the nerve center of the new economy. To them came labor, capital, and raw materials; from them finished products were dispersed. They became great shipping points, manufacturing centers, and accumulations of capital, skill, and managerial ability. The core of the city was business, around which other human activities arose to fashion a social and cultural as well as an economic community. These industrial centers attracted millions of people from abroad and from the American countryside.

From a culture based on largely agrarian, provincial attitudes and institutions, with small factories, subsistence farming, and local control had come a rapidly emerging, urban, cosmopolitan society, dominated by large-scale manufacturing and farming and governed by largely invisible forces, symbolized by corporations. No part of society remained untouched or unaffected.

Many different groups reacted to these changes and in a variety of ways. Social critics recoiled at the blatant materialism that seemed to be engulfing the country. Craftsmen experienced an accelerated de-skilling process and grew more dependent while receiving less pay. They formed a variety of labor organizations, among them the National Labor Union (1866–1872), the Knights of Labor (1869), and the American Federation of Labor (1886). Other workers affiliated with the Socialist Party of America (1901), and the Industrial Workers of the World (1905), which took the radical path of attempting to overturn capitalism. Small farmers expressed their frustration through the Grange movement of the 1870s and the Populist campaigns of the 1890s. Fearing the loss of self-sufficiency and control and feeling bewildered, they attacked "the money market, the banking and currency system, and more precisely the 'capitalists' who financed business." American society appeared to be poised for major social conflict; as Hays points out:

> The discontent of workers and farmers intensified a growing social cleavage in the United States in the last third of the nineteenth century. The gulf between rich and poor, who did not share in the nation's growing wealth, rapidly widened. On the one hand, the wealthy spent their fortunes on "conspicuous consumption." On the other, the urban masses lived in poverty, in slums "across the tracks." Farmers were no longer looked upon as respected yeomen. They were seen as "hicks" and "hayseeds" whose occupation seemed never to promise an urban standard of living. Immigration intensified this gulf, adding to the ranks of the urban poor and sharpening the contrast between the native American working class and the foreign urban workingman.

A series of labor confrontations exploded across the nation: the national railroad strike of 1877, the Haymarket Square massacre of 1886 in Chicago, the bloody Homestead steel strike of 1892 outside of Pittsburgh, the violent Pullman railroad car strike of 1894, based in Chicago, the Lawrence, Massachusetts, textile strike of 1912 involving 10,000 strikers, and the Paterson, New Jersey, silk textile strike of 1913 in which 25,000 workers walked out.[5] Labor conflict now assumed a mass character, with tens of thousands of workers striking in protest over low wages and dangerous or poor working conditions, and increasingly ended in armed violence, with injuries and deaths. American society seemed to be in the grip of an unprecedented social crisis.

There were attempts to ameliorate some of the social conditions that had bred this crisis. The Progressive movement, as the various reforms became called, was not monolithic; it had "local, state, and national manifestations," but it was, nevertheless, a largely urban phenomenon. Progressive reform was broad in scope. It included political reform, in favoring the political remedies of initiative, referendum, recall procedures (and popular election of senators); municipal reform in its attacks on "urban political machines and corruption"; business reform and trust busting in its championship of "regulation of public utilities" and general "curtailment of corporate power"; and social reform in the form of the "Americanization of the immigrant" and "regulation of child and women labor." Progressivism cut across political party lines. Theodore Roosevelt, a Republican president, and Woodrow Wilson, a Democratic president, served as "symbolic leaders of the movement."[6] The Progressive era was a complex time. It was marked by wide-ranging reforms, but positive progress was made only in some areas; other aspects of society seemed to regress.

School reform was an important component of the Progressive movement and proved to be as timely and wide ranging as the broader movement. During the Progressive era, school enrollment, which had been increasing steadily throughout the nineteenth century, shot up. "In Cleveland, enrollments increased from 45,000 to over 145,000 between 1900 and 1930." Similar increases occurred in other cities: Detroit from 30,000 to 250,000, Atlanta from 14,000 to 64,000, and San Francisco from 37,000 to 64,000. Educators and society as a whole had to address this flood of children overwhelming the public school classrooms.[7] Under Progressive school reform, the child-centered approach became institutionalized, the administration of education through an expanded school bureaucracy and a broader curriculum were introduced, and the basic functions of public schooling were expanded and intensified.

THE MOSAIC OF THE PROGRESSIVE EDUCATION MOVEMENT

In *The Transformation of the School: Progressivism in American Education*, a widely cited history of the period, Lawrence A. Cremin identifies a number of influences on the reform movement in the schools. Muckrakers made Americans aware of conditions in the schools, and reformers used education experimentally as a means of relieving social problems.

Muckrakers and Social Reformers

Many contemporary critics wrote sensational books and articles in this period that portrayed horrible social environments, exploitative business practices, and corrupt political deals. In *The Jungle* (1906), Upton Sinclair, intending to convey the plight of immigrant workers, alerted the American public to poor sanitation in uninspected meatpacking plants. In *History of the Standard Oil Company* (1904), Ida Tarbell attacked the monopolistic business practices of J. D. Rockefeller. Lincoln Steffens contributed a series of articles to *McClure's* magazine uncovering illegal city government practices, later published in book form as *The Shame of the Cities* (1904).[8] Muckrakers' writings also made Americans aware of the types of lives led by urban children and the shortcomings of public schools.

Jacob Riis, a pioneer photojournalist, used his camera to expose the severe living conditions in New York's ghettoes in the late 1880s. His first book, *How the Other Half Lives* (1890), received wide circulation and gained significant attention, including that of Theodore Roosevelt. The tone of the narrative that accompanied the photographs was highly moralistic and ethnocentric, since Riis's focus was on the newly arriving immigrants and their children. His study comprehensively treated such social issues as tenements, poverty, intemperance, sweatshops, crime, working women, child labor, youth gangs, and general ghetto culture.

Riis devoted three separate chapters to the children he found, describing crowded living conditions, the lack of play areas, poor sanitation and health, inadequate nutrition, unsafe environments, and neglectful parents. His treatment of abandoned babies, or "foundlings," was most poignant: "Seventy-two dead babies were picked up in the streets last year. Some of them were doubtless put out by very poor parents to save funeral expenses. In hard times the numbers of dead and live foundlings always increases very noticeably." Riis also recounted how "dirty" and "ragged" children fetched "beer for their elders" and "slept in the streets at night." He described how a truant officer "came upon a little party of four [boys] drinking beer out of the cover of a milk can. . . . " In the spirit of comradery, they offered to share their liquid libation with the officer. Riis described the conditions of homeless children and exposed how frequently children gambled. Finally, most of the children he met were illiterate or semiliterate at best.

Riis generally condemned the lack of "home" life for these children and blamed the parents. He also expressed outrage at the widespread child abuse he observed. As Riis concluded: "Nothing is now better understood than that the rescue of the children is the key to the problem of city poverty." They could only be saved, he emphasized, by philanthropic efforts and schooling. The public schools and teachers needed to assume many of the responsibilities of families and parents, teaching children such basics as washing with soap and water.[9]

Could the public schools indeed save these children? Joseph Mayer Rice, another muckraker, embarked on what was to become a famous study in 1892. Commissioned by the editor of *Forum* magazine, Rice "was to prepare a firsthand appraisal of American public education. From Boston to Washington, from New York to St. Louis, he was to visit classrooms, talk with teachers, attend school board meetings, and interview parents." Between January and June, he traveled to thirty-six cities and collected data, including 1,200 interviews with teachers. His articles, which began to appear in October, painted a largely negative picture of America's urban schools. He discovered little, or no, qualified supervision as well as uncovered ill-prepared instructors and dreary pedagogy. Politicians hired classroom teachers and principals based on their party affiliation and loyalty, corrupting the educational process. The classroom routine proved to be boring, dominated by dull drill and repetition, stern instructors, and frequent punishment. In the schools he witnessed, Rice wrote that the "years of childhood are converted into years of slavery." On the other hand, Rice did find a few schools and classrooms devoted to the well-being of children and committed to creative pedagogy. Minneapolis teachers focused on children as the center of the educational process; in Indianapolis instructors experimented with an integrated curriculum. Other schools introduced "drawing, painting, and clay modeling" as well as "nature study" and "social activities."[10] Rice's expose had a significant impact by drawing the public's attention to the shortcomings of many of America's public schools. His articles, of course, also drew the ire of angry educators.

Educational changes appeared to be in the offing. Some of these came directly from community social reform efforts, such as those initiated by Jane Addams. Born in 1860, in Cedarville, Illinois, to an affluent Quaker family, Addams attended the local one-room schoolhouse and graduated from the Rockford Female Seminary in 1881. She successfully completed one year of medical studies at the Pennsylvania Woman's Medical College in Philadelphia before withdrawing because of illness. While touring Europe in 1888, Addams visited Toynbee Hall in London, where male university students worked among the poor. Impressed with this social reform effort, she decided to replicate it in the United States, but with the aid of university women. She wanted to establish "reform centers, or 'settlements,' to bridge the social gulf that had opened up in American cities as a result of the expansion of industrialism and the immigration which it sucked in."

Addams founded Hull House in 1889, one of the "earliest" settlement houses, in a poor and working-class immigrant neighborhood in Chicago. There she maintained a program she called "socialized education." Addams believed that a utilitarian and enriching education was the main means of humanizing industrial capitalism. This community-based approach to education in an urban setting democratized learning by bringing it to the people. Hull House hosted a popular lecture series that drew several hundred people to each presentation. The topics covered history, politics, astronomy, and culture. Hull House also sponsored literature clubs that studied Shakespeare, Browning, and Plato, among other authors. Members of the boys club worked in Hull House's wood, metal, and electrical shops and learned photography and bricklaying. As Addams reasoned: "While these classes in no sense provided a trade training, they often enable a boy to discover his aptitudes and help him in the selection of what he 'wants to be' by reducing the trades to embryonic forms." These wholesome and practical activities lured boys off the streets, keeping them out of trouble through positive and potentially long-lasting influences. Finally, Hull House included a gymnasium and kindergarten and held adult classes in nutrition, English language, drama, "domestic training," and child care.

The settlement house movement became widespread; there were over 100 of them nationwide by 1900. "Addams became the leader of this movement, and in 1911 was elected the first head of the National Federation of Settlements, a position she held until 1935." Settlement houses, Hull House in particular, served as a mode of social reform. Settlement workers, later known as "social workers," attempted to ameliorate myriad social problems: among them, poor housing, untreated sewerage, contaminated water, and juvenile delinquency.[11] Education was one of their most important and potent social weapons. The notion of schooling as the center of an urban community grew out of these early experiments. John Dewey, the leading Progressive philosopher of education, would acknowledge the influence of Addams and Hull House in forming his views of the social role of education.

Philosophy and Principles

Progressive educational reform attempted to break previous patterns of haphazard financial support, irregular school attendance, low graduation rates, ill-trained teachers, and the absence of curriculum and building standards and supervision. The goal of Progressive educational reform was to have educational practice be guided by informed and well-trained teachers who would rely on clear theories to bring rationality to classroom practice. Some of the movement's pedagogical ideas grew out of classroom experiments. In other cases, they developed out of a synthesis of existing ideas. A standardized, organized, and cohesive system of public education would result, all of it guided by dedicated and visionary educational managers. During this period of educational ferment, many of these theories became institutionalized and universalized.

Father of Progressive Education

Francis W. Parker has been labeled the "father of the Progressive Education Movement." His influence certainly was fundamental and pervasive. Born in New Hampshire in 1837, he became a schoolmaster at age sixteen. Despite limited formal schooling, he became a principal in Carrollton, Illinois, five years later, where he proved to be highly successful, working with students and gaining community support. As a pro-Lincoln Republican and with antislavery views, he returned to New Hampshire at the beginning of the Civil War and enlisted in the army. Parker saw action as early as 1861 and throughout the war, receiving a serious gunshot wound in 1864. At war's end, he had been promoted through the ranks to colonel.

Parker returned to the classroom as a principal in Manchester, New Hampshire. He grew dissatisfied with the unsystematic routine of schooling he found. Borrowing ideas from both the military and the factory, he introduced teacher specialization, the grouping of students, and general standardization. With his success in Manchester, Parker accepted another principal's position in Dayton, Ohio, where he further refined his pedagogical beliefs. Dayton had a rather innovative school district; the Dayton schools had instituted coeducation and sponsored a public school library. Parker's opposition to memorization and drill, tests, and grades crystallized. The strong-willed educator, who antagonized school board members both in Manchester and Dayton, nevertheless continued to be successful. In 1869, the school board appointed him as principal of Dayton's first public normal school.

Three years later, Parker resigned his position in Dayton and, in order to gain some college education experience, enrolled at the University of Berlin. His educational notions matured as he observed the Prussian influence on German schools. Although Parker rejected what he perceived as "German authoritarianism" in that country's schools, he embraced other European concepts. "He visited the schools of Switzerland, France, Italy, and Holland. He singled out the schools of Switzerland and France as superior to those in America." Parker studied Johann Heinrich Pestalozzi's philosophy of natural education, Johann Friedrich Herbart's educational ideals of interest-centered pedagogy guided by scientific principles, and Friedrich Froebel's pioneering efforts with kindergartens in the village of Blankenburg. Parker saw democracy and common schooling as linked, a link crucial to his educational views.[12]

Parker instituted these fresh and innovative ideas of student participation and a general student-centeredness guided by well-conceived and planned lessons when he became superintendent of the Quincy, Massachusetts, schools in 1875, where they became known as the "Quincy System." He continued to find American teaching methods highly mechanical, focused as they were on regimented memorization and drill. Parker created kindergartens, relied on the object method, connected arithmetic with real-life situations, introduced field trips, allowed students to draw pictures, and stressed the individuality of each child.[13] "In Quincy, Massachusetts, he had started reading and language arts programs based on what today would be called a combined whole-language, phonetic approach." By 1879, his innovative teaching methods had gained national attention, with thousands of visitors descending on the Quincy's schools to observe firsthand this new education.[14]

In 1880, Parker resigned from the Quincy superintendency to accept a supervisor's position in the much-vaunted Boston school district, where he oversaw forty-two primary schools. But he encountered a great deal of skepticism, resistance, and criticism in Boston; his novel practices did not sit well with that city's entrenched educators. Frustrated with this opposition, Parker accepted the principalship of the Cook County Normal School located near Chicago in 1883. There his teaching ideas came to fruition and became legitimized. There too he could train disciples by shaping the pedagogical ideals and skills of aspiring teachers, thus broadening his influence. Parker saw public schooling as a natural part of the democratic process; independent and critical thinking was the heart of a healthy democratic society. Traditional educational methods he saw as aristocratic and artificial; memorization inhibited freedom of thought. At the Normal School, Parker began by purging all vestiges of "traditional education." He banned report cards. In place of an approach centered on subject matter, he demanded a student-centered perspective. "Parker saw education as a science which required special training." He expected that teachers become involved in the community in order to know their children better and to interact with their families. Although opponents branded Parker's practices as anti-intellectual, his practice school became a mecca for innovative educators, among them John Dewey.[15]

"An Embryonic Society"

Through his prolific writings, John Dewey became the leading American educational philosopher and established the intellectual foundation for the Progressive education movement. Born in 1859 in Burlington, Vermont, he was steeped in the New England, small-town, democratic tradition. He attended the local public school and graduated from high school at age fifteen, but saw his school experiences as boring. Dewey completed his undergraduate studies at the University of Vermont in 1879 and then taught a variety of high school subjects, first in Oil City, Pennsylvania, and then in Charlotte, Vermont, earning his master's degree in philosophy at the University of Vermont in 1881. He began doctoral studies at Johns Hopkins the following year.

Dewey completed his doctoral degree in philosophy and began to teach at the University of Michigan in 1884. In 1894, Dewey left to teach at the University of Chicago, where he began to take a serious and lifelong interest in the philosophy of education. Chicago's dynamic intellectual and educational environment proved to be stimulating and influential. When he arrived in Chicago, he visited the practice school at Francis W. Parker's Cook County Normal School. Dewey, impressed with what he saw, enrolled his own children. He had also visited Jane Addams's Hull House in 1892, where he became a frequent visitor, giving talks for Hull House's popular lecture series. Dewey joined Hull House's Board of Trustees in 1895, and developed a close intellectual and personal relationship with Addams. At Hull House, he observed her concept of socialized education in action.

In 1896, influenced by Parker's practice school, Dewey opened a "laboratory school" at the University of Chicago. It stressed experimentation to test his "theories and their sociological implications." The entire setting focused on children's needs and interests. The traditional curriculum was discarded. Students began with the concrete and familiar, and moved outward physically and intellectually from their home life to the world. The children became involved with "conversations, constructive work, stories, songs, and games" as part of the daily classroom routine. They created miniature societies in their classrooms, building, among many other activities, grocery stores or farms. In each, they counted money to work on math concepts and skills and planted, cultivated, and harvested wheat and made bread from it to study botany and chemistry, among other subjects. The curriculum remained integrated, emphasizing a cooperative environment, yet became more formalized as children progressed. By 1904, when Dewey abandoned the University of Chicago for Teachers College, Columbia University, the laboratory school "had become the most interesting experimental venture in American education; indeed, there are those who insist that there has been nothing since to match it in excitement, quality, and contribution."[16]

By the time Dewey moved to Teachers College, he had become the "leading theoretician and spokesman" of the Progressive education movement. His philosophy is difficult to capture and encapsulate in a few short pages. "Dewey gathered, rearranged, and recreated elements of educational reform that had been at work for decades—and even centuries." He rekindled "democratic faith" in the common-school ideal inherited from Thomas Jefferson and Horace Mann as well as tapped the "romantic emphasis upon the needs and interests of the child," in the tradition of Jean-Jacques Rousseau, Johann Heinrich Pestalozzi, and Friedrich Froebel.[17] Dewey, according to Cremin, envisioned the school as a *legatee* institution, that is, as assuming the educational responsibilities of the family and workplace, and formalized this view through his philosophy.[18] He saw all education as social. In *School and Society* (1899), Dewey catalogued the fundamental social changes that had occurred during the nineteenth century. He noted the advances of industrial manufacturing, the expansion of overseas trade, and the expediting of communication and distribution. Widespread institutional growth resulted. As the material world became transformed, social reality also experienced change. According to Dewey, "[a] society is a number of people held together because they are working along common lines, in a common spirit, and with reference to common aims. The common needs and aims demand a growing interchange of thought and growing unity of sympathetic feeling." Society needed to recapture this sense of community within a fluid context and vast institutionalization. The socialization of the child, previously the family's domain, now had to occur largely through the school. Dewey saw the public school as a community builder, as a vehicle for a new society.[19]

In *My Pedagogic Creed* (1897), Dewey provided a definition of education as well as a bold and concise statement of his vision of the schooling process. Education represented a pervasive social experience, transcending school. The school, meanwhile, operated as a social institution, organic rather than artificial: "the school life should grow gradually out of the home life; that it should take up and continue the activities with which the child is already familiar in the home."[20] All school subjects should have meaning and connect to the child's social world in a natural way, which implied, of course, a break from the traditional liberal arts curriculum. Teaching methods should stress active and engaged learning, focus on the interests of the student, and encompass the emotional side of the child—the antithesis of the typical passive approaches of recitation, memorization, and drill used in the public schools at that time.[21]

Dewey outlined clearly the school's social role. In *School and Society*, he asserted that the school should serve as "a miniature community, an embryonic society." He argued that "[w]hen the school introduces and trains each child of society into membership within such a little community, saturating him with the spirit of service, and providing him with the instruments of effective self-direction, we shall have the deepest and best guarantee of a larger society which is worth, lovely, and harmonious."[22] In such school communities, students would learn the democratic process, lend assistance to one another, and exercise, according to historian Gerald L. Gutek, "a communal, or communitarian, core of beliefs and values."[23] Dewey's embryonic community not only "reflected" society but intended to "improve" it. Traditional schooling utilized passive teaching methods, maintained a staid, abstract, and narrow curriculum, relied solely on the teacher, and focused on the textbook. Dewey saw all of this shifting to a child-centered approach and attitude.

This educational philosophy became the foundation for a new perception of schooling, one which saw schooling as fluid and reflective of broad and ongoing social transformations. As families and the world around them changed, as children changed, so should the schools. Schooling also served as a vehicle of social reform, preparing students to enter the world and improve it.

The Progressive Education Association

Many of the Progressive education movement's ideals took institutional form in the Progressive Education Association (PEA), which was founded in 1919 in Washington, D.C. The association had explicit principles: *freedom to develop naturally; interest, the motive of all work; the teacher a guide, not a task master; scientific study of pupil development; greater attention to all that affects the child's physical development; the progressive school, a leader in education movements.* These comprehensive principles reflected concern for the child's intellectual, moral, social, physical, and emotional growth. Harvard's Charles W. Eliot served as the first honorary president, and the PEA held annual meetings and published a journal, *Progressive Education*, beginning in 1924. Dewey succeeded him in 1927 and retained the post until his death in 1952. Membership amounted to 6,000 in 1928 and climbed to over 10,000 in 1938. The association proved to be enormously successful in promoting Progressive education's platform. The PEA became the "principal voice of the movement during the period between the wars."[24]

The Progressive education movement was not, however, monolithic. Many, often competing, strains of "Progressive" education emerged and gained footholds.

Child-Centered Progressives

Since schooling should be child centered, then schools had to be reconfigured. New developmental stages had to be addressed and incorporated into educational institutions. Schooling began to extend downward, to early childhood, and upward, to adolescence. During the Progressive era, early childhood education became readily available in the form of public school kindergartens, the culmination a long institutionalization process.

Early Childhood

Kindergarten had a unique evolution. German immigrants introduced it to the United States, the American middle class adopted it and Americanized it, and educators imposed it on poor immigrant and working-class children to assimilate them. Although "several of the people who had actively promoted the infant schools in the 1830s were also active in the kindergarten movement in the 1860s and 1870s," kindergarten changed from at first being play oriented, a naturalistic setting, to being focused on schooling, an institutional environment.[25]

German Antecedents

In 1856, Margarethr Meyer Schurz, a student of Friedrich Froebel, the German kindergarten pioneer, opened the first kindergarten in the United States, in Watertown, Wisconsin. German American communities in Detroit, Louisville, Milwaukee, Newark, and New York City, opened German-speaking kindergartens throughout the early 1870s and published kindergarten manuals. To accommodate the steady growth of this educational movement, Maria Boelte and John Kraus opened the New York Normal Training School for Kindergarten Teachers, Kindergarten and Adjoining Classes, a two-year course of study that followed Froebelian principles.[26]

Froebel was a disciple of Swiss educator Johann Heinrich Pestalozzi. During the early 1800s, Froebel advocated a naturalistic approach to education both in schooling experiments he undertook and in his writings. He rejected the commonly held "notion of child depravity and the need for prescriptive schooling." Unlike many of his contemporaries, he praised children's play and encouraged it. "In fact, his kindergarten was an institution founded on play. Through play, . . . children exhibit their simple and natural life. In games, they imitate adult activities and practice social and moral values." The teacher served as a facilitator who provided the environment and materials necessary for this active classroom to unfold. Teacher guidance was required, however. "Without some planned guidance by the teacher, children's whims can degenerate into aimless activities." The instructor introduced "songs, stories, and games." Froebel's instructional materials included "gifts," which consisted of "cubes, spheres, and cylinders," and occupations, which used "clay, sand, cardboard, and mud" to shape and create new things. His emphasis on occupations was related to extending children's social world from family membership to their future work lives; thus play replicated adulthood. Children who made mud pies duplicated the cooking process they witnessed in the family. "Play, construction, and modeling" prepared them "for an industrious, diligent life. By conceiving of God as the eternal Creator who works through eternity to manifest His thoughts into concrete entities, Froebel drew a close relationship between religion and work." In many ways, the kindergarten served as a substitute for the family.[27]

American Adaptions.   The kindergarten spread rapidly through American cities during the 1860s and 1870s. However, American parents disliked what they perceived as German rigidity as well as "German songs, games, and folk stories." Furthermore, a basic philosophical tension developed between an academic emphasis, generally American in origin, and a stress on play, the Froebelian approach.[28] In 1860, Elizabeth Peabody, a strict Froebelian, opened the "first English-speaking kindergarten in America in Boston." A supporter of the infant schools, she participated in the formation of the American Froebelian Society, later the American Froebel Union, in 1877. "Peabody used the early nineteenth-century ideology of domesticity and 'women's sphere' to promote kindergartening as an organization for American women." Finally, she believed that kindergartens should remain private institutions, separate from public schools, to avoid the artificialness of traditional schoolwork. Susan Blow also contributed to the "Americanization of the kindergarten" through her activities in the St. Louis schools, supported by William Torrey Harris, the highly visible superintendent of that city's public schools. Blow, who had visited kindergartens in Germany, began a kindergarten in one of the school buildings during the

1872–73 school year. The concept quickly became popular and soon spread throughout the other schools in the city, growing from 68 students in 1873 to 7,828 seven years later. Concerns about cost prompted Harris, with Blow's support, to institute double sessions each day. Blow and Harris modified Froebel's original approach. They deemphasized play and stressed socialization. Harris, in particular, held doubts about the family's ability to properly socialize children. Kindergartens could operate as surrogate family settings, preparing children for the typical school environment. According to Barbara Beatty's historical analysis, the kindergarten became "more a mental refuge and academic and civic training ground than a playground or garden."

These kindergartens remained semiprivate ventures, since the public school charged parents a one-dollar fee for their five-year-olds.[29] The concept of free kindergartens gained popularity as the movement gradually expanded during the late nineteenth century. How did the kindergartens succeed when the infant schools had failed? For one thing, some basic notions of early childhood had changed. According to historian Caroline Winterer:

> What had seemed a peculiarity in the 1820s—that young children might learn best what they learned themselves—seemed only natural late in the century. Also, the kindergartens accepted no children under the age of about four, thus mitigating the threat to the family implicit in the low admission ages of the infant schools. Finally, the kindergartens reveal the extent to which American views had changed in regard to the capacity of young children to engage in intellectual activity.

The emphasis on play also proved to be significant. It was a commonly held belief in the United States at the time that rigorous schooling before seven years old led to insanity.[30]

Educational reformers founded charity kindergartens in New York City and the Boston area in 1877. In Massachusetts, "kindergartens were torn between conservative Froebelians and more modern methods." By the 1880s and 1890s, the free kindergarten movement shifted to the West and consequently began to adopt a distinct American character. "In the Chicago area, kindergarteners Anna Bryan, Alice Putnam, and Elizabeth Harris collaborated with Progressive educators Francis Parker and John Dewey and advocated change or compromise." Putnam had "attended a summer school Parker ran on Martha's Vineyard." His innovative approaches so impressed her that "she helped Parker gain appointment as principal of Cook County Normal School in Chicago." Putnam enrolled her daughters at that institution's model school and became a kindergarten instructor there, training future teachers. She also taught kindergarten classes at Jane Addams's Hull House and participated in the founding of the Chicago Free Kindergarten Association and the Chicago Kindergarten Club. In the San Francisco slums, "Kate Douglas Wiggin and her sister Nora Archibald Smith developed an ideology of children's rights that contributed to rationales for universal public kindergartens." In 1878, Wiggin had begun to teach at the Silver Street charity kindergarten. The children generally came from poor and working-class immigrant families. "The reports of the Public Kindergarten Society of San Francisco, which supported Silver Street, documented the cost-effectiveness of kindergartening as an antidote to urban problems, and Wiggin's kindergarten became known in transforming the lives of urban families." This widespread acceptance of kindergartens transformed the philosophy and pedagogy behind the concept. Beatty summarizes:

> Froebelian pedagogy began to change as teachers in these free kindergartens began ministering to young children's physical as well as educational needs and educating mothers from different cultural and social-class backgrounds. Academicians and educators began looking to science to create rationally structured educational institutions and scientific pedagogy designed to deal with the problems created by industrialization and urbanization.

Froebel's romantic notions about the value of young children's play thus began to be replaced by an emphasis on socialization and preparation for schooling.

Anna Bryan, who played an important role in establishing the Louisville Free Kindergarten Association in 1877, both promoted free kindergartens and continued the trend toward Americanization. "One of the association's early reports discusses the efficiency of kindergartens as a means of preventing urban crime, promoting 'the public good, on the side of law, order and commercial property,' and combating the 'poisonous atmosphere' of some homes." Bryan also broke from "Froebelian orthodoxy" by encouraging pedagogical experimentation. Patty Smith Hill, who worked with Bryan in Louisville, Kentucky, further modified Bryan's ideas by connecting "pedagogical innovation and political progressivism."

Kindergarten as Assimilation.

The kindergarten movement, as we have seen, had largely urban roots. "In the late 1880s, the movement to establish public kindergartens that had begun in German-American St. Louis in the 1870s spread to Boston, Chicago, San Francisco, New York, and other cities and towns in the northeastern, midwestern, western, and mid-Atlantic states. Only the South and Southwest were slow to join the campaign, and rural areas everywhere lagged behind the rest of the country." This growth proved to be remarkable. In 1898, 200,000 children attended kindergarten; by 1910, this figure had virtually doubled. School districts reduced costs by implementing two shifts. "A 1915 Bureau of Education survey reported that by the 1911–12 school year, 546 of 867 school systems had instituted morning and afternoon kindergartens."

Purged of German culture, freely accessible, and academically and socially oriented, the kindergarten was transformed yet again. The emphasis on socialization increased as many public schools absorbed the charity and private kindergartens and as the growing number of southern and eastern European immigrants and their children residing in American cities alarmed many native-born Americans. With the onset of World War I, the presence of millions of foreigners caused Americans to look to the schools as instruments of acculturation. The process began with kindergarten. Educators increasingly saw kindergartens as having an important role in assimilation—instilling patriotism, teaching English, and promoting American culture. Among African American children, however, particularly in the South, the kindergarten movement seriously lagged behind the rest of the country; no kindergartens existed for them in 1901. Even as private kindergartens began to appear, whether in the North or the South, "vocational education seems to have won out over Froebelianism in most kindergartens for African American children." Because of perceived racial inferiority, educators saw such training as more appropriate than play. Many of the activities stressed work-type skills such as washing, gardening, ironing, "janitorial" duties, and "house cleaning" to prepare these children to assume menial, low-paying jobs in a segregated society.

In general, as the number of kindergartens increased and enrollment grew, and as cultural demands and the theories of scientific behaviorism grew, emphasis on social and cognitive skills gradually displaced Froebel's idealism and emphasis on play. "Worksheets appeared in kindergartens, and 'reading readiness' and other skill-oriented assignments were added to kindergarten curricula, reducing the time available for play and other nonacademic activities." Early childhood educational reform therefore was ultimately a tool of broad social reform. It echoed the concerns of earlier common-school reformers and was consistent as well with the persistent trend of the school displacing the family as educator. The historical continuity is evident: education continued to become institutionalized and to primarily address social needs. This "Gilded Age charity for the children of the urban poor and their families, who were thought to be individually at fault for their own degraded social position," evolved into a comprehensive Progressive social program, offering a variety of educational services. Kindergarten promoters saw their mission as shaping family culture and roles. They endeavored to train mothers to be caring, gentle, and nurturing, to fulfill their domestic role, and to socialize young children to be loyal citizens and productive workers. Stable family structures and social conformity, after all, ensured a smooth-running society.[31]

Adolescence

Because of Progressive educational reform, America's public schools not only extended formal education to younger children but expanded it for older children as well. High school enrollment climbed from 6.7 percent in 1890 to 32.3 percent by 1920. Jurgen Herbst points to three key causes for this phenomenon. First, for female students with "career motivations," the high schools were acceptable training venues in their normal school departments for young women to become elementary school teachers and in their business departments for new opportunities as secretaries and telephone operators, among other jobs. This finishing school approach did not threaten the existing cult of domesticity. Second, for males, a high school education facilitated the "acquisition of cultural property," that is, "speech patterns, tastes, manners, style, academic credentials," paramount for middle-class status. Thus the high school experience contributed to social mobility. The third, more general, reason, was "the democratic imperative," which Herbst sees as the "parental desire to see their children advance socially and economically combined with the schoolmen's ambition to expand their sphere of influence."[32] Accommodating so many young people generated a new pedagogical outlook, leading to the formal acceptance of adolescence as a stage of growth and development.

Coeducation became a common high school experience beginning in the late nineteenth century, and by the early twentieth century females easily outnumbered males. Boys, as we saw in Chapter 6, usually abandoned schooling in order to work; middle-class girls, with few nonmanual work options, typically remained in school. "Middle-class parents of girls were among the high school's most ardent supporters, and girls from such families could arguably be seen as the mainstay of the institution." In strictly academic subjects, female secondary students commonly performed at least as well as the males, if not better. Girls generally maintained a lower failure rate than boys and usually served as class valedictorians.[33] Changes in the nineteenth-century, middle-class family culture and size encouraged this trend. "Declining birthrates and the availability of cheap Irish servants cut into some of the traditional functions of teenage girls." To "fill up time," they attended high school to become cultured ladies in conformity to the reigning cult of domesticity. "Possession of an educated daughter became a sort of prestige symbol, a crude form of conspicuous consumption." In addition to the drop in birthrates, shrinking sibling age ranges and extended longevity reshaped the family and its internal dynamics. A smaller, more intimate, nuclear family unit, for historian Joseph Kett, "nurtured a more self-conscious approach to the socialization of children; adolescent rearing became as important as child rearing." This new perception of children introduced "passive and receptive stances rather than active purposive ones" within the household, and had broader implications: "Unproductive dependent" youth, so rare in the early 1800s, appeared somewhat common by 1900.[34]

There were several causes—technological, legal, and cultural—behind the waning of child labor and the extension of schooling. "By the 1920s," according to historian David Nasaw, "the children of the city had been pushed to the side by the automobile, which cut off their play and work space, by tougher and better-enforced child labor laws, and by adults who moved into the trades they once monopolized."[35] Furthermore, much improved "compulsory education laws further accelerated the unemployment of children." All of these factors explain the ebbing of child labor, since "effective federal regulation of child labor was only obtained after the Great Depression, first with the National Industrial Recovery Act and in 1938 with the Fair Labor Standards Act, which introduced the section on child labor." Viviana Zelizer's historical research views the changes from a slightly different stance. Beyond "the effect of structural, economic, and technological changes on child labor trends," a growing unskilled labor supply squeezed children out of the workplace while rising real income allowed families to keep their children in school. These factors combined to transform "children's economic roles." Children thus became "emotional and moral assets" rather than raw economic partners. Their future rather than the family's immediate survival began to take precedence.[36] The collective decision-making process within the family is again evident. For instance, Chicago's school enrollment between 1880 and 1930 increased for all ethnic, racial, and social-class groups. In 1930, 97 percent of the 7 to 13 age group went to school, 94.6 percent of the 14 to 15 age group, and 56.6 percent for the 16 to 17 age group. These figures reflect a new attitude toward the relationship among families, work, and schooling. Parents began to recognize the "significance of educational credentials in a wage labor system," and enrolled their children in school to enhance their "economic welfare."[37]

The origins of the idea of adolescence as a separate stage of development appeared between 1840 and 1880. Institutional formalization, according to Kett, changed how youths were perceived. As age grading evolved, teenagers became identified with the high school years. However, the concept of development played only a minor role. "A bureaucratic preference for order and efficiency and the logic of institutional change were the motivating forces." Ability grouping thus fell victim to "age-segregation"; school authorities sorted out younger and older children at each level simply for the sake of "systematization." The term *adolescence*, a generally "unfamiliar" one, "began to acquire more specific meanings toward the middle of the nineteenth century."[38]

G. Stanley Hall's two-volume 1904 work, *Adolescence: Its Psychology, and Its Relations to Anthropology, Sex, Crime, Religion, and Education*, which formalized this new field of child study, gave intellectual legitimacy to the necessity of schooling this age group. "While many educators and child advocates were suspicious of Hall's curious blend of science, romanticism, repression, and permissiveness, his basic idea of the 'sanctity' of adolescence was tremendously influential" and inspired a movement to "order . . . the experiences of young people." For Hall, high schools should teach practical rather than abstract knowledge and serve a social instead of an intellectual role. Schools were thus encouraged to assume more of the family's responsibilities, further marginalizing the family as an institution of education. Unexpectedly, adolescents became disconnected from their traditional family setting: "For adolescents, the most important changes centered on the high school, which was gradually assuming a crucial role in the adolescent life course."[39]

The 1900s therefore became "the century of adolescence."[40] Between 1900 and 1930, Progressive educators expanded the curriculum to accommodate the high school's new social and educational role. Historian Jeffrey Mirel makes a salient point: "These curricular changes were part of the larger process of economic and educational change in which preparation for work eventually supplanted actual engagement in work as the primary vocational experience of adolescents."[41] The identification of adolescence as a separate stage of development contributed to changes in the understanding of the relationship between school and work, spawned and stimulated the growth of a vital youth culture, and profoundly transformed the high school as an institution, as we shall see.

Social Reconstructionism

Some Progressive educators believed that the child-centered emphasis did not go far enough to reform society. George S. Counts, more than any other Progressive educator, embodied this social reconstructionist perspective, much of which reflected the profound social and economic transformations he had witnessed in his own life. Born in 1889 on a farm near Baldwin, Kansas, he grew up in a close-knit family that traced its ancestry to colonial New England and Virginia. In his autobiography, Counts recalled working hard as a child, cleaning the stable, plowing fields, and cultivating and harvesting crops, among many other tasks. He attended a one-room rural school, graduated from high school in 1907, and enrolled at Baker University in Baldwin for undergraduate work. In 1911, after graduation, Counts remained in Kansas to teach high school science and mathematics, and the following year became a principal at another high school. He began graduate studies at the University of Chicago in 1913, earning his doctorate in education three years later. He taught at five different institutions of higher education until 1927, when he became a professor at Teachers College, Columbia University. Here he became a close friend of John Dewey.

Counts's outlook matured and his scholarship blossomed at Teachers College. Raised, in his words, "in the tradition of the American frontier," he categorized himself as a combination of a "Jeffersonian Democrat" and a "Lincolnian Republican." Raised in a rural agrarian cultural environment, Counts saw "urbanized and industrialized society" as a major threat to democracy, as "outlined in the Bill of Rights and the Declaration of Independence." For him, "organized education served the purposes of democracy—

democracy conceived both as social ends and as social means." His studies of school board composition, in the *Social Composition of Boards of Education* (1927), and social class, in the *Selective Character of American Secondary Education* (1924), revealed that "our 'common school' was controlled by the middle and upper classes and that high school, in spite of its phenomenal growth after 1890, remained down to 1920 largely a school for sons and daughters of the more fortunate." (The latter study will be examined in detail in Chapter 8.) Counts further argued that the American Federation of Teachers (AFT) was synonymous with democracy in its mobilizing and defending of classroom teachers. He served as the AFT's president in 1939, 1940, and 1941.[42]

In his 1932 polemic *Dare the School Build a New Social Order?*, originally delivered as a provocative speech at the annual meeting of the Progressive Education Association, Counts proposed a radical social reform mission for the public schools to overcome social-class inequalities as well inaugurated the social reconstruction movement. He criticized the Progressive education movement as dominated by, in his words, the "liberal-minded upper class." These Progressives maintained "an inordinate emphasis on the child and child interests," with an unclear and undirected commitment to a better society. Counts proposed a break from the child-centered approach, which appeared to be too tentative. As he stated it, "progressive education wishes to build a new world but refuses to be held accountable for the kind of world it builds." He preferred a direct relationship between schools and society, with the schools generating genuine reform. The school's role and process grew from social needs, in other words: "If the schools are to be really effective, they must become centers for the building, and not merely the contemplation, of our civilization."

And this civilization was experiencing a crisis. Counts noted the tragic impact of the Great Depression and how it exacerbated the huge gap between the rich and the poor and the general conditions of an unequal distribution of wealth:

> . . . breakfastless children march to school past bankrupt shops laden with rich foods gathered from the ends of the earth; . . . great captains of industry close factories without warning and dismiss the workmen by whose labors they have amassed huge fortunes through the years; . . . the wages paid to the workers are too meager to enable them to buy back the goods they produce. . . .

Capitalism was failing. It was "cruel and inhuman." Counts cast this social criticism in the context of democracy: "A society fashioned in harmony with the American democratic tradition would combat all forces tending to produce social distinctions and class; repress every form of privilege and economic parasitism." He proposed a society committed to cooperation rather than competition, "careful planning" rather than laissez faire, a "socialized economy" rather than "private capitalism." School teachers had to assert their power to shape young minds about the defects of society and the means to correct them.[43]

In sum, with the onset of corporate capitalism, Counts argued that the family's educational role had receded while the school's mission had expanded. The educational process had moved from an informal, organic experience to a formal, institutional one. A fluid and increasingly insecure society dictated that the school could no longer be separate from "political, social, and economic life." "Counts censured progressive education for lacking a social program, ignoring the problems of cultural transition and economic depression, and continuing to rely on the child-centered school." It conveyed a "false notion of freedom" in a society dominated by inequality. Schooling was not to be intellectually abstract, detached from social reality, but primarily committed to socialization, focusing on the cultural induction of children into "group life." Counts "firmly advocated social planning" and schooling played a key role in it. "Counts affirmed that the school chart a program of social reconstruction" to assure democracy and equality, a vague sense of "democratic collectivism."[44]

"Administrative Progressives"

As the functions of schooling multiplied and as the ages of students extended downward and upward, the management of this educational process grew more complex and challenging. Educators recognized the need for rationalizing the entire operation of schooling, and many of them quickly, and unquestionably, adopted management techniques from the corporate world. These focused on efficiency through consolidation and supervision and were implemented first in urban school districts and then in the rural areas of the country.

Urban Schools

Rural school reform took the form of district consolidation; in urban school districts, efficiency appeared to dominate the administrative agenda. This was achieved through centralization and scientific management and followed similar reforms undertaken in municipal government.

Centralization.   Municipal reform undertaken during the Progressive era reveals the complexity and contradictions of the movement. Reform rhetoric appeared to have a legitimate basis—corruption seemed to be rampant in city governments. Powerful political party machines were apparent threats to democratic institutions. Samuel Hays reveals a less obvious side of this reform effort in this classic historic analysis: "Although reformers used the ideology of popular government, they in no sense meant that all segments of society should be involved equally in municipal decision-making. They meant that their concept of the city's welfare would be best achieved if the business community controlled city government." The business and professional elite (i.e., bank presidents, corporate officers and executives, physicians, and attorneys) and urban chambers of commerce as well as the likes of John D. Rockefeller in New York City, George Eastman in Rochester, New York, and John H. Patterson in Dayton, Ohio, either endorsed or spearheaded the reform movement of city governance throughout the country. They used political corruption as the reason, and they opposed the concept and practice of a pluralistic and highly decentralized ward system of municipal decision making.

At that time, all city politics was localized. Residents were represented by a city council elected at the ward level. These "ward bosses,"—grocers, saloon keepers, clerks, small business owners, and skilled and unskilled laborers—reflected the backgrounds of their communities. Voters had ready access to their duly elected representatives on the streets and in the neighborhoods to voice needs and register complaints. These ward officials in turn focused on the particular needs of their constituencies at city hall to ensure their reelection.

Frustrated with this parochialism and seeming inefficiency, reformers campaigned for a rational and centralized form of city management. "The movement for reform in municipal government, therefore, constituted an attempt by upper-class, advanced professional, and large-business groups to take formal political power from previously dominant lower- and middle-class elements so that they might advance their own conceptions of desirable political policy." Invoking the need to eradicate political corruption, and ultimately to rescue democratic ideals and institutions, municipal reformers purposefully eroded the concept and practice of representative government by leading a successful campaign for the appointment of city executives in the form of city managers or commissioners. They replaced ward elections of city council members with citywide elections, or the outright appointment of city council members.[45] These new government officials, of course, no longer felt any loyalty or obligation to a local constituency. In this way, municipal, citywide progress could be made. The new, centralized, hierarchical municipal form of governance now concentrated power in a highly efficient manner to facilitate the needs of the business and professional elite.

A similar process unfolded in school governance. A variety of governance structures existed throughout the nation. In Nashville and Milwaukee, the authority of the school boards overlapped with the authority and responsibilities of city councils, officials, and politicians. However, until the Progressive era, large cities usually maintained a decentralized, ward approach to school management. New York City and Chicago did have a central school board with members elected from individual wards but it proved to be too large and unwieldy. Many other cities, like Buffalo and Pittsburgh, were divided into subdistricts, which had complete autonomy to raise taxes, hire teachers, and construct and maintain buildings. Localized control thus diffused the power over making school decisions. Schools were tailored to community needs. Proponents defended this model of "participatory democracy," while "administrative progressive," borrowing the same rhetoric and tactics used in civic reform, attacked it as corrupt, parochial, and inefficient.

Administrative progressives successfully campaigned and ultimately implemented "a relatively closed system of politics in which power and initiative flowed from the top down, and administrative law or system took the place of decisions by elected officials." Under the Progressive education movement, urban boards became centralized and power became concentrated. Between 1893 and 1913, the average number of members on school boards shrank by more than 50 percent, from 21.5 to 10.2. A hierarchical structure ensured, proponents believed, a smooth-running bureaucracy run by educational experts.[46] Not only did the size of school boards shrink, but their composition experienced a profound change. A 1911 pamphlet published by the Voters' League of Pittsburgh urged people *not* to cast their ballots for unskilled and skilled workers, "small shopkeepers," and clerks for that city's school board since they lacked the educational background and "business training" necessary for administering "the affairs of an educational system." On the other hand, the pamphlet promoted "men prominent throughout the city in business life" and "in professional occupations." In some cases, citizens no longer elected school board members. For instance, judges in the court of common pleas appointed school board members in Pittsburgh.[47]

George S. Count's famous 1927 study, *The Social Composition of Boards of Education: A Study in the Social Control of Public Education*, clearly illustrated the consequences of this transformation. After researching 532 city school boards in all regions of the United States, he found that the typical urban school board member tended to be middle-aged, male, and highly educated. More important, 76 percent of school board members came from the upper social strata. Bankers, brokers, manufacturers, merchants, engineers, managers, and attorneys now dominated city school boards. As Counts summarized it, "[t]he outstanding conclusion to be drawn from this study of the occupations of the members of boards of education is that control of education and the formulation of educational policy are entrusted very largely to representatives of the more favored classes."[48] The majority of citizens—the poor, the working class, and immigrants—had been methodically excluded from school decisions affecting their children.

Progressive reformers resolutely believed that the private-sector expertise, achievements, and experience of the business and professional elite would result in equal success for the schools by operating them like corporations. Business philosophy and policies, as a result, were readily and enthusiastically embraced.[49] None proved more popular than business efficiency theory and methods.

Scientific Management.

Frederick Winslow Taylor created a revolution in business decision making and in industrial production with his concept of scientific management, which introduced efficiency methods into the workplace, cutting manufacturing costs and increasing profits. Taylor believed inefficient and lazy workers caused low productivity and waste. To combat this, management first had to break down the entire work process into simplified and standardized tasks and second provide close oversight and supervision of workers. When applied to business operations, this approach seemed to be highly successful, and it quickly became popular in the second decade of the twentieth century. "In the flood of enthusiasm, an attempt was made to apply the principles of scientific management to many aspects of American life, including the army and navy, the legal profession, the home, the family, the household, the church, and last but not least, to education."

As we saw earlier in this chapter, frustration with public schooling mounted during the late nineteenth and early twentieth centuries. Muckrakers claimed that schools wasted resources and revenue and failed to prepare students for useful occupations. "Gradually the criticism grew in volume, reaching a peak in the spring, summer, and fall of 1912. In these months a series of sensational articles were published in two of the popular journals with tremendous circulation, the *Saturday Evening Post* and the *Ladies' Home Journal*." Educators felt vulnerable, and they quickly embraced scientific management as a panacea. They equated the school board with a corporate board of directors and the superintendent with the chief executive officer. Viewing the school as a factory, educators saw the building principal acting as a shop foreman, the teachers as workers, and the children as products. The entire educational process became objectified. A whole class of educators was created who made decisions and initiated policies that significantly affected the schooling process and routine and who yet were not in the classrooms themselves. Educational bureaucrats implemented standardized tests, school surveys, efficiency ratings, and record-keeping requirements. They cut expenses by decreasing the number of teachers and increasing class size. Cost and efficiency, not educational philosophy, drove many school decisions and policies. Historian Raymond E. Callahan concludes that the "adoption of business values and practices in educational administration" was complete by 1930, when "school administrators perceived themselves as business managers, or, as they would say, 'school executives' rather than as scholars and educational philosophers"[50] This mentality still drives most school decisions.

The Gary Plan.   The Gary Plan, or platoon system, best illustrates the imposition of efficiency principles and methods on the schools. The plan used the school plant at full capacity and, at the same time, offered a richer variety of educational activities. William A. Wirt introduced the system as superintendent of the Gary, Indiana, schools. Wirt, born in a farming community near Markle, Indiana, in 1874, graduated from high school in 1892. He did not graduate from De Paul University until 1899 because he was working as a high school principal. He also attended summer classes at the University of Chicago, where he became exposed to "John Dewey's school innovations" and "to the public playground at Hull House." Wirt became superintendent of the Bluffton, Indiana, school district in 1899 and began to sketch the outline for his new school system. Agreeing to become superintendent in Gary in 1907, he fully developed and implemented his ideas in that immigrant, working-class steel town.[51]

Through his platoon system, Wirt ensured the "economical" use of entire school buildings, elementary through secondary. "This would be done through a departmentalized system in which the students moved from room to room. The plan was arranged so that all of the rooms, either home rooms or special rooms, were in constant use." Schools operated not only during the day but in the evening hours, becoming community social centers and holding adult classes much in the Hull House tradition. This improved "school machine," in Wirt's words, reduced the cost of "school plants and the actual per pupil cost of school maintenance" while at the same time permitted the addition of "manual training, nature study, music, drawing, playground and gymnasium equipment and specially trained teachers for each of these departments."[52] Gary's schools stressed preparation for work and Americanization; Wirt referred to high school diplomas as "work certificates."[53]

The Gary Plan attracted significant attention and was widely adopted by efficiency-minded school administrators, who could now justify any community's investment in its school plant. According to Ron Cohen's historical analysis of the experience, the platoon system provided the best of all worlds: "to most outsiders the work-study-play system—an efficient school organization combined with an enriched program—exemplified the illusive search for order, cost, savings, as well as expanded municipal services during the Progressive Period."[54] Child-centered Progressives endorsed it as well. None other than John Dewey and his daughter Evelyn gave Wirt high marks in their coauthored book, *Schools of Tomorrow*, first published in 1915. They praised Wirt's ability to "obtain" the

> necessary economy by using a building for twice as many pupils as the ordinary building is supposed to be able to take care of. There are two schools in every house, one from eight to three and the other from nine to four, and each takes its turn at the regular classrooms during alternate hours, the remaining half of the day being spent in the various occupations that make Gary unique. In this way enough money is saved to equip shops and pay extra teachers for the subjects that supplement the regular curriculum, and to pay for the extra sessions.[55]

During his Gary superintendency, Wirt also served as a paid consultant in New York City, Cleveland, and Minneapolis, implementing his educational system in those cities. "By

1929 the plan (or variations of it) was being used in 1,068 schools in 202 cities—schools with an estimated enrollment of 730,000 pupils."[56]

Rural Schools

The Progressive education movement largely began as an urban phenomenon, but reformers also turned their attention to rural schools. Until the middle of the twentieth century, for the most part cities had the best public schools in the nation. Because of a rich tax base, urban districts built the most elaborate facilities, attracted the best teachers, paid the highest salaries, and generally spent the most to educate children. Except for neighborhoods where the poor and minorities resided, city schools served as the hallmark of public education.[57]

Country schools, regardless of region, lagged behind their urban counterparts. The disparity was sharpest in the South. Most of the population resided in rural areas—70 to 90 percent. Rural children attended makeshift structures that lacked consistent maintenance. "Stumps, briars, or honeysuckle covered many a schoolyard, and the public road was the playground. At the Pamlico, North Carolina, school the house which belonged to the children in winter was turned over to goats for the other eight months." In 1907, Georgia's rural districts spent $3.77 per child "enrolled, in a term of 103 days, while town systems spent $12.72 per child in a term of 170 days."[58] African Americans, most of whom resided in the South prior to World War I, fared much worse.

Early twentieth-century country schools, like their nineteenth-century predecessors, focused on the "maintenance and reproduction of a common cultural identity." Local communities still managed to control schooling and determine what children actually learned. Schooling served to preserve local mores more than introduce children to new ideas. The lack of a coherent system and the dominance of an informal, largely local, decision-making process seemed to create an intellectual deficit. McGuffey's Readers remained in wide use, and in the Midwest and southern California these were supplemented by an irregular assortment of schoolbooks. Thus rural schools lacked academic uniformity. Memorization and recitation endured, dominating the daily classroom routine, and teachers persevered by meting out large doses of corporal punishment.[59] These schools also served as the centers of their communities, operating like an "enlarged family."[60] They welcomed weekend events, such as May festivals and community picnics; sponsored plays, musical performances, and the ever-popular spelling bees; and hosted monthly "family nights."

Community came at a price, of course, following a long rural tradition. "The exclusion of African American, Chinese, and Indian children from schools throughout the West in the nineteenth century was a powerful means of maintaining a cohesive, monocultural world." Rural instructors continued to face tight social controls. There was no escape. Rural and small-town school boards enforced strict limits on the personal and professional lives of female teachers, and their duties remained custodial as well as instructional. Through the interwar years of the twentieth century, female teachers still could not use makeup, wear sleeveless dresses or other immodest clothing, drink alcoholic beverages, play cards, and marry, dance, or smoke.[61]

The mere act of teaching proved to be an ordeal in many ways. The typical southern rural instructor walked 5.6 miles to her school and taught "seven different subjects" each day. Throughout the rural United States, teachers coped with multigraded one- and two-room schoolhouses. Daily nuisances added to the strain. In the West, rattlesnakes defiantly assumed residence in the local school's outhouse, leaving the instructor and her students to carefully extricate or exterminate them. Lottie Ross, a rural Oklahoma teacher carried a pistol at school, ever wary of strangers riding up to the lonely schoolhouse on horseback.[62]

For children, schooling was part of a long day and not without its daily challenges and possible dangers. Like their nineteenth-century counterparts, farm and ranch children began their days at dawn with a variety of chores, ate breakfast, then walked to school carrying their lunches in tin pails. "In the heavily settled states of the Midwest, such as Michigan, Ohio, and Illinois, only rarely did a rural pupil have to walk a distance greater than three miles. . . . In the states of the trans-Mississippi West, such the Dakotas and Nebraska, distances of more than three miles were common." Because of poor weather, swollen creeks, and other dangers, such as wolves, school began when the majority of students arrived. Others casually drifted in throughout the day. The trip home occasionally proved no less arduous; historian Paul Theobald describes one infamous incident:

> Sometime in mid-March, 1920, Hazel Miner, age sixteen, was driving a buggy home from school outside of Center, North Dakota. Her younger brother and sister (aged nine and eleven) accompanied her. The Miner children were caught in extreme cold, and when the buggy overturned, conditions were so bad that help could not get to them. Hazel put her brother and sister in the shelter provided by the overturned buggy, but this did not stop the wind from blowing off the blankets they used to cover themselves. Finally, she used her own overcoat to cover her siblings, and additionally, she laid her own body over them. The next day, Hazel was found frozen to death, but her siblings survived.

Walking these distances each day to and from the country school was not the only physical demand on the children. In most cases, the children's day ended only after completing hours of more chores at home. They ate dinner, completed their lessons, and went to bed. Because of the endless demands of farm and ranch work, rural attendance, which had been less than 50 percent during the pre–Civil War years, rarely exceeded 67 percent by World War I.[63] Schooling often took a back seat to work.

Progressive Reform.   Throughout the Progressive era, school reformers campaigned to improve rural education. A year-long study of rural schools commissioned by the National Education Association and conducted by the Committee of Twelve reported in 1896 that "no doubt the country school has points of advantage over the city schools . . . but on the whole it is inferior. The typical 'little red schoolhouse,' so invested with sentimentality, is a costly and unsatisfactory institution of education." Reformers implied a "small school" was a "poor school" lacking adequate resources, run by poor teachers, and treasuring provincialism in its simplicity.[64] "The Committee found that in 1890 an average of $13.23 had been spent on rural schoolchildren as opposed to the $28.87 spent on individual urban students."[65] The existence of so many tiny schools, irregularly and unevenly funded and crudely operated, ensured a lack of uniform education for children. Reformers thus held the typical country school, regardless of region, in low regard; in the early twentieth century, it was an anachronism.

In their often overexuberant commitment to "professionalism," rural school reformers, like their urban colleagues, approached schooling as a "business" and commonly borrowed corporate forms of centralized "management" that required trained experts to run the schools, not semiliterate amateurs. Their reform agenda demanded that they "centralize, bureaucratize, and systemize the schools." Uniformity was intended to provide equal schooling for all children, and efficiency methods were to eliminate redundancy of facilities, teachers, and costs as well as pool resources to provide a richer selection and wider variety of educational programs. Such changes had a price, however. The drive for standardization meant that community control would be sacrificed. Three key strategies evolved: preserve rural culture, institutionalize and formalize teacher supervision, and introduce an efficient decision-making apparatus and reduce costs. The latter two strategies assumed greater state control over the affairs of local schools, a transfer of power that turned out to be only gradual and incremental. The school modernization process moved ahead, nevertheless.

The Country Life Movement.   Rural to urban migration, which had begun in the 1830s and 1840s, continued unchecked throughout the nineteenth century and early decades of the twentieth. In the early 1800s, some 90 percent of this nation's population resided in the hinterland; by 1900, this figure had dropped to 60 percent and would continue to decline. Many people, most notably President Theodore Roosevelt, feared that the passing of this era and the loss of the "wholesomeness" of agrarian life would unduly harm the national character, destroying a significant part of the American heritage. Roosevelt appointed the Country Life Commission in 1908 to study this problem. "Liberty Hyde Bailey, professor of agriculture at Cornell University and one-time Michigan farm boy" headed the commission. After a year of study, the commission concluded "that in spite of the unprecedented rural prosperity there was much wrong with life in agrarian America. Intemperance, poor sanitation, poor roads, poor communication facilities, poor leadership, and a poor social life . . . were responsible for the declining farm population." The commission's report especially condemned rural education, claiming a dire need for agricultural training. Much in the framework of Progressive education, the report argued that "rural education must be related to living in order to keep farm boys and girls on the farms. . . . "[66] It should "dignify rural life." This gave impetus to reform-minded educators, who campaigned for these curricular changes throughout the Midwest.

However, the Country Life movement never fully met its goals. On the one hand, it stimulated the creation of rural organizations like the Boy and Girl scouts, Young Men's Christian Association, and 4-H clubs; initiated, in 1914, agricultural extension programs; aided communication by expanding mail delivery and access to telephones; and encouraged electrification. On the other hand, school reform efforts were largely unsuccessful. Many farmers opposed agricultural education, preferring that their children study academic subjects. But the Country Life movement failed to stem the rural-to-urban flow because rural life and the quality of country education did not cause this migration.[67] The commission had missed the point. The transformation of family farming into commercial agriculture, with unpredictable domestic and foreign markets, caused farmers to abandon the uncertainty and stress of rural work and migrate to cities in the hope of finding better economic opportunities in steel mills, automobile factories, and service industries.

Supervision.   Progressive educators also installed a system of supervision in their attempts to improve rural schools. School authority began to shift from the local township to the county. This transfer of power had actually begun in the Midwest as early as the 1860s; it occurred much later in states like California. There, women served in many administrative roles at first. "In 1902 . . . twenty-two women and thirty-five men were voted in as county superintendents of schools statewide." In the Midwest, however, women largely had subordinate roles in the public schools.[68]

On the surface, it seemed that the installation of an educational hierarchy reduced democratic participation. However, Theobald argues persuasively that it did not; in its initial stage, it acted to expand participation in some ways. Small, closed, community-based districts too often resorted to undemocratic means in making decisions and implementing policy, barring many groups from participating in school affairs. Midwestern "Yankee settlers" excluded the children of Norwegian and German immigrants, or saw that they were segregated for "language reasons." Wealthier community members exerted the most influence, sometimes arranging to have the schoolhouse located near their homes to shorten their children's daily journey. "Ironically," Theobald concludes, "it often took an undemocratic, centralized, bureaucratic school governance system, in this instance the appointed office of the state superintendent, to persuade local residents to behave democratically."[69]

The supervisory criteria that were implemented typically followed proven business, scientifically based methods, that is, observation of teachers and ultimately controlling how they worked and what they taught. State education authorities in California created publications for rural teachers and sponsored "the establishment of rural teachers clubs and groups," all of which was intended to disseminate knowledge of innovative teaching methods, share information, and generally systematize diverse and diffuse country schools. Publications stressed a standard Progressive pedagogical agenda: learner-centeredness, group activities, projects, various modes of student expression, and, guided by the Country Life movement, nature study, among many other initiatives.

Classroom instructors responded to supervision with ambivalence. Some resented it. Even through the interwar years, many isolated and small, ungraded, unsupervised, one- and two-room schoolhouses allowed creative teachers a great deal of "freedom" and flexibility to be "innovative." These instructors felt constrained and imposed on by the encroaching systemization and the bureaucratization that went with it.[70] Age grading, for example, introduced a rigid approach to schooling and undercut a teacher's own sense of who would be promoted and who would be retained. In the intimate setting of the small rural school, the instructor's flexibility permitted "the strengths and weaknesses of the students in the country school [to be] labeled according to the teacher's best judgement, and accommodations made for each students' capabilities insofar as that was possible."[71] But many teachers welcomed outside supervision because it introduced and spread new teaching ideas. Rural teachers throughout the nation in 1900 acted in a largely autonomous manner, but regardless of their perceptions or feelings, "by 1950 they found themselves almost at the bottom of a towering structure of administrative and supervisory experts."[72]

Consolidation.   Rural school mergers, strongly advocated by the Country Life Commission, proceeded at a much slower and irregular pace than did the introduction of supervision. As we saw in Chapter 6, the idea of establishing a public school bureaucracy sprouted during the nineteenth century. Similarly, the process of school consolidation originated, in Massachusetts, in 1869. By the early twentieth century, "educational experts had advocated consolidation as the solution to the 'rural school problem,' . . . arguing that larger schools offered more opportunities for children, that isolated teachers were unprofessional, and that larger administrative units were cheaper and more efficient."[73]

Consolidation exerted a major influence on the development of southern rural schools. "School consolidation in the South was one of the most successful reforms in the entire progressive reform movement."[74] Southern school reform, as we touched on in Chapter 6, moved that region's schools from the common-school to the modern graded-school era. In North Carolina, "[b]y 1925, the one-room common school, with its potbellied stove and homemade benches, had lost its place in all but the most isolated communities." At the elementary level, such "classification" and "ranking" of students in the educational process reflected, according to James L. Leloudis's historical analysis, the impact of the market economy on the New South. Rural schooling began to become highly formalized, organized, and standardized, with attendance record keeping, testing, and student evaluation. Classroom pedagogy changed, borrowing from Progressive philosophy. Finally, the schools now emphasized values like punctuality, regular attendance, citizenship, and competition, all useful in the new political economy.[75]

In the Midwest, school mergers had proceeded slowly and unevenly up to 1910, largely stymied by local resistance. Ten years later, though, Ohio, Indiana, and Illinois began to close local, usually "township" schools to reduce redundancy in taxing and expenditures and to "convey" students by wagon to a "centralized school."

> In both Ohio and Indiana, large, well-lighted, properly ventilated schoolhouses had been built to replace the one-room buildings that had served the people so long. The new schools had, or would have, libraries, the best educational apparatus available, and even some rooms for laboratories for conducting agricultural experiments. They were completely graded and thoroughly supervised by a principal who watched over four or five teachers who were much better prepared than any teacher the little school districts could afford.

School mergers reduced the number of teachers and lowered the costs of school building maintenance, and thus easily offset the new transportation expenses. Consolidation, proponents asserted, also facilitated closer supervision of children. Adult wagon drivers now escorted them to and from school. All students arrived on time, their attendance improved, and they all came to school during inclement weather.[76] In an effort to bring uniformity to the educational process, free textbooks, were introduced, though this proved to be slow and gradual. Schools also erected playground equipment for the children. Wisconsin's rural communities finally submitted to school mergers in 1909, although some districts stalled "until well in the 1920s."[77] "In short, the consolidated schools, economical and efficient, were as good as urban schools, and yet they could be established in the pure open country," offering the best of both worlds. "So the case for consolidation—from conveyance, to cost, to the conservation of country life—was made, and in no place did it receive a more enthusiastic reception than among Midwestern educators who had tried so long to solve the problem of rural education."[78]

These reforms threatened local control, beliefs, and values. To the bewilderment of school reformers, "country people," especially in the Midwest, resisted the trend toward uniformity. Local communities did not want to surrender their authority over the schools. "The impetus to consolidate rural schools almost always came from outside the rural community."[79] Their resistance was based on the results that had been achieved with their existing school system. In 1900, the Midwest claimed a 96 percent literacy rate, higher than any other region. Many communities attributed this to the diligence of able teachers, not fancy equipment, new-fangled instructional methods, and palatial school buildings. Communities also feared loss of authority over their children that transportation to distant schools implied. This was a particularly thorny issue when children were conveyed to a school centrally located in a nearby town. Town life and culture made farmers uneasy, and they were concerned about the possible deleterious influence of new values and bad habits, like smoking and "uncouth language."[80] At bottom, the problem rested on the fact that Progressive values, based on an urban-industrial context, stressed "individualism, competition, efficiency, and specialization." These values threatened the traditional agrarian values of "communalism, cooperation, tradition, and diversification."[81] In addition, the lengthened school day—because of longer commutes—was especially troublesome because the children were less able to complete their farm chores.

Temporarily, then, school consolidation languished. In 1920, 65 percent of the rural population opposed the merger of schools and districts. The state governments of Minnesota, Missouri, and Ohio even resorted to financial inducements to lure school districts into consolidation. Consolidation was delayed further by the Great Depression, which inflicted economic hardship and created a scarcity of valuable resources, and World War II, which diverted attention and priorities abroad. Thus, the one-room schoolhouse endured well into the 1940s. But these events eventually dealt the final blow to the rural school. The Depression caused demographic upheavals. Rural people were forced to abandon farm work to find employment in the cities, and the war lured people to urban areas with the higher wages offered by the armament industries and into the armed forces. These men and women rarely returned to their rural roots. In the 1940s, the rural Midwestern counties, typically having more than 100 independent one-room schools, merged to form, usually, a couple of dozen large school districts. School buses, which had been introduced in the 1920s, transported students over longer distances to centrally located and larger school buildings. The number of one-room schoolhouses nationwide declined from 200,000 in 1920 to 114,000 in 1940, and finally dropped dramatically to 20,000 by 1960. The physical size of school districts grew accordingly, with their number plummeting from about 120,000 in 1940 to approximately 40,000 in 1960. The custom of walking to a rural school virtually disappeared, and the physical and psychological distance between home and school increased.

As historian Kathleen Weiler points out, consolidation shifted the school environment, in states like California, from female dominated to male dominated. With the transformation of small, local, community schools to formalized, business like educational plants, male district superintendents and building principals supplanted their female colleagues. Weiler correctly argues that a crucial trade-off occurred, that is, consolidation largely liberated female teachers from the personal constraints imposed on them by local, provincial school boards, but it cost women their autonomy and power as administrators. They now became completely subordinate in male-governed schools.

In sum, the passing of the era of traditional rural education was a mixture of nostalgia and progress.[82]

Scientific Progressives

Along with the idea of managing schools like a business came the scientific approach to managing students. The most efficient means to mass educate them—just like products in an assembly line—required specialization. To best utilize scarce resources, schools began to differentiate among children by assigning them to specific academic tracks based on supposedly objective, scientific, standardized tests. The belief that drove all of this was that not all students were equal, and it was rarely challenged. "Simple reason decreed that the public schools should prepare some students directly for subordinate roles in the economy while it screened out those fit for further training in higher education."[83] This belief was predicated on the idea of "native intelligence," that is, that all intellectual ability was inherent. Nature dictated one's intellectual potential, not the environment. Nurture played a minor role, if any, in cultivating intelligence.

World War I stimulated the process of intellectual differentiation. War mobilization faced the United States Army with the formidable task of quickly categorizing millions of new recruits; an objective instrument was required to complete this task efficiently. The government commissioned an esteemed group of psychologists, including Robert Yerkes, Henry H. Goddard, and Lewis M. Terman, among others, to develop this instrument. Assembling at the Vineland Institute in New Jersey, the leading establishment for the study of the mentally retarded, on May 28, 1917, the group worked intensely on an intelligence test, which it presented to the Army on July 7. The Army tested and sorted 2 million soldiers with it. "The criterion used in the Army was ability to be a good soldier, which meant the ability to function well in a highly disciplined and highly stratified social organization." The intelligence test appeared to have even broader educational and social applications. "Robert Yerkes, head of the U.S. Army psychology team, wrote after the war, 'Great will be our good fortune if the lesson in human engineering which the war has taught is carried over directly and effectively into our civil institutions and activities.' The school, of course, was included in this dream of human engineering." Virtually the same test and directions were used in the public schools following the war—in 1920 alone 2 million children were tested.[84]

The Army's use of the intelligence test revealed apparent correlations between intelligence and occupation; as a result, test results began to be used in the schools for vocational guidance to classify students for jobs for which they had innate predilections. As Terman wrote in *Intelligence Tests and School Reorganization* in 1923:

> At every step in the child's progress the school should take account of his vocational possibilities. . . . Intelligence tests can tell us whether a child's native brightness corresponds more nearly to the median of (1) the professional classes, (2) those in the semi-professional pursuits, (3) ordinary skilled workers, (4) semi-skilled workers, or (5) unskilled laborers. This information will be a great value in planning the education of a particular child and also in planning the differentiated curriculum here recommended.

Terman further maintained that test scores should *not* be shared with students or parents: "If this rule is ever broken, it should be in the case of pupils in the upper grades or high school who test high but lack self-confidence or do not apply themselves diligently." Intelligence tests became the most widely used instrument to sort students into homogeneous academic groups, or tracks, that conformed to their ascribed abilities.[85]

The classification process which became universal, sparked an intense debate. Opponents maintained that placing complete reliance on intelligence testing, and especially on heredity as the source of intelligence, and on the sorting process that resulted undercut the very basis of democracy. "Mental tests suggested that not all men were equal or capable of being equal." Further, the academic segregation that occurred usually followed racial, ethnic, and social-class lines. "The common argument for those who had faith in the reliability of intelligence tests was that the poor were poor because of low intelligence and that blacks had not significantly progressed in American society because their race was genetically inferior."[86] Terman, a pioneer in intelligence testing and a proponent of the concept of innate ability, studied 1,000 gifted children and concluded in a 1924 article, "Conservation of Talent," that

> children of so many superiorities could hardly have acquired them all through environmental influences. Nor have they, for their heredity, too, is demonstrably superior. More than 50 percent . . . have sprung from the top 4 percent or 5 percent of the vocational hierarchy. The professional and semi-professional classes account for more than 80 percent. The unskilled labor classes furnish but a paltry 1 percent or 2 percent. One fourth of our children have at least one parent who is a college graduate. The average schooling for parents is about 12 grades completed as compared with 6 for the general population.[87]

This type of attitude and this kind of research led to a very new definition of schooling. It now served, through differentiated programs of study, only to prepare students for futures that matched their specific abilities. The debate over testing and tracking remained largely unresolved, and the public schools continued to employ intelligence tests and the tracking process for decades.

Some took this notion of innate ability a step further. Goddard, another leader of the intelligence-testing advocates, argued for an "aristocracy in democracy" in his 1920 book *Human Efficiency and Levels of Intelligence*. Because of below-average intelligence, the majority of people should not be permitted to vote. As he stated it, "while we believe in democracy, we may nevertheless admit that we have been too free with the franchise and it would seem a self-evident fact that the feebleminded should not be allowed to take part in civic affairs; should not be allowed to vote."[88] Carl Brigham, another noted psychologist, contended in his influential 1923 book *A Study of American Intelligence* that ethnic and social differences, based on the outcomes of the original Army intelligence tests, appeared to exist. He claimed that Americans of northern and western European descent scored higher than immigrants from southern and eastern Europe. In addition, European Americans earned higher test scores than African Americans. However, Brigham conveniently overlooked the fact that southern whites scored lowest of all European groups and received lower test results than northern African Americans. Existing prejudices, validated by a seemingly scientific process, led to the belief that certain ethnic and racial groups were, by nature, inferior in general intellectual ability. Brigham, fearful that "American intelligence is declining, and will proceed with an accelerating rate as the racial admixture becomes more and more extensive . . . " called for highly restrictive and selective immigration laws in order to prevent this country's physical stock and intellectual potential from deteriorating more.[89] Brigham's views lent credence to the congressional 1924 Johnson–Reed Act, which severely restricted immigration. We will return to this act in the next chapter.

The Special Child

The use of scientific measures to explain "individual differences" facilitated the segregation of special-needs students.[90] Alfred Binet's intelligence scale, known as the *Stanford–Binet Individual Test of Intelligence*, became the objective and scientific means of evaluating intelligence. According to historian Margaret A. Winzer, a new set of categories emerged based on mental age: idiots up to two years; "imbeciles" between three and seven years, "morons" between seven and twelve years, and "backward," with an intelligence quotient between 70 and 90. "Morons constituted the largest number of the mentally retarded population and were seen as the ones chiefly responsible for the antisocial behavior attributed to the group as a whole." Backward children, Goddard asserted, accounted for "14 percent of the general school population."[91] These findings dovetailed perfectly with school policy.

Compulsory attendance laws enacted by the states during the late nineteenth and early twentieth centuries forced urban public schools to confront the issue of exceptional children. To mitigate classroom behavior problems, assuage teacher complaints, and ease building principals' concerns about control, urban school officials established separate classrooms for the these children; "that is, segregation of selected pupils in special classrooms."[92] The segregating of exceptional children was most common in urban school districts, which instituted special schools as well as separate classes. Rural schools lacked the resources to accommodate these children. Boston had established separate and "ungraded" classes as early as 1879 and expanded them greatly over the next twenty years. Prior to the introduction of standardized mental tests, the city's schools had no fixed criteria for isolating these students. Overaged students, immigrant children, and those with poor behavior found themselves assigned to ungraded classrooms. "In effect, then, the ungraded classes became a catchall for students who for whatever reason could not perform satisfactorily in the regular grades as well as for older children who needed to learn basic skills but also, it was believed, had to be kept apart from younger pupils." Ordinary classrooms ran smoother and teachers operated more efficiently without the distractions of these children.[93]

"By 1911 more than one hundred large city school systems had established special schools and special classes for disabled children, and a number of states had begun to subsidize special programs by paying the excess costs special classes entailed."[94] In Baltimore, enrollment in special schools and classes grew slowly but steadily during the 1920s, from 1,421 in 1926 to 2,722 in 1929. Enrollment jumped to 10,956 in 1936 because of the Great Depression which reflected the general overall increase in school attendance because of a lack of jobs. "Compulsory attendance laws did not eliminate exclusionary practices; they merely changed the form of exclusion to in-school segregation." Administrators located special classes in school basements and former closets and generally secreted these children away in somewhat remote and bleak areas of buildings, totally separating them from the rest of their peers in all ways. Special education students, most of them from poor or working-class backgrounds, became stigmatized as a result.[95]

DAY ELEMENTARY SCHOOLS. UNGRADED CLASSES. "MOTOR METHOD"
OF TEACHING UNGRADED CHILDREN. "THE WORKING HAND
MAKES STRONG THE WORKING MIND"

(c. 1916) New York City Board of Educational Archives, Milbank Memorial Library, Teachers College, Columbia University.

Progressive educational philosophy had many crosscurrents. As we have seen, proponents of the child-centered approach focused on the student, social reconstructionists were trying to establish a radically new society, administrative progressives promoted efficiency, and scientific progressives touted tracking and segregation. The result of all these reform efforts was diverse curricula. Previously, the humanistic curriculum, stressing the traditional Western liberal arts subjects, had been followed. Three new curricula emerged in the Progressive era. The developmentalists, "infused with romantic ideas about childhood" and influenced by educational psychology, wanted the educational process to follow "the lines of a natural order of development in the child." Social meliorists promoted "the schools as a major, perhaps the principal, force for social change and social justice." Those educators who focused on social efficiency envisioned a new technological society that "needed a far greater specialization of skills in the curriculum . . . than had heretofore prevailed." What unfolded in the twentieth century was a "loose" and untidy "compromise" among these forces.[96] However, the dominant theme was differentiation, as we will see in the next chapter.

PROFESSIONALS OR WORKERS?

Speaking at the 1904 annual meeting of the National Education Association (NEA) in St. Louis, Margaret Haley railed against the imposition of the corporate model of decision making on the public schools:

> Two ideals are struggling for supremacy in American life today: one the industrial ideal, culminating thru [sic] the supremacy of commercialism, which subordinates the worker to the product and the machine; the other, the ideal of democracy, the ideal of educators, which places humanity above all machines, and demands that all activity shall be the expression of life. . . . Today, teachers of America, we stand at the parting of the ways.

Her speech, titled "Why Teachers Should Organize," expressed fear that classroom instructors would become subservient, students would be dehumanized, and the educational process would suffer primarily because of the influence of administrative progressives.[97] Progressive philosophy had moved the child to the center of the educational process as well as redefined and expanded the school curriculum. The teaching process and the instructor's role in the classroom, school, and community had altered as a consequence. With the public schools assuming additional social responsibilities, the teacher's functions increased and grew complex and demanding. Further, although some elements of the Progressive movement seemed to elevate the professional status of classroom instructors, highlighting their expertise, the scientific management aspect appeared to reduce them to mere workers in the assembly line that was school.

Thus, the Progressive education movement had brought to the surface two conflicting visions of the teacher's role during the early twentieth century. One role was that of the professional educator, an image that had begun during the common-school period. By the early 1900s, the NEA equated teachers with physicians and attorneys; like them, teachers commanded a special body of knowledge, acted above politics and special interests, and related to students as patients and clients. Another image, which took root in the 1890s and was eventually institutionalized in the American Federation of Teachers (AFT) union, was that teachers were more similar to blue-collar workers in their low pay, poor working conditions, job insecurity, few, if any, job benefits, subordinate decision-making role in the burgeoning school bureaucracy, and therefore their need to resort to direct action. Thus, the NEA and the AFT embraced profoundly different philosophies about teacher welfare and rights.

"Unquestioned Obedience"

As the public school system formalized and expanded during the latter half of the nineteenth century, educators saw the need for a professional organization. The National Teachers Association (NTA) emerged in 1857. Belying its name, however, it was run by male administrators, both at the public school and college levels, relegating female classroom instructors to mere spectators. The NTA evolved into the NEA in 1870. Although "women were granted the right to hold office," through the late nineteenth and early twentieth centuries female teachers made little headway in leadership positions. This generated some internal tensions. Male administrators comprised "50 percent" of the association's "active membership." But female instructors who dominated the public school workforce and swelled the NEA's annual summer meetings, only comprised "11 percent" of its actual membership.[98]

Administrators not only were the majority of the membership but commanded the NEA's philosophy, which was based on a hierarchy of authority. In 1908, William Estabrook Chancellor, superintendent of the Washington, DC, school district, proclaimed a separate "class of school directors, administrators, and supervisors, whose function is management rather than instruction." School administrators made decisions and teachers implemented them. Aaron Gove, Denver school superintendent, described this relationship: "The instruments used for that execution, namely the teachers, are furnished to this executive officer, who is instructed to use them in the performance of his duties, he having the knowledge and skill and ability to select given instruments for given purposes in order to obtain the results." William C. Bagley, a pioneer of school administration, wrote in his 1910 book *Classroom Management* that the ideal classroom instructor displayed "unquestioned obedience" to such authority.[99] The association further maintained that all educators were professionals, an attitude clearly stated in its constitution and charter: "That the purpose and object of the corporation shall be to elevate the character and advance the interests of the profession of teaching and to promote the cause of education in the United States."[100] The NEA advanced the general betterment of education and ignored the particular needs of teachers. As a result, this administrator-dominated organization implemented few, if any, initiatives regarding teacher welfare.

While the male-dominated NEA appeared to be careening headlong into a direct confrontation with female elementary teachers, the Chicago Teachers Federation (CTF), founded in 1897, excluded administrators and addressed teacher issues directly. Scientific management and its centralization of educational decision making that purposely borrowing the corporate model of business organization proved to be the most pressing problem. Catherine Goggin, an elementary instructor, CTF charter member, and its second president, steered the fledgling organization to an activist and political path. Margaret Haley, Goggin's colleague and another elementary teacher, gave the CTF high visibility. As "early feminists," these "two women shared a belief that women were destined to assume a political role in American life, and together they generated a charismatic leadership that inspired literally thousands of public school teachers across the nation."[101] These early leaders had widely divergent backgrounds and contrasting styles. Goggin, born in New York state in 1855, came from a somewhat affluent and genteel situation. She was related to one of Chicago's more popular and powerful judges, attended Chicago's best public high school, and carried on a family tradition of teaching. Before her premature death in 1916 in a streetcar accident, Goggin quietly guided CTF policies and strategy. Her genial and persuasive personality stood in sharp contrast to Haley's fiery and confrontational methods. Born in 1861, Haley had to begin teaching at age sixteen in rural Illinois because of her father's work and business failures. She moved to Chicago in 1882 and taught at an elementary school located in one of the poorer sections of that city. In January 1900, Haley became CTF's full-time "business representative."[102]

Under the leadership of Goggin and Haley, the CTF waged aggressive campaigns for teacher benefits and spearheaded social reforms. They fought for pensions and led a successful legal battle against several of Chicago's prominent corporations that were paying taxes substantially below their real property value or no taxes whatsoever. More revenue thus became available to the schools and for salaries. "Margaret Haley traveled to

Baltimore, Philadelphia, and Boston during the Chicago tax campaign. In each city, she found a basis for uniting the women teachers to obtain better wages."[103] In 1902, now with 5,000 members, the CTF formally affiliated with the Chicago Federation of Labor, linking it directly to labor unionism. Furthermore, "the CTF . . . supported many reform movements including woman suffrage, municipal ownership of public utilities, direct primaries, the popular election of United States's senators, and referendum and recall."[104] Goggin and Haley wanted the NEA to recognize the needs of public school instructors, to protect them, and to promote benefits for them. The association, which had an organizational structure that reflected specific educational interests, such as research and safety, did not have a classroom teacher division. Led by Haley, the CTF began to challenge the NEA's leadership as early as the 1901 annual meeting, calling attention to the hardships of teachers. At first, the association's patriarchs patronized her and belittled her efforts. In time, they began to view the CTF with horror; outraged, they denounced it as a radical and irresponsible organization, rebuked Haley, and defended scientific management. "In the period between 1913 and 1922, professionalism and unionism became two opposing forces, not because they were inherently in opposition but because unionism was so adamantly opposed by the new administrative Progressives within the NEA."[105]

"Factoryizing Education"

Teacher organizing efforts were not confined to Chicago; similar activities were unfolding in cities of varying sizes and in regions throughout the nation. Teachers in Atlanta, Boston, Butte, Montana, Cleveland, Gary, Indiana, New York City, Oklahoma, Philadelphia, and Scranton, Pennsylvania, St. Paul, Minnesota, San Francisco, and Washington, DC all created their own organizations. Male instructors were included. These scattered efforts coalesced on April 15, 1916 when various teacher groups met in Chicago to organize the American Federation of Teachers. The American Federation of Labor (AFL) granted the AFT an official charter. At the official ceremony, Samuel Gompers, AFL president, welcomed classroom teachers into the fold of national labor.

Like the CTF, the AFT in its early years preferred to be affiliated with the NEA and reform it from within, persuading it to focus on teacher issues. Indeed, feeling pressure, association leaders created the Department of Classroom Teachers in 1913 and mandated the election of female presidents during alternate terms. In 1922, after an aggressive recruiting campaign, it claimed some 100,000 members. Nevertheless, entrenched association leaders doggedly refused to have anything to do with unions in general and the subject of teacher welfare in particular. By 1921, the AFT and the NEA operated as rivals.[106]

The fledgling AFT suffered from internal discord and weaknesses as well as entrenched opposition, which severely limited its effectiveness. Federation members elected Charles Stillman of the Chicago Federation of Men Teachers as the first president, a rebuke to Haley and her Progressive agenda. Haley opposed " 'factoryizing education,' making the teacher an automaton, a mere factory hand . . . ," but with the transfer of power, the needs of female elementary teachers became subordinate to those of male secondary instructors, who were generally in favor of the scientific management approach. Tensions grew between these two factions. The AFT further lost its militant edge by aligning with AFL leaders and their policies, among them supporting U.S. entrance into World War I, which Haley vehemently opposed. In addition, the federation was organizationally diffuse. From the beginning, the AFT had been a loose confederation of local, usually urban, teacher organizations. Their autonomy impaired the development of a coherent national teachers union. Finally, and ironically, the AFT maintained a no-strike policy.[107] Despite the relative meekness of the AFT, school boards across the nation lashed out at it and its members. When the Chicago Board of Education prohibited union affiliation for classroom instructors in 1915, Haley withdrew Local #1 of the CTF from the AFT the following year, which significantly depleted its membership. "In 1920, the San Francisco Board of Education warned teachers that union membership would cost them their jobs while the same ruling was made in St. Louis. In May of the that same year, eighty-two members of the local in Lancaster, Pennsylvania, were dropped by the board of education."[108]

The Lowest Bidder

The weakness and turbulence of teacher organizations prevented them from having an impact on low salaries and differentiation based on both race and gender. Although in northern cities, few, if any, salary inequalities existed between races, this was not the case in the South. "By 1914, Richmond's white teachers earned $91.10 a month, while their black peers got $58.90. In Montgomery in 1890, white faculty members averaged $60 monthly; blacks received just $38, and the highest-paid black instructor made 20 percent less than the lowest salaried white teacher."[109] As we saw in Chapter 5, female instructors, generally speaking, received less than their male counterparts, with a few exceptions. In addition, urban teachers usually were assigned academic responsibilities based on gender. Male teachers usually taught at the secondary levels while female instructors dominated the elementary grades. Salary differentiation reflected these academic levels, with secondary paid higher than elementary. Urban and rural pay differences existed as well; city teachers generally received more money than rural and small-town instructors. Thus, many urban female teachers received higher salaries than their rural male counterparts. At the very bottom of the educational pay scale nationwide, were rural, female, southern, African American instructors.[110]

The Great Depression was devastating for teachers. Rural teachers received an average of $650 a year (southern African American instructors earned $524). In urban school districts, "[f]rom 1929–30 to 1933–34, average teachers' salaries dropped from $1,420 to $1,227" while superintendents earned about $4,000 a year. Insecurity grew. Classroom instructors and school administrators alike lost their jobs. Class size ballooned. When the Chicago schools ran out of money, the board paid its teachers with scrip, a virtually worthless IOU. Thousands of the city's teachers stormed the banks on April 1933 demanding cash for their scrip. Classroom instructors in other states and cities likewise protested, often successfully.[111] Teachers' personal and academic freedoms also suffered during this time because of weak and ineffective teacher organizations. A contract in a small North Carolina town stipulated the following behaviors for its female instructors:

> I promise to abstain from all dancing, immodest dressing, and other conduct unbecoming a teacher and a lady.
> I promise not to go out with any young men except as it may be necessary to stimulate Sunday School work.

I promise not to fall in love, to become engaged or secretly marry. . . .

I promise to sleep at least eight hours each night, to eat carefully, to take every precaution to keep in the best of health and spirits in order that I may be better able to render efficient service to my pupils. . . . [112]

These conditions, when coupled with the Red scare of the late 1930s, as we will see in Chapter 10, deprived public teachers of many basic civil rights.

In the late 1920s, George S. Counts expressed serious concern about education's obsession with the business mentality and its methods. The concentration of power in a hierarchical system of decision making, dominated at the school board level by a conservative business and professional elite, constituted a serious threat to academic freedom for teachers and students alike. As defenders of the status quo, school board members did not tolerate new or challenging ideas. School boards across the country consequently opposed teacher unions and teacher power in any form.[113]

Teacher organizations appeared, coalesced, and in some cases grew during the Progressive era. Most classroom instructors saw themselves as respected professionals; some viewed themselves as lowly workers. Most accepted administrative reform as an enlightened expression of professionalism; a few opposed it as an impediment to teaching and learning. Regardless of the perspective, the once-autonomous schoolteacher was now directed by indiscriminate policies set by a largely unseen source. The only power they had seemed to be limited to the confines of their classrooms, and even that power was constrained. The situation would change markedly after World War II.

CONCLUSIONS

The Progressive education movement inaugurated the modern American public-school system, philosophically, institutionally, professionally, and even architecturally. At the beginning of that era, in 1880, "an American averaged less than three full years of schooling." Only 1 million school-aged children attended the public schools that year. By 1920, the figure had climbed to 21 million.[114] By that time, schools had adopted a myriad of functions, assuming responsibility for the intellectual, vocational, physical, emotional, and psychological needs of children. Too many children, however, did not benefit from these changes. In some cases, Progressive school reform actually limited their educational experience rather than broadened it. Instead of liberating them, schooling actually restricted their opportunities by segregating them in specialized academic programs.

ACTIVITIES FOR FURTHER EXPLORATION

1. What was a muckraker? To capture the flavor of the work of Progressive journalist–muckraker Lincoln Steffens, "*The Shame of the Cities*: Steffens on Urban Blight" and "Lincoln Steffens Exposes 'Tweed Days in St. Louis' " can be found at http://chnm.gmu.edu/us/many.taf. What is the tone of Steffens's findings? At this same

Web site you can also examine the work of Jacob Riis, "Jacob Riis Tours New York City's Fourth Ward." Another site, http://www.yale.edu/amstud/inforev/riis/title.html, displays photographs from *How the Other Half Lives: Studies Among the Tenements of New York* as well as the accompanying text. Please be aware that Riis reflects the perspectives of that time; that is, you will find ethnocentric as well as racial commentary by the author.

2. To gain better insight into the influence of romantic thinkers on the Progressive education movement, see an analysis of Jean-Jaques Rousseau's naturalistic approach to child raising at http://www.infed.org/thinkers/et-rous.htm.

3. Frederich Froebel's biographical background as well as other information related to his influence can be found at http://www.infed.org/thinkers/et-froeb.htm.

4. How do present day classroom practices compare to those advocated by the Progressive education movement? Review the principles of the Progressive Education Association in light of today's practices. How many seem to still exist? How have others changed? Consider William H. Kirkpatrick's 1918 article " 'The Project Method': Child-Centeredness in Progressive Education" at http://chnm.gmu.edu/us/many.taf compared to " 'A Modern School': Abraham Flexner Outlines Progressive Education."

5. Should anyone be permitted to serve on school boards and make important educational decisions? School governance changed profoundly during the Progressive era; much of that legacy remains. Observe a local school board meeting. Interview a local school district superintendent or board member to gain insight into their "insider" experiences and expertise.

6. What is your response to the classic nurture–nature debate? Review the following documents: " 'The March of the Psychos': Measuring Intelligence in the Army"; "In Defense of IQ Testing: Lewis Replies to Critics"; " 'The Facts Must Be Faced': Intelligence Is Destiny," and "Debunking Intelligence Experts: Walter Lippmann Speaks Out," among others, at http://chnm.gmu.edu/us/many.taf.

7. Do you think that there should be teacher unions? Teacher organizations and unions became prominent during the Progressive era. Margaret Haley, an elementary classroom instructor, played a crucial role in the development of the American Federation of Teachers (AFT). For a brief biography and further details about her views, refer to the following Web site: http://www.aft.org/history/afthist/oconnor/oconnor/sld003.htm. Additional historical information about the AFT can be located at the federation's main Web site: http://aft.org/about/proud.html.

NOTES AND SOURCES

In order to condense endnotes, the first work cited is the primary one, usually the source of any direct quotes. Subsequent references serve as supplementary, or additional, sources of paraphrased information and/or alternative historical interpretations.

1. Mayer's shocking, yet comical, description is quoted in Barbara Finkelstein, *Governing the Young: Teacher Behavior in Popular Primary Schools in* *Nineteenth-Century United States* (New York: Falmer Press, 1989), p. 54. Finkelstein cites excerpts from Mayer's book on pp. 320–327.

2. Richard O. Boyer and Herbert M. Morais, *Labor's Untold Story* (New York: United Electrical, Radio & Machine Workers of America, 1976), p. 134.

3. The quotes in these paragraphs are from Samuel P. Hays, *Response to Industrialism, 1885–1914* (Chicago: University of Chicago Press, 1957), pp. 4–8, 13–15.

4. David B. Tyack, *The One Best System: A History of American Urban Education* (Cambridge, MA: Harvard University Press, 1974), p. 30.

5. The quotes in these paragraphs are from Hays, *Response to Industrialism*, pp. 17, 37, 40, 41, 43. Also, see Boyer and Morais *Labor's Untold Story*, pp. 60, 91, 125–126.

6. Gerald N. Grob and George Athan Billias, *Interpretations of American History: Patterns and Perspective, since 1877* (New York: Free Press, 1987), pp. 230, 231, 245.

7. Jeffrey E. Mirel, "Progressive School Reform in Comparative Perspective," in *Southern Cities, Southern Schools: Public Education in the Urban South*, eds. David N. Plank and Rick Ginsberg (Westport, CT: Greenwood Press, 1990), p. 161.

8. Lincoln Steffens, *The Shame of the Cities* (New York: McClure, Phillips & Co., 1904; rpt. New York: Hill and Wang, 1988.

9. Jacob A. Riis, *How the Other Half Lives* (New York: Charles Scribner's Sons, 1890; rpt. New York: Dover Publications, 1971), pp. vii, 91, 136–138, 143, 145–146, 148, 156.

10. The first quote in this paragraph is from Lawrence A. Cremin, *The Transformation of the School: Progressivism in American Education* (New York: Vintage Books, 1964), pp. 4, 5. Also, see David B. Tyack, *The One Best System*, pp. 55–56; Rice is quoted on p. 82. Refer as well to Finkelstein, *Governing the Young*, pp. 320–327.

11. The quotes in these paragraphs are from G. J. Barker-Benfield, "Jane Addams," in *Portraits of American Women: From Settlement to the Present*, eds. G. J. Barker-Benfield and Catherine Clinton (New York: St. Martin's Press, 1991), pp. 339–341. Also consult Cremin, *The Transformation of the School*, pp. 60–61; Ellen Condliffe Lagemann, ed., *Jane Addams on Education* (New York: Teachers College Press, 1985), pp. 11–12, 15, 16, 171, 174, 176, 178, 180, 185. Addams's quote is from Lagemann, p. 179.

12. The quotes and much of the biographical information in these paragraphs are from Jack K.

Campbell, *Colonel Francis W. Parker: The Children's Crusader* (New York: Teachers College Press, 1967), pp. 1, 3, 10, 13–14, 15–18, 34, 40–41, 45, 48–49, 50, 52–53, 63, 68, 70–72. Refer as well to Barbara Beatty, *Preschool Education in America: The Culture of Young Children from the Colonial Era to the Present* (New Haven, CT: Yale University Press, 1995), pp. 84–85; Gerald L. Gutek, *A History of the Western Educational Experience* (Prospect Heights, IL: Waveland Press, 1995), pp. 223–225, 257, 394–396; James L. Leloudis, *Schooling the New South: Pedagogy, Self, and Society in North Carolina, 1880–1920* (Chapel Hill, NC: University of North Carolina Press, 1996), p. 28.

13. Leloudis, *Schooling the New South*, p. 28. Also, refer to Campbell, *Colonel Francis W. Parker*, pp. 73, 78, 79, 80, 81, 82.

14. Beatty, *Preschool Education in America*, pp. 84–85. See, likewise, Campbell, *Colonel Francis W. Parker*, p. 87.

15. Campbell, *Colonel Francis W. Parker*, pp. 91, 106–107, 113, 118, 121, 130–131, 135, 140, 141. Refer as well to Leloudis, *Schooling the New South*, p. 28.

16. The quotes in these paragraphs are from Cremin, *The Transformation of the School*, pp. 125, 135, 136, 137, 138. Refer as well to Jane M. Dewey, "Biography of John Dewey," in *The Philosophy of John Dewey*, ed. Paul A. Schlipp (New York: Tudor Publishing Co., 1951), pp. 3, 5, 9, 10, 13, 19, 24, 27, 28, 29, 30, 34; Gerald L. Gutek, "John Dewey: Pragmatist Philosopher and Progressive Educator," in *Historical and Philosophical Foundations of Education: A Biographical Introduction* (Upper Saddle River, NJ: Merrill, 1997), pp. 319–320; Lagemann, *Jane Addams*, pp. 28–29. Herbart M. Kliebard, *The Struggle for the American Curriculum, 1983–1958* (Boston: Routledge & Kegan Paul, 1986), devotes an entire chapter to "The Curriculum of the Dewey School," see in particular, pp. 63, 69.

17. Martin S. Dworkin, *Dewey on Education: Selections* (New York: Teachers College Press, 1959), pp. 9, 17. Also see Jane M. Dewey, "Biography of John Dewey," p. 34; William J. Reese, "The Origins of Progressive Education," *History of Education Quarterly*, 41 (Spring 2001), pp. 1–24.

18. Cremin, *The Transformation of the School*, p. 117.

19. John Dewey, "The School and Society," in *Dewey on Education: Selections*, ed. Martin S. Dworkin (New York: Teachers College Press, 1959), pp. 38, 39.

20. John Dewey, "My Pedagogic Creed," in *Dewey on Education*, p. 23.

21. Cremin, *Transformation of the School*, p. 118; Dewey, "My Pedagogic Creed," p. 27.

22. Dewey, "School and Society," p. 41, 49.

23. Gutek, "John Dewey," p. 325.

24. Cremin, *Transformation of the School*, pp. 118, 241, 243–245, 247, 249, 257.

25. Caroline Winterer, "Avoiding a 'Hothouse System of Education': Nineteenth-Century Early Childhood Education from the Infant Schools to the Kindergartens," *History of Education Quarterly* (Fall 1992), p. 290. See as well Barbarba Beatty, " 'The Letter Killeth': Americanization and Multicultural Education in Kindergartens in the United States, 1856–1920," in *Kindergartens and Cultures: The Global Diffusion of an Idea*, ed. Roberta Wollons (New Haven, CT: Yale University Press, 2000), pp. 42–43, 45.

26. Beatty, *Preschool Education in America*, pp. 53, 54–56, 57; Beatty, " 'The Letter Killeth,' " p. 44; Selwyn K. Troen, *The Public and the Schools: Shaping the St. Louis System, 1838–1920* (Columbia, MO: University of Missouri Press, 1975), p. 99.

27. This biographical information on Froebel and the quotes are from Gutek, *A History of the Western Educational Experience*, pp. 260, 261, 262, 264. Also refer to Winterer, "Avoiding a 'Hothouse System of Education,' " p. 300; Wollons, *Kindergartens and Cultures,* pp. 2, 3.

28. Beatty, " 'The Letter Killeth,' " pp. 45, 46.

29. Beatty, *Preschool Education in America*, pp. 58–59, 61, 64–67. See as well Beatty, " 'The Letter Killeth,' " p. 46; Troen, *The Public and the Schools*, pp. 99, 102, 103, 107, 108; Winterer, "Avoiding a 'Hothouse System of Education,' " pp. 301, 310.

30. Winterer, "Avoiding a 'Hothouse System of Education,' " pp. 291, 304–306.

31. This section relies heavily for its quotes and information on Beatty, *Preschool Education in America*, pp. 72–74, 81–85, 89, 95, 99–101, 105, 108–109, 119–120, 124, 128, 134. Refer, likewise, to Beatty, " 'The Letter Killeth,' " pp. 47–48, 50–51, 54; Troen, *The Public and the Schools*, p. 102. According to Troen, p. 108, the St. Louis school district began to admit African American children in 1881.

32. Jurgen Herbst, *The Once and Future School: Three Hundred and Fifty Years of American Secondary Education* (New York: Routledge, 1996), pp. 93, 94.

33. David B. Tyack and Elisabeth Hansot, *Learning Together: A History of Coeducation in American Public Schools* (New Haven, CT: Yale University Press, 1990), pp. 114, 132–134, 137, 138.

34. Joseph Kett, *Rites of Passage: Adolescence in America, 1790 to the Present* (New York: Basic Books, 1977), pp. 138, 232, 233. Also, refer to Barbara Welter, "The Cult of True Womanhood: 1820–1860," *American Quarterly*, 18 (Summer 1966): pp. 151–174. Some parts of this section on adolescence, although reordered, are taken from Richard J. Altenbaugh, David E. Engel, and Don T. Martin, *Caring for Kids: A Critical Study of Urban School Leavers* (London: Falmer Press, 1995), pp. 35–42.

35. David Nasaw, *Children of the City: At Work and At Play* (New York: Oxford University Press, 1985), p. 187. Marvin Lazerson and W. Norton Grubb, eds., *American Education and Vocationalism: A Documentary History, 1870–1970* (New York: Teachers College Press, 1974), pp. 21–22.

36. Viviana Zelizer, *Pricing the Priceless Child: The Changing Social Value of Children* (New York: Basic Books, 1985), pp. 62–63, 65, 112. Also refer to Joseph M. Hawes, *The Children's Rights Movement: A History of Advocacy and Protection* (Boston: Twayne Publishers, 1991), pp. 52–53.

37. David Hogan, "Education and the Making of the Chicago Working Class, 1880–1930," *History of Education Quarterly*, 18 (Fall 1978), pp. 227, 231, 255.

38. Kett, *Rites of Passage*, pp. 3, 127.

39. Jeffrey E. Mirel, "Adolescence in Twentieth-Century America," in *Encyclopedia of Adolescence*, eds. R. M. Lerner, A. C. Peterson, and J. Brooks-Gunn (New York: Garland Publishing, 1991), pp. 1153, 1155–56. Also refer to Charles E. Strickland and Charles Burgess, *Health, Growth, and Heredity: G. Stanley Hall on Natural Education* (New York: Teachers College Press, 1965), pp. 22–23, 149; John Demos, *Past, Present, and Personal: The Family and the Life course in American History* (New York: Oxford University Press, 1986), p. 94; Joel Spring, "Youth Culture in the United States," in *Roots of Crisis: American Education in the Twentieth Century*, eds. Clarence J. Karier, Paul Violas, and Joel Spring (Chicago: Rand McNally, 1973), p. 199.

40. Philippe Aries, *Centuries of Childhood: A Social History of Family Life* (New York: Vintage Books, 1962), p. 30.

41. Mirel, "Adolescence," pp. 1154, 1157; Spring, "Youth Culture," pp. 201, 205.

42. George S. Counts, "A Humble Autobiography," in *Leaders in American Education: The Seventieth Yearbook of the National Society for the Study of Education*, ed. Herman C. Richey (Chicago: University of Chicago Press, 1971), pp. 151–153, 157–160, 163, 164, 170.

43. George S. Counts, *Dare the School Build a New Social Order?* (New York: John Day Co., 1932: rpt. New York: Arno Press, 1969), pp. 7–8, 10, 23–25, 31, 33–34, 37, 41, 47–48.

44. Gerald L. Gutek, *The Educational Theory of George S. Counts* (Columbus, OH: Ohio State University Press, 1970), pp. 5, 6, 21, 52, 62, 64, 104.

45. Samuel P. Hays, "The Politics of Reform in Municipal Government in the Progressive Era," in *Interpretations of American History: Patterns and Perspectives*. Volume 2. Eds. Gerald N. Grob and George Athan Billias (New York: Free Press, 1987), pp. 251–253, 255–256, 258–259.

46. The quotes in these paragraphs are from Tyack, *The One Best System*, pp. 37, 88, 89, 127, 141, 146, 147. Also refer to George S. Counts, *The Social Composition of Boards of Education* (Chicago: University of Chicago, 1927; rpt., New York: Arno Press, 1969), p. 12; Hays, "The Politics of Reform," p. 255.

47. The pamphlet is quoted in Hays, "The Politics of Reform," pp. 257–258. See also p. 261.

48. Counts, *Social Composition*, p. 74.

49. Tyack, *The One Best System*, p. 131.

50. The quotes in these paragraphs are from Raymond E. Callahan, *Education and the Cult of Efficiency: A Study of the Social Forces That Have Shaped the Administration of the Public Schools* (Chicago: University of Chicago Press, 1962), pp. vii, 23, 25, 28–34, 47, 90, 97, 99. For a full explication of scientific management, see Frederick Winslow Taylor, *The Principles of Scientific Management* (1911; rpt. New York: W. W. Norton, 1967). Refer as well to Richard J. Altenbaugh, "Teachers and the Workplace," in *The Teacher's Voice: A Social History of Teaching in Twentieth-Century America*, ed. Richard J. Altenbaugh (London: Falmer Press, 1992), pp. 157–161.

51. Ronald D. Cohen, *Children of the Mill: Schooling and Society in Gary, Indiana, 1906–1960* (Bloomington, IN: Indiana University Press, 1990), pp. 1–2, 5. Also refer to Callahan, *Education and the Cult of Efficiency*, pp. 128–129. Historiographic debate exists over the Gary Plan. Cremin, *Transformation of the School*, romanticizes the platoon system, relating it to Dewey's influences. Callahan, *Education and the Cult of Efficiency*, criticizes the Gary Plan, seeing it rooted in scientific management. Cohen shows both sides of this system and elucidates these interpretive differences on p. ix–x.

52. Wirt is quoted in Callahan, *Education and the Cult of Efficiency*, p. 130; refer too to p. 129. See also Cohen, *Children of the Mill*, p. 14.

53. Wirt here is quoted in Cohen, *Children of the Mill*, p. 28.

54. Cohen, *Children of the Mill*, p. 49.

55. John Dewey and Evelyn Dewey, *Schools of Tomorrow* (New York: E.P. Dutton & Co., 1962), p. 132.

56. Callahan, *Cult of Efficiency*, p. 130. Also see Cohen, *Children of the Mill*, pp. 49–50.

57. Jeffrey E. Mirel, *The Rise and Fall of an Urban School System: Detroit, 1907–81* (Ann Arbor, MI: University of Michigan Press, 1993), p. vii.

58. Louis R. Harlan, *Separate and Unequal: Public School Campaigns and Racism in the Southern Seaboard States, 1901–1915* (New York: Atheneum, 1969), pp. 21, 224. Refer as well to Spencer J. Maxcy, "Progressivism and Rural Education in the Deep South, 1900–1950," in *Education and the Rise of the New South*, eds. Ronald K. Goodenow and Arthur O. White (Boston: G. K. Hall, 1981), pp. 48, 163.

59. Kathleen Weiler, *Country Schoolwomen: Teaching in Rural California, 1850–1950* (Stanford, CA: Stanford University Press, 1998), pp. 95–96, 171. See also Maxcy, "Progressivism and Rural Education in the Deep South," p. 48; Wayne E. Fuller, *The Old Country School: The Story of Rural Education in the Middle West* (Chicago: University of Chicago Press, 1982), pp. 10, 11–12, 13, 93–96.

60. Fuller, *Old Country School*, p. 7.

61. Weiler, *Country Schoolwomen*, pp. 26, 96, 100, 171, 174, 175, 176, 177, 178. Also see Fuller, *Old Country School*, p. 212.

62. Maxcy, "Progressivism and Rural Education in the Deep South," p. 69. Refer as well to Weiler, *Country*

Schoolwomen, pp. 189, 191; Courtney A. Vaughn-Roberson, "Sometimes Independent But Never Equal—Women Teachers, 1900–1950," *Pacific Historical Review*, 53 (February 1984), p. 46.

63. Paul Theobald, *Call School: Rural Education in the Midwest to 1918* (Carbondale, IL: Southern Illinois University Press, 1995), pp. 102, 104, 105–106, 118–119.

64. Fuller, *Old Country School*, p. 111. The Committee of Twelve report is quoted from Fuller, pp. 101–102. See also Theobald, *Call School*, p. 162.

65. Theobald, *Call School*, p. 162.

66. Fuller, *Old Country School*, pp. 106, 108, 219–221. Also see Theobald, *Call School*, pp. 161, 163; Weiler, *Country Schoolwomen*, p. 61; Tyack, *The One Best System*, p. 23.

67. Theobald, *Call School*, pp. 170–172; Fuller, *Old Country School*, pp. 225, 226.

68. Weiler, *Country Schoolwomen*, pp. 67, 134. See also Fuller, *Old Country School*, p. 133; Theobald, *Call School*, pp. 66–67, 100.

69. Theobald, *Call School*, pp. 70, 71, 73–74. Theobald and Fuller, *Old Country School*, p. 107, profoundly disagree about the impact of the school bureaucracy on the democratic process. Theobald sees it as having a democratic influence; Fuller asserts that it imposed an undemocratic structure.

70. The quotes in these paragraphs are from Weiler, *Country Schoolwomen*, pp. 20, 66, 71, 73, 75, 119, 192, 199. Also refer to Maxcy, "Progressivism and Rural Education in the Deep South," p. 60.

71. Fuller, *Old Country School*, p. 196.

72. Maxcy, "Progressivism and Rural Education in the Deep South," p. 65.

73. Weiler, *Country Schoolwomen*, pp. 234–235. See as well Theobald, *Call School*, p. 174; Fuller, *Old Country School*, p. 228.

74. Maxcy, "Progressivism and Rural Education in the Deep South," 53.

75. Leloudis, *Schooling the New South*, pp. 24, 25, 30, 229. Refer also to Maxcy, "Progressivism and Rural Education in the Deep South," p. 52.

76. Fuller, *Old Country School*, pp. 228–229, 231–232.

77. Theobald, *Call School*, pp. 85, 86, 90.

78. Fuller, *Old Country School*, p. 232.

79. Tyack, *The One Best System*, p. 25. Also, see Cremin, *Transformation of the School*, pp. 275, 291.

80. Fuller, *Old Country School*, pp. 191, 235–236.

81. Theobald, *Call School*, p. 2.

82. Cremin, *Transformation of the School*, pp. 274–275; Fuller, *Old Country School*, pp. 1–2, 238, 245; Maxcy, "Progressivism and Rural Education in the Deep South," p. 52; Theobald, *Call School*, p. 177; Tyack, *The One Best System*, p. 25; Weiler, *Country Schoolwomen*, pp. 239, 244–245, 250.

83. Tyack, *The One Best System*, pp. 182, 188, 189.

84. The quotes in these paragraphs are from Edgar B. Gumbert and Joel H. Spring, *The Superschool and the Superstate: American Education in the Twentieth Century, 1918–1970* (New York: John Wiley & Sons, 1974), pp. 90–94. Also, refer to Robert L. Osgood, *For "Children Who Vary from the Normal Type": Special Education in Boston, 1838–1930* (Washington, DC: Gallaudet University Press, 2000), pp. 54, 55–56; Tyack, *The One Best System*, p. 207.

85. Terman is quoted in Clarence J. Karier, *Shaping the American Educational State, 1900 to the Present* (New York: Free Press, 1975), pp. 163, 172. Also, see Clarence J. Karier, "Testing for Order and Control in the Corporate Liberal State," in *Roots of Crisis: American Education in the Twentieth Century*, eds. Clarence J. Karier, Paul Violas, and Joel Spring (Chicago: Rand McNally, 1973), pp. 108–137. Refer as well to Tyack, *The One Best System*, pp. 204, 205, 208.

86. Gumbert and Spring, *The Superschool and the Superstate*, pp. 99, 100.

87. Terman is quoted in Karier, *Shaping the American Educational State*, p. 188.

88. Goddard is quoted in Karier, *Shaping the American Educational State*, p. 167.

89. Brigham is quoted in Karier, *Shaping the American Educational State*, p. 214. See also Gumbert and Spring, *The Superschool and the Superstate*, pp. 106–107; Osgood, *For "Children Who Vary from the Norm,"* pp. 55–56, and Tyack, *The One Best System*, p. 205.

90. Joseph L. Tropea, "Bureaucratic Order and Special Children: Urban Schools, 1890s–1940s," *History of Education Quarterly*, (Spring 1987), p. 39.

91. Margaret A. Winzer, *The History of Special Education: From Isolation to Integration* (Washington, DC: Gallaudet University Press, 1993), pp. 269, 272.

92. Tropea, "Bureaucratic Order and Special Children," pp. 31–32. Refer as well to Osgood, *For "Children Who Vary from the Norm,"* p. 57; Winzer, *History of Special Education*, pp. 323, 328–329, 331–332.

93. Osgood, *For "Children Who Vary from the Norm,"* pp. 76–77, 79, 80–81, 92.

94. Winzer, *History of Special Education*, pp. 314–315. See also Osgood, *For "Children Who Vary from the Norm,"* p. 59.

95. Tropea, "Bureaucratic Order and Special Children," pp. 34, 46, 48. Also refer to Barry M. Franklin, "Progressivism and Curriculum Differentiation: Special Classes in the Atlanta Public Schools, 1898–1923," *History of Education Quarterly*, 29 (Winter 1989), p. 591; Winzer, *History of Special Education*, p. 370.

96. Kliebard, *Struggle for the American Curriculum*, pp. 27–29.

97. Haley's speech is widely quoted. This excerpt is from Robert L. Reid, ed., *Battleground: The Autobiography of Margaret A. Haley* (Urbana, IL: University of Illinois Press, 1982), pp. 286–287. See as well Nancy Hoffman, *Woman's "True Profession": Voices from the History of Teaching* (Old Westbury, NY: Feminist Press, 1981), pp. 289–295; Marjorie Murphy, *Blackboard Unions: The AFT and the NEA, 1900–1980* (Ithaca, NY: Cornell University Press, 1990), p. 58.

98. The quotes in these paragraphs are from Murphy, *Blackboard Unions*, pp. 47, 48–49, 50, 52. Refer also to Wayne J. Urban, *Why Teachers Organized* (Detroit, MI: Wayne State University Press, 1982), p. 111.

99. Chancellor, Gove, and Bagley are quoted in Altenbaugh, "Teachers and the Workplace," pp. 158, 159, 160. See as well William E. Eaton, *The American Federation of Teachers, 1916–1961* (Carbondale, IL: Southern Illinois University Press, 1975), p. 23.

100. Edgar B. Wesley, *NEA: The First Hundred Years* (New York: Harper & Brothers, 1957), pp. 22–23.

101. Murphy, *Blackboard Unions*, p. 64. Also, see Eaton, *The American Federation of Teachers*, p. 5; Reid, *Battleground*, p. 33.

102. Reid, *Battleground*, pp. vii, viii. Refer as well to Murphy, *Blackboard Unions*, pp. 63, 64; Kate Rousmaniere, "Catharine Goggin," in

Historical Dictionary of American Education, ed. Richard J. Altenbaugh (Westport, CT: Greenwood Press, 1999), pp. 156, 157.

103. Murphy, *Blackboard Unions*, pp. 65, 66. See likewise Eaton, *American Federation of Teachers*, p. 5; Reid, *Battleground*, p. xi.

104. Eaton, *American Federation of Teachers*, pp. 6, 7. Murphy, *Blackboard Unions*, p. 67, and Reid, *Battleground*, p. xii, also describe the significance of the CFT's affiliation with the Chicago Federation of Labor.

105. Murphy, *Blackboard Unions*, pp. 53, 54, 55, 58–59, 81. See also Eaton, *American Federation of Teachers*, pp. 10–11.

106. Eaton, *American Federation of Teachers*, pp. 12, 14–19; Murphy, *Blackboard Unions*, pp. 80, 84; Reid, *Battleground*, pp. xxvii, xxx; Urban, *Why Teachers Organized*, pp. 113, 115, 134.

107. Haley is quoted in Reid, *Battleground*, p. 283; also see pp. xxviii, xxix. Refer as well to Eaton, *American Federation of Teachers*, pp. 16–17; Murphy, *Blackboard Unions*, pp. 80, 84–85; Urban, *Why Teachers Organized*, pp. 135, 136, 138.

108. Eaton, *American Federation of Teachers*, p. 20. See as well Murphy, *Blackboard Unions*, pp. 85–86; Reid, *Battleground*, pp. xvii, xviii.

109. Michael W. Homel, "Two Worlds of Race? Urban Blacks and the Public Schools, North and South, 1865–1940," in *Southern Cities, Southern Schools: Public Education in the Urban South*, eds. David N. Plank and Rick Ginsberg (Westport, CT: Greenwood Press, 1990), p. 247.

110. James L. Leloudis, *Schooling the New South*, p. 187.

111. David Tyack, Robert Lowe, and Elisabeth Hansot, *Public Schools in Hard Times: The Great Depression and Recent Years* (Cambridge, MA: Harvard University Press, 1984), pp. 32, 37, 39, 42–45.

112. These rules are quoted in Eaton, *American Federation of Teachers*, p. 23.

113. Counts, *Social Composition*, pp. 91–92; Callahan, *Cult of Efficiency*, pp. 120–122.

114. Neil G. McCluskey, *Catholic Education in America: A Documentary History* (New York: Teachers College Press, 1964), pp. 25, 30–31.

8

Universal and Equal Schooling?

Progressive reform, as we have seen, introduced the modern public-school system. It broadened the educational goals and curriculum for students and profoundly changed public schooling through its student-centered pedagogy. In spite of the best intentions of reform-minded educators, however, many children failed to experience positive results from Progressive philosophy and teaching methods. Progressive educational reform limited educational experiences for some poor and working-class children, girls, and many ethnic minorities. Furthermore, African American and Native American children were simply excluded from these innovations.

This chapter analyzes the role of social class, gender, ethnicity, and race in this time period to provide insight into the complexity and conflicts introduced by school reform and by broad social prejudices. Too often, public schooling did not transform lives or liberate children. It did not equip many children with the knowledge and skills necessary to pursue the American dream, achieve social mobility, or expand their intellects. It did operate in a concerted fashion to socialize groups of American children for prescribed social roles. We further attempt in this chapter to capture the struggles of parents and communities to ensure equal access and equal treatment of their children in the schools. In a few cases, various groups actually abandoned the public schools to create and support their own, alternative educational institutions.

"OUR CHILDREN ARE BEING TRAINED LIKE DOGS AND PONIES": THE SCHOOLING OF THE POOR AND WORKING CLASS

Race and ethnicity shaped educational policies and practices, but the social-class background of children influenced their schooling experiences as well. During the late nineteenth and early twentieth centuries, the demand for vocational education began to blur the separation between the workplace and

227

schooling. Not only did this trend continue the slow undermining of the family as the primary educator but it resulted in conflict over the fundamental issue of democracy in American schools. "What emerged was a redefinition of the idea of equality of educational opportunity and a rejection of the common-school ideal."[1]

Vocational Education and Tracking

Vocational education grew out of Progressive educational reform and began with the manual training concept. Its growth was driven by two forces: educational philosophy and business priorities.

Academic Motives

Many educators saw vocational education as an improvement over the traditional, one-dimensional academic emphasis of the typical American school curriculum. The 1876 Centennial Exposition in Philadelphia hosted a Russian display featuring "instructive shop training" created at the Moscow Imperial Technical School. Many leading American educators immediately embraced the concept and viewed such handwork as part of the larger educational process.[2]

Calvin Woodward developed an educational philosophy and program around this new idea at Washington University in St. Louis. It was not narrow training for work but part of general education. He argued for the synthesis of mental and manual labor. In an 1883 speech to the National Teachers Association, Woodward criticized present-day schooling as "boring" and "monotonous." He saw numerous benefits to manual training: "boys" would stay in school, "better intellectual development" would occur, occupations would be wisely chosen, "material success for the individual and for the community" would result, and social class tensions would be reduced.[3] This was all embodied in the Manual Training School, which he opened at the university in 1880. The curriculum of his three-year secondary school included traditional academic subjects as well as manual skills, such as wood turning, forge work, and brazing and soldering. As historian Lawrence Cremin summarizes it, "the goal of the course was liberal rather than vocational; the emphasis throughout was to be on education rather than production for sale, or principle rather than narrow skill, an art rather than the tradesman's competence." Through this approach, as Woodward put it, the "whole boy" would be educated.[4]

The concept of manual training evolved to assume a broad social and educational reform agenda. "The industrial education movement involved child labor and compulsory education movements, the junior high movement, vocational guidance, and neighborhood school concept and more, the very way Americans had traditionally conceived of the public schools." The rhetoric in support of the movement often stressed a child-centered approach. Schooling would serve as a bridge to a job and perhaps meaningful work. Work training in the nurturing environment of the public schools would be very different from the exploitative child labor systems in the factories, mines, and fields. Compulsory attendance also fit into the scheme. "Public elementary school enrollment climbed from about 12,500,000 in 1900 to 16,000,000 in 1910, while the average number of days per pupil per semester climbed in this decade from 86.3 to 113."[5] Yet the high rate of school leaving at the secondary level still troubled educators. In 1910, the National Education Association

(NEA) released its "Report of the Committee on the Place of Industries in Public Education." The NEA supported the general notion of vocational education at the secondary level, beginning in the seventh grade, but its attempt in the report to reconcile the notions of democracy and differentiated curricula largely failed.[6]

Progressive school reformers distorted the clear linkages between economic conditions and attendance. They deemphasized poverty as the cause of school leaving, believing it was caused by boredom instead. The economic opportunities offered by industrial education, advocates reasoned, would hold students in school. "Child-labor reform groups and reformist educators played down the poverty motive and stressed the dissatisfaction of the child with his [sic] schooling, since to do so strengthened their claims that children did not really work"; that is, the notion that leaving school created poverty superseded the idea that poverty caused school leaving. Reformers' arguments that vocational education provided opportunities to working-class and poor children, who would now have something to strive for and so would remain in school succeeded.[7] Furthermore, educators pointed out, only 5 percent of school-aged students pursued higher education. The vast majority, 95 percent, entered the industrial workforce. "For the children of the masses the whole system of public education had to be reshaped along vocational lines to help them better to adjust to the life they were destined to lead."[8]

Schooling for Profit

The second impetus for the introduction of vocational education in the public schools was that many industrial leaders wanted more productive workers. The National Association of Manufacturers (NAM) campaigned for industrial training from its founding in 1896. In the 1890s, emphasis shifted from mere manual training to outright vocational education: "where manual training had proposed to train the hand in order to perfect a general cultural education, vocational education intended to prepare its students for specific jobs." Foreign economic competition, especially with Germany, fueled NAM's educational goal. The association's Committee on Industrial Education issued two reports, one in 1905 and another in 1912, stating its position. In the first report, NAM supported industrial education for several reasons: in addressing the high rate of school leaving, it argued that industrial training would make the dropouts employable; it attacked the American Federation of Labor's (AFL) apprenticeship system as a monopoly and restriction of industrial training— vocational education promised a sufficient and continuous supply of skilled workers; finally, industrial education was a "national necessity" in order to compete economically with other nations. A sense of urgency, if not crisis, permeated the report. The 1912 report identified workers with machinery and promoted the production of "human capital." It pointed to adolescence as the ideal time for the creation of this human capital and said it was a "mistake" for the "State," or government, to lose "control and direction" of its youth. "Germany, France, Belgium, Australia, and Switzerland save, and infinitely strengthen and develop, the manhood and efficiency of their people, by retaining an educational control through these years."[9]

Another organization, the National Society for the Promotion of Industrial Education (NSPIE), an amalgamation of educators and industrialists formed in 1906, maintained a clear mission: "to unite the many forces making toward industrial education the country over."[10] The NSPIE's cooperative education plan was one of the early formalized expressions of special education for poor and working-class adolescents; it linked the public school classroom to the factory shop floor. The NSPIE developed thirteen cooperative industrial schools in eastern industrial centers. In Beverly, Massachusetts, the Union Shoe Company began to train high school students at its plant in 1909. The line between schooling and work became indistinct; students enrolled in the program attended classes while working up to fifty hours a week. According to Paul McBride's analysis, this arrangement proved to be highly profitable. The state and local authorities reimbursed the company for many of its fixed costs, while the company paid the students only 25 percent of the regular wage scale. Finally, "the company made at least normal profits from all the shoes which it purchased from the students at established prices."

In Fitchburg, Massachusetts, "educators designed the high school course to produce the 'right attitude' in the co-op students." In English class, students read *Romance of Industry and Invention*, *Romance of Modern Electricity*, *Romance of Modern Manufacturing*, *Story of the Railroad*, *Careers of Danger and Daring*, and other histories of "successful men." The Fitchburg school also established rigid guidelines to be observed by the students while they worked at the factory: "Remember the object of work is production. . . . It is your business to get along with the workmen and foremen; not theirs to get along with you. . . . Don't be a kicker and don't continually bother your foreman for higher wages." "The educators and industrialist," McBride summarizes, "carefully planned the academic education for the participants in the industrial program to instill obedience and docility." Manufacturers especially preferred this narrow training and socialization for the future workers.[11]

The AFL, on the other hand, approached the whole notion of vocational education cautiously and at first opposed it. Federation leaders recognized the arguments for it as antilabor and viewed vocational schools as, in their words, "scab hatcheries." In 1908, the AFL's Executive Council appointed John Mitchell, former president of the United Mine Workers, to chair its Committee on Education, which was investigating industrial education. In its 1910 report, the committee condemned private efforts, such as cooperative education, as exploitative and supported instead public sponsorship of vocational education. The key point in the report is that the federation endorsed vocational education: "Our boys and girls must leave school thoroughly prepared by industrial training to do well [sic] some kind of productive work. A healthy community is impossible without the union of the schoolhouse, the home, and workshop." In 1915, the AFL reasserted its support of public-school-sponsored vocational education in the *Report of the Commission on Industrial Relations*. In the end, the federation took an accommodationist approach, cooperating in this matter in order to blunt business's crass approach, and supported the creation of the comprehensive high school, which would have both academic and vocational tracks and thus lessen the impact of the segregation of students.[12]

There was substantial rural support for vocational education as well. Both the Grange and the Association of Agricultural and Experimental Stations campaigned throughout the late 1800s and early 1900s for the incorporation of agricultural education in the schools. Thus, both urban and rural interests argued for some form of vocational education. As Cremin summarizes:

> The two streams tended to run parallel during the first years of the twentieth century; but the National Society for the Promotion of Industrial Education did its work well, and after

1906 they began to converge. Groups that were at best strange political bedfellows found themselves lobbying together in Congress toward the common goal of a federal vocational education bill.[13]

The NEA, the Chamber of Commerce, and the AFL joined in this lobbying effort, and a general consensus seemed to exist among educational, business, labor, and agricultural groups. In 1917, Congress passed the Smith–Hughes Act. This act "confirmed more than innovated"; it standardized and accelerated the vocational education movement.[14] Training the working class through vocational education programs became virtually universal. "Vocational students constituted approximately 25 percent of the total high school population in New York City during 1909, about 57 percent in Cincinnati during 1911, 33 percent in Chicago during 1913, and 56 percent in Elyria, Ohio, during 1918." The 1917 Smith–Hughes Act had indeed legitimized the juxtaposition of schooling with work.[15]

The institutionalization of vocational education resulted in the creation of the junior high school, vocational guidance, and standardized testing. With most students abandoning their schooling by the eighth grade, vocational education needed to be introduced somewhat earlier in order to retain them. The junior high, an intermediate level of schooling, was developed to introduce vocational training at an earlier age. The differentiation process that separated out students for manual or for academic pursuits, which they would then pursue at the comprehensive high school, was thus pushed further down the educational ladder. Vocational guidance was introduced to serve as the sorting mechanism. "Children needed direction; industry needed recruits. Out of these imperatives came the vocational guidance movement. The two movements went hand in hand. The same faces were active in both movements; their objectives were identical."[16] Standardized testing facilitated the administration of this "increasingly differentiated system."[17] As a result, vocational education students were segregated from their academic counterparts at an even earlier age than before.

In a famous 1922 sociological study, *The Selective Character of American Secondary Education*, George S. Counts analyzed how quickly tracking became institutionalized. Using statistics from four different cities—Bridgeport, Connecticut; Mt. Vernon, New York; St. Louis; and Seattle—he documented the rapid growth in high school enrollment, attendance, and completion. Counts found that secondary enrollment followed social-class lines. Students from middle-class backgrounds, whose parents were in largely white-collar occupations, enrolled more often. He also discovered a similar pattern for attendance and graduation. Finally, Counts analyzed how high schools sorted students into college-bound, academic tracks or work-oriented, vocational courses of study. Middle-class boys and girls studied academic subjects far more often than their blue-collar counterparts, if the latter were in school at all. Counts concluded: "While the establishment of the free public high school marked an extraordinary educational advance, it did not by any means equalize educational opportunity;" rather, it "reflects the inequalities of family means. . . ."[18]

Opportunity or Differentiation?

The comprehensive high school, it was hoped, would mitigate social-class segregation by mixing students together in a single building. Students enrolled in different courses of study could mingle in elective subjects, at lunch and assemblies, and during extracurricular activities. The Progressive education movement introduced the concept of the comprehensive high school in order to integrate secondary education into the common-school continuum. "Americans now believed that all, or at least nearly all, young people could and should benefit from high school attendance." The Commission on the Reorganization of Secondary Education marked this transition by refuting the narrow academic perspective of the Committee of Ten's 1893 report. The commission's most significant work was its 1918 *Cardinal Principles of Secondary Education*, which furnished "the basic curriculum guidelines and the institutional framework for the public secondary schools" that continue to this day. The guidelines encompassed the basic academic subjects as well as health, physical education, vocational education, civic education, the arts, and character development, all in a coeducational setting. "By 1920 the publication of the *Cardinal Principles* and the incorporation of vocational education in the programs of the comprehensive high schools had put American secondary education on a new course. The high school set out to transform itself from a school for a selected few into a home for many."[19]

However, the impact of vocational education on school policy and practice, as described by Marvin Lazerson and W. Norton Grubb, "served to break down the common school ideology and the practice of a common educational system for all pupils; after vocational education had differentiated pupils according to future occupations, other forms of differentiation—ability grouping being the most widespread—were introduced into the schools."[20] Vocational education transformed the purpose of schooling. It was no longer a vehicle for social mobility but rather operated to rigidify social classes. This fact did not go unrecognized or unopposed.

A New Social Order

Radicals formed their own interpretations of the relationship between schooling and working-class children. In 1922, James H. Maurer, socialist president of the Pennsylvania Federation of Labor, criticized the schooling process as unabashed social control.

> The individuality of the student is suppressed. The attempt is made to mold all minds by the same pattern and independence, originality, and self-reliance are discouraged. Our children are being trained like dogs and ponies, not developed as individuals. Such methods, together with the vicious propaganda on social and economic questions to which the children are subjected, produce just the results that the conservative and reactionary elements of the country want, namely, uniformity of thought and conduct, no originality or self-reliance except for money-making schemes, a worshipful attitude toward those who have wealth and power, intolerance for anything that the business element condemns, and ignorance of the great social and economic forces that are shaping the destinies of all of us.[21]

Furthermore, schools preached the rhetoric of social mobility but prepared workers' children for manual labor.

"Kiddie Socialists"

Many workers loyal to the Socialist Party of America, which was organized in 1901 long before the Bolshevik Revolution, saw public education as highly ideological. They responded by demanding and creating their own classes and schools, which served children, adolescents, and adults, as well, and in numerous cases throve. Between 1900 and 1920, workers ran some 100 socialist Sunday schools across the nation for children ranging in age from five to fourteen. "They were organized in sixty-four cities and towns in twenty states and the District of Columbia." The title "Sunday school" belied their purpose: They had a focused and intense political and ideological function rather than a religious one in that they methodically opposed the capitalist ideology touted in the public schools.

Teachers and students usually spent two hours every Sunday morning meeting in cramped, rented halls or the local Socialist Party headquarters. The part-time instructors, generally female, came from working-class backgrounds, worked full time during the week at their regular jobs, and were active in the party. Lacking any formal college education, they received irregular and infrequent training as teachers. An average of forty students attended each week. Known as "good rebels," "little comrades," or "kiddie socialists," they likewise claimed working-class roots and came from the neighborhood or local community. About an equal number of boys and girls attended.

The Sunday school classes offered many different educational activities. Children sang songs, danced, played games, performed pageants and plays, participated in athletic events, recited poems, organized and held benefits for strikers, wrote and sent letters to jailed political prisoners, celebrated the May Day holiday, read such publications as John Spargo's *Socialist Readings for Children* and the *Young Socialist's Magazine*, and attended socialist meetings. All of the lessons and subject matter were designed to counter bourgeois tenets through the study of strikes, factory work, health issues, the press, the legal system, and noted individuals like Karl Marx and Abraham Lincoln.

Many problems plagued the Sunday schools. There was a constant shortage of teachers and a perpetual struggle to find funding for supplies and facilities.[22] Finally, following the Russian Revolution in 1917, they faced harassment as the first of many Red scares began.

Workers' Education

There were other, more mainstream educational classes and institutions for working-class adolescents and adults, which were inspired by the British Workers' Education Association and by the indigenous American socialist movement, which dated from the mid-1800s. Although these efforts for workers were as various as they were widespread, three basic and distinct models emerged during the early twentieth century: union-sponsored programs, university-related classes, and independent schools.

The International Ladies' Garment Workers Union (ILGWU), founded in 1900, led all other unions in sponsoring classes and workshops. By 1916, the ILGWU had fully committed itself to various educational activities, mainly in New York City. The largely socialist union endeavored to develop labor leaders and activists in order to strengthen union organizing campaigns. Its three-part educational program consisted of University Centers, the Workers' University, and Extension Centers. The University Centers were neighborhood part-time evening classes that met in local public school buildings to teach English to mostly immigrant workers along with other general academic subjects. The Workers' University, held at a public high school, offered more advanced study, which was limited to 350 part-time students a term. The Extension Division was a less-formal learning experience centered around community plays, concerts, lectures, and libraries. The union offered all of these opportunities at no charge. Eventually, the union grew wary of the more radical educational activities that were taking place under its auspices, fearing they might pose a threat to its leadership, and it turned to institutions of higher education to adopt the programs.

Colleges and universities indeed sponsored educational programs for workers. Bryn Mawr College, located near Philadelphia, pioneered the Summer School for Women Workers in 1921. Its goals and course of study were apolitical and focused on individual enrichment. The intent was to allow working women to leave the grim toil and dreary lives temporarily behind for a serene summer in a pastoral setting. Another program, the University of Wisconsin School for Workers, opened in 1923. It had a moderately militant agenda at first, but it soon became formally integrated into the university and was transformed almost completely into a labor relations course that discouraged class confrontation while encouraging labor–management cooperation. Such college and university efforts usually needed some sort of union support.

Finally, the American labor colleges were independent of union and university institutional and ideological constraints, and these colleges became the most radical form of workers' education. Schools like Work Peoples' College, founded in 1903 in Duluth, Minnesota, Brookwood Labor College, opened in 1921 in Katonah, New York, and Commonwealth College, organized in 1923 and later located near Mena, Arkansas, had distinctly socialist ideological roots. They strived, first, to train labor leaders and activists to organize workers, expand unions, and influence the local, state, and federal governments. Through such direct-action strategies, these schools hoped to create a new social order based on social democracy not corporate capitalism. These full-time residential schools combined academic studies with work in a communal setting. Although by 1941, they were gone, driven into extinction by internal ideological bickering, union attacks, and government harassment, their legacy remained. From them came numerous leaders and activists of the Congress of Industrial Organizations, which organized millions of unskilled industrial workers during the 1930s.[23]

Thus social class shaped educational policy and practice in fundamental and lasting ways. Vocational education was intended to train more productive workers for private industry, at public expense. In the process, working-class children were too often relegated to their parents' occupations. The result was economic reproduction, not social mobility. In quite similar ways, gender also shaped the educational experience.

SPECIAL SCHOOLING FOR WOMEN

During the latter half of the nineteenth century, high school boys and girls studied the same subjects together. Girls made up 57 percent of high school enrollment nationwide at the turn of the century. According to historian John Rury's careful research, "[t]he years extending from about 1870 to 1900 may have marked the first general period of gender equality in the history of American secondary education." In that environment, young women commonly outperformed their male classmates in academic subjects, particularly in the sciences, always dominated the graduation class, and typically were the class valedictorians. "In Cincinnati, for instance, girls outnumbered boys in the top ten ranked graduates from both the city's high schools for most of the years between 1870 and 1885." The overwhelming majority of these young women came from white, middle-class families whose fathers worked in white-collar occupations. Immigrant and working-class girls rarely attended high school. Female high school enrollments ranked the highest in the Northeast and lowest in the South; the West had relatively high female enrollments as well.

Rury's historical analysis reveals that these young women did not attend high school to obtain a job. What, then, motivated them to enroll and graduate? First, girls attended high school for social reasons, to interact with friends of both sexes, and second, the academic experience was an important attraction as well. They were serious students. "The high school typically was an academically elite institution, notwithstanding democratic rhetoric about its social purposes, and students whose grades fell below a certain level often were expelled summarily." Parents and teachers had high expectations, and the young women responded. Simply put, these middle-class girls attended high school in the late nineteenth century because they "enjoyed it." As Rury expresses it:

> High school was a place where close relationships were forged, where inspiring teachers were encountered, and possibly where a future spouse was to be found. It presented an opportunity to escape the narrow definition of domesticity, which had constrained the lives of previous generations of women, but in a manner that posed little threat to the Victorian sensibilities of middle-class parents.

In sum, these young women derived positive social and intellectual rewards from their high school experience.

The outstanding academic performance, impeccable behavior, and excellent attendance records of middle-class nineteenth-century high school girls made them "almost perfect students." They seemed to thrive in the coeducational environment. But there were many critics of identical coeducation, and, as earlier with the common schools, it came under attack.

Forces Undermining Identical Coeducation

Morality was, of course, a persistent concern. Opponents of coeducation feared that flirting between boys and girls would result in promiscuous behavior. After all, future mothers had to remain "morally pure."[24] There were two other, more provocative, arguments: "ovaries and algebra" and the "woman peril."

"Ovaries and Algebra"

In his 1873 book, *Sex in Education; or, a Fair Chance for Girls*, Dr. Edward H. Clarke, Harvard Medical School, asserted that girls did not lack intellectual ability, but the strain of intense study and the pressure of academic competition would be detrimental to their delicate physiological development. Blood that should flow to their reproductive organs during this vital stage of life was instead diverted to their brains. Their reproductive organs would shrivel as a result, he argued, possibly leading to sterility. Clarke stated that the only solution was to separate girls from boys in high school, that is, to basically eradicate identical coeducation. Young women should have special schooling to prepare them for their traditional domestic roles. Historians David Tyack and Elisabeth Hansot describe Clarke's views: "girls should have schooling that was adapted to their 'periodicity' and to their future lives as wives and mothers. [Clarke] believed they should receive monthly rest periods, work a third less than boys on their studies, pursue a less demanding curriculum, and above all be spared the threat of competition with boys." Clarke's book had a wide readership and was reprinted seventeen times in thirteen years.

Psychologist G. Stanley Hall's highly influential work *Adolescence: Its Psychology, and Its Relations to Anthropology, Sex, Crime, Religion, and Education*, published in 1904, echoed many of Clarke's earlier warnings and prescriptions. Hall contended that females and males were socially as well as biologically different and that therefore girls should avoid demanding academic subjects. He further proposed that girls and boys be separated. His ideal school for girls would accommodate monthly rest periods during menstruation, stress light but healthy exercise, focus on domestic skills, and only lightly touch on academic studies. All of this was intended to carefully prepare these young women to become proper and effective wives and mothers. Thus, identical coeducation was bad for girls.

Woman Peril

A second attack on coeducation focused on what was perceived as the woman peril. Critics like Hall contended that the preponderance of female teachers and students in the school environment was detrimental to boys. "The women were feminizing the boys . . . and the girls were shaming the boys by outperforming them in academic competition." This would ultimately produce male graduates who possessed female qualities, such as passiveness, timidity, and compliance, characteristics that were totally inappropriate for this nation's future political, economic, and intellectual leaders. Moreover, many male educators believed something was wrong with high schools if girls outperformed boys academically. Feminized schools ruined boys. "The advocates of a more masculine high school wanted to rid the curriculum of its sissy tinge, hire more men teachers, and in some cases to abolish coeducation itself by resegregating high schools and making them fit places for boys." Hall promoted corporal punishment to toughen boys and establish their virility. None other than Theodore Roosevelt praised Hall for his "sound common sense, decency, and manliness."[25]

Changes in the labor market also eroded support for identical coeducation. Between 1890 and 1910, the number of working women jumped from 829,373 to 2,380,914. But more important was the shift in the nature of women's work, which between 1890 and 1930 changed from manual labor to white-collar work, particularly office work. Female office workers—stenographers, typists, bookkeepers, secretaries, cashiers, and clerks—formed the fastest-growing segment of the female labor force, and by 1930, 40 percent of the female labor force nationwide was employed in this type of white-collar work. Women did not necessarily abandon manufacturing and domestic work for office jobs; rather, more women entering the workforce pursued white-collar employment. In 1930, 25 percent of all women worked.[26]

Gender-Differentiated Schooling

The various social forces that supported differentiated high school education for girls collectively altered coeducation. Girls had to be relieved of strenuous academic competition with boys, boys would naturally perform better academically in a masculinized setting, and finally young women needed to be specially trained for their new world of work. Various groups and educators had protested against student tracking based on race, ethnicity, and social-class background. But, according to Tyack and Hansot, "[d]ifferentiation by gender, by contrast, aroused relatively little dissent."

Gender-differentiated schooling assumed different forms. Separate girls and boys schools were an obvious option. Atlanta, Baltimore, Boston, Louisville, New York City, and Philadelphia all established sex-segregated high schools. During the early 1900s, separate academic classes were another alternative. These appeared in Chicago, Everett and Seattle, Washington, Riverside, California, and South Bend, Indiana. Under this approach, English classes set higher expectations for girls while science courses lowered requirements for them and diluted content. Meanwhile, educators adjusted history, mathematics, and science classes to be more demanding for boys. Most such experiments "fizzled," however.

Elective subjects offered yet another approach. As the number of required courses declined and electives increased, fewer young women enrolled in academically rigorous and "alien" academic subjects, like algebra. Tyack and Hansot describe how one school district created "special electives:"

> In 1915 the high school in San Jose, California, offered a course in physics for girls, in which the students learned about the mechanics of plumbing, vacuum cleaners, and sewing machines; the principles of sound "underlying the art of music"; and the properties of light as they applied to "the illuminating power of wall surfaces, the efficacy of lamps, and a comparison of colors."

Such courses were virtually bereft of any intellectual substance and did not prepare girls for college but rather for domestic roles.[27]

Vocational education was a fourth, and obvious, means of segregating high school girls and boys. "The vocational education movement in the United States," according to historian Jane Bernard-Powers, "marked a turning point in public education for young women, when sex segregation and the treatment of women based on their special characteristics and needs became a formal agenda of the public schools."[28] With the passage of the 1917 Smith–Hughes Act, many female students found themselves formally consigned to courses of study in home economics, trade or industrial education, and commercial education.

Home Economics

To some extent, domestic science was a continuation of Catharine Beecher's concept of " 'domestic feminism,' which advocated new roles for women while upholding the traditional female domestic vocations of wifery and motherhood." But there was a difference, as Rury points out: "While the domestic feminists had been especially concerned with establishing women's intellectual and social equality, participants in the home economics movement were interested in equipping women to address a variety of social problems from the vantage of home." Such "social feminism" coupled woman's equality with a "peculiarly female contribution to social reform."[29]

Home economics thus addressed an emerging social problem: the growing number of working women. Conservative critics claimed that working women contributed to the disintegration of the American family, which, in turn, led to an increase in crime, especially prostitution; poor parenting, with unsupervised children on the streets; and high divorce rates. Divorces had increased 600 percent between 1860 and 1920; in 1920 there were 7.7 divorces per 1,000 marriages. In 1912, an alarmed Carroll Page, Republican Senator from Vermont, proclaimed in Congress that "probably 50 percent of all divorces would have been avoided had the girls been good cooks, good housewives, and good mothers." He expressed little doubt about the social role of women: "the Almighty has ordained that women do the housework and the man do the work which he does." Of all of the vocational educational programs implemented for girls, domestic science received the most enthusiastic support.[30]

Homemaking and child rearing, it was asserted, required systematic study and formal training, rather than haphazard informal lessons handed down from mother to daughter. Pseudo-scientific principles and business-efficiency models validated homemaking as a professional pursuit. In 1910, the National Education Association released a report, "Vocational Education of Females," that articulated educational goals and recommended an educational program for female students. "The girls of our schools will be the wives and mothers of the next generation and the courses of study should be so laid out that these

"Cooking Class Making Salads" John Hay School, Chicago, IL (c. 1929). Courtesy of Library of Congress, Prints and Photographs Division.

girls will lead happier and richer lives and will be more successful as the future homemakers of our cities." The report recommended that girls enroll in courses stressing "homemaking training" or training for "distinctly feminine occupations."[31]

By the 1930s, 80 percent of junior high schools required girls to take home economics. At the high school level, however, success proved to be elusive. Only 26 percent of young high school women nationwide enrolled in domestic science classes. Home economics classes held little appeal, representing nothing more than dreary and redundant courses in cooking and sewing. Regionally, the West and South claimed an average enrollment of 33 and 32 percent, respectively. The Great Lakes region had the lowest enrollment, with 24 percent. Enrollments were highest among working-class, ethnic, and racial groups. "In the South in 1931, 85 percent of black high-school girls were required to take home economics, compared to only 30 percent of white girls." Southern schools prepared these young women to serve as hired domestics and cooks. For immigrant female students, domestic science courses served as part of the broader Americanization program.[32]

Trade Education

With more women entering the workforce, both the National Women's Trade Union League and the National Society for the Promotion of Industrial Education campaigned "for equal and coeducational trade education in all fields" so that "women should be free to choose and enter virtually any occupations, even those traditionally held only by men." This resulted in high school classes that strongly resembled home economics, but with the addition of dressmaking, millinery, power sewing, and tailoring. Proponents and educators did not want the skills taught to stray too far from the traditional domestic realm. Trade education largely proved to be a failure. Less than 1 percent of high school girls nationwide enrolled in industrial education classes during the 1920s. The Northeast and West each had a 4 percent enrollment, and the South enrolled only 0.3 percent of female students. Most of the girls in these courses resided in large cities, such as New York and Philadelphia. Enrollments remained low because most industrial jobs available to women were unskilled. Moreover, many poor and working-class girls had abandoned schooling before high school to go to work, thus limiting the number of students available for these classes.[33]

Secretarial Science

Commercial education proved to be the most successful form of vocational education for girls. The demands of the labor market fueled this success. "As clerical work became more routine, and as the number of clerical workers increased dramatically, employers turned to the schools to find suitably trained personnel.[34] The white-collar jobs naturally required a higher level of literacy and social graces, and so girls came to be the majority in business education classes. "By 1922, they accounted for 63 percent in bookkeeping, 76 percent in shorthand, and 70 percent in typing." The Northeast, at 27 percent, had the highest enrollment, while the South, with 6 percent, had the lowest rate. Commercial education became successful because parents and students alike perceived it as a means of social mobility. Office work was acceptable middle-class employment. While home economics prepared girls for the kitchen and trade education trained them for blue-collar jobs, commercial education enabled them to enter business offices as white-collar employees.

Even with their irregular degrees of success, these three educational programs had a cumulative effect. They discouraged girls from enrolling in academic courses. All served the goal of differentiating high school education for young women and separating them from their male classmates. Special education for females was not new. Beginning with the early republican period, public schooling had embraced a form of vocational education for girls, that is, practical schooling that would make them better wives and mothers. The common-school movement expanded on this concept by designating teaching as a natural avocation for women, "whose aims were thought to be similar to those of mothers."[35] Although home economics, trade education, and commercial education proved to be far less successful than their supporters had hoped, the fact is that high school girls participated less in academic courses. "Female enrollment rates in algebra fell by nearly a third between 1900 and 1928, and enrollment in physics dropped by 80 percent."[36] Little would change over the next few decades as the schools deliberately prepared adolescent women for narrow roles and dead-end jobs.

"EQUAL BUT SEPARATE?"

In Chapter 6, we explored the social context of the Reconstruction period and the educational outcomes. By the end of the nineteenth century, many of the social barriers that had emerged after the Civil War became legalized and institutionalized. "Separate but equal" became the law of the land in the first half of the twentieth century. African Americans, who continued to strive for equality, thus were placed under an even heavier educational burden.

Plessy v. Ferguson and *De Jure* Segregation

On the surface, Reconstruction seemed to create some hope for political, social, and economic equality for African Americans in the New South. The Thirteenth Amendment, ratified in 1865, abolished slavery; the Fourteenth Amendment, ratified in 1868, conferred citizenship on former slaves and defined due process; and the Fifteenth Amendment, ratified in 1870, granted suffrage. The United States Congress also passed the Civil Rights Act of 1875.

However, persistent southern hostility to racial equality caused many of these measures, and their implicit fundamental political aims, to come under assault. In 1873, the first of the legal challenges attacked the Thirteenth Amendment, particularly its application to civil rights. In what became known as the infamous Slaughterhouse Cases, the United States Supreme Court restricted the federal government's role in guaranteeing citizenship rights by narrowly defining them, that is, equal rights did not apply to involuntary servitude. Ten years later, the Supreme Court declared the Civil Rights Act of 1875 unconstitutional. It ruled that private individuals *could* discriminate.[37] The federal government therefore gradually retreated from the enforcement of civil rights by eroding the very measures created to protect them. The new legal environment thus created, one vehemently opposed to racial equality, placed no apparent federal restrictions or interference on the Jim Crow laws passed by the southern states. "The South, beginning in 1887, enacted rigid laws establishing racial separation 'in the courts, schools and libraries, in parks, theatres, hotels and residential districts, in hospitals, insane asylums—everywhere, including on sidewalks and in cemetaries.' "[38]

A group of African Americans in New Orleans created a well-conceived and systematic strategy to overturn Louisiana's 1890 segregation act, which required "equal but separate accommodations" on passenger trains, that ultimately challenged such laws throughout the South. This group planned to undermine the practice of separate railroad facilities using the strategy of intrastate and interstate travel. On June 7, 1892, Homer Plessy purchased a train ticket in New Orleans to travel to Covington, Louisiana. According to Louisiana state law, since one of his great-grandparents was African American, Plessy was deemed African American. He boarded the "white" railroad car; the conductor ordered him to vacate his seat in the white car and sit in the "colored" car. Plessy refused, and the police arrested and jailed him.[39] Meanwhile, Daniel F. Desdunes, also one-eighth African American, likewise tested the Louisiana segregation statute by purchasing a train ticket for a destination outside of that state. He, too, boarded a white car and was arrested. Judge John Howard Ferguson "ruled that the law was unconstitutional on interstate trains because of the federal government's power to regulate interstate commerce. . . . " Plessy's case, however, had a different outcome with Judge Ferguson. Plessy's attorney based his client's case on the Thirteenth and Fourteenth amendments. Ferguson ruled that intrastate travel did not come under the auspices of the federal government and therefore the Louisiana law was constitutional.[40] Plessy had thus violated Louisiana law. The plaintiff appealed the case and it worked its way through the appellate courts.

On May 18, 1896, the United States Supreme Court upheld Louisiana's segregation statute. The Court invoked the earlier Slaughterhouse and Civil Rights Act decisions and refuted Plessy's use of the Thirteenth and Fourteenth amendments. It cited the 1849 *Roberts v. Boston* case, which had pioneered the equal but separate concept. The justices, however, conveniently overlooked the fact that the Massachusetts General Court had reversed *Roberts* through subsequent legislation in 1855, as we saw in Chapter 4. Finally, the Court concluded that racial inequality represented a social construction and could not be simply and artificially overcome by passing laws to require otherwise: "If one race be inferior to the other socially, the Constitution of the United States cannot put them upon the same plane."[41] Only one justice dissented. Because of this landmark decision, de jure segregation became the law of the land. The impact on education was immense.

Schools

Southern African American schools did not fare well under de jure segregation. Any success they had was the result of great sacrifice on the part of African American communities throughout the South. In turn-of-the century North Carolina, white landowner opposition to African American education stemmed from the fear that educated African Americans would be unfit for manual labor. The "old attitude of master and slave" endured.[42] Southern states contributed as little as possible to African American common schools. "In the South as a whole, expenditures that had been approximately in the proportion of $3.00 per head for whites and $2.00 for blacks in the 1870s became by 1930 a proportion of $7.00 for whites and $2.00 for blacks." There were also fewer schools. In 1900, only 36 percent of African American children aged five to fourteen attended school, and the overwhelming majority of southern schools maintained a school year of less than six months for African Americans. South Carolina opened its African American schools for 30 days a year; Alabama in 1910 reluctantly supported a 90-day academic year. Secondary education was scarce. No rural African American school had more than seven grades. Finally, Georgia's African American teachers received about one-half of the salary paid to their white counterparts. W. E. B. DuBois described this policy of inferior education as "enforced ignorance."[43]

Southern African American common schools were established on the basis of northern philanthropic support and enormous sacrifices on the part of African Americans themselves. The General Education Board and the Southern Education Board, as we saw in Chapter 6, exerted a great deal of influence on southern educational reform and particularly on African American education. In the latter case, their influence could be characterized as "racial paternalism."[44] In 1907, Anna T. Jeanes, a Philadelphia Quaker, created a foundation to underwrite the hiring of teachers and supervisors for "elementary industrial work" in the classrooms. Julius Rosenwald, president of Sears, Roebuck and Company in Chicago, heavily influenced by Booker T. Washington's philosophy and efforts and a trustee of Tuskegee Normal and Industrial Institute, created in 1914 a fund to subsidize the construction of school buildings. According to historian James D. Anderson, "[t]his project launched one of the largest and most dramatic rural school construction programs of the era, resulting by 1932 in the building of 4,977 rural black schools with a pupil seating capacity of 663,615." But the Rosenwald school construction program double-taxed southern African Americans because they had to provide a share of the building costs; the Rosenwald Fund gave only a partial subsidy.

African Americans went to extreme lengths to send their children to schools. They donated what little cash they had. They also double-taxed themselves, as we saw, to subsidize schools for their children. Furthermore, African Americans had to contribute "land, labor, and building materials" whenever possible because of southern white opposition. "This alternative to state-financed public education was necessary because in the early twentieth century whites all over the South seized the school funds belonging to the disenfranchised black citizens, gerrymandered school districts so as to exclude blacks from certain local tax benefits, and expounded a racist ideology to provide a moral justification of unequal treatment."

The impact of such racism on African American secondary education was especially significant. The African American high school remained an exclusively urban phenomenon and came into being largely after 1920. As we saw in Chapter 6, general high school enrollment had grown steadily and dramatically. While only 3 percent of adolescent-aged children attended high school in 1880, this figure grew to 47 percent in 1930 and jumped to 60 percent in 1934. The South, however, tended to lag behind the rest of the country; it had 38 percent high school enrollment in 1930, and most of these students were white. In 1890, less than 1 percent of southern African Americans were enrolled in secondary institutions. Progress was slow. "Although in 1910 black children represented 29 percent of the total secondary school population, they constituted only 5 percent of the pupils enrolled in the secondary grades of southern public schools." Mississippi had the worst record in the South. The strongest opposition to African American secondary education came from "planters and their white working-class allies." Anderson states that "they used their influence in state and local governments to exclude black youth from the system of public secondary education." The struggle to provide secondary education for African American children became intense. Between 1880 and 1920, "the few black public high schools that did exist . . . were the result of joint efforts of local black leaders and urban white southerners."[45] And many of these carried the title of "training school" because that was the only label southern whites would accept, for it connoted vocational training rather than academic education, which was regarded as an unsuitable pursuit for African American children.[46]

Many academic high schools for African Americans were the direct result of the persistent efforts of African American communities. In Augusta, Georgia, African Americans assumed responsibility for the Freedmen's Bureau schools after the bureau's withdrawal in 1867. Using its own resources, the community supported these elementary schools until 1873, when they were absorbed by the public-school system. Because of the African American commitment to the schools, "initially, the black public schools were considered superior to the schools available to whites," a short-lived situation since white public officials devoted the most resources to white schools. After Augusta's African Americans submitted several petitions to the school board, and after parents promised to pay part of the tuition out of their own pockets, they persuaded the school board to open a high school for their children. The E. A. Ware High School opened in the fall of 1880, but it only offered the eighth grade, and suffered from chronic understaffing and the lack of basic resources—a sufficient number of desks, for example. The white community generally opposed secondary education for African American children. "Some questioned the wisdom of providing 'higher' schooling for blacks, and almost all resented being taxed to provide it." African Americans through the years persistently appealed to the school board for "another teacher, a longer school year, additional space, and better maintenance for the school." In spite of steady enrollment and the payment by African American parents of more than their share through tuition fees in addition to school taxes, the school board closed the school in 1897. The African American community ultimately filed suit. The case reached the federal Supreme Court in 1899; in *Cumming v. School Board of Richmond* the Court ruled against the plaintiffs.[47] Anderson argues that this decision "violated the separate but equal principle" because it "meant that southern school boards did not have to offer public secondary education for black youth."

After 1926, industrial education was the primary form of secondary schooling for African Americans. The Rosenwald Fund was the leading subsidizer of this type of education. However, in many cases, "black citizens, taxpayers, and educators outmaneuvered the philanthropists." They resisted economic reproduction. Parents had higher aspirations for their children; they wanted them to advance to more prestigious and better-paying occupations—no easy task. By the mid-1930s, 54 percent of southern white children attended high school, yet only 20 percent of southern African Americans did.[48] Thus, as happened in Augusta, Georgia, African American communities often assumed sole responsibility for providing secondary education for their children. This is exactly what happened in Caswell County, North Carolina, in the thirties.

Responses

The limits imposed by school segregation did not cause African Americans to give up. Their struggles against the restrictions found many forms of expression and the community, in its persistence and resourcefulness, proved to be a formidable force. African

Americans in southern cities successfully campaigned for the hiring of African American teachers. "By 1911, Atlanta schools employed eighty black faculty members, and they comprised an important part of the city's black economic and institutional life." This was a typical southern urban experience; Richmond, Raleigh, Charleston, and New Orleans employed African American instructors in their segregated schools.[49] There was certainly an unequal distribution of educational resources. However, despite that difficulty and other, almost insurmountable odds, African Americans managed, in some cases, to provide a solid education for their children.

Vanessa Siddle Walker describes in detail such an experience in her study of the Caswell County Training School (CCTS) in the Piedmont Region of North Carolina. Caswell County provided no high school education for African American children until "advocates" intervened. "In general, these advocates were parents and community leaders who interposed themselves between the needs of the Negro community and the power of the white school board. . . . " They resorted to a variety of tactics to generate support and acquire resources for the education of their children. This activism led to the creation of Caswell County's first African American high school in Yanceyville. Because of long-term resistance from the local white school board, Yanceyville's school principal, N. L. Dillard, and community supporters resorted to a surreptitious strategy to create the school. Beginning in the 1930–31 school year, an eighth grade was added to Yanceyville elementary school. "Each year a higher grade was added using the local student population." This gradual and subtle approach went unnoticed by the white school board. By 1933, the higher grades were in place and fully operational, and Yanceyville's African American community appealed directly to the state education board for recognition. A community member donated a stake-bed truck in order to provide state-mandated countywide transportation. Later, a bus body was installed on that truck frame, at the expense of the school's supporters, in order to raise attendance and to conform to state regulations. The school soon met state requirements and was granted authority by the local school board to hire more high school instructors and expand its facilities. The state accredited the high school during the 1934–35 school year, and it officially became the Caswell Community Training School. While allowing the word *training* to be inserted into the name of its school, the community resisted the imposition of the "industrial-school" model so common at that time (see Chapter 6). Some agricultural training did indeed occur in this rural setting, but most of CCTS's formal curriculum focused on academic subjects.

High school enrollment at CCTS had more than doubled by the 1937–38 school year, reaching 333 students. Beginning in the late 1930s, African American advocates petitioned and lobbied both the local board and state officials for the construction of a new high school building. Supporters even donated the lumber, but the local school board diverted it to a white school. War shortages further delayed the community's building plans, but by 1948 it had succeeded and a construction contract was signed. When the school board then attempted to locate the new school on an undesirable, if not unsafe, piece of property, some in the community fought back and employed a legal representative to reach a settlement. The new school opened in 1951.

Supporters contributed to the school through an active PTA, which furnished a variety of supplies, equipment, and services to partially compensate for deficiencies in public financial support. The PTA provided musical instruments, office furniture, a public-address system, mimeograph machine, typewriter, library books, and science equipment, among many other items. In many ways, the parents double-taxed themselves to educate their children. Further, they contributed free labor toward school maintenance, planting grass and painting. Finally, parents regularly attended plays and graduations, helped with school parties, and worked in the classrooms with teachers. Thus Yanceyville's African American community along with Dillard and the school's classroom instructors created a supportive and enriching educational environment and a student-centered approach. The principal, guidance counselor, and teachers fostered close relationships with the students, welcoming them into their homes and devoting themselves to their development and growth in all ways. CCTS's classroom instructors were all college graduates and virtually all possessed the state's highest-rated teaching certificates, unlike their white counterparts in the county schools. CCTS sponsored extracurricular activities; its debate team won a state championship in 1941. Recognizing its academic excellence, the Southern Association of Schools and Colleges accredited CCTS in 1954. The county's white high school remained unaccredited.[50]

CCTS unfortunately was the exception to the rule: secondary education for southern African Americans remained scarce and inadequate. As Anderson somberly concludes: "For blacks in the South, the struggle to attain public high schools for the majority of their high school age children would continue beyond the post–World War II era. While American youth in general were being pushed into high schools, southern black youth, a sizable minority of black high school age children in America, were being locked out of the nation's public high schools."[51]

De jure segregation resulted in an unequal distribution of educational resources; African American schools received only a fraction of the school funds. Nevertheless, African American parents and educators in many southern communities, such as Caswell County, Washington, DC, Atlanta, Baltimore, Little Rock, and other cities, overcame great obstacles to provide an excellent education for their children. This exacted much sacrifice and included many setbacks; still, they persisted. "Caring adults gave individual concern, personal time, and so forth to help ensure a learning environment in which African American children would succeed. Despite the difficulties they faced and the poverty with which they had to work, it must be said that they experienced no poverty of spirit."[52] African American communities, parents, and educators did not readily accept the restrictive conditions in the South. According to historian James L. Leoudis,

> Accommodation was not to be misread as acquiescence. . . . For most African Americans, the choice at hand was never a simple matter of agitation versus passivity. Instead, they adopted a more subtle strategy of survival, one that acknowledged the reality of white rule but at the same time searched the crevices of white supremacy for every opportunity for black power and self-determination. In the affairs of daily life, resistance and collaboration were not so much at odds as tightly interwoven.

Their successes did not consist of just their day-to-day educational victories, for their rewards would be greater. The schools they had made great sacrifices to support helped to educate a new generation of African Americans, one that would challenge the institution of after World War II.[53]

The Northern Experience

The practice of de jure segregation in the South limited educational opportunities for African American children, as we have seen. Abandoning the South to move North always held out the promise of equal education and social betterment, but, as many African Americans soon discovered, the dream did not match the reality.

The Great Migration

During the latter half of the nineteenth century and the first decade of the twentieth century, the regional distribution of African Americans remained fairly stable. A "steady trickle" of southerners migrated northward to seek economic and educational opportunities and to escape racial oppression. This all changed with the Great Migration. "From 1916 through 1918 that trickle became a flood that brought hundreds of thousands of blacks to the North." The outbreak of World War I was the trigger for this significant demographic event. To meet war orders, northern industry significantly expanded its production capacity, resulting in a sharp demand for labor. However, war mobilization, the expansion of the armed forces, and the cessation of European emigration due to military hostilities faced northern industrialists with a severe labor shortage. Southern African Americans provided a pool of untapped labor that northern employers could exploit.[54]

The labor agents employers sent South found a willing audience. Since the Civil War, southern African Americans had followed an intraregional migration strategy in order to survive economic insecurity. As agricultural workers, they migrated according to the season within the rural South as well as sought temporary employment in southern towns and cities. There men worked in sawmills, lumber camps, turpentine plants, steel mills, on railroads, and as longshoremen; women toiled as domestics. As a result, the African American urban population steadily grew in the South between 1880 and 1910.[55] For racially oppressed, exploited, and chronically poor southern African Americans, the lure of a better future for their children, the promise of higher wages, and the hope of steady work naturally led them to adopt an interregional migration pattern; they moved northward. "Between 1910 and 1920 the black population of Chicago increased from 44,000 to 109,000; in New York from 92,000 to 152,000; in Detroit from 6,000 to 41,000; and in Philadelphia from 84,000 to 134,000." They found work in the iron, steel, railroad, automotive, shipbuilding, transportation, and meat-packing industries. According to labor historian Philip S. Foner, this marked the birth of the African American "industrial working class in the United States."[56] Serious racial conflict soon broke out, however.

Racial Tensions

As soon as the war ended, northern industries reduced production, welcomed the returning veterans back to work, and fired or demoted many of their African American employees. "The 1921 economic depression made the situation even more acute for black workers. In Detroit, black unemployment rates were five times as high as those of white workers and twice as high as those of foreign-born workers."[57] Worse yet, as the African American population grew in northern cities, racial tensions intensified, resulting in violent riots. "Whites who had looked kindly upon blacks in distant Dixie and who had tolerated the small minority settlement of the nineteenth century felt threatened as the number of black migrants swelled."[58] The brutal conflict in East St. Louis in July 1917 resulted in the deaths of nine whites and about forty African Americans. Historian William M. Tuttle, Jr., summarizes the scene:

> Whites put torches to the homes of black people, leaving them with the choice of burning alive or fleeing to risk death by gunfire. Black women and children died along with their men; clubbed, shot, and stabbed, wounded and dying blacks lay in the streets. Others were lynched, including some who were already dead from other injuries. One black man had suffered severe head wounds; but, as he was not dead yet, the mob decided to hang him.

Race riots continued to increase in number and intensity, breaking out in twenty-five towns nationwide between April and October of 1919 alone. All were provoked by whites. Chicago had the bloodiest conflict. When an angry white killed an African American boy swimming at a segregated, white beach on Lake Michigan in July 1919, a long and devastating race riot erupted, resulting in 38 dead, 537 wounded, and hundreds made homeless because of the destruction. White hostility did not dissipate after the initial confrontation and found countless outlets afterward. Chicago's press continued to inflame the situation by publishing disparaging accounts of that city's African American citizens, which whipped up racist attitudes. Whites bombed African American residences.[59] Finally, the schools became an arena for venting northern white racism.

De Facto School Segregation

Historian Michael Homel has carefully chronicled the growing segregation of Chicago's schools because of the Great Migration and its violent aftermath. Chicago is an especially important city to study since it was this nation's second-largest city until the 1980s and a major manufacturing and financial center. Homel analyzes how Chicago's public schools went from exclusion to integration and finally to permanent segregation of African American children. Until the mid-1800s, that city flatly refused to educate African American children. In 1849 and 1851, city statutes were passed that finally permitted African American school attendance, and those children shared the classrooms with their white counterparts, although residential patterns ensured that some schools were predominantly African American. With the coming of the Civil War, racial attitudes intensified and in 1863 the Illinois legislature, dominated by Democrats, mandated segregated schools in Chicago. African American parents protested; most refused to send their children to the designated "Colored School." The following year, a Republican legislature banned school segregation. "During the last three decades of the nineteenth century, black pupils not only attended classes with whites but did so on relatively amiable terms."

The Great Migration altered all of this. By 1920, African Americans comprised 4.1 percent of Chicago's population. Just between 1910 and 1920, the increase had amounted to 148 percent. This had a profound effect on the city's schools. "While total school attendance in Chicago advanced 26.4 percent between 1910 and 1920, the figure for blacks jumped 185.2 percent. Despite the gains in black enrollment, however, classrooms remained racially mixed." African American teachers also freely participated in this integrated school system. Their numbers steadily increased to a total of forty-one in 1917, with most teaching in "predominantly or exclusively" white schools. School administrators supported these assignments when white parents occasionally complained. Nevertheless, "mass migration, combined with black confinement to specific blocks and neighborhoods, was concentrating black pupil enrollment in certain school districts" within Chicago—the early outlines of a segregated urban school system began to take shape.

Within a year after the July 1919 race riot, many of Chicago's white residents began a long and ultimately successful campaign to formally segregate the public schools. The school segregation that had started to emerge earlier out of residential patterns soon assumed a clear, institutionalized form as white parents increasingly complained to school administrators about the growing presence of African American children and teachers in the classrooms. School officials gradually buckled under the pressure. By manipulating school district boundaries, pupil transfers, and instructional assignments, among other policies, school segregation in Chicago was slowly formalized. African American teachers thus soon found themselves working in completely segregated schools. "By 1930, 85.4 percent of the city's black instructors served in schools with 90–100 percent black pupil enrollments." In the 1930s separate schooling grew in Chicago. During that decade, "the list of segregated black schools expanded from six to twenty-six (twenty-three grade schools, two junior highs, and Phillips High), and the proportion of black pupils in segregated buildings more than doubled to 82.4 percent." This distribution of students intensified in the 1930s as the city's African American population continued to increase.

Separate schooling was not equal. African American children attended old, deteriorating school buildings, often with cesspools nearby, filthy drinking fountains, and unsanitary kitchens, sat in cramped, overcrowded classrooms, received outdated textbooks, and had insufficient supplies. White teachers resented being assigned to these schools and usually took out their displeasure on the children. The gap in funding between white and African American schools became pronounced between 1920 and 1940: The 2 percent difference that existed in 1920 had grown to 16 percent by 1940. "In 1920 and 1925, blacks enjoyed the best pupil–teacher ratio of any group studied. Thereafter, however, the ghetto lost so much ground relative to white communities that by 1940 it ranked last." Because of overcrowding and the use of double shifts to cope with it, Chicago's African American children on a daily basis attended school less than southern African American students. Migrants decades earlier had fled the segregated South to seek better social, economic, and educational opportunities, only to find, more often than not, similar, if not worse, school conditions for their children in Chicago.

Responses

That city's African Americans protested segregation through their civic organizations, all of which, including the NAACP, persisted in their demand for integrated schools. They saw little difference between the segregated schools in Chicago and those in Alabama, Mississippi, and the rest of the South. Their efforts frustrated, they directed their energies at gaining school board representation and improving school facilities and conditions. The mayor appointed all school board members. After a long political campaign, in 1939 Chicago's Association of Colored Women and the city's Urban League finally succeeded in getting an African American appointed. These two organizations also assisted in local community protests, which occasionally succeeded in relieving school overcrowding. Changes were successfully brought about in tracking as well. As in the South, northern urban school authorities often assigned African American students to vocational courses. After World War I, African Americans campaigned against vocational education in Gary, Indiana, New York City, and Chicago. Furthermore, Chicago's politicians "helped expand the black teaching force during the 1920s and secured physical improvements at South Side schools" as well as lent their support to the school board campaign. At the grassroots level, local parents organized outside the Parent Teacher Association. In 1940, at one school they "criticized the lack of a playground, gym, and assembly hall, denounced the double shifts and supplies' shortages, and called for the transfer of the principal, whom they accused of denigrating area residents." Nevertheless, there was little progress overall. African Americans won occasional and isolated battles, but Chicago's schools generally remained segregated and their children failed to receive an equal education. White racism remained powerful and intransigent.

There are two ongoing questions that arise from Chicago's experience: Has the pattern endured and how widespread was it? First, about present-day Chicago, Homel stresses "many of the patterns that took shape in the 1920s and 1930s remain intact. The most important of these is racial segregation." White flight during the 1950s and 1960s solidified the racial isolation of African Americans. By the 1980s, African Americans made up 61 percent of Chicago's public school enrollment. Overcrowding, double shifts, overlarge classes, uncertified teachers, and unequal funding continue to characterize African American schooling in Chicago. Second, the pattern appeared to be common in many northern cities: Dayton, Ohio, Gary and Indianapolis, Indiana, New York City, and Topeka, Kansas all had mostly segregated schools. Cincinnati and Philadelphia operated both segregated elementary and integrated secondary schools. Northern public school districts, therefore, offered African American children fewer opportunities for equal education than they offered white children. This historical pattern persists to this day.[60]

Whether residing in the South or in the North, African American children faced unequal public schooling through the first half of the twentieth century. Racial segregation became either official and formal by law or occurred unofficially and informally as the result of residential patterns. Whatever the case, it became a sanctioned school practice, dooming African American children to an inferior educational experience and ultimately denying them social betterment. African American organizations, however, continued to denounce segregation and actively oppose it as a social and education policy; they fought for their equal rights as American citizens. They were not alone in their struggle.

"THE PROBLEM OF INDIAN ADMINISTRATION": FROM ASSIMILATION TO CULTURAL SENSITIVITY AND BACK AGAIN

Racist attitudes continued to deprive Native Americans of equal schooling and social and economic opportunities. Following World War I, Secretary of the Interior Hubert Work charged the Committee of One Hundred to review the federal government's policies toward Native Americans. This group of leading figures, including many Native Americans, issued a report that called for widespread reform, improvements in facilities and teachers, and wider access to public schools. The Secretary of the Interior commissioned the Brookings Institute to produce yet another review in 1926. Lewis Meriam chaired that committee, which visited sixty-four boarding schools. It found ill-nourished students, poor housing, overcrowded conditions, and extremely poor hygiene facilities, with the consequence that many students contracted serious diseases. The resulting comprehensive analysis, "The Problem of Indian Administration," known as the Meriam Report was issued in 1928 and widely condemned federal policies regarding Native Americans. "Based on the teachings of John Dewey and other Progressive educators, the Meriam Report pointed out shocking conditions in boarding schools, recommended not sending elementary-age children to boarding schools and urged an increase in the number of day schools." Little positive change occurred immediately, however. Because of budget cuts during the Warren G. Harding and Calvin Coolidge administrations, conditions went unimproved and boarding school students continued to succumb to many illnesses, often dying, because of poor living conditions, overwork, and a poor diet. The flogging of Native American students continued, and many schools contained locked rooms, or "jails," for punishing children.[61]

From Assimilation to Cultural Sensitivity . . .

President Franklin D. Roosevelt's New Deal administration, which assumed office after the 1932 election, initiated "a reversal of the policy of assimilation." Roosevelt appointed Harold Ickes as Secretary of the Interior. Ickes, in turn, selected John Collier to serve as Commissioner of Indian Affairs. Collier, a proponent of Progressive education, implemented the Meriam Report's recommendations. In 1936, Collier appointed Willard Walcott Beatty, a staunch Progressive and former president of the Progressive Education Association, as director of Bureau of Indian Affairs's (BIA) Indian Education.[62]

Three significant educational changes were implemented: an emphasis on community day schools, the reform of boarding schools, and the stressing of Native American culture in the classroom. The government began to close many boarding schools and simultaneously build numerous community day schools, "allowing Indian children to go to school and remain with their home areas." Native American leaders preferred community schools because they wanted to preserve their cultures. As a result, by 1941, more children attended the day schools than the boarding schools. During the 1930s, Beatty also reformed the boarding schools. He dispensed with the military atmosphere and regimented pedagogical style. He also attempted to improve living conditions at these institutions. And sensitivity to Native American cultures became an important component of the educational process. Collier ordered that Native American religious practices be permitted in all of the government's schools. He further encouraged the revival of Southwestern Native American art; the Santa Fe boarding school sponsored the first formal art class. Meanwhile, "Beatty started some of the first bilingual and English as a Second Language training programs in the United States." Finally, both Beatty and Collier attempted to revise the training programs for Anglo teachers of Native American children, stressing sensitivity, bilingualism, and native culture, as well as preparing Native American instructors.[63]

. . . And Back Again

The Johnson–O'Malley Act, passed in 1934, facilitated the transfer of Native American education from federal control to the public-school system; funding was funneled through state departments of education. Public-school enrollment increased as a result. "In 1930 federal schools accounted for 39 percent of total enrollment of Indian children in school. . . . By 1970 . . . 65 percent of all children in school were attending public school." This shift did not benefit the children, however. By the early 1940s, with state authority superseding federal oversight, the conditions for the education of Native American children had suffered a setback. Ill-prepared teachers and insensitive communities reversed the cross-cultural progress that had been accomplished in the federal schools.[64] "Indian children in some schools studied history from books that depicted Indians as savages. High dropout rates or apathy usually resulted from this type of miseducation."[65] The cross-cultural reforms that had been introduced into the federal schools also proved to be short-lived because of the outbreak of World War II, which dried up government funding for such domestic efforts.[66] "Because of the disruptions caused by World War II, there were more Indian students out of school in 1946 than in 1928."[67] Some 40,000 went to work in the war industries, while 24,000 joined the armed services. Finally, as historian Margaret Connell Szasz points out, Beatty shifted federal policies "from cross-cultural education, which emphasized both Indian and non-Indian value systems, to education for assimilation, which trained young Indians for urban life where they would be assimilated into mainstream society."

But a long-term and positive phenomenon came out of this period: Following the war, Native American leadership became more assertive regarding education. Returning veterans brought different perspectives and experiences back to their reservations that mainly served to emphasize the value of education. "Many tribes began to encourage their high school graduates to go on to college by setting aside tribal funds for scholarships. In addition, some tribes requested that the federal government improve their existing school facilities." The Navajo, the largest tribal nation, were the most assertive; the tribe sent delegates to Washington to demand better education for its children. Beatty responded by expanding educational opportunities and programs for the Navajo. For the most part, though, most Native American children faced a bad educational situation.

In April of 1961, the largest pan-tribal meeting ever was held in Chicago to protest prolonged poverty, poor housing, persistent and widespread disease, abysmal health care, and, of course, inadequate and unequal education. To exacerbate matters, leading Congressional politicians throughout the 1950s and early 1960s campaigned to end all federal commitments to Native Americans. This became known as the "termination policy," yet another attempt to forcibly assimilate Native Americans. At the Chicago meeting, Native American leaders advocated their needs, opposed termination, and developed strategies to assume self-determination and shake off paternalistic federal policies and traditions.

Thus, there were four distinct periods in Native American educational policy, according to Szasz. Assimilation was the first goal of federal policy towards Native Americans. During the 1920s and 1930s, many government officials began to support the preservation of tribal cultures. Beginning in the 1940s, authorities reversed themselves and reinstituted the goal of acculturation along Anglo lines. Finally, in the 1960s, the emergence of Native American leadership and the findings of key government reports shifted educational policy to self-determination.[68] We will explore this last trend in Chapter 10.

"THE CULTURE FACTORY": IMMIGRANT CHILDREN IN SCHOOL

Race was not the only barrier to equal education. Ethnicity, as we will see in the next two sections, was also a significant barrier. The process of Americanization through education, practiced by often self-righteous teachers and facilitated by an ethnocentric curriculum, was manifestly insensitive to other cultures. European and Latino/Latina immigrants responded in a variety of ways to these attempts to assimilate their children.

Mass Migration

One of the greatest voluntary worldwide migrations occurred between 1880 and 1930. This later movement differed both quantitatively and qualitatively from earlier emigration from northern and western Europe. During this period, 27 million southern and eastern Europeans emigrated to the United States. Italians were the largest group: "Between 1876 and 1930 more than 5,000,000 Italians sailed for the United States." Most of them were from southern Italy, and they came to escape poverty, disease, and overpopulation. Jews comprised the second-largest ethnic group. More than 2,000,000 emigrated from eastern Europe—"more than 70 percent of these coming from Russia"—to escape religious persecution and violent pogroms. Slavic immigrants, consisting of Russians, Ukrainians, Slovaks, Slovenes, Poles, Croatians, Serbs, and Bulgarians, added another 4 million. Other ethnic groups included Magyars, Greeks, Portugese, Czechs, Armenians, and Syrians. Immigrants tended to settle in the Northeast and upper Midwest. "According to the census records of 1910, about three-quarters of the population of New York City, Chicago, Detroit, Cleveland, and Boston consisted of immigrants and their children."[69]

Certain factors both pushed and pulled this massive, international migration. As we have seen, many fled political and religious oppression. Other immigrants abandoned poor social and economic conditions, lured to the United States by labor agents falsely promising them high wages and permanent jobs, if not riches. Regardless of the reason, all of these immigrants became industrial fuel for America's rapidly expanding industries. Men, women, and children found work in mines, textile mills, garment factories, iron and steel mills, and on railroads, usually as low-paid, unskilled laborers. "The great Carnegie Pittsburgh plants employed 14,359 common laborers, 11,694 of them South and East Europeans." American employers exploited them unmercifully. These peasant families needed $15.00 per week to survive; they earned an average of $12.50 a week. They also faced highly dangerous workplace conditions. "Nearly 25 percent of the recent immigrants employed at the Carnegie Steel Works were injured or killed each year between 1907 and 1910, 3,723 in all."[70]

Reaction and Assimilation

The immigrants brought various religions, languages, alphabets, and values with them, and even looked different, with their dark complexions, hair, and eyes. Native-born Americans reacted in a contradictory way. On the one hand, they welcomed the cheap labor and happily exploited it. On the other hand, they recoiled in fear and disgust at this flood of inferior peoples. Americans "despised" the Italians the most. "Old-stock Americans called them wops, dagos, and guineas and referred to them as the 'Chinese of

Europe' and 'just as bad as Negroes.' In the South some Italians were forced to attend all-black schools, and in both the North and South they were victimized by brutality." Jews were equally hated. Facing long-entrenched anti-Semitism, they were not permitted the right to vote in every state until the late 1800s. "By the Progressive era, open discrimination prevailed in housing and employment. Hotels displayed signs proclaiming 'No Jews Allowed,' and job advertisements specified 'Christians Only.' "[71]

These nativistic attitudes sparked an intense program of Americanization, and the public schools became culture factories, assimilating immigrants, in a highly self-righteous campaign to save American society from the polyglot flood of inferior cultures. Immigrants had to be culturally converted, not only to protect this society but to save them from themselves. Many educators approached the challenge with missionary zeal. Professor John L. Hart, principal of the New Jersey Normal School, a teacher-training institution, reflected this prevalent attitude in his 1879 book *In the School-Room*:

> About one-half of our poor can neither read nor write, have never been in any school, and know little, positively nothing, of the doctrines of the Christian religion, or of moral duties, or of any higher pleasures than beer-drinking and spirit-drinking, and the grossest sensual indulgence. . . . They have unclear, indefinable ideas of all around them; they eat, drink, breed, work, and die; and while they pass through their brute-like existence here, the rich and more intelligent classes are obliged to guard them with police and standing armies, and to cover the land with prisons, cages, and all kinds of receptacles for the perpetrators of crime.

Hart proclaimed that the schools could solve this dire social and cultural crisis by instilling immigrant children with Anglo-Protestant values. "He argued that 'schoolhouses are cheaper than jails' and that 'teachers and books are better security than handcuffs and policemen.' "[72]

Hart's was not an isolated opinion. Marion Brown, principal of the City Normal School in New Orleans, delivered a speech at the annual meeting of the National Education Association in 1900 that proclaimed the ideal "American type" as "Anglo-Saxon." However, she lamented that "the American of pure Anglo-Saxon descent was rare" because southern and eastern European immigrants and their children now dominated America's largest cities. "In Boston," she added, "out of 1,230 boys in the Eliot School, 602 were born in Europe; the parents of 1,117 were born in Europe; only 16 could find that one of their four grandparents was born in America." This cultural mix created "discipline and teaching" problems. Brown explicated this by proceeding to stereotype Italian children as excitable, Spanish as lazy, Irish as mischievous, and the Teutons as slow but tenacious. She labeled many immigrants as "flotsam and jetsam" and viewed their children as "frequently defective physically and morally." Brown summed up the key social and educational issue facing the nation: These immigrants and "their children are the greatest problem we have." Her solution proved to be clear and simple. Teachers served as the representatives of traditional American culture. Their mission was serious: Lead immigrant children "to the Anglo-Saxon standard, train them to self-control that means freedom, the love of country that foreshadows the brotherhood of man, the developing personality of that can take only justice and right as its standard."[73]

Hart's and Brown's declarations reflected the prevailing hostility, if not the superiority, native-born Americans felt toward southern and eastern Europeans. They wanted to use the public schools to drive a cultural wedge between immigrant parents and their children, and this quickly became the dominant educational policy and was translated into classroom practice. Socialization through assimilation became the primary mission of America's urban public schools. English served as the sole language of instruction and students only learned about one culture. As in the mid-1800s, this intolerance set the stage for cultural conflict.

"... I come back to Italy"

Human agency played a key role in the Americanization process, with a rich variety of immigrant responses. Many ethnic groups enthusiastically embraced the acculturation process, or at least attempted to come to terms with it, in their pursuit of the American dream. This was especially true of Russian Jews. In other cases, immigrants resisted assimilation by holding on to their culture. Some responded by returning to Europe. Depending on the ethnic group, repatriation figures varied sharply. "Intelligent estimates of how many foreigners returned to their native countries range from a high of nearly 90 percent for the Balkan peoples to a low of 5 percent for Jews." Italians proved to be the most mobile group—many literally commuted across the Atlantic Ocean, especially between 1908 and 1916, although some, disillusioned with American society, completely abandoned it and returned home.[74] One Italian boy who had lived in Rochester, New York, expressed his feelings of alienation in a poem, written in 1908:

> *Nothing job, nothing job,*
> *I come back to Italy;*
> *Nothing job, nothing job,*
> *Adieu land northerly. . .*
>
> *Nothing job, nothing job,*
> *O! sweet sky of my Italy;*
> *Nothing job, nothing job,*
> *How cold in this country. . . .*
>
> *Nothing job, nothing job,*
> *I return to Italy;*
> *Comrades, laborers, good-bye;*
> *Adieu, land of "Fourth of July."*[75]

While American society exploited most immigrants, some ethnic groups turned the tables and got all they could out of this society, returning to their homelands with precious cash to purchase property.

The immigrants who remained in the United States and resisted the acculturation process did not view their old and rich cultures as inferior—just the opposite; they saw American culture as inferior. Gabro Karabin, born of Croatian parents in McKeesport, Pennsylvania, a steel town near Pittsburgh, later expressed the immigrant's view of this cultural conflict:

Around Pittsburgh, the Croat is commonplace and at no time distinctive. As people think of us, we are cultureless, creedless, and colorless in life, though in reality we possess a positive and almost excessive amount of these qualities. Among ourselves, it is known that we keep our culture to ourselves because of the heterogeneous and unwholesome grain of that about us. . . . We are, in the light of general impression, just another type of laboring foreigner . . . fit only as industrial fuel.[76]

Some immigrants, therefore, made the conscious decision to remain in the United States and at the same time preserve their culture, its language, religion, and institutions in the face of intense Americanization. The public school, of course, was an important battleground in this struggle.

The Public Schools

The overwhelming number of immigrant children who descended on the schools strained the public education system enormously. In New York City, school enrollment increased by more than 50 percent between 1899 and 1914. With classrooms typically holding sixty to eighty students, the New York public schools denied admission to between 60,000 and 75,000 students in 1905. Historians Michael Olneck and Marvin Lazerson have analyzed the academic achievement of two groups of these immigrant children—Southern Italians and Russian Jews. There was wide variation in the academic performance of these children because their cultural groups responded differently to the assimilation practices of the American public schools. Olneck and Lazerson specifically examine grade-retention rates for the elementary level as well as high school attendance and completion rates.

Southern Italian students had the worst achievement record of all school-aged children, while Russian-Jewish students proved to be the most academically successful. In 1908, Southern Italians had the highest average percentage of retention in grade of all nationalities, including native-born white and African American children, in Boston, Chicago, and New York City. In that same year, Southern Italians in those cities also sent the smallest percentage of eighth graders to high school—with only 23 percent. Few Italians graduated from high school. Meanwhile, in that era Russian Jews had the lowest rate of grade retention and the highest percentage of students going to high school among all other ethnic groups. Furthermore, they graduated the most students, in some cases outstripping the percentage of native-born white students.

What accounts for these sharply divergent school performances? "Both groups arrived in the United States at roughly the same time (1880–1930), were poor upon arrival, spoke little English, and settled in close proximity to one another along the eastern seaboard." Olneck and Lazerson conclude that "cultural values" best explain these varied school performances. "Russian-Jewish culture prepared that group to fare very well in terms of educational success, and Southern Italian culture was at odds with the demands of formal schooling in America." First, Russian Jews valued studying and learning and had founded religious schools in Russia. Education conferred social status. This "respect for learning" was "transplanted" to the United States and was made manifest in the public schools. Second, Russian Jewish parents embraced the American dream, "and enthusiastically entrusted their children" to the public schools. Third, Russian Jewish parents had high expectations for their children and encouraged "successful school performances." Fourth, Russian Jewish parents believed in the future of their children and sacrificed to keep them in school. Fathers worked two jobs, or mothers worked, or older siblings forsook their schooling to earn money and ensure schooling for their younger brothers and sisters.

Southern Italian values and attitudes, in contrast were confrontational toward American culture and the goals of the public school. Long suspicious of religious and governmental institutions in southern Italy, these immigrants transplanted these views largely intact to the United States. They therefore distrusted the public schools, which they correctly perceived as a threat to their culture. Southern Italians also viewed the family as the core social and educational institution in their culture; "it was the sole refuge within which trust and loyalty could be cultivated." Italians used the nuclear as well as the extended family as the source of economic, social, and emotional support, and members were obligated to it. Thus, "the family required complete allegiance, viewed the outside world as off-limits, and discouraged independence and autonomy by its members." The Southern Italian family proved to be the most intransigent social institution the American public schools had ever encountered. It effectively blunted the Americanization process. Italian culture and language endured for three generations, well into the 1950s. However, cultural preservation came at the high price of limited schooling.[77]

The Catholic Parochial Schools

Millions of immigrants, in spite of the relentless efforts of assimilationists, mostly preferred to preserve their cultures. Religion and language were the pillars of these cultures. As a result, enrollment at Roman Catholic parish schools increased sharply. "The ethnic Catholic school was a key element in the rapid growth of parochial education for fifty years following the Civil War." Ethnic parochial schools began with German Catholic and Lutheran immigrants in the 1830s and 1840s, as we saw in Chapter 4. These groups wished to preserve their German language and their religion. At the turn of the century, Polish, Bohemian, Slovakian, and Ukrainian Catholic immigrants also wanted "to sustain cultural, linguistic, and religious values in the next generation." Polish immigrants proved to be the most devoted to their own culture. "By 1910, the Poles had established more than 350 parish schools in more than a dozen states."[78] Catholic school enrollment in general more than doubled between 1900 and 1920, rising from 854,523 to 1,800,000.[79] In Chicago, by 1920, there were 196 parochial schools with 112,735 students, including secondary schools. The Catholic Church also established universities, nursery schools, settlement houses, vacation schools, and adult education classes. "The histories of all these varied activities, from the elementary school to the university, from the settlement house to the adult education center, from the parish library to the boy scout troop, lead to one indisputable conclusion: The Church attempted to construct a Catholic education island within Chicago." As a result, Chicago eventually hosted the "largest Catholic school system the world had ever seen."[80]

This growth continued across the nation, but the goal of cultural preservation was pushed aside by the Catholic hierarchy, who, like their public school counterparts, pressed for Americanization. American society in general, caught up especially in the frenzied xenophobia of World War I, also pressured ethnic parochial schools to assimilate immigrant children. And as American-born priests and nuns replaced their immigrant predecessors at the parish level, language and cultural preservation became less important. "By the 1930s, native language and culture had become extracurricular subjects in most parochial schools and dropped altogether at some of these institutions."[81] The popularity of Catholic education nevertheless continued. "In 1963, some 5.5 million youngsters, 14 percent of the nation's school population, were enrolled in 10,633 Catholic elementary schools and 2,502 Catholic secondary schools. . . . " Urban areas had huge parish school enrollments. The parochial schools in Dubuque, Iowa, enrolled 61 percent of that city's school-aged population, Pittsburgh enrolled 42 percent, Philadelphia claimed 39 percent, Chicago absorbed 33 percent, and St. Louis accounted for 25 percent.[82]

Meanwhile, some nativists found the school-based process of Americanization to be insufficient and too time-consuming. After years of public appeals and lobbying Congress, they succeeded in passing laws that at the worst excluded immigrants and at the best sharply restricted the kinds of newcomers allowed into the country. As early as 1882, Congress began this exclusion process by banning Chinese immigration. A 1917 law went further, virtually excluding all Asian immigrants. In 1921, Congress passed the first immigration restriction law for Europeans, setting a limit of 358,000 per year that continued on a year-by-year basis until 1924, when Congress passed the draconian Johnson–Reed Act. "It cut the number of immigrants to 2 percent of the foreign-born of that group based on the 1890 census, and this further discriminated against southern and eastern nations, which is exactly what Congress wanted to do." Congress also totally banned all Asians that same year. By 1929, when the Johnson–Reed Act was fully implemented, only 153,714 newcomers entered the country, most of them from northern and western Europe. "The act ended the virtually free immigration policy."[83] The process of Americanization forged ahead for those immigrants already here, unchallenged by new waves of immigrants seeking opportunities and freedom for their children.

SCHOOLING FOR MEXICAN AMERICANS

Immigrants not only sailed over the Atlantic Ocean but crossed the Rio Grande River. Spanish Americans, as we have seen, had resided throughout the Southwest since the 1500s. A trickle of Mexican immigrants had entered the United States in the late nineteenth century, but economic and political changes in both the United States and Mexico caused them to enter this country in unprecedented numbers during the first three decades of the twentieth century.

Among the changes that encouraged Mexican immigration was the rapid and extensive construction of railroads in the Southwest by such companies as the Southern Pacific and the Santa Fe railroads. Large numbers of workers were required and the increased demand for labor had to be met by a new source. The Asian workers who had previously been involved in railroad construction had been excluded by the federal government. Chinese and Japanese immigration had been curtailed in 1882 and 1907, respectively, and all Asian immigration in 1917. The outbreak of World War I cut European emigration, and the Johnson–Reed Act further restricted the influx following the war. Southwestern railroad employers turned south to fill the void.[84] Another construction boom followed the passage of the Newlands Reclamation Act of 1902, which authorized the construction of reservoirs to provide irrigation water. Such "irrigation projects 'revolutionized' agriculture," creating an "economic boom" in the Southwest. "From almost no such production in 1900, the Southwest by 1929 was responsible for 40 percent of America's total fruit and vegetable output."[85] Growers created the "factory farm" system to supply inexpensive produce.[86] This, in turn, required cheap labor on a massive scale.

Employment agencies, working on commission, aggressively recruited workers in Mexico and signed them to labor contracts with American companies. This defied the contract-labor law of 1885, which forbade such practices. In short, employers through their labor agents encouraged border crossings to ensure a supply of cheap, unskilled labor and ever-greater profits.

Dire conditions in Mexico also stimulated emigration. The weak Mexican economy, depressed wages, and serious inflation coupled with the turmoil of the Mexican Revolution, which began in 1910, pushed poor agricultural peasants in northern Mexico to cross the border, seeking better opportunities and more security for themselves and their families.[87] Mexican immigration fluctuated between 11,000 and 22,000 per year until World War I. Until then, most Mexicans settled in rural areas of the Southwest, but the labor needs of war industries drew them to cities, thus beginning the long trend toward the urbanization of Mexican Americans. Immigration jumped to 29,000 in 1919 and climbed to 88,000 in 1924. In 1890, Mexicans in the Southwest had numbered 75,368, "or 1.9 percent of the total population," but by 1930 that figure had "increased to 1,282,882, or 9.6 percent. . . . " The number of immigrants dropped precipitously during the Great Depression to an average of about 1,500 per year because the United States forcibly deported more than 400,000 Mexicans, many of them United States citizens, between 1929 and 1934. High unemployment during the depression made them the scapegoats for a sagging economy. The flow of immigration increased once again during World War II with the *bracero* program, which actively recruited Mexican laborers to work in the labor-starved war industries, yet it never exceeded 6,500 a year.[88]

Anglo society responded to Mexican immigrants and well-established Mexican American citizens in the same way it did to other immigrant groups: It embarked on a long campaign of Americanization. Schools again became the main vehicle for assimilation.

During the Progressive era, as we saw in Chapter 7, public schooling expanded and became systemized, and during this period, the establishment of segregated schools for Mexican American children was formalized. Mexican American education, according to historian Gilbert Gonzalez, can be separated into four distinct historical periods: (1) 1900 to 1950, the "era of de jure segregation"; (2) 1950 to 1965, marked by de facto segregation; (3) 1965 to 1975, a period of "militant and reformist" activities; and (4) since 1975, a period characterized by "conservative retrenchment." In this section, we will focus on the first period, returning to the others in subsequent chapters.

Gonzalez also describes three types of experiences within the Mexican immigrant community: "the urban working class, the occasional migrant class, and the truly migratory class." All three conditions reflected family needs, and the proportions of immigrants within them changed over time. "In 1930, about half of the Mexican population resided in rural, or semi-rural, regions; by 1950 that figure decreased to only one-third." Urban children, at one end of the spectrum, had a relatively permanent residence and attended largely segregated schools. Because of compulsory attendance laws, these students, usually attained some secondary schooling. Rural agricultural children, at the other end of the spectrum, were indigent and mobile and received irregular schooling at best. They rarely progressed beyond the fifth grade. They usually worked in the fields with their parents in order to earn the income necessary for their families' survival. Schools that taught immigrant children usually dismissed early to accommodate the needs of employers. In some communities, schools barred admission to migrant children. Regardless of where they lived or their circumstances, Mexican American children were usually segregated, Americanized, and tracked into vocational programs.[89]

De Jure Segregation

From the beginning, public and parochial schools segregated Mexican children throughout the Southwest. Texas is a clear illustration of the establishment of de jure segregation. The growing Mexican population in Texas forced state education officials to establish uniform policies. "The number of counties where *Tejanos* comprised 50 percent or more of the total scholastic population jumped from twenty-three in 1922 to thirty-one in 1928." Urban areas as well as rural ones were affected. A previously local matter had now become a statewide concern. State educators in Texas, as well as those throughout the Southwest, relied on two rationales to justify the segregation of Mexican American students. First, the "pedagogical rationalization" for segregation argued that it helped Mexican children with their so-called language deficiencies and irregular attendance. Second, Anglo parents objected to their children mixing with the "inferior" Mexicans, who, to make matters worse, often had lice, were dirty, and smelled.[90] "By 1930, 85 percent of Mexican children in the Southwest were attending either segregated classrooms or entirely separate schools." Even in segregated systems, few Mexicans attended, let alone completed, high school. For example, San Antonio's elementary schools in 1934 enrolled 11,000 Mexican children, while its high schools had only 250 Mexican students, an extremely high attrition rate.[91]

A small minority of Mexican American children actually attended school, and even when they did, it was on an irregular basis. Many school districts provided no schooling for them whatsoever. Local Texas growers generally opposed schooling for Mexicans. They feared that educated Mexicans might favor unionization. They also thought that education spoiled Mexican Americans for work. As one employer pontificated: "I am for education and educating my own children, but the Mexicans . . . get some education and then they can't labor. . . . They think it is a disgrace to work. . . . The illiterates make the best farm labor." Still other growers opposed schooling for Mexican Americans because they viewed them as too "inferior" to be properly educated.[92]

Americanization

Public school educators implemented a rigid assimilation program in response to the large influx of Mexican immigrant children. They based their approach on long-entrenched "stereotypes of Mexicans as dirty, shiftless, lazy, irresponsible, unambitious, thriftless, fatalistic, selfish, promiscuous, and prone to drinking, violence, and criminal behavior."[93] The 1910 *Report of the Immigration Commission* took the pessimistic view that Mexican immigrants, were "backward."[94] In some school districts, such as Los Angeles and Oakland, California, departments of Americanization or immigration education were created to train classroom instructors how to assimilate Mexican children. The primary focus, as we saw earlier, was on language instruction, specifically the purging of Spanish. Public schools also inculcated Anglo values. Specific teaching methods included conducting morning inspections for cleanliness, encouraging children to ridicule their dirty classmates, and taking students on field trips to visit "model" American homes to illustrate proper housekeeping and correct furnishings. Roman Catholic parochial schools likewise implemented an

Americanization program. According to Gonzalez, cultural conversion set the educational agenda for Mexican children, but educators never intended to use Americanization to integrate them into the larger Anglo society. In fact, an unintended outcome was that segregation actually acted to reinforce Mexican culture.

Vocational Education

American schools throughout the Southwest placed virtually all Mexican students in domestic, industrial, and agricultural education programs. Los Angeles school officials, in particular, impressed by the Tuskegee model of manual training, applied it to Mexican American children. In predominantly Mexican schools, this program began at the elementary level and continued through the secondary grades. Girls learned domestic and child-rearing skills; boys enrolled in industrial and agricultural courses. Educators guided Mexican American girls into home economics classes at a younger age than Anglo girls because of their early dropout rate. They believed such classes would Americanize the Mexican girls and prepare them to be domestics and waitresses, as well as to be better wives and mothers.[95]

Intelligence and other standardized tests conferred a scientific legitimacy on tracking Mexican American students into vocational education programs. Study after study seemed to verify that Mexicans suffered from inferior intelligence. One researcher even claimed that "Mexican children, as a group, had an IQ of 78.1." As historian Ruben Donato points out, such "objective" instruments were not the only tools used for tracking. "Although 'specific tests' were used to guide youths into vocational tracks, teacher judgement, student grades, student behavior, and student social and ethnic backgrounds were also used as sorting devices."[96] Thus, while seemingly objective and scientific on the surface, the academic sorting process proved to be highly subjective and biased.

Finally, the conditions under which Mexican American children received their schooling were poor. Too often, they attended overcrowded schools housed in dilapidated buildings, had few, if any, resources, and were under the supervision of unqualified teachers. Their schooling obliterated any hope of social mobility; it served only to reproduce the economic position of their parents.[97]

Responses

Mexican Americans recognized these educational inequalities and many challenged the discriminatory policies and practices. These were scattered efforts at first, but over the decades, and through the influence of larger social forces, these efforts assumed a more formal organization and an intellectual basis. "The Chicano community fought segregation, inferior schools and education, the discrimination of IQ exams, poor teaching, the lack of Mexican teachers, and the socialization process which condemned them to failure and then conditioned them to accept it."

Early Activities

As early as 1900, "Mexicans turned to the arena of education which next to labor has been their most intense battleground." They focused on school segregation. Mexican parents in

San Angelo, in west Texas, boycotted the schools, protesting the segregation of their children in second-rate facilities, "thus denying state aid to the school district."[98] Mexican Americans also opposed unequal education through the courts. In 1931, the Mexican American community in Lemon Grove, California, near San Diego, mobilized protests against the segregated school there, boycotted it, and filed suit. The court, in *Alvarez v. Lemon Grove*, ruled in favor of the plaintiffs. This proved to be the "first successful desegregation case in the United States." This victory was limited, however; it "had only local repercussions."[99] In Los Angeles, which in the 1930s had the largest concentration of Mexicans in the United States, the Mexican community fought back by establishing a variety of mutual aid societies to attempt to preserve Mexican language, folklore, music, and dance. But in spite of this impressive network of cultural activities, Mexican children there still faced poor schooling.

Organizational Efforts

By the late 1920s and early 1930s, the Mexican American community throughout the Southwest began to assume some permanence and coherence. "The new generation of Chicanos was not as preoccupied with returning to Mexico as earlier generations of Mexicans had been." They preferred to acquire the rights of American citizens. Throughout the 1930s and 1940s, Mexican newspapers in Los Angeles protested segregation.[100] And Mexican Americans not only voiced their complaints publicly, they organized to fight inequality. In south and central Texas, *Tejanos* faced the serious problems of discrimination, beatings and lynchings by vigilantes, and harassment and threats from law enforcement agencies like the Texas Rangers. In 1929, a group of middle-class Mexican Americans organized the League of United Latin American Citizens (LULAC) to actively seek redress through the American political system. LULAC attacked school segregation through the courts as early as 1930, a frustrating effort as it turned out. LULAC did achieve success in pressuring local boards to provide schooling for Mexican American children, in lobbying Texas state legislators for better educational financing in 1937, in its general campaign against school discrimination and overcrowding during the 1930s, and in promoting school attendance and parent–teacher organizations within Mexican American communities.

World War II brought significant changes in the community. The lure of labor-starved war industries accelerated the urbanization of Mexican Americans in the Southwest. Yet fundamental Anglo attitudes did not change. At best "discrimination" endured and at worst outright "hostility" erupted, as in the Zoot Suit Riots in Los Angeles during the summer of 1943. All of this despite the fact that between 375,000 and 500,000 Mexican Americans served in the armed forces. "Mexican Americans received more Congressional Medals of Honor, Distinguished Service Crosses . . . Infantry Medals of Honor, Silver Stars, and Bronze Stars . . . than any other ethnic group in the United States." When the veterans returned to the United States, they brought with them a more intense sense of citizenship, concern about civil rights, and a clearer concept of the importance of political awareness. "Having fought a war against Hitler's theories of Aryan supremacy, the returning veterans realized that they now had to fight against similar practices at home." The American G.I. Forum, created March 26, 1948, in Texas, joined forces with LULAC to campaign for equal educational opportunity and specifically attacked school segregation.[101] Leadership came from other quarters as well.

Intellectual Leadership

George I. Sánchez, an educational sociologist and prolific author, provided significant intellectual and legal leadership to many Mexican American campaigns for educational equality. Born in Albuquerque, New Mexico, in 1906, he became a rural school teacher in 1923 and eventually became principal and superintendent. During the summer months, Sánchez attended the University of New Mexico, from which he graduated in 1930. Receiving a fellowship to the University of Texas-Austin, he earned a master's degree in educational psychology in 1931. Four years later Sánchez completed his doctorate in educational administration at the University of California-Berkeley. He returned to New Mexico and became director of the Division of Information and Statistics in that state's Department of Education, and in 1935 accepted a faculty position at the University of New Mexico. He moved to the University of Texas-Austin in 1940, where he taught until his death in 1972.

Sánchez used his research and writings to criticize the lack of educational opportunities for Mexican American children. He saw the historical treatment of Mexican Americans as the root of the problem. He argued that Mexican Americans were a "colonized people" who had suffered discrimination in the Southwest since the Mexican War. As historian Mario Garcia interprets Sánchez, "Anglo society, ethnocentric in character, refused to recognize and validate the existence of a significant number of culturally different groups such as Mexican Americans." Anglo society consequently segregated and Americanized them. "In a 1948 article, 'Spanish Name Spells Discrimination,' [Sánchez] made it very clear that segregation in the southwestern schools was based on race and ethnicity and not on any other factor." Thus Sánchez attacked the established rationale for the separation of Mexicans. He supported school integration, but within a pluralistic setting to allow Mexican American children to retain their cultural identity. This approach agreed with his notions of democracy. Sánchez also attacked intelligence tests for their cultural and racial biases and challenged their scientific basis. Writing in 1944, Sánchez asserted that "the educational backwardness of a people is not an inherent or biological characteristic." Rather, he saw the environment as a crucial variable. Furthermore, he became an early proponent of bilingualism. Public school inflexibility over language condemned Spanish-speaking children to failure. As he wrote in 1954, "I sometimes wonder if the problem of bilingualism is not as much due to the language handicap of the educator as it is that of the child." Finally, Sánchez acted on his beliefs—he served as president of LULAC in 1941.[102]

Mendez v. Westminister School District

In addition to fighting many local school segregation cases in Texas during the war, LULAC assisted in a famous California court case, *Mendez v. Westminister*, which had been brought by Mexican Americans in several school districts in Orange County. The Santa Ana school district had segregated Mexican school children since the early years of the twentieth century. In spite of repeated complaints by Mexican parents, this practice continued until 1943, when parents petitioned the school board to transfer their children to better facilities. Clearly, separate was not equal. "The pay for teachers at the Mexican schools, on the average, ranged from $80 to $100 less per year than teachers at Anglo schools. The principal at the Mexican school received $135 less per year than principals at the Anglo schools." The buildings set aside for Mexican American students were inferior; in one case, a building had been condemned but was still used. The school board refused the parents' petition. A similar situation existed in the nearby community of Westminister. In 1944, the Mendez family attempted to enroll their children in the school closest to their home and were refused by school officials because that school was reserved for Anglo children. After some frustrating delays, the Mendez family joined with families in Santa Ana and other local school districts and "filed suit in the Ninth Federal District Court seeking an immediate injunction against the segregation of Mexican schoolchildren."[103] On April 17, 1947, the court ruled in favor of the plaintiffs, arguing that the schools violated the "equal protection clause of the Fourteenth Amendment."[104] The decision turned out to have far-reaching consequences. As Gonzalez points out, *Mendez* was the first stage in the process of overturning the *Plessy v. Ferguson* doctrine of 'separate but equal.' " Thurgood Marshall and other attorneys in the National Association for the Advancement of Colored People followed this case very closely.[105]

Texas school officials circumvented the *Mendez* ruling by denying that segregation occurred because of race or ethnicity. They asserted that it existed for pedagogical reasons only, to address the "English language deficiencies" of the children. This, of course, was loosely interpreted to justify segregation at all grade levels, not just in the primary grades. LULAC and the G.I. Forum challenged this disingenuous policy. Basing their case on California's *Mendez* decision, *Tejanos* filed suit in May of 1948 in *Delgado v. Bastrep Independent School District*. The federal district court ruled for the plaintiffs but still permitted segregation in first grade for "instructional purposes." Although they had successfully reversed state policy of segregation, Mexican Americans confronted intransigency; local school districts in Texas simply refused to comply with the ruling. When Mexican Americans complained, some districts resorted to school-choice policies to further subvert desegregation.[106]

Thus, despite court victories and other successes, not much appeared to change. Mexican Americans seemed to face the same educational fate of other minorities: segregation, assimilation, and vocational education. But, through the early half of the twentieth century, they had come so far as to stage early community protests, create a formal organizational structure, successfully utilize the judicial system, and lay a solid intellectual foundation for their positions.

CONCLUSIONS

This chapter has attempted to complete the picture of Progressive educational reform. While some children experienced positive changes, others, because of their social class, gender, race, or ethnicity, did not. Public schooling became an instrument for ensuring inequality rather than assuring opportunity. This was in direct conflict with basic notions of American democracy. Age-old prejudices exacerbated by misinformed scientific theories caused an unequal and separatist system to become institutionalized during the early decades of the twentieth century. Although recognized and often challenged, the system would remain unchanged until mid-century.

ACTIVITIES FOR FURTHER EXPLORATION

1. Does vocational education for school-aged boys and girls provide opportunities or limit them? Create a list of pros and cons. The public schools were not the only supporters of "domestic science," other educational forums touted it as well. Popular magazines like *Good Housekeeping* and *Ladies Home Journal* offered advice to ensure that homemakers performed their tasks in an efficient manner. See "The New Middle-Class Housekeeping: 'How I Keep House without a Maid?' " " 'More Work for Mother?' Scientific Management At Home," and "The 'One Best Way' to Wash: A Home Economist Explains" at http://chnm.gmu.edu/us/many.taf.

2. It is always preferable to examine and analyze primary documents for yourself in order to investigate an historian's interpretation. To sample the federal Supreme Court decisions referred to in this chapter, see the following Web site: http://supct.law.cornell.edu/supct/cases/name.htm.

3. To gain further historical insight into the sequence of events in African American history, refer to the "Timeline of African American History": http://lcweb2.loc.gov/ammem/aap/timeline.html. As we saw in this chapter, the Great Migration profoundly shaped northern American culture. A wide range of oral histories can be found at http://chnm.gmu.edu/us/many.taf, which reconstruct this complex and sometimes harrowing experience. Many African American newspapers claimed that there were new opportunities in the North: " 'The Negro and the War': Reports in African American Newspapers." There was another side to this experience, of course; recollections of the race riots can be found in oral histories, both in text and audio formats: " 'Defending Greenwood': A Survivor Recalls the Tulsa Race Riot of 1921"; " 'Says Lax Conditions Caused Race Riots': *Chicago Daily News* and Carl Sandburg Report the Chicago Race Riot of 1919." Some migrants, disillusioned by their northern experiences, yearned to return to the South: " 'Cotton Belt Blues': Lizzie Miles's Blues Song."

4. How is racism learned? The popular media has helped to influence the public through popular films, beginning with the 1915 release of *The Birth of a Nation*, which portrayed African Americans in a negative manner and made heroes of members of the Ku Klux Klan. Refer to "An NAACP Official Calls for Censorship of *The Birth of a Nation*" at http://chnm.gmu.edu/us/many.taf.

5. How did Native Americans respond to the Reorganization Act of 1934? John Collier's goals can be found in " 'We Took Away Their Best Lands, Broke Treaties'; John Collier Promises to Reform Indian Policy" and " 'A Bill of Rights for the Indians': John Collier Envisions an Indian New Deal." You can hear an opposing view through the oral histories of two Native Americans, " 'It Didn't Pan Out as We Thought It Was Going to': Amos Owen on the Indian Reorganization Act" and " 'It Set the Indian Aside as a Problem': A Sioux Attorney Criticizes the Indian Reorganization Act." All of these documents can be found at http://chnm.gmu.edu/us/many.taf.

6. The reaction to immigrants proved to be multifaceted. Native-born Americans certainly discriminated against European immigrants. Who else migrated to northern cities during World War I, and what were their experiences? In addition to the recruitment of

Mexican immigrants, industry's efforts to compensate for the severe labor shortage by also recruiting Puerto Rican immigrants were supported by the federal government. For this experience, see, among other documents, " 'Such Cases of Outrageous Unspeakable Abuse . . .': A Puerto Rican Migrant Protests Labor Conditions During World War I." European immigrants themselves were intolerant of Puerto Rican workers. An audio and text version of a Puerto Rican immigrant's recollections, " 'I Was More of a Citizen': A Puerto-Rican Garment Worker Describes Discrimination in the 1920s," among others, can be found at http://chnm.gmu.edu/us/many.taf. Use these primary documents and historical insights by the participants themselves as a focus for discussion of the complex social impact immigration had on society, particularly its effect on school policy.

VIDEO EXPLORATION

A fourteen-minute clip (starting at 87 minutes and ending at 101 minutes) from the video *Surviving Columbus* (Alexandria, VA: PBS Home Video, 1992) illustrates the federal government's termination and relocation policies and their impact on the North American Pueblo culture.

NOTES AND SOURCES

In order to condense endnotes, the first work cited is the primary one, usually the source of any direct quotes. Subsequent references serve as supplementary, or additional, sources of paraphrased information and/or alternative historical interpretations.

1. Marvin Lazerson and W. Norton Grubb, eds., *American Education and Vocationalism: A Documentary History, 1870–1970* (New York: Teachers College Press, 1974), p. 24.
2. Lawrence A. Cremin, *The Transformation of the School: Progressivism in American Education, 1876–1957* (New York: Vintage Books, 1961), p. 24. Also see Sol Cohen, "The Industrial Education Movement, 1906–1917," *American Quarterly*, 20 (1968), p. 95.
3. The quotes in this paragraph are from Calvin M. Woodward, "The Fruits of Manual Training," in *American Education and Vocationalism* eds. Marvin Lazerson and W. Norton Grubb, pp. 60–65. Also, refer to Lazerson and Grub, pp. 4, 5; Cremin, pp. 27–28.
4. Cremin, *The Transformation of the School*, p. 28. Woodward is also quoted on p. 28.
5. Cohen, "The Industrial Education Movement," pp. 96, 97.
6. National Education Association, "Report of the Committee on the Place of Industries in Public Education," in *American Education and Vocationalism*, eds. Marvin Lazerson and W. Norton Grubb, p. 87.
7. David L. Angus, "The Dropout Problem: An Interpretive History" (Ph.D. diss., Ohio State University, 1965), pp. 40, 45. This paragraph is taken from Richard J. Altenbaugh, David E. Engel, and Don T. Martin, *Caring for Kids: A Critical Study of Urban School Leavers* (London: Falmer Press, 1995), pp. 38–39. Also see Cohen, "The Industrial Education Movement," pp. 98–99.
8. Cohen, "The Industrial Education Movement," p. 99.

9. National Association of Manufacturers, "Reports of the Committee on Industrial Education (1905, 1912)," in *American Education and Vocationalism,* eds. Marvin Lazerson and W. Norton Grubb, pp. 88, 89, 91, 92, 93, 94. Also see, Cremin, *The Transformation of the School,* p. 38.

10. The NSPIE is quoted in Cremin, *The Transformation of the School,* p. 39.

11. Paul W. McBride, "The Co-Op Industrial Education Experience, 1900–1917," *History of Education Quarterly,* 14 (Summer 1974), pp. 211–212, 213, 215, 218. The quotes are on p. 215. Refer as well to Richard J. Altenbaugh, " 'Forming the Structure of the New Society Within the Shell of the Old': A Study of Three Labor Colleges and Their Contributions to the American Labor Movement" (Ph.D. diss., University of Pittsburgh, 1980), pp. 41–44; Cohen, "The Industrial Education Movement," p. 15; Jurgen Herbst, *The Once and Future School: Three Hundred and Fifty Years of American Secondary Education* (New York: Routledge, 1996), pp. 133, 135; Paul C. Violas, *The Training of the Urban Working Class: A History* (Chicago: Rand McNally, 1978), pp. 169–192.

12. The first quote is from Lazerson and Grubb, p. 20. Also see pp. 21, 111. American Federation of Labor, "Reports of the Committee on Industrial Education (1910) and Commission on Industrial Relations (1915)," in *American Education and Vocationalism,* eds. Marvin Lazerson and W. Norton Grubb, p. 110. Finally, refer to Cremin, *The Transformation of the School,* pp. 39–41.

13. Cremin, *The Transformation of the School,* pp. 50, 56.

14. Cohen, "The Industrial Education Movement," p. 96. Lazerson and Grubb, p. 28.

15. Violas, *Training of the Urban Working Class,* p. 15.

16. Cohen, "The Industrial Education Movement," p. 103.

17. Lazerson and Grubb, *American Education and Vocationalism,* p. 39.

18. George S. Counts, *The Selective Character of American Secondary Education* (1922; rpt. New York: Arno Press, 1969), pp. 3–4, 15, 33, 37, 56–57, 148.

19. The quotes in this paragraph are from Herbst, *The Once and Future School,* pp. 143, 146–149, 157. Refer as well to Herbert M. Kliebard, *The Struggle for the American Curriculum, 1893–1958*

(Boston: Routledge & Kegan Paul, 1986), pp. 113, 114, 115.

20. Lazerson and Grubb, *American Education and Vocationalism,* p. 39. Also see Cohen, "The Industrial Education Movement," pp. 106–108.

21. James H. Maurer, "Labor's Demand for Its Own Schools," *Nation,* 115 (Sept. 1922), pp. 276–278. Refer as well to Richard J. Altenbaugh, " 'Our children are being prepared like dogs and ponies': Schooling, Social Control, and the Working Class," *History of Education Quarterly,* 21 (Summer 1981), pp. 213–222.

22. Kenneth Teitelbaum, *Schooling for "Good Rebels": Socialist Education for Children in the United States, 1900–1920* (Philadelphia: Temple University Press, 1993), pp. 12, 37, 91, 92, 104, 105, 106, 110, 111, 113, 124, 125, 131, 132, 133, 137, 140, 152, 153, 155, 163. See likewise Kenneth Teitelbaum and William J. Reese, "American Socialist Pedagogy and Experimentation in the Progressive Era: The Socialist Sunday School," *History of Education Quarterly,* 23 (Winter 1983), pp. 429–454.

23. Richard J. Altenbaugh, *Education for Struggle: The American Labor Colleges of the 1920s and 1930s* (Philadelphia: Temple University Press, 1990), pp. 33, 34, 36–37, 47, 48, 49, 50–53, 59–60, 71, 81, 92–94. Also refer to Chapters 5, 6, 7.

24. The quotes in these paragraphs are from John L. Rury, *Education and Women's Work: Female Schooling and the Division of Labor in Urban American, 1870–1930* (Albany, NY: State University of New York Press, 1991), pp. 12, 18, 24, 28, 36, 37–38, 43, 46, 57, 60, 63–64, 70, 81, 87, 118. See as well, Kim Tolley, "Science for Ladies, Classics for Gentlemen: A Comparative Analysis of Scientific Subjects in the Curricula of Boys' and Girls' Secondary Schools in the United States, 1794–1850," *History of Education Quarterly,* 36 (Summer 1996), pp. 129–153.

25. The quotes in these paragraphs are from David B. Tyack and Elisabeth Hansot, *Learning Together: A History of Coeducation in the American Public Schools* (New Haven, CT: Yale University Press, 1990), pp. 146, 148, 149, 150, 154, 155, 160–161, 165, 166; Roosevelt is quoted on p. 161. Also, refer to Rury, *Education and Women's Work,* pp. 23, 25–26, 158; Sue Zschoche, "Dr. Clarke Revisited: Science, True Womanhood, and Female Collegiate Education," *History of Education Quarterly,* 29 (Winter 1989), pp. 545, 546, 556.

26. Jane-Bernard Powers, *The "Girl Question" in Education: Vocational Education for Young Women in the Progressive Era* (London: Falmer Press, 1992), pp. 10, 17, 40; Tyack and Hansot, *Learning Together*, pp. 203–204, 207, 212; Rury, *Education and Women's Work*, pp. 91, 93, 94.

27. The quotes in these paragraphs are from Tyack and Hansot, *Learning Together*, pp. 164, 169, 180–181, 182. Also refer to Rury, *Education and Women's Work*, pp. 39, 40, 157.

28. Bernard-Powers, *The "Girl Question"*, p. 2. Also, see Rury, *Education and Women's Work*, pp. 131, 132.

29. Rury, *Education and Women's Work*, pp. 12–13, 136, 140.

30. Bernard-Powers, *The "Girl Question"*, pp. 10, 17, 72. Page is quoted in Bernard-Powers, pp. 17, 59 and in Tyack and Hansot, *Learning Together*, p. 217.

31. National Education Association, "Vocational Education of Females," in *American Education and Vocationalism*, eds. Marvin Lazerson and W. Norton Grubb, pp. 114, 115. Also, see Bernard-Powers, *"The Girl Question"*, pp. 14–15.

32. Tyack and Hansot, *Learning Together*, p. 220. Refer also to Bernard-Powers, *"The Girl Question"*, pp. 72, 88–91, 94–95; Rury, *Education and Women's Work*, p. 165.

33. Tyack and Hansot, *Learning Together*, p. 203. Also see Bernard-Powers, *"The Girl Question"*, pp. 53–55, 102–103; Rury, *Education and Women's Work*, pp. 153, 154, 170.

34. Rury, *Education and Women's Work*, p. 114.

35. Tyack and Hansot, *Learning Together*, pp. 208, 213, 215; the quote is from p. 212. Also refer to Bernard-Powers, *The "Girl Question"*, pp. 40, 113; Rury, *Education and Women's Work*, p. 167.

36. Rury, *Education and Women's Work*, p. 157.

37. Gary Orfield, Susan E. Eaton et al., *Dismantling Desegregation: The Quiet Reversal of Brown v. Board of Education* (New York: New Press, 1996), p. 34; *Plessy v. Ferguson*, 163 U.S. 537 (1896), p. 542; Brook Thomas, ed., *Plessy v. Ferguson: A Brief History with Documents* (Boston: Bedford Books, 1997), pp. 11, 16, 19, 24; J. Harvie Wilkinson, III, *From Brown to Bakke: The Supreme Court and School Integration, 1954–1978* (New York: Oxford University Press, 1976), pp. 11, 14, 16–17, 18. For southern periodization, see John Hardin Best, "Education in the Forming of the American South,"

38. Wilkinson, *From Brown to Bakke*, p. 17.

39. *Plessy v. Ferguson*, pp. 538–39, 540, 542. Refer to Thomas, *Plessy v. Ferguson*, pp. 3–4, 6, as well.

40. Thomas, *Plessy v. Ferguson*, p. 5.

41. *Plessy v. Ferguson*, p. 552; Orfield et al., *Dismantling Desegregation*, p. 27.

42. Louis R. Harlan, *Separate and Unequal: Public School Campaigns and Racism in the Southern Seaboard States, 1901–1915* (New York: Atheneum, 1969), p. 70. See also James L. Leloudis, *Schooling in the New South: Pedagogy, Self, and Society in North Carolina* (Chapel Hill, NC: University of North Carolina Press, 1996), p. 178.

43. R. Freeman Butts, *Public Education in the United States: From Revolution to Reform* (New York: Holt, Rinehart and Winston, 1978), pp. 252–253. Also refer to James D. Anderson, *The Education of Blacks in the South, 1860–1935* (Chapel Hill, NC: University of North Carolina Press, 1988), pp. 150, 186, and Harlan, *Separate and Unequal*, pp. 13, 109, 110, 204, 209, 239, 246; Orfield et al., *Dismantling Desegregation*, p. 36; Leloudis, *Schooling in the New South*, p. 226. Du Bois is quoted in Harlan, p. 13.

44. Leloudis, *Schooling in the New South*, p. 224.

45. The quotes in these paragraphs are from Anderson, *Education of Blacks*, p. 152, 153, 154, 156, 187, 188, 197, 198. See as well Harlan, *Separate and Unequal*, pp. 86, 87, 239; Leloudis, *Schooling in the New South*, pp. 185–186, 211, 214, 224, 226–227.

46. Harlan, *Separate and Unequal*, p. 234.

47. June O. Patton, "The Black Community of Augusta and the Struggle for Ware High School, 1880–1899," in *New Perspectives on Black Educational History*, eds. Vincent P. Franklin and James D. Anderson (Boston: G.K. Hall & Co., 1978), pp. 49, 50, 51, 52, 54.

48. Anderson, *Education of Blacks*, pp. 188, 192, 211, 224, 235. See also Orfield et al., *Dismantling Desegregation*, p. 35.

49. Michael W. Homel, "Two Worlds of Race? Urban Blacks and the Public Schools, North and South, 1865–1940," in *Southern Cities, Southern Schools: Public Education in the Urban South*, eds. David N. Plank and Rick Ginsberg (Westport, CT: Greenwood Press, 1990), p. 245.

History of Education Quarterly, 36 (Spring 1996), pp. 47, 48.

50. Vanessa Siddle Walker, *Their Highest Potential: An African American School Community in the Segregated South* (Chapel Hill, NC: University of North Carolina Press, 1996), pp. 3, 6, 19, 30–33, 35–36, 45, 53–69, 74–75, 78–79, 96, 98–99, 102–103, 105, 117, 124, 143.

51. Anderson, *Education of Blacks*, p. 236.

52. Walker, *Their Highest Potential*, pp. 201, 216–217.

53. Leloudis, *Schooling in the New South*, pp. 180, 227, 228.

54. Philip S. Foner, *Organized Labor and the Black Worker, 1619–1973* (New York: International Publishers, 1976), p. 129.

55. Peter Gottlieb, *Making Their Own Way: Southern Blacks' Migration to Pittsburgh, 1916–30* (Urbana, IL: University of Illinois Press, 1987), pp. 12–13, 23, 25, 31.

56. Foner, *Organized Labor*, p. 131. Refer as well to Philip T. K. Daniel, "A History of Discrimination Against Black Students in Chicago Secondary Schools," *History of Education Quarterly*, 20 (Summer 1980), pp. 150, 151; Gottlieb, *Making Their Own Way*, p. 32; Leloudis, *Schooling the New South*, p. 212.

57. Foner, *Organized Labor*, p. 132.

58. Michael W. Homel, *Down From Equality: Black Chicagoans and the Public Schools, 1920–41* (Urbana, IL: University of Illinois Press, 1984), p. 5.

59. William M. Tuttle, Jr., *Race Riot: Chicago in the Red Summer of 1919* (New York: Atheneum, 1985), pp. 5, 12–13, 14, 242, 249, 250. Also refer to Elliot Rudwick, *Race Riot in East St. Louis: July 2, 1917* (Urbana, IL: University of Illinois Press, 1982) for a detailed account of that conflict.

60. The quotes and much of the information in these paragraphs are from Homel, *Down From Equality*, pp. 2–7, 22, 27, 28, 32, 34, 59, 62, 66, 69, 70, 73, 83–84, 136, 144, 147, 148, 151–152, 158, 161, 178. See also Daniel, "A History of Discrimination Against Black Students," pp. 147, 148, 149, 151, 152, 157–158; Homel, "Two Worlds of Race?", pp. 241, 242, 252–253; Leloudis, *Schooling the New South*, pp. 213, 178, 187–188, 189–190; John L. Rury and Frank A. Cassell, eds., *Seeds of Crisis: Public Schooling in Milwaukee since 1920* (Madison, WI: University of Wisconsin Press, 1993); David B. Tyack, *The One Best System: A History of American Urban Education* (Cambridge, MA: Harvard University Press, 1974), pp. 222, 226–228.

61. Jon Reyhner and Jeanne Eder, *A History of Indian Education* (Billings, MT: Eastern Montana College,

1989), pp. 100, 102, 104. Refer as well to Brenda J. Child, *Boarding School Seasons: American Indian Families, 1900–1940* (Lincoln, NE: University of Nebraska Press, 1998), pp. 32, 33, 37, 38; David H. DeJong, *Promises of the Past: A History of Indian Education* (Golden, CO: North American Press, 1993); Margaret Connell Szasz, *Education and the American Indian: The Road to Self-Determination Since 1928* (Albuquerque, NM: University of New Mexico Press, 1999), pp. 13, 16, 17, 18, 19, 20. DeJong, pp. 135–159, quotes the entire Meriam Report.

62. Szasz, *Education and the American Indian*, pp. 38–40, 48. See also Reyhner and Eder, *History of Indian Education*, pp. 104, 106.

63. Reyhner and Eder, *History of Indian Education*, pp. 105, 106, 107–108. Also refer to DeJong, *Promises of the Past*, pp. 154–155, 158; Szasz, *Education and the American Indian*, pp. 48, 55, 57, 61, 62, 64, 67, 70, 72–73, 75.

64. Szasz, *Education and the American Indian*, pp. 89, 92, 100, 105.

65. DeJong, *Promises of the Past*, p. 176, 177, 178.

66. Szasz, *Education and the American Indian*, p. 80, 81, 106, 109. Refer likewise to Reyhner and Eder, *History of Indian Education*, p. 109.

67. Reyhner and Eder, *History of Indian Education*, pp. 109, 102.

68. Szasz, *Education and the American Indian*, pp. 4, 106–108, 114–117. Also, see DeJong, *Promises of the Past*, p. 161–162. The Chicago meeting and the "termination policy" are treated in great detail in Thomas Clarkin, *Federal Indian Policy in the Kennedy and Johnson Administrations, 1961–1969* (Albuquerque, NM: University of New Mexico Press, 2001), pp. 1, 2, 3, 5, 9–10.

69. Leonard Dinnerstein and David M. Reimers, *Ethnic Americans: A History of Immigration* (New York: Harper & Row, 1988), pp. 43, 44, 45–46, 47. Tyack, *The One Best System*, p. 230.

70. Herbert G. Gutman, "Work, Culture, and Society in Industrializing America, 1815–1919," *American Historical Review*, 78 (1973), p. 553. Also see Dinnerstein and Reimers, *Ethnic Americans*, pp. 51–52.

71. Dinnerstein and Reimers, *Ethnic Americans*, pp. 48, 49.

72. Hart is quoted in Gutman, "Work, Culture, and Society," p. 585.

73. Brown is quoted in Clarence J. Karier, *Shaping the American Educational State, 1900 to the Present* (New

York: Free Press, 1975), pp. 255, 270, 271, 273, 274. Also refer to Richard J. Altenbaugh, "Italian and Mexican Responses to Schooling: Assimilation or Resistance?" in *Class, Culture, and Race in American Schools: A Handbook*, ed. Stanley W. Rothstein (Westport, CT: Greenwood Press, 1995), pp. 91–106; Tyack, *The One Best System*, p. 235. Gilbert G. Gonzalez, *Chicano Education in the Era of Segregation* (Philadelphia: Balch Institute, 1990), p. 35, sees Americanization as cultural conformity and as applying to all immigrants, regardless of origin.

74. Dinnerstein and Reimers, *Ethnic Americans*, pp. 46, 47.

75. This poem is quoted in Gutman, "Work, Culture, and Society," p. 554.

76. Quoted in Gutman, "Work, Culture, and Society," p. 586.

77. The quotes and information in these paragraphs are from Michael R. Olneck and Marvin Lazerson, "The School Achievement of Immigrant Children: 1900–1930," *History of Education Quarterly*, 14 (Winter 1974), p. 458, 459, 460, 462, 464, 472–474, 475, 476. Also, refer to Tyack, *The One Best System*, pp. 230, 243, 248–254. For excellent historical background on the Italian family, see Virginia Yans-McLaughlin, *Family and Community: Italian Immigrants in Buffalo, 1880–1930* (Ithaca, NY: Cornell University Press, 1977); Richard J. Altenbaugh, "Urban Immigrant Families: A Comparative Study of Italians and Mexicans," in *The American Family: Historical Perspectives*, eds. Jean E. Hunter and Paul T. Mason (Pittsburgh, PA: Duquesne University Press, 1991), as well as Richard J. Altenbaugh, "Italian and Mexican Responses to Schooling: Assimilation or Resistance?" in *Class, Culture, and Race in American Schools: A Handbook*, ed. Stanley W. Rothstein (Westport, CT: Greenwood Press, 1995).

78. Timothy Walch, *Parish School: American Catholic Parochial Education from Colonial Times to the Present* (New York: Crossroad Publishing Company, 1996), pp. 76, 77, 79, 82.

79. Neil G. McCluskey, *Catholic Education in America: A Documentary History* (New York: Teachers College Press, 1964), p. 25.

80. James W. Sanders, *The Education of an Urban Minority: Catholics in Chicago* (New York: Oxford University Press, 1977), pp. 3, 4, 12.

81. Walch, *Parish School*, pp. 81.

82. McCluskey, *Catholic Education*, p. 1; Walch, *Parish School*, pp. 1–2.

83. Dinnerstein and Reimers, *Ethnic Americans*, pp. 76–77.

84. Mark Reisler, *By the Sweat of Their Brow: Mexican Immigrant Labor in the United States, 1900–1940* (Westport, CT: Greenwood Press, 1976), pp. 3, 6; Joan W. Moore, *Mexican Americans* (Englewood Cliffs, NJ: Prentice-Hall, 1976), pp. 22, 39; Guadalupe San Miguel, Jr., *"Let All of Them Take Heed": Mexican Americans and the Campaign for Educational Equality in Texas, 1910–1981* (Austin, TX: University of Texas Press, 1987), p. 13.

85. Reisler, *By the Sweat of Their Brow*, pp. 4, 5, 6.

86. Moore, *Mexican Americans*, p. 21. Refer as well to Ruben Donato, *The Other Struggle for Equal Schools: Mexican Americans during the Civil Rights Era* (Albany, NY: State University of New York Press, 1997), p. 38; Victoria-Maria MacDonald, "Hispanic, Latino, Chicano, or 'Other'?": Deconstructing the Relationship between Historians and Hispanic-American Educational History," *History of Education Quarterly*, 41 (Fall 2001), pp. 407–408.

87. Reisler, *By the Sweat of Their Brow*, pp. 8–10, 14–15; San Miguel, Jr., *"Let All of Them Take Heed,"* pp. 14–15.

88. San Miguel, Jr., *"Let All of Them Take Heed,"* pp. 16–17. Also see Moore, *Mexican Americans*, pp. 25, 41, 42; Rudolfo Acuña, *Occupied America: A History of Chicanos* (New York: Harper & Row Publishers, 1981), pp. 127, 136, 138, 140, 144; Donato, *The Other Struggle*, pp. 39, 40, 41; Gilbert G. Gonzalez, "Segregation and the Education of Mexican Children, 1900–1940," in *The Elusive Quest for Equality: 150 Years of Chicano/Chicana Education*, ed. Jose F. Moreno (Cambridge, MA: Harvard University Press, 1999), pp. 53–54.

89. The periodization, quotes, and information in these paragraphs are from Gonzalez, *Chicano Education in the Era of Segregation*, pp. 13–14, 30, 68, 94, 95–96. Also see Donato, *The Other Struggle*, pp. 15, 31–32. Donato sets up the structure of segregation, Americanization, and vocational education. Gonzalez in *Chicano Education* and "Segregation and the Education of Mexican Children," pp. 56, 67, likewise structures his analysis around the same three educational experiences.

90. San Miguel, Jr., *"Let All of Them Take Heed,"* pp. 19, 20, 24, 55. Refer as well to Mario T. Garcia,

Mexican Americans: Leadership, Ideology, and Identity, 1930–1960 (New Havens, CT: Yale University Press, 1989), p. 265; Gonzalez, *Chicano Education*, p. 22; Moore, *Mexican Americans*, p. 81.

91. Donato, *The Other Struggle*, pp. 12–13, 16. See also Gonzalez, *Chicano Education*, p. 21; Acuña, *Occupied America*, pp. 304, 310, 311; San Miguel, Jr., *"Let All of Them Take Heed,"* p. 56.

92. San Miguel, Jr., *"Let All of Them Take Heed,"* pp. 51. The grower's quote is on that page.

93. Gonzalez, *Chicano Education*, p. 36. Also, see Donato, *The Other Struggle*, p. 15; San Miguel, Jr., *"Let All of Them Take Heed"*, pp. 33, 35.

94. Acuña, *Occupied America*, p. 128.

95. Gonzalez, *Chicano Education*, pp. 35, 38, 39–40, 48–49, 77, 84–85, 86, 88–89. Refer as well to Donato, *The Other Struggle*, pp. 19, 22; Gonzalez, "Segregation and the Education of Mexican Children," pp. 56, 58; Moore, *Mexican Americans*, pp. 88–91.

96. The researcher's quote is from Donato, *The Other Struggle*, p. 26. Also see p. 21. Gonzalez, *Chicano Education*, pp. 61, 63, 99; San Miguel, Jr., *"Let All of Them Take Heed,"* pp. 46–47.

97. Gilbert G. Gonzalez, "Segregation and the Education of Mexican Children," p. 70.

98. Acuña, *Occupied America*, pp. 303, 304.

99. The quotes in these paragraphs are from Donato, *The Other Struggle*, p. 2. Also see Acuña, *Occupied America*, p. 318; Gonzalez, *Chicano Education*,

p. 28; Gonzalez, "Segregation and the Education of Mexican Children," p. 71.

100. Acuña, *Occupied America*, pp. 311, 316, 317–318.

101. The quotes in these paragraphs are from San Miguel, Jr., *"Let All of Them Take Heed,"* pp. 67–68, 70, 80, 81, 82, 83, 84, 113, 114, 115, 116, 117. Refer as well to Acuña, *Occupied America*, pp. 323, 326; Gonzalez, "Segregation and the Education of Mexican Children," p. 71.

102. The quotes in these paragraphs are from Garcia, *Mexican Americans*, pp. 252–254, 256, 265, 266, 267, 271; Sánchez is quoted on pp. 257, 262. Refer also to Gonzalez, *Chicano Education*, pp. 49, 52, 54, 58, 59; San Miguel, Jr., *"Let All of Them Take Heed,"* pp. 95, 98, 100–101. According to MacDonald, "Hispanic, Chicano, Latino, or 'Others?,'" p. 377, Sánchez's influence proved to be long-term and significant.

103. Gonzalez, *Chicano Education*, pp. 136, 137–138, 142, 143, 147, 148, 150, 151. See as well San Miguel, Jr., *"Let All of Them Take Heed,"* p. 119.

104. San Miguel, Jr., *"Let All of Them Take Heed,"* p. 119.

105. Gonzalez, *Chicano Education*, pp. 28, 153. Also refer to Acuña, *Occupied America*, p. 330; Gonzalez, "Segregation and the Education of Mexican Children," p. 73.

106. San Miguel, Jr., *"Let All of Them Take Heed,"* pp. 120–121, 123, 125, 126, 128. Refer as well to Donato, *The Other Struggle*, p. 2; Acuña, *Occupied America*, p. 330.

9

Schooling, Ideology, and National Policy

eginning in the 1930s, international events began to intrude on the world of America's public schools. As we saw in earlier chapters, the pattern of American education generally unfolded at the local level, whether rural or urban. Parents, school reformers, clergy, and businesspeople shaped schools to meet their community's distinct needs. By the mid-nineteenth century, schools began to informally reflect regional patterns. And by the turn of the century, schools and school culture began to adopt the more formal and institutionalized patterns mandated by state departments of education or policymakers in Washington, DC. Influences exerted on the schools thus remained largely domestic ones, even though they had over time shifted from local levels to remote, if not invisible, decision markers in far away places. During the early twentieth century, international events also began to play a significant role in school affairs. This chapter attempts to trace how these increasingly distant social forces affected all facets of American society, including school policies and practices as well as the culture of America's youth.

ECONOMIC UPHEAVAL AND TOTAL WARFARE

The Great Depression, often thought to have begun with the 1929 stock market crash, actually had much older and deeper roots. Throughout the 1920s, a gradually failing agricultural sector, victim of collapsing crop prices, foreshadowed the financial and industrial crisis of 1929. At the onset of this economic cataclysm, 5,761 banks failed. "Industrial production dropped by almost 50 percent. By 1933 there were anywhere from 12,000,000 to 17,000,000 unemployed." Those who did have work found themselves grossly underemployed, working three-day weeks or just part-time, and received little pay due to drastic wage and salary reductions. The social upheaval was as disastrous as the economic one. People unable to maintain their mortgage or rent payments were physically removed from their homes and apartments by the authorities; they and their belongings were literally put out on the sidewalks, a humiliating experience. Auctioneers sold off the failed farms and mortgaged equipment of bankrupt farmers. Homelessness reached record highs—200,000 children alone had no shelter of any kind. This was an economic and social cataclysm on an unprecedented scale.[1]

World War II broke out during the depression. Japan's militaristic adventures in Asia began in the early 1930s, at the same time as Fascism took hold in Italy and Nazism in Germany. During the latter half of the 1930s, the Germans began their military advance in Europe and war broke out. The United States remained diplomatically neutral, but the attack by Japanese naval forces of Pearl Harbor on December 7, 1941, changed all of that. America mobilized its industrial and human resources, shifted its industrial production from civilian to military, and recruited men and women for the armed forces.

The Great Depression and World War II both affected the lives of America's children significantly. The developmental stage of adolescence became a permanent part of American culture during these two decades. Conceptualized during the Progressive era, this stage of childhood continued to be studied in the 1930s and 1940s. Recognition as a separate, unique stage of development was clearly established during the 1950s and 1960s.

Adolescent Culture

As we have said, the concept of adolescence originated with the Progressive education movement. It began to emerge as a separate, widely accepted stage of childhood in the 1920s and 1930s among affluent European American families whose parents could afford not to send their children to work. The high school served as the petri dish for the growth of youth culture. Adolescent immigrants attended high school depending on the values of their culture, as we saw in the case of Russian Jews and southern Italians. Mexican Americans had little or no access to secondary education. Race and social class played a role, too. Japanese American youths had their schooling rudely interrupted by wartime internment. African American adolescents rarely had opportunities to attend high school, especially in the South where it was available only in isolated situations. Poor and working-class adolescents in general had to work. Thus, the twentieth-century phenomenon of adolescence unfolded unevenly and in fits and starts.

"Brother, Can You Spare A Dime?"

Although youth fads began to appear in the 1920s, the Great Depression served as the "turning point in the history of adolescence." According to historian Jeffrey Mirel, "by destroying the youth labor market, the depression had closed off virtually every legitimate avenue except the high school through which adolescents could grow to adulthood."[2]

Hobo Kids.   The experiences of youth during these times of economic and social calamity were sometimes traumatic. Many modern observers have described the nuclear family during the depression in romantic terms, as a tight-knit unit pulling together to survive economic emergency. This was not always the case. Severe economic pressure and poverty proved corrosive to many American families. "Men withdrew from family life or turned violent; women exhausted themselves trying to 'take up the slack' both financially and emotionally, or they belittled their husbands as failures. . . . " Children faced an insecure present with little, or no, hope for a better future. Frustrated, distraught, and hungry parents sometimes abused their children. In too many cases, the children's basic protection failed them. Families disintegrated. Parents sometimes told their children to abandon the family, perhaps hoping they would find a better life but too often to have one less mouth to feed. The poverty rate among children rose to 14 percent. To avoid being a further burden on their families, many youths simply ran away from home, hitching rides on railroad trains.[3]

Some 250,000 boys and girls, white and African American and as young as eight years old, became drifters; the homeless, then referred to as "hoboes," came from a variety of backgrounds. Children of unemployed miners and factory workers, struggling farmers, and even "prosperous" physicians rode the rails, or hitchhiked across the nation. According to Errol Lincoln Uys's account: "While one road kid in five was on a summer adventure, most teenagers riding the rails left home to seek work. Some were high school dropouts, but many had graduated only to find their local job prospects were nil. They joined the mass of migrant job seekers estimated in 1933 to be as many as four million. It was a desperate world of cut-throat competition, where a boy or girl had to hustle for the lowliest job." And they traveled thousands of miles in search of work.

These children faced serious injury or even death sneaking rides on moving trains. The margin for error was too narrow to just blithely hop on and off. Some lost their limbs or lives falling from freight cars. Others suffocated in locked box cars. Because of exposure to the weather and inadequate clothing, many became deathly ill. Many suffered from malnutrition. They faced other dangers as well. Most communities greeted these "vagrants" with hostility. The local police met trains and drove the children out of town. Police officers beat boys at the railroad yards. Sixteen-year-old John Kercsi recalled the attack on him by a railway goon, a hired security guard who carried a billy club and sometimes a shotgun: "I fell to the ground and covered my head with my arms. He kept yelling at me and kicking me repeatedly. . . . " Girls, who made up about 10 percent of these youthful transients, often disguised themselves as boys to avoid aggressive advances from older male hoboes and rape. Some of the young male wanderers offered protection to them. In other cases, the girls ably defended themselves. One boy hobo recalled an incident on a boxcar to Idaho: ". . . one of the girls took out a gun and shot three of the five crows sitting on the telegraph wire. Everyone had respect for them after that." Many young females carried knives. Young boys also had to fend off unwanted sexual advances from older men. Sixteen-year-old Jan van Hee remembered his close call with a hobo predator: "He was dragging me by the collar, slapping me around, and telling me what he was going to do to me. Next thing I knew this bunch of kids came to my rescue. There were about a dozen of them, the youngest around twelve years. They took care of my attacker, stepping on his face and beating him severely." African American drifters encountered "brutal" racism, usually from white adults, who harassed and sometimes beat them. But African American children occasionally found comradeship with their white peers. "Because of their shared privations, hoboes were generally tolerant of minorities in their midst."

This "adolescent army" found only temporary jobs. They swept floors, shoveled coal, harvested crops, dug ditches, paved roads, mined silver, washed dishes, caught rattlesnakes, fought forest fires, and repaired railroad tracks. Too often, they found themselves begging for food in the streets. Some of these children received kind treatment on the road. Individuals and families showed pity, feeding, clothing, and sometimes providing them with shelter. Local organizations also tried to help. "At the Community Lodge in Los Angeles, 623 boys who applied for shelter in the five months ending in March 31, 1932, came from forty-five states and the District of Columbia." But individuals could only do so much with extremely limited resources, and local relief agencies often became overtaxed by the flood of needy children.

New Deal Youth Programs.   The "young nomads" ultimately attracted the attention of government officials and policymakers.[4] "The idea that a generation might have no ties to the past and no faith in the future was frightening. Youth had the energy and the anger to spark a social revolution—or at least a full-fledged explosion in the streets." The National

Youth Administration (NYA) and the Civilian Conservation Corps (CCC) were established by President Franklin D. Roosevelt's administration to address the specific problem of unemployed youth. The NYA focused on youths between sixteen and twenty-five years of age; its program, "the first of its kind at the federal level," combined schooling with job training and character building. Historian Grace Palladino summarizes: "Sponsoring resident training camps and work projects designed to encourage the poorest youth to become self-sufficient, it also offered short-term courses in child care, car mechanics, commercial art, and a host of academic and practical subjects." NYA staff members taught poor children middle-class values through team sports, hygiene classes, and savings plans.[5]

The CCC, created in 1933, focused on young men and women between eighteen and twenty-one years of age and served some 2,500,000 youths over ten years. The CCC fed, clothed, provided shelter and paid $30.00 a month, which was sent home to the parents. Known as the "Tree Army," the CCC organized corps of youths, in military fashion, to work on rural conservation projects. Ernest Amundsen described his CCC experiences at West Yellowstone:

> We worked on Forest Service roads. A dump truck hauled loads of gravel. Left-handed boys had to shovel on the right-hand side and right-handers on the left side. The boss did this with whatever tools we were using. I learned to use a shovel, ax, saw, pick, and other tools left-handed. I also learned not to drink whiskey like you drink beer, and how to play poker and how not to play poker.

In spite of the difficult work, the CCC proved to be a lifesaver for many American youths. World War II eventually absorbed most of these young people; many of them enlisted voluntarily. This still left younger itinerants without any apparent social support systems.[6]

The High School as Custodian.   The depression's high rate of unemployment boosted school attendance; there was a 64 percent enrollment rate for fourteen- to seventeen-year-olds. In 1929, 4,800,000 students attended secondary school; only ten years later, this figure had jumped to 7.1 million by 1939. Historian David Angus adds that "thousands of children went to school simply because there was no place else to go. The schoolroom was warm, if not necessarily friendly, and often the school lunch, perhaps paid for out of the teacher's pocket, was the closest thing to a complete meal the child received. The school became, in many communities, a relief agency; with classes of fifty and sixty in rooms designed to seat thirty-five, it could hardly have been more than this."[7] Idleness and hunger thus drove children to attend school.

In the depression, the "youth problem" was no longer child labor, but youth unemployment. Mirel and Angus note a "profound and permanent shift in the basic relationships between youth, schools, and unemployment." In order to attract and retain students, school officials began to shift curricular emphasis. National leaders like Charles M. Prosser, an advocate of secondary vocational education and executive secretary of the National Society for the Promotion of Industrial Education, supported a "life-education curriculum in which vocational education played a diminished role." The rationale for this approach stemmed from the perceived death of entrepreneurship and the emergence of persistent unemployment, with school leavers threatening to become a "permanent underclass."

Thus, in the Detroit schools, the majority of students now enrolled in practical, if mundane, courses like "Personal Service," in which they studied diet, etiquette, and dating. The results were dramatic: "While high school enrollments rose in Detroit by 61 percent from 1929 to 1939, the number of graduates increased by 237 percent." The schools, in this case, appeared to be successful in withdrawing students from the labor market. Mirel and Angus, generalizing from this depression-era Detroit school experience, maintain that educators "shifted the purpose of their institutions away from college and vocational preparation and toward custodianship of the young based on the conviction that there were not meaningful jobs for them and that their task was to adjust youth to that state of affairs."[8] American public high schools simply came to be warehouses for adolescents.

Increasing high school enrollment encouraged the development of a distinct adolescent culture, which became prevalent following World War II, when the term *teenager* first appeared. Grace Palladino sees the historical unfolding of "teenage culture" as involving "family restructuring," with adolescents assuming a passive, dependent role in the family; "institution building," with the expansion and maturation of the high school; and "market expansion," with American business targeting adolescents as a new source of consumers.

The Birth of Andy Hardy.   White middle-class high school youths during the 1930s were the first to show signs of the new teenage culture. *Andy Hardy*, a famous 1930s character in a series of movies, the son of a small-town judge, proved to be an enigma to his straight-laced, doting parents. Andy's irrepressible energy, his social popularity, many school activities and adventures, and his steady girlfriend appeared to be alien to them. Since his was the first full-fledged adolescent generation, they struggled to tolerate his youthful shenanigans. Although a somewhat irritating character, Andy's adventures nevertheless projected a wholesome image of American youth.

Still, adolescents began to assert themselves and deviated markedly from G. Stanley Hall's ideal of "sheltered adolescence." "By the 1930s, high school students seemed more convinced than ever that experimentation was a normal part of growing up." They smoked cigarettes, which alarmed many adults, who saw smoking as inevitably leading to an immoral life. The first antismoking campaign resulted. Dances, parties, and dates became part of the adolescent world and lexicon. Parents began to confer allowances, with which teens purchased cosmetics and clothes, and fret over necking and petting. By the end of the decade, adolescent socializing had assumed significant importance in this developmental stage.

The American "Teenager"

The 1940s were a watershed for teen culture. As the decade unfolded, several distinct aspects of the adolescent experience became clear.[9] Some of these were holdovers from the thirties; others related directly to the war. Of course, many girls and boys joined the armed forces and others found work in the war industries, which contributed to higher school leaving rates during this period. Still other American adolescents found themselves taken from their families and homes because of their racial background. Adult American society began to perceive the new youth culture as vulnerable to criminal temptations, a serious and growing social problem. And during the late 1940s, corporations recognized adolescents as a profitable market niche.

War Heroes and Heroines

Military mobilization required millions of recruits. Teens entered the armed services either involuntarily through the military draft or voluntarily through enlistment. Roger Tuttrup dropped out of high school and enlisted, at age seventeen, in the Marine Corps. He had tried earlier, at fifteen and sixteen, lying about his age. As he recalls, "I wanted to be a hero, let's face it. I was havin' trouble in school. . . . The war'd been goin' on for two years. I didn't wanna miss it, for Chrissake." Tuttrup later participated in the bloody invasion of Okinawa and was sent to China to support Chiang Kai-shek's ill-fated effort to rule that country. Eighty percent of E. B. Sledge's Marine division during the Guadalcanal campaign "was less than twenty-one years of age." He recounts the brutality of war and how it made "mild-mannered kids" into "twentieth-century savages" in order to survive.[10] In spite of the desperate need for war industry workers and inductees, government officials encouraged students, especially males, to remain in school. "If the war taught the federal government anything, it was that too many potential draftees were unprepared—both physically or mentally—to withstand the rigors of war."[11]

On the domestic front, war production needs created an ominous shortage of workers for industry. The federal government appealed to women's patriotism to take their places on assembly lines for the manufacture of planes, tanks, ships, and other war materiel. "Rosie the riveter" was born. Employers enticed married women with children to fill the need for labor by providing emergency nursery schools, the first federally subsidized preschool program. Companies recruited female adolescents as well. The federal government made it easy for them by lowering the "age limit for the employment of women from eighteen to sixteen years."[12] Because military mobilization created so many employment opportunities and deregulation opened the factory doors, many youths once again chose work over schooling. Their participation in the workforce increased by 300 percent, to 3 million. School leaving rates therefore increased: "After decades of phenomenal increase, high school enrollments declined by nearly a million from 1940 to 1943."[13] Publicity campaigns and new regulations reaped predictable results: "At the peak of wartime production in 1945, 19.5 million women [of all ages] were actually earning wages."[14]

At the age of eighteen, Peggy Terry began work in an ammunition factory in Viola, Kentucky. Her job consisted of standing at a conveyer belt to assemble artillery shells. Peggy recalls incredibly dangerous working conditions. The chemical tetryl covered the workers with an orange coating from head to foot. "We never questioned. None of us ever asked, What is this? Is this harmful? We simply didn't think about it." The munitions workers constantly inhaled caustic paint fumes, causing Peggy to recollect that "it burned the nose and throat. Oh, it was difficult to breathe." Finally, she barely escaped a horrible and instant death when a detonator fell to the floor, almost exploding.[15] The war, however, produced heroes and heroines in other, less legitimate and moral, ways.

Prisoners in Their Own Land: The Plight of Japanese American Children

Japanese American young people had profoundly different experiences from those of other groups following the bombing of Pearl Harbor on December 7, 1941. Although President Franklin D. Roosevelt did not officially issue relocation orders until February 19, 1942, FBI agents, suspicious of the loyalty of Japanese American citizens, began to round them up as early as the evening of December 7. Throughout the West coast, families were split up and sent to guarded camps. "Ten internment camps were established in California, Idaho, Utah, Arizona, Wyoming, Colorado, and Arkansas, eventually holding 120,000 persons." Some 66 percent of the internees were U.S. citizens; children comprised about 25 percent of this total.[16]

Reaction to the presence of Japanese Americans was not surprising, but the severity of it was. Some 200,000 Japanese had emigrated to Hawaii between 1885 and 1924 to escape the 1885 famine in Japan as well as to take advantage of job opportunities. They also emigrated to the mainland, principally California, during this same period. As in Hawaii, they came for agricultural labor, "but in a decade or so, many had become owners of their farms." The migration was atypical, however: "The Japanese government controlled the quality of the immigrants. They had to pass strict health examinations. Educational qualifications were prescribed. All in all, they were a highly select group." Moreover, the Japanese and U.S. governments worked together to resolve many delicate, and potentially volatile, international and diplomatic issues involving the treatment of Japanese immigrants. Beginning in 1893, and subsequently in 1905, 1907, and 1909, San Francisco school officials had attempted to segregate Japanese students. The Japanese government protested. In every case, Washington intervened and managed to overturn these decisions. The Gentlemen's Agreement of 1907 arranged between Japan and the United States banned the further emigration of farm laborers; only affluent Japanese immigrants sailed to American shores between 1908 and 1924.[17]

Anti-Japanese feelings continued to gain momentum in California; the presence of so many Japanese made native-born Americans uncomfortable. "The fear was expressed in the 'yellow peril' scare just after 1900. The yellow peril was a visionary invasion of the United States by hordes of Asians." White prejudice against Chinese immigrants, mitigated somewhat by the 1882 Chinese Exclusion Act, was now transferred to the Japanese.[18] This racism assumed many forms. Led by federal, state, and local politicians and trade unions, the Asiatic Exclusion League was organized in 1905 in San Francisco. "In California, the Land Laws of 1913 and 1920 were designed specifically to limit the freedom of Japanese Americans to own or lease farm land." Ultimately, the Oriental Exclusion Act of 1924 eliminated any further Asian migration.[19] Such restrictions naturally spilled over into the public schools. Although Japanese American students consistently maintained outstanding academic and extracurricular records in the schools, many communities managed to relegate most of them to separate schools. The San Francisco school board instituted such a policy in 1906. "Of the city's 25,000 schoolchildren only 93 were Japanese, but the public was outraged at reports that older Japanese boys were sitting next to little white girls in class."[20]

The Japanese placed a high value on education. Immigrant parents, or Issei, not only insisted that their children attend public schools to pursue economic opportunity and social mobility but also sent them to private Japanese-language schools. Japanese communities had created 268 such schools throughout California by 1940, less to preserve the language than to strengthen "ethnic ties", as historian David Yoo asserts. The Issei saw this two-pronged educational process as creating a "bridge" between the two cultures. Over the decades, the Japanese established a vibrant and rich subculture in the United States, creating and supporting Buddhist and Christian religious institutions and maintaining a string of Japanese- and English-language newspapers.

The total ban on immigration, Japanese American academic achievement, and persistent school assimilation efforts were not enough to persuade the dominant European American society to accept Japanese Americans. As one California Nisei—American-born Japanese—recounted: "In going through high school and college, I can't recall how many times I was cast aside just because I am a Japanese. I was barred from parties, dances, swimming pools, etc. . . . Truly American is for Americans and all other races are not given its [sic] chance." Prevailing racist attitudes prevented education from assuring success and eventual acceptance. Many college-educated Nisei found themselves relegated to menial jobs, such as working at family fruit stands, well beneath their abilities and training. "Hard work, playing by the rules, and investment in education guaranteed nothing."

When the Japanese Imperial forces invaded Manchuria in 1931, anti-Japanese attitudes became inflamed. Throughout the 1930s, American newspaper writers expressed sympathy for China's plight. American consumers boycotted Japanese goods, such as silk stockings. Americans also often vented their anger against the Nisei themselves. Violence even erupted between Chinese Americans and Japanese Americans in San Francisco and Sacramento. "In early October 1937, fists flew between Chinese and Japanese American youths at Central High School in Los Angeles . . . sixty-five American-born Chinese and thirty-five Nisei fought in the schoolyard. . . . " The bombing of Pearl Harbor by the Japanese Imperial Navy unleashed yet another round of bitter anti-Japanese feelings. Federal authorities swooped down on all Issei and Nisei in California. With only a few days notice, they had to surrender all of their property. Yoo outlines two stages of incarceration. Officials first transported Japanese Americans to "assembly" or "relocation" centers and then transferred them to "concentration camps."[21]

Relocation Centers.   The race track at Santa Anita, California, was the assembly area for 18,000 Japanese Americans. The authorities controlled all aspects of their lives from then on. They censored the center's newsletter and focused the schools completely on Americanization. Officials also "harassed" Buddhists; their non-Christian religion was seen as un-American.[22] Peter Ota, who lived in Los Angeles and was fifteen years old at the time, recalls that the arrest of his father and emotional breakdown of his mother due to the shock and trauma of relocation, which left him and his twelve-year-old sister parentless. "In April 1942, we were evacuated to Santa Anita. At the time we didn't know where we were going, how long we'd be gone. We didn't know what to take. . . . Only what you could carry." Nisei children faced an uncertain future, full of confusion, went through frightening, if not horrific, experiences. "Santa Anita," he continues, "was a race track. The horse stables were converted into living quarters. . . . The people in the stables had to live with the stench. Everything was communal. . . . When you went to the toilet, it was communal. It was very embarrassing for women especially. The parent lost control of the child." Yuriko Hohri, who lived in Long Beach, California was also sent to Santa Anita in early 1942 at the age of twelve. She, like Peter and his sister, endured filthy conditions at the track. "We lived in a horse stable. We filled a cheesecloth bag with straw—our mattress. . . . The floors were asphalt. I do remember what we called stinky bugs. They were crunchy, like cockroaches, large, black." She recalls irregular, "informal" schooling. The federal government eventually shipped Yuriko and her family to an internment camp in the swamp lands of Arkansas.[23]

Concentration Camps.   The ten, highly isolated, inland internment centers became labeled as concentration camps. They were surrounded by tall fences and barbed wire, guarded by armed sentries and guard towers with machine guns, and scanned by search-lights. Inmates lived in crude tar-papered barracks and used communal toilet facilities. There was little privacy, and regimentation reigned.[24]

Imprisoned Japanese adults, attempting to recapture some sense of order, began to hold classes for the children, which were taught by college-educated Nisei and generally focused on traditional school subjects. The War Relocation Authority (WRA) soon replaced the Japanese teachers with European American instructors. "Many of the schools focused on the fundamentals of reading, writing, and arithmetic but did so in ways that stressed an appreciation of the English language and American democracy." These camp schools had few, if any, desks and chalkboards. Not all students had books. The buildings themselves were poorly constructed and maintained. The student-to-teacher ratio, at 48:1 for the elementary grades and 35:1 for the secondary levels, easily exceeded the national average. Finally, teacher turnover proved to be frequent, with average tenure amounting to only five months.[25]

Peter Ota and his sister were eventually reunited with their father and shipped to a permanent "prison" camp in Colorado. Here they attended a makeshift school, with Peter describing a cruel irony: "School in camp was a joke. Let's say it was loose. If you wanted to study, fine. If you didn't, who cared? . . . One of our basic subjects was American history. They talked about freedom all the time."[26] Many children like Peter became bored and dis-illusioned. The gulf between youth and adult culture widened. With thousands of Nisei youths concentrated in one place, their allegiances began to shift. Their parents, lacking control of their own lives, lost authority over their children, and the two generations tended to drift apart. The promotion of democracy by their instructors in this coercive set-ting proved to be too much to endure for many of the young people. Students recognized and verbalized the hypocrisy. Camp officials, viewed as symbols of the tragedy, found themselves likewise unable to assert control, especially after 1944. Nisei teens opposed their repression: "seven young Nisei students at the Minidoka concentration camp school declared their solidarity with African Americans . . . and Native Americans." Other young Nisei prisoners even resorted to mass boycotts of classes, vandalism, and finally the cre-ation of their own Japanese language and culture schools. Still others preferred to work in the sugar beet fields rather than attend high school classes, or they generally misbehaved and were labeled as juvenile delinquents.[27]

Restitution.   Some Japanese American prisoners challenged their treatment as uncon-stitutional through court suits, but the U.S. Supreme Court upheld the federal govern-ment's actions in two cases, *Hirabayashi* in 1943 and *Korematsu* in 1944. Others—about 20,000 Nisei youths—joined the United States Armed Forces. They worked in intelligence to decipher "captured Japanese documents, interrogated prisoners of war, and even slipped behind enemy lines."[28] "The famous all-Japanese 442nd Regimental Combat Team won numerous decorations for its heroic deeds in Italy and Germany."[29]

After the war, hostility toward Japanese Americans did not dissipate. A few Nisei, fear-ful or bitter, "renounced their American citizenship and returned to Japan," but most chose "to return to California."[30] They were unwelcome. They "faced arson fires, threats, shootings, and acts of terrorism."[31] Veterans' organizations boycotted Japanese American businesses and banned Nisei war veterans from the American Legion. "Bumper stickers appeared declaring 'No Japs Wanted in California.'" Such ill feelings lingered for some time, but the 1952 McCarran–Walter Immigration Act reversed the "ban on Asian immigrants" and American citizenship for them. By the 1960s, racial tensions finally began to abate. Ultimately, in 1988, the federal government admitted its culpability in the tragic incarceration of Japanese American citizens during the war and provided some financial restitution to the survivors and their families.[32]

Japanese American children learned during World War II that American society maintained a double standard for citizenship and civil rights. German and Italian Americans did not suffer the same fate as Japanese Americans, yet the United States fought against Nazi Germany and fascist Italy as well as a militaristic Japan. They also experienced schooling as a tool of indoctrination. Finally, they learned that adolescence was not the same experience for all.

"A Nation of Criminals": The Origins of Juvenile Delinquency

By 1943, juvenile delinquency, the third aspect of teen experience, had become a universal adult concern. Delinquency had always existed, but the war redefined it. The disruptions in family life, with fathers serving in the military and mothers working in armaments factories, gave American youths a new-found freedom, "and they *were* getting into trouble." Police and juvenile court officials complained about teenage drinking, smoking, vandalism, auto theft, petting, and, for the first time, drug abuse, in the form of "reefers." A flood of magazine articles and radio programs exaggerated and sensationalized the topic. The U.S. Senate held hearings on delinquency in 1943. However, as in all cases, and as Palladino emphasizes, "this apparent epidemic of juvenile delinquency had as much to do with adult perceptions of teenage behavior as it did with a rise in criminal behavior." Parents, teachers, and adults in general often lumped disrespect, insolence, and back talk in with juvenile delinquency. No one could readily explain the phenomenon of deteriorating adolescent behavior. Many critics pointed to selfish and greedy parents, especially working mothers who seemed to prefer devoting time and energy to earning money by working in the war industries than properly raising their children. Other observers complained about indulgent parents who never seemed to resort to strict discipline or stiff punishment. Still others, looking for simplistic causes, blamed the negative influences of comic books, movies, and "swing music" for the unfavorable shift in adolescent behavior. This concern extended well after the war, into the 1950s.

Jitterbugging Youths

The advent of "bobby soxers" in the 1940s seemed a natural evolution of teen behavior during the previous decade, but the older generation sharply disapproved of the teenage passion for swing music. "In their saddle shoes, skirts, and sweaters, they became the new symbol of high school life, one that was identified with music, fads, and fun." The very future of society, in adult eyes, appeared to be surely bleak. Adults disliked the frivolous and uninhibited attitude of the bobby soxers, "their obvious obsession with crass commercial culture and their deliberate waste of precious leisure time." High school students in general became known as *teenagers*, "tied to the new high school world of dating, driving, music, and enjoyment."

A development related to this new teenage culture was the targeting of marketing campaigns toward this age group. Palladino argues that during this period, the adolescent began to be regarded as a major consumer. "Envisioning the teenage market as an after-school extension of a home-economics class, pioneer promoters took it for granted that adults could shape teenage tastes and steer young consumers along appropriate wholesome paths—a theory known at the time as character building." Popular magazines, such as *Seventeen*, "offered solid advice to middle-class adolescents about preparing for college and future careers" while at the same time "encouraged teenagers to define themselves through their appearance (and dates) and ensure their status as successful teens by purchasing the products they saw advertised in the pages." So began the manipulation of this age group by the corporate world.

The war had certainly disrupted families and temporarily interrupted the steady growth in secondary enrollment. This proved especially true for Nisei children. However, and generally speaking, adolescent culture, which had first made its appearance in the 1930s, firmly established itself among affluent European American youths by the end of the 1940s. Certainly the high school served as the incubator, providing the environment for the emergence of a previously nonexistent adolescent culture. "There would be no going back to the prewar days, when teenagers had to fight for their right to a social life. During the war, they had experienced a level of personal freedom that they did not intend to relinquish now." Adults did not react rationally to the growing independence of youths.[33] The adolescent experience during the 1940s encompassed battlefields, armaments factories, concentration camps, peer groups, and Madison Avenue. The film image of "Andy Hardy" remained alive and well; although a wholesome image, it nevertheless irritated adults, but it was one they could live with. The teens of the 1940s annoyed parents, teachers, and other adults by flaunting both their authority and notions of social conformity, but they did not arrogantly confront the adult world as their successors would in the 1950s or gleefully disparage it as their counterparts would in the 1960s.

"WE WILL BURY YOU"—IDEOLOGY, SCHOOL POLICY, AND THE COLD WAR

In a famous speech at the University of Missouri in March 1946: Winston Churchill warned "From Stettin in the Baltic to Trieste in the Adriatic, an iron curtain has descended across the continent."[34] The Cold War had begun. Instead of basking in the peace following World War II, the United States and its allies embarked on a fifty-year ideological confrontation with the Union of Soviet Socialist Republics (USSR) and the communist world in general. Espionage, armed conventional conflicts, and repeated nuclear brinkmanship all combined to create fear, insecurity, and paranoia.

International crises seemed to unfold in rapid-fire succession. Soviet-backed guerillas led a civil war in Greece in 1947. It was then that President Harry S. Truman issued the Truman Doctrine, implementing the official U.S. policy of containment to counter Stalinist infiltration and aggression wherever it threatened. The Berlin Crisis followed in 1948 over the USSR eleven-month blockade of that city. One year later the communist Chinese took control of the mainland. And that same year the Soviet Union exploded its first atomic bomb, sending shivers through the American public. The bloody Korean Conflict ignited in 1950 between North Korean and Chinese troops and United Nations' forces, a war that lasted until 1953. U.S. support for the traumatic and costly decades-long Vietnam War also began during the fifties. The construction of the odious Berlin Wall in 1961 and the dangerous Cuban missile crisis in 1962 further marked the ideological and military skirmishes that continued to unfold until the early 1990s. Tensions between the USSR and the United States were perhaps best symbolized by Nikita S. Khrushchev, the Soviet premier, at the conclusion of a 1956 reception for Western diplomats in Moscow, where he blurted out his infamous line: ". . . Whether you like it or not, history is on our side. We will bury you." He meant that the Soviet Union would ultimately win the ideological contest. The touchy Western diplomats who stormed out in protest believed that Khrushchev had threatened their countries with military annihilation.[35] The Cold War in many ways was a mix of irrationality and pathos.

Unprecedented military mobilization occurred. "In the twenty-five years from the end of World War II to the 1970s, the United States federal government spend a thousand billion dollars for military purposes. It trained a standing army of 3,000,000 men; it built 400 major and 3,000 minor military bases in 30 countries overseas, and it placed 7,000 tactical weapons in Europe."[36] Ultimately, the Cold War's almost half-century ideological struggle permeated all aspects of American culture. On the one hand, the entire society permanently prepared for conventional and eventual nuclear warfare while, on the other hand, it operated in fear, if not outright terror, of the consequences of a military holocaust no one would win.

The ideological, strategic, and military conflict between the United States and the communist world thus brought profound changes to America, including its schools. Moreover, the growth and increasing diversity of the high school population and the emergence of an affluent society had a strong effect on student culture.

The Red Scare

Americans not only dreaded the enemy without but feared the betrayer within. At times, paranoia gripped American society. Political witch hunts and the unveiling of conspiracies became frequent preoccupations of the public and politicians alike. These activities, which monopolized the attention of two generations of Americans, exacted an enormous toll in resources, emotions, and lives. The public schools were swept up in these often tragic events.

The United States first became fixated on the "communist threat" following the 1917 Russian Revolution. The Bolsheviks' usurpation of power filled Americans with fear and hysteria. Between 1919 and 1920, U.S. Attorney General A. Mitchell Palmer basically ignored the Bill of Rights and ordered the arrest and deportation of alleged immigrant radicals sympathetic to the communist cause. The second Red scare occurred in the late 1930s when Texas Democrat Martin Dies chaired the House Committee on Un-American Activities (HUAC), a committee newly established to investigate communist influence in American society. Dies, as did other southern politicians who "opposed New Deal reforms," accused the American Civil Liberties Union, Boy Scouts, and Girl Scouts, among others, of serving as communist fronts. Dies also devoted a great deal of attention to the American Federation of Teachers (AFT), which he believed was infested with communists. As a result, the federation, rather than take a stand on protecting academic freedom, purged in 1941 three major locals suspected of having communist leanings, including the large New York City local. The union's action reduced AFT membership by one-third, jeopardizing its very existence.[37] These Red scares, however, paled in comparison to what occurred during the late 1940s and early 1950s.

The manipulative and media-savvy Senator Joseph McCarthy, a Republican from Wisconsin, led HUAC on an infamous pursuit of purported communist conspiracies. A dangerous political demagogue, McCarthy convened high-profile hearings and publicized HUAC's efforts to expose supposed Red spies within the American government. "Between 1945 and 1957 HUAC . . . held in excess of 230 hearings and gathered the official testimony of more than 3,000 people, of whom more than 100 individuals were cited for contempt." HUAC investigations knew no bounds—it even accused the Department of Defense and the U.S. Army of being infiltrated. HUAC proclaimed that the Cold War operated as a propaganda war as much as it did a desperate strategic and military contest for influence and power. The Red scare placed restrictions on all of the media, especially many Hollywood writers, directors, and producers accused of being procommunist. The ruthless inquisition, spearheaded by narrow ideological dogma and anti-intellectualism, extended to the schools. According to historian Stephen J. Foster, "over 100 school teachers had been dismissed for non-cooperation with Congressional committees" in 1953. The Philadelphia School District alone fired twenty-six teachers.

Barbed-Wire Schools

Many individuals and organizations attacked the public schools during this time: overzealous patriots, paranoid free-enterprise proponents, self-righteous Christians, and finally pathological populists, who opposed taxes in all forms, especially for subsidizing schools. Such organizations as the Friends of the Public Schools, the Committee for Constitutional Government, the Guardians of American Education, Sons and Daughters of the American Revolution, and most Republican and conservative Democratic politicians, wrapping themselves in the flag, attacked "teaching methods and textbooks commonly used in the schools," and teachers themselves and accused the National Education Association of being communist at worst and pink (i.e., liberal) at best.

The National Council for American Education (NCAE), organized by Allen Zoll in 1948, was the most insidious Red-scare organization that focused on the schools. Zoll, according to Foster's account, was "anti-Semitic," "racist," and an ultraconservative Christian who wanted to purge subversion from the public schools. He vehemently attacked the public school curriculum, textbooks, and teachers. The NCAE published dozens of critical pamphlets and booklets on such themes as "How Red Are the Schools?" "Progressive Education Increases Juvenile Delinquency," "Progressive Education Increases Socialism," and "The Commies Are After Your Kids."[38] Critics attacked classroom practices, subject matter, and teacher loyalty. Schools, in addition, focused on preparing children for the atomic Armageddon.

You Don't Teach Good.   Anticommunist zealots excoriated Progressive educational philosophy and practices, which were seen as undermining national interests, and insisted on replacing them with traditional means of instruction and narrow academic content.

Kitty Jones's 1956 polemic, *Progressive Education is REDucation*, was one of the most vitriolic examples of these attacks. "Critics indicted" progressive teachers as " 'little red hens' poisoning young minds with communistic ideology."[39] Teachers felt compelled to alter how and what they taught. They grew more teacher-centered rather than student-centered; they resorted to conveying simple "fundamentals" and the "3R's." Classroom instructors, in short, retreated to "self-censorship" to avoid controversy and harassment.[40] The curriculum took on decidedly anticommunist slant. "Children were being taught in school that 'communists are bad men that want to kill us'; they then might overhear their parents remark that 'the neighbor who raises questions about the local civilian defense program is probably a communist!' " There was no sober analyzing of the policies of the Soviet Union and the People's Republic of China.[41] The communist world was simply viewed as monolithic and a threat. Schools waged ideological warfare through the minds of children.

Don't Judge a Book by Its Cover.   Textbooks, already closely monitored according to historian Joel Spring, came under even more scrutiny. As far back as the 1920s, pressure groups had attempted to shape the content of schoolbooks. The American Legion and Daughters of the American Revolution (DAR) wanted texts to promote nationalism and unquestioned loyalty; the Women's Christian Temperance Union pushed for the condemnation of alcohol in textbooks; and Christian groups opposed any mention of evolution in them. Business organizations such as the U.S. Chamber of Commerce and the National Association of Manufacturers denounced liberal public education in general and textbooks in particular. In 1939, the conservative Hearst newspaper chain and *Forbes* magazine attacked Harold Rugg's social studies books as anticapitalist. Millions of children in some 5,000 schools read Rugg's popular series. Opposition to them grew more intense in 1940 when patriotic organizations, such as the American Legion and DAR, assailed Rugg's books for being un-American. Small-town communities burned his books and school boards across the country banned them. Sales subsequently plummeted "from 289,000 copies in 1938 to 21,000 copies in 1944, to virtual elimination by the early 1950s." As the United States entered World War II, propaganda and censorship became routine and acceptable in American schools, and the campaign continued after the war. In the late 1940s, the Conference of American Small Business Organizations (CASBO) assumed leader-ship; CASBO also condemned texts that seemed to criticize free enterprise.[42]

During the 1950s, the era of HUAC and McCarthy, assaults on textbooks intensified throughout the nation. Anticommunists deemed that Frank Abbott Magruder's social studies textbook *American Government* promoted "totalitarianism" by its supposedly sympathetic portrayal of the Soviet Union and mobilized parents to pounce on it in "Englewood, New Jersey; Port Washington, Long Island; and Washington, D.C."; Eventually the book was banished in "Richland, Washington; Houston, Texas; Little Rock, Arkansas; Lafayette, Indiana; and the entire state of Georgia." Schools all over the country were purging books; some communities even resorted to burning so-called subversive books. Hysteria replaced common sense. The state of Indiana attempted to ban *Robin Hood* from schools because it smacked of communism—he and his band of merry men supported Karl Marx's concept of the redistribution of wealth in stealing from the rich and giving to the poor. To maintain sales and profits, cautious textbook publishers marketed politically safe—that is, bland, uncontroversial, and ultrapatriotic—books for use in America's classrooms.[43]

"You read books, eh?"
(April 24, 1949, by
Herbert Block,
Washington Post)
Courtesy of the Library
of Congress Prints and
Photographs Division.

Who Is Teaching Your Child?   It was not only textbooks that came under attack. Federal and state politicos expressed fundamental doubts about the loyalties of America's teachers. Their supposedly questionable patriotism made the public schools potentially subversive institutions. Many state legislatures revived the requirement of teacher loyalty oaths, a practice that harkened back to colonial times when some colonies required allegiance to be declared to the King of England. Twenty-five states had required loyalty oaths during World War I, and twenty required them again in the 1930s. Concern over communist sedition during the late 1940s and early 1950s produced demands for yet another round of loyalty oaths. Some of the oaths required at this time actually restricted what classroom instructors could teach. Foster states, "loyalty oaths and loyalty legislation were being used as a means to further discredit teachers, to place them under constant public supervision, and to undermine their academic and personal freedoms." School districts blacklisted teachers suspected of left-wing sympathies. Estimates are that 600 were fired nationwide—most were liberal.[44]

A general fear gripped many American teachers. Some of them, out of a sense of patriotism, willingly submitted to taking the oaths. Most felt coerced, especially urban instructors. A few teachers resisted at first. In Pittsburgh, Helen Darby, who had held a high-security position as a cryptographer during World War II, balked at taking the oath:

> We were all required a loath of loyalty [she laughs] . . . an oath of loyalty. I loathed it. I took it under duress and I resented it for this reason. I had just spent three years in the Navy and I felt that it was self-evident that I was a loyal American citizen. I had taken an oath when I joined the armed services. I thought it was an insult. . . . It was a fear. Oh, yes, it was a great fear, and so people did not talk much about it.

Sometimes loyalty oaths had tragic results: "Minnie Gertrude, a New York City instructor, grew despondent because of an investigation of her political past and committed suicide."[45]

Duck and Cover!   The USSR exploded its first atomic bomb on August 29, 1949. With a sense of emergency, President Truman created the Federal Civil Defense Administration (FCDA) the following year, which was intended to alert American citizens to the dangers of atomic attack from the Soviet Union. "The Atomic Energy Commission misled the public in its informational literature, minimizing the real and known effects of atomic radiation and working itself with faulty scientific appreciation of the medical effects of radiation exposure." In simple terms, the commission persuaded the American people they could survive an atomic war, if proper precautions were taken. The FCDA focused its campaign on the public schools. As President Truman declared, "Education is our first line of defense." Civil defense education had begun.

Schools dutifully prepared their students for the impending atomic cataclysm. Air raid drills began nationwide during the 1950–51 school year in cities. The Los Angeles schools conducted its drills on a weekly basis. Routinized, as if practicing a common fire drill, urban pupils quickly retreated with their teachers to school basements, which served as civil defense shelters, and lined up next to boxes containing cots, blankets, water bottles, cans of food, and medical supplies. In Newton, Massachusetts, one "kindergarten teacher had her children decorate the bomb shelter as a 'reading den,' papering the brick walls with their drawings and placing small chairs around the room." In 1951, New York City issued metal name tags to each schoolchild; Seattle, San Francisco, and Philadelphia, among others, followed suit. These durable markers functioned much as military "dog tags," since they would survive undamaged and so identify the little vaporized victim. The FCDA published 3 million copies of a comic book featuring "Bert the Turtle," who demonstrated the proper measures to take in order to survive an atomic blast. He told children that all they had to do was "duck and cover." The FCDA also produced an animated film, *Duck and Cover*, starring Bert. When given the signal by their teachers, children deftly ducked under their skimpy and fragile desks and covered their heads; in other schools they huddled together in hallways. Some home economics courses taught young women how to stock and decorate their bomb shelters.

Like the nation at large, the public schools adopted a siege mentality; this however, became intensified in the schools. The classroom routine grew more regimented. The scope of content shrunk. Teachers feared for their livelihood. The cumulative psychological toll on children, who year after year practiced air raid drills, witnessed parents and neighbors constructing underground concrete bunkers to serve as atomic bomb shelters, and read about the evil Soviets in the their textbooks remains unclear. Perpetual "anxiety" and "uncertainty," according to historian JoAnne Brown, had to exact a high price.

Certainly all of the measures taken to meet the perceived communist threat—censorship, loyalty oaths, even civil defense—conveyed a "dangerous and widespread psychology of repression."[46] The sacrifice of academic freedom did indeed cheat students, in different and costly ways, of their ability to learn. In the final reckoning, anticommunist, cold war hysteria did much to damage the nation and its institutions. It ruined lives. It made a mockery of the U.S. Constitution. "McCarthyism was amazingly effective. It produced one of the most severe episodes of political repression the United States ever experienced." This long period of largely unsubstantiated accusations created an atmosphere of fundamental distrust and restricted creative and intellectual experimentation and exploration. It thus severely harmed American public education. The federal government finally admitted its wrongdoings when it censured Senator Joseph McCarthy in 1954, thus bringing the worst chapter in this country's history of Red scares to an ignominious close.[47]

The Generation Gap

A distinct youth culture first emerged in the 1930s and assumed some key traits and patterns in the 1940s, as we have seen. "Youth culture is defined by those distinctive behavior patterns that children and adolescents develop, often in opposition to the power of adults and their institutions." This culture, like any other culture, assumed its own "attitudes, values, beliefs, and behavior patterns," as well as symbols and language. Peer conformity, rebellion against adult culture, idealism, and a sense of immortality were the chief aspects of American youth culture.[48] Just the sheer number of adolescents attending high school following World War II set the stage for its development into a full-blown culture.

Since the colonial era American birthrates had steadily declined, but this all changed after World War II. Beginning in 1947, there was a dramatic increase, unprecedented in scale, which continued until 1962. "Nearly twice as many children were born in 1956 as were born in 1936." The children born during this fifteen-year period became known as the "baby boomers." Neither society nor the schools had ever encountered so many youths. Their numbers served to significantly shape American culture: they expanded markets for goods as well as created entirely new ones in clothing, cars, and other consumables; they challenged the "older generation's" values; and they reshaped schooling. The overcrowding that resulted created an immediate and serious crisis in the schools. The economic upheaval of the Great Depression had dried up funds for school construction, while defense demands during World War II had diverted precious revenue to more pressing needs. By the 1950s, with a flood of students, America was faced with either old and dilapidated schools or a severe shortage of classrooms. "By 1957 the United States Office of Education was estimating that the school year had started with a shortage of 247,000 classrooms. This figure did not take into account the nearly 100,000 more estimated as necessary to replace existing classrooms that were unsuitable and unsafe." That same year some 840,000 students attended school "on a shift or some other part-time basis."[49]

The high school became the "inescapable institution" for American adolescents during the 1950s.[50] Graduation rates surpassed the 50 percent mark for the first time in history. Although recognition of adolescence as a distinct life stage did not come all at once and everywhere—it was given more quickly in small cities and towns than in rural and metropolitan areas and was interrupted by the demands of World War II—by mid-century it appeared to be widely acknowledged. "In the three decades after 1920, virtually every state extended legal protection provided by the juvenile court to those between sixteen and eighteen or twenty. In effect, adolescence became a legal as well as a social category."[51]

Rebels

The 1950s proved to be a pivotal decade for adolescence. Growing affluence and the unprecedented numbers of working-class and minority children attending high school changed the entire "nature" and "appeal" of teenage culture. The gap between youth and middle-class adult cultures, which had begun during the 1940s, continued to widen. According to Palladino, the rebelliousness of rock 'n' roll and Elvis Presley replaced the wholesomeness of bobby soxers and *Seventeen* as teenage symbols. Rock 'n' roll's direct roots in African American rhythm and blues music shocked white middle-class adults. Its popularity proved to be instantaneous and pervasive among adolescents. Radio disc jockeys promoted it and mass concerts were popular. Adults objected to its raw emphasis on rhythm and its suggestive lyrics; they feared a total breakdown of traditional morals and society. "It celebrated the wrong kind of values (and the wrong kind of people) and promoted a hedonistic view of life that mocked the very notion of wholesome adolescence." Adults condemned "rock 'n' roll as the devil's music" and denounced "teenage fans as delinquents," which reflected their fears of minority and working-class cultures.[52] Meanwhile, teenagers reveled in their rebel image.

Elvis Presley's stardom became a national controversy and introduced a shrill tone to the debate over rock 'n' roll. Teens adored him and mimicked his dress and provocative on-stage moves; many adults were intimidated by his influence. The clergy attacked Elvis in sermons, a Florida judge threatened to arrest him, newspapers linked him to marijuana. His commercial success was, however, indisputable. Elvis's regalia flooded stores and teens enthusiastically purchased it—with their parents' money, of course. "There were t-shirts, hats, black denim trousers, magazines, mittens, stationary, and charm bracelets, all properly licensed and bearing a picture of the newly crowned king of rock 'n' roll."[53] The commercial sector exploited the opportunity at every turn. Such films as *Rock Around the Clock* appealed to the teen market; television introduced *American Bandstand*. Teenage girls were the targets of cosmetics ads, which encouraged them to construct their identities around products. For young women, appearance became "commodified" and was the means of capturing the perfect love, husband, marriage, and family. "High schools became an important place to be seen, perhaps one of the main attractions of attending high school." Consumerism even extended to younger children in unprecedented ways. Coonskin caps were marketed to exploit children's fixation on the Walt Disney film *Davey Crocket*, and toys were sold during cartoon television shows every Saturday morning. Commercialization became a powerful force in the lives of children. In 1959, teenage consumers spent $10 billion, "most of it going to the entertainment industry".[54] In the process, as rock 'n' roll and its stars became legitimized, as youth fads became popular, adolescent culture became more acceptable.

But not to some. "To no one's surprise, teenage rebels resurrected the 1940's specter of juvenile delinquency, largely because they looked the part." Boys wore black leather jackets and blue jeans, combed their unconventionally long hair in ducktail style, and defiantly smoked cigarettes; girls applied excessive makeup, dressed in tight skirts, and seemed to be a bit too familiar with the boys. Concerned adults warned that cruising, hanging out, drinking beer, going steady, and sitting in cars in the dark at drive-in movies led teens to illegal or immoral behavior. Scores of books and magazine and newspaper articles fretted over the appearance and insolence of teenagers; the public blamed permissive parents, fussed over the demise of the American family, and declared a general decline in society's values. Adult concerns of the 1940s became the adult fears of the fifties.[55]

These fears were confirmed by the soaring rate of teenage pregnancy during the 1950s. "In 1957, 97 out of every 1,000 girls aged fifteen to nineteen gave birth, compared to only 52 of every 1,000 in 1983. A surprising number of these births were illegitimate, although 1950 census codes made it impossible to identify an unmarried mother if she lived at home with her parents." Adoption also masked this social issue.[56] Female teens received mixed social messages: Appear and act sexually desirable but do not engage in sex. Young women were, therefore, supposed to look like Marilyn Monroe but act like Doris Day. These were the "good girls." While pressured to remain virgins, teen rebelliousness meant testing the taboo of sex. Those who did became labeled as "bad girls."[57]

Holy Censorship, Batman!   Jitters over a perceived communist threat, apprehension over the perceived disintegration of the American family, and alarm over teenage delinquency all contributed to cries for censorship during the 1950s. Mainly, the target was popular culture. Statistics on juvenile delinquency, which had steadily declined from 1945 to 1953, suddenly showed an increase. This rise was blamed on the commercialization of youth. For many, the media—namely music, movies, television, and comic books—were responsible for this negative result. The Senate's Kefauver investigation, which began in 1953, heard witnesses testify that rock 'n' roll, movies, and comic books caused the disgusting behavior of youth. Movies encouraged teenage disobedience and diminished family values. Several communities and organizations banned violent, youth-oriented films like *The Wild One* (1953), *Blackboard Jungle* (1955), and *Rebel Without a Cause* (1955). Some believed these movies portrayed delinquency in a positive way and, in turn, might encourage gullible teenagers to imitate such behavior and thus create problems for schoolteachers and administrators and society in general. Television, the new medium, likewise seemed to these critics to promote wanton violence. As early as 1947, the American Bar Association spoke out in opposition to media's influence on children. Catholic organizations and the National Parent Teachers Association condemned television for promoting violence. According to the Kefauver Committee, the media came between parents and their children. Even such a childhood staple as comic books came under close scrutiny. Dr. Frederic Wertham, a psychiatrist, assailed them in his polemical *Seduction of the Innocent* (1954). "Comics not only encouraged violence, but also racism, sexism, historical falsification, even homosexual conduct. . . . " They portrayed pornographic images. Organizations like the American Legion and the Junior Chamber of Commerce clamored for action. "[B]y 1955 thirteen states had passed legislation regulating crime and horror comics."[58]

Adolescents learned their lessons well from sources other than the school. The commercial market proved to be an efficient and effective source of instruction, and the high school began to lose its authority as the educator of this age group. This development was an educational watershed. Parents had been gradually supplanted in their role as educators of their children by the institutionalization of the process in the public schools. But television especially intensified the influence of the commercial market on the lives of American youths, diminishing the influence of the school. Teenagers and increasingly younger children were influenced by television's Saturday morning cartoons and commercials from which they received training as consumers. This immersion in materialism was largely unregulated and unmonitored.

Hippies

The youth culture of the 1950s was further refined in the 1960s, setting a pattern that would continue to the present. Baby boomers reached adolescence during the sixties, and the sheer size of this group fundamentally altered American culture. "There were 22 million teenagers in 1964, and their numbers were increasing three times as fast as the overall population. . . . " More of them attended school and eventually college than ever before, producing an unprecedented "education gap" between generations. They were also a huge consumer market, spending $13 million a year on such things as records, clothes, soft drinks, and movie tickets. They were so influential that the Ford and Chrysler companies even devoted entirely new car models, the Mustang and the Barracuda, respectively, to this young and affluent group of consumers. These vehicles embodied, as well as reinforced, the freedom, power, independence, and energy of teenagers.

During the 1960s, youth culture became firmly and permanently entrenched. The Beatles symbolized a three-decade transition—"from bobby soxers, to rock 'n' rollers, to middle-class rebels." General irreverence fed teenage defiance. According to Palladino, adolescents "worried about nuclear war, despised their parents' racism, and rejected the notion of taking their place in the adult rat race. They were looking for stimulation, not security. They demanded social justice, not the privileges of class. And they looked forward to college as a place to try out new ways of living and learning, not as a passport to conventional service." The gap between generations was never wider than in the late 1960s. Nonconformity to their parents' mores and values began to assume extreme forms. Long hair, radical politics, raw music, and drug use all represented youth's flaunting of convention. Adults, the guardians of mainstream culture, responded either with rage or fear, or were simply bewildered by the counterculture. Neither parents nor educators had a clue about how to explain teenage culture, let alone properly respond to it. As Palladino concludes, "from that point forward, teenagers began to shape their own space and chart their own futures without reference to their parents' plans."

Today, big business sees children as a large and profitable market niche. Adolescents as young as middle-school age own their own telephones, VCRs, stereos, computers, televisions, game systems, and designer clothes and shoes.[59] And in a highly credentialized society, too few view schooling as an intellectual challenge, but rather as part of an institutional journey, or rite of passage, or simply a place where they could hang out and socialize. In sum, adolescents now base much of their decision making on peer acceptance rather than on their parents' values, at least for a while. Adolescent culture has also become hostile to schooling. Academic achievement seldom confers peer acceptance. High achievers, known as "geeks" or "nerds," suffer social rejection. The most extreme expressions of this counterculture are juvenile delinquency and gangs. While both of these manifestations of youth rebellion have always existed, beginning in the 1950s gangs became predatory and aggressive, unlike their more protective and generally defensive nineteenth- and early twentieth-century predecessors. Another change has been the lengthening of the period of adolescence. Since the 1930s, the age considered as the beginning of adolescence has steadily dropped; it now includes twelve- and thirteen-year-olds.[60]

The high school has attempted to compete for attention and influence by assuming a complex array of functions. It continues to take up the largest portion of teenagers' time and to provide education and socialization in their broadest forms with academic and vocational training; the high school has also taken on psychological counseling, suicide and substance abuse intervention, sex education, birth control clinics, and child care, among other functions. Measured against these efforts is the increasingly questionable influence on children's lives of largely unregulated commercial interests, all in the name of profit. With the many different social and educational institutions—families, peers, schools, and corporations—competing for their attention, the educational environment of American children and adolescents indeed appears to be complex and fraught with conflict.

CONCLUSIONS

World affairs such as the Great Depression, World War II, and the Cold War rudely and permanently imposed the world scene onto American schools. Previously, local concerns had dictated parochial educational institutions, but international economic, military, and ideological events came to supplant community priorities and domestic needs. For the first time in American educational history, distant turmoil shaped school policies and practices. The school culture underwent fundamental changes. Poverty, although certainly not a stranger historically in childhood and adolescence, became an enduring part of it, one which the schools had to confront on a daily basis, starting in the 1930s. The federal government recognized that it had a role—albeit limited—in alleviating the problem. Decision makers also recognized how the public schools could be used to serve national interests and policies. The public schools were not only a source of "manpower" for military and economic needs but could ensure as well ideological hegemony.

The school environment grew more complex. Common schools characterized education in the nineteenth century; secondary education characterized the twentieth. Schooling now appeared to be indispensable as a bridge to employment instead of an indulgent option. As a result, enrollment, attendance, and graduation increased.

With more of America's children in school for longer periods of time, a separate youth culture that confronted adult institutions, values, and mores developed. However, much of this was misconstrued. Adults too often confused a maturing adolescent culture with juvenile delinquency. Particularly during the 1950s, middle-class adults feared that children were adopting lower-class habits and values—they simplistically labeled this different agenda as juvenile delinquency. But the generation gap had indeed widened. Teen behavior had abruptly dispensed with white, middle-class norms. By 1960, adult fixation on youth deviancy waned as the period of schooling lengthened and the reality of a distinct youth culture became accepted.[61]

In sum, the public schools assumed a more central economic, political, and social role generally in American society and particularly in children's lives during the latter half of the twentieth century. This had an unintended outcome. Although academic credentials had become a necessity and the duration of formal education increased, the schools became battlegrounds for unfulfilled dreams and ideals during the latter decades of the twentieth century.

ACTIVITIES FOR FURTHER EXPLORATION

1. Adolescents, as we saw, made up a significant part of the military forces during World War II. What did these young people learn? In addition to the recollections of Roger Tuttrup and E. B. Sledge, you can hear another Marine's actual battle experiences at the front in Guam. Refer to " 'We Need to Exterminate Them': A Marine Describes the Battle of Guam." A Japanese soldier's perspective is expressed through a poem, "A Japanese Soldier Describes the Horrors of Guadalcanal." These primary sources can be located at http://chnm.gmu.edu/us/many.taf.

2. For additional information about and photographs of the incarceration of Japanese American children during World War II, consult the following Web site: www.pbs.org/childofcamp/history/index.html. The actual executive order, the text of the U.S. Supreme Court decision in *Korematsu v. United States*, and a oral history of a resentful Nisei as well as other documents treating Japanese internment can be located at http://chnm.gmu.edu/us/many.taf.

VIDEO EXPLORATIONS

1. View excerpts of an "Andy Hardy" film and list and discuss, with classmates, distinct symbols of adolescent culture that first emerged during the 1930s. Compare and contrast this with *The Wild One* from the 1950s.

2. The films *Blackboard Jungle* and *Breakfast Club* can be used to compare conflicts with adult authority in the high school of the 1950s and 1980s, respectively. What are the differences? Similarities?

3. The atomic threat and Cold War mobilization influenced the schools during the 1950s, and the public schools trained children how to respond to an atomic war. A unique film, *Atomic Café* (New York: First Run Features, 1993), contains actual footage from government archives and various civil defense agencies intended to educate Americans about the survivability of atomic warfare. The last ten minutes specifically focus on atomic bomb drills in the public schools.

4. The 1950s was an important decade for American youths. The major features of that decade included the advent of the baby boomers, atomic bomb drills in the midst of

the Cold War, the continuing development of adolescent culture, the growth in high school graduation, and the profound counterreaction to Progressive education, among many others. That decade also saw the beginning of the eradication of polio, with the public schools used as the main sites for testing and eventual inoculation, thus formalizing the custom of school immunization that continues to this day and encompasses many other childhood diseases. The film *A Paralyzing Fear: The Story of Polio in America* (Alexandria, VA: PBS Home Video, 1998), provides a comprehensive historical overview of the origins and impact of polio. Selected clips show "iron lungs," polio's impact on children, schools, communities, and families, and of course the public school campaign.

NOTES AND SOURCES

In order to condense endnotes, the first work cited is the primary one, usually the source of any direct quotes. Subsequent references serve as supplementary, or additional, sources of paraphrased information and/or alternative historical interpretations.

1. Richard O. Boyer and Herbert M. Morais, *Labor's Untold Story* (New York: United Electrical, Radio & Machine Workers of America, 1976), pp. 249, 250, 251. Also, refer to Irving Bernstein, *The Lean Years: A History of the American Worker, 1920–1933* (Boston: Houghton Mifflin Company, 1960), pp. 48, 255, 259; Errol Lincoln Uys, *Riding the Rails: Teenagers on the Move During the Great Depression* (New York: TV Books, 1999), p. 47.

2. Jeffrey E. Mirel, "Adolescence in Twentieth-Century America," in *Encyclopedia of Adolescence*, eds. R. M. Lerner, A. C. Peterson, and J. Brooks-Gunn (New York: Garland Publishing, 1991), pp. 1158–1159. This material is taken from Richard J. Altenbaugh, David E. Engel, and Don T. Martin, *Caring for Kids: A Critical Study of Urban School Leavers* (London: Falmer Press, 1995), pp. 39–41. Also see Joel Spring, "Youth Culture in the United States," in *Roots of Crisis: American Education in the Twentieth Century*, eds. Clarence J. Karier, Paul Violas, and Joel Spring (Chicago: Rand McNally, 1973), pp. 205, 207–210.

3. Stephanie Coontz, *The Way We Never Were: American Families and the Nostalgia Trap* (New York: Basic Books, 1992), p. 14. Refer as well to Uys, *Riding the Rails*, pp. 11, 22, 23, 26, 53–54, 56, 57, 141–142.

4. The quotes and information in these paragraphs are from Uys, *Riding the Rails*, p. 9, 11, 13, 15, 21, 27–29, 31–33, 60, 62, 93, 95, 99, 102, 105, 107, 109–110, 113–117, 119, 139–140, 146, 155–171, 207–211, 213. Kersci and van Hee are quoted on pp. 119 and 196, respectively.

5. Grace Palladino, *Teenagers: An American History* (New York: Basic Books, 1996), pp. 37, 39–40. Also see Uys, *Riding the Rails*, pp. 21, 41, 42.

6. Uys, *Riding the Rails*, pp. 43, 231, 233. Amundsen is quoted on p. 232.

7. David L. Angus, "The Dropout Problem: An Interpretive History" (Ph.D. diss., Ohio State University, 1965), pp. 65, 66. See as well Lawrence A. Cremin, *The Transformation of the School: Progressivism in American Education, 1876–1957* (New York: Vintage Books, 1964), p. 274.

8. Jeffrey E. Mirel and David L. Angus, "Youth, Work, and Schooling in the Great Depression," *Journal of Early Adolescence* 5 (1985), pp. 490, 499, 501, 502.

9. The quotes in these paragraphs are from Palladino, *Teenagers*, pp. xii, xxi, 4, 5, 6, 7, 9, 12, 25, 28, 30. Palladino describes three distinct adolescent trends in her analysis of the 1940s in Chapters 4, 5, 6, and 7. I have added a fourth.

10. Studs Terkel, *"The Good War": An Oral History of World War Two* (New York: Ballantine Books, 1984), pp. 56–57, 171, 174.

11. Palladino, *Teenagers*, pp. 66, 71.

12. Alice Kessler-Harris, *Out to Work: A History of Wage-Earning Women in the United States* (New York: Oxford University Press, 1982), p. 275. See as well Barbara Beatty, *Preschool Education in America: The Culture of Young Children from the Colonial Era to the Present* (New Haven, CT: Yale University Press, 1995), pp. 186–192.

13. Angus, "The Dropout Problem," p. 87. Also see James Gilbert, *A Cycle of Outrage: America's Reaction to the Juvenile Delinquent in the 1950s* (New York: Oxford University Press, 1986), p. 19.

14. Kessler-Harris, *Out to Work*, p. 276. Also refer to Lynn Y. Weiner, *From Working Girl to Working Mother: The Female Labor Force in the United States, 1820–1980* (Chapel Hill, NC: University of North Carolina Press, 1985), pp. 95, 110–111.

15. Terkel, "The Good War," pp. 105, 106.

16. Eric Foner and John A. Garraty, eds., *The Reader's Companion to American History* (Boston: Houghton Mifflin, 1991), p. 589. See as well Thomas James, *Exile Within: The Schooling of Japanese Americans, 1942–1945* (Cambridge, MA: Harvard University Press, 1987), p. 3; Meyer Weinberg, *Asian-American Education: Historical Background and Current Realities* (Mahwah, NJ: Lawrence Erlbaum Associates, 1997), p. 46.

17. Weinberg, *Asian-American Education*, pp. 46, 52–53, 58. Refer also to Leonard Dinnerstein and David M. Reimers, *Ethnic Americans: A History of Immigration* (New York: Harper & Row, 1988), p. 66.

18. Dinnerstein and Reimers, *Ethnic Americans*, pp. 60, 65. Also see James, *Exile Within*, p. 14, 17.

19. Weinberg, *Asian-American Education*, p. 53. Also see Dinnerstein and Reimers, *Ethnic Americans*, pp. 65–66, 85.

20. Dinnerstein and Reimers, *Ethnic Americans*, p. 66. Refer as well to Weinberg, *Asian-American Education*, pp. 54, 55, 56.

21. David K. Yoo, *Growing Up Nisei: Race, Generation, and Culture among Japanese Americans of California, 1924–49* (Urbana, IL: University of Illinois Press, 2000), pp. 24–25, 28, 31, 36, 39, 50, 70, 87–88, 89, 96. The quote of the California Nisei is from p. 27. Also refer to Dinnerstein and Reimers, *Ethnic Americans*, p. 82; James, *Exile Within*,

pp. 10, 11, 12; Weinberg, *Asian-American Education*, pp. 57, 64.

22. Yoo, *Growing Up Nisei*, pp. 96, 97, 98–99, 100, 101.

23. Terkel, "The Good War," pp. 27, 31, 32, 33.

24. James, *Exile Within*, pp. 25, 30, 35, 43; Weinberg, *Asian-American Education*, pp. 59, 60; Yoo, *Growing Up Nisei*, p. 103.

25. Yoo, *Growing Up Nisei*, pp. 103, 106, 107–108. Also refer to James, *Exile Within*, pp. 43, 46; Weinberg, *Asian-American Education*, pp. 60–61.

26. Terkel, "The Good War," pp. 28, 29.

27. Weinberg, *Asian-American Education*, pp. 61–62, 67. See likewise James *Exile Within*, pp. 62–63, 115–116, 140–141, 142, 149; Yoo, *Growing Up Nisei*, p. 103, 109, 110.

28. Yoo, *Growing Up Nisei*, p. 104. Refer also to Dinnerstein and Reimers, *Ethnic Americans*, p. 83; Weinberg, *Asian-American Education*, p. 60.

29. Foner and Garraty, *Reader's Companion*, p. 589.

30. Dinnerstein and Reimers, *Ethnic Americans*, p. 83. Also see Weinberg, *Asian-American Education*, p. 64.

31. Yoo, *Growing Up Nisei*, p. 136.

32. Dinnerstein and Reimers, *Ethnic Americans*, pp. 83–84. Likewise refer to Weinberg, *Asian-American Education*, p. 64.

33. The quotes and much of the information in these paragraphs are from Palladino, *Teenagers*, p. xvi, xvii, 51–52, 81–83, 93. Gilbert, *A Cycle of Outrage*, p. 25, 28, 32, 40, provides a similar interpretation of the perceptions of juvenile delinquency. The "nation of criminals" quote is on p. 29. And see Elaine Tyler May, *Homeward Bound: American Families in the Cold War Era* (New York: Basic Books, 1988), pp. 74–75.

34. Churchill's speech is quoted in Margaret Truman, *Harry S. Truman* (New York: William Morrow & Co., Inc., 1973), p. 312.

35. Khrushchev is quoted in William J. Thompson, *Khrushchev: A Political Life* (London: Macmillan Press, 1995), p. 171. See also Ellen W. Schrecker, *No Ivory Tower: McCarthyism and the Universities* (New York: Oxford University Press, 1986), pp. 4, 7; Kenneth P. O'Donnell and David F. Powers, *"Johnny, We Hardly Knew Ye": Memories of John Fitzgerald Kennedy* (Boston: Little, Brown and Co., 1970), p. 284.

36. Stuart J. Foster, *Red Alert! Educators Confront the Red Scare in American Public Schools, 1947–1954* (New York: Peter Lang, 2000), p. 12.

37. David M. Oshinsky, *A Conspiracy So Immense: The World of Joe McCarthy* (New York: Free Press, 1983), pp. 85, 87–88, 92. Refer as well to William E. Eaton, *The American Federation of Teachers, 1916–1961* (Carbondale, IL: Southern Illinois Press, 1975), pp. 101–102, 120–121; Marjorie Murphy, *Blackboard Unions: The AFT and the NEA, 1900–1980* (Ithaca, NY: Cornell University Press, 1990), pp. 167, 171; Paul C. Violas, "Academic Freedom and the Public School Teacher, 1930–1960," in Karier, Violas, Spring, eds., *Roots of Crisis*, pp. 165, 170, 173–176.

38. The quotes in these paragraphs are from Foster, *Red Alert!*, pp. 1, 15, 52–53, 54–55, 57, 62, 63, 64, 65, 86, 87, 111. See also JoAnne Brown, " 'A Is for Atom, B Is for Bomb': Civil Defense in American Public Education, 1948–1963," *Journal of American Education* 75 (June 1988), p. 73; Murphy, *Blackboard Unions*, p. 193; Oshinsky, *A Conspiracy So Immense*, pp. 189–190; Schrecker, *No Ivory Tower*, p. 8; Joel Spring, *The Sorting Machine: National Education Policy Since 1945* (New York: David McKay Co., 1976), pp. 8–9; Joel Spring, *Images of American Life: A History of Ideological Management in Schools, Movies, Radio, and Television* (Albany, NY: State University of New York Press, 1992), p. 179.

39. Brown, " 'A Is for *Atom, B* Is for *Bomb*'," p. 71. Likewise consult Spring, *Images of American Life*, p. 175.

40. Foster, *Red Alert!*, pp. 2, 20, 83–85, 181, 183, 184.

41. Brown, " 'A Is for *Atom, B* Is for *Bomb*'," p. 75.

42. Foster, *Red Alert!*, pp. 92, 93, 95. Refer as well to Spring, *Images of American Life*, pp. 43, 45, 46, 47, 131, 132–133, 134, 138–139; David B. Tyack, Robert Lowe, and Elisabeth Hansot, *Public Schools in Hard Times: The Great Depression and Recent Years* (Cambridge, MA: Harvard University Press, 1984), p. 65.

43. Spring, *Sorting Machine*, p. 14. Spring, *Images of American Life*, p. 135, 176–177. Also refer to Foster, *Red Alert!* pp. 1, 185–186.

44. Foster, *Red Alert!*, pp. 90, 100, 101, 126, 127, 128, 181. See as well Spring, *Images of American Life*, pp. 127–128; Violas, "Academic Freedom and the Public School Teacher," p. 165.

45. Richard J. Altenbaugh, "Oral History, American Teachers and a Social History of Schooling: An Emerging Agenda," *Cambridge Journal of Education*, 27 (November 1997), p. 322. The quote from Helen Darby is also from this page.

46. The quotes in these paragraphs are from Brown, " 'A Is for *Atom, B* Is for *Bomb*'," pp. 68–69, 70, 71, 75, 77, 78, 79, 80, 81, 83, 84. Truman is quoted on p. 74. Also see Foster, *Red Alert!*, p. 17; May, *Homeward Bound*, pp. 104–107.

47. Schrecker, *No Ivory Tower*, p. 9. See as well Oshinsky, *A Conspiracy So Immense*, pp. 491–492.

48. Kathleen Bennett deMarrais and Margaret D. LeCompte, *The Way Schools Work: A Sociological Analysis* (White Plains, NY: Longman Press, 1995), pp. 85–90.

49. Eaton, *American Federation of Teachers*, pp. 153–154. May, *Homeward Bound*, devotes Chapter 6 to the causes and patterns of the baby-boom phenomenon.

50. Mirel, "Adolescence in Twentieth-Century America," pp. 1159–1160.

51. Joseph Kett, *Rites of Passage: Adolescence in America, 1790 to the Present* (New York: Basic Books, 1977), p. 245.

52. Palladino, *Teenagers*, pp. xviii, 114–115, 127. See likewise Wini Breines, *Young, White, and Miserable: Growing Up Female in the Fifties* (Boston: Beacon Press, 1992), pp. 19–20; Gilbert, *A Cycle of Outrage*, pp. 18–19.

53. Palladino, *Teenagers*, pp. 129, 131. Refer as well to Gilbert, *A Cycle of Outrage*, p. 15.

54. Breines, *Young, White, and Miserable*, p. 92, 105–106. Refer as well to Gilbert, A *Cycle of Outrage*, p. 15.

55. Palladino, *Teenagers*, pp. xviii, 132–133, 158, 159, 160. Also see Gilbert, *A Cycle of Outrage*, pp. 15, 64, 103.

56. Coontz, *The Way We Never Were*, p. 39.

57. Breines, *Young, White, and Miserable*, pp. 86–87, 92, 97, 101, 103, 113.

58. Ronald D. Cohen, "*The Delinquents*: Censorship and Youth Culture in Recent U.S. History," *History of Education Quarterly*, 37 (Fall 1997), pp. 258, 259–260, 261–262, 264, 269. Refer as well to Palladino, *Teenagers*, pp. xvii, 158, 159, 160; Spring, *Images of American Life*, pp. 185–86, 188, 196. See Gilbert, *A Cycle of Outrage*, Chapter 11, for a complete analysis of the "juvenile delinquency" films. Also, refer to pp. 3, 64, 80–81, 89–111, 143, 156.

59. The quotes in these paragraphs are from Palladino, *Teenagers*, pp. xix, 194, 195, 197, 201, 202, 225, 232. Also see Joel Spring, "Youth Culture in the United States," in Karier, Violas, and Spring, eds., *Roots of Crisis*, p. 213.

60. Kett, *Rites of Passage*, pp. 265–266; Mirel, "Adolescence in Twentieth-Century America," pp. 1159, 1162; Sherman Dorn, "Origins of the "Dropout Problem," *History of Education Quarterly* 33 (Fall 1993), pp. 353–374; Gary G. Wehlage, Robert A. Rutter, Gregory A. Smith, Nancy Lesko, and Ricardo R. Fernandez, *Reducing the Risk: Schools as Communities of Support* (London: Falmer Press, 1989), pp. 2–3.

61. Gilbert, *A Cycle of Outrage*, pp. 13, 18, 79.

IV

The Continuing Struggle for the Public School Ideal and Future Challenges

CHAPTER

10

Civil Rights and Public Schooling

I n the period that followed the economic cataclysm of the Great Depression and the tragedies of global warfare the international distractions of the Cold War were not the only problems facing American society. There were as well serious domestic social issues centering around race, ethnicity, and gender, problems that had been building up for a long time. The long-standing policy of segregation in the American public school system reflected society's broad racial and ethnic intolerance. America had fought fervently and sacrificed greatly to protect its democratic heritage during World War II, but it found itself facing a contradiction: It sent its children to a publicly subsidized institution that upheld and taught democratic principles yet practiced and perpetuated inequality. The struggle of African Americans against discrimination and for equal treatment in the schools and in society as a whole spearheaded the civil rights movement. Other racial, ethnic, and gender groups became swept up in this movement to achieve the American ideal of equality. Eventually, teacher and student rights were caught up in the movement. This chapter describes the degree of progress that has been made toward achieving the ideal of public education—and also how much remains to be done.

"SEPARATE EDUCATIONAL FACILITIES ARE INHERENTLY UNEQUAL"

Largely due to the federal Supreme Court's decision in *Plessy v. Ferguson*, racism during the first three decades of the twentieth century had never been more virulent. By World War I, a "reported" 1,100 lynchings of African Americans had occurred in both the North and South. Following the war, the Ku Klux Klan grew alarmingly to over 100,000 members throughout the Northeast, South, Midwest, and Northwest. "It declared itself against Negroes [*sic*], Japanese, and other Orientals, Roman Catholics, Jews, and all foreign-born persons." Klan members were elected to public office, and the organization generally exerted a great deal of influence. It directed much of its "wrath" at African Americans. "More than seventy Negroes were lynched during the first year of the postwar period. Ten Negro soldiers, still in their uniforms, were lynched. . . . Fourteen Negroes were burned publicly, eleven of them were burned alive."[1]

The Grand Strategy

African American intellectuals based at Howard University's Law School began a long campaign to erase discrimination by attacking *Plessy,* the powerful legal ruling that had cut off fundamental civil rights for African Americans, particularly access to equal education. They worked through the organizational structure of the National Association for the Advancement of Colored People (NAACP). According to Richard Kluger's thorough historical account, in the early 1930s NAACP strategists devised a clever, subtle, yet rather moderate plan to attack de jure segregation: First, they would confront the "equal" component and second, tackle the "separate" concept. Separate southern schools clearly failed to provide equal education, thus the policy of de jure segregation, although pervasive and entrenched, appeared to be vulnerable. "By moderate Supreme Court decisions requiring the South to draw up fair laws to administer them in a way to provide truly equal schools, the NAACP would improve Negro education and in the process put so much financial pressure on the white community that in time it would be forced to abandon the far more costly dual system and integrate the schools."

"Mr. Civil Rights"

Thurgood Marshall led the NAACP's Legal Defense and Educational Fund (LDF), which had been created in 1939, in a series of court cases that chipped away at "separate but equal." Marshall was born and raised in Baltimore, Maryland, of middle-class parents. In 1925, he enrolled at Lincoln University, an all-male, African American liberal arts college located in eastern Pennsylvania and known as the "Black Princeton," where he "excelled" on the college debate team. After graduation, he enrolled at Howard University's Law School, where he was a remarkable student, becoming the "top ranking student in his class."

After completing his legal studies, Marshall went to work for the NAACP's Baltimore branch, eventually becoming head of the LDF in 1939. During the 1930s and 1940s, he traveled tirelessly throughout the country arguing civil rights cases and fulfilling the NAACP's methodical strategy for deconstructing insidious de jure segregation. He was under constant threat for his activities and survived a near-fatal beating. By the late 1940s, Marshall had become known as "Mr. Civil Rights."

The Long Road to Brown

The NAACP's legal strategy began to bear fruit. In 1936, the courts forced the University of Maryland Law School to admit an African American student, since that state had failed to provide a "separate" law school. Two years later, the U.S. Supreme Court rendered a similar decision against the University of Missouri Law School; that state too had neglected to provide a separate law school of "equal" caliber. Similar higher education segregation cases were ruled on in Texas and Oklahoma in 1950. "Equal facilities" represented a "precondition to sanctioning the separation of the races."

The post–World War II period forced American society to confront a conundrum. The nation had fought and sacrificed to destroy Hitler's racial policies and practices of Aryan supremacy, which had cost millions of innocent lives, yet it maintained a similar posture of racial superiority toward 10 percent of its citizens. The Cold War brought this social issue into even sharper focus. The United States opposed the totalitarian government of the Soviet Union and promoted democracy and equality throughout the world. But at home the country failed to uphold these political and social ideals—a contradiction the Soviets fully exploited in their propaganda. America could not self-righteously promote itself as the world's ideological role model when it had laws that ensured racial inequality and condoned intolerance within its own borders. It simply did not practice what it preached.

Aware of these contradictions, President Harry S. Truman took unprecedented leadership in delivering equal rights to African Americans, albeit in limited situations. His administration supported court cases filed by the NAACP, fought against segregated housing, ended segregation in all branches of the federal government, including the armed forces, and pushed for antilynching legislation. By the late 1940s, the U.S. Supreme Court had outlawed segregated housing established through racial covenants. Truman's activities in this area lost him the support of southern Democrats (known as Dixiecrats), but he still won the 1948 presidential election.

Oliver Brown et al. v. Board of Education of Topeka, Kansas

Led by its famous civil rights attorney, Thurgood Marshall, the NAACP aggressively sought out test cases with the aim of ultimately overturning public school segregation.[2] Since the "equal" component of *Plessy* had been effectively undermined through a long series of court rulings, Marshall turned his attention to obliterating the "separate" concept of "separate but equal." NAACP attorneys did not have far to look for a case. Segregation was, of course, deeply ingrained in American culture and in its institutions. In 1950, African Americans comprised approximately 10 percent of the nation's total population, but they were not evenly distributed. About 23 percent of them resided in the South. Even within that region residential patterns varied. African Americans, for example, accounted for 50 percent of Mississippi's population. Seventeen states maintained school segregation laws; "eleven were from the old Confederacy." Only two states, Delaware and Kansas, were not southern.[3]

Marshall wanted to end "doghouse education," as he termed it, in the South. "In 1945, the South was spending twice as much to educate each white child as it was per black child. It was investing four times as much in white plants, paying white teachers salaries 30 percent higher. . . . " In Clarendon County, South Carolina, the school board during the 1949–50 school year spent $179 on each white student and only $43 for each African American child. African American school buildings lacked lunch rooms, custodial services, a sufficient number of desks, and many extracurricular activities. Children also had to cope with poor sanitation conditions. Many African American students had to resort to using a galvanized bucket with a common dipper for drinking while white children had water fountains. In some cases, shacks served as schools for African Americans. They attended school only from three to six months a year, depending on the needs of the local white landowners who employed them.[4]

School conditions in the North and West were only marginally better. Those regions "distanced" African Americans "without segregation statutes. In the North, the barrier was housing, potentially the most effective of all." The cumulative effect of northern de facto separation and "attitudinal racism" proved to be just as devastating as southern de jure segregation.[5] "Oklahoma was so vehement in its opposition to biracial schools that its laws called for a fine from $100 to $500 a day against any institution that instructed whites and blacks together, and any student attending such a school could be fined five to twenty dollars a day."

Topeka, Kansas, had always been a "Jim Crow town." In 1941, local African Americans won a court suit against the creation of segregated junior high schools. The school district promptly fired eight African American instructors; students would be integrated but not teachers. Furthermore, both the supposedly integrated junior and senior high schools remained intensely segregated. The district assigned and enforced separate cafeteria seating, assemblies, sports teams, and academic tracks. The elementary schools remained segregated. Kenneth McFarland, Topeka's school superintendent through the 1940s and 1950s, "invoked" Booker T. Washington regarding race relations. Thus the racial status quo appeared to be secure in Topeka's schools.

In 1950, Oliver Brown attempted to enroll his seven-year-old daughter, Linda, at a white elementary school close to her home. The school refused to admit her, forcing her to walk several blocks through dangerous railway yards to catch a bus to her segregated school an additional thirty-minute ride away. The NAACP filed suit on behalf of Oliver and Leola Brown and their daughter, Linda. Thurgood Marshall threw the full weight of the LDF into this case.

The federal Supreme Court heard the first set of arguments in the case on December 9, 1952. The *Brown* case was a class-action suit that consisted of school segregation lawsuits from South Carolina, Delaware, Virginia, Washington, DC, and, of course, Topeka, Kansas. The NAACP's position emphasized the psychological impact of social separation of the races on African American children. An "unhappy" Delaware child recalled, " 'I travel thirty miles a day to school. . . . The white school is twelve blocks away.' The buses were often late and caused them to miss classes, some of them said. One thirteen-year-old reported, 'When we get on the bus, the white children [outside] look at us and laugh.' The tensions produced between the races by enforced segregation were apparent. . . ."[6] After more than a year of deliberation and further arguments, the Supreme Court's Chief Justice, Earl Warren, read the decision on May 17, 1954:

> . . . Does segregation of children in public schools solely on the basis of race, even though the physical facilities and other "tangible" factors may be equal, deprive the minority group of equal educational opportunities? We believe it does. . . .
>
> We conclude that in the field of public education the doctrine of "separate but equal" has no place. Separate educational facilities are inherently unequal.

For the Court, any sense of "separation" created a permanent feeling of "inferiority."[7]

It is extremely important to note that the *Brown* decision itself did not mark the end of school segregation; rather, it signaled the beginning of a long struggle to achieve the elusive goal of integration. *Brown* could not exorcize the deep-seated racism in American society, a tragic flaw that persists to this day. Over the decades, racism would assume novel and less visible forms than segregated schools. The *Brown* decision was thus just the beginning of a new series of struggles.

School desegregation moved ahead slowly, evoking a great deal of emotion and racial conflict. Legal historian J. Harvie Wilkinson, III, divides its progress into five distinct chronological stages, which facilitate historical analysis of this experience: absolute defiance (1955–1959); token compliance (1959–1964); modest compliance (1964–1968); massive integration (1968–1974); and resegregation.[8] Most of the attention focused on the South in the beginning. After 1970, desegregation efforts were concentrated in the North and West.

Absolute Defiance (1955–1959)

The South reacted immediately to the Court's decision in *Brown*. Southern governors gave vent to their outrage and opposition. By the spring of 1956, 101 southern Congressmen had endorsed the "Southern Manifesto," which defied the *Brown* ruling. They maintained that states' rights superceded federal authority. Some southern communities stubbornly refused to submit to school desegregation and resorted to confrontation and even school closures. Therefore, beginning in the 1950s, African American children had a very different experience from their white counterparts. What happened in Little Rock, Arkansas, became the most well-known and infamous episode in the frustrating school desegregation effort.

The Little Rock Nine

Staunch segregationists implemented a two-stage strategy to prevent integration of Little Rock's Central High School. First, they attempted to prevent African American students from even entering the school building. Second, having failed in that, they tried to drive them out of the school. All of this involved brutal, terrorist tactics.

Sixteen African American students had originally applied to attend Central High School during the 1957–58 school year but, fearful for their safety, the number soon dwindled to nine. They all came from middle-class backgrounds since their parents were teachers or preachers, and all planned to attend college. Governor Orval Faubus, using states' rights as his weapon, refused to desegregate Central High or any other public school. On September 3, 1957, in a show of strength, he ordered the Arkansas National Guard to prevent the nine African American teenagers from entering Little Rock's high school. The students, later known as the "Little Rock Nine," became symbols of the struggles of African American children everywhere for desegregated schools.

Melba Pattillo Beals recalls in her autobiography her first day of school. A violent confrontation awaited her and the other eight students. The National Guard blocked the school's entrance as planned. The local police, although visible, stood passively by. Meanwhile, Melba and her mother barely escaped death that day. A furious mob of white segregationists drove them from the school grounds. Melba describes the terror she felt:

> The men chasing us were joined by another carrying a rope. At times, our pursuers were so close I could look back and see the anger in their eyes. Mama's pace slowed, and one man came close enough to touch her. He grabbed her by the arm but instead tugged at her

blouse. The fabric ripped, and he fell backward. Mama stepped out of her high-heeled shoes, leaving them behind, her pace quickening in stocking feet.

They just managed to return to their house safely; it was sprayed with bullets that evening. The nine students tried to re-enter the high school through the side entrance twenty days later. Although they initially succeeded, hostile white students spat on Melba and slapped her as she was escorted to her homeroom. Students openly threatened her in class; most teachers refused to discipline, or even silence, her tormentors. The unruly crowd outside of the building and the heckling white students inside it created so much turmoil and posed such a threat that the nine African American students were secretly removed from the school by noon. While certainly discouraged, Melba, her mother, and her grandmother remained resolute.

The next day, September 24, 1957, a "reluctant" President Dwight D. Eisenhower ordered 1,200 troops from the crack 101st Airborne Division to Little Rock to quell tensions and enforce the federal court's decision. They arrived the following day and escorted all nine students through the front door of Central High School. Although federal troops accompanied the students everyday through the school's hallways, from class to class, white students continued their defiant taunting. During classes, students pelted Melba with pencils and chanted racial epithets. White students knocked her down and kicked her in the hallways and on the staircases. One student even stabbed her with a thin iron rod attached to a Confederate flag. By the beginning of October, white students' racial attitudes had grown more intense and their actions even bolder and more dangerous. Melba recollects how she was nearly blinded by an assailant while she was walking through the hallway between classes: "The boy flashed a shiny black object in my face. The sudden pain in my eyes was so intense, so sharp, I thought I'd die. It was like nothing I'd ever felt before. I couldn't hear or see anything except the throbbing, searing fire centered in my eyes. I heard myself cry out as I let go of everything to clutch my face." Only the quick wits and instant response of her Airborne bodyguard, who flushed the caustic liquid out of her eyes, saved Melba's eyesight. When the federal government began to gradually withdraw the 101st Airborne Division, the attacks increased, undeterred by any punishment from school administrators. Intimidated by segregationist pressure and threats, the administrators had completely lost control of the school.[9] Sympathetic white students also suffered at the racists' hands. "Students seen talking with blacks in the halls received threatening phone calls at home."[10] Segregationists even pressured the local school board to blackmail Melba's mother. In April, the school superintendent threatened to terminate her teaching contract unless she withdrew Melba from Central High School. She refused and, because of heavy and sympathetic national newspaper coverage, was reluctantly rehired.

The stress of the relentless daily harassment and media attention took its toll on the Little Rock Nine. They gradually withdrew emotionally and became pessimistic about the entire desegregation process and its goals. Minnijean Brown, one of the nine African American students, lost her composure during lunchtime in the cafeteria. She threw a bowl of chile on two boys who had blocked her access to a table. School administrators immediately suspended her. After a second similar incident in which she attempted to defend herself, the school expelled her on February 18, 1958. The school rarely, if ever, punished the white perpetrators.

The Little Rock Nine endured; eight of them completed that tumultuous school year. The entire episode ended ignominiously, though. Rather than cave in to federal authority and mandate integration, Governor Faubus simply closed all schools for the entire 1958–59 academic year.[11] This was not an uncommon southern strategy. The community of Prince Edward County, Virginia, also defied desegregation by closing its public schools. Between 1959 and 1963, white students attended hastily organized private schools housed in churches and rented stores, while African American children went without schooling altogether.[12] Thus, hostility and intransigence marked the initial period of desegregation. Stalling tactics characterized the next phase.

Token Compliance (1959–1964)

The desegregation process moved at a snail's pace. "Only 11 percent of almost seven thousand school districts in the South and border states had integrated by 1961."[13] Most southern communities decided to comply superficially by instituting a policy of "tokenism." In response to the *Brown* ruling, ten southern states split legal hairs by implementing "pupil placement statutes." Local white school authorities "assigned" students to schools, minimizing, of course, the number of African Americans enrolled in white schools. As a result, Charlotte, North Carolina, "had three blacks in white schools in 1957–58, four in 1958–59, and exactly one in 1959–60." No whites were sent to African American schools. As Wilkinson asserts, "blacks bore the brunt. In many ways the tokenism of 1960 was no better than the segregation prior to 1954. In some ways it was worse. It was certainly just as profitless; the mass of black schoolchildren still lacked an equal education."[14]

Modest Compliance (1964–1968)

By the mid-1960s, the South had resorted to yet another clever strategy to forestall total desegregation: "local option," otherwise known as "open enrollment."[15] This proto-school-choice plan promoted the ideal of parents selecting schools for their children. In reality, choice was not made available to "all" families. This scheme ensured minimum enrollments of African American children because "white children did not choose to go to black schools. And doubtless due to ancient southern mores, many Negroes [*sic*] did not select white schools." Finally, school authorities created numerous impediments to discourage African American enrollment in white schools.[16] Thus little real progress occurred. "By 1964, only one-fifteenth of southern black children attended integrated schools." Enraged African American leaders demanded equality. While a series of court cases dismantled the so-called freedom-of-choice policy, "northern segregation . . . was virtually untouched until the mid-1970s."[17]

The "American South"

A major breakthrough was made when President John F. Kennedy's administration adopted an aggressive civil rights strategy. On June 19, 1963, Kennedy sent a comprehensive civil rights bill to Congress, an action that sparked instant opposition from Dixiecrats. Intensive lobbying efforts by the Kennedy administration and the emotional aftermath of the President's assassination in November led Congress to pass the Civil Rights Act in June

1964. By outlawing discrimination, this act provided more tools for desegregating society as a whole, particularly the schools. It authorized the U.S. Department of Justice to file suit in discrimination cases and the Office of Education to draw "up guidelines for desegregation in response to the Act."[18]

Due to this legislation, both the judicial and the executive branches of the federal government now required the South to desegregate in a comprehensive, rather than a piece-meal, manner. For the first time, the entire federal government seemed to be mobilized against segregation. Schools had to desegregate the student body, faculty, staff, athletics and other activities, as well as redistribute equipment and library resources.

The commitment of President Lyndon B. Johnson, Kennedy's successor, to equal rights and his masterful ability to successfully lobby Congress resulted in a flurry of legislation favorable to integration. The most important of these laws was the 1965 Elementary and Secondary Education Act, which proved to be a powerful piece of legislation by, as historian Richard Kluger explicates it,

> making sizeable federal funds available to local school districts and providing the government with a mighty financial club to enforce compliance with the desegregation orders of the federal courts; under the 1964 Act, any state or local government practicing discrimination was not eligible to receive federal aid. The education bill was part of a proliferating series of imaginative new federal programs aimed at declaring war on poverty and ignorance. Together—aid to schools, Model Cities, the Office of Economic Opportunity, VISTA, Head Start and others—Johnson labeled them steppingstones to a Great Society. . . . No sector of the nation stood to gain more from the Great Society than black America.

Finally, Johnson appointed Thurgood Marshall to the Supreme Court in 1967.[19] Subsequent administrations, however, turned out to be neglectful of civil rights at best or embarked on purposeful deconstruction at worst.

Massive Integration (1968–1974)

The period beginning in 1968 saw mixed results. On the one hand, it was an era of mass integration; on the other hand, it marked the start of a long and effective campaign to abandon school desegregation. A sea change had begun.

Some momentum from the equal rights legislation of the early 1960s carried integration efforts forward for a while. Years of enforcement of the Civil Rights Act by the Department of Justice produced significant results. "By 1970, the schools in the South, which had been almost totally segregated in the early 1960s, were far more desegregated than those in any other region. The few years of active enforcement had had huge impacts."[20] During the 1968 presidential election campaign, however, candidate Richard M. Nixon, an advocate of states' rights, won over southern voters. After his victory, the federal government started to retreat on all social matters. "He began by phasing out the anti-poverty programs as rapidly as feasible. Away with Model Cities and offices of economic opportunity and all such inflationary flotsam. He slashed federal spending for education and school lunches." Nixon's administration also proved to be "obstructionist" regarding school desegregation. Finally, during his truncated term in office, he appointed staunch conservatives to the federal Supreme Court, profoundly shaping its outlook on civil rights.[21] In many ways, then, the southern campaign to desegregate the public schools ended in 1968. Efforts at integration then began to focus on the North and the West.

School Busing

In an effort to overcome segregation based on residential patterns, the U.S. Supreme Court, in 1970 introduced the policy of school busing in *Swann v. Charlotte–Mecklenberg Board of Education*. Although this case directly affected the Charlotte, North Carolina, school district, it proved to be a turning point in desegregation. "The school issue now became a national one, because busing was meant not to remedy a particularly southern obstruction but to overcome the chief problem of the urban metropolis: racially separate patterns of housing."

Busing itself had been done for decades. It was used, as we have seen, to facilitate school consolidation in many rural areas of the United States. "By 1970, busing had become the means of daily transportation for over 18,000,000 pupils, almost 40 percent of the nation's schoolchildren." Busing had also been used to maintain segregation. School officials in Selma, Alabama, bused African American students on a fifty-mile round-trip to a separate school, passing a white school on the way. An African American student who resided in White Sulphur Springs, West Virginia, rode 108 miles round-trip. "The boy lived four blocks from a white school." No one worried about safety, or appeared concerned about inconvenience, or even expressed a preference for neighborhood schools. Only when busing was proposed for desegregation did white parents complain, protest, and eventually riot.

The federal court system ordered busing in Raleigh, North Carolina, Richmond, Virginia, and Louisville, Kentucky. Rather than submit their children to desegregation, white families quickly abandoned the cities for the suburbs or enrolled them in private or parochial schools. "In 1970, Richmond's first year of busing, the city's school population was 35 percent white; by 1976, the seventh year of busing, it was less than 20 percent and heading downward." School busing was a highly inflammatory issue during the early 1970s. Tens of thousands of people expressed their opposition by flooding the Supreme Court with complaint letters or petitions. President Nixon publicly expressed his opposition to busing for school desegregation.[22] However, contrary to popular perceptions and media coverage, busing proved to be a highly successful means of desegregating the schools. "By the 1972–73 school year, 46.3 percent of the black children in the eleven southern states were attending schools in which the majority of children were white. No other sector of the nation had achieved anything near that degree of desegregation."[23]

When the courts ordered busing for northern and western cities, the desegregation argument intensified. Segregated schools and housing had long been traditions in the North. "Indiana . . . had a statute authorizing segregated schools as late as 1949." Residential housing patterns anchored the rigid system of segregation throughout the North and the West, the latter having the most segregated systems in the nation. "The Civil Rights Commission reported that in 1972, 83.5 percent of New York City blacks attended schools more than half black." Los Angeles and Chicago had even worse records.[24] In 1972, the federal Supreme Court, in *Keyes v. School District No. 1*, ordered busing in Denver to facilitate desegregation. The courts subsequently ordered busing in city after city: Baltimore, Cleveland, Detroit, Indianapolis, and Kansas City, among others. The 1970

Swann ruling, which mandated busing as a means of integrating public schools, and the 1972 *Keyes* decision, which ordered the desegregation of northern schools, "extended" the scope of *Brown*.[25]

Busing in Boston

The North fought back. Boston, the oldest public school system in the country and the first school district to officially desegregate its public schools in 1855, became a violent battleground and ironic symbol of opposition to school busing in the 1974–75 school year, earning the title of "the Little Rock of the North." Race was not the only issue in Boston; social class was another flash point.

Segregation in Boston typified that of other northern cities. "By 1973 . . . fully 85 percent of Boston blacks were in schools with a black majority, over half in schools 90 percent black."[26] And those schools hosted deplorable conditions. In 1967, Jonathan Kozol published a widely popular and poignant book, *Death at an Early Age: The Destruction of the Hearts and Minds of Negro Children in the Boston Public Schools*. It graphically recounted his experiences as a teacher in one of Boston's ghetto elementary schools. Because of overcrowding, he had to teach his fourth grade class in a corner of the school's auditorium, where other classes and clubs were meeting simultaneously. With as many as 120 students and teachers in the same room at the same time, the noise reached unbearable levels. The school building itself was in a dilapidated state. Windows fell from rotted frames, and broken windows went unrepaired. Old chalkboards were barely usable because they had so many scratches and cracks. Kozol also described insensitive and punitive teachers. Many of the white instructors uttered racist epithets among themselves. Building principals and classroom teachers beat children with "bamboo whips" in the school's basement. The severity of one such use of corporal punishment sent one child to the hospital. Kozol characterized teacher–student relationships in such segregated schools as the "slave master and black child feeling." These conditions and attitudes proved to be pervasive throughout the Boston school system. That district spent less on African American children: "10 percent lower textbook expenditures . . . 19 percent lower library and reference book expenditures . . . 27 percent lower health expenditures per pupil."[27]

The NAACP began to complain to the Boston School Committee about de facto school segregation and inferior conditions in the early 1960s; the district's officials remained indifferent. A federal judge ultimately ordered busing for the blue-collar neighborhoods of South Boston and Charlestown. South Boston's white residents boycotted the schools and stoned the buses transporting African American students to South Boston High School, many of whom were cut by the broken glass. Enraged Charlestown whites screamed racial epithets at the African American children bused into their community. Tensions mounted. A large white protest was held in October 1974; an African American student was stabbed at Hyde Park High School on October 15. Despite Governor Francis Sargent's calling out the National Guard, the number of racially motivated fights exploded, with both whites and African Americans sustaining injuries. Such "incidences of racial violence persisted at a high level and did not taper off until the 1980s."[28]

South Boston's residents also directed their anger and frustration at the city's wealthier white neighborhoods, which, because of their affluence, power, and influence, had managed to avoid school desegregation and busing. South Boston's poorer whites resented this hypocrisy. "[B]using suffered an unpardonable, class double standard. Perhaps," Wilkinson continues, "Boston suggests the way we handle racial problems in this country: by leaving poor blacks and working-class whites to trench warfare, while most of middle-class America remains comfortably quartered outside of the battle zone."[29] In addition to racial and social rage, progress towards school integration began to encounter numerous legal impediments.

The Retreat from Brown

The federal Supreme Court's 1973 ruling in *San Antonio School District v. Rodriguez*, which allowed the practice of unequal school funding to continue in that city, began to turn matters around from a judicial standpoint for the Nixon administration. The Court had, in essence condoned school inequality. Any further attempts to extend the *Brown* decision would slam into the brick wall of *Rodriguez*. In 1974, the Supreme Court's decision in *Milliken v. Bradley* marked for all intents and purposes the official beginning of the end of desegregation efforts in the North. White flight and political realignments had left Detroit's public schools unable to implement desegregation and other improvements. The NAACP filed suit to institute busing across city lines to largely white suburbs to undermine de facto segregation. But the Court struck down such interdistrict busing strategies, leaving intradistrict busing intact; that is, busing could only occur within city limits. Justice Thurgood Marshall dissented, calling this decision a "giant step backward."[30] As Kluger concludes, "*Rodriguez* . . . had approved unequal schools; now, in the Detroit case, the Court was accepting separate ones as well."[31]

This Court ruling crippled any future attempts at effective and thorough urban racial integration. "The outcome in *Milliken* reflected Nixon's goal of weakening desegregation requirements. His four [Supreme Court] appointees made up four of the five votes to protect the suburbs." Nixon furthermore supported a Constitutional amendment outlawing school busing for desegregation purposes.[32] The *Milliken* decision encouraged white flight from the cities to the suburbs, thus reifying residential patterns of racial separation and guaranteeing segregated public schools. Separate but equal had now returned in the resilient form of de facto segregation.[33]

Resegregation

Nixon's federal Supreme Court appointments coupled with those of Republican Presidents Ronald Reagan and George Bush ensured a conservative judiciary. Even Democratic President Jimmy Carter appeared to be ambivalent about desegregation. The Reagan administration that took office in 1980 "denounced desegregation." The lack of commitment from the executive branch and obstructionist decisions by the judicial branch signaled the end of the integration movement and ultimately restored segregated public schools. The Supreme Court rulings in *Riddick v. School Board of the City of Norfolk (VA)* in 1986, *Board of Education of Oklahoma v. Dowell* in 1991, and *Freeman v. Pitts* in 1992 collectively accepted the intent—not the success—of desegregation as sufficient and approved partial school integration, thus releasing districts from "desegregation responsibilities." *Missouri v. Jenkins* in 1995 virtually gutted the *Brown* decision by prohibiting "voluntary" desegregation and removing federal support for desegregation. According to Gary

Orfield, a hundred years after the 1896 *Plessy v. Ferguson* decision, the American public schools had come full circle to racial separation.[34]

Orfield's extensive research sheds a great deal of light on this issue. Segregation not only represents a racial and ethnic phenomenon but maintains social-class barriers as well. "National data show that most segregated African-American and Latino schools are dominated by poor children but that 96 percent of white schools have middle-class majorities." Furthermore, there are sharp and, in some cases, ironic regional variations in current segregation patterns. "Both African-American and Latino students . . . continue to face the most intense segregation in the Northeast. Millions of African-American children in the southern and border states attend schools that are still well-integrated decades after the first court orders."[35]

Resegregation represents a tragic situation because school integration efforts since the 1950s had made many gains. During the fifties, "less than 50 percent of young black adults were high school or GED graduates, but by 1993, this figure had risen to 83 percent, close to the white completion rate." African American students had also closed the gap with their white counterparts in standardized test scores. And public national surveys in the 1990s showed majority support for desegregation in general and busing in particular.[36] Nonetheless, school segregation remains at the dawning of the twenty-first century. Separate and unequal educational facilities and resources are a fact of life. Some progress has been made, but only after a long struggle and great sacrifice. Unless American society commits to true integration, the public schools will continue to be separate and unequal.

"You Little Mexicans"

As we have seen, segregation does not apply only to the African American educational experience. Mexican Americans also faced a great deal of conflict and many setbacks as they pursued equal education for their children. As you may recall from Chapter 8, historian Gilbert Gonzales described four distinct periods of Chicano education: "de jure segregation" (1900–1950), "de facto segregation" (1950–1965), "militant and reformist" activities (1965–1975), and "conservative retrenchment" (1975–).[37] We focused on the first period in that chapter; we will examine the remaining three periods in this section.

"De facto Segregation" (1950–1965)

Although the California court case *Mendez v. Westminister* officially ended de jure segregation in 1947, as we saw in Chapter 8, Mexican American children nevertheless continued to attend separate schools throughout the Southwest. By the 1960s, "[n]early half of all Chicana/o students in the Southwest attended elementary and secondary schools in which the Chicana/o enrollment was over 50 percent of the total student body." In other cases, Mexican American pupils were segregated from Anglo students in the same classrooms. Tracking represented yet another form of segregation and it continued well into the 1960s. Schools disproportionately channeled Mexican students into vocational programs or special education classes.[38]

Chicana/o students also faced other educational problems. Treated as intellectually and culturally inferior and taught in English only, Mexican students fell behind in their studies. The English-only policy was strictly enforced. As one former student recalled, "In Texas the teacher beats you for using Spanish in school to remind you that you are an American. Your friends beat you after school to remind you that you are Mexican." Most students became alienated from school after being retained in the same grade year after year, disengaged from their incomprehensible academic studies, and ultimately abandoned their schooling altogether. In 1950, Mexican Americans in Los Angeles, Chicago, and Texas averaged only seven years of schooling, with as few as four in rural Texas.[39]

"Militant and Reformist" Activities (1965–1975)

Partially in response to clearly inferior and unequal schooling, "many Chicanas/os in the 1960s embraced a nationalist perspective and militancy to bring about educational, political, and social reform." These activities became a part of the larger civil rights movement and general social activism typical of that period. This militant spirit was cast broadly, encompassing the unionization of migrant workers, the assertion of Mexican American political rights, and control over education. More importantly during this period, the Mexican American campaign for equal rights shifted from the local to the national level.[40]

Mexican American migration from the rural United States to the cities had brought about fundamental changes. "In the 1950 and 1960 census Chicanos were the least urbanized of the racial groups of the Southwest; the 1970 census showed that they were the most urbanized." This was especially apparent in Los Angeles County, where the Latino/a population between 1960 and 1970 "increased from 576,716 to 1,228,595, an increase of 113 percent"; growth that was due less to immigration and more to an increase in the birthrate.[41] This concentration of an American-born population fostered the development of a sense of community and solidarity, which rallied around the civil rights guaranteed American citizens in the Constitution.

Schooling certainly became a major component of the Mexican American political agenda. Activists saw the public schools as part of an elaborate mechanism of cultural repression and decided to oppose the system. "In 1968, well over 10,000 Chicana/o students walked out of the East Los Angeles high schools to protest inferior schooling conditions." This action sparked similar walkouts in "Crystal City and San Antonio, Texas; Denver, Colorado; and Phoenix, Arizona." They had grown weary of being schooled for subordinate economic and social positions because of their racial and ethnic background. Patssi Valdez recalled a home economics teacher berating her class: "You little Mexicans, you better learn and pay attention. This class is very important because . . . most of you are going to be cooking and cleaning for other people."[42] Activists in Texas created the Mexican American Legal Defense Fund (MALDEF) in 1968 to achieve better education for Chicano/a children. Patterned after the NAACP's Legal Defense Fund and subsidized by the Ford Foundation, MALDEF's aggressive litigation strategy broke from the patient political style of the League of United Latin American Citizens (LULAC) and the G.I. Forum. MALDEF pursued a variety of goals, among them equalized school financing, desegregation, and bilingual education.

School Funding

The policy of inadequately financing Mexican American schools dated back to the early years of the twentieth century; it led, of course, to extremely poor educational facilities. The 1971 court case of *Serrano v. Priest* challenged California's practice of providing inferior schooling for Mexican American students. The California courts ruled that the funding plan, based largely on local property taxes, was indeed unequal. This case established that school financing was a state responsibility. When this issue was argued at the federal level, however, its ultimate resolution proved to be elusive. In *San Antonio Independent School District v. Rodriguez*, MALDEF attacked unequal school funding in Texas. The state courts in 1971 ruled the "Texas school finance system unconstitutional under the equal protection clause of the Fourteenth Amendment." When it considered the case on appeal two years later, the U.S. Supreme Court did not see a federal role and remanded it to the state level.[43] The policy of unequal school financing, as a result, continued. For researcher Dolores Delgado Bernal, the cumulative effect of these two court cases "signaled the end of an era of progressive change and set the tone for educational inequality during the 1980s and 1990s." Unequal funding continues to plague America's public schools, as we shall see in Chapter 11.

Desegregation

Segregation was a stubborn problem for Mexican Americans. "By the 1970s, more Chicana/o students attended second-rate segregated schools than at the time of the 1947 *Mendez* decision."[44] In 1968, MALDEF filed an important desegregation suit, *Cisneros v. Corpus Christi Independent School District*, in the federal court in Corpus Christi, Texas. MALDEF's brief cited the 1954 *Brown* ruling as a precedent. MALDEF won the *Cisneros* decision; for the first time the courts acknowledged Mexican Americans as a minority group, not as part of the European American majority. The judge in this case ruled that Mexican Americans represented a minority because of their "physical characteristics, their Spanish language, their Catholic religion, their distinct culture, and their Spanish surnames. . . ." The judge further ordered a desegregation plan for Corpus Christi. Subsequent appeals, however, somewhat muddied the waters until the federal Supreme Court clarified matters in its 1975 *Keyes* desegregation ruling by including Mexican American as well as African American students. Mexican Americans now officially became an "identifiable minority" and eligible for desegregation plans.[45]

Bilingual Education

The campaign for bilingual education elicited the most reaction from the European American majority. "The assertion of cultural rights was in many ways the most threatening aspect of the movement to Anglo-Americans, for many viewed such demands as subversive." The public schools served as a crucial socialization agent—upholding the decades-old tradition of the culture factory—Americanizing native-born and foreign-born children alike. Cultural education efforts, like bilingual education, represented, in the words of historian Rodolfo Acuña, the "antithesis . . . of American public education in that it counteracts ethnocentrism. American education espoused democracy while discouraging political dissent. . . . [I]t rejected any pedagogy which questioned the supremacy of the English language or the superiority of American institutions and culture. The speaking of Spanish or any foreign language was viewed as deviant behavior."[46]

The surge into southern Florida in the late 1950s of Cuban refugees fleeing Fidel Castro's takeover introduced bilingual education into the Dade County schools, which were flooded by Spanish-speaking children. Bilingual education was begun only as a local, stopgap measure; it was not intended as a permanent long-term policy. Broader application of bilingual education policies was given impetus by national legislation. The Bilingual Education Act, or Title VII of the Elementary and Secondary Education Act, became law in 1968. "Title VII did not mandate bilingual education, but provided funds for districts to establish programs that used primary language instruction to assist limited English proficient children." Congress reauthorized Title VII and broadened its scope in 1974, 1978, 1984, and 1988.[47] Ultimately, the judicial process paved the way for the implementation of bilingual education. The 1974 U.S. Supreme Court decision in *Lau v. Nichols*, a case that MALDEF participated in and supported, ordered language considerations for Chinese children enrolled in San Francisco's public schools. This ruling had a far-reaching effect. The following year the Department of Health, Education, and Welfare and the Office of Civil Rights issued bilingual education guidelines. *Lau* also served as the precedent upon which New York City's Puerto Rican community negotiated for bilingual education programs. Finally, bilingual education made progress at the state level. Following the lead of Massachusetts in 1971, within ten years all fifty states had implemented bilingual education policies.[48]

What impact did these decade-long militant activities have on the educational conditions of Mexican American children? Deeply entrenched social prejudices prevented substantial progress. The U.S. Commission on Civil Rights, after a five-year study, released its conclusions about the education of southwestern Mexican Americans in 1974:

> The findings of this report reflect more than inadequacies regarding the specific conditions and practices examined. They reflect a systematic failure of the educational process, which not only ignores the educational needs of Chicano students but also suppresses their culture and stifles their hopes and ambitions. In a very real sense, the Chicano is the excluded student.

By the mid-1970s, therefore, the educational record remained very poor for Latinos/as, particularly Mexican Americans. "Some 24 percent of persons of Mexican origin twenty-five years old and over had completed fewer than five years of school in March, 1976, whereas 18.7 percent of Puerto Ricans, 9.5 of the Cuban, 7 percent of the other Spanish, and only 3.8 percent of the total population had received less than five years of schooling." Only 67 percent of all Mexican American students graduated from high school at that time.[49] These conditions would only modestly improve during the 1980s and 1990s.

"Conservative Retrenchment"

The conservative backlash that began during the mid-1970s gained momentum and intensified during President Reagan's administration. Equity programs across the board came under attack, and support for bilingual education declined sharply. "Title VII bilingual education funding was cut from $167 million in 1980 to $133 million in 1986."[50] In

1981, a "Constitutional English Language Amendment" was proposed to Congress. Conservatives also assailed affirmative action in hiring and education, calling it reverse discrimination.[51] Not only did neglect and obstructionism appear at the federal level but it occurred at the local and state levels as well. "Between 1973 and 1980 local and state school officials, with the support of the executive and legislative branches of the federal government, used all legal remedies at their disposal to halt the dismantling of segregated schools," according to historian Guadalupe San Miguel, Jr. He continues, "[a] larger percentage of Mexican Americans was in segregated schools in 1980 after a decade of litigation than in 1970, and little change in their scholastic achievement had resulted." Schools continued to assign Chicano/a children at a disproportionate rate to special education classes.[52] Bilingual education continues to suffer setbacks at the state level. In 1998, California's voters approved Proposition 227, which mandated an English-only approach to the schools. "Today, Proposition 227 represents a distinct cultural attack on Chicanas/os and other Latinas/os, and creates yet another educational barrier imposed on Chicana/o students."

Disagreements among Mexican Americans themselves have stalled progress. To some, bilingual education and desegregation appeared to be mutually exclusive policies. On the one hand, bilingual education programs separated Mexican American children from students of other ethnic and racial backgrounds. On the other hand, integration dispersed Chicano/a children throughout the schools and thus failed to address their language needs and undermined their cultural heritage. Unsympathetic educators have easily manipulated this dilemma, as Bernal explains:

> . . . education policymakers who opposed bilingual education could avoid it by scattering limited-English-proficient students throughout their districts in the name of desegregation. At the same time, someone who opposed mixing White and Chicana/o students in the same classroom could use the opportunity to segregate Chicana/o students in bilingual classrooms, thus using the same old racially motivated rationale for separating Mexican children from White students based on their perceived language deficiency.

MALDEF has maintained that both goals are compatible.

By the mid-1980s, although there had been a gradual intergenerational increase in schooling among Mexican Americans, they had achieved a median of only nine years of schooling. The 2000 census indicated that Latinos/Latinas no longer constituted the second-largest minority after African Americans—both groups were equal numerically— yet, generally speaking, at the beginning of the twenty-first century, educational progress among Mexican American children can be best summarized as "modest."[53] They are not alone.

"Bury My Heart at Wounded Knee"

In March and April of 1973, a tense, thirty-seven-day confrontation flared up between Native Americans and federal agents at Wounded Knee, South Dakota, the site of an infamous 1890 slaughter of Native Americans by the U.S. Army. The "siege" was intended to symbolize the centuries of Native American anger over the injustices, including genocide, that had been committed against them.[54] As we have seen, education never had been a source of opportunity for them, but a means of further repression through acculturation. Native Americans wanted to change that legacy.

A Policy Shift in Native American Schooling

A long and sustained period of reform in government policies toward Native Americans resumed in the 1960s. Progress toward self-determination came from two quarters: the federal government and Native Americans themselves. In 1961, some 9,000 Native American students could not attend school because of a shortage of classrooms, teachers, and equipment. Although educational funding increased dramatically between 1961 and 1963, because of a sharp increase in enrollment, little real progress occurred. In 1965, about 8,600 Native American children still had no access to school, and the assimilationist curriculum remained intact. A task force appointed by President Kennedy stated the need for bilingual education, yet, while "sympathetic" to Native American issues, the Kennedy administration offered little in tangible results or programs.

President Johnson's "War on Poverty," part of his Great Society agenda, was not aimed directly at Native Americans but it did benefit them. The Economic Opportunity Act of 1964, created, among many antipoverty programs the Office of Economic Opportunity (OEO). As the overseer of antipoverty efforts, "OEO was the first federal program created in the 1960s supporting the principle of Indian self-determination." It provided leadership training and opportunities, furnished legal services, improved housing, and established Head Start programs for pre-school-aged children.[55] In 1966, Johnson became the first President to appoint a Native American as Commissioner of Indian Affairs. Both the Kennedy and Johnson administrations increased expenditures for Native American education, constructing new school buildings, adding libraries to existing ones, and providing equipment and supplies. In 1966, Title I funds became available through the Elementary and Secondary Education Act for schools under the authority of the Bureau of Indian Affairs (BIA). "Kindergarten and special education programs became common in the 1970s." By the late 1960s, the notion of self-determination had gained momentum. Both Presidents Johnson, in 1968, and Nixon, in 1970, supported tribal self-determination.[56]

The influential 1969 Kennedy Report, *Indian Education: A National Tragedy*, in many ways echoed the 1928 Meriam Report but was even more critical of government policies regarding Native American education. In short, the report called them an abysmal failure. Unacceptably high levels of illiteracy and poverty plagued Native Americans. Public schools clung to a belief in the inferiority of Native Americans and too often presented negative stereotypes. Children suffered through a culturally insensitive curriculum, read biased and distorted textbooks, too often were placed in remedial or special education classes, struggled with English-only instruction, and abandoned their schooling at alarming rates. The federal day and boarding schools under the auspices of BIA did not come out much better. They were inadequately funded, struggled under the burden of a wasteful and inefficient bureaucracy, emphasized vocational education, had overcrowded classrooms and a high turnover in non-Native-American teachers, used strict discipline, and offered few social and extracurricular activities. The Kennedy Report recommended a culturally sensitive curriculum, increased funding, and greater attention to Native American affairs in general. These recommendations were insufficient by themselves, however, for "from 1783 to 1971 the government had run the show."[57]

A new generation of Native Americans had assumed a new role in educational issues and in establishing goals for self-determination in general. They were also using new strategies to achieve their goals. They

> had grown weary of government excuses and government promises. They were not con-cerned with *why* the government had failed in its educational programs. Their concern was *that* the government had failed. For almost a century the education offered to them in fed-eral and public schools had failed to recognize their cultures and had disregarded the right of parents and leaders to have a voice in policy formation and administration. Their goal was to revise this education to respond to their needs and be shaped and directed by their own people.

These new leaders generally became more actively involved; they bypassed the bureau-cracy and appealed directly to Congress and the general public. They also created organi-zations to pursue their demands. In 1969, they founded the National Indian Education Association.[58] The Coalition of Indian-Controlled School Boards, formed in 1971, "testi-fied before congressional committees and lobbied Congress," and members of the American Indian Movement (AIM) protested by taking over the BIA headquarters building in Washington, DC, in 1972. "On a more local level, AIM organized a number of high school sitins and walkouts with the purpose of getting more classes in Indian culture and history and more Indian involvement in school administration."[59] As historian Margaret Connell Szasz points out, "[t]he significant feature of almost all of these new organizations was that they were concerned with Indian control of education."[60]

Beginning with the Indian Education Act of 1972, legislation gradually ceded control of education to Native Americans. In 1975, Congress enacted the Indian Self-Determination and Education Assistance Act, whose purpose was "to promote maximum Indian participation in the government and education of Indian people" and "to support the right of Indians to control their own educational activities." The Nixon, Ford, and Carter administrations all fostered Indian self-determination.[61]

Community Control of Schools

The Rough Rock Demonstration School exemplified the drive for community-controlled Native American education. Opened in 1966 on the Navajo reservation in Arizona, the school taught Navajo and English and generally stressed Navajo culture and encouraged parental involvement. Nothing like it had existed since the tribally controlled schools sponsored by the Five Civilized Tribes in the nineteenth century.

As we saw in Chapter 2, prior to European contact the Native American educational process relied on the entire tribal community. The European model of schooling attempted to alter this by introducing the concept of a single "educator." But by the 1970s, through self-determination efforts, that is, through the involvement of parents and community par-ticipation, Native Americans began to restore the cultural roots of their education.[62] Although the Rough Rock school achieved a great deal of success from a cultural stand-point, the dream of Native American control of education remained less than completely fulfilled. The BIA still assumed most of the authority over the allocation of education funds, and because of uneven and irregular funding, the school remained fiscally vulner-able. This "led to a high annual turnover in teaching staff." Some parental resistance and poor transportation contributed to attendance problems, as well. Nevertheless, such schools "have been active forces in community development and the maintenance of tribal culture through the offering of course work in Indian history and culture."[63]

A Dream Deferred?

The attitudes and policies of the Reagan administration toward Native Americans were a significant setback. This administration tried to negate all of the nineteenth-century treaties in which the federal government guaranteed schooling in exchange for land "in perpetuity." It also moved to make all decisions regarding Native American education unilaterally. The BIA closed all of the boarding schools that had been "Indianized." Native American leaders responded by lobbying Congress and generally asserting their influence in Washington, DC. In April 1994, President Bill Clinton, through an executive order, reversed many of the Reagan administration's policies and further agreed to recognize Native American tribes and negotiate with them as sovereign nations. In 1998, Clinton signed yet another executive order to initiate improvements in Native American schooling.[64] Thus, after centuries of armed conflict, land appropriation, and cultural oppression, Native Americans continue to struggle to retain some control over their lives. What does the future hold for the next generation of Native Americans?

THE DEMISE OF JUNE CLEAVER?: GENDER IN THE CLASSROOM

Mrs. June Cleaver, the wife/mother character in the popular 1950s television program *Leave It to Beaver*, epitomized the romantic image of the ideal American family. As the maternal parent, she remained at home, devotedly maintaining the household and lovingly raising her children. She appeared always well groomed; she wore makeup, jewelry, and high heels when cooking meals and doing other household chores; she seemed to be perpetually cheerful and calm and often intervened on behalf of the children with their father, who was usually portrayed as relaxing comfortably in his easy chair and wearing a white shirt and tie, sweater, and slippers. This contrived image—that of perfect domesticity—did not necessarily reflect reality. By the mid-twentieth century, women's work world had changed drastically, although gradually and subtly. The number of working women overall and particularly married working women had been increasing since 1900. This "has been a long-term consequence of maturing industrial capitalism, originating in rising real wages, shifts in the demand for labor, greater education for women, and better control over childbearing. It is an international, not just an American, phenomenon and has taken place in countries with a wide variety of cultural attitudes towards women."

In the United States, necessity and consumerism played significant roles in this trend. For decades, sheer need to provide the basic essentials of life had driven poor and working-class women out of the home to ensure the very survival of their families. The decade of the 1960s represented a milestone because highly educated women began to enter the workplace in unprecedented numbers. They were no longer content with being relegated to the home. Thus, both material and psychological needs contributed to the ongoing trend of working wives and mothers. Consumerism, too, drove women to work. The acquisition of goods and services is an integral part of the American lifestyle and a mainstay of modern capitalism. Beginning in the 1920s, an economy centered around personal consumption unfolded, and this trend continued throughout the twentieth century. Although interrupted by the Great Depression and World War II, mass consumerism made a strong recovery in the late 1940s. "It was the marketing strategists of the 1950s, not the 'permissive' child-care ideologues or political subversives of the 1960s, who first attempted to bypass parental authority and 'pander' to American youth." By the 1960s, advertising campaigns were routinely injecting sexual overtones to attract youthful attention to products. As those children grew into adults, they demonstrated how well trained they had been by their informal consumer education. In sum, the labor market and the consumer economy were more critical in removing wives and mothers from the home more than any other factor. The trend has become a decades-long phenomenon. Feminism neither destroyed domesticity nor altered women's work roles. The free market system, more than any other single factor, transformed women's work lives.[65]

The feminist movement that emerged during the late 1960s and early 1970s was only one in a series of women's struggles for equal rights and was only part of the long-term change in their status. Throughout American history, "[t]he issue of women's rights challenged the basic premise of domestic ideology, the separation of male and female spheres, by demanding equality of participation in public activities." From the Seneca Falls Declaration of Rights of Women in 1848 to the leadership provided by Elizabeth Cady Stanton and Susan B. Anthony, who founded the National Woman Suffrage Association and fought to have the Fifteenth Amendment include women's right to vote, to the suffrage campaign that resulted in the ratification of the Nineteenth Amendment in 1920 after fifty-two years of struggle, women had persistently sought political, social, and economic reform. What made the most recent gender reform movement unique was its focus on schooling.

The Girl Next Door?

The popular 1950s perception of and prescription for American women confined them solely to the household to serve as the "partner" of their upwardly mobile husbands and nurturers of their ever-growing brood of children. The reality, though, was very different. While white, affluent women might fit into the neatly defined female role, they were the exception, not the rule. In fact, many American families entered the middle class on the backs of their working mothers. Most of the jobs they held followed conventional female work patterns, such as nursing, clerical work, and teaching. "In contradiction to the privatized images of family life and the glorification of motherhood, white married women with children entered the labor force at an accelerating rate. From 1950 to 1960 their labor force participation rate grew from 17 to 30 percent."

An impetus for reform emerged from this growing group of working women as well as from traditional feminist organizations, women's union activities, the rise of the lesbian consciousness movement, minority women who had achieved a high profile in the civil rights movement, and women's campaigns for peace in the face of the threat of nuclear holocaust. The first signal of a federal role in equal rights for women was President Kennedy's appointment of Esther Peterson as head of the Department of Labor's Women's Bureau. A Presidential Commission on female discrimination followed, and in 1963 Congress passed the Equal Pay Act. "The same year the commission issued its report, Betty

Friedan published her book *The Feminine Mystique*." In it she blamed "educators, advertisers, Freudian psychologists, and functionalist sociologists for forcing women out of public life and into a passive and infantilizing domesticity. . . ."

This most recent feminist movement gained momentum throughout the 1960s. The 1964 Civil Rights Act included Title VII, which prohibited sexual discrimination in employment, and was supported by the National Woman's Party and pushed by congresswomen. "Once the Civil Rights Act passed, the newly created Equal Employment Opportunity Commission (EEOC) found itself flooded with women's grievances." To gain additional political clout, representatives from such organizations as the League of Women Voters, the American Association of University Women, and the United Auto Workers, among others, used the proceeds from Friedan's popular book to create the National Organization of Women (NOW) in 1966. The following year, NOW endorsed a Bill of Rights for Women that called for an Equal Rights Amendment (ERA) to the Constitution. The women's movement and its organizations, continuing to evolve, became more assertive in political campaigns. Under this pressure, Congress ultimately passed the ERA in 1972 and sent it to the states for ratification. A year later, the U.S. Supreme Court issued a landmark decision, *Roe v. Wade*, permitting legal abortions.[66] The women's comprehensive strategy, covering political, economic, social, and biological rights, also was aimed at the impact of schooling on women.

Schooling for Girls

As we saw in Chapter 8, coeducation by itself did not ensure equal treatment for girls. By the 1970s, feminists came to understand the power of schooling, both in its content and teaching methods, in shaping traditional female roles. "Institutionalized discrimination and cultural prejudice" limited female educational opportunities.[67] Discrimination was evident in both the formal and the hidden curriculum.

Gender socialization began at the elementary level and permeated the child's entire educational experience. Schoolbooks in particular promoted sexual stereotypes. Basal readers, regardless of publisher, portrayed traditional occupations and traits. Stories typically depicted adult males as scientists, archeologists, firefighters, and police officers, and females as nurses, teachers, and mothers. These books also characterized boys as clever, resourceful, persistent, and brave, and girls as helpful, obedient, compliant, dependent, and emotional. The illustrations supported these distortions—boys were taller than girls or girls were omitted altogether. One 1973 study of elementary readers found that 79 percent of the drawings focused on male figures. Nonfiction reading books followed a similar pattern. Seventy-five percent of the biographies read by schoolchildren celebrated male accomplishments.[68]

As students moved into the upper grades, much of the formal curriculum followed the same process of socialization, but even more obviously. Counselors guided girls into home economics and English courses and directed boys into wood and metal shops or academic subjects. History textbooks also maintained a male bias. "Women on Words and Images," a NOW task force, observed in its study that "[g]overnmental leaders as disparate as Alexander the Great, George Washington, and Franklin Delano Roosevelt are portrayed. Yet, women of power such as Cleopatra, Queen Elizabeth I, or Queen Victoria never appear."[69] These serious omissions led students to believe that males alone shaped human history. Thus, through tracking and required reading, female and male students learned their social roles in powerful ways. They were either physically segregated, studying separate programs, or learned together, absorbing biased information. More subtle means of socialization existed as well.

The informal, hidden curriculum, consisting of "implicit messages given to students about socially legitimated or 'proper' behavior, differential power, social evaluation, what kinds of knowledge exists, which kinds are valued by whom, and how students are valued in their own right," played a vital part in the socialization process.[70] First, a school's "authority structure" defined superordinate and subordinate gender roles. Men comprised the overwhelming majority of school administrators, while women served as classroom instructors. Students of all ages witnessed daily the respect and deference given by females to their male superiors. Gender determined power, they learned. Second, teachers' casual interactions with students defined gender roles in almost imperceptible, but compelling, ways. Whether female or male, classroom instructors generally devoted more attention to boys, scolding them for inappropriate conduct and rewarding them for work well done. "One consequence might be a cumulative increase in independent autonomous behavior for boys as they are disapproved, praised, listened to, and taught more actively by the teacher. Another might be a lowering of self-esteem generally for girls as they receive less attention and are criticized more for their lack of knowledge and skill."[71]

In the decades since the 1970s, the formal curriculum's gender socialization mechanisms have been partially adjusted. "In 1972 Congress passed Title IX of the Education Amendments to the Civil Rights Act to address issues of sex discrimination in educational programs that received federal funding." This effectively ended sexual discrimination through academic tracking. Textbook content, too, now offers a more balanced approach. According to a 1987 study, "[o]ut of 1,121 stories, females were portrayed in 37 occupations, compared with 5 occupations in 1961–1963 readers and 23 occupations in 1969–1971 readers." Yet the hidden curriculum still operates largely unfettered. In part, this reflects the defensive mode the women's movement has adopted.

Patriarchy's Resilience

During the 1970s, an antifeminist countermovement emerged, led by women who opposed equal rights and often invoked fundamentalist Christian values that prescribed the female roles of obedient wife and full-time mother to support their views. The ratification of the ERA lost momentum by 1975 as a result of the countermovement's efforts. After much political wrangling, Congress reluctantly extended the ratification period, but to no avail. The Reagan political agenda opposed the ERA, and in 1982 it died. At that time as well, Reagan's conservative posture encouraged an active and visible antiabortion crusade, which was also driven by religious imperatives.

Schooling for female students has improved, but it has failed in its goal of achieving equality. According to recent research, girls continue to lose self-esteem as they progress through schooling. Because they lack intellectual confidence, they tend to participate less than boys in programs for the gifted and they avoid math and science courses. Female students also score lower on the Scholastic Aptitude Test. And the school's "implicit" messages continue. The "educational harem"—male administrators and female teachers—endures.

Elementary instructors too often select girls to clean the blackboards and neaten the class-room and ask boys to perform more physical chores. And teachers at all levels still devote more attention, positive and negative, to their male students.[72]

TEACHER POWER

A number of problems that plagued the public schools during the late 1940s and early 1950s established the deep-seated conditions for the growth of teacher militancy. First, school buildings were deteriorating. The economic calamity of the Great Depression virtu-ally eliminated school construction, and national security needs during World War II diverted valuable resources to the armed services. By the middle of the century, America had old and often dilapidated schools overcrowded by record-breaking enrollments due to the postwar baby boom. Teachers felt overburdened by the poor working conditions and the increased demands made upon them.

Second, the Red scare of the 1940s and 1950s, as we saw in Chapter 9, made teachers feel largely defenseless. Instructors united in an assertive organization might have been able to repulse such assaults on basic freedoms, but such an organization did not exist. Although the National Education Association (NEA) established the National Council for the Defense of Democracy Through Education in 1941 to address issues of academic free-dom, during the intense Red scare of the late 1940s and early 1950s, that commission walked a tightrope. It opposed communism but somehow wanted to defend academic freedom. It could never quite resolve this dilemma. Its efforts, therefore, were limited and ineffective—teachers were fired, blacklisted, or censored.

Third, increasing school consolidation alienated teachers. The number of school dis-tricts had declined from about 120,000 in 1940 to some 42,000 in 1960. Larger districts transformed formerly personal and informal relations into impersonal and formal bureau-cratic routines. Growing school bureaucracies also diminished the stature of the individual instructor, causing intense feelings of isolation.

Fourth, the credential requirements for prospective educators had become tougher through the decades. At the beginning of the century, a two-year normal school education often sufficed. During the Progressive era, four-year baccalaureate programs became the norm. Following World War II, many states began to mandate graduate work for certifica-tion. This translated into higher tuition expenses for pre-service and in-service teachers and more time required for learning how and what to teach. Classroom instructors believed their monetary reward should be commensurate with the cost and time they had expended to earn and maintain a teaching license.

Fifth, this was not to be. Teachers continued to earn meager incomes. During the 1933–34 school year, the nationwide average teacher salary amounted to $1,227. "In 1941 . . . the average salary of an American public school teacher was $1,470. In contrast, the average salary for a lawyer or a doctor in independent practice amounted to $4,794 and $5,047 respectively." The average federal government employee received an annual income of $4,150. To make matters worse, "[b]etween 1939 and 1946 the average indus-trial workers' income rose 80 percent in real terms, while the average income for a class-room teacher fell 20 percent."[73] Many teachers subsequently abandoned the classroom for more lucrative careers in the private sector. "And leave they did. Despite increased enroll-ments, there were 50,000 fewer teachers in 1943–44 than there had been in 1939–40."

Sixth, the absence of job security contributed to this outflow. In the 1940s, fewer than half of America's instructors claimed the luxury of tenure; many worked on one-year contracts. The feeling of permanence proved to be even more elusive for female teachers. Some 60 percent of school districts nationwide still fired female instructors who married.

Meanwhile, and seventh, males for the first time since the early nineteenth century entered the teaching force in increasing numbers. The G.I. Bill, which offered war veterans the benefit of a free higher education, stimulated this influx. The presence of more males placed school districts in an unexpected and vulnerable bargaining position. Boards of education traditionally paid female teachers lower salaries than their male counterparts because, it was reasoned, men had families to support. With more male teachers entering the classroom, salary demands for instructors increased. School districts had painted themselves into a corner.[74]

Finally, the civil rights movement contributed to the emergence of teacher militancy in both indirect and direct ways. The American Federation of Teachers (AFT) had a long record of support for equality. As early as the 1930s, the federation denounced discrimination, and by 1951 the "Executive Council voted not to charter new locals that were segregated." The AFT also endorsed the *Brown* decision and mandated integration of all locals a year later. The large Atlanta local refused and was purged; the federation likewise expelled other locals. "By the beginning of 1958 the AFT claimed it had lost close to 7,000 members or 14 percent of its membership because of its stand on integration." It had to expand its constituency or cease to exist. The NEA, meanwhile, tolerated dual affiliates until 1966 when association members forced its leaders to endorse integration of all locals. Regardless of their parent organization, public school teachers throughout the 1950s and early 1960s had witnessed the successes of the civil rights movement and realized the effectiveness of collective, nonviolent action.

STRIKE!

Teacher attitudes began to change gradually in the fifteen years following World War II; many began to resort to aggressive tactics to seek solutions. Classroom instructors started to question, and even challenge, the old traditions of personal and professional control by communities and school officials, which was manifested through job insecurity, low pay, and the denial of academic freedom. In rapid succession, teachers asserted themselves in remarkable ways. Classroom instructors in Cicero, Illinois, in 1941 signed the first collective bargaining agreement for teachers in American history. Two years later, teachers in Norwalk, Connecticut, refused to sign annual contracts and insisted on better pay and work conditions. In 1947, in the first official teacher strike in America, Buffalo's instructors held out for higher salaries. This was followed by a teachers' walkout in Minneapolis in 1948 and in Oglesby, Illinois, in 1949. Since both the NEA and the AFT opposed strikes, these actions were grassroots efforts in which teachers joined together to collectively protest low pay and poor working conditions. They did this without any significant organizational support and in defiance of the state laws of the time, which forbade public employee strikes.

What happened in New York City during the early 1960s was a culmination of the various conditions that teachers all over the country had endured—and it was the birth of teacher power. New York City, which had the largest school district in the country, became the site of the first massive and most visible teacher strike. The New York Teachers Guild had replaced the allegedly communist locals purged by the AFT in 1941. During the 1950s, the federation, with financial assistance from the AFL-CIO, launched a membership campaign to enlarge the guild, and by 1960 it had become the United Federation of Teachers (UFT), a combination of the city's various teacher groups.

City teachers took an aggressive posture. They faced a number of poor working conditions. Among them, elementary instructors had to toil straight through the day with no lunch break. In the fall of 1960, New York's public school teachers petitioned the school board for a collective bargaining election; the board refused. The teachers staged a one-day walkout on November 7, and the board conceded. The following spring, classroom instructors voted for the UFT as their bargaining agent. The UFT proceeded with negotiations but the board stalled. Finally, on April 12, 1962, with negotiations stalled, some 20,000 teachers struck. Since public employee walkouts were forbidden in New York State, the school board fired the teachers. However, the UFT won a swift and decisive victory when, on the next day, the mayor and governor intervened and the school board agreed to terms. In the end, the school board rehired the striking teachers, as well as granted a lunch break, sick pay for substitute teachers, dues checkoff, and a pay raise.

United Federation of Teachers Celebrate Bargaining Contract, New York City Labor Day Parade, Sept. 1961. United Federation of Teachers Archives, UFT Photo Collection, Robert F. Wagner Labor Archives, New York University.

A new era had begun. The success of the confrontation and one-day walkout in New York City opened the floodgates throughout the nation. Public school instructors organized effective unions, negotiated contracts, and initiated strikes, if necessary. "Collective bargaining changed the fundamental relationship between teachers and administrators. It promised teachers more say in the conduct of their work, more pay, and greater job security." Moreover, existing teacher organizations themselves were transformed. The AFT supported collective bargaining; the NEA opposed it, but not for long. By the late 1960s, the association expelled all of its school administrators and became an organization for teachers only. It adopted a policy of collective bargaining and strike action. "By the late seventies, 72 percent of all public school teachers were members of some form of union that represented them at the bargaining table."[75] Today, the NEA and the AFT are the largest unions in the country and wield significant political clout.

Despite their new militancy, classroom teachers continue to be paid unevenly and to receive relatively low salaries. Great disparities exist on a regional basis. During the 1993–94 school year, public school instructors earned an average annual salary of $37,701 nationwide. However, mid-Atlantic teachers—Delaware, the District of Columbia, Maryland, New Jersey, New York, and Pennsylvania—made an average of $46,132, the highest salary in the nation. This was followed in order by New England, the Far West, the Great Lakes, and the Plains states. Instructors employed in the Rocky Mountains, Southeast, and Southwest received the lowest salaries at $31,650, $31,642, and $31,446, respectively.[76] In sum, teachers earn higher salaries where their organizations have been the strongest and most assertive. But the pay that classroom instructors receive pales in comparison to that of other professions that require equal preparation.

"SCHOOL OFFICIALS DO NOT POSSESS ABSOLUTE AUTHORITY OVER THEIR STUDENTS"

Should school-aged children be permitted to exercise their civil rights? As we have seen from the historical record, students of all ages have been afforded few, if any, rights. But, as we have also seen, the public schools from the beginning have been given the responsibility of preparing loyal citizens for a democratic republic. Among others, Thomas Jefferson, Horace Mann, and John Dewey, to different degrees, stressed this function of schooling. In the classroom, pupils have been taught about the citizenship rights guaranteed in the U.S. Constitution, which encompassed fundamental civil rights like religious worship and freedom of speech, yet through school policies and daily practices they have learned something entirely different. The assertive nature of youth culture during the 1960s challenged these disparities. This section analyzes how by the middle of the twentieth century public school students in different parts of the country finally acquired some basic liberties.

Freedom of Religious Practice

Religion, as we have seen, was an integral part of the schooling experience from the colonial period onward. Driven by native-Protestant ideology, religion continued to be part of schooling through the common-school era. Public schoolbooks contained ample references to Christianity and lessons in religious values. There was not, however, always a consensus on this matter.

Protecting students' freedom of religion and freedom from religion has been a long and earnest campaign. During the mid-1800s, Irish Roman Catholics, appalled at the sectarianism of America's public schools, created and supported parochial schools. Subsequent immigrant groups likewise opened their own religious schools. In mid-nineteenth-century Chicago, as we saw in Chapter 4, a variety of religious groups successfully "de-Protestantized" that city's public schools. Campaigns for religious freedom continued into the twentieth century, focusing on the seemingly benign patriotic ritual of the Pledge of Allegiance and the long tradition of reciting the Lord's Prayer and reading the King James version of the Bible in classrooms.

The Pledge of Allegiance

The introduction of the Pledge of Allegiance in classrooms coincided with the introduction of American flags in public schools during the 1890s when the emphasis on assimilation of the growing and feared horde of southern and eastern Europeans flooding into the United States was at its strongest. In 1892, the pledge became a formal part of the daily school routine to promote nationalism and patriotism. The pledge was revised in 1923 and 1924 and was "incorporated into the Flag Code, a U.S. law. . . . " Congress added the phrase "under God" in 1954.[77]

Religious Protests   The earliest student resistance to participation in the pledge was based on religious convictions. The Minersville School District in Pennsylvania required all students and teachers to take part in this particular ceremony every day. The Gobitis family, members of the Jehovah's Witnesses, thought the pledge directly contradicted their literal interpretation of the Bible. "Lillian Gobitis, aged twelve, and her brother William, aged ten, were expelled from the public schools of Minersville . . . for refusing to salute the national flag. . . . " Their father withdrew them from the public school system and enrolled them in a private school to avoid this offensive ritual. Wanting his children to be readmitted to the Minersville public schools, he also sued the school district to enjoin it from continuing this ceremony.

The lower courts upheld Gobitis's complaint, but the federal Supreme Court on June 3, 1940, thought differently. While First Amendment rights remained sacrosanct, "national cohesion" too proved to be important: "The mere possession of religious convictions which contradict the relevant concerns of a political society does not relieve the citizen from the discharge of political responsibilities." According to the High Court, no conflict of interest existed here; no individual rights appeared to be violated. While the school district compelled a loyalty oath, it did not prohibit the Gobitis children from practicing their religion. The school district's action, therefore, did *not* violate the due process clause of the Fourteenth Amendment either. "National unity is the basis of national security," the Court declared in *Minersville School District v. Gobitis*.[78] However, the Court reversed this decision in 1943, in the midst of World War II.

Based on the *Gobitis* ruling, the West Virginia Board of Education, in January 1942, mandated that all children enrolled in that state's public school system recite the Pledge of

Allegiance. The board further stipulated that any student or students who refused would be expelled from school until they complied. Meanwhile, those children would be deemed delinquent and could be sent to a reform school. The board would also enact a system of daily fines against the recalcitrant students' parents and even threatened jail sentences. Once again, parents who were members of the Jehovah's Witnesses denomination objected to this law and its draconian punishments. The pledge ceremony, they claimed, violated their religious principles; namely, it assaulted one of the Ten Commandments: "Thou shalt not make unto thee any craven image. . . . " They viewed the American flag as a "craven image." As a result, their children refused to participate and remained passively seated during the daily recitation of the pledge. Their actions did not interfere with those of the other students. The Jehovah's Witnesses's legal challenge focused on the Fourteenth Amendment: Did the state in passing and enforcing a compulsory declaration of "belief" violate individual freedoms guaranteed in the First Amendment?

In *West Virginia State Board of Education v. Barnette*, the federal Supreme Court ruled for the defendants. First, it invoked the power of the Fourteenth Amendment, which "protects the citizen against the State itself and all of its creatures—Boards of Education not excepted." The state thus could not undermine First Amendment privileges guaranteed by the U.S. Constitution. Second, the Court condemned punishment of individuals who refused to conform: "Those who begin coercive elimination of dissent soon find themselves exterminating dissenters. Compulsory unification of opinion achieves only the unanimity of the graveyard." This, of course, reinforced First Amendment freedoms. Third, the Court sharply criticized the notion of mandated loyalty: "If there is a fixed star in our Constitutional constellation, it is that no official, high or petty, can prescribe what shall be orthodox in politics, nationalism, religion, or other matters of opinion or force citizens to confess by word or act their faith therein." This proved to be a sore point among the Justices. As their opinion stressed, "Words uttered under coercion are proof of loyalty to nothing but self interest, love of country must spring from willing hearts and free minds. . . . "[79] Within the context of a bloody world conflict, combating Fascist powers that were murdering millions of political dissenters and methodically obliterating millions of European Jews, freedom superseded all other values. The United States government not only had to fight oppression abroad but had to confront it at home.

Political Opposition   The right to refuse the Pledge of Allegiance on religious grounds eventually became a general exemption. In the 1973 case *Goetz v. Ansell*, which involved the North Colonie Central School District in Latham, New York, Theodore Goetz, a senior honor student and class president, chose not to stand during the school's morning pledge exercise; rather, he sat quietly and passively. He did not think that "liberty and justice" existed for "all in the United States" and refused to participate in what he saw as a politically hypocritical ritual. School regulations did not compel actual participation but mandated that all students either stand respectfully or leave the room during the pledge. The U.S. Second Court of Appeals ruled for Goetz, citing federal Supreme Court cases *Barnette* and *Tinker v. Des Moines Independent Community School District*, which declared that freedom of speech rights existed for public school students. The court also referred to another high-profile Supreme Court case, *Abington v. Schempp*, which outlawed religious ceremonies in public schools.[80]

Prayers and Bible Reading

Many public schools throughout the country had long maintained the practice of opening the school day with a reading from the King James version of the Bible. In Pennsylvania, the state legislature had mandated Bible reading in the schools in 1913. A 1959 state law mandated a reading of ten verses at the beginning of each school day. The law further stipulated that "[a]ny child shall be excused from such Bible reading, or attending such Bible reading, upon the written request of his parent or guardian." The Abington School District, located near Germantown, Pennsylvania, adhered to the statute. The Schempp family, members of the Unitarian Church, who sent their children to the Abington schools objected to this religious activity. They filed suit claiming that such Bible reading violated the Fourteenth Amendment. Their children had been deprived of their First Amendment right of religious freedom without due process. The Schempps contended that the "religious doctrines purveyed by a literal reading of the Bible '. . . were contrary to the religious beliefs which they held and to their familial teaching.' " The lower court upheld their complaint. The school district appealed and the federal Supreme Court ruled for the Schempps on June 17, 1963.

This seemingly isolated case revealed how broadly opposed school-sponsored Bible reading was. An unlikely coalition had formed among Christians, non-Christians, and nonbelievers. Christians had filed the Pennsylvania complaint, and the American Jewish Committee and the Synagogue Council of America supported it. The High Court also accepted testimony from Jewish scholars. One of the class-action cases brought in *Schempp* emanated from Baltimore, Maryland, where Madalyn Murray, an atheist, filed suit protesting state sponsorship of religion. Finally, the Supreme Court heard cases from sixteen different states, among them a number from the Bible Belt.

The U.S. Supreme Court ruled that Bible reading represented a compulsory religious ceremony. The fact that children could be excused from this ritual failed to "mitigate it because of the fear of social ostracism from their peers and disapproval from their teachers. As the Court stated it: "The exercises are held in the school buildings and perforce are conducted by and under the authority of the local school authorities and during the school sessions." The Court also made the point that governments at all levels had to remain religiously impartial: "In the relationship between man and religion, the State is firmly committed to a position of neutrality." Third, the Supreme Court did not preclude the study of comparative religion or religious literature as part of an intellectual activity in school subjects like history or English. Finally, the Court did not see this decision as opposing religion or promoting a "religion of secularism."[81]

Following the *Engel v. Vitale* decision in New York forbidding the recitation of prayers and the *Schempp* decision outlawing Bible reading, the public schools became a secular institution in recognition of the country's religious pluralism. Historian Neil McCluskey describes it this way: "the process of total secularization of the common school has been a consistent one—the working out of an inner logic whose final outcome is not yet in view. . . . America's public schools are no longer either Protestant or Christian. They are no longer religiously oriented. They are officially secular."[82] In answer to the question of whether the public schools must therefore be antireligious, the Supreme Court directed that the public education system must maintain a neutral stand toward all religious matters. In a society that was growing increasingly diverse racially, ethnically, and religiously, the public schools must remain neutral concerning such a sensitive, emotional, and potentially volatile matter. This is not a new idea. Thomas Jefferson (see Chapter 3) certainly anticipated religious conflict unless sectarianism was avoided, and John Dewey's humanist agenda (in Chapter 7) avoided religious issues by focusing on a larger, social mission.

Freedom of Speech

Regardless of the historical period, schools had never permitted students to express their own political views. Thomas Jefferson had endorsed debate over a variety of political ideals, but the public school system that evolved traditionally avoided, if not suppressed, nonconformity or apparent lack of patriotism. The public schools acted to transmit existing values, both moral and political. But by the mid-twentieth century, students, aided by increasing access to information through technology, challenged the conformity that had been required of them. But theirs proved to be a Pyrrhic victory.

"A Silent, Passive Expression of Opinion?"

As the U.S. military commitment to the Vietnam war steadily increased during the 1960s, student protests on college campuses and public demonstrations, including high-profile marches in Washington, DC, also intensified throughout the nation. Inspired by these events, three Des Moines, Iowa, public school students, Christopher Eckhardt, John Tinker, and his sister Mary Beth Tinker, decided to likewise express their disapproval of the war. With their parents' support and guidance—Mr. Tinker was a Methodist minister and ardent opponent of the war—they agreed to wear black armbands on December 16, 1965, in their respective school buildings. Before that date, they had attempted to place an announcement of their planned dissent in the school newspaper.

What had begun as a seemingly benign and somewhat obscure expression of opposition to the war quickly assumed larger implications. School district administrators acted decisively to quash the publication of the student article and stifle the demonstration. They reasoned that the symbolic protest would be disruptive. They "adopted a policy that any student wearing an armband to school would be asked to remove it, and if he [sic] refused he would be suspended until he returned without the armband." However, this action contradicted usual school policy and practice, which permitted the wearing of black armbands for such purposes as mourning the lack of school spirit and expressing sympathy with the civil rights movement. The display of political buttons, the Nazi Iron Cross, and religious symbols was tolerated as well. A double standard was clearly operating here. Making matters worse was the fact that many teachers used their classes as forums to condemn antiwar demonstrations and students threatened the protestors with physical retribution if they proceeded with their plans.[83]

The students' protest demonstration commenced on schedule. Christopher Eckhardt converted the planned protest into an act of "civil disobedience," voluntarily and directly reporting to the principal's office when he arrived at Theodore Roosevelt High School. The vice principal and a student advisor asked him to remove the armband because it violated school rules; he disobeyed. They threatened suspension in order to intimidate him; he remained intractable. They even resorted to veiled physical threats of student retaliation to frighten him; he still refused. Those administrators officially suspended Eckhardt and sent him home, warning him never to return to school. Mary Beth Tinker was suspended on the spot when she attended Warren Harding Junior High School that day. The next day, December 17, John Tinker wore his armband to North High School and, though he encountered a less hostile reception, he was nevertheless sent home.

This incident created considerable acrimony in the community at an overflowing and raucous school board meeting on December 20, the community appeared to be divided over the armband issue. One side defended the right of freedom of expression; others saw the armbands as disrespectful to school authority. School board members themselves seemed to be split over the rule imposed by the district's administrators and postponed its final decision until after the holiday break. Finally, on January 3, 1966, the board voted to uphold the administrators' decision prohibiting the wearing of antiwar armbands.

This modest local protest attracted national attention. The *New York Times* and CBS reported on it. The Iowa Civil Liberties Union (ICLU) came forward with legal advice and services for the Eckhardt and Tinker families and initiated litigation. The federal district court upheld the school board's decision, but the ICLU pursued the case to the U.S. Supreme Court, where it resulted in the landmark decision *Tinker v. Des Moines Independent Community School District*.[84]

"Pure Speech"

The Court delivered its opinion on February 24, 1969, ruling for the plaintiffs. First, and foremost, the justices declared that this case illustrated "pure speech." The public school setting can in no way infringe on that right: "It can be argued that neither students or teachers shed their constitutional rights to freedom or expression at the schoolhouse gate." Second, this "silent, passive expression of opinion" did not disrupt schooling, that is, it failed to interfere with the rights of other students to education. Third, the Court condemned the school district's double standard of prohibiting the wearing of antiwar armbands while permitting the display of religious and political symbols like the Iron Cross, "traditionally a symbol of Nazism." As the justices asserted: "In our system, state-operated schools may not be enclaves of totalitarianism. School officials do not possess absolute authority over their students." Differences must be tolerated. The educational process actually thrived on the "robust exchange of ideas," both inside and outside of the classroom.[85] However, students did not retain the right of free speech for very long.

The Retreat to Paternalism

Conservative presidential administrations and their conservative Supreme Court appointees "undercut" much of the *Tinker* decision during the 1980s. The 1984 Court opinion in an indirectly related case, *New Jersey v. T.L.O*, ruled that school officials did not need a search warrant for student property, such as purses. This was a threat to "juvenile privacy" and established limits on student rights. More directly, the justices agreed two years later in *Fraser v. Bethel S.D. No 403* that school administrators could suspend a student "for employing sexual innuendos in a speech before a school assembly." Free speech were thus confined to some parts of the school building and not others, to some activities but not all. Finally, in *Hazelwood School District v. Kublmeier* (1988), the Supreme Court declared that school officials could censor student newspapers. "The Court considered the paper 'school sponsored expression,' in contrast to the 'personal expression' permitted in the Court in the 1969 *Tinker* decision." The effect of these cases was to cast a "chilling effect" on student freedoms. Adolescents could thus practice *freedom of expression* under close adult supervision, a highly paternalistic and contradictory approach.[86]

Thus rather than encouraging preparation for responsible citizenship through the exercise of basic civil rights, secondary schools hold adolescents back in a dependent and subordinate position. Their rights are postponed until they graduate, turn eighteen, and vote. But one might well ask whether they have been equipped to properly perform this important civic duty.

SPECIAL EDUCATION

Following World War II, many developments brought about gradual changes in the treatment of exceptional children. Demands for labor, technology, and other innovations began to erode impediments for many. The labor shortage in military production gave opportunities to retarded workers, who proved to be capable and productive. The development of small hearing aids and the availability of guide dogs and better long canes helped mitigate physical barriers and encourage participation in everyday activities. Moreover, the school enrollment boom of the post-war years increased the number of exceptional children enrolled by 47 percent. School administrators began to revise the traditional special education curriculum, which had relied on repetition, low expectations, and crafts. Finally, parents of special needs children became mobilized for the first time in the 1940s. They created organizations and began to lobby state legislatures, with some success. "By 1946 there were well over a hundred laws in the United States dealing with the education of exceptional children."[87]

"Parent Activism"

It was mainly the local efforts of parents in the 1940s and 1950s that sparked the campaign for the education of exceptional children that eventually spread to the state and federal governments. Up to this point, retarded children were either committed to an institution or cared for at home. "In the 1950s, mental retardation—like death or old age—was virtually dismissed as an irreversible or minimally treatable condition." Parents thus organized to better their children's lives.

The Parents Council for Retarded Children, organized in 1951 in Rhode Island, was typical of this "parent activism." It was the result of early networking efforts by parents of retarded children in order to share information, a pattern that had occurred in other states—Massachusetts, Minnesota, New Jersey, and New York—throughout the 1940s. The Rhode Island group began to sponsor meetings to focus on education and consciousness-raising. This activity quickly led to lobbying activities. Working tirelessly and selflessly throughout the 1950s, the council gained the support of John E. Fogarty, a

Rhode Island Representative in the U.S. Congress by inviting him to their meetings. "His legislative influence resulted in the creation of clinics, sheltered workshops, special education classes, and special education training; the liberalization of . . . discriminatory immigration laws; and the funding of major medical research into the causes (and thus the means) of retardation." Council efforts produced other tangible and local benefits. "A diagnostic clinic was opened, recreational programs were funded, scout troops and camps were begun, sheltered workshops were put into operation, and special classes were developed." Ultimately, in 1967, the "parents' movement" influenced the funding of the Rhode Island Office of Mental Retardation.[88]

As a result of efforts like these across the country, attitudes toward exceptional children began to change to acceptance during the 1950s. Parents continued to organize, creating the National Association for Retarded Children. Lobbying strategies became formalized. And enrollment of exceptional children in school continued to climb: "between 1948 and 1968 the number of children in public school special education classes in the United States went from 357,000 to 2,252,000. . . . " The groundwork had been laid.

The efforts on behalf of exceptional children were absorbed into the broader civil rights campaigns of the 1960s. President Kennedy approved the creation of the Division of Handicapped Children and Youth in 1963 and initiated federally sponsored research programs and conferences, bringing the issue to national attention. Furthermore, studies of exceptional children found that special classes had a disproportionate share of poor and minority students, placed there for allegedly academic reasons. In fact, these classrooms were simply "dumping grounds." For almost half a century, special education children had been segregated in schools, where the care they received was merely custodial. Teachers and administrators had low expectations of them. But the parents of these children now began to pursue litigation. As Margaret A. Winzer's historical account summarizes it: "From the mid-1960s on there was a series of cases in federal courts attacking special education on various fronts. The arguments presented to the courts focused on five points: that tests were inappropriate, that parental involvement was lacking, that special education itself was inadequate, that placement was inadequate, and that placement stigmatized children." During the 1960s, humanitarian motives fostered the policy of "normalization," that is, allowing exceptional children the opportunity to participate in all aspects of life including school. This led to "mainstreaming," which ended the policy of educational segregation. Decades of work culminated in the 1975 Public Law 94–142, the Education of All Handicapped Children Act.[89] The mainstreaming of exceptional children now became school policy.

But segregation continued. Some teachers and administrators circumvented the law by removing "difficult" children from regular classes by declaring them "behavior" problems. Schools also resorted to suspensions, which rose steadily through the 1960s. The outcasts, with a great deal of unsupervised time on their hands, often committed crimes such as shoplifting, creating headaches for local police and increasing the crime rate. Furthermore, many urban school systems introduced security forces to maintain order and control behavior problems. As historian Joseph L. Tropea concludes, "[l]owered performance expectations, segregation in special classes, and exclusion generated poor performance, negative school experiences, and limited future possibilities." Consequently, Tropea continues, "order within the urban schools was secured at the cost of future deviance and conflict."[90]

CONCLUSIONS

The practice of public schooling too often fell short of its promise: Instead of providing opportunity, it restricted the lives of many racial and ethnic minorities as well as women; instead of ensuring academic and religious freedoms, it stifled teachers and students alike; instead of fulfilling the American dream, it thwarted it. As so often in the past, only continuous struggle broadened, or at least maintained, educational opportunity. The civil rights movement that began in the 1930s had fought to ensure equal schooling for all children. Some progress was achieved, but too often it proved to be short-lived or insufficient.

ACTIVITIES FOR FURTHER EXPLORATION

1. How tolerant is American society in general? How tolerant are the public schools? Write a short reaction essay responding to these questions.

2. It is always preferable to examine and analyze primary documents for yourself in order to investigate historians' interpretations. To sample the federal Supreme Court decisions referred to in this chapter, see the following Web site: http://supct.law. cornell.edu/supct/cases/name.htm. To view the *Barnette* decision, see http://usinfo. state.gov/usa/infousa/facts/democrac/46.htm: the *Brown* decision can be found at http://usinfo.state.gov/usa/infousa/facts/democrac/36.htm.

3. To gain further historical insight into the sequence of events in African American history, refer to the "Timeline of African-American History," http://lcweb2.loc.gov/ ammem/aap/timeline.html. The Civil Rights Act of 1991 can be found at http:// www.law.ou.edu/hist.

4. Should teachers be permitted to strike? Interview practicing teachers and school administrators about their views on teacher unions and strikes. Are teachers' salaries sufficient? Check the most recent press releases regarding teacher salaries at http:// aft.org/press/2001/051601.html.

5. Should the federal government play a role in providing equal educational opportunity? What is your view? What are the views of others?

VIDEO EXPLORATIONS

1. The video series *Eyes on the Prize: America's Civil Rights Years* (Alexandria, VA: PBS Video, 1986) is a solid recounting of the civil rights movement, with original film footage and interviews of the historic participants. The first thirty-five minutes of "Episode 2: Fighting Back (1957–62)" depict the early years of school desegregation in the South, focusing on the Little Rock experience.

2. The video *The Hispanic Americans: Hispanic Education at the Crossroads* (Princeton, NJ: Films for the Humanities & Sciences, 1998) illustrates the impact on and conflict over culture and language faced by Cuban, Puerto Rican, and Mexican American children in the public schools. How does multicultural education fit into this conflict? How does assimilation affect it?

3. A glimpse of the Native American self-determination campaign can be found in the final twenty minutes of the video *Surviving Columbus* (Alexandria, VA: PBS Home Video, 1992). This segment completes the film, parts of which have been referred to in previous chapters, and provides a cohesive view of the cultural conflicts one tribe, the Pueblos, experienced.

NOTES AND SOURCES

In order to condense endnotes, the first work cited is the primary one, usually the source of any direct quotes. Subsequent references serve as supplementary, or additional, sources of paraphrased information and/or alternative historical interpretations.

1. John Hope Franklin, *From Slavery to Freedom: A History of Negro Americans* (New York: Alfred A. Knopf, 1980), pp. 346–347.

2. The quotes and much of the information in these paragraphs come from Richard Kluger, *Simple Justice: The History of* Brown v. Board of Education *and Black Americans' Struggle for Equality* (New York: Vintage Books, 1977), pp. 12, 18–19, 134–136, 177–178, 180, 184, 192–193, 212–213, 221–223, 226, 255. Kluger presents the most comprehensive and readable account of the historical background of the famous *Brown* decision. "Mr. Civil Rights" is quoted on p. 272. Also see J. Harvie Wilkinson, III, *From* Brown *to* Bakke: *The Supreme Court and School Integration, 1954–1978* (New York: Oxford University Press, 1976), p. 23.

3. Wilkinson, *From* Brown *to* Bakke, pp. 49, 51.

4. Kluger, *Simple Justice*, pp. 8, 11, 256, 332, 702. Marshall is quoted on p. 302.

5. Wilkinson, *From* Brown *to* Bakke, pp. 54, 55.

6. These paragraphs draw heavily on Kluger, *Simple Justice*, pp. 258, 374–375, 379, 381–383, 393, 395, 408–410, 408, 443. See as well Wilkinson, *From* Brown *to* Bakke, p. 23.

7. *Brown v. Board of Education*, 347 U.S. 483 (1954), pp. 363–364.

8. Wilkinson, *From* Brown *to* Bakke, p. 78, provides an extremely useful periodization with which to analyze the post-*Brown* era. Gary Orfield, "Politics Matters: Educational Policy and Chicano Students," in *The Elusive Quest for Educational Equality: 150 Years of Chicano/Chicana Education*, ed. Jose F. Moreno (Cambridge: Harvard Educational Review, 1999), pp. 111–112, offers a similar periodization.

9. Melba Pattillo Beals, *Warriors Don't Cry: A Searing Memoir of the Battle to Integrate Little Rock's Central High* (New York: Washington Square Press, 1994), pp. 1–2, 24–25, 51, 64–65, 111–112, 117, 151, 173, 184–187. Refer as well to Wilkinson, *From* Brown *to* Bakke, p. 90; Grace Palladino, *Teenagers: An American History* (New York: Basic Books, 1996), p. 182.

10. Palladino, *Teenagers*, pp. 184–185.

11. Beals, *Warriors Don't Cry*, pp. 193–194, 205–206, 243, 285, 294, 306–307.

12. Wilkinson, *From* Brown *to* Bakke, pp. 83, 98–99.

13. Palladino, *Teenagers*, p. 185.

14. Wilkinson, *From* Brown *to* Bakke, pp. 83, 84, 85, 86.

15. Kluger, *Simple Justice*, p. 752.

16. Wilkinson, *From* Brown *to* Bakke, pp. 108, 109, 110.

17. Gary Orfield, "Turning Back to Segregation," in Gary Orfield, Susan E. Eaton et al., eds., *Dismantling Desegregation: The Quiet Reversal of* Brown v. Board of Education (New York: The New Press, 1996), pp. 7–8. Refer as well to Kluger, *Simple Justice*, p. 758, 766; Wilkinson, *From* Brown *to* Bakke, pp. 111, 112.

18. Wilkinson, *From* Brown *to* Bakke, pp. 103, 104. Also, see Kluger, *Simple Justice*, pp. 755, 759. For southern periodization, see John Hardin Best, "Education in the Forming of the American South," *History of Education Quarterly* 36 (Spring 1996), pp. 47, 48.

19. Kluger, *Simple Justice*, pp. 759, 760. See as well Orfield, "Turning Back to Segregation," in Orfield, Eaton et al., *Desmantling Desegregation*, p. 8.

20. Orfield, "Turning Back to Segregation," in Orfield, Eaton et al., eds., *Dismantling Desegregation*, p. 8.

21. Kluger, *Simple Justice*, pp. 763, 764. Refer also to Orfield, "Turning Back to Segregation," in Orfield, Eaton et al., eds., *Dismantling Desegregation*, pp. 6, 15.

22. Wilkinson, *From* Brown *to* Bakke, pp. 126, 134–136, 150, 151–152, 175, 179, 180. Kluger, *Simple Justice*, pp. 765–766, 768, covers similar material.

23. Kluger, *Simple Justice*, p. 768. Also, see Wilkinson, *From* Brown *to* Bakke, pp. 158, 159.

24. Wilkinson, *From* Brown *to* Bakke, pp. 194, 195, 202.

25. Gary Orfield, "*Plessy* Parallels: Back to Traditional Assumptions," in Orfield, Eaton, et al., eds., *Dismantling Desegregation*, p. 30. Refer as well to Orfield, Eaton et al., eds., *Dismantling Desegregation*, p. xxi; Kluger, *Simple Justice*, p. 768; Wilkinson, *From* Brown *to* Bakke, pp. 195, 202.

26. Wilkinson, *From* Brown *to* Bakke, p. 203.

27. Jonathan Kozol, *Death at an Early Age: The Destruction of the Hearts and Minds of Negro Children in the Boston Public Schools* (New York: Bantam Books, 1970), pp. 9, 11–12, 21, 29, 30, 31, 33, 34, 36, 42, 54.

28. Ronald P. Formisano, *Boston Against Busing: Race, Class, and Ethnicity in the 1960s and 1970s* (Chapel Hill, NC: University of North Carolina Press, 1991), pp. 1, 2, 11. Formisano's study is a highly detailed account of Boston's complex desegregation effort. Also see Wilkinson, *From* Brown *to* Bakke, p. 207.

29. Wilkinson, *From* Brown *to* Bakke, p. 213. Again, refer to Formisano, *Boston Against Busing*, for a thorough study of Boston's busing experience.

30. Marshall is quoted in Orfield, "*Plessy* Parallels," p. 29. See as well Orfield, "Turning Back to Segregation," in Orfield, Eaton et al., eds., *Dismantling Desegregation*, pp. 2, 10; Formisano, *Boston Against Busing*, p. 12; Kluger, *Simple Justice*, pp. 771–772; and Jeffrey E. Mirel's thorough analysis of Detroit's educational history, *The Rise and Fall of an Urban School System: Detroit, 1907–81*

(Ann Arbor, MI: University of Michigan Press, 1993).

31. Kluger, *Simple Justice*, pp. 769–770, 771–772, 773.

32. Orfield, "Turning Back to Segregation," in Orfield, Eaton et al., eds., *Dismantling Desegregation*, pp. 12, 13.

33. Orfield, "*Plessy* Parallels," in Orfield, Eaton et al., eds., *Dismantling Desegregation*, p. 30; Kluger, *Simple Justice*, p. 773.

34. Orfield, "*Plessy* Parallels," pp. 27, 45, 50; "Turning Back to Segregation," pp. 1, 3, 4; "Unexpected Costs and Uncertain Gains of Dismantling Desegregation," p. 75; in Orfield, Eaton et al., eds., *Dismantling Desegregation*.

35. Orfield, "The Growth of Segregation: African Americans, Latinos, and Unequal Education," pp. 53, 57–58; "Unexpected Costs and Uncertain Gains," p. 104; in Orfield, Eaton et al., eds., *Dismantling Desegregation*.

36. Orfield, "*Plessy* Parallels," p, 23; "Unexpected Costs and Uncertain Gains," pp. 85, 86, 197, 108; in Orfield, Eaton et al., eds., *Dismantling Desegregation*.

37. Gilbert G. Gonzalez, *Chicano Education in the Era of Segregation* (Philadelphia: Balch Institute, 1990), pp. 13–14. Gonzalez's periodization matches that of Dolores Delgado Bernal, "Chicana/o Education from the Civil Rights Era to the Present," in Moreno, ed., *The Elusive Quest for Equality*, pp. 77–108. See likewise Victoria-Maria MacDonald, "Hispanic, Latino, Chicano, or 'Other?' ": Deconstructing the Relationship between Historians and Hispanic-American Educational History," *History of Education Quarterly*, 41 (Fall 2001), pp. 402, 404.

38. Bernal, "Chicana/o Education," in Moreno, ed., *The Elusive Quest for Equality*, pp. 78, 79, 80, 81–82.

39. The quote is from Joan W. Moore, *Mexican Americans* (Englewood Cliffs, NJ: Prentice-Hall, 1976), pp. 124, 125. Also, see Rodolfo Acuña, *Occupied America: A History of Chicanos* (New York: Harper & Row, 1981), p. 267; Bernal, "Chicana/o Education," in Moreno, ed., *The Elusive Quest for Equality*, p. 81.

40. Bernal, "Chicana/o Education," in Moreno, ed., *The Elusive Quest for Equality*, pp. 82–83. Refer as well to Guadalupe San Miguel, Jr., "*Let All of Them Take Heed*": *Mexican Americans and the Campaign for Educational Equality in Texas, 1910–1981* (Austin, TX: University of Texas Press, 1987), pp. 166–167,

as well as MacDonald's critique in "Hispanic, Latino, Chicano, or 'Other?' ":, pp. 403–402.

41. Acuña, *Occupied America*, pp. 170, 387. Likewise see Bernal, "Chicana/o Education," in Moreno, ed., *The Elusive Quest for Equality*, p. 82.

42. Bernal, "Chicana/o Education," in Moreno, ed., *The Elusive Quest for Equality*, p. 83; Valdez is quoted on pp. 83–84. Also refer to San Miguel, "*Let All of Them Take Heed*," p. 192.

43. The quote and much of the information in these paragraphs draw on San Miguel, "*Let All of Them Take Heed*," pp. 53–54, 169, 171–174. See also Acuña, *Occupied America*, p. 351; Bernal, "Chicana/o Education," in Moreno, ed., *The Elusive Quest for Equality*, pp. 82, 92.

44. The last two quotes are from Bernal, "Chicana/o Education," in Moreno, ed., *The Elusive Quest for Equality*, pp. 89, 92–93.

45. San Miguel, "*Let All of Them Take Heed*," pp. 177–178, 180–181. Refer as well to Bernal, "Chicana/o Education," in Moreno, ed., *The Elusive Quest for Equality*, pp. 89–90.

46. Acuña, *Occupied America*, p. 394.

47. Judith Lessow-Hurley, *Foundations of Dual Language Instruction* (New York: Longman Press, 1990), pp. 11, 111, 115. Also, see David Ballesteros, "Bilingual-Bicultural Education: A Must for Chicanos," in *The Chicanos: As We See Ourselves*, ed. Arnufo D. Trejo (Tucson, AZ: University of Arizona Press, 1980), p. 153; San Miguel, "*Let All of Them Take Heed*," p. 192.

48. Ballesteros, "Bilingual-Bicultural Education," in Trejo, ed., *The Chicanas*, pp. 158–159; Angela L. Carrasquillo, *Hispanic Children and Youth in the United States: A Resource Guide* (New York: Garland Publishing, 1991), pp. 115, 116–117; Lessow-Hurley, *Foundations of Dual Language Instruction*, pp. 11, 115–116, 117; San Miguel, "*Let All of Them Take Heed*," pp. 181, 183.

49. Alfredo Mirande and Evanelina Enriquez, *La Chicana: The Mexican-American Woman* (Chicago: University of Chicago Press, 1979), pp. 123, 124, 126; the report is quoted on p. 132. Refer as well to Moore, *Mexican Americans*, p. 66.

50. Bernal, "Chicana/o Education," in Moreno, ed., *The Elusive Quest for Equality*, p. 91. See as well Carrasquillo, *Hispanic Children and Youth*, p. 119.

51. Carrasquillo, *Hispanic Children and Youth*, p. 128. Likewise refer to Bernal, "Chicana/o Education," in Moreno, ed., *The Elusive Quest for Equality*, p. 89.

52. San Miguel, "*Let All of Them Take Heed*," pp. 185–186. Also see Carrasquillo, *Hispanic Children and Youth*, p. 106.

53. Bernal, "Chicana/o Education," in Moreno, ed., *The Elusive Quest for Equality*, pp. 90–91, 100–101. Refer as well to "Broken Promises: Resegregation in Norfolk, Virgina," in Orfield, Eaton et al., eds., *Dismantling Desegregation*, pp. 116–118; Susan E. Keefe, and Amado M. Padilla, *Chicano Ethnicity* (Albuquerque, NM: University of New Mexico Press, 1987), pp. 37–38; Lessow-Hurley, *Foundations of Dual Language Instruction*, p. 119; San Miguel, "*Let All of Them Take Heed*," pp. 184–185.

54. Margaret Connell Szasz, *Education and the American Indian: The Road to Self-Determination Since 1928* (Albuquerque, NM: University of New Mexico Press, 1999), p. 143. Also see Dee Brown, *Bury My Heart at Wounded Knee: An Indian History of the American West* (New York: Bantam Books, 1970).

55. Thomas Clarkin, *Federal Indian Policy in the Kennedy and Johnson Administrations, 1961–1969* (Albuquerque, NM: University of New Mexico Press, 2001), pp. 76, 77, 79, 110, 125, 137–138.

56. Jon Reyhner and Jeanne Eder, *A History of Indian Education* (Billings, MT: Eastern Montana College, 1989), p. 117. Also see Clarkin, *Federal Indian Policy*, pp. 270–71; David H. DeJong, *Promises of the Past: A History of Indian Education* (Golden, CO: North American Press, 1993), p. 228; Reyhner and Eder, *A History of Indian Education*, p. 117; Szasz, *Education and the American Indian*, pp. 141, 144, 146, 147.

57. DeJong, *Promises of the Past*, pp. 196–227, quotes the entire Kennedy Report. Also, refer to Szasz, *Education and the American Indian*, pp. 150–151.

58. Szasz, *Education and the American Indian*, pp. 138, 155, 158, 159, 160, 193.

59. Reyhner and Eder, *A History of Indian Education*, p. 124. Refer as well to Szasz, *Education and the American Indian*, pp. 143, 161.

60. Szasz, *Education and the American Indian*, p. 162.

61. Reyhner and Eder, *A History of Indian Education*, p. 125. See also DeJong, *Promises of the Past*, p. 229; Szasz, *Education and the American Indian*, pp. 197, 212.

62. Most of the information in these paragraphs is from Szasz, *Education and the American Indian*, pp. 153, 155, 171–172, 204–205. Also consult Clarkin, *Federal Indian Policy*, p. 236; DeJong, *Promises of the Past*, p. 229; Reyhner and Eder, *A History of Indian Education*, pp. 126–127.

63. Reyhner and Eder, *A History of Indian Education*, pp. 127, 128, 132. Refer as well to DeJong, *Promises of the Past*, pp. 238, 239, 267.

64. Szasz, *Education and the American Indian*, pp. 201, 212, 213, 216, 223–224, 232.

65. The quotes in these paragraphs are from Stephanie Coontz, *The Way We Never Were: American Families and the Nostalgia Trap* (New York: Basic Books, 1992), pp. 150, 156–157 163, 169–173. Labor historians provide an insightful perspective about working women in general and working wives and mothers in particular. See Alice Kessler-Harris, *Out to Work: A History of Wage-Earning Women in the United States* (New York: Oxford University Press, 1982), pp. 300–319; Lois Scharf, *To Work and To Wed: Female Employment, Feminism, and the Great Depression* (Westport, CT: Greenwood Press, 1980), 159–165; Lynn Y. Weiner, *From Working Girl to Working Mother: The Female Labor Force in the United States, 1820–1980* (Chapel Hill, NC: University of North Carolina Press, 1985), pp. 83–118.

66. The quotes in these paragraphs are from Sara M. Evans, *Born for Liberty: A History of Women in America* (New York: Free Press, 1997), pp. 94, 102–103, 123, 172, 225, 249, 252–253, 257–259, 264, 274–277, 288, 290–291. Also refer to Carl N. Degler, *At Odds: Women and the Family in America from the Revolution to the Present* (Oxford: Oxford University Press, 1981), pp. 175, 190, 330, 342, 360, 441, 443–446.

67. Judith Stacey, Susan Bereaud, and Joan Daniels, eds., *And Jill Came Tumbling After: Sexism in American Education* (New York: Dell Publishing Co., 1974), pp. 17–18.

68. Elizabeth Fisher, "Children's Books: The Second Sex, Junior Division," in Stacey, Bereaud, and Daniels, eds., *And Jill Came Tumbling After*, pp. 116–117, 118, 119, 120. Women on Words and Images, "Look Jane Look, See Sex Stereotypes," in Stacey, Bereaud, and Daniels, eds., *And Jill Came Tumbling After*, pp. 160, 161, 162, 163, 170, 171, 172; Michigan Women's Commission, *Sex Discrimination in an Elementary Reading Program* (Lansing, MI: Michigan Women's Commission, 1974), pp. 8, 13, 29, 35.

69. Women on Words and Images, "Look Jane Look," in Stacey, Bereaud, and Daniels, eds., *And Jill Came Tumbling After*, pp. 173–174.

70. Kathleen Bennett deMarrais and Margaret D. LeCompte, *The Way Schools Work: A Sociological Analysis of Education* (New York: Longman, 1999), p. 242.

71. Pauline S. Sears and David H. Feldman, "Teacher Interactions with Boys and Girls," in Stacey, Bereaud, and Daniels, eds., *And Jill Came Tumbling After*, pp. 148, 149, 150. See as well Betty Levy, "Do Schools Sell Girls Short?" in Stacey, Bereaud, and Daniels, eds., *And Jill Came Tumbling After*, pp. 143–144, 145.

72. deMarrais and LeCompte, *The Way Schools Work*, pp. 299–300, 303, 306, 307, 313, 315. Consult as well Degler, *At Odds*, p. 446; Evans, *Born for Liberty*, pp. 304–306, 309.

73. Stuart J. Foster, *Red Alert! Educators Confront the Red Scare in American Public Schools, 1947–1954* (New York: Peter Lang, 2000), pp. 25, 32, 33, 39, 47, 48, 187–188, 193, 194, 204. Also refer to Marjorie Murphy, *Blackboard Unions: The AFT and the NEA, 1900–1980* (Ithaca, NY: Cornell University Press, 1990), pp. 139–140, 210.

74. William E. Eaton, *The American Federation of Teachers, 1916–1961* (Carbondale, IL: Southern Illinois University Press, 1975), pp. 139–140, 153, 155, 157. See as well Murphy, *Blackboard Unions*, p. 212; Foster, *Red Alert!*, p. 48.

75. The quotes and much of the information in these paragraphs are from Murphy, *Blackboard Unions*, pp. 197–201, 205, 209–210, 213, 215–217. Also see Eaton, *American Federation of Teachers*, pp. 141–142, 144, 146–147, 150–151, 159–160, 162–163, 165.

76. deMarrais and LeCompte, *The Way Schools Work*, pp. 174–175.

77. Eugene F. Provenzo, Jr., and Asterie Bakker Provenzo, "Columbus and the Pledge," *American School Board Journal* (October 1991), p. 25.

78. *Minersville School District, Board of Education of Minersvile School District v. Gobitis*, 310 U.S. 586 (1940), pp. 591, 592, 594–595.

79. *West Virginia State Board of Education v. Barnette*, 319 U.S. 624 (1942), pp. 627–631, 637, 641, 644.

80. *Goetz v. Ansell*, 477 F.2d 636 (1973), p. 636.

81. *School District of Abington Township v. Schempp*, 374 U.S. 203 (1963), pp. 203–206, 208, 211, 225–226. See also Louise Gilchriese Walsh and Matthew J. Walsh, *History and Organization of Education in Pennsylvania* (Indiana, PA: R. S. Grosse Print Shop, 1930), p. 260.

82. Neil G. McCluskey, *Catholic Education in America: A Documentary History* (New York: Teachers College Press, 1964), p. 20.

83. *Tinker v. Des Moines Independent Community School District*, 393 U.S. 503 (1969), p. 504. Also refer to John W. Johnson, *The Struggle for Student Rights: Tinker v. Des Moines and the 1960s* (Lawrence, KS: University Press of Kansas, 1997), pp. 6–7, 7–8, 73, 98, 103. Johnson provides an excellent and comprehensive analysis of the *Tinker* case, placing it into historical context and giving it a human face.

84. Johnson, *Struggle for Student Rights*, pp. 8–9, 16–20, 25, 29, 31–32, 36, 45, 49, 66. Refer also to *Tinker v. Des Moines*, p. 504.

85. *Tinker v. Des Moines*, pp. 505, 506, 508, 510, 511, 512–513, 514. See also Johnson, *Struggle for Student Rights*, pp. 67, 79, 171, 172, 173.

86. Johnson, *Struggle for Student Rights*, pp. 206, 207, 208, 209, 211.

87. Margaret A. Winzer, *The History of Special Education: From Isolation to Integration* (Washington, DC: Gallaudet University Press, 1993), pp. 372, 373, 374, 375.

88. The information and quotes in this paragraph are from Barbara Blair, "Parents Council for Retarded Children and Social Change in Rhode Island, 1951–1970," *Rhode Island History* 40 (1981), pp. 145–146, 150–151, 153, 156–159.

89. Winzer, *History of Special Education*, pp. 375–377, 379–382. See also deMarrais and LeCompte, *The Way Schools Work*, p. 273; Joseph L. Tropea, "Bureaucratic Order and Special Children: Urban Schools, 1950s–1960s," *History of Education Quarterly* 27 (Fall 1987), pp. 340, 341, 343.

90. Tropea, "Bureaucratic Order and Special Children," pp. 344, 347, 357–358, 360, 361.

11

School Reform and Public Reaction

You Get What You Pay For: School Funding and Inequality

The Continuing Struggle for the Public School Ideal

The headline on the August 22, 2000, edition of *USA Today* screamed "School Rolls Hit Record." The article, based on a U.S. Department of Education report, claimed that 53 million children would be enrolled in America's public and private schools at the beginning of the 2000–2001 school year. Not only would this represent a record-high enrollment but this huge figure would be outstripped in the near future. Unprecedented growth had already produced serious problems, such as severe teacher and administrative shortages, overcrowded classrooms, and an insufficient number of school buildings, and assured that conditions would further deteriorate in the years ahead. Other significant changes included a declining proportion of European American students and a rapid increase of minority children. The article predicted a 60 percent increase in Latino/Latina student enrollment alone.[1] Clearly, the American public schools would continue to be dynamic and influential institutions.

This chapter attempts to draw together many of the themes that we have explored thus far. As we have seen, public schooling has been often beset with conflict over issues of race, gender, ethnicity, and social class. The promise of public schooling has not always matched reality, causing over time different groups either to wage reform campaigns within the public system or seek alternative educational experiences. As our society becomes more diverse, the public school system must decide if it will break from tradition and employ a policy of tolerance.

What is taught in schools has also generated serious disagreements. Over the centuries, the school's curriculum gradually became formalized and expanded to offer an at times bewildering array of courses at different academic and vocational levels for children with a variety of abilities. The schools have further been used to convey many different values: patriotic chauvinism and cosmopolitanism, individualism and teamwork, competition and cooperation, Christianity and secularism. What is taught and discussed in the classroom is supposedly rooted in our basic Constitutional right to freedom of speech. Some groups and communities, however, think otherwise.

At the same time as public schools have assumed increasing social and educational responsibilities, families have either willingly surrendered some of these duties or school officials have usurped them—sometimes in the cause of nationalism, sometimes for the sake of social and economic stability, sometimes to ensure cultural continuity, and sometimes because of professional self-righteousness. The result of all of these changes is that the public schools have become highly integrated into this country's social, economic, and political systems. Groups from different political, economic, and ideological camps have vied to shape the schools according to their goals and images, creating a seemingly endless cycle of reform and reaction.

The complex mission of the public system and its dismaying array of responsibilities will cause it to face many more challenges and criticisms—some old and some new. The story is far from over.

E Pluribus Unum?

The United States has never been as diverse as it is today. The scope and complexity of immigration and of demographic changes grow each year. Over 16,000,000 immigrants entered this country between 1971 and 1994. "In the 1980s, half as many people emigrated from Europe to the United States as in the 1960s; more than five times as many came from Asia; twice as many from Mexico, the Caribbean and Central America; and nearly four times as many from Africa—including as many from Nigeria as from Greece." Specifically, almost 6 million of the immigrants, or about 38 percent, came from Asian countries like China, Japan, India, Korea, the Philippines, and Vietnam. The impact of this has already been significant, and it will continue to resonate throughout our society. European Americans now constitute a minority in major cities like El Paso and San Antonio, Texas, Los Angeles, and Miami. In California in 1990, European Americans made up 57 percent of the population; Hispanics, African Americans, and Asian Americans made up the rest.[2]

Children of color will very soon make up the majority of the public school population. Between 1972 and 1992, African American public school enrollment increased 3 percent, Latino/Latina enrollment jumped 89 percent, and European American enrollment fell 14 percent. "A dramatic drop in white birth rate" accounted for much of this demographic shift in the student population. During the early years of the twenty-first century, minority children comprise about 40 percent of all students enrolled in the public schools nationwide. The racial shift is especially noticeable in large urban school districts, which have experienced most of the urban-to-suburban movement by European American middle-class families.[3] This section wrestles with the reality of a multicultural society and how cultural differences, largely based on race and language, will shape public education policy and practice through the twenty-first century.

The Forgotten Immigrants

Today, Asian immigration has reached unprecedented levels. The Chinese account for the largest group of Asian immigrants, totaling over 1,500,000 by 1994. Almost 1,000,000 of those have entered this country since 1971.[4] Yet the United States has an abysmal record of intolerance toward Asian Americans in general and Chinese Americans in particular, despite the fact that the Chinese are the oldest group of Asian immigrants. Chinese immigrants began to trickle into various Spanish and English North American colonial settlements during the late eighteenth and early nineteenth centuries. Industrial development, railroad construction, the growth of commercial agriculture, and the expansion of mining required a cheap source of unskilled labor. Chinese immigrants, fleeing political turmoil in China and seeking better economic opportunities here, began to enter the United States in large numbers in 1850. By 1882, 332,000 Chinese had emigrated, most entering through the port of San Francisco.[5]

The Chinese faced serious discrimination from the beginning. They worked at the most menial of jobs and were often treated little better than slaves. "The Chinese were accused of having low morals, specifically of practicing prostitution and smoking opium, of low health standards, and of corrupt influences and practices." These beliefs, coupled with the ongoing large influx of Chinese immigrants and the economic recession of the 1870s, fueled hostility among Western whites, particularly Californian residents. In 1871, a Los Angeles mob killed nineteen Chinese immigrants. Whites campaigned for the total exclusion of Chinese immigrants, and the effort succeeded in 1882 with the passage by the United States Congress of the Chinese Exclusion Act. In a further response to racism, federal and state laws forbade naturalization for those Chinese already residing here. The political actions seemed to legitimize anti-Chinese sentiments, which sparked even more riots in Seattle and Tacoma, Washington, and Utah. The prejudice, discrimination, and stereotyping continued well into the twentieth century.[6]

Chinese organizations fought back. "Chinatown leaders frequently petitioned for more equitable treatment." Chinese-language newspapers and magazines contained editorials and articles criticizing discrimination. Chinese Americans also initiated numerous court cases to secure their U.S. citizenship. Nevertheless, they continued to encounter segregation in virtually all aspects of their lives, including schooling.[7]

Schooling

Because of state law and local restrictions, "Chinese-American children in San Francisco had no legal claim to a public education from 1871 through 1884." Only after winning a court suit in 1885 could they attend a segregated school located in Chinatown, which had only five grade levels and where the educational agenda focused on Americanization.[8] Chinese immigrants resisted general assimilation. They attempted to preserve their culture by establishing their own cultural institutions and schools in Chinatowns scattered throughout the United States. The first school opened in San Francisco in 1888. Nevertheless, their children, because of the overwhelming influence of the American culture and its various institutions, began the long process of assimilation, and the use of the Chinese language declined. "The degree of Americanization was not uniform throughout the community, which reflected a wide variety of combinations of Chinese and western ways."[9] Schooling was a continuing source of conflict. By the 1920s, when Chinese public school enrollment outstripped the space allocated by San Francisco's school authorities, Chinese American children were finally allowed to attend public schools outside of Chinatown. Segregation persisted, however. The school district hired a few American-born

Chinese Student with American Flag (date unknown). Woman's American Baptist Home Mission Society, Courtesy of Tedd Levy.

Chinese American bilingual instructors, but the majority of the teachers remained insensitive, if not downright biased. The curriculum continued to emphasize Americanization.

Discrimination eased somewhat following World War II, and more and better employment and educational opportunities gradually became available. Chinese immigration began again, but slowly, though some federal authorities and politicians were alarmed about the potential for communist infiltration. Education remained a problem: "In 1969, some 85 percent of Chinatown's people had never attended high school. . . ." In 1970, the Chinese American community filed suit to force attention to be paid to the language needs of its children. Four years later, the U.S. Supreme Court in *Lau v. Nichols* ruled for the plaintiffs, ensuring proper staffing and addressing of curricular needs.[10] As we shall see, this landmark ruling had a broad and significant impact, for it helped to usher in the era of modern bilingual education.

The 1965 Immigration Act eased quota restrictions, and Asian immigrants once again began to enter this country in large numbers. Most of them have been highly educated, middle-class professionals. "Generally, Asian-Americans have the highest median income and academic credentials of any racial or ethnic group."[11] By 1980, the United States had the largest Chinese population of "any nation outside Asia."[12]

Bilingual Education

Bilingual education as a concept and in practice has existed, officially and unofficially since colonial times. German-speaking settlers' use of their native language was widely tolerated and was even recognized by the Continental Congress. As early as 1840, Cincinnati's German residents managed to introduce German at elementary school levels after lobbying the Ohio state legislature. "The resulting schools were bilingual: at first children learned reading, grammar, and spelling in both English and German in the primary grades, moving onto instruction in English in arithmetic, geography, and other subjects." By mid-century, Germans in Baltimore, Indianapolis, and St. Louis had similar success in introducing their language into the schools. As historian David B. Tyack points out, this bilingual effort helped "to preserve their culture."[13] Other immigrant groups used a similar approach. "In the nineteenth century, non-English or dual language instruction was offered in more than a dozen states in a variety of languages including Dutch, German, Swedish, Norwegian, Danish, Polish, Italian, Czech, French, and Spanish." Furthermore, bilingualism existed not only among European immigrants; many members of Native American tribes were bilingual during the nineteenth century. Oklahoma's Cherokees had a high rate of English literacy.

General antiforeign feelings, particularly anti-German ones during World War I, eliminated linguistic tolerance. "At the turn of the century, only 14 of the 45 states mandated English as the sole language of instruction in the schools. By 1923, a total of 34 of the 48 states had English-only instructional policies." For patriotic and nativistic reasons, foreign-language instruction in general became taboo. But all of this changed again in the 1940s. World War II and the Cold War caused multilingualism to be regarded as an important component of national defense. The National Defense Education Act of 1958 encouraged foreign-language instruction. The civil rights movement and growing pride in "ethnic identity" in the 1960s gave additional support to proficiency in more than one language. President Lyndon B. Johnson's attempt to "equalize educational opportunities" in the 1965 Elementary and Secondary Education Act (ESEA) paved the way for the passage of the Bilingual Education Act, Title VII of the ESEA, in 1968—a law strongly supported by Hispanic activists, as we saw in Chapter 10. "Title VII was directed at children from environments where the dominant language was not English and at those whose families had incomes of less than $3,000 per year." The passage of Title VII was followed, as we have seen, by the federal Supreme Court case *Lau v. Nichols*, initiated by Chinese Americans. "In 1969, plaintiffs representing 1,800 language minority children in the San Francisco Unified School District sued the district, claiming that limited English proficient children were being denied equal educational opportunity in English-only classrooms." The Court's favorable ruling in 1974 led to the amending of the Bilingual Education Act in 1978 to include Native American children.

As we saw in Chapter 10, the state of Massachusetts pioneered mandated bilingual education in 1971. "By 1983, bilingual education was permitted in all 50 states, and 9 states had laws requiring some from of dual language instruction for students with limited

English proficiency."[14] Congress extended the Bilingual Education Act in 1984 and "currently funds maintenance, . . . transitional, and immersion bilingual programs." The maintenance approach preserves the native language while teaching English as a second language, developing both languages. The transitional emphasis teaches English as quickly as possible with little, or no, regard for the native language. "While children are taught extensively in their native language during their first year of school, instruction in English is quickly phased in so that by about fourth grade all instruction is in English. Transitional programs do little to promote native language skills."

The transitional approach has been used most commonly with Native American children and has proven to be mostly unsuccessful. Language immersion involves teachers speaking only "the languages to be learned to the children." Typically, this approach has been used to some effect to teach Spanish, French, German, or Latin to English-speaking students who have elected to learn a second language. It is, however, the most culturally insensitive approach for teaching native-speaking children English. Native Americans "tend to lose their first language skills in immersion programs." As historians Jon Reyhner and Jeanne Eder summarize: "Subtractive educational programs that sought to replace native language and culture with the English language and culture cause minority students to fail while additive educational program teaching English language and culture in addition to native language and culture created conditions for students to succeed in their schoolwork."

During the 1980s, various tribes, such as the Northern Ute and Navajo nations, required native-language instruction in their schools. Tribes also mandated that teachers be prepared in these languages. In 1990, President George Bush signed the Native American Languages Act, which "preserves, protects, and promotes" tribal languages, finally reversing a centuries-old practice and eliminating language instruction as a tool of assimilation. As Reyhner and Eder conclude: "The current tribal interest in Indian languages and cultures has not been promoted as a substitute for the study of the English language and European culture but as a supplement."[15]

Cultural Backlash

Opposition to bilingual education is predicted on two basic arguments. "Language parochialism" regards "multilingualism" as useless, if not "harmful." This view rejects a cosmopolitan vision of American society and distrusts a multinational perspective on the world. It stems from a degree of insecurity. "Language elitism" totally opposes multilingualism and regards English as *the* national language; it is afraid that bilingualism may cause national fragmentation. Both viewpoints, of course, are contrary to the educational policies and practices of most other nations, which require the acquisition of two or more languages before graduation from secondary institutions. Opposition to bilingualism rests on a belief in the relationship between language and loyalty and concern over the connection between language and national unity. Much of this opposition, of course, revives age-old arguments over assimilation. The attacks on bilingual education are intended to undermine the concept and implementation of multiculturalism in place of the school's traditional assimilationist role. The conflict between Americanization and pluralism, as in the past, will intensify as the country becomes more diverse. It is worth noting, as researcher Judith Lessow-Hurley points out, that by the end of the twentieth century, "only 14 percent of the population had Anglo-Saxon heritage."[16]

Diversity once again challenges American society and its educational institutions. Some recent events are significant. In 1994, California passed Proposition 187, which barred children who were "reasonably suspected" of being "illegal aliens" from attending the public schools. Mexican Americans mobilized opposition to this vaguely worded statute, and the Mexican-American Legal Defense Fund, League of United Latin American Citizens, and the American Civil Liberties Union successfully challenged the measure in court a year after its passage.[17] As this country grows more ethnically and racially diverse, how will the public schools respond? Will they continue in their historical role as a tool of Americanization? Or, in view of the recent emphasis on multicultural education, will they tolerate, if not honor, other cultures? In sum, how tolerant is our society and its public education system? What have we learned from the past to assist us in creating educational policies and practices that will match our ideals of democracy and equality?

"THE MONSTERS NEXT DOOR": AMERICAN YOUTH VIOLENCE

The May 3, 1999, cover of *Time* magazine shrieked, "The Monsters Next Door," a headline referring to the tragic slayings at Columbine High School in Colorado which had occurred on April 20. The special issue reported the killing of twelve students and one teacher and the wounding of a number of others by two troubled students. They fired 900 rounds of ammunition from semiautomatic weapons and a shotgun, as well as planted thirty bombs, in a careful and methodical assault on students and teachers. *Time* devoted several articles in the issue to analyzing the effectiveness of school security measures, the role of parents, the impact of student cliques, the availability of guns and other weapons, and the influence of a media fixated on violence.[18]

This incident of school violence in an affluent suburban community came on the heels of the previous year's shootings in seemingly remote and safe rural and suburban middle and high schools in places like Arkansas, Oregon, and Pennsylvania. The nation found itself in the grips of deep angst. Countless talk shows and broadcasts and forests of newsprint were devoted to deep soul searching. But what many analysts and policymakers overlooked was the fact that school violence was not new. As we saw in Chapter 5, school violence plagued the schools throughout the nineteenth century. And in Chapter 9, we noted that juvenile delinquency played a prominent role in the adolescent experience of the twentieth-century. School violence is, in short, a long-term and deep-seated problem.

"A Nation of Jailers"

Much of what occurred in rural and suburban schools in the 1990s had been foreshadowed in urban schools. Through the 1970s and 1980s, the media often reported acts of gang violence, but it was often dismissed as an aberration, endemic to the pathology of urban environments. More important, when African American and Latino/Latina youths were perpetrators as well as victims of this violence, American society as a whole did not seem to be alarmed. The general response was to pass stiffer crime laws and construct more prisons to incarcerate juvenile offenders.

Politicians and the media contend that the results of this policy are reflected in the decline in the U.S. crime rate. If so, this has occurred at a high cost. The cover of the November 13, 2000, issue of *Newsweek* announced "America's Prison Generation." More and more youths are now treated as adult criminals and receive heavy sentences. Because of a recent referendum, California "in the next five years will send an estimated 5,600 youths to adult prisons who normally would have gone to the Youth Authority or county jails." While California leads the nation with almost 250,000 prisoners, the United States outstrips the world, with some 2,000,000 inmates in jails and prisons—a jump from 500,000 in 1980. "We have become, to put it bluntly, a nation of jailers."

Imprisonment has proven to be an expensive way to reduce crime. "Between 1985 and 1996, total expenditures on state-prison activities more than doubled, going from just under $13 billion to over $27 billion." On an individual basis, it costs about $71,000 a year to "house an inmate in New York's Rikers Island." Furthermore, a disproportionate number of those incarcerated are minority youths. Too often unable to afford competent legal aid, they receive sentences based on flimsy charges while white youths who can hire attorneys escape prison. The epidemic of imprisonment has placed a heavy burden on family life by separating children from their parents. And the rate of recidivism remains high. The dip in crime may be an illusion; as prisoners are released, crime rates could increase.[19]

America cannot simply solve youth violence by condemning children to prisons where they are treated as adults. This social problem runs deep and requires more than just imprisonment. Only when violence struck rural and suburban schools, when it occurred among white children, did society begin to realize how widespread and deeply entrenched it was and turn to addressing its causes.

School Safety

Violence is too often an integral part of American childhood. Homicide has now replaced motor vehicle accidents as the leading cause of death among children under the age of one. According to sociologists Kathleen Bennett deMarrais and Margaret D. LeCompte, a child younger than five is murdered every fourteen hours. "Homicide is the third leading cause of death for all children between the ages of 5 and 14; the second leading cause of death for all young people between the ages of 10 and 24; the leading cause of death among African Americans of both sexes between the ages of 15 and 34." In Chicago's inner city, 74 percent of children have witnessed a shooting, stabbing, or robbery. Youth violence has reached unprecedented proportions because of gradual escalation and social denial. "Every year since 1950, the number of American children gunned down has doubled." When this violence overflows into the public schools, it threatens one of America's fundamental institutions. Everyday 135,000 children take a gun to school.[20]

In spite of these staggering statistics and the impression given by sensationalized media treatment, the fact is that school violence in general has declined in the United States since 1993. "Targeted violence," that is, a planned action with prechosen targets, although rare, is the type of violence that has received high-profile coverage from the media, which feeds the public's anxiety and paranoia. Such violence represents an act of "revenge," focusing on specific school administrators, or teachers, or students. It is not gang- or drug-related violence and is not restricted to any region of the country, with incidents reported in twenty-six states. A gender element does exist: All of the attackers have been males between the ages of 11 and 21. Beyond this, no generalizations can be made.[21]

School violence is a complex phenomenon that cannot be simply and quickly solved. It stems from the confluence of many and various educational and social issues. First, the school consolidation that began during the Progressive era has produced larger school districts and school buildings. The rationale for this was to expand the number and variety of academic courses and extracurricular activities for students. But an uneasy trade-off developed. On the one hand, school buildings would become larger and so house more students and offer them access to richer programs and more resources. However, in reality, cost-effectiveness was the reason for consolidation to a greater degree than educational philosophy. Efficiency dictated that redundant programs be eliminated. Little actual enrichment, in fact, occurred. The large, factorylike environments that resulted caused many students to feel alienated from school life and their peers. High schools warehousing more than 1,000 students claim the highest dropout rates; those enrolling only a few hundred maintain the best school retention records. "Small school buildings remain flexible, foster a more personal relationship between teachers and students, and appear more committed to nurturing students."[22]

Second, society in its determination to minimize school expenditures through consolidation also appears reluctant to adequately subsidize school personnel. This is a salient point. The perpetrators of targeted violence in all cases informed peers ahead of time of their intent, but adolescent–adult bureaucratic "barriers" prevented communication between students in the know and school officials. The ratio of students to counselors nationwide ranges from 350:1 to 420:1.[23] Students who most need counseling rarely, if ever, have access to it. Couple this with the fact that the typical middle and high school teacher sees between 100 and 180 students each day, and it is little wonder that many serious emotional and social needs go unattended and that too little personal communication occurs. Too many adolescents who desperately need adult intervention rarely receive it because educators are overburdened.

Third, the callous commercialization of American youth for the sake of profit breeds the wrong values and encourages inappropriate behaviors. As we saw, this began in the 1940s when businesses began to target adolescents as consumers. Over the decades, this trend has reached crass proportions, and there is little, or no, regard for children's developmental needs. Violent movies and video games send the wrong messages to youth.

Fourth, the easy availability of firearms to American children of all ages is conducive to brutal solutions to social conflicts between peers. As Bennett deMarrais and LeCompte point out, "there are more gun dealers in the U.S. (284,000) than gas stations; there are 211 million firearms circulating among the American public." Most perpetrators of targeted violence had experience with firearms, and the overwhelming majority had access to them, a tragic commentary on our so-called Constitutional right to "bear arms."[24]

Finally, quick fixes, such as metal detectors and student profiling, will not eliminate targeted violence in schools. According to a report by the U.S. Secret Service, there is no "typical" attacker. They have no particular racial or ethnic background; come from a variety of family environments, functional as well as dysfunctional, traditional and untraditional; have different academic records; and have a wide range in social contacts with peers, from loners to highly sociable.[25] Thus, how can a common profile of a student attacker be deduced?

Must we learn to live with the "Columbine Effect," as the March 19, 2001, cover of *Time* magazine termed it in reporting on yet another school shooting, the eighth since Columbine, that had occurred at Santana High School in Santee, California, on March 5, 2001.[26] As American children spend more time in school, as the number of adolescents continues to grow through the next two decades, as schools increasingly become the arenas for youth violence, this society needs to understand that wrong-headed policies have to be addressed. Instead of relying on educational philosophy, the business notion of cost efficiency, a legacy of the efficiency movement that dominated the twentieth century, continues to drive school policy. Society can no longer afford to be frugal with its schools. Public education is not a business. A child's life is precious, too dear, to be cheapened by the shortsightedness of a perspective that it is in some way a "business investment."

ACADEMIC FREEDOM OR CENSORSHIP?

School knowledge has a powerful and lasting effect on children. Should schools and teachers have the right to teach anything? Or should what students learn be restricted? These crucial questions have been debated from the beginning, as we have seen, and revolve around the idea that all knowledge is socially constructed. The function of education during the colonial period was to convert students to a distinct religious doctrine, or at least ensure their knowledge of it. The American Revolution introduced political education to the schools, and industrial capitalism inserted economic values and vocational training. An increasingly diverse society required a more outward-looking and less narrow environment, leading to the present-day trend of multiculturalism.

The means to control the knowledge that schools convey has, over time, assumed many different forms. In the past, local communities exerted a powerful influence over teachers. In other cases, interest groups have restricted the content of textbooks or the curriculum itself has been attacked. Censorship remains a serious problem that must be faced, for it challenges the basic notion of intellectual freedom. At the same time, in a society that has increasing access to information through electronic media, what is taught must be balanced by a responsible approach to what is appropriate for children to learn. All of this is fraught with conflict.

Teachers

Classroom instructors have always felt constrained in their teaching activities. We saw this with accounts of various limitations, such as religious background and conduct, imposed on teachers' personal and professional lives. Female instructors in particular were powerfully affected by such constraints. Moreover, the restrictions placed on teachers are not relegated to the distant past; rather, they assumed subtle forms in the early twentieth century.

In 1936, Howard K. Beale, in his pioneer nationwide study of academic freedom, *Are American Teachers Free?*, characterized the relationship between teachers and their communities as that of conformity, meaning that the community shaped racial perceptions, galvanized teachers' roles, and restricted religious values, among other social and political prescriptions. The school operated as a cultural repository while the teacher served as a "paid agent of cultural diffusion."[27] Thus, the teacher functioned neither as an autonomous professional nor as an enlightened intellectual, both in the classroom and out of it. Social norms, more than credentials, county exams, and state certification codes, regulated the teacher's professional and private life.

The influence of communities appeared to be so pervasive and effective that Beale encountered almost insurmountable problems in merely collecting data for his study. He identified the obstacles as teachers' fears and administrators' reticence in responding to questions about "ideas," like the League of Nations, socialism, income taxes, social and political equality for "Negoes," as well as "personal conduct," such as attending the theater, smoking, dancing, and union membership. Classroom instructors generally seemed to be intimidated, if not downright frightened, and chose to remain silent. "The multiplicity of examples of fears of teachers about supplying facts is in itself eloquent testimony to the lack of freedom in the schools." In some cases, a surprised Beale found that many teachers expressed intolerance of their colleagues' nonconformities and identified instead with the norms of their communities. In other instances, a frustrated Beale pointed to the fact that too many teachers lacked a cosmopolitan perspective and thus failed to realize that their communities' conventional ideas, values, and routines inhibited their freedoms: "Thousands of teachers are utterly uninformed and unaware of anything outside of the textbooks and minutiae of small-town life." A universal, hierarchical bureaucratic structure reinforced provincialism. Beale discovered many authoritarian-minded school administrators: "They are not interested in freedom. One characteristic of the successful administrator is skill in avoiding trouble. . . . In general, superintendents and school board members seem to feel . . . that it is impudent for anyone to question or enquire into their motives."[28]

Tradition, ideology, patriotism, personal relationships, and racism all trespassed on teachers' rights, Beale discovered. Although the nineteenth-century's legacy regarding academic freedom was far from faultless, as we have seen, the pressure to conform took on an ominous tone through much of the first half of the twentieth century. The biological theory of evolution, which called into question religious dogma; the political ideology of communism, which challenged capitalist beliefs; and the profound social change of pluralism, which overwhelmed this once relatively homogeneous nation with ethnic, religious, and racial diversity, challenged many groups, including religious, business, and patriotic associations, which stubbornly clung to the status quo. Some organizations, like the Ku Klux Klan (KKK), attacked the stance of teachers and their curricula over these provocative issues. The modest progress that teachers had achieved toward academic freedom was threatened. One observer lamented in 1939, "Even today . . . the freedom which teachers enjoy in many communities depends to a large degree upon their intelligence, information, and tact."[29]

Religion was a particularly touchy subject. Beale noted that Americans despised irreligion. Largely Protestant, they saw religious education as moral and civic imperatives as well as an integral part of American culture and tradition. As a result, in 1926, eleven (mostly southern) states required Bible reading in the schools and strictly enforced this law. Delaware specified fines and dismissal for teachers who violated the law. The schools used the King James version of the Bible, and most Protestants failed to see this choice as a sectarian act. Catholic, Jewish, and agnostic parents felt otherwise. Parental protests and legal actions, especially in heterogeneous communities like large cities, often caused schools to excuse children from these services. Yet unlike their students, teachers faced coercion, that is, "the alternative of the exclusion from teaching or else going through the motions of religious forms that are to him [sic] a mockery." In more homogeneous, and particularly evangelical religious settings, attitudes appeared to be stronger and more rigid, and Catholic public school instructors were special targets: "In 1915 about 100 hundred

Catholic teachers were dismissed in Denver, Colorado. In 1913 two women were dropped from the schools of Charlotte, North Carolina, because of the Catholic issue." During the 1920s, the KKK included Catholic public school instructors among its targets in its campaigns of prejudice and harassment.[30]

Community constraints shadowed teachers outside of the classroom as well, and these on occasion assumed abstract and subtle forms. Instructors had to maintain impeccably moral lives as defined by the values of a particular locale. After World War I, big-city school districts appeared to be the most tolerant, yet in many states school buildings were used for temperance meetings, which were often led by teachers. Small towns and rural areas expected teachers to devote personal time to church attendance, Sunday-school instruction, and other such wholesome activities. And while these communities presupposed that their classroom instructors would be civic-minded, they frowned on teachers' participation in political campaigns, especially those that flouted local customs. Teacher complaints and tenure laws, passed by different states during the 1930s, alleviated some of these restrictions but failed to eradicate them.[31]

Only the teacher union movement, as we saw in Chapter 10, finally gave public school instructors the ability to shield themselves from such professional and personal restrictions. Nevertheless, since the 1960s, many communities and states throughout the nation have either prohibited unions or eroded their power through legislation. Furthermore, indirect constraints on the academic freedom of teachers have been accomplished through censorship of textbooks and library books and by curricular proscriptions.

A Little Knowledge Can Be a Dangerous Thing

Like the personal and professional lives of teachers, the content of schoolbooks has also always been controlled in terms of the economic, political, and moral messages they conveyed, as we have seen. Concerns over ideology were especially strong during the twentieth century. During the 1930s and 1940s, Harold Rugg's popular social studies series dared to stray from the doctrine of unfettered capitalism. His detractors claimed that the series championed communism, and it subsequently disappeared from public school classrooms.

From the colonial period onward, schools have espoused religious values using both teachers, who were to be models of morality, and schoolbooks, which boldly proselytized for Protestantism. The increasingly diverse society of the early twentieth century had caused the extremely pious McGuffey Readers to become less blatantly Christian—while still maintaining a highly moralistic tone—through a series of revised editions. But schoolbooks never became completely secularized—in fact, until the mid-twentieth century passages from the King James version of the Bible were still being read in public school classrooms—nor were they permitted to deviate from some central Christian beliefs. Censorship is not confined to the distant past: It occurs frequently today and for many of the same reasons. It has "increased dramatically since 1980," pushed by religious fundamentalists. Leaders of this movement recognize neither the concept nor the practice of academic freedom. As researcher Joan Delfattore asserts, fundamentalists saw—and continue to see—"public education" as "the enemy of Christian parents."[32]

Dictating what schoolbooks can and cannot contain attacks the heart of the educational process. "It is estimated . . . that 75 percent of the time elementary and secondary students are in classrooms and 90 percent of their time on homework is spent with text materials." Limitations placed on textbooks thus often are meant to limit the school curriculum. Much of what American children learn comes from these books. But concerns about ideology and religion govern their content, too often restricting their scope.

"America the Beautiful"

Textbooks are highly "political," according to sociologist Michael W. Apple, who believes intense "ideological pressures" are brought to bear on textbook writing and adoption. The result is a cleansed version of American history and society, especially in high school texts.[33] Researcher James W. Loewen condemns secondary social studies textbooks for their purposeful "misteaching of" American history. They deemphasize "controversial issues" and emphasize hagiography—great American heroes—avoid reflection and critical thinking, stress the memorization of facts, and focus on teaching "nationalism." "In sum, startling errors of omission and distortion mar American histories." History textbooks offer a bland, unblemished, and largely ethnocentric picture of American history, intent on "indoctrinating blind patriotism."[34]

"One Nation Under God"

Religious ideology has also been a powerful force in controlling the content of textbooks, as we have mentioned. The most publicized challenge, *Mozert v. Hawkins County Public Schools*, occurred in Tennessee and culminated in a 1986 state supreme court ruling. The issues in this case arose over an elementary reading series published in 1980. Some parents protested the inclusion of creative, science fiction stories in which characters communicated through mental telepathy and of stories with "minorities, foreigners, environmentalists, women in nontraditional roles, and open-ended value judgments without clear right and wrong answers." They also complained about stories in the readers that they interpreted as promoting gun control, globalism, vegetarianism, different religions, and peace over war. These parents also targeted *The Wizard of Oz* because it advanced "secular humanism" and "satanism." In sum, these religious fundamentalists refused to allow their children to stray from a literal interpretation of the Bible and its authority in all things and to use their imaginations and creative reasoning to consider and solve problems. Tennessee's high court ruled for the school district, but the plaintiffs ultimately won. The textbook publisher crumbled under the pressure of censorship and purged the "objectionable" material from the reading series in subsequent editions.

This and other judicial defeats caused fundamentalists across the nation to alter their strategies. They ran for school boards and won. As board directors, they could directly control the selection of classroom reading materials. A long list of literary classics were consequently banned. Delfattore reports: "John Steinbeck's novel *The Grapes of Wrath*, which was one of the most challenged books in American schools in the 1980s, was usually attacked for the use of profane language. It also presents capitalism in a negative light, and several groups of fundamentalist textbook activists have maintained that support for free enterprise is part of their religion." Christian fundamentalists challenged other textbooks. Science books that taught evolution and literary works that contained "profanity" or "sexual references" came under attack. A fundamentalist school superintendent in Florida banned classics like "Sophocles's *Oedipus Rex*; Chaucer's *Canterbury Tales*; Shakespeare's *Twelfth Night*, *The Merchant of Venice*, *King Lear*, and *Hamlet*," among other renowned works. Throughout the 1990s, censorship organizations attacked fairy tales, stories that contained "witches and ghosts," and anything that might be loosely interpreted as promulgating the "occult." Generally speaking, Delfattore says that such censorship campaigns "promote hostility between parents and the public schools. . . ."[35]

Business Is Good: Textbook Self-Censorship

How can we account for the successful control of school textbook content? Much of it can be explained as plain and simple business decisions. Textbook publishing, a highly competitive business, has a narrow profit margin. In order to sustain earnings, schoolbook publishers must be sensitive to their customers' demands. Twenty-three, mostly southern and western, states adopt textbooks on a statewide basis, and conservative Texas represents the largest single market. Together, these states wield undue influence over schoolbook content. "Since this is the case, the political and ideological climate of these primarily southern states often determines the content and form of the purchased curriculum throughout the rest of the nation."[36]

What You Don't Know Can't Hurt You

Like textbooks, the school curriculum has been circumscribed since colonial times. Through the nineteenth century, much of it dwelled on religious matters and there was little serious conflict. Even the gradual integration of secular knowledge, such as history and foreign languages, raised little controversy; however, scientific information did. Beginning in the early twentieth century, what constituted science in the public schools aroused extremely emotional and highly visible debates. Religious conservatives focused on Charles Darwin's theory of evolution. The battles over the teaching of his theory that followed seemed to be endless and continued into the twenty-first century.

Monkey Business

"In 1919, sixty years after the publication of *The Origin of the Species*, the World's Christian Fundamentals Association (WCFA) was formed to oppose the teaching of evolution in American public schools." Popular culture distorted Darwin's evolutionary theory into one of an oversimplified linear progression from apes to human beings. The WCFA lobbied many states to pass antievolution statutes, eventually known as "monkey laws." By the early 1920s, many school districts across the nation had restricted what teachers could say about evolution. In 1923, the state legislatures of Florida and Oklahoma passed antievolution laws forbidding its teaching in public schools. Tennessee's 1925 Butler Act stated: "it shall be unlawful for any [public school] teacher to teach any theory that denies the story of the Divine Creation of man as taught in the Bible, and to teach instead that man has descended from a lower order of animals." That same year Dayton, Tennessee, authorities arrested John Thomas Scopes, a first-year high school physics instructor and football coach, for his naive defense of the teaching of evolution. The 1914 text he used in class, *Civic Biology*, lumped humans in with the mammals. The American Civil Liberties Union defended him in one of the century's most notorious academic freedom cases, the Scopes trial or "monkey trial." The national media sensationalized this case, and farcical atmosphere surrounded the trial. To boost its sagging economy, the town of Dayton promoted the twelve-day trial. The local court found Scopes guilty and the judge fined him $100; the state supreme court overturned the lower court's conviction. But Tennessee's antievolution law remained in effect; it was repealed only in 1967.[37]

The ambiguous decision in the Scopes trial did not resolve a fundamental question: "Did tax-supported schools have the right to teach children truths that controverted the beliefs of their parents?"[38] Thus, not for the first time, as we have seen, the basic educational institutions of family and public school clashed over values. The very same confrontation occurred again forty years later. Following Tennessee's monkey trial, Arkansas had also passed an antievolutionary resolution, in 1928. This statute remained in effect until 1968 when the federal Supreme Court overturned it. During the 1965–66 school year, the Little Rock School District adopted a biology textbook that included evolution. Susan Epperson, a tenth-grade biology instructor at Central High School, fearing that she would be fired for teaching evolution, filed suit, "seeking a declaration that the Arkansas statute is void. . . . " The lower court ruled in her favor; on appeal the Arkansas Supreme Court decided for the state. The case ultimately reached the U.S. Supreme Court in 1968, and the Court ruled that the law was unconstitutional: "Government in our democracy, state and national, must be neutral in matters of religious theory, doctrine, and practice. It may not be hostile to any religion or to the advocacy of no-religion; and it may not aid, foster, or promote one religion or religious theory against another or even against the militant opposite."[39]

Nevertheless, the debate over evolution continued. The banning of school prayers gave rise to the Creation Research Society in 1963, which was founded to promote creation science. As late as 1967, prior to its repeal, Tennessee's Butler Act was used against teacher Gary L. Scott. "In 1974, Tennessee lawmakers required equal emphasis be given in biology texts for various theories or origins. The alternatives, in particular, meant the Genesis account. Arkansas and Louisiana enacted similar legislation in 1981." The revival of religious fundamentalism in the 1980s and 1990s caused the teaching of evolution to once again come under attack—with President Ronald Reagan's endorsement. In 1998, at least seven, mostly southern, states did not include the teaching of evolution in their science curriculum guidelines.[40]

"I Don't Think We're in Kansas Anymore"

In 1999, the Kansas state school board expunged evolution from the required science curriculum and adopted instead creationism. Religious proponents of creationism argued that human evolutionary theory was based on conjecture rather than evidence. They also opposed the "big-bang" theory of the creation of the universe on the grounds that it had no provable scientific basis and that fossil records failed to substantiate evolutionary development. Creationists argued against evolution as a "state-sanctioned theory of origins that is taught in the textbooks and classrooms of American public schools," and that the "misguided duty" of "elite" evolutionists "is to indoctrinate students in evolutionary theory while protecting them from error." "Atheism," to them, was nothing more than an extension of evolution. In sum, evolution "is bad science, bad education and a violation of the academic and religious freedom of both teachers and students."[41]

In Kansas, faith triumphed over empiricism; religious beliefs were equated with scientific evidence. From a legal point of view, the Kansas school board's action violated the

Constitutional separation between religion and the state by basing what was taught in its public schools on religious absolutism instead of scientific knowledge. This debate over scientific knowledge versus religious beliefs is neither isolated nor new. Voters in Kansas ousted the creation science advocates from the state school board in 2000 and so reversed the decision, but the situation in Kansas was not unique: Eighteen other states in 2000 either ignored the theory of evolution or relegated it to a minor part of the science curriculum.[42] Thus, some 150 years after the publication of Darwin's groundbreaking work, the controversy over evolution continues.

The relationship among families, religion, and schools has undergone profound change. During the colonial period, these institutions seemed to be tightly intertwined, and their close connection resulted in a consensus on what was to be taught in school. At the dawning of the twenty-first century, these three social institutions seemed to be bogged down in strident, and at times apparently irreconcilable, conflict. Serious and fundamental epistemological questions thus remain unresolved. Should schools merely transmit knowledge and values from one generation to the next, maintaining an intellectual stasis? Or should schools be providing a learning environment in which children can engage new ideas and different perspectives, preparing them for a changing world?

SCHOOL CRISES?

The American public schools have continuously operated in an environment of crisis and contradiction. We have seen how American society historically has appointed its schools to solve social problems and, at the same time, condemned them for failing its children. The very foundation of the public schools rested on the perception that there were serious social, economic, and political problems that had to be addressed. Horace Mann and other school reformers complained that America's families were failing to meet their educational responsibilities and believed that the existing private and quasi-public schools could not shoulder the responsibility. Again, during the Progressive era, reformers criticized both the family and the schools for not properly preparing children for an increasingly diverse and industrialized society. In the last half of the twentieth century, educational philosophies oscillated between conservatism and liberalism, inciting the public, frustrating parents, and bewildering educators.

The End of Progressive Education

Sustained and effective attacks on Progressive educational philosophy and practice started in earnest during the late 1940s. A number of critical studies began to appear: Bernard Iddings Bell, *Crisis in Education: A Challenge to American Complacency* (1949); Mortimer Smith, *And Madly Teach: A Layman Looks at Public School Education* (1949) and *The Diminished Mind: A Study of Planned Mediocrity in Our Public Schools* (1954); Albert Lynd, *Quackery in the Public Schools* (1953); Robert Hutchins, *The Conflict in Education* (1953); and Paul Wooding, *Let's Talk Sense about Our Schools* (1953). Generally speaking, these books assailed the schools for lacking a clear intellectual focus, which created ill-prepared students. Incompetent teachers were blamed for the crisis. The critics, mostly academics, called for broad reforms that would stress basic skills and academic excellence as well as rigorous teacher training. Of all of the detractors, "it was Bestor whose attacks were destined to exert the most telling impact on the progressivist movement."[43] In his 1953 *Educational Wastelands: The Retreat from Learning in Our Public Schools,* Arthur Bestor condemned Progressive education for stressing teaching methods instead of academic substance, bemoaned the lack of rigorous intellectual education, and ridiculed teacher training. Bestor advocated traditional liberal arts subjects, upheld the goal of a "disciplined mind," supported the reorganization of teacher education, called for high academic standards, and demanded intense examinations of all students.[44]

Blaming Progressive education for educational deficiencies, however, was not founded on fact. The Progressive philosophy was not as widespread as many believed. Throughout the twentieth century, teachers had only rarely implemented student-centered methods, especially at the secondary level, and most school administrators gave them only superficial support. Consequently, classroom instructors often resorted to conventional, teacher-centered methods, even though Progressive education proved to be effective where it took root. The famous Eight-Year Study, conducted between 1932 and 1940, found that college students who had graduated from such "experimental" high schools outperformed their traditionally trained peers. The outbreak of World War II had unfortunately distracted public attention from the report's findings.

The Commies are Coming

The Soviet Union's launching of Sputnik in 1957 seemed to confirm the sorry state of American schooling to its critics. In spite of evidence to the contrary, they claimed that the United States school system had lost the technological race to the Soviets, and they blamed Progressive educational philosophy for this supposed defeat. Supporters' response was anemic—the Progressive Education Association folded that same year.[45] In sum, by the 1950s, the schools were deemed too liberal and failing in the attempt to prepare our children for the Cold War and the life-and-death ideological and technological global struggle with the Soviet Union.

Ironically, tracking, an offshoot of the Progressive education movement, was recommended as the way to challenge academically able students. In 1958, Vice Admiral Hyman G. Rickover published *Education and Freedom,* which attacked the mediocrity of public education and argued that the sorry state of affairs ultimately threatened national security because the United States was losing the technological race with the USSR. He blamed "professional educators" for this impending disaster. Unlike Bestor though, Rickover called for increased sorting of students by ability level; he proposed the development of "an intellectual elite." This "aristocracy of talent" would save the nation.

James B. Conant's 1959 work, *The American High School Today,* also supported the concept of sorting students by ability. To provide more resources to those with the greatest ability, he encouraged school consolidation. Conant's goal was to train the top 10 percent of America's students exceptionally well. The public schools would sort out the most gifted students through such objective means as IQ tests and allocate a large proportion of resources to their education. This elite group would become the intellectual leaders of the country. To maintain the illusion of a "democratic community," Conant recommended that such streaming occur within a comprehensive high school, which would allow for the superficial mixing of students of different ability.[46] Those students who were not being prepared for higher education would be trained for work. As Conant noted two years after the publication of *The American High School Today*, "two-thirds of the male dropouts did not have jobs and about half of the high school graduates did not have jobs." High schools needed to prepare students for work. Sidney Marland, United States Commissioner of Education, became a leading proponent of career education. A student's entire twelve-year career, he persuasively reasoned in 1971, should be marked by a single purpose: preparation for work. This approach would permeate the K–12 curriculum and drive students' course choices at the secondary level.[47]

Thus, instead of promoting intellectual growth and exploration, learning for the sake of learning, and education as self-fulfillment, the educational process was to serve the need for human capital, either military and strategic or economic. In doing so, the system would come up against the fundamental democratic ideal of freedom. Schooling, in the end, became merely a means to advance the nation's needs or secure a job. American children became human capital.

Schooling Is Too Rigid

During the following decade, liberal critics took aim at the harshness, sterility, and rigidity of the overly academic schooling that resulted from Conant's and others' reforms. Liberal authorities denounced the schools for providing environments not conducive to learning and a pedagogy that stifled creativity and thinking; schools were, in short, too traditional. Charles Silberman's 1970 critique *Crisis in the Classroom: The Remaking of American Education* attacked the conservative reforms of the 1950s and early 1960s. "They placed almost all emphasis on subject matter, i.e., on creating 'great compositions,' and for the most part ignored the needs of individual children."

Silberman's study examined the purposes of public education as well as its teaching methods and curriculum. He generally saw schools as "grim, joyless places," having "oppressive and petty rules," and characterized them as "intellectually sterile and esthetically barren" and "uncivil," breeding "contempt for children." He catalogued the public school's main ailments. Unequal schooling topped his list. Teachers treated affluent students better than poor ones and maintained different expectations for each group. Race and ethnicity were also factors in this unequal treatment. This attitude generated a "self-fulfilling prophecy." Next, Silberman targeted the social control function of schooling. In his view, schools were committed to socializing children instead of liberating them intellectually and socially. "The most important characteristic schools share in common is a preoccupation with order and control." Thus, schools were oppressive environments. In order to progress and ultimately succeed, students had "to subordinate" their "own interests and desires to those of the teachers." Silberman particularly criticized the heavy use of multiple-choice tests at all levels, which required rote memorization and regurgitation and discouraged retention or meaningful learning, as part of this environment of control and intellectual sterility.

Silberman called for an open approach, an "informal classroom" that would focus on humanistic concerns. Intellectual development would follow naturally. To support his claims, he invoked John Dewey's work as well as contemporary English examples of open schooling. These classrooms fostered cooperative, active learning and placed heavy emphasis on kinesthetics. "Flexibility" was a key concept. Silberman described American classrooms that used informal methods. The elementary classrooms included learning centers where students, either in groups or individually, could study writing, science, reading, spelling, and mathematics. Self-directed, children in these classrooms were busy learning, with teachers assisting small groups and individuals. Instructors also worked in teams and classrooms combined different age groups. In secondary classrooms, independent study allowed students to pursue interests in a concentrated, subject-centered manner. Students also pursued their studies using resources outside of the school classroom.[48] In sum, Silberman attacked the authoritarian, curriculum-based approach and promoted a democratic, learner-centered ideal.

In 1969, Neil Postman and Charles Weingartner published *Teaching As a Subversive Activity*, a book that was part of the liberal critique of schooling typical of that era. Taking a quasi-Progressive education perspective, these authors wanted schooling to become relevant and meaningful, attuned to the speed and complexity of social change. Postman and Weingartner attacked the existing curriculum as constricting, abstract, and provincial and the reduction of knowledge to nothing more than trivia; they criticized the assembly-line environment of schools, assailed the teacher-centered approach that made students passive memorizers, and deplored the school's insistence on intellectual conformity. They advocated instead teaching that promoted active thinking and problem solving; they wanted students to challenge the intellectual canon. To achieve this goal, they called upon schools and teachers to banish textbooks, integrate the curriculum, and eliminate all tests and grades. Schools should be centers of learning, focusing on students' intellectual growth.[49]

Schooling Is Not Rigorous Enough

By the time of the nation's bicentennial, conservative critics were attacking American public schools for declining standardized test scores and ignoring the "basics." These criticisms gained momentum, achieving focus and legitimacy in the 1983 U.S. Department of Education report *A Nation At Risk: The Imperatives for Educational Reform*, which was issued by the Reagan administration. It comprehensively damned the public schools: ". . . the educational foundations of our society are presently being eroded by a rising tide of mediocrity that threatens our very future as a Nation and as a people. . . . If an unfriendly power had attempted to impose on America the mediocre educational performance that exists today, we might well have viewed it as an act of war." The report expressed alarm at falling standardized test scores, bemoaned the absence of high academic standards, denounced the curriculum as dilated, and accused teachers of being ill prepared, incompetent, and unmotivated. It claimed that the scores on the Scholastic Aptitude Test (SAT) had steadily declined since 1963 and that science and math skills had eroded generally. The report devoted a great deal of attention to secondary education. It criticized soft electives, like cooking and driver's education, and recommended more rigorous academic studies, like math and foreign languages. Furthermore, school textbooks had been "dumbed down" and teachers assigned too little homework. Teacher-bashing was the final component of this picture of school failure: "Too many teachers are being drawn from the bottom quarter of graduating high school and college students." Poor training by mediocre colleges of education only compounded the problem; insufficient teacher compensation meant that the trend would continue. This nation was simply not attracting the brightest and best to teach its children. The report concluded that the public schools failed to adequately instruct children to face a more demanding, competitive, and technological world, and ultimately these poorly prepared workers impaired America's ability to compete with such economic powerhouses as Japan and Germany: "What was unimaginable a generation ago has begun to occur—others are matching and surpassing our educational attainments." A failing public school system explained our poor economic performance and relegated us to second-rate status as a nation. Only a completely reformed school system, or a totally new one, would graduate better trained and more productive workers to ensure this country's economic superiority.[50]

This report unleashed a series of other high-profile studies, among them Ernest Boyer's *High School: A Report on Secondary Education in America* (1983) and Theodore Sizer's *Horace's Compromise: The Dilemma of the American High School* (1984), which focused on deficiencies at the secondary level. Others, like John Goodlad's *A Place Called School: Prospects for the Future* (1983), provided a comprehensive overview of troubled American schools. E. D. Hirsch in *Cultural Literacy* (1987) and Allan Bloom in *The Closing of the American Mind* (1987) eulogized the demise of Western culture among American youth. William Bennett, Secretary of Education in the Reagan administration, labeled the Chicago public school system as this country's worst when he visited that city in 1987. Collectively, these critics painted a grim picture of America's public schools. The media uncritically sensationalized these attacks.

Relentless and organized conservative criticism continued through the 1990s, eroding the credibility of the public schools. Conservative detractors labeled the public schools a monopoly. They opposed additional funding, claiming that the "educational establishment" wasted it, and touted the successes of private schooling. They offered school vouchers as the only solution. Vouchers would introduce the efficiencies of the free-market system. They would destroy public school dominance and permit parents to actively participate in their children's schooling and to demand quality schools, which would force both public and private schools to compete for money, in terms of vouchers, and thereby improve education. These critics, in short, wanted, at worst, to dismantle the American public school system or, at best, fundamentally alter its functions.[51] This stance begs the question: Is the American public education system that poor?

Are the Public Schools Failing?

Accusations about the collapse of the public schools and appeals for school improvement appeared to be ideologically driven. In their 1995 study *The Manufactured Crisis: Myths, Frauds, and the Attack on America's Public Schools*, David C. Berliner and Bruce J. Biddle offer both a very different and provocative perspective. They contend that there has been an organized campaign of unsubstantiated claims; few of the critical reports ever supplied supporting evidence of the decline in America's public schools. In some cases, a barefaced and systematic "disinformation campaign" had been used.

The Manufactured Crisis was not an accidental event. Rather, it appeared within a specific historical context and was led by identifiable critics whose political goals could be furthered by scapegoating educators. It was also supported from its inception by an assortment of questionable techniques—including misleading methods for analyzing data, distorting reports of findings, and suppressing contradictory evidence. Moreover, it was tied to misguided schemes for "reforming" education—schemes that would, if adopted, seriously damage American schools.

Berliner and Biddle supply evidence to refute the critics' charges and make the following conclusions, among others, about American schooling and education in general: (1) "Standardized test data reveal *no* recent drop in student achievement," and, in fact, "indicate modest recent *gains*." (2) Students are not dumber. "The number of students expected to have IQs of 130 or higher—a typical cutoff point for defining giftedness in many school districts throughout the nation—is now about *seven* times greater than it was for the generation now retiring from leadership positions in the country and often complaining about the poor performance of today's youth." (3) American school students compete quite well on an international basis. This issue has been obfuscated. Either the statistical basis of these comparisons of standardized test scores has been faulty, or positive information has been suppressed. (4) Americans *are* satisfied with the public schools. Seventy-two percent of parents assign their local schools an "A" or "B" grade. (5) Private schools are not inherently superior to public schools. In many cases, public school standardized test scores are higher than private ones. In sum, Department of Education bureaucrats and other politicians, according to Berliner and Biddle, have buried or distorted studies, such as the Sandia Report, that substantially refute negative analyses of the state of American schooling.

Given these counterarguments and opposing data, why have the public schools been so vilified? Why has this program of disinformation unfolded? Berliner and Biddle offer some compelling answers. First, many politicians, often private school graduates themselves and whose children are enrolled in them, feel no loyalty to the concept of public education. They have attacked the public schools to distract the American public from their political shortcomings or failure to address serious domestic social problems. As we have seen, schools and teachers have historically served as scapegoats. Second, Presidents Reagan and Bush (1988–1992) went along with the desires of influential and powerful "business leaders" who wanted the schools to educate and train a workforce for them at no charge. The third, and most insidious, motive was profits. Public school districts typically have multimillion dollar budgets and oversee extensive facilities. These publicly subsidized assets could earn significant profits if private corporations were to take control of them. While educational quality and children's welfare would be paid lip service, public schools could be exploited for profit paid for by taxpayers' money.[52]

Other studies demonstrate that the American public schools are succeeding quite well, under the circumstances. Gerald Bracey, for example, has published several articles that both refute critics' charges of school failure and report on public school successes. He points out that high school graduation is at an "all-time high." Furthermore, SAT scores have not plummeted: "In the past decade, the number of scorers above 650 on the SAT has grown on both the verbal section and the math one." Bracey also sheds light on the educational structure and process in other countries to explain why some differences in educational achievement may exist as well as to defend American educational performance. On the one hand, countries like Korea and Japan have school years of 220 and 243 days, respectively. The United States averages only 180 days. A longer school year implies, of course, a greater financial commitment to education. This society simply does not fund its schools adequately. At best, U.S. education rates average compared to other countries and at worst "places near the bottom." On the other hand, we outstrip other countries in providing educational opportunities. China has yet to institute universal elementary education, and both Great Britain and Germany assign their students to tracks at early ages. "Currently, 68 percent of college-aged students are enrolled in postsecondary institutions. This is double the rate of Japan and Germany and triple the rate for the United Kingdom."[53] These data are not intended to be chauvinistic or to disparage the education efforts of other nations. Little can be gained from taking that approach. They simply offer a very different, and perhaps more balanced, perspective from which to conduct an honest debate over educational policies and the state of American public education.

Family Values

Some politicians and pundits have blamed so-called school failure, and America's social ills in general, on the decline of the American family. This argument, too, has been exaggerated or distorted. There is an illusion that the family of the vague past was a model of virtue that we have drifted away from and that today's social and education problems and crises are due to the poor condition of the modern family. If this society can only find its way back to the structure and function of the ideal American family, critics argue, then all difficulties will be solved. If we fail, then America is doomed. Thus, a simple return to "family values," whatever they may be, is the sure and simple answer to all problems. But many studies have directly challenged both the purported domestic crisis and the myth of the ideal American family of the past. As researcher Stephanie Coontz states, "our recurring search for a traditional family model denies the diversity of family life, both past and present, and leads to false generalizations about the past as well as wildly exaggerated claims about the present and future."[54]

Separate Spheres?

The nostalgic myth of the American family centers on a cohesive, nuclear unit with a paternal working parent. This ideal was part of the model of the cult of domesticity that became prevalent around the mid-1800s. As we have seen, the model was rarely achieved and only existed in affluent families who could afford the luxury of a "stay-at-home" wife and mother. In time, even this became nothing more than a stereotype: ". . . in the years following World War II, many women were not white, middle-class, married, and suburban; and many white, middle-class, married, suburban women were neither wholly domestic or quiescent."[55] As we found in our earlier historical analysis, in too many cases, women and children whether native-born or immigrant, had to work to ensure the very survival of the family, Native American families had to surrender their children to government authorities, African American families had to withstand the atrocities of slavery and then discrimination, and Asian American families had to face incredible prejudice. In the case of Japanese

American families, they even faced the horrors of concentration camps. Where then was the "ideal" American family? What were *the* "family values?" Was the American family really "better" in the past?

Even the decade of the 1950s, the purported golden-era of families, the period idolized in television shows like *Father Knows Best*, *Ozzie and Harriet*, and *Leave It to Beaver*, in numerous ways was a "deviant decade," according to Coontz's interpretation. Except for that decade, many characteristics of the American family have actually changed very little. "Today's diversity of family forms, rates of premarital pregnancy, productive labor of wives, and prevalence of blended families, for example, would all look much more familiar to colonial Americans than would the 1950's patterns."[56] What was behind this aberration in the structure and role of the family during this decade? What accounts for the "in-between generation" who married and raised families during the 1950s, embraced "traditional" gender roles, and bucked the historical pattern?

"Those who came of age during and after World War II were the most marrying generation on record: 96.4 percent of the women and 94.1 percent of the men." Birthrates also reached unprecedented heights. The phenomenon unfolded over several decades and reflected the economic insecurity of the Great Depression, the threat of national obliteration during World War II, the horror of atomic cataclysm during the 1950s, the intense conformity demanded by an expanding corporate world, and the ongoing pressures of materialism and consumerism. These new conditions dictated a unique institutional response; that is, once again the family adapted to a challenging situation. Individuals felt vulnerable and insecure, so they created and maintained families like never before to act as a fortress to fend off a terrifying, overwhelming, and alienating reality. It represented a defensive strategy on the part of individuals to shield themselves from a new and unsure world. This experience did not represent an inherent part of American culture.[57]

Mrs. June Cleaver, the quintessential wife/mother symbol in *Leave It to Beaver*, did not succumb to the lures of the new feminist movement, as we saw in Chapter 10. Feminism did not represent an antifamily force, nor did it serve as the impetus for the growing number of working wives and mothers. Betty Friedan's 1963 book *The Feminist Mystique* certainly influenced women's perspectives, but it was not the cause of the reemergence of the campaign for female equality. As historian Joanne Meyerowitz points out, the foundation for this most recent upsurge was laid during the 1950s, for that decade did not necessarily represent a period of conservative, traditional feminine values.[58]

The typical image of the 1950s invokes affluence, families, security, confidence, and a placid time when everyone seemed to be content. It was supposedly the era of white, middle-class America: the ideal, comfortable family living blissfully in the clean suburbs, owning one or two cars, barbecuing in the neat, well-manicured backyard, and parenting well-behaved and respectful children. In reality, it was a complex and enigmatic decade, a period of tremendous economic and social change: "from production to consumption, from saving to spending, from city to suburb, from blue- to white-collar employment, and from an adult to a youth culture." And by the late 1950s and early 1960s, the supposedly safe, secure, and tranquil domestic life of middle-class America began to show signs of stress. Homophobia abounded; parents fretted over the declining authority they seemed to wield over their teenagers; society fixated on juvenile delinquency; communists appeared to be everywhere; and everyone feared an atomic holocaust. American society, according to sociologist Wini Breines, appeared to be committed to containing not only foreign aggression but domestic change, constricting women's roles, segregating African Americans, and suppressing youthful independence; conformity proved to be the rule of the day.

A number of studies of women relegated to being wives and mothers reported dissatisfaction; women increasingly sought psychiatric help in order to cope with their lives. The family, supposedly a source of happiness, was a source of a great deal of frustration for them. They felt trapped, with no other choices, and they repressed these feelings of discontent. Women felt unfulfilled; their joy was supposed to be found in providing comfort for their husbands and in his professional success, the raising of their children, and the appearance of their homes. Females were also supposed to smother their sexual drives and suppress their dreams of achievement. Middle-class women therefore were to have limited aspirations. Boys went to college; girls simply graduated from high school. Parents did not want their daughters to be too smart, that is, "geniuses" or "brains." If they were, they would become social outcasts, misfits, "old maids."[59]

In fact, Mrs. Cleaver did not exist. She was a fictitious wife and mother in a make-believe television program who lived in a contrived nuclear family in a nonexistent house surrounded by the proverbial white picket fence that was fabricated on a studio lot. When and where she existed in reality was an exception in American life, a rare and fleeting phenomenon in the long span of American history, and she did not necessarily stand for domestic perfection. Hence, attacks on the decline of the family and the poor academic performance of children that resulted from the absence of mothers in the home are unfounded, if not distorted.

The father's role during the 1950s did not appear to be ideal either. The growth of the suburbs and the "cult of success" that offered social status and mobility caused fathers to work further away from their homes—to the extent that they almost led separate lives. They became, as a result, weekend parents. "Since such fathers spent so little time at home, they could not acquire savvy and skills in 'domestic employments.'" "Patterns" of fatherhood have changed markedly, as we have seen, and they will assuredly continue to change. Historian John Demos remarks, "[f]atherhood, as history reminds us, is a cultural invention."[60] As American society changes, so will the image and role of the father.

If indeed an educational crisis exists in this nation's schools, it cannot be blamed on the sudden collapse of the American family. The American family of the past, generally speaking, was, according to Coontz, no better than its modern counterpart. We have lost the benefit of historical perspective. The modern American family is just as cohesive, if not more so, as it always has been. The modern divorce rate in the United States is often criticized for corroding the very foundation of the nation, but this country has had the highest divorce rate in the world since colonial times. It is true that divorce rates increased through the first half of the twentieth century, but much of this was due to women opting out of marriage because of cruelty. It is also true that by the early 1980s this country had a 50 percent rate of divorce. Nevertheless, throughout the twentieth century, the United States continued to prosper and in spite of major wars and economic turmoil.

Furthermore, families have never provided better care for children. "As late as 1940, 10 percent of American children did not live with either parent, compared with only one in twenty-five today." Prior to the 1920s, child support did not exist; divorced fathers simply had no legal financial obligations toward their children. In addition, the incidence of child abuse was far worse in the past.[61] The mistreatment of children, as Demos reminds us, has always existed and has been most prevalent during the "past two or three centuries," although actual historical records reach back only about 150 years. From these records it is clear that social and economic upheavals, that is, economic dependence, depersonalization, and alienation arising from the introduction of industrial production, growth of urbanization, implementation of the assembly line, and the rise of corporate bureaucracies, have created the conditions for abuse. It is also clear that society now sees such treatment of children as an outrage, rather than as a common parenting practice.[62] Thus, the modern American family appears to be an improvement over its antecedents. Its current failures to completely fulfill its responsibilities reflect society's lack of will to provide the institutional support it needs.

Home Sweet Home

Can the modern family solve all child-raising and educational problems? The current record is not promising. One in seven Americans claims to have been sexually abused as a child; one in six were physically abused. Ten percent of newborns are exposed to some kind of illicit drug. The United States maintains the worst vaccination rate in the Western hemisphere except for Bolivia and Haiti. According to the U.S. Surgeon General, women face more danger at home because of spousal abuse than on city streets. Given this dubious record, should the inviolable right of families to control over their children be further strengthened? The claims that a conspiracy exists in which the "modern state" is attempting to control families are exaggerated. The nuclear family retains most of its autonomy and parental authority, as Coontz points out. "It is also clear, however, that a man's claim to absolute rule in his household is no longer accepted: the castle is not supposed to have a torture chamber." With new laws instituted during the 1960s, child and spousal abuse will not be tolerated as they were in the past.

In the final reckoning, compelling Americans to simply reembrace "family values" will not solve this society's serious social issues. This is a false hope, mere demagogic rhetoric, a placebo for real institution building, a smoke-and-mirrors approach to resolving serious and complex problems. These are society's challenges; they cannot be solved by the family or the public school system alone. Proposing such a hollow solution as "family values" may actually do more harm. As Coontz concludes, "[t]he problem is not to berate people for abandoning past family values, nor to exhort them to adopt better values in the future—the problem is to build better institutions and social support networks that allow people to act on their best values rather than on their worst ones." Although critics presume "that parents have primary control over how their children turn out," they do *not*. "The idea that there is one single blueprint for parents to follow, one family form that always produces well-adjusted children, or one 'normal' set of family arrangements and interactions is not true now and never has been." This is a powerful notion. The American family is not declining or failing, American society is not disintegrating, America's youth is not defective, and the public schools are not at their nadir.

Family issues and relationships have been terribly oversimplified. No one historical period hosted the ideal family—or school. Except for the overall long-term decrease in the birthrate, American families have rarely shared typical characteristics—in fact, families have been highly varied. And if the roles of individual members have changed, they have not necessarily done so for the worst. The family's educational role has certainly experienced some transformations, shifting this responsibility largely to the schools. Even so, the schools can do only so much given the resources available. Social and educational institutions never develop in a linear fashion reflecting steady progress and improvement or, for that matter, decline. Rather, as human creations, with human flaws and strengths, they change in accordance with social developments. As society grows more diverse, as work continues to change, these institutions will undergo even more transformations and increase in complexity.[63]

Education in the United States is neither in a "golden" era nor is it in the dire straights some detractors claim. The educational process is certainly in a state of flux—constantly so as we have seen. As society changes, so will its public schools and other educational institutions, like the family. The fundamental philosophical dilemma remains: Do the schools operate to preserve values and customs, or do the public schools exist to prepare students for change?

The emphasis of educational policy on educational excellence since the early 1980s has pushed into the shadows persistent and glaring educational inequalities. The unrelenting campaign for higher standardized test scores can be viewed as a subtle attack on school desegregation and bilingual education. The policy of promoting higher academic standards to the point of neglecting fundamental educational inequalities will surely result in failure.[64]

YOU GET WHAT YOU PAY FOR: SCHOOL FUNDING AND INEQUALITY

One thing is certain: "Educational deficits," where they exist, are due more to poverty than to failed schools or poor family values. This society seems to resist helping its poor children by providing well-financed, well-equipped, and well-functioning schools. As Coontz asserts, American society must "care" for "all" of its children.[65] However, we continue to face the enduring and complex issue of school funding. Equal educational opportunity, that is, providing educational excellence to all children, simply cannot exist while different amounts of money are spent on the schools. This problem stems from the tradition of subsidizing public education through local property taxes. If a community has high property values, then it can afford to devote more money to its children's schooling. If a community's real estate is valued low, then it is sharply restricted in what it can spend on its children's education.

Equalizing school funding represents the "most pressing civil rights issue facing the school systems. . . . "[66] Jonathan Kozol's poignant *Savage Inequalities*, which won wide acclaim, brought this issue to the public's attention. During the late 1980s, he visited schools in Illinois, New Jersey, New York, Ohio, and Texas and found different levels of funding and concomitant unequal school conditions. He described school conditions in some places that were akin to those in underdeveloped countries. In East St. Louis, Illinois, Kozol found extremely poor conditions. Perpetual sewage problems plagued East St. Louis Senior High School. Class sizes averaged thirty-five students, science laboratories were ill equipped, and teachers lacked rudimentary supplies like chalk and paper. The New York

City school district had converted a former skating rink into an elementary school; the classrooms were overcrowded and windowless. Worse, the district failed to supply enough textbooks for all of the students. The inequality Kozol discovered proved to be pervasive, and not only did too many African American and Latino/a schoolchildren suffer but poor white students did as well.[67] This is not a new social and educational issue.

As we saw in Chapter 10, the whole concept of equalizing school funding was relegated to the state level for litigation some thirty years ago. California's famous court case *Serrano v. Priest* (1971) was the first of such cases that were argued at the state level. The *Rodriguez* case, involving the San Antonio school district, followed. It went to the federal Supreme Court, which ruled in 1973 that there was no federal jurisdiction in school financing complaints, since education was "not among the rights explicitly protected by the federal Constitution." State constitutions did, however, contain clauses requiring "the legislatures to establish a 'uniform system of public schools' or to provide a 'thorough and efficient,' 'ample' or 'adequate' education. During the late twentieth century, plaintiffs won 15 of 22 major state court decisions." These included Montana (1989), Idaho (1993), Arizona (1994), New York (1995), Maryland (1996), Ohio (1997), and North Carolina (1997).[68] Nonetheless, public school financing remains significantly uneven throughout the country, thus denying equal educational opportunities to America's poor children.

THE CONTINUING STRUGGLE FOR THE PUBLIC SCHOOL IDEAL

This history of education textbook celebrates the ideal of the public school, the notion that there should be schooling for all of America's children, regardless of their physical, emotional, and intellectual abilities, their gender, and their ethnic, social-class, or racial backgrounds. Certainly flawed, suffering from the frailties typical of all human institutions, the public schools must be accessible to every child who appears at its doors.

As we have seen, this has not always happened. In fact, by this point, this interpretation of the history of education has either disillusioned you or inspired you. In the former case, the public schools appear on the surface to have failed miserably. They remain largely segregated and unequal. In too many instances they have restricted opportunities rather than expanded them. The concept of the value of diversity has remained fragile at best. And some school administrators and classroom teachers seem to be either incompetent or unprofessional. However, we must remember history's lessons. As a social institution, the public schools reflect society's values. If equality of opportunity fails in society at large, then how can we expect it to flourish at school? If society is intolerant, then why should the schools be any different? And finally, if society undervalues educators while assigning them more and more responsibilities and continues to be stingy with funding, then why should "the best and the brightest" remain in education for very long, if they enter the classroom at all? The schools not only reflect society's values but serve as the battleground for some of its most bitter conflicts.

When, on the other hand, the public schools have become more equal, provided opportunities, encouraged tolerance, and welcomed creative and committed school personnel, it has been because of the long struggle, incredible sacrifice, and persistent vigilance of a variety of individuals and groups. Between 1988 and 1998, for example, preprimary enrollment (ages three through five) jumped from 34 to 51 percent. Enrollments at the elementary and secondary levels during that same period increased by 18 and 14 percent, respectively. Since 1980, the public schools have expanded services to special needs children and now accommodate 13 percent of them. While school consolidation has grown, the student–instructor ratio has dropped from 22.3 in 1970 to 16.8 in 1998. The academic achievement gaps between African American and Latino/a students and their European American counterparts has narrowed somewhat since 1970, and the same can be said for achievement differences between female and male students.[69] A greater number of children than ever have access to schooling, school personnel have never been more qualified, and the participation of the schools in critical social debates certainly has been a function, in some cases, of efforts, to change prevailing biases and challenge the status quo. Therefore, reality has not always matched the ideal of education, but the ideal is worth the struggle. And much remains to be done.

In some ways, the future looks grim for public education. In this era of educational fads and quick fixes, like vouchers, privatization, and standardized tests, largely dictated by a business mentality, the whole concept of public education is threatened. The influence of corporate business values on the schools throughout the twentieth century has harmed children more often than it has helped them. In the 1920s, business efficiency theories and practices placed financial costs above the educational and social needs of children. As the century wore on, schools imbued with such business values regimented children in dehumanized warehouselike settings, stressed conformity, subordinated teachers, and marginalized parents and the local community. By mid-century, corporations exploited children as a commercial market, and they continue to do so, manipulating their values and outlooks for sheer profit. Business was incredibly-successful in training children to be insatiable and eager consumers. By the end of the twentieth century, it had crept indirectly and directly into the classroom. The guns that children have used to shoot each other were sources of profit to corporations and gun dealers. And America's media assisted in the violence by introducing it to children through movies, television, and video games. Tens of thousands of students begin their school day as captive and passive viewers of television programs, replete with commercials hawking products, in their very classrooms. The values that such economic activity represents—conformity rather than individuality, competition rather than cooperation, greed over sharing, and consumption rather than preservation—stifle rather than encourage debate, undermine the basic notions of democracy, and attack the very heart of our country's unique political foundation—capitalism, it seems, has triumphed over republicanism.

Vouchers, which commodify education; privatization, which sees education as another source of profits; and accountability, which threatens academic freedom, will not fulfill the promise of "free" schooling. Voucher proponents, assuming a free-market philosophy, claim that schools would improve by competing with one another for customers, much like car manufacturers. But can children test drive their education? Privatization supporters see schooling as a source of profit, one that would use revenue in a more efficient manner, with less waste. But who could afford the luxury model? The mid-size? The compact version? Standardized test disciples see objective, scientifically based scores as a way of ensuring quality, that is, as a measure of successful schooling and particularly teaching. But how long does the "warranty" last? One year? Five years? Twelve years? Or a lifetime? Worse yet, standardized tests stress memorization and regurgitation, not the critical thinking that challenges the status quo, not the analytical reasoning that feeds intellectual growth.

Can a public education system continue to survive in such a climate? Can a vital democratic culture endure? We cannot afford to sacrifice the public school ideal; we must work to improve it, learning from the efforts of those who preceded us. Too much is at stake.

ACTIVITIES FOR FURTHER EXPLORATION

1. How will twenty-first-century European Americans perceive Chinese immigrants? The historical record is not encouraging. The nineteenth-century Chinese immigrant experience has received little attention in our school textbooks. To gain firsthand, and various, perspectives see " 'Rock Springs is Killed': White Reaction to the Rock Springs Riot," " 'To This We Dissented': The Rock Springs Riot," and "Fair's Fair: McDonnell Argues for Acceptance of Aliens" at http://chnm.gmu.edu/us/many.taf.

2. For the full text of the *Lau* and *Rodriguez* cases, see the following Web site: http://supct.law.cornell.edu/supct/cases/name.htm.

3. What are the pros and cons of bilingual education? How does it fit into the multicultural education agenda? How does the English-only school curriculum enacted in California affect the future of bilingual education?

4. How can you as an educator cope with school violence? A wide selection of web sites provides further insight into this issue; see, for example, the National Center for Education Statistics: http://pde.org/resources.htm. The "Gun-Free Schools Act of 1994" can be found at http://www.lrp.com/ed/freelib/free_state/bu20892.htm. And the American Psychological Association provides a list of "warning signs": http://pde.org/resources.htm.

5. Are smaller school settings better? If so, for whom? If not, why?

6. For a classroom instructor, where is the line between censorship and academic freedom? Refer to the Web site: http://www.ala.org/bbooks and review the list of banned books compiled by the American Library Association as you ponder this question.

7. When did the feminist movement begin? And what do we learn in school about it? The women's movement has a long and rich history. Abortion rights and birth control have been integral parts of this ongoing campaign and shed a different light on the role of women and the traditional concept of families. This is not a new issue. For example, either read or listen to "A Woman Recounts Her Twelve Abortions in Turn-of-the-[Twentieth] Century New York" and review " 'A Less Reliable Form of Birth Control': Miriam Allen deFord Describes Her Introduction to Contraception in 1914" and " 'I Limited My Own Family': Memoir of a 1920s Birth Control Activist." Voting rights was another crucial issue, not easily accepted by some, see "More Logic, Less Feeling: Senator Vest Nixes Woman Suffrage" and, for an opposing view, "Suffrage On Stage: Marie Jenney Howe Parodies the Opposition." All of these original documents can be found at http://chnm.gmu.edu/us/many.taf.

8. Will Americans pay more for better schooling? Interview classmates, parents, and grandparents to compile a response to this question.

9. What drives educational policy? Educational philosophy/theory or finances? Write a brief response to this question.

10. What is the function of public schooling? Has your view changed since you first answered this question in Chapter 1?

VIDEO EXPLORATIONS

1. What subjects and materials should be included in the public school curriculum? The first part of the video *Battle Over the Books: Censorship in American Schools* (Princeton, NJ: Films for the Humanities, 1994) generates discussion and debate about the conflict of values in the public schools and the restriction of reading material. It also links nicely to Professor Joan Delfattore's research findings in *What Johnny Shouldn't Read: Textbook Censorship in America* (New Haven, CT: Yale University Press, 1992). The American Library Association maintains an updated list of banned books at its Web site: http://www.ala.org/bbooks. In addition to the banning of a variety of books, many communities have proscribed any material dealing with homosexuality. Homophobia has existed since the early years of the twentieth century. " 'No Snuggling!' Sex Talks to Young Girls," at http://chnm.gmu.edu/us/many.taf, reveals this long-standing sexual prejudice. After viewing the film and digesting the Web site document, separate into groups to define the limits, if any, of academic freedom in the classroom.

2. The video *Investigative Reports: Teenagers Under the Gun* (New York: Arts & Entertainment Television Network, 1996) provides background about school violence, its causes, solutions, civil rights abuses, and the media's sensationalization of this tragic experience.

3. Which is more important, academic standards or equality? Does the *Standardized Aptitude Test* ensure a meritocracy? The role of standardized tests undergoes an in-depth scrutiny, within the context of the demise of affirmative action, in a 'Frontline' special, "*Secrets of the SAT*" (Alexandria, VA: PBS Home Video, 1999). A Web site, wysiwyg://17http://www.pbs.org/wgbh/pages/frontline/shows/sats/, accompanies this video.

4. For a close look at the difference in the quality of schooling, see *Unequal Education* (Princeton, NJ: Films for the Humanities, 1994), a Bill Moyer PBS special. The first part focuses on Kozol's findings by videotaping the experiences of two students who attend two differently funded schools. The second part involves a debate between Jonathan Kozol and John Chubb, author of *Politics, Markets, and America's Schools*, over the school voucher issue. Although this video has a 1994 copyright, it remains quite useful for providing further, concrete insight into the consequences of unequal school funding as well as a summary of the debates over school vouchers.

NOTES AND SOURCES

In order to condense endnotes, the first work cited is the primary one, usually the source of any direct quotes. Subsequent references serve as supplementary, or additional, sources of paraphrased information and/or alternative historical interpretations.

1. Tamara Henry, "School Rolls Hit Record," *USA Today*, 22 August 2000, Sec. A, p. 1.
2. Sam Roberts, *Who We Are: A Portrait of America Based on the Latest U.S. Census* (New York: Times Books, 1993), pp. 62, 73, 81. Also, refer to Meyer Weinberg, *Asian-American Education: Historical Background and Current Realities* (Mahwah, NJ: Lawrence Erlbaum Associates, 1997), pp. 3, 63, 68, 76; Judith Lessow-Hurley, *The Foundations of Dual Language Instruction* (New York: Longman Press, 1990), p. 137.
3. Gary Orfield, Susan E. Eaton et al., *Dismantling Desegregation: The Quiet Reversal of Brown v. Board of Education* (New York: New Press, 1996), pp. 62, 63. Also see Angela L. Carrasquillo, *Hispanic Children and Youth in the United States: A Resource Guide* (New York: Garland Publishing, 1991), pp. 89–90.
4. Weinberg, *Asian-American Education*, p. 3.
5. H. M. Lai, "Chinese," in *Harvard Encyclopedia of American Ethnic Groups*, ed. Stephan Thernstrom (Cambridge, MA: Harvard University Press, 1980), pp. 218, 219; Weinberg, *Asian-American Education*, p. 3.
6. Leonard Dinnerstein and David M. Reimers, *Ethnic Americans: A History of Immigration* (New York: Harper & Row, 1988), pp. 63, 64, 65. Refer as well to Weinberg, *Asian-American Education*, p. 18; Lai, "Chinese," in *Harvard Encyclopedia*, ed. Stephan Thernstrom, p. 220; Dale R. Steiner, *Of Thee We Sing: Immigrants and American History* (San Diego, CA: Harcourt Brace Jovanovich, 1987), p. 149.
7. Lai, "Chinese," in *Harvard Encyclopedia*, ed. Stephan Thernstrom, p. 223.
8. Weinberg, *Asian-American Education*, pp. 18, 19, 21.
9. Lai, "Chinese," in *Harvard Encylopedia*, ed. Stephan Thernstrom, p. 225.
10. Weinberg, *Asian-American Education*, pp. 19, 22, 25, 26, 28. Also, see Lai, "Chinese," in *Harvard Encyclopedia*, ed. Stephan Thernstrom, pp. 226, 227.
11. Roberts, *Who We Are*, p. 82. Refer as well to Weinberg, *Asian-American Education*, p. 24.
12. Lai, "Chinese," in *Harvard Encyclopedia*, ed. Stephan Thernstrom, pp. 228, 229, 230. See also Joe R. Feagin, *Racial and Ethnic Relations* (Englewood Cliffs, NJ: Prentice-Hall, 1989), pp. 330–340.
13. David B. Tyack, *The One Best System: A History of American Urban Education* (Cambridge, MA: Harvard University Press, 1974), pp. 106, 107, 108. Also see Lessow-Hurley, *Foundations of Dual Language Instruction*, pp. 9, 10; Carrasquillo, *Hispanic Children and Youth in the United States*, p. 115.
14. The quotes in these paragraphs are from Lessow-Hurley, *Foundations of Dual Language Instruction*, p. 9, 10, 11, 109, 110, 113–114, 115. See as well Carrasquillo, *Hispanic Children and Youth in the United States*, p. 10; Jon Reyhner and Jeanne Eder, *A History of Indian Education* (Billings, MT: Eastern Montana College, 1989), p. 132.
15. The quotes in these paragraphs are from Reyhner and Eder, *History of Indian Education*, pp. 132, 133, 134, 135–136, 137.
16. Lessow-Hurley, *Foundations of Dual Language Instruction*, p. 127, 132–133, 136–137, 140.
17. Dolores Delgado Bernal, "Chicana/o Education from the Civil Rights Era to the Present," in *The Elusive Quest for Equality: 150 Years of Chicano/Chicana Education*, ed. Jose F. Moreno (Cambridge, MA: Harvard Educational Review, 1999), p. 98; the phrases are quoted on p. 97. Also see Loucas Petronicolos and William S. New, "Anti-Immigrant Legislation, Social Justice, and the Right to Equal Educational Opportunity," *American Educational Research Journal*, 36 (Fall 1999), pp. 374, 375, 377.
18. *Time*, 3 May 1999, pp. 20–52.
19. Ellis Cose, "The Prison Paradox," *Newsweek*, 13 November 2000, pp. 40–49.
20. The quotes and information in these paragraphs draw on Kathleen Bennett deMarrais and Margaret D. LeCompte, *The Way Schools Work: A Sociological Analysis of Education* (New York: Longman Press, 1999), p. 116. Refer as well to Stephanie Coontz, *The Way We Never Were: American Families and the Nostalgia Trap* (New York: Basic Books, 1992), pp. 2–3.

21. U.S. Secret Service National Threat Assessment Center and U.S. Department of Education, "Safe School Initiative: An Interim Report on the Prevention of Targeted Violence in Schools" (Washington, DC: National Threat Assessment Center, 2000), pp. 1, 2, 3, 5.

22. Richard J. Altenbaugh, David E. Engel, and Don T. Martin, *Caring About Kids: A Critical Study of Urban School Leavers* (London: Falmer Press, 1995), p. 162.

23. U.S. Secret Service National Threat Assessment Center and U.S. Department of Education, "Safe School Initiative," p. 4. Also see Bennett deMarrais and LeCompte, *The Way Schools Work*, p. 116.

24. Bennett deMarrais and LeCompte, *The Way Schools Work*, p. 116. Refer as well to U.S. Secret Service National Threat Assessment Center and U.S. Department of Education, "Safe School Initiative," p. 6.

25. U.S. Secret Service National Threat Assessment Center and U.S. Department of Education, "Safe School Initiative," p. 5.

26. *Time*, 19 March 2001, pp. 22–35.

27. The material in this section is taken from Richard J. Altenbaugh, ed., *The Teacher's Voice: A Social History of Teaching in Twentieth-Century America* (London: Falmer Press, 1992), pp. 60–61. The quote is from Willard Waller, *The Sociology of Teaching* (New York: Russell and Russell, 1932), p. 40. Howard K. Beale, *Are American Teachers Free? An Analysis of Restraints upon the Freedom of Teaching in American Schools* (New York: Charles Scribner's & Sons, 1936).

28. Beale, *Are American Teachers Free?*, pp. x, xi, xii–xiii, xiv, xvi, 785–791.

29. Willard S. Elsbree, *The American Teacher: Evolution of a Profession in a Democracy* (New York: American Book Co., 1939; rpt. Westport, CT: Greenwood Press, 1970), p. 543. Beale, *Are American Teachers Free?*, passim.

30. Beale, *Are American Teachers Free?*, pp. 211, 218, 223.

31. Elsbree, *The American Teacher*, pp. 535, 541–543.

32. Joan Delfattore, *What Johnny Shouldn't Read: Textbook Censorship in America* (New Haven, CT: Yale University Press, 1992), pp. 5, 19–20, 67.

33. Michael W. Apple, *Teachers and Texts: A Political Economy of Class and Gender Relations in Education* (New York: Routledge & Kegan Paul, 1986), pp. 82, 85.

34. James W. Loewen, *Lies My Teacher Told Me: Everything Your American History Textbook Got Wrong* (New York: New Press, 1995), pp. 2, 3, 4, 5, 9.

35. The quotes and information in these paragraphs are from Delfattore, *What Johnny Shouldn't Read*, pp. 14, 36–37, 46–48, 60, 77, 81, 82, 90, 91, 100–107, 109, 113, 168, 170, 171.

36. Apple, *Teachers and Textbooks*, pp. 91–92, 97, 98, 99. Also see Delfattore, *What Johnny Shouldn't Read*, pp. 89, 121, 138, 143, 147, 149, 153, 154, 155, 156.

37. Delfattore, *What Johnny Shouldn't Read*, pp. 91–92. Tennessee's antievolutionary law is quoted on p. 91 in Delfattore and on p. 45 in Lawrence A. Cremin, *American Education: The Metropolitan Experience, 1876–1980* (New York: Harper & Row, 1988). Cremin treats the entire Scopes case in great detail, pp. 44–49. Refer as well to Edward Caudill's overview in *The Scopes Trial: A Photographic History* (Knoxville, TN: University of Tennessee Press, 2000), pp. 1, 2, 5–6, 7, 18, 19; Constance Areson Clark, "Evolution for John Doe: Pictures, the Public, and the Scopes Trial Debate," *Journal of American History*, 87 (March 2001), pp. 1275–1276, 1279, 1285–1287, 1290–1291, 1303.

38. Cremin, *American Education: The Metropolitan Experience*, p. 49.

39. *Epperson v. Arkansas* 393 U.S. 97, pp. 100, 101, 103–104.

40. Caudill, *Scopes Trial*, p. 19. Also see the comments by Jess Fox Mayshark, pp. 58, 65–66, 67, 71, 73, 87, in that same publication.

41. Duane Gish, *Teaching Creation Science in Public Schools* (El Cajo, CA: Institute for Creation Research, 1995), pp. v, vi, 35, 61.

42. Mary Beth Marklein, "19 States Get a Bad Grade for Their Teaching of Evolution," *USA Today*, 27 September 2000, Section D, p. 11.

43. Lawrence A. Cremin, *The Transformation of the School: Progressivism in American Education, 1876–1957* (New York: Vintage Books, 1964), pp. 339–340, 343–344. See as well Diane Ravitch, *The Troubled Crusade: American Education, 1945–1980* (New York: Basic Books, 1983), p. 70; Joel Spring, *The Sorting Machine: National Educational Policy Since 1945* (New York: David McKay Co., 1976), pp. 23–24, 27.

44. Arthur Bestor, *Educational Wastelands: The Retreat from Learning in Our Public Schools*, (1953 rpt. Urbana, II: University of Illinois Press, 1985), p. 59. Also refer to Cremin, *Transformation of the Schools*, pp. 344–347; Spring, *Sorting Machine*, pp. 15–16, 20–21, 22.

45. Cremin, *Transformation of the Schools*, pp. 251–256, 347; Larry Cuban, *How Teachers Taught: Constancy and Change in American Classrooms, 1880–1990* (New York: Teachers College Press, 1993).

46. Spring, *Sorting Machine*, pp. 32–33, 35, 36, 37, 46, 47–48. See as well Joel Spring, *Images of American Life: A History of Ideological Management in Schools, Movies, Radio, and Television* (Albany, NY: State University of New York Press, 1992), pp. 167–169.

47. James B. Conant, "Slums and Suburbs," in *American Education and Vocationalism: A Documentary History, 1870–1970*, eds. Marvin Lazerson and W. Norton Grubb. (New York: Teachers College Press, 1974), p. 161. Refer also to Sidney P. Marland, Jr., "Career Education," in *American Education and Vocationalism*, pp. 174–176.

48. Charles E. Silberman, *Crisis in the Classroom: The Remaking of American Education* (New York: Vintage Books, 1970), pp. 5, 10, 84, 89, 91, 98, 151, 176, 180, 220, 221, 296, 343, 345.

49. Neil Postman and Charles Weingartner, *Teaching as a Subversive Activity* (New York: Delta Publishing, 1969), pp. xiv, pp. 137–138.

50. National Commission on Excellence in Education. *A Nation At Risk: The Imperatives for Education Reform* (Washington, DC: U.S. Department of Education, 1983), pp. 5, 8, 9, 21, 22.

51. Paul E. Peterson, "Are Big City Schools Holding Their Own?" in *Seeds of Crisis: Public Schooling in Milwaukee since 1920*, eds. John L. Rury and Frank A. Cassell (Madison, WI: University of Wisconsin Press, 1993), pp. 269–301. Refer as well to Ernest Boyer, *High School: A Report on Secondary Education in America* (New York: Harper & Row, 1983); Theodore Sizer, *Horace's Compromise: The Dilemma of the American High School* (Boston: Houghton Mifflin Co., 1984); John Goodlad, *A Place Called School: Prospects for the Future* (New York: McGraw-Hill, 1983); E. D. Hirsch, *Cultural Literacy* (Boston: Houghton Mifflin Co., 1987); Allan Bloom, *The Closing of the American Mind* (New York: Simon & Schuster, 1987); "Chicago's Schools Hit as Worst," *Chicago Tribune*, November 7, 1987, p. 1; Jeffrey Mirel, *The Rise and Fall of an Urban School System: Detroit, 1907–81* (Ann Arbor, MI: University of Michigan Press, 1993), p. 399.

52. David C. Berliner and Bruce J. Biddle, *The Manufactured Crisis: Myths, Fraud, and the Attack on America's Public Schools* (Reading, MA: Addison-Wesley. Co., 1995), pp. 3, 4, 14, 26, 44, 63, 112–113, 114–115, 122–123, 147–148, 149–150.

53. Bracey has written a series of reports: "The Condition of Public Education," *Phi Delta Kappan* (October 1991), pp. 106, 113, 114; "The Second Bracey Report on the Condition of Public Education," *Phi Delta Kappan* (October 1992), p. 108; "The Third Bracey Report on the Condition of Public Education," *Phi Delta Kappan* (October 1993), p. 106; "The Fourth Bracey Report on the Condition of Public Education," *Phi Delta Kappan* (October 1994).

54. Coontz, *The Way We Never Were*, p. 14. Refer as well to John Demos's analysis in *Past, Present, and Personal: The Family and the Life Course in American History* (New York: Oxford University Press, 1986), pp. 25, 38.

55. Joanne Meyerowitz, "Women and Gender in Postwar America, 1945–1960," in *Not June Cleaver: Women and Gender in Postwar America, 1945–1960*, ed. Joanne Meyerowitz (Philadelphia: Temple University Press, 1994), pp. 1, 2.

56. Coontz, *The Way We Never Were*, pp. 25, 183.

57. Elaine Tyler May, *Homeward Bound: American Families in the Cold War Era* (New York: Basic Books, 1988), pp. 5–6, 9, 13, 20, 22, 24, 26, 38, 39, 53, 58, 87, 90–91.

58. Meyerowitz, "Women and Gender," in *Not June Cleaver*, ed. Joanne Meyerowitz, pp. 3, 5. See as well May, *Homeward Bound*, pp. 189–191, 193, 196–197, 199, 203, 209, 211–212.

59. The quotes in these paragraphs are from Wini Breines, *Young, White, and Miserable: Growing Up Female in the Fifties* (Boston: Beacon Press, 1992), pp. 2, 8–9, 50, 52–54, 57, 68, 73–74.

60. Demos, *Past, Present, and Personal*, pp. 61, 64.

61. Coontz, *The Way We Never Were*, pp. 2–3, 4, 15, 66. Refer likewise to Glenda Riley, *Divorce: An American Tradition* (Lincoln, NE: University of Nebraska Press, 1991), pp. 133, 156, 159.

62. Demos, *Past, Present, and Personal*, pp. 71–72, 83, 84, 87.

63. The quotes and information in these paragraphs draw on Coontz, *The Way We Never Were*, pp. 2–3, 22, 141, 144, 193–194, 207, 209, 225, 228, 229.

64. Gary Orfield, "Policy Matters: Educational Policy and Chicano Students," in *The Elusive Quest for Equality: 150 Years of Chicano/Chicana Education*, ed. Jose F. Moreno (Cambridge, MA: Harvard Educational Review, 1999); p. 112.

65. Coontz, *The Way We Never Were*, pp. 229, 231.

66. Deborah A. Verstegen, "The New Wave of School Finance Litigation," *Phi Delta Kappan*, (November 1994), p. 243.

67. Jonathan Kozol, *Savage Inequalities: Children in America's Schools* (New York: Crown Publishers, 1991), pp. 23, 24, 85, 86–87.

68. Michael A. Rebell, "Fiscal Equity Litigation and the Democratic Imperative," *Studies in Judicial Remedies and Public Engagement*, Vol. 1, No. 2 (New York: Campaign for Fiscal Equity, Inc., 1998), pp. 2, 3, 4, 21.

69. *Digest of Education Statistics*, http://nces.ed.gov

G L O S S A R Y[1]

Academies: Private, denominational, educational institutions that emerged toward the end of the eighteenth century and continued to exert influence well into the nineteenth century. These numerous institutions, which existed throughout the United States, offered an assortment of schooling at various levels—elementary, secondary, and higher education. Public high schools, which proliferated during the late nineteenth and early twentieth centuries, eventually replaced academies.

Acculturation: Involves the learning of a culture, encompassing its values, beliefs, language, heritage, religion, traditions, etc., either voluntarily or involuntarily, formally or informally.

Bilingual Education: In spite of a heterogeneous society, the United States has rarely supported the teaching of non-English in its public schools. German immigrants appeared to be the strongest proponents of bilingual education, to preserve their European culture, dating back to colonial times. At the local levels, some non-English languages were allowed throughout the nineteenth century. However, the xenophobia of World War I created an environment of intolerance for any "un-American" cultural artifact such as language. Because of the civil rights campaigns of Latinos/as, Chinese-Americans, and Native Americans, the U.S. Congress passed the Bilingual Education Act, or Title VII of the Elementary and Secondary Education Act, in 1968. And the federal Supreme Court mandated bilingual education in its 1974 decision, *Lau v. Nichols*. Federal legislation re-authorized Title VII and broadened its scope in 1974, 1978, 1984, and 1988. Bilingual education is not monolithic, and involves diverse theories and approaches like maintenance, transitional, and immersion.

Braceros: Mexican workers who entered the United States as part of an agreement between the Mexican and United States governments between 1942 and 1947 to fill a worker shortage during the wartime economy. Responding to pressure from American employers, the United States Congress extended this immigrant worker program to 1964. Many employers exploited the immigrant Mexican workers who participated in this program.

Californio: Native-born Californians of Spanish descent, dating to the colonial period.

Calvinism: During the early 1500s in Geneva, Switzerland, John Calvin formally proposed the three basic tenets of a reformed Protestantism: predestination, that is, God grants grace to the chosen, or elect; literal translation of the Bible; and a

Christian community operating in unison. These served as the theological basis for Puritanism.

Charity schools: A largely urban phenomenon of the early nineteenth century, these schools provided free schooling to children of families unable to afford the fees of private schools typical at the time. Philanthropists and charitable societies provided most of the revenue necessary to operate them, although some public funding existed. These schools attempted to teach poor children the virtues of obedience, morality, temperance, and work, values that their largely indigent and allegedly immoral parents failed to convey. These philanthropic organizations, like the well-known New York City Free School Society, assumed a missionary zeal and self-righteous posture in their social reform efforts.

Coeducation: First emerged during the colonial period in dame schools, which catered to toddlers and very young children. Local district grammar schools gradually began to admit girls in the late eighteenth and early nineteenth centuries; this coeducational setting became formalized with the emergence of the common-school movement. Female students eventually dominated high school enrollment and outperformed their male counterparts academically through the early years of the twentieth century. Although consensus largely prevailed, some resistance to coeducation existed at different times and in various forms.

Common schools: The Commonwealth of Massachusetts, in 1837, is credited with inaugurating the first state-supported school system. Free schooling thus became available at the grammar school level with access "common" to all, generally emphasizing a "common" set of "American" political, economic, and religious values.

Corporate capitalism: The economic system that transformed industrial capitalism, beginning in the late nineteenth century. Business organization generally shifted from individual ownership and partnerships to large, impersonal arrangements based on the accumulation of capital through the sale of stocks and bonds to fund the manufacturing process. Large-scale production, with factories and plants housing 10,000 to 30,000 unskilled workers, replaced the small workplaces that had accommodated only a few dozen employees. Management superseded worker authority, efficiency dictated the work process, a bureaucratic hierarchy emerged, and worker insecurity and alienation grew. Economies of scale afforded profit and drove competitors into bankruptcy or consolidation. As a result, wealth became concentrated in fewer hands.

Dame schools: These emerged during the early colonial period as an informal and popular means of providing care for extremely young children. For a fee, a village widow or mother, often with children of her own, supplied adult supervision and taught rudimentary literacy skills in her own home. This domestic setting appealed to many parents as an appropriate setting for young children unable to work in the fields, especially during the summer months. Dame schools quietly and subtly introduced early forms of coeducation as well as the concept of female instructors. By the late eighteenth century, some communities provided subsidies and instituted some regulations for dame schools. The institution had largely disappeared by the early 1800s, when primary schools became more widespread and available.

De facto segregation: A pattern of separate schooling that occurs due to restricted residential areas, enforced by social patterns, prejudices, and biases.

De jure segregation: A separate schooling system growing out of local, state, or federal law or judicial statutes or rulings.

Female seminaries: These pioneered female education during the first half of the nineteenth century. Usually private institutions, they provided an exclusively female, boarding-school setting; focused on a rigorous, academic program of study; hired female teachers; and established many other precedents, such as inaugurating early teacher training. During the latter half of the nineteenth century, they either evolved into private female colleges or disappeared entirely, displaced by public high schools.

Freethinkers: Individuals who do not hold any particular spiritual views, maintain any specific pietistic practices, or affiliate with any formal religious denomination. Often regarded as irreligious or atheist, they are anticlerical deists.

Grammar schools: A colonial, private, European educational institution that served to prepare scholars for college by teaching the traditional classical liberal arts curriculum. The inception of the common schools during the first half of the nineteenth century and the appearance of public high schools during the second half of that century marginalized the grammar school.

Hispano: Native-born New Mexicans of Spanish descent, dating to the colonial period.

Human agency: History and events shaped by human actions, whether individual or collective activities; overt or covert efforts; compliant or resistant behaviors.

Industrial capitalism: The economic system that displaced merchant capitalism, beginning in late-eighteenth-century Great Britain. Often solely associated with the mechanization of production, industrial capitalism introduced rigid and distinct social-class relationships as well as profoundly transformed social values and institutions. The need for carefully trained skilled labor shrank ever so gradually throughout the nineteenth century to a reliance on a largely unskilled workforce. Artificially driven production, dependent on clocks, supplanted a natural rhythm of work; timed labor superseded task-oriented work; highly supervised, crowded factories replaced individual workshops; total economic dependence destroyed any semblance of independence; and the demand for cheap labor, i.e., child and women workers, eroded the organic family structure. The new factory owners laid the foundation for the modern middle class, or bourgeoisie.

Infant schools: An early childhood institution, imported from England and maintained through philanthropic support, that appeared in many American cities during the 1820s and 1830s. With missionary zeal these schools socialized young children of the poor and taught them morality, obedience, and discipline, to save them from a perceived corrupt environment created by their seemingly slothful, indigent, and intemperate parents.

Issei: Japanese immigrants who settled in Hawaii and California, as well as other West Coast states, during the late nineteenth and early twentieth centuries.

Jehovah's Witnesses: A religious denomination originated in a Bible study group in Allegheny (Pittsburgh), Pennsylvania, during the 1870s. In the view of the Jehovah's Witnesses, the outbreak of World War I in 1914 marked the transition point from human domination to Christ's reign on Earth. The wars, pestilence, and natural disasters since that war represent the dawn of a new epoch, Christ's signs of the last days. The Jehovah's Witnesses are an inclusive denomination and a worldwide movement focused on strict Bible study.

King James Bible: Published in 1611, this definitive English translation of the Bible was commissioned by King James Charles Stuart, successor to Queen Elizabeth. He employed fifty-four translators proficient in Hebrew, Aramaic, and Greek, among other languages. It became widely—if not universally—used by a variety of Protestant sects.

Lancaster system: Acknowledged as the first mass education "system" to be used in late eighteenth- and early nineteenth-century America. Created by Joseph Lancaster in England, and generally used in urban charity schools, it fit perfectly into the new industrial age. English and American factories spewed forth finished products in ever increasing numbers, operated efficiently, followed a rigid authoritarian hierarchy, and reduced costs. With the factory as its model, philanthropic societies funded Lancaster schools that hosted 100–300 poor children crowded into a single cavernous room. Monitors, often former students themselves, supervised the intense educational routine through drill, regimentation, and marching. The monitors, in turn, were directed by a master, seated on an elevated platform so he could oversee the entire educational operation.

Merchant capitalism: The economic system that gradually replaced European feudalism from the fifteenth through the seventeenth centuries. Merchant capitalism, based on private ownership and property, proved to be dynamic, generating wealth and power from risk, effort, and achievement, while feudalism remained rooted in a static aristocratic class, relying on inherited, or anointed, status. Merchant capitalists, creating the outlines of an emerging, urban middle class, acquired social esteem and capital through profits earned from national and international trade and commerce. Skilled workers handcrafted many of the goods exchanged in the trade process.

Mestizo/a: A person of mixed blood, usually referring to individuals of both Spanish and Native American descent.

Monitorial system: See Lancaster System.

Multiculturalism: An offshoot of cultural pluralism, first proposed in 1915 by Horace M. Kallen and revived during the 1960s' racial and ethnic civil rights campaigns. It supports the application of democratic principles to a heterogenous society consisting of different racial and ethnic groups, in which each group is equal. It values the rich cultural contributions of diverse groups and sees American society enriched by the contributions of various, unique cultural values, beliefs, languages, and institutions. This cosmopolitan perspective celebrates cultural differences in contrast to chauvinistic practice of imposing a single, narrow, and ethnocentric definition of culture.

Nat Turner revolt: Part of a long tradition of slave rebellions. Nat Turner in 1831 led a group of up to eighty slaves in attacking numerous farms in Virginia. Retribution proved to be swift and vicious. Because of this insurrection, a deep fear gripped the South, causing many of those states to pass a series of severe and restrictive slave laws.

Nisei: Japanese Americans born in the United States; the children of "Issei," Japanese immigrants.

Normal school: Initial nineteenth-century teacher training institutions that borrowed European precedents. The earliest American normal schools began as private academies and seminaries at the beginning of the nineteenth century. With the inception of the "common schools" in 1837, state-subsidized normal schools began to appear in many states. Transformed to multipurpose universities during the middle of the twentieth century, most still exist to this day, albeit with little emphasis on teacher education.

Pan-Protestantism: A universal set of Christian values, beliefs, and morals that transcends various Protestant denominations, this perspective deliberately excluded Roman Catholicism, Lutheranism, and Judaism. The "common schools" from the mid-nineteenth to the mid-twentieth centuries were used to promote Protestant hegemony blatantly through daily readings from the King James Bible and/or recitation of the Lord's Prayer and subtly through assigned readings and screening of teachers' spiritual backgrounds, rarely tolerating other Christian and non-Christian religious tenets.

Pauper schools: Refer to Charity schools.

Progressive education: A complex and enigmatic school reform movement dating to between 1890 and 1920 that introduced the basic philosophies, curricula, teaching methods, classroom and school routines, architectural trends, and governance structures of the modern public school system. Different philosophical strains of Progressivism emerged–child-centered, administrative, scientific, social reconstructionist–many of which worked at cross-purposes.

Reformation: A Christian religious reform movement that began in sixteenth-century Europe which attempted to address grievances against the Roman Catholic Church, and resulted in the creation of numerous and various Protestant denominations after many devastating wars and bloody conflicts.

Romanticism/Romantics: Artists, thinkers, and activists who embraced the late-eighteenth- and early-nineteenth-century European Romantic movement, which idealized a past in which society followed organic, or natural, human patterns in contrast to modern patterns of industrial growth, burgeoning cities, and impersonal and artificial bureaucratic institutional settings. Romantics often became involved in utopian movements to recapture this "perfect" lifestyle.

Sunday schools: Began as a charity school effort during the late eighteenth century and subsidized by philanthropic groups to teach literacy to children of the urban poor.

Since children worked six days a week, Sunday was the only day available for them to attend reading and writing classes. As the common schools gained popularity during the early nineteenth century, Sunday schools de-emphasized literacy training, came under denominational auspices, and solely taught religious doctrine.

Tejanos: Native-born Texans of Spanish descent, dating to the colonial period.

NOTES AND SOURCES

1. For additional information about these terms, events, concepts, etc., refer to Mitchell and Robert E. Salsbury, eds., *Multicultural Education in the United States: A Guide to Polices and Programs in the Fifty States* (Westport, CT: Greenwood Press, 2000); Richard J. Altenbaugh, ed., *The Historical Dictionary of American Education* (Westport, CT: Greenwood Press, 1999) as well as Eric Foner and John A Garrity, eds., *The Reader's Companion to American History* (Boston: Houghton Mifflin, 1991); Stephan Thernstrom, ed., *Harvard Encyclopedia of American Ethnic Groups* (Cambridge: Harvard University Press, 1980).

A U T H O R I N D E X

SUBJECT INDEX